DAVIES

PRINCIPLES OF TAX LAW

AUSTRALIA
LBC Information Services
Sydney

CANADA and USA
Carswell
Toronto, Ontario

NEW ZEALAND
Brooker's
Auckland

SINGAPORE and MALAYSIA
Thomson Information (S.E. Asia)
Singapore

DAVIES

PRINCIPLES
OF
TAX LAW

THIRD EDITION

by

Professor David W. Williams, LL.M., Ph.D., A.T.I.I., SOLICITOR
*Deputy Director of the Centre for Commercial Law Studies,
Queen Mary & Westfield College*

Professor Geoffrey K. Morse, LL.B., BARRISTER
Head of the Department of Law, University of Nottingham

David Salter, LL.B., SOLICITOR
Senior Lecturer in Law, University of Birmingham

LONDON
SWEET & MAXWELL
1996

First Edition (1980) Introduction to Revenue Law by F.R. Davies
Second Edition (1985) Introduction to Revenue Law by
F.R. Davies, David Williams and Geoffrey Morse

*Published in 1996 by Sweet & Maxwell Limited of
100 Avenue Road, London, NW3 3PF
Typeset by York House Typographic Ltd, London W13 8NT
Printed in England by Clays Ltd, St Ives plc*

No natural forests were destroyed to
make this product; only farmed timber was used and replanted.
A CIP catalogue record for this book is available
from the British Library.

ISBN 0 421 570 90 3

© Sweet & Maxwell
1996

All rights reserved. No part of this publication may be reproduced
or transmitted in any form, or by any means stored in any
retrieval system of any nature without prior written permission,
except for permitted fair dealing under the Copyright, Designs and
Patents Act 1988, or in accordance with the terms of a licence
issued by the Copyright Licensing Agency in respect of
photocopying and/or reprographic reproduction. Application for
permission for other use of copyright material including
permission to reproduce extracts in other published works shall be
made to the publishers. Full acknowledgement of author,
publisher and source must be given.

PREFACE TO THE THIRD EDITION

The first lesson in coming to terms with tax law is that you cannot really understand tax if you only look at the surface. The second lesson, which is linked to the first, is that it is also impossible to come to terms with the subject unless it is looked at as a whole. It is unfortunately the case that most lawyers – and most accountants – only learn bits about tax and so see it as a series of unconnected and incomprehensible codes. Our hope in rewriting this book is that, in demonstrating that there are underlying principles in tax law, just as in any other area of the law, it will help you see the subject as a whole and put the often complex specialised provisions into context.

There is much criticism of the British tax systems (to call it one system would be, of course, to oversimplify). They are said to be too complex, too obscure, etc ... the list is long. One reason for the perceived complexity is that people insist on looking at the surface rather than the structure. They look for the rules, not the principles. If they are tax officials they look for £££ when that is not always appropriate. If they are taxpayers, they want to know what the tax officials think of the rules, rather than asking what is appropriate. Politicians are, sadly, not ones to look for the principles of taxation. The result is that we have the tax systems we deserve – a mess, where at times even the word system is misleading. These are strong words, perhaps. But we challenge anyone to be complimentary about the combined amendments to United Kingdom law brought forward in the Finance Acts 1992 to 1996.

Tax work is like dentistry. Leave things alone, and the result is pain. Yet behind the decay of neglect is a system that can still bite. Our hope is that this introduction will help you work through the detritus to the solid underlying structure. We hope also that it removes the fear factor (the analogy with dentistry also hold good) from the study of tax. If it does, it will repay your efforts – materially as well as intellectually. In the first edition, this is what Ron Davies wanted. He was ahead of his time in trying to debunk the mystery and the jargon. We have tried to follow his lead in this third edition. In doing so we have received considerable help from colleagues, including Colin Manchester and Julia Kerr of the University of

Preface to the Third Edition

Birmingham and David Ormerod of the University of Nottingham. We would also like to thank our respective secretaries for all their assistance in the writing process and Carolyn Morse who applied a classicist's brain to the page proofs.

There have been a horrifying number of changes of detail since the last edition, but we intend this book to be up to date to the Finance Act 1996 and cases decided to June 1996. The information on self-assessment has been produced in consultation with the Inland Revenue. The rest is up to you – good luck!

Geoffrey Morse
David Williams
David Salter

PREFACE TO THE FIRST EDITION

This book is in one sense a very ambitious project; I embarked on it with the ambition to prove that Aristotle was wrong when he said: 'It is not possible to state simply that which in itself is not simple.'

Well, of course, Aristotle is right and the trick cannot be done. But something can be done. As George Orwell nearly said, 'All writers on revenue law are equal in obscurity, but some are more equal than others.' I aim to be less equal. This book tries to take the mystique out of revenue law. It aims to provide a more relaxed exposition of the subject than is elsewhere available. Above all, the book aims to take the fear out of revenue law. Some people have a sort of mental or emotional blockage about tax. When I left the Bar and went into the Civil Service I was horrified to find myself posted to the Inland Revenue Solicitor's Office. But it turned out to be quite painless. I stayed there for 12 years. Then I went into university teaching.

What this book cannot do is to take the slog out of revenue law. It is not an easy subject: in fact it is mighty difficult. A good book helps; a good teacher helps; discussion with fellow-students helps; but what really counts is the *thinking* that you do 'in the silence of your lonely room'.

The book has very few footnotes. The point of this is to try to maintain (so far as the subject-matter allows) a narrative flow. In particular there are no footnotes for the citation of cases. After each case mentioned in the text there is the date of the case and, if it was decided in a court higher than the High Court, an abbreviation showing *what* court; 'C.A.' for Court of Appeal, 'H.L.' for House of Lords. A full citation for each case is given in the Table of Cases at the front of the book.

Writing a book on revenue law is like trying to take a photograph of a restless child – the blighter won't stand still for more than a moment. The moment I have tried to catch is September 30, 1979.

F.R.D.

CONTENTS

Preface v
Preface to First Edition vii
Table of Cases xi
Table of Statutes xxiii
Table of Statutory Instruments xxxv

PART ONE INTRODUCTORY

| Chapter 1 | How Tax Ticks | 3 |
| Chapter 2 | Handling Tax Laws | 21 |

PART TWO TAXATION OF INCOME

Chapter 3	The Mechanics of Income Tax	51
Chapter 4	Capital and Income	64
Chapter 5	Income from a Trade or Profession	69
Chapter 6	Income from an Employment	99
Chapter 7	Casual Earnings	132
Chapter 8	Income from Land	135
Chapter 9	Capital Allowances	146
Chapter 10	Losses	156
Chapter 11	Taxation of Income Under Case III of Schedule D	162
Chapter 12	Trusts and Estates	177
Chapter 13	Settlements: Anti Avoidance Rules	183
Chapter 14	The Taxation of Individuals	190
Chapter 15	National Insurance Contributions	209

PART THREE TAXATION OF CAPITAL GAINS

Chapter 16	Capital Gains Tax	219
Chapter 17	Computing Gains and Losses	250
Chapter 18	Exemptions and Reliefs	265

CONTENTS

PART FOUR CORPORATION TAX

Chapter 19	Taxation of Companies and Shareholders	281
Chapter 20	Corporation Tax	288
Chapter 21	Close Companies	308

PART FIVE INHERITANCE TAX

Chapter 22	The Evolution of Inheritance Tax	321
Chapter 23	Chargeable Transfers	324
Chapter 24	Exemptions and Reliefs	339
Chapter 25	Computation	358
Chapter 26	Settled Property	373
Chapter 27	Liability and Incidence	398
Chapter 28	Administration and Collection	404

PART SIX VALUE ADDED TAX

| Chapter 29 | Value Added Tax | 411 |
| Chapter 30 | VAT Rates and Problems | 434 |

PART SEVEN STAMP DUTIES

| Chapter 31 | Stamp Duties | 447 |

PART EIGHT INTERNATIONAL ASPECTS

| Chapter 32 | International Aspects | 459 |

Index   476

TABLE OF CASES

ABERDEEN CONSTRUCTION GROUP LTD v. IRC [1978] A.C. 885;
[1978] 2 W.L.R. 648; [1978] 1 All E.R. 962, H.L. 252
Akbarali v. Brent London Borough Council [1983] 2 A.C. 309;
[1983] 2 W.L.R. 16; [1983] 1 All E.R. 226, H.L. 460, 463
Alexander v. IRC [1991] S.T.C. 112, C.A. 368
Alloway v. Phillips [1980] 1 W.L.R. 888; [1980] 3 All E.R. 138,
C.A. 133
Anglo-Pension Oil Co. Ltd v. Dale [1932] 1 K.B. 124 86
Apple and Pear Development Corporation v. Customs and Excise
Commissioners [1988] 2 All E.R. 922, European Ct 28, 413, 420
Atkinson v. Daucer [1988] S.T.C. 758 275
Att.-Gen. v. Seccombe [1991] 2 K.B. 688 332

B.S.C. FOOTWEAR LTD v. RIDGWAY [1972] A.C. 544; [1971] 2
W.L.R. 1313, H.L. 81
Baker v. Archer-Shee [1927] A.C. 844 177
Ball v. Johnson [1971] T.R. 147 105
— v. National & Grindlay's Bank [1973] Ch. 127; [1972] 3 W.L.R.
17; [1971] 3 All E.R. 485 294
Baron Inglewood v. IRC. *See* Inglewood (Lord) v. IRC
Batey v. Wakefield [1982] 1 All E.R. 61, C.A. 269
Beauchamp v. F.W. Woolworth plc [1990] 1 A.C. 478; [1989] 1
W.L.R. 1, H.L. 86
Beecham Group Ltd v. Fair (H.M. Inspector of Taxes) (1984) 57
T.C. 733 130
Benham's Will Trusts, Re (1995) 401
Bennett v. IRC [1995] S.T.C. 54 342
Bentley v. Pike (1981) 53 T.C. 590 250
Bentleys, Stokes & London v. Beeson [1952] 2 All E.R. 82, C.A. ... 87, 89
Bird v. IRC [1989] A.C. 300, H.L. 31
Blackpool Marton Rotary Club v. Martin (Inspector of Taxes) 62
T.C. 686, C.A. 281
Blount v. Blount [1916] 1 K.B. 230 171
Bond (Inspector of Taxes) v. Pickford [1983] S.T.C. 517, C.A. 248
Booth v. Ellard [1980] 1 W.L.R. 1443; [1980] 3 All E.R. 569,
C.A. 242, 243
Booth (E.V.) Holdings Ltd v. Buckwell (1980) 53 T.C. 425 252

TABLE OF CASES

Bowden v. Russell & Russell [1965] 1 W.L.R. 711; [1965] 2 All
E.R. 258 88
British Insulated and Helsby Cables Ltd v. Atherton [1926] A.C.
205, H.L. 86
British Salmson Aero Engines Ltd v. IRC [1938] 2 K.B. 482, C.A. ... 85
British Transport Commission v. Gourley [1956] A.C. 185; [1956]
2 W.L.R. 41; [1955] 3 All E.R. 796, H.L. 127
Brown v. Bullock [1961] 1 W.L.R. 1095, C.A. 118
— v. National Provident Institution [1921] 2 A.C. 222, H.L. 27
Buccleuch v. IRC [1967] 1 A.C. 506; [1967] 2 W.L.R. 207; [1967]
1 All E.R. 129, H.L. 371
Butler v. Evans [1980] S.T.C. 613 225

CAIRNS V. MACDIARMID (INSPECTOR OF TAXES) [1983] S.T.C. 178,
C.A. 163
Calvert v. Wainwright [1947] K.B. 526; [1947] 1 All E.R. 282 .. 105, 106
Campbell v. IRC [1970] A.C. 77; [1968] 3 W.L.R. 1025, H.L. 165
Campbell Connelly & Co. Ltd v. Barnett (Inspector of Taxes)
[1993] S.T.C. 50, C.A. 273
Capcount Trading v. Evans (Inspector of Taxes) [1993] 2 All E.R.
125, C.A. 250
Carr (Inspector of Taxes) v. Sayer [1992] S.T.C. 396 154
Carson v. Peter Cheyney's Executor [1959] A.C. 412; [1958] 3
W.L.R. 740; [1958] 3 All E.R. 573, H.L. 96
Cenlon Finance Co. v. Ellwood [1962] A.C. 782; [1962] 2 W.L.R.
871; [1962] 1 All E.R. 854, H.L. 53
Chaloner (Inspector of Taxes) v. Pellipar Investments Ltd [1996]
S.T.C. 234 229
Chancery Lane Safe Deposit and Offices Co. Ltd v. IRC (1996)
C.I.R. 64 170
Chinn v. Collins [1981] A.C. 533; [1981] 2 W.L.R. 14; [1981] 1
All E.R. 189, H.L. 183
Clark (Inspector of Taxes) v. Oceanic Contractors Inc. [1983] A.C.
130 27
Clarke v. Mayo [1994] S.T.C. 570 275
Clore, dec'd (No. 3), Re [1985] 1 W.L.R. 1290; [1985] 2 All E.R.
819 .... 399, 404
Cole Bros v. Phillips [1982] 1 W.L.R. 1450; [1982] 2 All E.R. 247,
H.L. 150
Collins v. Addies (Inspector of Taxes) [1992] S.T.C. 746 316
Colquhoun v. Brooks (1889) 14 App. Cas. 493 .... 69, 469
Commissioner of Taxation v. Squatting Investment Co. Ltd [1954]
A.C. 182, P.C. 80
Congreve v. IRC [1948] 1 All E.R. 948, H.L. 474
Conservative and Unionist Central Office v. Burrell [1982] 1
W.L.R. 522; [1982] 2 All E.R. 1 .... 31, 281

xii

TABLE OF CASES

Cooke (Inspector of Taxes) v. Blacklaws (1984) 58 T.C. 255 103
Copol Clothing Ltd v. Hindmarch (Inspector of Taxes) [1984] 1
  W.L.R. 411, C.A. 154
Corbett v. IRC [1938] 1 K.B. 567 177
Couch (Inspector of Taxes) v. Administrators of the Estate of
  Caton *The Times*, December 28, 1995 253
Counters Fitzwilliam v. IRC [1993] 1 W.L.R. 1189; [1993] 3 All
  E.R. 184, H.L. 42, 383
Craven (Inspector of Taxes) v. White [1988] 3 W.L.R. 423; [1988]
  3 All E.R. 495, H.L. 42
Crowe v. Appleby [1975] 1 W.L.R. 1539; [1975] 3 All E.R. 529 243
Customs and Excise Commissioners v. Oliver [1980] 1 All E.R.
  353 416
— v. Professional Footballers' Association [1993] 1 W.L.R. 153,
  H.L. 420
— v. Robert Gordon's College unreported, H.L., 1995

DAPHNE V. SHAW (1926) 43 T.L.R. 45 150
Davenport (Inspector of Taxes) v. Chilver [1983] Ch. 293; [1983] 3
  W.L.R. 481 .... 229, 230
Davis v. Powell [1977] 1 W.L.R. 258; [1977] 1 All E.R. 471 230
De Beers Consolidated Mines v. Howe [1906] A.C. 455 462
Drummond (Inspector of Taxes) v. Austin-Brown (1983) 58 T.C.
  67 230
Duple Motor Bodies v. Ostime. *See* Ostime v. Duple Motor Bodies
Dyer v. Dorset County Council [1988] 3 W.L.R. 213, C.A. 269

EDWARDS V. BAIRSTOW AND HARRISON [1956] A.C. 14; [1955] 3
  W.L.R. 410; [1955] 3 All E.R. 48, H.L. 18, 56, 72, 101
— v. Clinch [1981] Ch. 1; [1981] 3 W.L.R. 707; [1981] 3 All E.R.
  543; [1982] A.C. 845, H.L. 100
Eilbeck v. Rawling [1982] A.C. 300; [1981] 2 W.L.R. 449; [1981]
  1 All E.R. 865, H.L. 252
Ellesmere v. IRC [1918] 2 K.B. 795 367
Emmerson v. Computer Time International [1977] 1 W.L.R. 734;
  [1977] 2 All E.R. 545, C.A. 251
Ensign Tankers (Leasing) Limited v. Stokes (Inspector of Taxes)
  [1992] 1 A.C. 655; [1992] 2 W.L.R. 469; [1992] 2 All E.R.
  275, H.L. 39, 42, 43, 72
Erichsen v. Last (1881) 8 Q.B.D. 414 72
Ewart v. Taylor (Inspector of Taxes) [1983] S.T.C. 721 248

FALL V. HITCHEN [1973] 1 W.L.R. 286; [1973] 1 All E.R. 368 102
Falmer Jeans Ltd v. Rodin (Inspector of Taxes) [1990] S.T.C. 270 .. 297
Ferguson v. IRC [1970] A.C. 442; [1969] 2 W.L.R. 1116; [1969] 1
  All E.R. 1025, H.L. 171, 172

TABLE OF CASES

Fetherstonhaugh v. IRC [1985] Ch. 1; [1984] 3 W.L.R. 212, C.A. .. 348
Fielder (Inspector of Taxes) v. Vedlynn Ltd [1992] S.T.C. 553 251
Fitzleet Estates v. Cherry [1977] 1 W.L.R. 1345; [1977] 3 All E.R. 996, H.L. 170
Fitzpatrick v. IRC (No. 2) [1994] 1 W.L.R. 306; [1994] 1 All E.R. 673, H.L. 119
Floor v. Davis [1980] A.C. 695; [1979] 2 W.L.R. 830; [1979] 2 All E.R. 677, H.L. 238
Frankland v. IRC (1996) 354, 391
Frost v. Feltham [1981] 1 W.L.R. 452 200
Furniss v. Dawson [1984] A.C. 474; [1984] 2 W.L.R. 226; [1984] 1 All E.R. 530, H.L. 42, 45, 144

G v. G. (1975) 6 Fam. Law 8 353
Gallagher v. Jones (Inspector of Taxes) [1994] Ch. 107; [1994] 2 W.L.R. 160, C.A. 76
Glantre Engineering v. Goodhand (Inspector of Taxes) [1983] 1 All E.R. 542, D.C. 57
Global Plant v. Secretary of State for Social Security [1972] 1 Q.B. 139; [1971] 3 W.L.R. 269 101
Golding (Inspector of Taxes) v. Kaufman (1984) 58 T.C. 296 237
Gordon v. IRC [1991] S.T.C. 174 273
Government of India v. Taylor. See India (Government of) v. Taylor
Graham v. Greene [1925] 2 K.B. 37 75
Gray v. IRC [1994] S.T.C. 360, C.A. 371
Great Western Railway Co. v. Bater [1922] A.C. 1 100
Grey v. Tiley (1932) 16 T.C. 414 133
Griffin (Inspector of Taxes) v. Craig-Harvey [1993] S.T.C. 54 271

HALL (INSPECTOR OF TAXES) V. LORIMER [1994] 1 W.L.R. 209; [1994] 1 All E.R. 250, C.A. 103
Hamblett v. Godfrey (Inspector of Taxes) [1987] 1 W.L.R. 357; [1987] 1 All E.R. 916, C.A. 105
Harthan v. Mason [1980] S.T.C. 94 242
Hatton v. IRC [1992] S.T.C. 140 327
Hayes' Will Trusts, Re [1971] 1 W.L.R. 758; [1971] 2 All E.R. 341 367
Hillyer v. Leeke [1976] S.T.C. 490 .... 89, 118
Hinton v. Maden & Ireland Ltd [1959] 1 W.L.R. 875; [1959] 3 All E.R. 356, H.L. 85
Hoare Trustees v. Gardner [1979] Ch. 110; [1978] 2 W.L.R. 832, 839; [1978] 1 All E.R. 791 247
Hochstrasser v. Mayes [1960] A.C. 376; [1960] 2 W.L.R. 63; [1959] 3 All E.R. 817, H.L. 103
Hoechst Finance Ltd v. Gumbrell (Inspector of Taxes) [1983] S.T.C. 150, C.A. 295

TABLE OF CASES

Honour (Inspector of Taxes) v. Norris [1992] E.G.C.S. 35 269
Horton v. Young [1972] Ch. 157; [1971] 5 W.L.R. 348; [1971] 3
  All E.R. 412, C.A. 90

ICI PLC v. COLMER (Inspector of Taxes) *The Times*, March 15,
  1996 298
India (Government of) v. Taylor [1955] A.C. 491; [1955] 2 W.L.R.
  303; [1955] 1 All E.R. 292, H.L. 27
Inglewood (Lord) v. IRC [1993] 1 W.L.R. 866, C.A. 394
Ingram v. IRC [1995] S.T.C. 564 334
IRC v. Barclay, Curle & Co. Ltd [1969] 1 W.L.R. 675; [1969] 1 All
  E.R. 732, H.L. 149
— v. Brander & Cruickshank [1971] 1 W.L.R. 212; [1971] 1 All
  E.R. 36, H.L. 103, 127, 426
— v. Church Commissioners for England [1977] A.C. 329, H.L. . 67, 166
— v. Clay [1914] 3 K.B. 466 368
— v. Cock, Russell & Co. Ltd [1949] 2 All E.R. 889 81
— v. Crawley [1987] S.T.C. 147 169
— v. Crossman [1937] A.C. 26 368
— v. Duke of Westminster [1936] A.C. 1, H.L. 42
— v. Green [1982] S.T.C. 485 270
— v. Land Securities Investment Trust Ltd [1969] 1 W.L.R. 604;
  [1969] 2 All E.R. 430, H.L. 166
— v. Livingston (1927) 11 T.C. 538 74
— v. Lord Rennell [1964] A.C. 173; [1963] 2 W.L.R. 745; [1963] 1
  All E.R. 803, H.L. 343
— v. Macpherson [1988] 2 W.L.R. 1261; [1988] 2 All E.R. 753,
  H.L. 327, 381, 391
— v. Maxse [1919] 1 K.B. 647 75
— v. National Book League [1957] Ch. 488; [1957] 3 W.L.R. 222;
  [1957] 2 All E.R. 644, C.A. 165
— v. National Federation of Self-Employed and Small Businesses
  [1982] A.C. 617; [1981] 2 W.L.R. 722; [1981] 2 All E.R. 93,
  H.L. 62
— v. Plummer [1980] A.C. 896; [1979] 3 W.L.R. 689; [1979] 3 All
  E.R. 775, H.L. 183
— v. Ramsay (1935) 20 T.C. 79 .... 166, 326
— v. Richard's Executors [1971] 1 W.L.R. 571, H.L. 252
— v. Scottish and Newcastle Breweries [1982] 1 W.L.R. 322;
  [1982] 2 All E.R. 230, H.L. 150
— v. Sheppard (No. 2) [1993] S.T.C. 240 286
— v. Slater (Helen) Charitable Trust [1982] Ch. 49; [1981] 3
  W.L.R. 377; [1981] 3 All E.R. 98, C.A. 278
— v. Spencer-Nairn [1991] S.T.C. 60 329
— v. Stannard [1984] 1 W.L.R. 1039; [1984] 2 All E.R. 105 399
— v. Stype Investments (Jersey) Ltd. *See* Clore, dec'd (No. 3), Re

xv

TABLE OF CASES

— v. Willoughby (1995) S.T.C. 143 .... 18, 40, 41, 43
— v. Wolfson [1949] 1 All E.R. 865, H.L. 185

JARMIN (INSPECTOR OF TAXES) v. RAWLINGS [1994] S.T.C. 1005 275
Jenkins (Inspector of Taxes) v. Brown [1989] 1 W.L.R. 1163 243
Johnston v. Britannia Airways *The Times*, July 20, 1994 77
Jonas v. Bamford [1973] S.T.C. 519 55
Jones v. Leeming [1930] A.C. 415 133
Jones (Samuel) & Co. (Devondale) Ltd v. IRC (1951) 32 T.C. 513 . 92

KELSALL PARSONS & Co. v. IRC (1938) 21 T.C. 608 78
Kidson v. MacDonald [1974] Ch. 339; [1974] 2 W.L.R. 566;
  [1974] 1 All E.R. 849 .... 28, 242
Kirby (Inspector of Taxes) v. Thorn EMI plc [1988] 1 W.L.R. 445;
  [1988] 2 All E.R. 947, C.A. 225, 229
Kirkham v. Williams (Inspector of Taxes) [1991] 1 W.L.R. 863,
  C.A. 75

LAKE v. LAKE [1989] S.T.C. 865 354
Law Shipping Co. Ltd v. IRC (1924) 12 T.C. 621 .... 92, 93
Leader v. Counsel [1942] 1 K.B. 364 133
Lennartz, H. v. Finanzamt Munchen III (C-97/90) [1991] C.C.R. I-
  3795; [1993] 3 C.M.L.R. 689 431
Letts v. IRC [1957] 1 W.L.R. 201; [1956] 3 All E.R. 588 332
Levene v. IRC [1928] A.C. 217 463
Lewis (Inspector of Taxes) v. Lady Rook [1992] 1 W.L.R. 662,
  C.A. 269
Lewis v. Walters (Inspector of Taxes) [1992] S.T.C. 97 255
Limmer Asphalte Paving Co. v. IRC (1872) L.R. 7 Exch. 211 449
London and Thames Haven Oil Wharves Ltd v. Attwooll [1967]
  Ch. 772; [1967] 2 W.L.R. 743; [1967] 2 All E.R. 124, C.A. 79
London County Council v. Attorney-General [1901] A.C. 26,
  H.L. 11, 64
Lord Fisher v. Customs and Excise Commissioners [1979]
  V.A.T.T.R. 227 425
Lowe v. Ashmore [1971] Ch. 545; [1970] 3 W.L.R. 998; [1971] 1
  All E.R. 1057 138
Lucas v. Cattell (1972) 48 T.C. 353 88
Lurcott v. Wakely & Wheeler [1911] 1 K.B. 905 92
Lynall v. IRC [1972] A.C. 680; [1971] 3 W.L.R. 759; [1971] 3 All
  E.R. 914 368
Lyon (Inspector of Taxes) v. Pettigrew (1985) 58 T.C. 452 232

McCLURE (INSPECTOR OF TAXES) v. PETRE [1988] 1 W.L.R. 1386 .. 138
Macfarlane v. IRC [1929] S.C. 453 179
McGowan v. Brown and Cousins [1977] 1 W.L.R. 1403; [1977] 3
  All E.R. 844 80

McGregor v. Adcock [1977] 1 W.L.R. 864; [1977] 3 All E.R. 65 275
Macpherson v. IRC. *See* IRC v. Macpherson
Makins v. Elson [1977] 1 W.L.R. 221; [1977] 1 All E.R. 572 268
Mallalieu v. Drummond [1983] 2 A.C. 861; [1983] 3 W.L.R. 409;
 [1983] 2 All E.R. 1095, H.L. 89, 90, 118
Mairs (Inspector of Taxes) v. Haughey [1994] 1 A.C. 303; [1993] 3
 W.L.R. 393; [1993] 3 All E.R. 801, H.L. (N.I.) 104
Markey (Inspector of Taxes) v. Saunders [1987] 1 W.L.R. 864 269
Marren v. Ingles [1980] 1 W.L.R. 983; [1980] 3 All E.R. 95, H.L. .. 229,
 232, 233
Marsden v. IRC [1965] 1 W.L.R. 734; [1965] 2 All E.R. 364 117
Marson v. Marriage [1980] S.T.C. 177 235
Marson (Inspector of Taxes) v. Morton [1986] 1 W.L.R. 1343 ... 73, 144
Martin v. Lowry [1927] A.C. 312 74
Mason v. Innes [1967] Ch. 1079; [1967] 3 W.L.R. 816; [1967] 2
 All E.R. 926, C.A. 83, 95
Miller v. IRC [1987] S.T.C. 108 377
Minden Trust (Cayman) Ltd v. IRC [1985] S.T.C. 758, C.A. 373
Mitchell and Edon v. Ross [1960] Ch. 498; [1960] 2 W.L.R. 766;
 [1960] 2 All E.R. 218, C.A. 102
Moodie v. IRC [1993] 1 W.L.R. 266; [1993] 2 All E.R. 49, H.L. 42
Moore v. Griffiths [1972] 1 W.L.R. 1024; [1972] 3 All E.R. 399 106
— v. Thompson (Inspector of Taxes) [1986] S.T.C. 170 268
Moore & Osborne v. IRC [1985] Ch. 32 377
Moorhouse v. Dooland [1955] Ch. 284; [1955] 2 W.L.R. 96;
 [1955] 1 All E.R. 93, C.A. 106
Munby v. Furlong [1977] Ch. 359; [1977] 3 W.L.R. 270; [1977] 2
 All E.R. 953, C.A. 150
Munro v. Commissioner of Stamp Duties [1934] A.C. 61 .... 333, 334
Murray v. Goodhews [1978] 1 W.L.R. 499; [1978] 2 All E.R. 40,
 C.A. 80

NATIONAL WATER COUNCIL v. CUSTOMS AND EXCISE COMMIS-
 SIONERS [1979] S.T.C. 157 430
Newsom v. Robertson [1953] Ch. 7; [1952] 2 All E.R. 728, C.A. ... 90
Nicholls v. IRC [1975] 1 W.L.R. 534; [1975] 2 All E.R. 120, C.A. . 333,
Nicoll v. Austin (1935) 19 T.C. 531 109

OAKES v. COMMISSIONER OF STAMP DUTIES OF NEW SOUTH
 WALES [1954] A.C. 57; [1953] 3 W.L.R. 1127; [1953] 2 All
 E.R. 1563 332
O'Brien v. Benson's Hosiery Ltd [1980] A.C. 562; [1979] 3 W.L.R.
 572; [1979] 3 All E.R. 652, H.L. 225, 226, 228, 229
Odeon Associated Cinemas Ltd v. Jones [1973] Ch. 288; [1972] 2
 W.L.R. 331; [1972] 1 All E.R. 681, C.A. 93, 251
O'Grady v. Bullcroft Main Collieries Ltd (1932) 17 T.C. 93 92

TABLE OF CASES

O'Kelly v. Trusthouse Forte [1984] Q.B. 90; [1983] 3 W.L.R. 605; [1983] 3 All E.R. 456, C.A. 101
Oram v. Johnson [1980] 1 W.L.R. 558; [1980] 2 All E.R. 1 252
Ostime v. Duple Motor Bodies [1961] 1 W.L.R. 739; [1961] 2 All E.R. 167, H.L. 82
Owen v. Elliott (Inspector of Taxes) [1990] Ch. 786; [1990] 3 W.L.R. 133, C.A. 270
— v. Pook [1969] 2 W.L.R. 775; [1969] 2 All E.R. 1, H.L. 107, 116, 120

PAGE (INSPECTOR OF TAXES) v. LOWTHER [1983] S.T.C. 799, C.A. .. 144
Park, dec'd (No. 2), Re [1972] Ch. 385; [1972] 2 W.L.R. 276; [1972] 1 All E.R. 394, C.A. 343
Parsons, Re [1943] Ch. 12 328
Partridge v. Mallandine (1886) 18 Q.B.D. 276 75
Pearson v. IRC [1981] A.C. 753; [1980] 2 W.L.R. 872; [1980] 2 All E.R. 479, H.L. 376, 377
Pepper (Inspector of Taxes) v. Daffurn [1993] S.T.C. 466 275
— v. Hart [1993] A.C. 593; [1992] 3 W.L.R. 1032; [1993] 1 All E.R. 42, H.L. 37, 40, 121
Pettit, Re [1922] 2 Ch. 765 172
Pexton v. Bell [1976] 1 W.L.R. 885; [1976] 2 All E.R. 914, C.A. 246
Pickford v. Quirke (1927) 13 T.C. 251 74
Pigott v. Staines Investments Co. Ltd [1995] S.T.C. 114 306
Pilkington v. Randall (1966) 42 T.C. 662, C.A. 144
Polsar Investments Netherlands BV v. Inspecteur der Invoerrechten en Accijnzen te Arnhem (C-60/90) [1991] E.C.R. I-3111 422
Prest v. Bettinson (1982) 82 T.C. 437 278

R. v. HUDSON [1956] 2 QB 252; [1956] 2 W.L.R. 914; [1956] 1 All E.R. 814; (1956) 40 Cr.App.R. 55, C.C.A. 59
— v. IRC, ex p. National Federation of Self-Employed and Small Businesses. *See* IRC v. National Federation of Self-Employed and Small Businesses
— v. Kensington Commissioners, ex p. Aramayo [1917] 1 K.B. 486 53
Ramsay v. IRC [1982] A.C. 300; [1981] 2 W.L.R. 449; [1981] 1 All E.R. 865, H.L. 40, 42
Ransom v. Higgs [1974] 1 W.L.R. 1594; [1974] 3 All E.R. 949, H.L. 72, 88
Ready Mixed Concrete (South East) v. Minister of Pensions and National Insurance [1968] 2 Q.B. 497; [1968] 2 W.L.R. 775 ... 101
Reckitt, Re [1932] 2 Ch. 144 172
Regent Oil Co. Ltd v. Strick [1966] A.C. 295; [1965] 3 W.L.R. 696; [1965] 3 All E.R. 174, H.L. 86
Rendell v. Went [1964] 1 W.L.R. 650; [1964] 2 All E.R. 464, H.L. 121

Table of Cases

Ricketts v. Colquhoun [1926] A.C. 1 .... 116, 117, 118
Robert Gordons College v. Customs and Excise Commissioners
  [1993] V.A.T.T.R. 159 43
Robinson v. Scott Bader Co. Ltd [1981] 1 W.L.R. 1135; [1981] 2
  All E.R. 1116, C.A. 290
Rolfe v. Nagel [1982] S.T.C. 53, C.A. 80
Roome v. Edwards [1982] A.C. 279; [1981] 2 W.L.R. 268; [1981]
  1 All E.R. 736, H.L. 247
Roskams v. Bennett (1950) 32 T.C. 129 118
Russell v. IRC [1988] 1 W.L.R. 834; [1988] 2 All E.R. 405 ...... 348, 354
Rutledge v. IRC (1929) 14 T.C. 490 73

Salt v. Chamberlain [1979] S.T.C. 750 73
Sansom v. Peay [1976] 1 W.L.R. 1073; [1976] 3 All E.R. 353;
  [1976] B.T.R. 259 270
Sargent v. Barnes [1978] 1 W.L.R. 823; [1978] 2 All E.R. 737 .... 90, 118
Savacentre Ltd v. IRC [1995] S.T.C. 867, C.A. 304
Schlumberger v. Customs and Excise Commissioners [1987] S.T.C.
  228 53
Scorer (Inspector of Taxes) v. Olin Energy Systems Ltd [1985] A.C.
  645; [1985] 2 W.L.R. 668; [1985] 2 All E.R. 375, H.L. 54
Scott v. Ricketts [1967] 1 W.L.R. 828; [1967] 2 All E.R. 1009,
  C.A. 133, 225
Secretan v. Hart [1969] 1 W.L.R. 1599; [1969] 3 All E.R. 1196 219
Seymour v. Reed [1927] A.C. 554 106
Shah v. Barnet London Borough Council. See Akbarali v. Brent
  London Borough Council
Sharkey v. Wernher [1956] A.C. 58; [1955] 3 W.L.R. 671; [1955] 3
  All E.R. 493, H.L. 82, 83, 233
Shilton v. Wilmshurst (Inspector of Taxes) [1991] 1 A.C. 684;
  [1991] 2 W.L.R. 530, H.L. 104
Shove v. Downs Surgical plc [1984] 1 All E.R. 7 128
Simpson v. Reynolds (John) & Co. (Insurances) Ltd [1975] 1
  W.L.R. 617; [1975] 2 All E.R. 88, C.A. 80
— v. Tate [1925] 2 K.B. 214 118
Smith (Inspector of Taxes) v. Abbott. See Fitzpatrick v. IRC (No. 2)
— v. Schofield (Inspector of Taxes) [1993] 1 W.L.R. 398, H.L. 263
Smiths Potato Estates Ltd v. Bolland [1948] A.C. 508; [1958] 2 All
  E.R. 367, H.L. 91
Spargo's case (1873) 8 Ch. App. 407 453
Staatssecretaris van Financien v. SAFE BV (C-320/88) [1990] I
  E.C.R. 285 418
Stainer's Executors v. Purchase [1952] A.C. 280, H.L. 96
Stamp Duties Commissioner of New South Wales v. Permanent
  Trustee Co. of New South Wales [1956] A.C. 512; [1956] 3
  W.L.R. 152; [1956] 2 All E.R. 512 332

TABLE OF CASES

Stanley v. IRC [1944] K.B. 255 180
Stanton v. Drayton Commercial Investment Co. Ltd [1983] A.C.
    501; [1982] 3 W.L.R. 214; [1982] 2 All E.R. 942, H.L. 252
Starke v. IRC [1995] S.T.C. 689, C.A. 350
Stenhouse's Trustees v. Lord Advocate [1984] S.T.C. 195 377
Stephens (Inspector of Taxes) v. T. Pittas Ltd (1983) 56 T.C. 722 ... 315
Stephenson v. Barclays Bank Trust Co. Ltd [1975] 1 W.L.R. 882;
    [1975] 1 All E.R. 625 242
Stevenson (Inspector of Taxes) v. Wishart [1987] 1 W.L.R. 1204;
    [1987] 2 All E.R. 428, C.A. 180
Strong & Co. Ltd v. Woodfield [1906] A.C. 448 89
Swales v. IRC [1984] 3 All E.R. 58 .... 377, 379, 395
Swires (Inspector of Taxes) v. Renton [1991] S.T.C. 490 248

TAYLOR v. GOOD [1974] 1 W.L.R. 556; [1974] 1 All E.R. 1137,
    C.A. 75
— v. Provan [1975] A.C. 194; [1974] 2 W.L.R. 394; [1974] 1 All
    E.R. 1201, H.L. 116, 117, 118, 120
Tennant v. Smith [1892] A.C. 150 .... 108, 212
Todd (Inspector of Taxes) v. Mudd [1987] S.T.C. 141 273
Tolsma v. Inspecteur der Omzetbelasting, Leenwarden (C-16/93),
    The Times, March 29, 1994 420
Tomlinson v. Glyn's Executor Co. [1970] Ch. 112; [1969] 3
    W.L.R. 310; [1970] 1 All E.R. 381 242
Tucker v. Granada Motorway Services Ltd [1979] 1 W.L.R. 683;
    [1979] 2 All E.R. 801, H.L. 86
Turner v. Follett [1973] S.T.C. 148, C.A. 226

VAN BOECKEL v. CUSTOMS AND EXCISE COMMISSIONERS [1981] 2
    All E.R. 505 53
Van den Berghs Ltd v. Clark, unreported, 1935 .... 64, 78
Varty v. Lynes [1976] 1 W.L.R. 1091; [1976] 3 All E.R. 447 270
Vertigan v. Brady (Inspector of Taxes) [1988] S.T.C. 91 114
Vesty v. IRC [1962] Ch. 861; [1962] 2 W.L.R. 221; [1961] 3 All
    E.R. 978 166
— v. — [1980] A.C. 1148; [1979] 3 W.L.R. 915; [1979] 3 All E.R.
    976, H.L. 474
Vickerman (Inspector of Taxes) v. Mason's P.R.s [1984] 2 All E.R.
    1 53
Vodafone Cellular Ltd v. Shaw [1995] S.T.C. 353 290

WALDING v. IRC [1996] S.T.C. 13 348
Walton v. IRC *The Times*, December 11, 1995 369
Wase v. Bourne [1996] S.T.C. 18 275
Watkins (Inspector of Taxes) v. Ashford Sparkes and Harward
    [1985] 1 W.L.R. 994; [1985] 2 All E.R. 916 89

Table of Cases

Watton (Inspector of Taxes) v. Tippett *The Times*, December 21, 1995 .... 228, 273
Weight v. Salmon (1935) 19 T.C. 174, H.L. 108
West v. Phillips (1958) 38 T.C. 203 74
Whitechapel Art Gallery v. Customs and Excise Commissioners [1986] 1 C.M.L.R. 79 425
Whitehouse v. Ellam [1995] S.T.C. 503 227
Wilkins v. Rogerson [1961] Ch. 133; [1961] 2 W.L.R. 102; [1961] 1 All E.R. 358, C.A. 108, 111, 121
Williams v. Bullivant [1983] S.T.C. 107 230
— v. Evans [1992] S.T.C. 498 273
Williams (Inspector of Taxes) v. Merrylees [1987] 1 W.L.R. 1511 .. 269
Wimpey International v. Warland [1989] S.T.C. 273, C.A. 149
Woolwich Building Society v. IRC [1993] A.C. 70; [1992] 3 W.L.R. 366; [1992] 3 All E.R. 737, H.L. 27
Worthing R.F.C. v. IRC [1987] 1 W.L.R. 1057, C.A. 281
Wright v. Boyce [1958] 1 W.L.R. 832; [1958] 2 All E.R. 703, C.A. 106

Yarmouth v. France (1887) 19 Q.B.D. 647 .... 149, 150
Young, Re (1875) 28 Ch. D. 705 461
Young and Young v. Phillips (Inspector of Taxes) (1984) 58 T.C. 232 224
Young and Woods Ltd v. West [1980] I.R.L.R. 201, C.A. 101
Yuill v. Fletcher (Inspector of Taxes) (1984) 58 T.C. 145, C.A. . 144, 145
— v. Wilson [1980] 1 W.L.R. 910; [1980] 3 All E.R. 7, H.L. 144, 145

Zim Properties Ltd v. Procter (Inspector of Taxes) (1984) 58 T.C. 371 .... 225, 227, 228

TABLE OF STATUTES

1803	Income Tax Act (43 Geo. 3, c. 122) 23, 24, 29, 46, 64	1925	Trustee Act (15 & 16 Geo. 5, c. 19)
	Scheds. A–E 29		s. 31 .... 178, 187, 377, 379, 395
1842	Income Tax Act (5 & 6 Vict., c. 35) 24		(i)(ii) 377
1853	Income Tax Act (16 & 17 Vict., c. 34) 24		s. 32 394
1880	Employers' Liability Act (43 & 44 Vict., c. 42) 149		Law of Property Act (15 & 16 Geo. 5, c. 20)
1890	Inland Revenue Regulation Act (53 & 54 Vict., c. 21) 14		s. 184 335
			Administration of Estates Act (15 & 16 Geo. 5, c. 23)
			s. 34 401
	Partnership Act (53 & 54 Vict., c. 39) 195		s. 47A 355
1891	Stamp Duties Management Act (54 & 55 Vict., c. 38) 447		Sched. 1 Pt. II 401
		1931	Finance Act (21 & 22 Geo. 5, c. 28)
	s. 1 447		s. 28 450
1891	Stamp Act (54 & 55 Vict., c. 39) 447	1934	Law Reform (Miscellaneous Provisions) Act (24 & 25 Geo. 5, c. 41) 163
	Pt. I 447		
	Pt. II 447		
	Pt. III 447	1936	Finance Act (26 Geo. 5 & 1 Edw. 8, c. 34) 24, 40
	s. 1 .... 29, 447		
	s. 14(4) 449, 447	1945	Income Tax Act (8 & 9 Geo. 6, c. 32) ... 146
	s. 59 453		
	s. 75(1) 455	1948	Agricultural Holdings Act (11 & 12 Geo. 6., c. 63) 230
	s. 122 447		
	Sched. 1 .. 447, 449, 454		
1894	Finance Act (57 & 58 Vict., c. 30) 26	1952	Income Tax Act (15 & 16 Geo. 6 & 1 Eliz. 2, c. 10) 24, 25, 40
1918	Income Tax Act (8 & 9 Geo. 5, c. 40) ... 24		

xxiii

Table of Statutes

1963	Finance Act (c. 25) 135, 136	1973	Social Security Act (c. 38) 209
1965	Finance Act (c. 25) 25	1974	Finance Act (c. 30) 26
	s. 90(1) 453	1975	Finance Act (c. 7) 336, 339, 349
1967	Leasehold Reform Act (c. 88) 255		ss. 39–42 336
1968	Capital Allowances Act (c. 3) 25		s. 39 336
1969	Finance Act (c. 32) 136, 297		s. 40 336
			s. 41 .... 336, 337
			s. 42 336
1970	Taxes Management Act (c. 9) .. 14, 17, 25, 220, 288		Social Security Act (c. 14) 25, 209
	s. 8 52		s. 2 214
	s. 9A(1) 61		s. 7 214
	s. 12B(1)(a) 62		Inheritance (Provision for Family and Dependants) Act (c. 63) 355
	s. 20 52		
	B(8) 52		
	s. 29 52		Finance Bill 336
	(1)(a) 52	1976	Finance Act (c. 40)
	(b) 52, 53		s. 115 337
	(3) 52, 54	1978	Theft Act (c. 31)
	(8) 65		s. 2(1)(c) 59
	s. 31 .... 17, 54		Finance Act (c. 42) 111
	s. 34 58		s. 31 236
	s. 36 58		s. 49 236
	s. 40 58	1979	Customs and Excise Management Act (c. 2) 13, 17
	s. 44 54		
	s. 50(6) 54		
	s. 54 .... 53, 54	1980	Housing Act (c. 51) 269
	s. 55 54	1982	Supply of Goods and Services Act (c. 29) 416
	s. 56 18		
	A 56		
	B 55		Finance Act (c. 39) 201
	D 55	1983	Oil Taxation Act (c. 56) 28
	s. 57 220		
	s. 59A 61	1984	Finance Act (c. 43) 147, 151
	s. 106(2) 171		
	Income and Corporation Taxes Act (c. 10) .. 24, 25, 40		Capital Transfer Tax Act (c. 51) 322
			Inheritance Tax Act (c. 51) 322, 325, 331, 336, 339, 363, 371, 373, 375, 379, 464, 467
1971	Finance Act (c. 68) 239		
1972	Finance Act (c. 41) 282		
	European Communities Act (c. 68) 465		Pt. III 373
			s. 1 .... 29, 324

TABLE OF STATUTES

1984	Inheritance Tax Act—contd	1984	Inheritance Tax Act—contd
	s. 2(1) 324		s. 43 .... 370, 373
	s. 3 358		s. 47 378
	s. 3(1) 324		s. 48 378
	(2) 325		(1)(a) 396
	(3) 326, 328, 391		s. 49 380
	(4) 381		(1) 378
	s. 3A 329		s. 50 375
	s. 4 .... 334, 352, 371,		(6) 370, 379
	380, 381		s. 51 .... 380, 381
	(1) 334		s. 52 .... 381, 385
	(2) 335		(1) 380
	s. 5 .. 345, 363, 378, 380		(2) 382
	(1) 327, 371		(3) 381, 390
	(2) 327		(4) 382
	(5) 365		s. 53(2) 382, 396
	s. 7(4) 359		(3) 383
	s. 10 353, 356, 391, 397		(4) 384
	(1) 328, 329		s. 54 383
	s. 11 .... 351, 352, 353		s. 54A 385
	(1) 352, 353		s. 54B 385
	(6) 353		s. 55 396
	s. 12 356		s. 56(2) 340
	s. 13 356		ss. 58–85 385
	s. 14 356		s. 58(1) 386, 391
	s. 15 .... 326, 356		s. 59 386
	s. 16 357		s. 60 387
	s. 17 353		s. 61 387
	s. 18 339		s. 64 387
	ss. 19–22 381		s. 65(1) 390
	s. 19 340		(2) 391
	s. 20 341		s. 66 388
	s. 21 341		(2) 389
	s. 22 .... 342, 343		(6) 390
	s. 23 344		s. 67 388
	s. 24 .... 344, 345		s. 68 391
	s. 24A 344		s. 69 392
	s. 25 344		s. 70 395
	s. 26 344		s. 71 .... 394, 395
	s. 26A 345		s. 76 391
	s. 27 347		s. 80 387
	s. 29A 353, 355		s. 90 384
	ss. 30–35 346		s. 91 379
	s. 31 395		s. 92 336
	ss. 36–42 402		s. 93 .... 353, 355
	s. 41 401		ss. 94–98 .... 336, 384

Table of Statutes

1984	Inheritance Tax Act—contd	1984	Inheritance Tax Act—contd
	s. 94 336		ss. 199–214 398
	s. 96 336		s. 199(3) 349
	s. 98 337		s. 202 336
	s. 99 384		s. 203 400
	s. 101 384		s. 204 400
	s. 102 .... 336, 337		s. 211 400
	ss. 103–114 347		ss. 215–261 404
	s. 104 366		s. 215 404
	s. 106 388		s. 216 404
	ss. 115–124 349		s. 218 405
	s. 115(2) 350		s. 219 405
	(3) 350		s. 220 405
	ss. 125–130 351		ss. 221–225 406
	s. 131 360		ss. 226–236 406
	s. 141 .... 346, 384		s. 237 407
	ss. 142–145 353		s. 238 407
	s. 142 .... 326, 354		s. 256 404
	(1) 353		s. 262 .... 336, 337
	s. 143 354		s. 263 .... 336, 338
	s. 144 354		s. 264 362
	s. 145 355		s. 265 361
	s. 150 347		s. 266(1) 362
	s. 152 345		(2) 362
	s. 154 345		s. 268 326
	s. 155 345		(2) 327
	s. 160 367		(3) 327
	s. 161 369		s. 272 .... 326, 327
	(1) 369		Chap. II 386
	s. 162(1) 366		Chap. III 386
	(2) 365		Sched. 1 359
	(5) 363		Sched. 3 . 344, 345, 347
	s. 163 369	1985	Companies Act (c. 6) . 291, 300
	s. 164 363		
	s. 165 363		s. 135 299
	s. 167 370		s. 741(2) 312
	s. 168 368		Finance Act (c. 21) 147
	s. 170 370		Housing Associations
	ss. 171–177 335		Act (c. 69) 344
	s. 171 371	1986	Finance Act (c. 41) 455
	(2) 335		s. 86(1) 455
	s. 172 .... 335, 371		s. 87 .... 447, 455
	s. 173 372		s. 99 455
	s. 176 370		s. 102 .... 331, 332
	ss. 178–189 371		s. 103 .... 365, 367
	ss. 190–198 371		(5) 365

Table of Statutes

1986 Finance Act—*contd*
Sched. 20   331, 333, 334
para. 6 333
1986 Insolvency Act (c. 45)
s. 341 347
1988 Income and
Corporation
Taxes Act (c. 1) 24,
25, 29, 40, 64,
65, 169, 190
Pt. XI 309
Pt. XV 183, 184, 189
s. 1 .... 26, 29, 31
s. 3 169
s. 5 59
ss. 6–14 288
s. 6 .. 26, 31, 64, 65, 281
s. 7(1) 167
s. 9 290
  (1) 281
s. 13A 309, 316
s. 14 .... 285, 289
  (2) 301
s. 15 (Sched. A) .. 64, 65,
132, 135, 137, 138,
139, 140, 141, 142,
143, 156, 192, 198,
290, 424, 468, 469
s. 17 (Sched. C) 64,
65, 292
s. 18 (Sched. D) .. 32, 66,
69, 70, 71, 84, 90, 101,
102, 103, 115, 116,
117, 127, 131, 132,
164, 198, 426, 469
  (1) 69
  (a)(ii) 469
  (2) 469
  (3) 69, 70, 162
  Case I .. 51, 59, 64,
  65, 66, 68, 69, 71,
  75, 82, 83, 84, 93,
  98, 99, 115, 132,
  133, 134, 136, 138,
  139, 140, 146, 156,
  157, 175, 190, 192,

1988 Income and Corporation
Taxes Act—*contd*
s. 18 Case I 196, 198,
215, 283, 284,
290, 291, 424,
469, 470
Case II 51, 59,
64, 65, 66, 69, 70,
75, 83, 84, 93, 98,
99, 100, 102, 115,
132, 133, 134, 146,
156, 157, 215, 283,
284, 424, 469
Case III 64, 65,
66, 132, 162, 163,
164, 165, 166, 167,
170, 173, 175, 180,
183, 189, 190, 192,
292, 296, 425, 469,
470
Case IV 31, 66,
132, 162, 292, 470, 471
Case V 31, 66,
132, 424, 469,
470, 471, 473
Case VI 64, 65,
96, 132, 133,
134, 137, 139,
140, 145, 156, 186,
187, 225, 297, 424,
471,
474, 475
s. 19 (Sched. E) 41,
59, 65, 66, 68, 70,
71, 83, 88, 90, 91,
99, 100, 101, 102,
103, 104, 105, 115,
116, 126, 127, 128,
129, 131, 192, 197,
211, 212, 283, 426,
462, 470, 471, 473
  (1) 99
Case I 99, 471,
472
Case II 99, 472
Case III 99, 472

xxvii

Table of Statutes

1988 Income and Corporation Taxes Act—*contd*
  s. 20 (Sched. F) . 66, 132, 193, 285, 286, 289, 296, 302, 303, 306, 473
  ss. 21–43 135
  s. 21(3) 139
  s. 25 140
  s. 28 140
  s. 32 .... 146, 153
  ss. 34–39 141
  s. 34 .... 141, 142
    (1) 141
    (2) 142
    (4) 142
    (5) 142
  s. 35 .... 141, 143, 284
  s. 36 .... 141, 143
  s. 38 142
  s. 45 303
  s. 46 282
  s. 53 75
  s. 61 95
  s. 63 .... 95, 284
  s. 64 166
  s. 69 133
  s. 74 84, 85, 87, 91, 140
    (a)–(q) 84, 85
    (a) 84, 85, 87, 91
    (b) 84
    (d) 85, 92
    (e) 84
    (f) 84, 85
    (g) 84, 92
    (k) 84
  s. 75 .... 140, 295
  s. 76 295
  s. 83 .... 84, 281
  s. 85A 113
  ss. 103–110 96
  s. 103 .... 96, 97
    (2) 96
  s. 104 .... 96, 97
  s. 107 134
  s. 110(3) 95
  s. 111 .... 195, 196

1988 Income and Corporation Taxes Act—*contd*
  s. 113(1) 196
  s. 119 162
  s. 120 162
  s. 125(1) 164
  s. 131(1) 65, 103, 107, 115
  s. 134 71
  s. 141 110
  s. 143 110
  s. 145 113
    (4) 114, 122
  s. 148 .... 127, 128
  ss. 153–168 119
  s. 153 .... 107, 120
  s. 154 121
  s. 155A 125
  s. 156 122
    (1) 121
  s. 157 .... 123, 213
  s. 158 124
  s. 159 124
  s. 159A 124
  s. 159AA 124
  s. 159AB 124
  s. 160 .... 124, 125
  s. 161(1) 124
  s. 162 125
  s. 163 122
  s. 166 120
  s. 168A 123
  s. 168F 124
  s. 185 112
  s. 186 111
  s. 188 127
  s. 198 .... 83, 107
    (1) 115
  s. 201 118
  s. 202B 130
  ss. 203F–203L 130
  s. 207A 285
  s. 208 303
  ss. 209–218 66
  s. 209(2)(a) 66
  s. 210 299

xxviii

Table of Statutes

1988 Income and Corporation
       Taxes Act—*contd*
       s. 211 299
       ss. 212–218 299
       ss. 213–218 301
       ss. 217–229 300
       s. 231 317
       s. 238(1) 302
       s. 239 303
           (2) 302
       s. 240 303
       s. 241(2) 304
           (3) 304, 305
       s. 242 304
       s. 243 305
       s. 247 305
       ss. 257–278 202
       s. 257(5) 203
       ss. 257A(2)–(5) 204
       s. 257BA 204
       s. 259(5) 204
       s. 275C 203
       s. 278 .... 202, 286
       s. 313 127
       s. 314 71
       s. 329 163
       s. 334 462
       s. 335 461
       s. 336 461
       ss. 337–347 288
       s. 338 .... 293, 294
           (3) 293, 294
           (4) 294
       s. 339 295
       s. 340 294
       s. 343 297
       s. 344 297
       s. 347A 163, 164,
                              184, 189
           (1) 164, 189
           (7) 164, 189
       s. 347B 166, 173
       s. 348 ..... 162, 164, 167,
                         168, 169, 170,
                                175, 294
           (1)(a) 168

1988 Income and Corporation
       Taxes Act—*contd*
       s. 349 .... 65, 159, 162,
                         164, 167, 168, 169,
                                170, 175, 294
           (2) 65, 175, 176
       s. 350 159
       s. 353 .... 125, 159
           (3) 199
       s. 380 ...... 157, 158, 159
       s. 381 161
       s. 384 .... 158, 296
       s. 385 ...... 158, 159, 160
           (4) 159
       s. 386 159
       s. 387 159
       s. 388 160
       s. 390 159
       ss. 393–413 288
       s. 393 296
           (9) 293, 296
       s. 393A 296
       s. 397 .... 158, 297
       s. 402 298
       s. 403(1) 298
           (7) 293
       ss. 414–417 310
       ss. 414–430 288
       ss. 419–422 315
       s. 477A 175, 176
       s. 480A 175, 176
       s. 483 303
       s. 503 139
       s. 504 139
       ss. 559–565 71
       s. 577 .... 84, 87
       s. 580(3) 127
       s. 592 .... 91, 129
           (4)–(6) 84
       s. 594 129
       s. 595 91
       s. 596 129
       s. 617 100
       ss. 619–629 97
       ss. 630–655 97
       s. 630

TABLE OF STATUTES

1988 Income and Corporation
Taxes Act—*contd*
ss. 639–646 129
s. 639 97
s. 641 98
s. 642 98
s. 643(2) 98
s. 656 .... 174, 175
s. 660A 184, 185,
186, 188, 189
(1) 185, 186,
187, 189
(2) 185
(3) 185
(4) 185
(5) 185
(6) 186
(8) 186, 189
(9) 189
(10) 185
s. 660B 184, 186,
187, 188
(1) 186
(2) 187
(3) 187
s. 660D(1) 186, 187
s. 660G(1) 183
s. 673 185
ss. 677–678 184
s. 677 ...... 187, 188, 314
(2) 188
(4) 188
(9) 187
(10) 187
s. 678 188
s. 686 .... 178, 186
(2)(b) 186
(6) 181
s. 687 179
s. 739 464
ss. 747–756 464
ss. 757 *et seq.* 465
s. 765 464
s. 768 295
s. 768A 296
s. 770 83

1988 Income and Corporation
Taxes Act—*contd*
s. 776 .... 41, 144, 145
(1) 144, 145
s. 779 144
s. 780 144
s. 787 199
s. 788 454
s. 790 457
s. 811 458
s. 817(1) 84
ss. 831–842A 279
s. 832 .... 31, 72
s. 833 197
(4)(c) 134
s. 835 ...... 169, 170, 190
s. 836 169
s. 837 114
Sched. 6 123
Sched. 6A 124
Sched. 9 .... 111, 112
Sched. 10 111
Finance Act (c. 39) 136,
162, 163, 166, 173, 174,
184, 189, 192, 198
s. 66 452
s. 78 113
s. 80 113
1989 Finance Act (c. 26) 58, 313
ss. 67–74 113
s. 67 113
s. 76 91
s. 178 .... 54, 62
Sched. 5 113
1990 Capital Allowances
Act (c. 1) 25, 147
s. 18 154
(7) 154
s. 24 151
s. 27 .... 146, 152
ss. 34–36 153
s. 37 153
s. 61 150
s. 67A 150
s. 79 151
ss. 84–97 154

Table of Statutes

1990 Capital Allowances Act—*contd*
   s. 140 157
   Sched. AA1 ..... 148, 150
   Finance Act (c. 29) 440, 447

1991 Finance Act (c. 31)
   s. 72 158

1992 Social Security (Contributions and Benefits) Act (c. 4) 25, 98, 209
   Pt. I 209
   s. 1(1) 209
   s. 2(1) 211
   s. 3(1) 211
   s. 6 211
   s. 10 213
   Social Security Administration Act (c. 5)
   s. 17 210
   s. 18 210

1992 Social Security Administration (Northern Ireland) Act (c. 8) 209
   Taxation of Chargeable Gains Act (c. 12) 31, 64, 220, 226, 255, 288, 464, 467
   s. 1(1) 222
   s. 2 473
     (1) 224
     (2) 223, 264
   s. 3 .... 221, 250
     (5)(a) 264
       (b) 264
     (7) 222
   s. 4 221
   s. 8 .... 281, 290
   s. 10(1) 224
     (4) 224
   s. 12(1) 224
   ss. 15–20 250

1992 Taxation of Chargeable Gains Act—*contd*
   s. 15(2) 222
   s. 16(1) 263
     (2) 263
   s. 17 .... 226, 227, 233, 251, 266, 273, 277
   s. 18(2) 227
     (3) 264
   s. 19(2) 229
     (5) 225
   s. 21(1) 224
     (b) 226
     (2) 228
   s. 22 229
     (1) 228, 229, 232, 233, 237
     (2) 229
   s. 23 231
   s. 24 237
     (1) 230
     (2) 230
   s. 28 232
   ss. 29–34 238
   s. 29 238
     (1) 250
   s. 30 238
   ss. 31–34 239
   s. 35 .... 250, 260
     (2) 260
     (5) 262
   ss. 37–52 250
   s. 37(1) 228
   s. 38(1) 251
     (4) 253
   s. 39 251
   s. 40 253
   s. 42 254
   s. 44(1) 254
   s. 45 272
   s. 48 .... 232, 233, 251
   ss. 53–57 .... 250, 256
   s. 53(1) 256
     (2A) 256
   s. 54 256
   s. 55 256

Table of Statutes

1992 Taxation of Chargeable
Gains Act—*contd*
s. 55(2) 261
s. 56 260
s. 58 239
s. 59 223
s. 60 .... 241, 242
    (1) 244
    (2) 241
s. 62 239
    (1) 239, 240
    (2) 241
    (4) 240
    (6)–(9) 240
s. 64(2) 240
    (3) 240
s. 68 241
s. 69 247
    (4) 249
s. 70 243
s. 71 246
    (1) ... 244, 245, 246,
                  247, 248
s. 72
    (1) 244, 245,
                 246, 247
    (4) 246
s. 73 246
    (1)(a) 245, 246
      (b) 245
s. 76(1) 248
    (2) 249
ss. 104–114 257
s. 107 259
s. 115 267
s. 117 .... 236, 267
s. 122 234
ss. 126–140 234
s. 132(3)(b) 236
s. 137 235
ss. 144–147 237
ss. 152–159 272
s. 155 273
s. 159 273
s. 161(1) 233
    (2) 234

1992 Taxation of Chargeable
Gains Act—*contd*
s. 161(3) 233
s. 162 .... 235, 273
s. 163 274
s. 164 274
ss. 164A–N 276
s. 165 277
s. 210 268
ss. 222–226 268
s. 222 270
    (6) 271
s. 223(4) 270
s. 224 270
    (3) 268
s. 225 270
s. 251 236
    (3) 237
    (4) 236
s. 253 236
s. 254 236
s. 256(1) 277
    (2) 277
s. 258 272
s. 260 266
s. 262 271
s. 271 129
    (1)(h) 98
s. 275 .... 224, 473
s. 286 227
    (2) 227
    (8) 227
s. 288(3) 221
Sched. 1
    para. 2 222
Sched. 2 .. 250, 262, 263
Sched. 3 .... 222, 250
Sched. 6 274
Sched. 7 255
Sched. 8
    para. 5(1) .. 228
Sched. 9 267
Finance Act (No. 2) (c.
    48) 55
s. 59 140
Sched. 10 140

1992	Tribunals and Inquiries Act (c. 53)	1994	Value Added Tax Act— *contd*
	s. 11 410		Sched. 1 423
1993	Finance Act (c. 34) 123, 124, 276		Sched. 2 442
			Sched. 3 442
1994	Finance Act (c. 9) ... 51, 61, 62, 95, 130, 166, 202, 456		Sched. 4 418
			para. 1 418
			para. 3 419
	s. 87 447		Sched. 5
	s. 117 148		para. 1 419
	s. 249 463		Sched. 8 .. 436, 437, 439
	Value Added Tax Act (c. 23) 409, 411, 415, 436		Sched. 9 .. 421, 437, 439
		1995	Finance Act (c. 4) . 51, 135, 136, 181, 183, 184, 187, 188, 189
	s. 1 29		
	s. 3(1) 414		s. 39(1) 137
	s. 4(1) 414		(2) 139
	(2) 414, 421		s. 154 350
	s. 5 418		s. 160 24
	(2) 414, 418	1996	Finance Act (c. 4) ... 34, 47, 162 192, 198, 281, 293, 422, 475
	s. 19 440		
	s. 26 429		
	s. 43 422		Pt. IV
	s. 83 .... 18, 413		Chap. II . 288, 291
	s. 84(4)(c) 430		s. 81 291
	s. 94 424		s. 82 291
	(4) 426		s. 83 291
	(5) 424		s. 85 291
	s. 96 419		s. 86 291

TABLE OF STATUTORY INSTRUMENTS

1975 Social Security (Credits) Regulations (S.I. 1975 No. 556) reg. 8 215
1978 Categorisation of Earners Regulations (S.I. 1978 No. 1689) 214
1979 Social Security (Contributions) Regulations (S.I. 1979 No. 591) 33, 210, 212
    reg. 19 212
        (1)(d) 212
    reg. 21 213
    reg. 22 213
1981 Capital Transfer Tax (Delivery of Accounts) Regulations (S.I. 1981 No. 880) 404
Capital Transfer Tax (Delivery of Accounts) (Scotland) Regulations (S.I. 1981 No. 881) 404
1987 Inheritance Tax (Double Charges Relief) Regulations (S.I. 1987 No. 1130) .. 366
1989 Taxes (Interest Rate) Regulations (S.I. 1989 No. 1297) 54
1991 Inheritance Tax (Delivery of Accounts) Regulations 1991 (S.I. 1991 No. 1248) 404
1994 Special Commissioners (Jurisdiction and Procedure) Regulations (S.I. 1994 No. 1811) 55
General Commissioners (Jurisdiction and Procedure) Regulations (S.I. 1994 No. 1812) 55
General and Special Commissioners (Amendment of Enactments) Regulations (S.I. 1994 No. 1813) ...55, 56
1995 VAT Regulations (S.I. 1995 No. 2518) 33

Part One

Introductory

Chapter 1

HOW TAX TICKS

The question "What is a tax?" is surprisingly difficult to answer. It is tempting to rely on the well-known reply of the child who was asked to define an elephant. "An elephant is large and grey, and lives in a herd of elephants." Some payments are not clearly one of the herd. This is so, for example, of the profits made on postage stamps or the fees paid to government for the right to operate independent television channels. Clarity is not helped because some politicians find it convenient to say that things are not tax when they certainly seem to look like taxes. An example is social security contributions.

Defining taxes

So, as the elephant definition does not seem to work, we must try to define a tax. A tax has three characteristics. It is *a compulsory levy imposed by an organ of government for public purposes.* The legal essence of this definition lies in the compulsion. Law requires that the payment be made. The political essence lies in the public purposes for which the payments are made. Even the definition reflects the disagreements that often take place about tax.

Another way to define taxes is by way of a list of levies that are, beyond doubt, taxes. Listing all the payments that might be regarded "currently" as taxes in force in the United Kingdom would be contentious and perhaps tedious. Here is a list of the principal taxes, in order of importance to government: income tax, value added tax, social security contributions, corporation tax, the national business rate, excise duties, council tax, capital gains tax, stamp duty (and stamp duty reserve tax), inheritance tax, petroleum revenue tax, vehicle excise duty, and insurance premium tax. We have left out customs duty? Yes and no: customs duties are European taxes, and there is now no British law imposing them. British customs officials are collecting them for the European Union. We should perhaps also include hidden taxes like the gas levy, national lottery levy, sugar levy, fossil fuel levy, and ports levy—but then it does get tedious.

3

How Tax Ticks

Why do we tax?

Before we look in detail at the present United Kingdom tax system, it is valuable to spend a little time thinking about tax policy. Why do we tax the way we do? What are the political, economic, social and administrative pressures that have contributed to the shape of our tax system?

The primary purpose of taxation is to raise revenue for government expenditure. The government can raise revenue by borrowing, by "printing" money, and by selling things, but in practice it is unavoidable that taxation should raise most of the government's fiscal requirements. The government spends part of the money on services which private enterprise cannot provide, such as defence and law and order. It also pays for services that it is thought are better provided on a universal basis, such as social security benefits, and education. Attitudes to taxation depend to some extent on the views of taxpayers as to the merits of these items of government expenditure. Do you, for example, think it the job of government to provide a health service, or consumer protection laws, or pensions? If raising money to pay for these things was the only reason for taxes, however, we could have a much simpler system. If we raised the rate of income tax by 2 per cent, we could abolish inheritance tax and capital gains tax and still make money. Or we could raise the rate of value added tax and abolish most of income tax. Would that be fair? Would it be efficient?

Another purpose behind taxation is the redistribution of wealth and income. Certain aspects of this idea are generally agreed. It is generally—but not universally—agreed that income tax should be "progressive", and that some government revenue should be spent on welfare services. This was a major reason why the poll tax was so unpopular. People thought it unfair that everyone should pay *the same* tax, whether they were rich or poor, just because they lived in the same town. An unpopular tax is a failure—it loses politicians votes, and it proves too expensive to collect. Of course, for any tax the questions of rate and amount are of immense importance. *How* progressive should income tax be? *How much* should be spent on social services? Once upon a time it was considered right that income tax had a top rate of 98 per cent. Does anyone think that right now? Few do, but "once upon a time" was only 20 years ago. Fashions change in tax as in all else.

Another purpose behind imposing taxes is control of the economy. Changes in taxation can and do affect the economy, but

4

control is also exercised by adjusting the money supply and credit. A good example of using tax to control behaviour is the use of customs duties. There used to be a very high customs duty on imported leather. The aim was to protect the Scottish leather industry. This tax was successful because it collected no money! This also shows that taxes are not used only to raise money. That is an important point. One main way in which taxes are used to influence people is by what is *not* taxed. For instance, we put value added tax on most things that people buy, but we do not tax medicines.

Taxes may also be used as a kind of social control. We see this idea concerning the taxing of alcohol and tobacco. More recently, politicians have decided that cars are less of a good thing, so they have started increasing the cost of petrol by increasing the tax on it.

We can also use taxes to make sure people pay the full price for something. This is the idea of a pollution tax. When I buy goods, I pay the price the seller asks. That makes the seller a profit and meets the costs. What if the seller has polluted the local area while making the goods? Perhaps the seller has made something that I am going to dump untidily when I have finished with it (like car tyres or plastic bags)? Taxes can be used to impose the cost of destroying the tyre and collecting up the bags. This is a matter of debate at present. It is not widely used as a form of tax in Britain. There is an informal levy imposed by sellers on the price of every tyre to pay for its destruction. In 1996 a landfill tax was introduced. Others may follow.

Principles of Taxation

Choices of taxes, and the reasons for taxes, is a fascinating topic of academic analysis and discussion. It leads on to an easy question that it is almost impossible to answer: what is the best form of tax? That debate was started in this country by a former customs official, Adam Smith in *The Wealth of Nations* (first published in 1776). Smith set out four "canons" that, in his view, lead to better taxes. In modified form, they still influence official thinking today. The four axioms are:

- people should contribute taxes in proportion to their incomes and wealth;
- taxes should be certain, not arbitrary;
- taxes should be levied in the most convenient way;
- the costs of imposing and collecting taxes should be kept minimal.

To this we must add a modern canon: taxes should be both convenient and competitive internationally. We are a trading nation, and we trade in a global economy.

Taxation, then, can be used for several purposes other than collection money. For more detailed discussion, see Kay and King, *The British Tax System*.[1] There is another side to the question of "better" taxes. If a tax operates in a certain way that they can sidestep (such as stamp duty taxing documents, but not oral transactions), people will change the way they do things to pay less tax. That is human nature. A tax that does not alter behaviour is said to be *neutral*. The aim of those designing taxes is to create neutral taxes, unless policy requires a tax to be non-neutral. In practice, taxes often have unintended side-effects. The United Kingdom suffers, some allege, from this problem of non-neutral taxes. This allegation is scrutinised closely in Kay and King's volume.

Is taxation fair?

Let us look at the tax system from the point of view of justice. The current thinking on this matter concentrates on *equity*, which in this context means fairness. *Horizontal equity* is the idea that people in equal circumstances should pay an equal amount of tax. *Vertical equity* means that people in different circumstances should pay an appropriately different amount of tax.

Horizontal equity commands strong support. It was the reason that Adam Smith invented income tax, and it is still a major reason for that form of tax today. Those with similar levels of income should pay similar levels of tax. Why should that be so? There are several ways of justifying the levels of tax paid by individuals. One economic view is the ability-to-pay argument. On that basis, those with equal ability to pay should pay equally. Another economic view is the benefit argument. Those who pay tax should do so according to the benefits they gain. Leaving aside personal circumstances (for example, that A needs more help than B because A is older/younger/less fit than B), again those with similar means should be paying similar taxes. The same result is achieved by taking the lawyer's view of fairness that "we are all equal before the law", or the democratic

---

[1] Oxford University Press (1995).

Principles of Taxation

view that we are all members of the same society, and are equal within it.

Vertical equity is much more controversial. It is generally agreed that the richer should pay more tax than the poorer. That was why so many people did not like the poll tax, and found it "unfair". Incidentally, they effectively threw out the benefit argument in so doing, and dismissed the "equal before the law" view as insufficient. But how much more should the richer be paying? Even with a proportional tax the richer do pay more than the poorer. If there were an income tax at a flat rate of 30 per cent, someone with an income of £100,000 would pay £30,000 in tax. This is more than the £300 that someone with an income of £1,000 would pay. Should the person with £100,000 pay more tax than the person with £1,000 not merely absolutely but also proportionally? This is where a progressive tax comes in. Instead of paying at 30 per cent, those on £100,000 income should pay rather more (at least, on part of their income), and those with £1,000 rather less. Again the details become as important as the principle. Precisely what percentage? And on precisely what part of the income? Why?

An important aspect of the justice—or otherwise—of the tax system is the *tax base*. The base of a tax means the thing, transaction, or amount on which the tax is raised. All taxes have bases—whether the base is you (in the case of a poll tax), your income, your wealth, the number of shoes you buy, or whatever. This means the precise boundary of what is taxed as distinct from what is not taxed. Let us take an example. Hal has £100,000 in hand. He uses it to buy a house in which he then lives, paying no rent. Cher also has £100,000 in hand. She spends it on buying company shares. She lives in a rented house. Hal pays no tax on the use he has made of his £100,000 (the occupation of his house). Cher does pay tax on the use she has made of her £100,000 (the dividends). Is this fair?

As Adam Smith pointed out, another aspect of justice is certainty. The tax system should be clear, so that a taxpayer can see in advance how much tax must be paid. Secondly, enforcement should be consistent and universal. There is nothing more destructive of taxpayer morality than the suspicion that others are not paying. If you pay only half your income tax because of a trick, why should I pay more than that? Equally, if you get some form of special allowance, why should I not get one too? But if neither of us understands the law, we do not know if we are paying enough. So, certainty also requires rules that can be understood. This thought leads to another of the paradoxes of tax. The simpler the rules are, the less fair they are (because they ignore justified differences). But the fairer they are, the more complex they are. The more complex they are, the harder they are to understand and put into effect. Therefore they are less certain and, arguably, therefore less fair. If both simplicity and complexity lead to unfairness, is there a happy medium?

Is taxation efficient?

The fourth Smithian canon is cost-effectiveness. The effectiveness of a tax system is partly a matter of success in enforcement, and partly a matter of the total cost of running it and complying with it. Some think that enforcement, in the case of income tax, is not showing a very high success rate. There has grown up what we call the black economy, meaning moonlighting and other forms of tax evasion. Moonlighting is the practice of earning and paying tax on a source of income properly, but then undertaking a second job without declaring the tax. Then there are the ghosts—those who do not appear on any tax department records, and therefore pay no tax. Or do they? In practice, they may pay no direct income tax, but they would be hard put also to avoid all VAT.

Currently, the cost of collecting the Inland Revenue taxes is about 2 per cent of the total net yield, and the cost of collecting the Customs and Excise duties varies from tax to tax. But, of course, this deals only with the direct government costs. There are also hidden *compliance costs*, that is, the costs incurred by taxpayers in paying taxes. Two notable examples of these compliance costs are the costs of an employer for staff hours acting as an unpaid collector of income tax for the Revenue under the PAYE system, and the costs of a trader in complying with the VAT system. Both may also incur substantial costs for professional assistance and advice concerning tax affairs.

There is also an even more deeply hidden cost, a kind of social cost, which the community as a whole pays as part of the price of taxation. What we have in mind is the expenditure (one might almost say waste) of brain-power. Some of the best brains in the country are exclusively devoted to tax matters; some on the Revenue side, some against the Revenue. This brain-power could be better employed in increasing the wealth, health or happiness of the community. In the past, this brain-drain was closely linked to the immensity of the rates of tax. If someone is asked to pay 98 per cent income tax, or even 75 per cent tax, there is a high premium on good advice to avoid it. If income tax had a maximum rate of, say, 10 per cent, much less time and effort would be devoted to escaping the tax. But what would the state stop doing in return?

As for the effects of taxation, we are afraid that this is a topic where asking questions is easier than answering them. Does a high rate of income tax encourage people to work harder or does it discourage them? Most people would say that it discourages them, that it is a disincentive. But it is quite possible to argue that, on the contrary, it spurs people on to earn more, so that even when the tax is paid they will have enough left to live on. Does a high rate of tax on business raise prices? Does a high rate of tax on individuals raise wages and salaries? No one seems to know the answers. A high *average* rate of tax is probably an incentive to work, whereas high *marginal* rates are disincentives.

Of course, the ideal position for the taxpayer confronted with this dilemma is to ensure that whatever others pay, I pay no more tax than I must. In considering this, it is very important to emphasise the distinction between *tax avoidance* and *tax evasion*. Tax avoidance is so arranging my affairs within the rules that I pay the smallest tax bill that is possible. This is perfectly lawful. Tax evasion is when you escape tax by unlawful means. This usually involves some form of dishonesty, ranging from omitting to state some item of income in a tax return to forging a document to create untrue "facts". It is not easy to see (and keep to) the distinction between evasion and avoidance—if needed, evasion involves some crime where avoidance involves no crime. Two factors blur this distinction in practice. First, some quite honourable people think that a tax crime is not "really" a crime at all. What is "really" wrong with omitting to mention in a tax return some jobbing gardening or book-reviewing done at weekends? We tend to think that what we do ourselves is not really criminal at all. What others do is always bigger and badder. The second factor is that crime versus no crime is not the last word on the subject. Elaborate schemes of tax avoidance that have no other purpose may not be criminal, but they are distasteful to many taxpayers and to some judges. Some schemes come near the line—so much so that a word has been coined for them, avoision.

Some taxes are more easily avoided than others. For example, income tax is more easily avoided than VAT. It is partly for this reason that governments have made a big switch from income tax to VAT. We did not have VAT as a tax in 1970. Just 25 years later is it our second biggest tax. Indeed, replacement of income tax by an expenditure tax is advocated in some quarters. The merits of this are said to be that it would be less easily avoided or evaded, it would encourage saving, and it would be cheaper to administer. (Remember that the cost of collecting Customs and Excise duties is less than the cost of collecting Inland Revenue taxes). On the other hand it contradicts the progressive principle. An expenditure tax hits the poor harder than it would hit the rich. So there are two strong ideas for the "reform" of taxation recently advocated which are in direct conflict of each other—the idea of an expenditure tax and the idea of a wealth tax. But neither actually exists.

International aspects

We added a new principle to those of Adam Smith. It is that our rules have to work in the international arena. There are two aspects to this. First, we are now part of the European Union, and must comply with its rules. Secondly, there is strong tax competition between states. Tax systems are as much part of the global marketplace as any other aspect of a country. Both are extremely important in any overall view of current British tax policy. There is another dilemma here: we must both join them and beat them.

Say it softly, but Britain's entry into the E.U. limited the powers of the British Parliament and Government in respect of taxation. Certain Articles of the E.C. Treaty prohibit rules of tax that would discriminate against persons in other Member States. Another Article provides for Member States to work towards tax harmonisation, at least on indirect taxes—those on goods. This movement has progressed farthest in the field of VAT. It is partly why VAT is now so important as a British tax, but it is not the only reason. For most of British—and before it, English—history, the extraordinary revenues of the Crown (as taxes were called) came from customs duties on imports, and from excises. Excises have now been replaced by VAT—a European tax. Customs have now been replaced by the Community customs regime. So much so is this that to call the relevant collection department "Her Majesty's Customs and Excise"—as we do—is a bit of a misnomer. It would be more accurate to call it "Her Majesty's VAT and Duties"—but it is nothing like as romantic. It would be even less romantic—and even more accurate to call it "Her Majesty's part of the European VAT and Duties". But that might invoke the response given to Alice by the Queen of Hearts.

Our direct taxes have not been affected by the rising tide of E.U. law. Well, even that is not true, as we shall see. We might avoid the E.U. tide. We cannot avoid the currents caused by global tax competition. Ours is a world of tax havens (or tax heavens as French students consistently mistranslate "paradis fiscaux"), customs unions, free trade zones, enterprise zones, special regimes, favourable treaty resorts, tax holidays, free depreciation regimes ... in short, a highly competitive marketplace. We shall return at the end of the book to some international issues that our tax system has to solve. But we must now begin at the beginning.

Introducing the Taxes

We want to finish this introduction, and start our detailed analysis of tax, by introducing the taxes dealt with in this book and then by referring generally to the kinds of taxes that exist, and the issues that each tax must tackle. We want to try to state in a very few words what it is that each tax is taxing.

First, **income tax**. Why? Because it is in government terms the largest revenue raiser, and therefore the most important tax. And because, with corporation tax, it is the most complex tax, and the hardest to understand. And because it involves significant efforts by lawyers and accountants to ensure that their clients comply with the law, and avoid its excesses. What does it tax? In a famous aphorism in *London County Council v. Attorney-General* (H.L.), Lord Macnaghten said: "Income tax, if I may be pardoned for saying so, is a tax on income." This is largely, but not absolutely, true. There are some items of income that are not taxed; for example, student grants. So income tax is not a tax on all income. On the other hand, there are some charges to income tax that are imposed on receipts that are not income tax receipts, but rather capital receipts. This is so, for example, of the taxing of premiums received on the leasing of land. Anyway, what is income? Such questions are why we wrote a good part of this book!

Secondly, **VAT** (which is what the Act imposing value added tax calls it, so we shall too). Why? Because it recently became the second most important tax in fiscal terms. Secondly, it has become the most litigated of the taxes, and is gaining in complexity and practical importance each year.

Thirdly, social security contributions (or **NI contributions** as everyone and everything except the law itself terms them), which are the third source of government finance, and, for most people, a second income tax. The law is less complex and comprehensive by far than income tax law, so requires less extended treatment.

How Tax Ticks

Fourthly, **capital gains tax (CGT)**. Its fiscal significance is trivial compared with the taxes so far listed. Nevertheless, its complexity—and therefore its nuisance value to lawyers—far outweighs its importance in filling a gap in the income tax. What it taxes is the gain represented by the difference between the price at which an item was acquired and the price at which it is sold. Since 1982 this taxes the *real* gain (taking account of inflation), not the *cash* gain.

Fifthly, **corporation tax**. This is simply the income tax and capital gains tax imposed on companies. Well, not simply—parts are fiendishly complicated, although we will try to avoid the worst of it!

Sixthly, **inheritance tax (IHT)** or, as it used to be called before they thought it fun to change its name, capital transfer tax. It still is a tax on capital transfers, and has never been a tax on inheritances, but what does that matter? It is a tax on transfers of property by certain gifts, by transfers into trust, and by operation of law on someone's death from that person's estate. Although whether or not it is accurately named does not matter, accurate advice on where it may affect capital transfers is important to many lawyers. Again we must examine it in detail.

Seventhly, **stamp duties** and the stamp duty reserve tax. These are taxes imposed upon certain specified documents and transactions, notably transfers of land (including house and other buildings) and transfer of shares. This is one of the simplest and most effective of taxes. But it can also add an unwanted extra layer of tax to formal transfers of property, and is again therefore of concern to property lawyers.

Collecting taxes

All these taxes, and all other taxes in Britain, can be grouped under three broad heads of taxation in terms of the way they are imposed and collected: withholding taxes, taxation related to particular transactions or their effects (called transactions taxes for short), and taxes based on profits or wealth of any kind (assessed taxes). British taxes are of all these kinds, frequently muddled up together.

A withholding tax is a tax imposed on the payer of a sum so that the recipient receives less than would otherwise be received. For example, someone paying patent royalties to another person will be required to deduct from that sum an amount equal to the basic rate of income tax. If this is done, the recipient is treated as having paid tax on those royalties. The tax authorities are always on the lookout for ways of increasing the payment of taxes at source in this way. Most income tax and NI contributions are now collected in this way through the PAYE system. Under most forms of withholding tax, the payer is liable to pay the tax to the tax authorities even though they did not deduct it from the payment and even though it was the *recipient* who was really supposed to be paying the tax.

Transactions taxes are those based on particular transactions or their results. VAT is usually imposed on any supply of goods or services made by a business. Stamp duty is imposed whenever a document is used (as it must be) to transfer land. Inheritance tax and capital gains tax can be regarded as being, in one sense, transactions taxes. But the charge on an estate at death is a sort of indirect wealth tax.

Assessed taxes are the most usual kinds of taxes in Britain. Income tax raises most of its money from the income of the employed, the self-employed and those with investment income. So does the National Insurance Fund through NI contributions. Then there are the special taxes like petroleum revenue tax.

Anatomy of a tax

Whichever form of tax we adopt, and whatever the fiscal or other reasons for its adoption, the lawyer's task is to identify when it is payable and when not. Tax law, or revenue law as many also call it, is there to define when taxes shall be charged. In respect of each tax this definition will contain the same elements:

- the tax base;
- the incidence (including the rate) of the tax; and
- the taxpayer, or person liable to pay.

The rate is often the most important politically or commercially, but rarely detains the lawyer long. The other issues need further thought.

The tax base, as we have seen already, is the asset, transaction, profit or other thing which is liable to the tax. This may be anything from a television to the net profits of a year's trading. Each tax will have a limited tax base, the limits being of two kinds: the general limits on that kind of tax, and specific exceptions. Clearly, the wider the tax base of a tax, the more revenue it will collect. The more exceptions that are allowed, the smaller the return from the tax.

Over the years, all our main taxes have become subject to important exceptions. This is partly because granting an exception is very easy politically, and votes are not easily won for removing it later. Nonetheless, in the last few years more attention has been turned to both the limits on the tax bases of our taxes and the width of exceptions. It has become commonplace to regard exceptions as tax expenditures, that is, subsidies created by the tax not collected. The cost of these tax expenditures has often been worked out. As a result, some longstanding exceptions and reliefs from tax have been removed, such as the life assurance relief that lasted from 1842 to 1984. This trend is continuing.

The second issue is the identity of the taxpayer. Economists talk of this as the incidence of the tax, distinguishing between the *formal incidence* of the tax (who is required by law to pay it) and the *effective incidence* (who ends up paying). Lawyers are concerned only with formal incidence. In most cases under modern laws different people can be made to pay in respect of some taxes, especially when withholding taxes are used to collect the tax. For example, if someone makes a gift of shares to someone else on which inheritance tax ought to be paid, the authorities can try to collect the tax from the donor, the recipient and most subsequent owners of the shares.

Tax Authorities

Two main government departments administer our taxes: the Inland Revenue and Customs and Excise. The Contributions Agency of the Department of Social Security has executive responsibility for collecting and accounting for NI contributions. Customs and Excise is responsible for VAT, but all the taxes described in this book apart from those are administered by the Inland Revenue.

The **Revenue** is more formally known as the Commissioners of Inland Revenue. The commissioners are appointed under the Inland Revenue Regulation Act 1890 for the collection and management of inland revenue. The powers of the commissioners to deal with income tax, corporation tax and capital gains tax are set out in the Taxes Management Act 1970. Formally, the care and management of these are in the hands of the commissioners acting together as the Board. The Board is based at Somerset House on the Strand in London.

The Revenue is run through the head office in London, supported by specialist offices (for example for stamp duty, petroleum revenue

Tax Authorities

tax, and valuation questions) with a national network of district offices under a regional structure. The main functions of the Revenue are divided into the inspection function and the collection function. Inspectors (known formally as Her Majesty's Inspectors of Taxes) are appointed for each district. Your local inspector will therefore be the inspector for the district responsible for collecting your taxes. For the self-employed this will be a local office (for example, Oxford). For employees, it is the office that deals with the employer (for example Wrexham 1, the office dealing with employers in part of London). The inspectors have the formal power to require information and make assessments. They are supported by specialist staff in the regional and national offices. The tax is collected by collectors of tax through a separate operation, much of which is now based in Scotland.

The processes of assessment and collection are part-way through a complete change. The traditional approach was "us and them", where all assessments and demands were made by inspectors or collectors and their staff, with the taxpayer supplying information or following procedures in a passive role. Over the last few years the whole of the revenue operation was being computerised and placed on a self-assessment basis. This has involved simplifying and codifying laws and practices. It also involves transferring the duty to decide tax liability to the taxpayer. Inspectors are being reallocated to advisory and enforcement duties, with the mechanical work being done by machine.

These processes of codification, mechanisation and self-assessment are also being adopted for NI contributions. At the same time the staff of the **Contributions Agency** are working more closely with the Revenue. Much of the collection work of contributions is performed by the Revenue on an agency basis.

Customs is the colloquial term used for Her Majesty's Commissioners of Customs and Excise. Tradition, and law, provides that they are appointed under the Great Seal of the United Kingdom. The pomp and circumstance perhaps reflects the long history of those officials, now presiding jointly over the oldest government department of all. In practical terms, the powers of Customs now come from two sources. The United Kingdom legislation is the Customs and Excise Management Act 1979. Powers for collection of customs itself, and aspects of the indirect taxes, arise directly under European Community law. In practice, customs officers have the widest powers of any government officials. This is because one part of their job is tackling smuggling, contraband, arms trading and, above all, illegal drugs sales. That part of their functions is separate from the VAT organisation. This is based at Southend, and is run through a national network of local VAT offices. The local office is responsible for all aspects of the operation of the tax locally, although it is supported by both national computer facilities and national staff. Most of the task of determining and collecting VAT is placed on those registered for VAT. The main job of VAT staff is therefore checking that the tax is being collected properly.

Why do we have two tax departments? Increasingly, countries are combining their tax departments into one, for example the Danish Customs and Tax Department. The more that tax administration becomes the province of the computer and self-assessment, the less sense it makes to have separate tax departments that may compete and may conflict. Nor does it make much sense to have different powers, or even different registration numbers, for different taxes. Once upon a time, the reason for different administration was a deliberate inbuilt inefficiency in the tax service, and the sharply different nature of customs work to tax work. Then there were several different sets of tax officials. The historic reasons for the different administrations have long ceased to provide justification of themselves for the current separation, but tradition is itself a powerful force in tax matters.

Controlling the tax authorities

It is important to note that each of the tax authorities is constrained to act only within the legislative powers at its disposal. As we explore in the next chapter, the United Kingdom has no constitution. It therefore has no constitutional limits on executive action. History is replete with examples of tax authorities being used to extract taxes for dubious official use. In most advanced states, there are therefore constitutional checks on such action. Lacking such limits in the United Kingdom, it has been left to judges to prevent the use of arbitrary power. They have been alert to ensure that a tax authority has clear legal authority both to collect a tax, and to carry out the procedures necessary to do this. Taxpayers have also been alert to ensure that any apparent stepping beyond the limits is challenged. The result is a developed administrative law of taxation. If you look at any book on constitutional and administrative law, you will see a significant number of tax cases cited. It is precisely because it is only through such cases that the balance has been struck between the Executive and the taxpayer.

Tax Authorities

At the same time, the fair enforcement of a tax such as income tax depends heavily on taxpayers honestly providing information about what they are earning. Authorities need strong powers to obtain information and collect taxes from those who do not comply readily or who are dishonest. A balance has to be struck between giving powers to the tax authorities on the one side, and on respecting rights of taxpayers on the other. In particular, individual taxpayers do not expect their privacy to be invaded by tax officers, nor do businesses wish to sacrifice commercial confidentiality. Both will want to be inconvenienced to the minimum extent by the process of collecting and paying taxes.

The balance is struck in three ways. First, the powers of the tax authorities are limited by law, and often subject to internal safeguards. These are found in the Taxes Management Act, the Customs and Excise Management Act, and the Acts providing for individual taxes. Secondly, a dispute about either the law or the facts (and often also the procedure) can be referred to independent tribunals and courts. Thirdly, independent reviewers can check the fairness and efficacy of administrative issues.

Tax appeals

Tax appeals against assessments to the Inland Revenue taxes go to appeal tribunals or to the courts. The appeal tribunals are, confusingly, called the General Commissioners and the Special Commissioners. General Commissioners (or, formally, Commissioners for the General Purposes of the Income Tax) are roughly the tax equivalent of a local magistrates' court. The Commissioners are often not experts in the law or tax, but are local people with financial ability and experience. They meet in divisions, each division having a clerk. Procedure is informal and to some extent varies from division to division. The Specials (Commissioners for the Special Purposes of the Income Tax) are based in London, although they also sit elsewhere. They are tax experts drawn both from the professions and from former Revenue officials, and sit singly. Their proceedings tend to be more formal.

There is a general right of appeal against any assessment to income tax, corporation tax or CGT given by section 31 of the Taxes Management Act. Taxpayers have a right to choose whether to appeal to the local General Commissioners or to refer the matter to the Specials. The two groups of Commissioners have the right to transfer cases between them. The Commissioners, when they hear a case, have the right to look anew at any matter of law or fact referred to them, and they can dismiss or alter any assessment in any way they consider to be justified.

Appeal from the Commissioners to the courts is only allowed on a question of law: section 56 of the Taxes Management Act. This is restrictive of the rights of the courts to interfere in the administration of taxes. It effectively prevents judges from deciding a tax case as such. The distinction between law and fact is, however, not an easy one. We explore it in the "Escape to Victory" decision in the next chapter, but you should also read *Edwards v. Bairstow* (1952). Appeals from the Commissioners are made by way of case stated to the Chancery Division.

Reports of the decisions of Commissioners have long been secret, as have the hearings. The taxpayer could technically release them, but hardly ever does. The Revenue never published them, and had no authority to do so. A recent change in the law allows selected decisions to be released for publication. Some are now published commercially as *Simons Tax Cases Special Commissioners' Decisions*.

VAT appeals go to the VAT and Duties Tribunal (VADT), mainly because of section 83 of the Value Added Tax Act. This contains a long, but by no means comprehensive, list of matters that can be appealed. The VADT headquarters is now at the same offices (in Bedford Square) as the Specials, and the President of the VADT is the same person as the Presiding Special Commissioner. There are also a growing number of individuals who are both VADT chairmen and Special Commissioners or Deputy Special Commissioners. However, there are also still considerable differences between the VADT and the Specials, so they cannot yet be regarded as a tax court. Procedure before a VADT can also be informal.

Appeals from the VADT are treated as appeals on administrative law and therefore go as part of the Crown Office list before the Queen's Bench Division. Consequently, they are heard by different judges to the income tax appeals. This sometimes leads to interesting contrasts of approach in the High Court between the two taxes on similar questions.

Appeals go from both divisions to the Court of Appeal and—often in tax cases—to the House of Lords. Cases may leapfrog direct to the Court of Appeal, as did *Willoughby* (1995) mentioned in the next chapter. If a point of European law is involved, cases can go direct to the European Court of Justice under Article 177 of the E.C. Treaty at any level. The VADT has referred several important issues direct to the ECJ without waiting for the British courts to be involved. The Commissioners and VADT also operate in Scotland and Northern Ireland, but appeals on questions of law go to the Scottish and northern courts. We discuss how this appeal system works in the next chapter.

Tax reviews

There are two more informal ways in which taxpayers can get cases reviewed. The first is to refer matters to the Revenue Adjudicator (who is also the Customs Adjudicator, and the Adjudicator for contributions questions). The office of adjudicator is informal, but provides a way in which a dissatisfied customer (as taxpayers are called in marketspeak) can get a file reopened and looked at afresh.

The Parliamentary Ombudsman provides a semi-formal method of reviewing complaints of taxpayers. The Parliamentary Ombudsman is an officer of parliament who has the specific job of investigating allegations that injustice has been caused to complainants by means of maladministration by a government department. Complaints to the Ombudsman are routed through the complainant's M.P. Complaints can result in financial redress. This may be appropriate where no formal appeal is possible, or where the Revenue or Customs have applied a rule in a way that may strictly be correct, but has worked unfairly (for example, they have enforced the rule unevenly).

The tax professions

Our final introductory topic is that of the professional status of those who advise on tax matters. The Revenue has its own high grade training operation, and Customs also does much training, but this training is aimed at the personnel of the tax departments.

Taxpayers' advisers may belong to several professions or to none. Unlike the legal profession, but following the general approach taken to accountants in the country, the tax profession is an open profession not a closed profession. This means that a tax practitioner does not need a specific qualification to deal with tax affairs. Qualifications are only needed to represent a taxpayer before an appeal tribunal, and there the qualifications of both lawyers and accountants are recognised.

More generally, the complexity of tax makes a professional training advisable to any tax practitioner. There are, however, three

How Tax Ticks

separate routes to such status. The only specialist body covering the full range of taxation is the Chartered Institute of Taxation, whose members style themselves tax practitioners. Many tax practitioners are also lawyers (perhaps associated with the Revenue Bar or specialist solicitors), or accountants (where they may be associated with the Tax Faculty established by the Institute of Chartered Accountants of England and Wales). More recently, an Institute of Indirect Tax Practitioners has been established. A fourth source of private tax practitioners is former staff of the tax departments. However, as the profession is an open one, so that no qualification is needed to claim expertise in tax, there is also a range of less formally qualified advisers, and also limited companies, operating in the field. As this book shows, it is increasingly difficult to justify expertise in the field without a formal qualification. In Germany, for example, where tax is largely a closed profession, it has been stated that no individual can properly claim to be an expert in the whole field of taxation. It could be argued that tax is noticeably more complicated in the United Kingdom than Germany.

Tax laws may be compared more with an iceberg than an elephant. They are certainly vast and often grey to the outsider. In practice, you will find that there is a lot more to it when you examine it closely than is seen by those who merely view it from a distance. Let us learn how to handle the ice.

Chapter 2

HANDLING TAX LAWS

Tax is often regarded as being about numbers. Tax law is about words. It is an odd thing that many lawyers seem worried about tax, because they are worried about the numbers, while many others are worried about tax, because they are worried about the words! What needs to be understood by many lawyers is that you can be a completely sound tax lawyer yet leave the numbers for others to work out. That is the approach taken in this book. Any examples will be simple ones! At the same time, it is of the highest importance that a tax lawyer is fully competent at interpreting and applying the laws that impose taxes. This is because, quite simply, every tax case is a case about statutory interpretation and application.

The purpose of this chapter is to make an initial survey of the raw material of a tax lawyer's work—the statutes and other materials to be used in finding out what the relevant tax law for a particular matter is, what that law means, and how it is to be applied. To do this we must first reflect on the history of tax law. Despite Mr Ford's views on such things, it is not bunk. We must also examine the territorial extent of the tax laws. Having set the scene, we look at the forms of tax legislation, and the current high levels of criticism about those forms. Another point of importance is finding out about the current law. Tax law changes with extreme rapidity, and to be out of date is easy but useless. How are tax questions researched? That we must explore. We then look at how the laws are handled—the methods of interpretation and application, including some thoughts on the use of techniques to avoid the application of tax laws. Some of what we say is relevant to the study of any statute law. That does not make it any less important. On the contrary, the techniques involved are central to a lawyer's skills, and repetition of them is always justified.

Handling Tax Laws

History

It is no coincidence that some of the oldest documents in existence are tax returns. We hold tax laws from over four millennia ago in the British Museum archives. Wherever there is social organisation, there is also tax, unless there is almost total slavery or serfdom. Even in the shorter history of England (and the much shorter history of Great Britain) taxation played a central role. It lay behind several rebellions (including, of course, that of the American colonies) and the failure of governments, both ancient and modern. We will not stray into those areas now, fascinating as they are, just for their own sake. Happily, others have chronicled the subject with care. Pre-eminent among recent historians is Basil Sabine, whose *History of Income Tax* and well-written contributions to the *British Tax Review* are of considerable help. Stephen Dowell's *History of Taxation*, written at the beginning of this century, spans the previous 600 years, but is sadly found in too few libraries.

Is not the history of tax yet more clutter in the study of a complex subject? We think not. We need to examine the backgrounds of our taxes. This is because some of them are old and understandable only in the context of their origins. Others of our taxes may be new but there are lessons to be learnt from previous experiments that are of continuing relevance.

The oldest taxes in this book are the stamp duties. These were introduced in 1694 by William of Orange. They were a direct import from his home territories. The proceeds were exported, in the shape of the English Navy, to fight the French. The taxes have changed little since, although technology is now overtaking them.

The next tax to be introduced was the income tax. Its proceeds were also exported to fight the French. It was adopted in 1799 as a temporary tax to finance the war against Napoleon. At the time, it replaced, and to some extent copied, what were known as the assessed taxes and land tax that had been used for over a century before. The need for new revenue was desperate. The usual practice until then had to be to tax things. In large part this was done by customs duties, the takings from which were reduced sharply by the war at sea. In Britain itself, the usual practice was to put excise taxes on things—windows, servants, tea, wigs—but these were not enough. Pitt therefore introduced a "contribution on property, profits and income". It was based on a voluntary declaration that the sum of money paid was "not less than ten per centum" of the contributor's income. Not surprisingly, it did not raise much. In

1802, after a lull in the fighting, the tax was repealed. In 1803, it was reintroduced by Addington in a more efficient form. So efficient, indeed, was it that the tax still has much of the form given it by the 1803 Act—and a surprising amount of the original wording. Addington's Act lasted to 1815, when peace finally arrived and the tax expired automatically. For 27 years, land taxes and trade taxes were again used, but they proved too weak a tax base for the emerging economy. In 1842 the income tax, still much in its 1803 form, was reintroduced as a temporary measure. The need for revenues might again have had something to do with ships, as that year we seized Hong Kong. Income tax has been with us ever since, although it is still in form a temporary measure.

During its long history the details of the income tax have been chopped and changed by governments. For example, in 1910 we needed some more ships, so a higher rate of tax (in the guise of supertax) was proposed. That is one reason why the present tax is so difficult to understand. It is not the work of any one committee or team of drafters, but a patchwork of the efforts of innumerable minds with differing and often unstated aims. Every so often, someone has a go at sorting it out, but they have rarely succeeded in changing much.

It was always thus. Back in 1752, Lord Chesterfield and other "backbench" reformers wanted to change the calendar to get rid of the extra 11 days that had crept into the measurement of the year under the Julian calendar. In those days the official year started on March 25 (Lady Day). Lord Chesterfield and colleagues got their way and, despite rioting, the middle of September (mid-year) was removed in 1752. The end of the year was left as March 24, 1753—except for the Treasury. Then, as now, to lose 11 days from a financial year was just too expensive. So the tax year continued to April 5, 1753. For income tax, it still does, 240 years later. With the daily revenue from the tax exceeding £1 billion, it is unlikely to change.

There have been some spirited attempts to knock the income tax into shape. A Royal Commission on Income Tax had a go in 1920 (Cmd. 615). A few changes followed. More ambitious was a Codification Committee in 1936 (Cmd. 5131). This conducted the monumental task of sieving through our then tax laws to find the principles and the problems. It is a fascinating study which still repays the reading, but it was never implemented. There was another Royal Commission in the early 1950s, reporting in 1953 (Cmd. 8671), 1954 (Cmd. 9105) and 1955 (Cmd. 9474). It led to several changes but no substantial restructuring. There was an unofficial attempt by a committee on the structure and reform of direct taxation (and published by the Institute for Fiscal Studies under that name), chaired by Sir James Meade, a Nobel Laureate in economics. It advocated scrapping income tax to replace it by an expenditure tax. It didn't happen. But the work had some effect, in particular invigorating economic thought about our taxes and spawning work such as the brilliant summary by Kay and King, *The British Tax System* (above). If anything beyond black letter law interests you, read it.

None of these initiatives did anything to improve the shape of the income tax. Finally (so far), a more serious attempt than most was started in 1995 when years of grumbling boiled up into a most unusual statutory requirement that something be done (see section 160 of the Finance Act 1995, passed against the wishes of the government). We will discuss below what is being attempted. But even this looks as though it will be a reform within the thinking imposed in 1803, and there is much caution in changing key terminology despite—or because of—the passage of two centuries. There is just a faint chance that now we don't need so many ships, the income tax (which was in essence always a war tax) may be allowed to fade away. Otherwise we may well enter the new millennium with a law framed by those whose thinking predated the French Empire. The inertia of a system that raises so much revenue is too great.

Only one improvement has been achieved over the years. This is the regular consolidation of the income tax. The 1842 Act did a bit of tidying, and some more was done in 1853. That was kept going until 1918 when, under the strains of yet another war, the laws were consolidated. The 1918 text was strengthened on several occasions (notably 1936 and during the next war). It lasted until 1952 when a new consolidation changed the structure of the tax and attempted to give it a more modern appearance. It was given another structure and another consolidation in 1970, and yet another structure and yet another consolidation in 1988. But until 1995, it had never been simplified, just allowed to grow. For example, by 1995 the 1988 Act had grown from 845 sections to over 1100, and 12 Schedules had been added to the original 31—with hundreds of pages of additional law in the Finance Acts passed since 1988. Hidden at the heart of it is still the old flagship of the Napoleonic fleet, the 1803 Act, never codified and never reformed. It still cruises on, as old as the *Victory*, but never dry-docked and with a hull encrusted with the sharp barnacles of decades of judicial precedent and corroded by decades

HISTORY

of administrative compromise. We must treat it, as the Navy treats the *Victory*, with the respect due to it. But we must not be surprised if it does not always feel as comfortable as a modern vessel.

Alongside the main Act are other supporting Acts. The 1970 consolidation split the 1952 Income Tax Act into three: an Income and Corporation Taxes Act (1970), a Taxes Management Act (1970) and a Capital Allowances Act (1968). The current Acts are now the 1988 Income and Corporation Taxes Act, the 1970 Taxes Management Act, and a 1990 Capital Allowances Act.

Compared with the old taxes, the other taxes in this volume are comparatively modern. Corporation tax was introduced in the Finance Act 1965, as a modernisation of a profits tax on companies introduced in the last world war. It was, despite its name, devised as a parasite on the income tax and integrated into the 1970 consolidation Act. It was reformed heavily in 1972, and again in the 1980s. Only in the last few years do we see it emerging as a separate tax, with separate rules for calculating income, rather that something best described as "the same, but different".

Capital gains tax (CGT) also appeared in 1965, in the wake of a Labour Party election victory in 1964, but succeeding to measures first introduced by the Conservatives in 1962. In reality, it was and is a device for plugging obvious gaps in the tax base of income tax. In some other countries it is part of the income tax. Maybe it should be here too.

Social security contributions, in their present form, came into being in 1973. The law was consolidated into a Social Security Act in 1975, and into a Social Security (Contributions and Benefits) Act 1992. The idea of special contributions towards funding social insurance dates back to 1911, when the idea was adopted from Germany. It was modified in 1948 after the last world war, and again in 1973 when the funding for social security was heavily in deficit. Since 1973, contributions on both employees and the self-employed have been a second form of income tax, but only since 1994 has any attempt been made to make the two taxes work together.

Value added tax (VAT) also appeared in 1973, but for a very different reason. VAT is a peace tax. Several of our taxes were introduced in order to help us beat our European neighbours. This one was introduced so we could join them. The adoption of VAT was a precondition of our entry into the European Community—now the European Union. It is the only permissible form of general indirect tax, or sales tax, in the Member States of the E.U. This is

25

because it proved to be the only major tax that could offer a neutral way of taxing production and consumption, and also handle international transactions neutrally. It was first introduced in the E.C. in 1967. Its main framework was established in 1977, and now applies not only in all E.U. states, but throughout Europe.

Inheritance tax (IHT) has a shorter but odder (and in one way longer) history. It was introduced in 1974 and 1975 as a tax called capital transfer tax, to replace estate duty (dating from 1894) and to succeed to a tradition of taxing estates on death which predates even William of Orange. It had its name changed in 1984 to the present title, although it was not changed into an inheritance tax. It has been reformed since then, but now looks in some ways rather more like the 1894 Act than the 1974 Act! It has been threatened recently with abolition, but then so have most of the other taxes in this list. If it is abolished, it will only be the third time in our history that an estate duty has been abolished. Each time it has reappeared in a new guise, and with the same problems.

History therefore offers us a range of taxes, some 20 years old and some over 200 years old. It confronts us with a range of approaches and a range of reasons for the form of tax used. More important to us as lawyers, it confronts us with a wide variety of language. Some is the product of the word-processor, while some is only a little younger than the later plays of Shakespeare. It also confronts us with old ideas in new shapes—but we must remember that they are old ideas if we are to treat them correctly.

One old idea is that taxes are annual. Parliament still has to re-enact the income tax legislation every year. If it does not, then there would be no income tax next year. Read section 1 of the Income and Corporation Taxes Act 1988. You will see that it does not operate unless in any year there is a Finance Act imposing the income tax. Then read section 6. You will see that no such provision is necessary for corporation tax. Nor is it a necessary approach for income tax, save for our history. Read the preamble to any Finance Act. You will see that taxes are still granted annually to the Crown, not imposed by it. It is, we are supposed to believe, a voluntary offering. This fiction has the consequence that the income tax this year is different to the income tax last year. Further, a judge cannot assume that there will be an income tax next year. So any case about income tax can only look at what happens this year. If, for example, tax is imposed on a form of income, that form of income must exist this year to be taxed. It is not enough that it existed last year, or might exist next year.

The judicial reaction to the annual nature of income tax is called the source doctrine: see *Brown v. National Provident Institution* (1912) (H.L.). The doctrine means that if, say, a trader retires in one year, and receives income in the next, that income can be taxed in neither year. It was not received in the first year. There was no trade in the second year. It will not surprise you to learn that there are statutory provisions designed to prevent tax avoidance this way, but the doctrine still remains.

Another old approach that also haunts us still is the schedular nature of taxation. Old taxes like the income tax, customs duties, excise taxes and the stamp duties were drawn up as lists: so much to pay on this, and so much to pay on that. They are what is called schedular taxes. Modern taxes like VAT are comprehensive taxes. With a schedular tax, the tax authorities can only collect tax if they can show that what they are trying to tax appears in the list of things to be taxed. There was an extra reason for this in England. Our older taxes emerged at a time when the Stuart kings had developed a habit of raising taxes without asking for parliamentary help. (Like their successors, they needed to raise money for ships.) This was not too popular and led to a change of government and the Bill of Rights. This said that taxes could only be imposed by assent of parliament. For a tax to be imposed, therefore, it has to be shown that parliament has agreed to it. Without clear authority, a tax cannot be raised. This old idea still receives warm support from the judges. Lord Goff said in *Woolwich Building Society v. IRC* (1992):

> "the retention by the state of taxes unlawfully exacted is particularly obnoxious, because it is one of the most fundamental principles of our law ... that taxes should not be levied without the authority of Parliament."

Geography

Our diversions into the past have forced us to talk about England and Britain as well as the United Kingdom. This is because taxes only apply to the territory whose government authorises them. This reflects international practice. One state will not enforce the tax laws of another state without express agreement. Our courts apply this rule: *Government of India v. Taylor* (1955). They also operate on the basis that United Kingdom tax laws apply only in the United Kingdom: *Clark v. Oceanic Contractors* (1983).

For tax purposes, the United Kingdom consists of its four constituent countries together, since 1973, with the territorial sea and continental shelf. This includes, of course, the North Sea oilfields. They have their own tax, the petroleum revenue tax. This is imposed by the Oil Taxation Act 1983. But it is too specialist for a principles book like this.

Even defining the extent of the United Kingdom causes problems in modern tax practice. First, the United Kingdom is legally a union formed of states with a single tax system, but three different legal systems: those of Scotland and Northern Ireland cannot be ignored in the detail of our taxes. In addition, the Scots and Northern Irish have their own appeal systems, generating separate precedents. They are subject only to the unifying influence of the House of Lords—and the European Court of Justice.

The problem of Scottish law is a real one. Its contract laws, property laws, divorce laws, trust laws, and laws of succession are different to those of England. Yet the tax laws are supposed to be enforced throughout the kingdom in an even-handed way. Sometimes this results in separate Scottish terms, or separate Scottish sections. Often the problem is ignored, and the judges are left to do the best they can. This may mean generalising not just the Scottish law, but the English law too: for example *Kidson v. MacDonald* (1974).

At the same time, we are now part of the European Union, and some of our taxes are European taxes, not merely United Kingdom taxes. The territorial boundaries are those of the E.U. not the United Kingdom. Equally, the laws are sometimes those of the Union and not of the Union (if you get my meaning). Take, for example, customs duties. These are now imposed by the Community Customs Code, which applies throughout the European Economic Area, and in Turkey too—19 states (plus a few small states like Monaco) with a common law. VAT applies throughout the European Union, partly again as a result of common laws. Each of the states has accepted that it will enforce the European taxes imposed by all the other member states. Here the old rules and assumptions have been swept away. Sometimes it is English rules that have to be ignored: see *Apple and Pear Development Corporation v. CEC* (1988).

"A Tax Shall Be Charged"

The key sections in any tax law are the charging sections. These are the sections that actually impose the tax. Take them out, and the rest is mere verbiage. They are often signalled by the draftsman stating unambiguously that "a tax shall be charged ... ". Look for

"A Tax Shall Be Charged"

this language in section 1 of the Stamp Act 1891, of the Value Added Tax Act 1994, of the Inheritance Tax Act 1984 or of the Income and Corporation Taxes Act 1988.

These are not the only charging sections in the Acts. Others are often found lurking in the more obscure parts of the Acts, particularly in the 1988 Taxes Act and its many amendments. The multiplicity of charging provisions is particularly important in the income tax and corporation tax. Look again at section 1. It refers us to "the Schedules". What are they? They are a throwback to the 1803 Act. Nowadays, Schedules are added at the ends of Acts and given arabic numerals to identify them. Not so two centuries ago. Then the Schedules appeared in the body of the text, after the sections incorporating them, and were given capital letters for identity. The 1803 Act contained several, though some merely contained procedural provisions. Schedules A to E, however, set out the basis of charge on different kinds of income. That form has been carried on without a break since then, even down to the inclusion of the Schedules in the body of the Act—despite a whole retinue of new-style Schedules at the end. And the Schedules are still divided into cases, just as they were then. Further, tax practitioners all talk of "Schedule E" rather than "the tax on earnings", or Case I instead of "taxation of trades". The shorthand is extremely useful.

Income tax used to be divided into five Schedules. These grew to six, then shrank to five in 1990, and to four in 1996: A, D, E and F. Of these, Schedules D and E are divided into cases. However, there are now only two Schedules that apply to companies: A and D. Let us explain:

Schedule A (in section 15) charges tax on the *annual profits or gains arising in respect of rents and receipts* from land in the United Kingdom. It replaced a former charge to tax on the value of ownership of land in 1963. Since 1995, Schedule A takes different forms for income tax and corporation tax.

Schedule B (repealed in 1990) charged tax on the occupation of commercial woodlands. It was not, in fact, an income tax but a property tax. In its last years it was a mere shadow of a former provision that had lasted in similar form from long before 1803.

Schedule C (repealed in 1996) charged tax on *profits arising from public revenue dividends*. So did Case III of Schedule D. Eventually, someone got round to rationalising this, and this Schedule was no more. A pity, perhaps, as it managed almost two centuries with hardly any litigation.

Schedule D (section 18) charges tax on a range of forms of property and profits.

Case I taxes the *annual profits or gains* from trades (including any employments and vocations of companies): (section 6).

Case II taxes the *annual profits or gains* from professions and vocations of individuals. As noted, these reciepts are caught under Case I for companies.

Case III taxes investment income or, as it puts it, *interest, annuities and other annual payments* plus discounts, and a variety of anti-avoidance charges. Since 1996, Case III has a different form for companies to that for individuals.

Case IV (abolished in 1996 for companies) is a charge on overseas income from securities. It has now been absorbed into Case III for corporation tax purposes.

Case V originally parallelled Case IV in charging overseas income from *possessions*. Now it stands alone for companies as the basis of charge for overseas income (although in practice the charging provisions are usually those in our double taxation agreements).

Case VI covers *any annual profits or gains not falling under any other Case of Schedule D, and not charged by virtue of Schedule A or E*. This sounds wider than the judges have let it be—and it is narrower for companies than individuals. It is a sweeper clause, rather than a major extra tax charge.

In the past, the Schedule has had Cases VII and VIII as well. You may still come across Case VIII in the cases. It was what is now Schedule A.

Schedule E (section 19) is fiscally the most important but legally the most obscure. It is a tax on all *offices or employments on emoluments therefrom*. If you have never heard of the gloriously ancient word "emoluments" before, you have now. It comes, of course, straight from 1803. This Schedule has three Cases, but their function is to deal with international aspects of employment rather than different kinds of income, so we will return to them later.

Schedule E, as we have noted, does not apply to companies.

Schedule F (section 20), is the newcomer, dating back only to the introduction of corporation tax. It is a tax on *all dividends and other distributions of companies* that are resident in the United Kingdom.

Taxes and Charging Provisions

It applies only to income tax, as United Kingdom companies do not pay tax on dividends received from other United Kingdom companies. (If you look carefully, you will see that Schedule F applies only to income tax, while the other Schedules apply to "tax".)

The remarks about corporation tax reflect that it is, from many points of view, a different tax to income tax. It also has a separate charging section, section 6.

Now read the list of Schedules again. Better still, read the sections in which these are contained. How many of them charge tax on *income*? Only two—Cases IV and V of Schedule D. What is more, you won't find a charge on income in either section 1 or section 6 either. The disparate phraseology of the income tax both causes and conceals problems, as we shall see later. Just to complicate things, most talk about profits and gains. So does the Taxation of Chargeable Gains Act 1992.

The Relationship Between Taxes and Charging Provisions

Faced with this battery of separate provisions, important questions arise. Can any form of income be charged under two cases, two Schedules, or even two taxes at the same time?

As regards income tax and corporation tax, only one can apply to any one taxpayer on any item of income. Corporation tax applies to companies (defined as bodies corporate by section 832), and income tax to anyone or anything that is not a body corporate. Income tax therefore covers trusts and partnerships. For a fascinating case that decided that the Conservative Party under Mrs Thatcher was not a body corporate (because it consisted of Mrs Thatcher!) see *Conservative Central Office v. Burrell* (1982). History does not record whether the tax inspector in that case was duly promoted.

There is also a clear ranking between income tax and capital gains tax (or the corporate equivalents). In every case, it must first be asked if income tax applies. Only if we conclude that it does not do we ask whether there is a charge to capital gains tax. A charge cannot arise to the two taxes at once. Case law establishes that the Revenue may raise alternative assessments under both taxes, but can only collect tax under one of them: *Bird v. IRC* (1989).

This rule of mutual exclusivity also applies to the income tax Schedules. Whatever may be the theoretical possibilities, a form of income can be charged under one Schedule only. If the legislation does not make clear which Schedule that should be, it will be for the judges to decide. The reason for this is that income tax is regarded as a single tax, not a series of taxes. It follows that only one set of provisions of that tax can apply to any taxable income at any one time. However, the judges do not apply that reasoning to overlap between rules within a single Schedule. If income falls within two cases of the same Schedule (usually Schedule D) it is for the Revenue to decide which applies, and there may be alternative assessments.

These rules are necessary because it is not clear from the words of the legislation alone that there is no overlap between the taxes, Schedules or cases. Any other rule would, in principle, be unfair. Note that the rule does not apply to other kinds of taxes. The relationship between VAT and income tax, for example, does not exist. It is therefore irrelevant in law that something is or is not subject to income tax for VAT purposes. This also applies to the stamp duties. In other words, the mutual exclusion rule only applies to similar taxes.

Tax Legislation

As we have seen, one of the few clear principles that can be said to be constitutional in the United Kingdom is the Bill of Rights of 1688/89 providing that taxes cannot be imposed save by consent of parliament. There is no common law of tax, nor any prerogative or other inherent rights to tax. Nor can taxes be imposed by treaty without parliamentary authority to recognise and collect them.

For this reason, we must locate the express authority of parliament to impose a tax on every occasion on which we wish to collect tax. If there is no authority, there is no liability to tax. Applying that approach to our tax laws may once have been a simple operation. Now it is enormously complicated. This is because there have been new tax provisions passed by parliament at least once a year for at least 130 years without any break. Since 1894 there has been at least one omnibus **Finance Act** each year. These have rarely shortened the extant law, even when taxes have been abolished.

The primary legislation imposing our main taxes is therefore of formidable dimensions. As indicated above, some sort of order has been imposed on parts of this vast array of provisions by a series of **Consolidation Acts**. But the laws have never been codified. This creates genuine problems of interpretation, as we note below. At the same time, it means that there is likely to be some provision covering most forms of income or transaction, and determining whether or not it comes within the tax. We cannot, however, assume this. Leaving aside, for the moment, the problems of interpreting tax laws, the rule remains that unless there is a provision that covers the income or transaction in point, no tax can be collected. At the heart of this process lies the simple fact that the purpose of a tax law is to impose tax on certain things, and not on other things. There may be a range of reasons why parliament has decided to do that. But, following the traditions of British legislation, the reasons why are normally left unstated. The question is always; "is this activity or thing within the scope of a taxing provision?"

Traditionally, parliament has added extra levels of complexity to the process of imposing taxes by insisting that all major rules of tax are imposed by primary legislation. **Delegated legislation** is therefore limited. This means that any significant detail must be set out in a section of an Act, not in delegated legislation. This rule was in particular applied to the income tax. There were good democratic reasons for this. Every word of every section of a Finance Act is open for political and technical debate and may be the subject of a separate vote. This is restricted in the case of Schedules to the decision whether a Schedule "stand part". It is even more restricted in the case of statutory instruments to a vote whether the instrument be (or not be) made. Despite, or perhaps because of, these limitations, much greater use is made of Schedules and statutory instruments in the more modern taxes. Much of VAT is, for example, to be found in the new VAT Regulations 1995, while many important aspects of National Insurance contribution law is found in the much amended Social Security (Contribution) Regulations 1979.

Nonetheless, it is a pretence to claim that there is an open technical debate on every tax provision. Time does not allow it. A few selected provisions are subject to a high profile political debate on the floor of the House of Commons. Other selected provisions are subject to more technical debate in the Finance Bill committee. Other provisions pass without comment. All provisions pass without comment in the House of Lords, because they are (since the Parliament Acts were passed) effectively debarred from interfering in tax laws. The fact that this results in what some regard as our most important laws being subject to the least thorough scrutiny by parliament is of course justified by an appeal to history and democracy. Perhaps that is another of the principles of our constitution. If so, perhaps, now that the Queen also pays taxes, we should change it.

Handling Tax Laws

Some of our tax laws receive even less parliamentary scrutiny. These are the rules imposed by the **European Union Treaties, Regulations and Directives**. Most important is the Community Customs Code (E.C. Council Regulation 2913/92). By virtue of the European Community Treaty (Article 189) it is directly effective in all Member States without further enactment. No pretence was made to enact it in the United Kingdom. VAT is also based on extensive E.C. law, although most of this is in the form of directives. Many of the provisions of these directives apply directly in the same way as provisions in regulations. This is so, even though a Finance Act provision says otherwise. Why? Because E.U. laws prevail over United Kingdom laws. Is that part of our constitution?

Of course, as all readers know, we don't have a **constitution**. In tax matters that is most important. Constitutions almost always contain rules limiting aspects of the right to impose taxes. We have no such rules. Even the simple rule in the Bill of Rights is no longer right unless we amend it to include tax laws imposed by the authority of the E.U. More generally, we can observe only that, constitutionally, parliament may choose to tax anything it wishes in any way it wishes, and under any name it wishes. Once it has so wished, we must pay. Or must we?

Before leaving the topic of tax legislation, we must notice another curiosity. This is the collection of **extra-statutory concessions** issued alongside all our main tax laws. ESCs, for short, are truly curious. They are not law, yet they prevail over the law in practice. The courts cannot enforce them or interpret them, because they have never been enacted, but yet they, arguably, can ensure that others enforce them. They exist in a sort of constitutional never-never land, supposedly authorised by ministers (who have no legal power to do it), and tolerated by a parliament that has no time to enact them (except when it does have time, as in the Finance Act 1996). In short, parliament, by an extrastatutory procedure, allows us to ignore its enactments. Against that, it is said that the system works. It is also argued that a lawyer who ignores any ESCs would be negligent to the client. If so, it is a curious law system indeed that holds a lawyer negligent for failing not to observe the law!

Even then, our list is not complete. The United Kingdom has ratified many dozen **double taxation agreements**. These are given formal effect as Orders in Council, each of which is then given precedence over internal law by general enabling provisions in the primary legislation for dealings between taxpayers and the United

Kingdom and the treaty partner. We note these in the final part of the book.

Finding the Law

The first rule in trying to find the current law imposing a tax is not to do so from the official versions of the law. Trying to establish, for example, the current extent of the stamp duties from the official texts of Acts of Parliament would mean reading some 110 Acts of Parliament, any one of which may have repealed something from its predecessors (and probably did). Even where there is a recent consolidation, this would be an excessively time-consuming occupation. It is also pointless, because there are splendid commercial consolidations of the law published annually by several publishers. One or other of these consolidations is indispensable for a proper study of tax law. They are even available on CD-Rom for those who think computers should replace books.

These commercial consolidations are particularly useful because they give the history of sections in the consolidation measures, and cross-reference texts to other relevant provisions. They also set out the S.I.s, the E.U. law, and the ESCs.

Using Tax Laws

There are traditionally two approaches to deciding how a tax law works. One is to try and determine its meaning. The other is to try and determine what the tax authorities think it means. These are often different things, and require different techniques. For a professional adviser, which is the appropriate technique depends on the client. One approach is to seek to establish with the maximum certainty whether the tax authorities will demand that a tax be levied on a transaction. The other approach is to form an independent view about whether tax applies, and be prepared to argue the point before the courts if necessary. But even the most law-abiding taxpayer is unlikely to do this to increase a personal tax bill. The first of these approaches is the process of *tax compliance*, that is, of ensuring that the law is obeyed at minimum cost and risk. The other is the process of *tax planning*, under which a taxpayer seeks to explore the law to mitigate a tax burden, or possibly to remove it altogether, within the terms of the law.

The development of *self-assessment* is causing these two traditional approaches to coalesce. The aim of self-assessment is to transfer to the taxpayer any decision about the extent to which something should be taxed. Decisions about the relevance of any tax provision to a set of facts, or of interpretation and application of the law to those facts, is for the taxpayer. Of course, tax officials will check on the accuracy of the taxpayer's judgment. Self-assessment has also made it more important for the tax authorities to clarify their own views on what taxpayers should be doing. We will look at how they make their views known first, and then how tax laws are interpreted.

The Official View

In addition to the laws themselves, the tax authorities must in a range of ways ensure that the laws actually work in practical terms. Both the Revenue and Customs have spent considerable time in recent years trying to do this. In part, they have been spurred on by the process of automation of our taxes. Computers demanding "yes or no" answers will not accept "perhaps", nor will they accept inconsistencies. In part, the deregulation initiative of government has contributed by focusing on the removal of excessive detail or procedure.

The Inland Revenue produce guidance and information to assist taxpayers, or their own staff, in several forms. Together these add up to a substantial body of published statements. However, in every case it must be remembered that these express only the Revenue's view of the law. Save as noted below, the guidance is always general, and does not relate to individual taxpayers. The cumulated texts of these forms of guidance are published in the commercial compilations of Revenue material.

Extra-statutory concessions. These were mentioned above together with the statutes from which they purport to derogate. In fact, ESCs as they are usually called, are a motley list of matters, some reflecting interpretations of the law, others examples of faulty procedures, and others aiming at dealing with gaps in the law. They are known by a code such as ESC A85 (removal expenses), because there are so many of them—209 in 1996.

Statements of practice. SPs, as they are known, were first issued in a methodical way in 1978, since when 176 have been issued (to 1996). They seek to apply the law (or ESCs), and can be quite lengthy. For example SP 5/95 on the taxation of insurance and personal pension scheme commission is 24 paragraphs long. Prior to 1978, these

The Official View

statements were often made through Parliament. SPs are published as Inland Revenue press releases.

Press releases. A steady stream of press releases are issued by the Revenue, covering all changes to a Finance Bill, SPs, announcements of other publications and background information. For those who like finding such things, they are also all on the Internet. Just try http.//www.col.gov.uk/coi/deptsGIR/GIR.html
The most important set of press releases are the huge bundle issued on the day of the budget announcement. These often include details left out of the Chancellor's speech.

Parliamentary proceedings. Ministerial statements and planted parliamentary questions have long been used for making minor announcements about taxes. Since 1978, this practice is less common, although answers to other PQs may still reveal interesting points. Parliament rarely debates the tax affairs of an individual (and when it does, ministers rarely do more than give general answers). The Finance Bill debates have gained a new importance since the decisions in *Pepper v. Hart* (1992), discussed under interpretation below. The adjudications of the Parliamentary Ombudsman on tax cases (published as House of Commons Papers), although also anonymous, give interesting insights to the otherwise mysterious workings of the tax authorities when things appear to have gone wrong.

The main parliamentary proceeding of relevance is the budget speech and debate each year. Along with this the Treasury publishes a "red book": the Budget Statement and Financial Forecast for the year. It is important background reading to the budget process. It is also available on the Internet at http//www.coi.gov.uk/coi/depts/GIR/GIR.html.

Tax Bulletin. First published in 1991, this regular publication states Revenue interpretations on difficult points, and some decisions on contentious issues. One commercial compendium listed 120 such rulings and decisions published by 1996.

Guidance leaflets. These have been published for many years, but they have gained considerably in appearance and readability since the Revenue started taking the Plain English Campaign seriously, and they now regularly win praise for clarity. Guidance is now issued with most standard forms (for example the coding notices sent to most individuals, and the annual returns). There are also a series of leaflets and booklets made generally available on a wide variety of issues. For example IR 20 deals with questions of residence, and is important enough to be referred to in context as the "Revenue code".

Instruction manuals. Open government appeared to take a step forward when, after long discussions, the Revenue agreed to publish its 48 volumes of instruction manuals to staff. However, what it actually did was to commission a private publisher to publish them, and a significant price was attached to each of the volumes. Although they are now technically available to everyone, we are reminded of the comment of the Irish judge, Mathew J., that "in England, justice is open to all—like the Ritz Hotel." It is certain that the authors of the manuals do not subscribe to the well-known philosophy of the founder of that hotel, Cesar Ritz, that "le client n'a jamais tort". The manuals are also available on CD-Rom.

Indirect guidance. The Inland Revenue also has the commendable habit of reaching agreement with taxpayer representatives and professional associations about the operation of the taxes in its charge. Agreements may be by way of a fairly formal statement of agreement with appropriate groups, or by way of a letter sent to a group in response. These sometimes receive restricted publication, but bodies such as the Tax Faculty of the Institute of Chartered Accountants, the Chartered Institute of Taxation and the Law Society's Revenue Law Committee regularly publish their own views, and exchanges with the Revenue, on points of law.

A similar list of sources could be prepared for the guidance given by Customs and Excise to deal with value added tax and by the Contributions Agency to deal with national insurance contributions. In recent years both have used similar series of press releases, interpretations, and publications, and engage in similar forms of indirect guidance.

Interpreting the Law

This should be the easy bit. It is not. Consider the following provisions:

> "*Interest* means both annual and yearly interest and interest other than annual or yearly interest."

"*Interest* includes dividends and any other return (however described) except a return consisting of an amount by which the amount payable on a security's redemption exceeds its issuing price."
"*Interest and dividends* do not include any interest or dividend which is a distribution"
"*Distribution* ... means ... any dividend payable by a company ... "
"*Trade* includes any trade, manufacture, adventure or concern in the nature of trade"
"*Trade* includes vocation and also includes an office or employment"
"*Profits* means income and chargeable gains"
"*Profits* or *gains* shall not include references to chargeable gains"
"*Income* includes any amount on which a charge to tax is authorised to be made under any of the provisions of this Act"

Rule number one of interpreting legislation should be to note the meanings given to the language by parliament. In tax law, as the above illustrations (all drawn from the Tax Acts) show, this has to be modified by two reflections. The first is that the definitions may themselves add no extra meaning. The second is that words change their meaning from one part to another of the tax legislation. Or, as T.S. Eliot observed, "words strain, crack and sometimes break, under the burden." The job of the lawyer is to ensure that any words that do suffer in this way are patched back up again.

Words can have two kinds of meaning: a technical meaning given by the judges as a matter of law, or "the ordinary English meaning". Which kind of meaning is given to a word is itself a decision of law, but decisions about the language of the tax laws are not consistent on this point. The *Ensign Tankers* case discussed below (see *Escape to Victory?*) illustrates this in the way it seeks to apply the simple word "trade". It also illustrates another dilemma of interpretation. If a word has an ordinary meaning, then it is for the tax authorities and the appeal tribunals to determine its meaning. It cannot be appealed to the higher courts, because it gives rise to no question of law. If, however, the word has a technical meaning, then that is a question of law and can be appealed to the courts. The *Ensign Tankers* case also illustrates this problem. How do we decide the meaning of a word?

Decisions on the meanings of words and the phrases in which they appear are guided by the rules of statutory interpretation. For a long time, judicial thinking was that tax laws should be interpreted strictly. Judges justified this by references to analogies with the criminal law and by reference to the Bill of Rights. The result could be an excessively literal reading of the words of a tax provision in isolation from its context. More recently, judges have been seeking to establish the view that interpreting tax statutes is no different from interpreting other legislation, save that the words have to be clear before tax can be imposed. The judgment of Lord Wilberforce in the *Ramsay* case (1981) is formative:

> "A subject is only to be taxed on clear words, not on 'intendment' or on the 'equity' of an Act. Any taxing Act of Parliament is to be construed in accordance with this principle. What are 'clear words' is to be ascertained on normal principles; these do not confine the courts to literal interpretation. There may, indeed should be, considered the context and scheme of the relevant Act as a whole, and its purpose may, indeed should be, regarded ... "

Unfortunately, this statement cannot be left without further comment. First, we must remind you that the Acts being interpreted are frequently consolidation measures. An attempt to look at the purpose of a consolidation measure means looking at the purpose of the provisions lying behind it. In a real sense, what the drafters have stitched together for presentational purposes have to be unstitched to establish what is meant. For an example of the complexities that result from such unstitching, see the Court of Appeal decision in *IRC v. Willoughby* (1995).

Part of the reason for the complexity in unstitching is the decision of the House of Lords in the tax case of *Pepper v. Hart* (1992). This decided that in cases of ambiguous language, it was proper to look to the record of the House of Commons for any ministerial statements about the intention of parliament behind a specific provision. In the *Willoughby* case, the logic of this was to look through not only the 1988 Act, but also the 1970 Act and the 1952 Act back to original enactment of the provision in question in 1936. While this might help deal with ambiguities, the resulting need to effectively ignore the consolidation measure for interpretation purposes is not conducive to an easy operation of the law. It means that a "proper" consolidation should identify where each part of the consolidated provision comes from. None of the consolidations currently available do this.

A second reason for complexity is the constant adjustment in the precise terms of sections to deal both with the need to counter avoidance, and the need to avoid injustice in special cases. Some sections have therefore seen considerable amendment during their working lives, including reshaping during the consolidation process.

Take the definition of "trade". In 1803, this was defined as including any trade, manufacture, art or mystery. The word was used in a phrase identical to that now in section 19 of the Taxes Act, but its statutory definition has changed. The words are the same as in 1803, but not the extended meaning. Had the relevant minister made its main meaning clear then, should we return to it now? Here again, we have the problem of some words and phrases being "ordinary" while others are "technical".

Because of the need to prevent avoidance, tax law is also at times aimed very widely. The sections in the *Willoughby* case are good examples. Another is section 776, which starts: "This section is enacted to prevent the avoidance of tax by persons concerned with land or the development of land." Does a statement like that make it easier to interpret a phrase such as "any arrangement ... effected as respects ... land which enables a gain to be realised by any indirect method ... by any person who is ... concerned in the arrangement"?

A further reason for complexity in interpretation is the influence of European Community law. Some parts of our law are now subject to reference to the European Court of Justice. It is their interpretation, and therefore their techniques of interpretation, that must prevail in these areas. This may lead to inconsistencies, where the courts find that the approach taken by the European Court is different to that which they would take in a purely national context. Given that VAT is a mixture of European and United Kingdom provisions, the result may be untidy. See, for an example, the House of Lords decision in *CEC v. Robert Gordon's College* (1995).

Applying the Law

A reference to the European Court emphasises another aspect of handling tax cases. The European Court takes the view that it can interpret E.C. law, but it cannot apply the law to the facts. In the United Kingdom, these two stages in a case are often conflated. Take, for example, the child's definition of an elephant as something large and grey and living in a herd of elephants. The definition is that it is large, grey, and sociable. Whether the group of creatures is a herd of elephants is an application of the law to the facts. Application of law to facts in tax matters can be an issue of considerable complexity. If you wish to see how difficult, take a piece of paper and draw a diagram on it of the transactions described by the House of Lords in *Ramsay v. IRC* (1981). Then try the same thing with the *Ensign Tankers* case discussed below.

Until the *Ramsay* case, judges would accept any series of transactions, however complicated, as something to be taken at face value. The underlying approach was one said to have been approved by the House of Lords in *IRC v. Duke of Westminster* (1936). It was that the *form* of a transaction should be followed, not its substance. That doctrine has been modified by a series of cases including the *Ramsay* and *Ensign Tankers* cases but of which the most important is another House of Lords case, *Furniss v. Dawson* (1984).

In *Furniss*, Lord Brightman, on behalf of the House, and following the lines already set out in *Ramsay*, propounded the rule that the court did not have to look at the form in isolation in certain series of transactions, or complex transactions. A broader view of the whole operation could be taken where the series was preordained, and where one or more steps in the series existed for no other purpose than tax avoidance. This broad view allowed the courts in both *Ramsay* and *Furniss* to look at what happened without getting caught up in the interstices of complex constructions which, in substance, had replaced much more straightforward transactions. A later House of Lords case, *Craven v. White* (1988) emphasised that the new approach only applied where the conditions were strictly met. A further decision of the House in *Countess Fitzwilliam v. IRC* (1993), stressed that the courts could look through a series of artificial transactions to the real transaction underneath if the conditions were met. However, this had to be done to the transactions as a whole, and the Revenue could not pick and chose parts of the series to look through, while taking other parts at face value. However, in *Moodie v. IRC* (1993), the House reaffirmed the underlying principle, and applied it notwithstanding an inconsistent decision of the House of an earlier date dealing with the transactions under question.

The fact that so many decisions of the House have concerned this issue in little more than a decade shows its importance. The precise extent of the operation of the new approach is still a little unclear, but it does allow judges to look through artificial schemes to the reality underneath. It also represents an attitude to the facts, rather than to the law, which has a wider implication of the kind shown in the *Ensign Tankers* case. It is that courts are encouraging the tax authorities to take a broad view of the facts, rather than a narrow view, and one which takes fully into account the need to be realistic about tax avoidance.

ESCAPE TO VICTORY?

Where does that leave tax planning? The *Robert Gordon* case suggests that it is alive and well for VAT purposes both in a straightforward way, and in less obvious ways. The *Willoughby* case provides a most interesting test of the extent of the legitimacy of tax avoidance where parliament has itself encouraged avoidance. *Ensign Tankers* suggests, however, that complicated manoeuvres which have little external effect save for alleged tax saving and which form a composite whole will save little direct tax. However, as *Ensign Tankers* shows only too well, the judicial process carries with it a level of uncertainty. It can also be time-consuming, and introduce inefficiency and inconsistency in an area where both add to the cost of an already costly process.

Escape to Victory?

The tale of how a tax appeal is handled is best told by a case study. The case chosen here is formally known as *Ensign Tankers (Leasing) Ltd v. Stokes (Inspector of Taxes)*. The reports of the case are at [1989] STC 705 (case stated by the Special Commissioners, and decision of Millet J.), [1991] STC 136 (decision of the Court of Appeal) and [1992] STC 226 (decision of the House of Lords). It came to be a most important decision on the boundary between acceptable and unacceptable tax avoidance. A little less usually for a tax case, the plot involves Michael Caine and Sylvester Stallone. How did they come to be involved with a tanker leasing company?

The story starts with an Inland Revenue Statement of Practice, SP 9/79. This announced the Revenue's view that the Revenue would accept claims for capital allowance for expenditure on plant in respect of the cost of master prints of films. In effect, this was a decision in favour of potential investors in the film industry, allowing them to write off against their profits (or claim losses) on the capital cost of producing the master print of any film for distribution. Ownership of the master print carries with it the rights to exploit and distribute the film.

A number of professional tax advisers were attracted by this statement of practice towards devising tax efficient ways of securing investment in the film industry. At the same time, the taxpayer company, previously a profitable leasing business, was finding it harder to make profits, and was looking to the film industry as a possible source of new business. As a result of complicated negotiations, the taxpayer company became a limited partner of a partnership known as the Victory Partnership with the intention of making a film called *Escape to Victory*. This was filmed in Hungary in 1980. Commercially, it proved a failure.

A little after filming started, a meeting took place in London of the limited partners of the Victory partnership at which 17 documents were completed. These included the partnership agreement and a series of loan and financial agreements. Through them, in broad terms, the partnership put up capital of $3.25 million, of which Ensign put up $2.38 million. A further $9.75 million was lent to the partnership by the film production company, funded by an American bank. This was a non-recourse loan, that is, the film production company could not demand repayment of the loan from the partnership, only from the proceeds of the film. The partnership bought the partly completed film from the production company, and agreed to pay the production company a fixed amount to finish the film. Under other provisions, the partnership were to have 25 per cent of the proceeds from the film, while the production company were to receive 75 per cent towards repayment of the loan to the partnership. In other words, the partnership put up about $3 million of the $13 million that the film was budgeted to cost, but came to own the film outright subject to charges on the proceeds from the film. In tax terms, therefore, the partnership could claim an allowance for the cost of its master print of *Escape to Victory*, although it would in due course be subject to tax on the whole proceeds of the film.

The secret of the scheme lay partly in its cash-flow advantages, and partly in the fact that the taxpayer could not lose from its investment after taking account of tax. This was because it received the benefits of its share of the tax allowances for making the film in 1980 as offsets to the considerable profits being made by the group of companies of which it was a member. It would be taxed only later if profits were made. If they were not made, it still received an allowance against tax for a sum equal to about four times its actual investment. This was because the corporation tax rate was then 52 per cent, so the company received a right to claim a loss worth more in tax terms than its original investment. (The full details of how this happened are in the 1986 report of the case.) The film, unfortunately, did make a loss, so the company claimed the tax allowances (a setoff against profits of about £5 million) in its 1980 tax returns. The inspector refused them. Why?

To claim the tax relief, the company had to show that the partnership was a person "carrying on a trade". In the inspector's view, the partnership was not doing that. It was engaging in tax avoidance, not trading. This view was accepted by the Special Commissioners in a lengthy decision made after 18 days of hearings in 1986. They rejected evidence of one of the key witnesses that the scheme was a commercial scheme and held, as a matter of law, that the partnership was not trading. They were asked to consider also whether the case fell within the principles of the decision in *Furniss v. Dawson*, and found on the facts that it did, but that this was not necessary to their decision.

The case went on appeal to the Chancery Division where it was heard by Millett J. for six days in 1989. He upheld the taxpayer's appeal on the ground that the Commissioners had reached a decision that no person acting judicially and properly instructed as to the law could have made. In particular, in his view the partnerships were trading. However, he could not make that finding of fact with authority, so the case had to go back to the Commissioners for a rehearing. This is a good illustration of a judge not being able to change a decision on the facts, but only to see if the Commissioners took a decision that was correct in law. It reflects the limits on the judicial role in section 56 of the Taxes Management Act 1970. It means that the result of a successful appeal is that the process of appeal must start again.

The Revenue (usually referred to, as in this case, as the Crown) appealed to the Court of Appeal. The case was heard by the Vice-Chancellor and two Lords Justice of Appeal over four days at the end of 1991. Put shortly, they allowed the appeal by the Crown, but also found that the Commissioners had made an error of law (identified by Millett J.) in their decision, so referred it back for rehearing. In the view of the Court of Appeal, Millett J. was wrong in saying that the only possible interpretation of the facts was different to the interpretation adopted by the Commissioners. So, in the view of the Court of Appeal, both lower levels of appeal had been wrong, and it was remitted to start again.

A little over a year later, the case was heard for a further six days before the House of Lords on an appeal and cross-appeal by both parties. The judgment of the House was given by Lord Templeman, a judge who earned during his judicial career a formidable reputation as a judge determined to see tax law applied with common sense and in the common interest. The other four members of the House agreed with his decision.

To Lord Templeman, the case was concerned about a tax avoidance scheme. His opinion on this issue should be read as a concise review of judicial thinking on tax avoidance (see pages 235 to 244 of the report). In forthright terms, Lord Templeman dismisses the operation of the scheme used by the taxpayer in this case as "play acting". Under his guidance, the House reached the decision that all three lower levels of appeal had been wrong. The case was therefore remitted to the Commissioners again, but this time with a direction to allow a claim for a loss equal to the actual amount put into the partnership (and lost) by the taxpayers—the sum of $2.38 million dollars, not the inflated sum the taxpayer had claimed, or the refusal of any claim by the inspector and Commissioners.

Thirty-four days of hearings therefore produced four different answers from the four levels of appeal, although three levels were merely, in the words of Lord Templeman, overseeing the task of the Commissioners to "find the facts and apply the law, subject to correction by the courts if they misapply the law." The answer, 12 years after the original taxable activity, was based to some extent on judicial decisions made after the deal was first incurred but equally was expressed as an interpretation of a simple word: *trade*. Who was right? Read the decisions for yourself and decide with which of the four levels of appeal you most agree. In one way, each of the four decisions could be said to be a permissible use of the accepted techniques of interpretation and application of the law (although, of course, the precedent system means that three are wrong, and only the last one is actually technically correct).

With which of the four decisions do you most readily sympathise? Why? That will tell you much about your own views on the taxing process. Whichever decision you do support, the story, which might be better entitled as *Escape To Where You Came From*, is also a comment on the weaknesses, as well as strengths, of a multi-layered system of tax appeals. What *does* the word "trade" mean? Perhaps the 1803 Act was right in including mysteries in its definition.

Making Things Better

At the time of writing, considerable thought is going into ways of improving our statute law and how we use it. One proposal is to rewrite the entirety of our statute laws (in tax only, we hasten to add!). The Inland Revenue published a report at the end of 1995, entitled *The Path to Tax Simplification*, exploring these issues. An independent and more wide-ranging committee, the Tax Law Review Committee, also reported at that time on methods of rewriting the law (in its *Series of Reports on Tax Legislation*). Both are full of ideas. Whether these ideas will improve the operation of our laws is a moot point. Some welcome the proposals, while others criticise them either as a waste of time or as an introduction of unwelcome uncertainty. The 1996 Finance Act certainly failed to show any major improvements. It was also longer than ever. We leave it for the reader to follow any progress that is made.

Part Two

Taxation of Income

CHAPTER 3

THE MECHANICS OF INCOME TAX

In this chapter we want to trace the steps in an income tax case. In practice the most litigated heads of income tax are Cases I and II of Schedule D, dealing with trades and professions. So let us look at the position of a trader. Traditionally, assessment by the Revenue rather than self-assessment by the taxpayer has been fundamental to the initiation and development of an income tax case. However, the Finance Act 1994 started, perhaps, the most important reform of personal tax administration when it outlined the structure of a system of self-assessment for income tax and capital gains tax which applies for the tax year 1996–97 and subsequent years.[1] It is essentially a system which gives those taxpayers who customarily completed a tax return (often traders and professionals) the opportunity to compute their own tax liability. Not surprisingly, a change of this magnitude has had considerable "knock-on" effects, perhaps the most significant of which is the move towards a current year basis of assessment for all sources of income so that ultimately the Revenue, in respect of a particular tax year, will be in a position to issue the taxpayer with a statement which shows all his income from whatever source in that year and present him with a corresponding tax bill. Many other facilitative measures have been taken, not the least of which on a practical level has been the design, after public consultation, of a purportedly user-friendly tax return form in readiness for April 1997!

An outline of the major features of self-assessment is given later in this chapter (below, pp. 60–62). Initially, however, due regard must be given to its forerunner (assessment by the Revenue), which we have loosely called the traditional approach. This approach continues to be germane to those tax years which precede the introduction of self-assessment and aspects of it, for example, the tax appeals system (and its operation) are also important to self-assessment.

---

[1] See also the Finance Act 1995 which contains provisions concerned with self-assessment and the PAYE system.

Further, it acts as a useful comparator for measuring the degree of change which self-assessment entails.

The Steps in an Income Tax Case

1. *The Traditional Approach*

Any person can be required by an inspector (under section 8 of the TMA 1970) to make a return disclosing "such information as may be required" for the purpose of assessing him to income tax. Of course, the Revenue may not know that a particular person is trading, and there is no doubt that some people get away with trading unknown to the Revenue for a long time. However, once the Revenue know that a person is trading they can serve a notice under section 8 on him requiring him to disclose the pertinent information.

In practice a trader submits a return which simply says "see accounts". And he (or his accountant) sends with the return a profit and loss account, a balance sheet and a "computation". This latter is simply an adjustment, bringing the commercial accounts into line with income tax requirements, the most common adjustment being that depreciation has to be added back for income tax purposes. The inspector can issue a notice requiring a person to deliver to him accounts, relevant documents, and such other particulars as are relevant to the trader's liability to tax (see section 20 of the TMA 1970). Information may also be gathered about the trader's income from other sources, although there may be limits on the availability of such information, *e.g.* where it is privileged (see section 20B(8)).

The next step is for the inspector to make an assessment on the trader. The normal time limit is six years. The inspector's powers to make an assessment come from section 29 of the TMA 1970. This gives the inspector a number of linked possibilities. If he is satisfied that the trader's return affords correct and complete information, "he shall make an assessment accordingly": section 29(1)(a). If dissatisfied with a return, or no return has been made, the inspector may make an assessment "to the best of his judgment": section 29(1)(b). This power is very important in practice to deal with recalcitrant traders, as we shall see in a moment. Finally, section 29(3) gives a power to assess to an inspector who "discovers" (a) non-assessed profits which should be assessed, (b) an insufficient assessment, or (c) excessive relief.

The Traditional Approach

"Discovers" has been treated by the courts as having a very wide meaning, "comes to the conclusion": *R. v. Kensington Commissioners, ex p. Aramayo* (1916) (H.L.). So, for example, the discovery power can be used to correct an under-assessment caused by bad arithmetic, even when the Revenue compounded this error with a second mistake, namely quoting the wrong part of the section as authority for their action! This sorry tale occurred in *Vickerman v. Mason's P.R.s* (1984). Further, the discovery need not be of new facts, and includes any case in which it newly appears that the trader has been undercharged (see *Cenlon Finance Ltd v. Ellwood* (1962) (H.L.)).

Let us return to the power to make what are usually called estimated assessments: section 29(1)(b). The inspector will use this if our trader fails to submit a return in time, or at all. The estimate will be based on the assumed income of the trader without allowances. The effect of an estimated assessment is normally to force the trader to appeal and produce a proper return. Of course, the trader may be content to pay the estimate.

The estimated assessment, as we have seen, is based on the inspector acting "to the best of his judgment". This should rule out wild guesses as to the trader's potential liability to tax, but there is hardly any income tax case law about the limits, if any, of the inspector's power. By contrast a similar power to assess for value added tax has been the subject of many tribunal decisions and the decision in *Van Boeckel v. CEC* (1981) shows there are clearly some limits (see also *Schlumberger v. CEC* (1987)).

If the trader does not appeal against the assessment and he does pay the amount charged by the assessment, that is the end of the matter. If he does not pay up, the Revenue can sue him. Or, instead of suing, the collector can distrain on the lands or goods of the debtor. Such a distress can be levied without the Revenue having first to obtain a judgment against the debtor; all they need is a finalised assessment, and a warrant issued by a justice of the peace.

If the trader does appeal against the assessment, the inspector may enter into an agreement with the trader that the assessment should be upheld or varied, or discharged or cancelled. Such an agreement has the same effect as a determination of the appeal by the Commissioners. This is covered by section 54 of the TMA 1970, which also gives the taxpayer a generous 30-day "cooling-off period" to resile from the agreement. On the other hand, it prevents a taxpayer from withdrawing an appeal until the inspector has had 30 days to consider preventing the withdrawal, and has chosen not to prevent it. It is thus possible for an inspector to force an appeal by a high estimated assessment, and then to prevent the taxpayer withdrawing the appeal. Where a point has been subject to an appeal, and, following disclosure of all material facts by the trader, the appeal was settled by a section 54 agreement, the Revenue cannot go back on that agreement by using section 29(3) (see *Scorer v. Olin Energy Systems Ltd* (1985) (H.L.)).

If there is no agreement between the trader and the inspector the appeal goes to the General (or Special) Commissioners. We have already seen that the "Generals" are the laymen and the "Specials" are the professionals (p.17). In theory, in most cases the taxpayer can choose freely which forum will hear his appeal: section 31. However, this choice may be overridden. An inspector can refer any appeal to the Generals notwithstanding the taxpayer's choice, and the Generals may ignore the election for the Specials unless there are substantive legal issues involved. Equally, where the taxpayer chooses the lay body, it can itself refer the matter instead to the professionals because of complexity or length: section 44.

In the past, appeals were often put in simply in order to delay the time at which the trader had to pay the tax. This tactic was virtually knocked out in 1975 when a new section 55 of the TMA 1970 was substituted. Thus the tax cannot be left wholly unpaid pending the hearing of an appeal. Payment is postponed only on that part of the tax as to which the Commissioners decide (or the inspector agrees with the taxpayer) that there are reasonable grounds for believing that the appellant is overcharged. The rest of the tax is due as though there had been no appeal. Interest is payable on tax which is overdue. The rate of interest is calculated in accordance with a formula, which is designed to align it with market rates (see section 178 of the Finance Act 1989 and S.I. 1989 No.1297). There is no income tax relief for the interest payments, so there is a pretty hefty inducement to pay tax promptly.

At the hearing of the appeal the onus is on the taxpayer. Section 50(6) of the TMA 1970 says: "If, on an appeal, it appears to the majority of the Commissioners present at the hearing, by examination of the appellant on oath or affirmation, or by other lawful evidence, that the appellant is overcharged by any assessment, the assessment shall be reduced accordingly, but otherwise every such assessment shall stand good." This is an enormously important point. It provides the Revenue with a very strong lever indeed with which to extract from the taxpayer all necessary information. The

The Traditional Approach

assessment is right unless it is shown by the taxpayer to be wrong. This is particularly important where the Revenue raise an assessment based on "best of judgment" or a "discovery". It may be that the Revenue can no more prove it right than the taxpayer can prove it wrong. It was emphasised in *Jonas v. Bamford* (1973) that that did not matter. So, in practice, a taxpayer who is shown to have means well in excess of that declared for tax will have to prove he gained them from betting or Great Aunt Maud. Mere assertion is not enough.

Once a taxpayer has given notice of appeal against an assessment he cannot withdraw his appeal without the agreement of the inspector. A reason for this rule is that on an appeal the assessment may actually be increased. But a taxpayer's appeal from the Commissioners to the court (see below) can be withdrawn in tax cases as in other branches of law.

The practice and procedure followed by Commissioners is governed by regulations made by the Lord Chancellor under section 56B of the TMA 1970 (introduced by the Finance Act (No. 2) 1992) and which are effective from September 1, 1994.[2] At the hearing before the Commissioners, normally the inspector appears for the Revenue and the trader may represent himself or be represented by a barrister, solicitor or accountant. For many years, hearings before the Commissioners were secret in the sense that they were not open to the public (nor to journalists) and in the sense that they were not reported. However, as a result of the regulations made in furtherance of section 56B, hearings before the Specials have, since 1994, usually been held in public (see S.I. 1994 No.1811, para.15), whilst the publication of reports of Specials' decisions is also sanctioned (see S.I. 1994 No.1811, para. 20, which gives effect to the enabling provision in section 56D of the TMA 1970 inserted by the Finance Act (No. 2) 1992). Reports of Specials' decisions have been published as part of *Simon's Weekly Tax Service* since mid–1995.

The Specials have been empowered since September 1994 to award costs where either party to a hearing has acted wholly unreasonably. The Generals have no power to award costs.

---

[2] See, the Special Commissioners (Jurisdiction and Procedure) Regulations 1994, S.I. 1994 No.1811, the General Commissioners (Jurisdiction and Procedure) Regulations 1994, S.I. 1994 No.1812 and the General and Special Commissioners (Amendment of Enactments) Regulations 1994, S.I. 1994 No.1813.

The Mechanics of Income Tax

An appeal lies from the Commissioners to the court, but only on a point of law, not on fact (see below for the importance of this).

Any party to proceedings before the Generals may, within 30 days of the Generals' decision, declare, in writing, dissatisfaction with that decision and require the Generals to "state and sign a case for the opinion of the High Court". The "Case Stated" is a document prepared by the Generals setting out their findings of fact, the contentions of the parties, and the Commissioners' conclusions of law. It is drafted in agreement with both the Revenue and the taxpayer. By this procedure of Case Stated an appeal is taken to the court. The Appeal is heard by a judge of the Chancery Division of the High Court. Thereafter, appeal lies from the Chancery judge to the Court of Appeal, and thence to the House of Lords in just the same way as in other branches of law.

Until September 1, 1994, appeals from decisions of the Specials also proceeded by way of the Case Stated procedure. Since then, however, a much simpler procedure has been used. Thus, either party to proceedings before the Specials may, on receipt of the written decision of the Specials, appeal, if dissatisfied, against that decision (see section 56A of the TMA 1970, as substituted by the General and Special Commissioners (Amendment of Enactments) Regulations, S.I. 1994 No.1813). In most cases, the appeal is heard initially (as with appeals from the Generals) by a judge of the Chancery Division of the High Court, although, exceptionally, an appeal may go direct to the Court of Appeal. Ultimately, the matter may be resolved on appeal by the House of Lords.

A high proportion of the cases heard in the House of Lords are tax cases. The reason is that often there is a great deal of money at stake, and even where it is more a question of principle than of money one of the litigants has an almost bottomless purse.

Law and Fact

It is very important to keep in mind the point made earlier that an appeal lies from the Commissioners to the court only on a point of law. The leading authority on this matter is *Edwards v. Bairstow and Harrison* (1956) (H.L.). The question at issue was whether certain transactions carried out by the respondents in relation to the buying and selling of textile machinery constituted an adventure in the nature of trade, in which case the profits were taxable, or whether they did not, in which case the profits were not taxable (though they would now be taxable as capital gains). The General

The Traditional Approach

Commissioners decided that there was no adventure in the nature of trade. The High Court and the Court of Appeal held that it was purely a question of fact and that the court could not interfere. But the House of Lords took a more robust stand. True, trade or no trade is a question of fact, but if the only reasonable conclusion to which the Commissioners could come on a consideration of all the facts contradicts the conclusion to which they did come, then their finding can be reversed by an appellate court. Naturally, this decision of the House of Lords greatly widened the scope for appealing from the Commissioners to the courts. But it still quite often happens that the court holds that it has no power to interfere with a decision of Commissioners because they are the sole judges of fact (see, for example, *Glantre v. Goodhand* (1983) (Schedule E)). It should be borne in mind that when this occurs the case is not much of an authority for the future. Where, on the other hand, the court does reverse a decision of Commissioners the judgment is of much greater authority.

Penalties and Criminal Proceedings

So far the litigation that we have been considering has been purely civil litigation; the taxpayer and the Revenue have been arguing as to which of them is right on the facts or on the law. But there can be criminal proceedings by the Revenue and also quasi-criminal proceedings for penalties. Proceedings for penalties usually arise out of "back duty cases", that is, instances where the Revenue are investigating the possibility that a person has not paid all the tax in the past that he should have paid.

PENALTIES

The Revenue may take penalty proceedings against a person in a number of different circumstances. The main instances are where a person has failed to make a return at all or where a person has made an incorrect return. The latter is much the more important in practice. A penalty is incurred if there is negligence or fraud—not otherwise. The maximum penalty is 100 per cent of the tax underpaid, *i.e.* the difference between the amount of tax payable and the lesser amount of tax which would have been payable if reliance had been placed on the incorrect return or accounts submitted. This penalty is additional to the tax itself. A person who knowingly assists in the preparation or delivery of an incorrect return or accounts may incur a penalty of up to £3,000.

The Board has a discretionary power to mitigate any penalty. At first sight it might seem that a penalty could be exacted from the taxpayer without making any assessment. But on reflection it is obvious that an assessment is needed in order to establish how much tax has been lost, and therefore how much the penalty should be. Normally, this kind of assessment will be based on the "best of judgment" power.

How far back can the Revenue go in making an assessment? The basic rule (in section 34 of the TMA 1970) is that an assessment may be made at any time not later than six years after the end of the chargeable period to which the assessment relates. This is called the "ordinary time limit". However, for many years, there was no time limit for making an assessment in cases of fraud or wilful default, although such an assessment could be made only with the leave of a General or Special Commissioner. Further, in cases of neglect the ordinary time limit could be extended to enable the Revenue to make an assessment (again with the leave of a General or Special Commissioner) for any of what were known as "earlier years". For years of assessment after 1982–83, however, a different regime applies under which there is a time limit of 20 years for assessments for tax lost because of fraudulent or negligent conduct (see section 36 of the TMA 1970, as substituted by the Finance Act 1989).[3] This period runs from the end of the year of assessment (or accounting period) to which the fraudulent or negligent conduct relates. An assessment may be made without seeking the leave of a General or Special Commissioner.

Assessments on the personal representatives of a deceased taxpayer are very much restricted. First, the time allowed for making an assessment shall in no case extend beyond the end of the third year following the year of assessment in which the death occurred. Secondly, when the deceased had been guilty of fraudulent or negligent conduct the Revenue can only go back as far as the year of assessment which ended not earlier than six years before the death (see section 40 of the TMA).

---

[3] A change prompted by proposals made by the Keith Committee. This Committee, which was chaired by the Scottish Law Lord, Lord Keith, was established in 1981 to review revenue enforcement powers. Its report was published in four volumes (volumes 1 and 2 in 1983; volumes 3 and 4 in 1984), and comprises an extremely clear and yet detailed survey of this fascinating topic.

The Traditional Approach

CRIMINAL PROCEEDINGS

Making a false statement to the Revenue (for example, in a tax return) is an offence chargeable on indictment or summarily under section 2(1)(c) of the Theft Act 1978: "where a person by any deception ... dishonestly obtains any exemption from or abatement of liability to make a payment ... he shall be guilty of an offence."

Making a false statement in a tax return with intent to defraud the Revenue is also an indictable offence at common law. The leading modern authority on this is *R. v. Hudson* (1956) (C.C.A.). This is the head under which the majority of Revenue prosecutions are brought.

Other heads under which criminal proceedings may be taken are forgery and perjury.

It is very rare for the Revenue to take criminal proceedings as a result of false tax returns. One reason for this dearth of criminal proceedings is that taxpayers are given an opportunity to settle. Bearing in mind that this totally avoids publicity and also allows taxpayers to avoid the full rigours of the penalty provisions, it is not surprising if taxpayers are often anxious to reach a settlement. Further, it would appear that the Revenue tend to the view that a prosecution should be undertaken only in serious cases.

Dates for Payment of Tax

The due dates for payments of income tax (after which interest generally begins to run on unpaid tax) are laid down in section 5 of the Taxes Act (as amended). The general rule is that tax becomes due on January 1 in the year of assessment or at the expiration of a period of 30 days beginning with the date of the issue of the notice of assessment, whichever is the later. But a special rule applies to tax charged on an individual or on a firm under Case I or Case II of Schedule D; here the tax is payable in two equal instalments on January 1 in the year of assessment (or at the expiration, if later, of the 30-day period mentioned above) and on the following July 1. There is a proviso to the effect that if the notice of assessment is not issued until after June 1 following the end of the year of assessment the general rule applies and the tax is due after 30 days (all in one amount, not in instalments). Tax under Schedule E is treated as due when it is deducted by the employer. Tax at the higher rate is due on December 1 following the end of the year for which it is assessed or at the end of the 30-day period mentioned above whichever is the later.

The Mechanics of Income Tax

2. Self-assessment

Return and Assessment

The introduction of the system of self-assessment gives the taxpayer the opportunity to compute his own tax bill. If the taxpayer opts to calculate the tax due, the tax return must be delivered by January 31 (the filing date) following the year of assessment and include an assessment of the taxpayer's liability to income tax (and capital gains tax) for that year.

When a taxpayer does not wish to calculate the tax due this will be done for him by a Revenue officer, provided the taxpayer delivers the return by September 30 following the year of assessment. If the return is filed after the earlier date of September 30, but without a completed "self-assessment" of the tax due, then in law the return is incomplete. In practice a Revenue officer will calculate the tax due, but the Revenue has indicated that it cannot guarantee to notify the taxpayer of the tax due in time for the January 31 payment date. If the tax due is paid late then interest and surcharge will be payable in the normal way.

Where a business is carried on in partnership a partnership return will be required. This partnership return will require details of the profits made by the partnership and of the shares of profit allocated to each partner. But no assessment will be made on the partnership and therefore there will be no joint liability for the tax due on partnership profits. Instead each partner will be required to include his share of the partnership profit in his own return (and self-assessment) and will be liable for the tax due on that share.

Sanctions against late filing of a return

If a return is not filed by the January 31 filing date an automatic penalty of £100 arises. If the return is still outstanding after six months a further fixed penalty of £100 will arise (unless a Revenue officer has obtained a direction that a daily penalty, of up to £60 a day, should apply instead).

When a taxpayer fails to file a return (and self-assessment) by the January 31 filing date a Revenue officer may make a determination of the tax due 'to the best of his information and belief'. This determination is then treated as the taxpayer's self-assessment for the relevant year until such time as the taxpayer actually files his return (and self-assessment). Superficially this resembles the traditional practice of raising estimated assessments (see above, p. 53).

But the determination is automatically replaced by the taxpayer's own self-assessment once filed.

Correction of Errors and the Power to make Enquiries

The Revenue may correct obvious errors in a taxpayer's self-assessment within nine months of the delivery of the return. Otherwise, the Revenue may only conduct an investigation into a return if a notice in writing is given to the taxpayer indicating the intention "to make enquiries into the return". The notice must be served usually within 12 months of the filing date (section 9A(1) of the TMA 1970, inserted by the Finance Act 1994). If such enquiries are undertaken, a taxpayer may be required by notice in writing to produce documents and accounts which might reasonably be required for the purpose of determining the accuracy of the return. A self-assessment may be amended in the light of information unearthed during an enquiry, although there is a right of appeal to the Commissioners against the amendment. On completion of an enquiry, no other enquiry into that return may be made, unless the Revenue "discovers" later an error in the return because of information not previously available or due to fraudulent or negligent conduct by the taxpayer. In such circumstances, the Revenue may raise an "old-style" discovery assessment against which the taxpayer may appeal to the Commissioners.

A taxpayer may amend his return within 12 months of the filing date, although this right is not exercisable during a Revenue enquiry.

Dates for Payment of Tax

For the tax year 1996–97 and subsequent years, the due date for payment of tax is January 31, following the end of the year of assessment. But provision is made for the Revenue to seek payments on account of two equal instalments payable on January 31 in the year of assessment and on the following July 31 (section 59A of the TMA 1970, inserted by the Finance Act 1994). Payments on account will not be sought where the taxpayer's income is mainly subject to deduction at source, *e.g.* under PAYE. When calculating the balancing payment due on January 31 following the year of assessment, credit is given for the tax paid on account and, depending on the circumstances, a further sum may be payable or a repayment made. Interest is payable on any payment which is overdue (whether a payment on account or a balancing payment) at a rate calculated in accordance with section 178 of the Finance Act 1989 (see above, p.54). Further, a surcharge of 5 per cent is levied if any balancing payment due on January 31 is not made by February 28, and an additional surcharge of 5 per cent is charged if the payment of tax due is still outstanding by July 31.

Duty to Keep and Preserve Records

Section 12B(1)(a) of the TMA 1970 (inserted by the Finance Act 1994) requires a taxpayer to keep all records which enable him to deliver a correct and complete return in a given tax year. For a trader, this includes details of all receipts and expenses of the trade and any supporting documentary evidence, *e.g.* accounts and books. Moreover, he must preserve those records for five years from the filing date (a "non-trader" must preserve records for one year from the filing date). Failure to keep or preserve records in this way will lead to the imposition of a penalty not exceeding £3,000.

Reviewing the Reviewers

One question of principle worth noting here is the extent to which the Revenue and their decisions can be appealed or reviewed. Some consideration has been given to the appellate system earlier in this chapter (below, pp. 54–56). An application by a taxpayer for judicial review may be appropriate in order to control improper conduct on the part of Revenue in dealing with the taxpayer's affairs (or, exceptionally, with other taxpayer's affairs, see *R. v. IRC, ex p. National Federation of Self-Employed and Small Businesses* (1982) (H.L.)), or by the Commissioners in the course of hearing an appeal. Where an application for judicial review is made, the court is exercising a supervisory as opposed to an appellate jurisdiction. It does not determine, facts nor does it become involved with the merits of the case. Its concern is to see if, on the facts presented to it, there has been a misuse of power which results in an injustice. For example, a court may be called upon to determine whether a decision taken by the Revenue was such that no authority acting reasonably and directing itself correctly as to the law could have reached it. A court, however, will only invoke its power of review when there is no alternative procedure available which is just as convenient and effective. Thus, if a matter is properly resolvable on appeal then this is the course which should be taken. For some instances where there is no remedy apart from judicial review, see Lord Woolf, "Tax and Judicial Review" [1993] B.T.R. 219.

Self Assessment

Allegations of maladministration may be pursued outside the courts. Thus, the Parliamentary Ombudsman may be called upon to investigate a taxpayer's grievance. Similarly, a matter may be referred to the Revenue Adjudicator who was appointed in 1993 by (although independent of) the Revenue in furtherance of the Taxpayer's Charter and whose remit is to consider complaints about the way in which the Revenue has dealt with a taxpayer's affairs.

Chapter 4

CAPITAL AND INCOME

A SEMANTIC NOTE

Income tax, Lord Macnaghten stated wittily, but inaccurately, in 1901 (*L.C.C. v. A.G.*) is a tax on income. Capital gains tax, we are told by the Taxation of Chargeable Gains Act 1992, is a tax on capital gains. But as long ago as 1935 Lord Macmillan helpfully advised us (in *Van den Berghs Ltd v. Clark*) that:

> "The Income Tax Acts nowhere define income any more than they define capital ... What constitutes income they discreetly refrain from saying ... Consequently it is to the decided cases one must go in search of light."

But wait a minute. In Chapter 2 we set out the wording of all the main charging sections of the Income Tax Acts. What is more, we asked you to reread the list. You will have found that the word "income" was rarely used. Instead, the 1988 Act spoke of "property, profits and gains" just as did the 1803 Act. In 1803 the tax was not called income tax at all. It was a "contribution" on "property, profits and gains". It still is.

Before we set off on our detailed exploration of income tax, we must take careful note of problems within the key words and phrases of the charging sections, and one fundamental problem behind them.

The problems within the words lie in the meanings of "income", "profits", "gains" and "annual". All these words are hopelessly ambiguous when taken out of their contexts, and their use must be carefully controlled. Take the word "profits". This is used in Schedule A, Schedule C,[1] Schedule D, Cases I, II, III and VI and section 6, the corporation tax charging section. Yet it means at least three different things. As used in the phrase "annual profits or gains" in

---

[1] Repealed in 1996.

Schedule D, Cases I and II it means *net profit*, that is, revenue income less revenue expenditure.[2] In Schedule C it meant *gross profits*, that is, revenue profits or income without any deduction for expenses. In Schedule D, Case VI it can mean *either* gross revenue income *or* net revenue income. Finally, to confuse us, "profits" in section 6 means both revenue and capital profits, that is, income and capital gains. We find the word again in section 131(1) in the definition of the key word of the charge to Schedule E, emoluments. Emoluments include "all ... profits whatsoever". What does it mean here? Our conclusions can best be summarised in the helpful words of section 29(8) of the Taxes Management Act 1970:

"... profits—

(a) in relation to income tax, means income,
(b) in relation to capital gains tax, means chargeable gains,
(c) in relation to corporation tax, means profits ... "

So now you know!

The same problems exist for "gains", a word which serves both as one of the key words of the charge to capital gains tax, whilst at the same time featuring prominently in a totally different sense in the Income Tax Acts.

"Annual" is also a chameleon word. It usually means "yearly" to the layman, as in the phrase "annual interest". Confusingly, the Taxes Act uses "annual interest" and "yearly interest" in relation to the same section, presumably meaning the same thing: see the marginal note to section 349 and section 349(2). What that same thing is has caused judges a lot of problems. Broadly, it has been held to be interest on a loan which may continue for more than a year, even if it does not do so in fact. "Annual payments" (as in sections 348 and 349 and Schedule D, Cases III and VI) are recurrent payments, that is, payments which continue beyond a year. By contrast the word takes a totally different meaning in the phrase "annual profits or gains". No recurrence is needed here. It means merely profits or gains *of a revenue or income nature*.

So we are back to the word "income". If "annual" is chameleon, we can only say "income" is kaleidoscopic. One must invoke the warning of Humpty Dumpty to Alice: "When *I* use a word it means just what I choose it to mean,—neither more nor less." At times it is used to mean *net* income, at other times *gross* income; elsewhere it

---

[2] Similarly, a *net profit* is taxable under Schedule A.

Capital and Income

means everything coming in, in a jurisdictional sense (as in Cases IV and V of Schedule D), that is, income remitted to the United Kingdom. In a general sense "income" in the phrase "income tax" means neither more nor less than those things which are caught by the charging sections of the Income Tax Acts.

These definitions can best be tested by reference to yet another meaning of income, that given by economists following Simons in 1938. He defined income as being the sum of the gain (or loss) in wealth over a set period, together with total expenditure incurred during that year. For example, if Shirley is worth £10,000 at the beginning of the year, and £20,000 at the end of the year, and has spent £5,000 during the year, then Shirley's income for the year is £15,000.

The charges to income tax can be both wider and narrower than this definition. It is, though, a very useful definition against which to judge the true scope of various charging provisions and, in particular, the limits on the charge on trading and similar income.

The closest that the charging sections come to the wide, Simons' definition is in Schedule E and Schedule F. Schedule F charges "dividends and other distributions". That phrase receives a very complicated definition in sections 209 to 218 of the Taxes Act 1988 (see pp. 296–305). All dividends are included, including a capital dividend: s.209(2)(a). Here it does not matter whether the receipt is revenue or capital for company law purposes: both are caught for tax.

The same is true for Schedule E, where "emoluments" are charged. This is a much wider word than "wages and salaries". Anything which arises "from" employment is, it seems, an emolument, whether or not it is income or capital in the sense used for Schedule D. Both Schedule E and Schedule F aim to catch everything that "comes in" to the taxpayer from the relevant sources. By contrast, Cases I, II and III of Schedule D catch "annual profits and gains", meaning net revenue income, as compared with capital receipts. But what is a capital receipt and what is capital?

Capital and Income

Some cases make a distinction between fixed capital and circulating capital. There is some value in this distinction, but it must be borne in mind that an item which would be fixed capital in one person's hands may be circulating capital in another person's hands. To take an example, a factory owned by X, a manufacturer, is fixed capital. If X sells the factory (because he no longer needs it) at a profit, the profit is of a capital nature and is not chargeable to income tax. A factory owned by Y, who makes his living by buying and selling factories, is circulating capital. If Y sells a factory, the receipt is trading income and is an item in calculating his taxable profit.

The distinction between capital receipts and income receipts has its parallel in a distinction between two kinds of expenditure. But because "income expenditure" would be rather an absurd expression, it is usual in this context to speak of capital expenditure and revenue expenditure ("revenue" with a small "r", of course). If X (above) buys a new factory, that is capital expenditure, and is not deductible in calculating X's income.[3] If Y (above) buys a factory that is revenue expenditure and is deductible.

At first sight one might think that a payment must either be capital in the hands of the payer and in the hands of the recipient, or it must be revenue in the hands of the payer and in the hands of the recipient. But this is not necessarily so. Suppose X (above) buys a factory from Y (above): X's payment is a capital payment, but Y's receipt is an income receipt. (For another instance of the principle see the House of Lords case of *IRC v. Church Commissioners for England* (1977).) And the converse may also occur: if Y buys a factory from X, Y's payment is revenue expenditure, but X's receipt is a capital receipt. This is a general point worth remembering. The nature of the payment does not determine the nature of the receipt, or vice versa.

At one time, if a receipt were held not to be an income receipt but a capital receipt, it was not chargeable to any tax at all. Nowadays a capital receipt may be, though not chargeable to income tax, chargeable to capital gains tax; taxes which remain distinct notwithstanding the fact that since 1988 capital gains have been taxed at the taxpayer's marginal rate of income tax.

As well as the distinction between income and capital, there is also a distinction between income (that is, taxable income) and casual receipts. Tips received by a taxi-driver are taxable; tips received by a nephew from an uncle are not. How does this difference arise? The explanation must lie in the source doctrine. The nephew has no source. The uncle is not a source, because a source must be a state of affairs which falls within one or other of the Schedules and Cases.

---

[3] But it may qualify for capital allowances: see Chap. 9.

CAPITAL AND INCOME

The taxi-driver's tips have a source which falls either within Schedule E or within Schedule D, Case I, depending on whether he is an employee (of a taxi company) or self-employed.

Most casual receipts (such as uncles' tips) are gifts. Here again (as with capital receipts) at one time gifts were not taxable at all, but now they may be chargeable to inheritance tax, and (if they are not in the form of money) to capital gains tax as well. For various reasons Uncle George's tip to little Bertie would almost certainly not be taxable, but in principle a gift is now capable of being taxed.

CHAPTER 5

INCOME FROM A TRADE OR PROFESSION

INTRODUCTORY

We now leave the more generalised aspects of income tax, and begin a study of each particular kind of income. It is convenient to begin with income from a trade or profession.

The basic section is section 18(1) of the Taxes Act. Section 18 sets out the broad provisions of Schedule D as a whole. So far as concerns trades and professions it provides that: "Tax under this Schedule shall be charged in respect of—(a) the annual profits or gains arising or accruing— ... to any person residing in the United Kingdom from any trade, profession or vocation, whether carried on in the United Kingdom or elsewhere ... " Section 18(3) sets out the various Cases of Schedule D and says that "The Cases are—Case I—tax in respect of any trade carried on in the United Kingdom or elsewhere; Case II—tax in respect of any profession or vocation not contained in any other Schedule ... "

It has been held by the House of Lords in *Colquhoun v. Brooks* (1889) that, despite the words "or elsewhere", Case I does not apply to a trade carried on *wholly* outside the United Kingdom. See further on this Chapter 32 below.

As we have seen, "profits" and "gains" (in this context) mean the same thing. It is legislative tautology. And the word "annual" carries very little weight. It only means that profits or gains, to be taxable, must be of an income nature; it does not mean that they must be recurrent.

What we must define are the words "trade" in Case I and "profession or vocation" in Case II. Each of these definitions, and Cases, presents in practice a major problem requiring considerable thought in drawing the lines around activities caught within the words. Apart from these problems, the principles of the two cases are broadly the same, although we will note a few differences.

The Case I problem is this: Is a given gain a trading gain or a capital gain? In the good old days a capital gain was entirely free of tax; since 1965 it has been subject to capital gains tax. Capital gains tax is distinct from income tax (this is unaffected by the unification of the rates of capital gains tax and income tax from 1988–89). Each tax has its own regime for the computation of gains/losses, and the characterisation of a particular gain/loss can have important repercussions for a taxpayer.

The Case II problem is this: Is a given person's exercise of his profession (or vocation) carried on within an office or employment, in which case he is to be taxed under Schedule E or is it carried on outside any office or employment, in which case he is to be taxed under Schedule D? Remember that section 18(3) in reference to Case II says "tax in respect of any profession or vocation not contained in any other Schedule". The issue is between Schedule D and Schedule E. It is nowadays accepted that the distinction falls to be made on the same principles as in the law of tort, and also employment law. In tort the distinction is important in connection with vicarious liability, and it is generally described as the distinction between a servant (or employee) and an independent contractor.

And in employment law the same distinction has led to considerable case law, especially on the questions of unfair dismissal and redundancy payments. In tax law it is described as the distinction between an employed person (Schedule E) and a self-employed person (Schedule D). In all contexts it is the distinction between a contract of service and a contract for services. For example, a solicitor in private practice,[1] either as sole principal or as a partner, is self-employed and falls under Schedule D. A solicitor engaged in local government or in central government or in, say, Unilever Limited, is employed and falls under Schedule E, and so does an employed solicitor in private practice; that is a person qualified as a solicitor who works otherwise than as a partner in a firm of solicitors. And, of course, the same person can be employed and self-employed at the same time.

Is there any importance in this distinction? Yes, there is. The tax rules are different as between Schedule D and Schedule E. In particular, a Schedule E earner is subject to PAYE and the rules governing his expenses are less generous.

---

[1] A solicitor is said to be "in private practice" in the same circumstances in which an accountant would be said to be "in public practice". Curious.

INTRODUCTORY

Although the advantages are not all one way, most people would rather be taxed under Schedule D than under Schedule E. On occasions, as the following instances illustrate, Parliament has intervened to determine whether liability to tax should be under Schedule D or E. One such instance concerns what is called "The Lump". The Lump means the men in the construction industry who, though performing the functions of employed persons, claim the status of self-employed persons by means of "labour only" sub-contracting. Several attempts at dealing with this situation have been made, and currently the position is governed by sections 559–565 of the Taxes Act. Except where a sub-contractor holds an "exemption certificate," the contractor must deduct from each payment that he makes to the sub-contractor a sum equal to the basic rate of tax, after allowing for the sub-contractor's expenditure on materials. So a sub-contractor, though nominally remaining under Schedule D, is to suffer deductions as though he were under Schedule E. That is the theory of the thing: in practice it does not always work very well.

Attention has also been directed towards "workers supplied by agencies." Section 134 of the Taxes Act provides that these workers shall be taxed under Schedule E. Examples of workers caught by this provision are secretaries, typists and nurses.

A third group of workers have been dealt with very differently indeed. These are "divers" and "diving supervisors". Section 314 of the Taxes Act provides that "the Income Tax Acts shall have effect as if the performance by [a diver or a diving supervisor of his duties] constituted the carrying on by him of a trade within Case I of Schedule D; and accordingly Schedule E shall not apply ... " This is the reverse of the treatment meted out to "The Lump" and to agency workers; it is a case not of treating self-employed persons as employed, but of treating employed persons as self-employed. One gathers that the reason for this generous treatment is the political or economic reason that if it were not done these divers and diving supervisors would leave the North Sea for sunnier places; sunnier fiscally speaking as well as climatically.

We shall return to the distinction between "employed" and "self-employed" when we come to deal with Schedule E in the next chapter.

We want to discuss more fully what we called (above) the Case I problem: Is a given gain a trading gain or a capital gain? Another way of putting the same question is, What is trading?

What is Trading?

There is a kind of definition of "trade" in section 832 of the Taxes Act. We say a "kind of definition" because it is one of those so-called definitions, common in tax legislation, which merely expand a word without defining it. "Trade", we are told, "includes every trade, manufacture, adventure or concern in the nature of trade." Notice that the last few words are "nature of trade", not "nature of *a* trade." Even so, this is little better than defining an elephant as being either an elephant or something which looks and behaves like an elephant.

Judges have also resisted giving an exhaustive definition to "trade", as widened by section 832. There is a very useful discussion of the concept, and its problems, in the anti-avoidance case of *Ransom v. Higgs* (1974) (H.L.). This concludes that it is possible for something to be a trade even though noone can actually give the trade a name; see also the consideration of *Ensign Tankers (Leasing) Ltd v. Stokes* in Chapter 2.

One other point to watch here is that the same person may be carrying on two or more separate trades at the same time, possibly in the same place. If so, it may be necessary for the trades to be taxed separately.

The question whether a particular person is or is not trading is a question of fact. It was neatly described in one case as "a compound fact made up of a variety of things"; *Erichsen v. Last* (1881). We will look in a moment at the variety of things that may bear on the decision, but first we want to draw attention again (as we did in Chapter 3) to the point that an appeal lies from the General or Special Commissioners to the High Court only on a point of law. At first sight, therefore, it would seem that a finding by the Commissioners that a person is trading (or is not trading) can never be reversed by the court. This is not so. Following the decision of the House of Lords in the case of *Edwards v. Bairstow and Harrison* (1956), the court can and will reverse the Commissioners' decision if it is of the opinion that (*per* Lord Radcliffe) "the facts found are such that no person acting judicially and properly instructed as to the relevant law could have come to the determination under appeal." His judgment in that case, with that of Viscount Simonds, repays close study.

The factors which bear on the question "Trade or No Trade" were graphically described by the 1954 Royal Commission on Taxation as "badges of trade". The Commission listed six badges of trade and though subsequent cases have indicated others those six are still the dominant factors. Quite a useful approach to the problem is to ask oneself, when considering a transaction or series of transactions, if it is not trading, what is it? The rival candidate is usually, though not always, investment. To purchase and subsequently realise an investment is not in itself trading. Another candidate is a hobby or private and non-commercial activities.

The first point to consider is the subject-matter of the realisation. Generally, if the subject-matter is such that the purchaser cannot either use it himself or derive an income from it or derive pleasure from it that points towards trading. Thus in *Rutledge v. IRC* (1929) the taxpayer, while in Berlin in connection with a cinema business, bought a million rolls of toilet paper for £1,000. Shortly after his return to England, he sold the whole lot to one purchaser at a profit of over £10,000. It was held that this was an adventure in the nature of trade. Notice that in this case, as in many others, the fact that there was only one transaction (a one-off job as the saying is) did not prevent its being held to be trading.[2] Contrast the case of *Salt v. Chamberlain* (1979). Mr Salt was one of those smitten by the computer "bug". He thought he had hit the jackpot with his by inventing a fool-proof method of investing in shares. He didn't and it wasn't. He lost a lot of money and tried to claim it as a trading loss. The court held that the shares were bought as investments. One test was whether the subject-matter itself produces income. Subsequently, however, in *Marson v. Morton* (1986) it was suggested that land could constitute an investment even though it was not income producing.

The second point is length of ownership. This is not a very compelling consideration, but there is something in it. A quick re-sale points towards trading but see also the fifth point, below.

The third point is repetition. Although, as we have seen, a single transaction can amount to trading, there are situations where a single transaction would not be trading but that kind of transaction

---

[2] There is a rumour amongst tax lawyers that this case should really be called the case of the *imaginary* toilet rolls. It is said that the taxpayer invented the story of the toilet rolls to explain an increase in wealth, in the same way as many, many taxpayers claim that their wealth has arisen from betting-winnings (which are not taxable). It is said that this taxpayer thought that the toilet roll story would not be taxable. It is the tax law equivalent of the alleged non-existent snail in the ginger beer bottle. Any student of tort law will be willing to explain this to the uninitiated.

repeated several times would be trading. In *Pickford v. Quirke* (1927) a director of a spinning company formed a syndicate which bought the shares of a mill-owning company and then sold the assets of that company at a profit. He then took part in three similar transactions, although the members of the syndicate were not always the same people. The Court of Appeal held that he was carrying on a trade, even though each transaction considered by itself was not an adventure in the nature of trade.

The fourth point is supplementary work in connection with the realised property. In *Martin v. Lowry* (1927) (H.L.) the taxpayer (who had had nothing to do with the linen trade) purchased from the Government its entire surplus stock of aeroplane linen, about 44 million yards. He found difficulty in selling it, and so he had to advertise extensively, rent offices and engage a manager and staff. He sold the linen to more than a thousand purchasers over a period of about 12 months and made a profit of between £1 and £2 million. It was held that the operations constituted trading. In *Martin v. Lowry* there was a very definite sales organisation, but there are cases where much more simple supplementary work has been held to make the transaction of buying and selling into trading. Thus in *IRC v. Livingston* (1927) three individuals, a ship-repairer, a blacksmith and a fish salesman's employee, who had not previously been connected with each other in business, bought a cargo steamer, converted it (partly by their own labour) into a steam drifter, and sold it at a profit. The Court of Session overruled a finding of no trade, and held that this transaction was the carrying-on of a trade.

The fifth point concerns the circumstances responsible for the realisation. There may be some explanation of why something is sold which negatives the idea of trading. In *West v. Phillips* (1958) a builder built some houses to hold as an investment and some for resale. Later on he decided to sell the investment houses, and he did so through the same organisation that sold his trading houses. The Special Commissioners held that there was trading, but the Court of Appeal reversed them, holding that the taxpayer decided to sell his investment houses because of rent control and the rising cost of repairs and higher taxation, and that in respect of the investment houses he was not trading.

The sixth point is motive. Although a trade may be held to exist even where there is no intention to make a profit, the absence of such an intention points against trading, whereas where there is such an intention that points towards trading. It is an important factor in a

What is Trading?

borderline case. Just such a case was *Taylor v. Good* (1973) where the taxpayer bought a house at an auction without really intending to, in the hope that he might live there. He later sold it, making a profit, but the Court of Appeal held he did not intend to trade when he bought it, and had not traded with it (see also *Kirkham v. Williams* (1991)).

So much for the case law on trading. Some activities have been declared by statute to be trading. The most important are farming and market gardening. Section 53 of the Taxes Act states that "All farming and market gardening in the United Kingdom shall be treated as the carrying on of a trade ... "

What is a Profession?

We must now turn to Case II, professions and vocations. Neither term is defined by the statutes, so the judges have done the job instead. In *IRC v. Maxse* is was said that the hallmark of a profession is the use of intellectual skill, with or without manual skills. In individual cases it will be a matter of fact whether, on balance, say a photographer running his own shop is a professional photographer taxable under Case II, or a trade taxable under Case I, or possibly both at the same time, because the trade is separate from the profession.

"Vocation" is a calling, the way in which someone spends his life. In ordinary speech it carries a rather starry-eyed idea of nurses or others dedicated to their work. This seems to mean that they carry on their work without worrying about mundane things like pay. But for tax purposes, it is somewhat ironic to find that the leading case on vocations is a case about a bookmaker. The case is *Partridge v. Mallandine* (1886). But, although the work of a bookmaker, a jockey and a racing tipster have all been held to be vocations, a full-time gambler is not! This was described in *Graham v. Greene* (1925), for the sensible reason (if illogical) that the Revenue would stand to lose far more than it gained from such people, because of loss claims! Anyway, betting and gaming taxes ensure such people contribute their share to the Exchequer.

The Computation of Profits

THE IMPORTANCE OF ACCOUNTS

What we have said so far may suggest that the charge to tax is concerned with individual items of income. This is true of value added tax, and in individual tricky cases for income tax, but not in the vast majority of income tax cases. Remember that there is a charge not on receipts, but on annual profits and gains.

The fundamental point about an assessment on this basis is that taxpayers need to produce a form of account in order to find out for themselves if they have made a profit. Likewise, the tax inspector needs the same information in broad terms, to provide a proper measure of profits for assessment purposes.

It is the professional task of accountants to produce accounts of profits and losses of income and expenditures, over a set period, usually a year. Professional accountants do this in accordance with the accepted practices of their profession, some of which have been formally laid down as statements of standard accounting practice (SSAPs) or as financial reporting standards (FRSs). An example of the former is SSAP 2, which sets out the fundamental accounting concepts that should guide the preparation of accounts.

Companies' accounts are limited by guidelines. All companies must produce and publish annual accounts which follow the forms and formats laid down in the Companies Acts. Furthermore, the accounts must be independently audited by professional auditors who must certify that the accounts comply with legal requirements, and also reflect a "true and fair view" of the company's profits for the period.

As the prestige of the accounting professions grows, and their role in tax matters also grows, so the question of relationship between tax law and accounting practices and principles becomes sharper. The underlying question of the relationship is whether evidence that proper principles of accounting practice requires that an item be dealt with in a certain way should be decisive of its treatment in tax law. For example, if accountancy principles treat an item as revenue expenditure, to be included in the profit and loss accounts, can the item be treated as a capital expense for tax purposes?

The answer to this question appears to be that courts will not readily accept that accounts prepared in accordance with accepted principles of commercial accountancy are not adequate for tax purposes as a true statement of the taxpayer's profits, etc. However, such accounts will not be acceptable for tax purposes to the extent that they or particular items contained within them conflict with any express or implied statutory rule or are contrary to principles established by case law. Although it is noteworthy in the latter respect that Sir Thomas Bingham M.R. in *Gallagher v. Jones* (1993) (C.A.) said:

The Computation of Profits

"I find it hard to understand how any judge-made rule could override the application of a generally accepted rule of commercial accountancy which (a) applied to the situation in question, (b) was not one of two or more rules applicable to the situation in question and (c) was not shown to be inconsistent with the true facts or otherwise inapt to determine the true profits or losses of the business."

If two or more principles of commercial accountancy either or any of which is generally accepted are pertinent in a particular case it is for the court, taking into account the professional evidence submitted to it, to determine what is the correct principle of commercial accountancy to apply—see, for example, *Johnston v. Britannia Airways Ltd* (1994).

For further consideration of these (and related) matters, see the special issue of the *British Tax Review* entitled *Accounting Standards and Taxable Profits* [1995] B.T.R. 433–524.

In the more workaday world of tax offices, if sensible-looking accounts are produced by respected accountants, they will usually be accepted without much problem, even if they do "try it on" from time to time.

Profit and loss accounts must follow a basic form, whatever precise rules deal with individual items. They must show the totals of relevant forms of income for the period and, against that, the totals of relevant expenditures. They must also show the opening and closing balances of trading stock (or opening and closing values of work in progress). The profit is the excess of income over expenditure, adjusted to reflect any increase or decrease in stock or work in progress between the start and end of the accounts period.

We will now examine the income tax rules determining what should be included as a trading receipt, how trading stock is handled and finally, what expenditures are allowable as deductions.[3]

TRADING RECEIPTS

The first question to be asked about any receipt is, is it a trading receipt or is it a capital receipt? The reader may wish to refer back at this point to Chapter 4 above.

---

[3] Broadly, these rules also apply where a trade is carried on by a company. In addition, for corporation tax purposes, the profit, losses and expenses relating to loan relationships entered into by companies for the purposes of a trade are treated as receipts or expenses of that trade (see below, p. 289).

In some circumstances the answer to the question is perfectly plain. Thus, if a manufacturer sells his factory because he has had a more up-to-date one built for him, it is clear that the proceeds of the sale constitute a capital receipt, which consequently does not enter into the computation of his profits for income tax purposes. It is equally plain that if the same manufacturer sells a widget[4] which has been made in his factory the proceeds of that sale constitute an income receipt which becomes an item in his income tax computation.

In other circumstances, however, the question "trading receipt or capital receipt?" is quite difficult to answer. This is particularly so where compensation is paid to a trader, and in cases of voluntary payments to traders.

Compensation

There is a mass of decided cases on this matter. We will look at three of them. In *Van den Berghs Ltd v. Clark* (1935) (H.L.) the appellant English company had entered into agreements with a competing Dutch company under which each company agreed to conduct its business on certain lines. After a dispute it was settled that the agreements should be terminated on condition that the Dutch company paid £450,000 to the English company. It was held that this was a capital receipt, and thus was not taxable. Lord Macmillan said that " ... the cancelled agreements related to the whole structure of the appellant's profit-making apparatus."

In *Kelsall Parsons & Co. v. IRC* (1938) the appellants were manufacturers' agents; they held contracts with several manufacturers under which they sold their products for a commission. One of these manufacturers wished to terminate its agency contract and it did so about 16 months before it was due to expire, paying Kelsall Parsons & Co. £1,500 as compensation. This sum was held to be an income receipt, and hence taxable. The loss of this one agency clearly did not relate to the whole structure of the appellants' profit-making apparatus. Lord Normand said (in the Court of Session): "The agency agreements, so far from being a fixed framework, are rather to be regarded as temporary and variable elements of the profit-making enterprise."

---

[4] "Widgets" are much beloved of American academic lawyers, but not many have crossed the Atlantic. They are simply unspecified units, and whether they are lollipops or lasers does not matter.

The Computation of Profits

In *London and Thames Haven Oil Wharves Ltd v. Attwooll* (1967) (C.A.) the taxpayer company owned a jetty which was seriously damaged by a tanker when it was coming alongside. The owners of the tanker paid a sum of money to the taxpayer of which part was apportioned to physical damage to the jetty and part to consequential damage, namely loss of use of the jetty during the 380 days taken up in repairing it. The Revenue did not seek to tax that part of the payment which was apportioned to physical damage, but it did seek to tax the part apportioned to consequential damage. The assessment was upheld by the Court of Appeal. Diplock L.J. gave a limpidly clear judgment. He said:

> "Where, pursuant to a legal right, a trader receives from another person compensation for the trader's failure to receive a sum of money which, if it had been received, would have been credited to the amount of profits (if any) arising in any year from the trade carried on by him at the time when the compensation is so received, the compensation is to be treated for income tax purposes in the same way as that sum of money would have been treated if it had been received instead of the compensation."

The Lord Justice went on to say that two questions have to be asked. First, was the compensation paid for the failure of the trader to receive a sum of money? If the answer to that is yes, there arises a second question: If that sum of money had been received by the trader would it have been credited to the amount of profits of the trader? The same question can be put more shortly, namely, would it have been an income receipt of the trade (and not a capital receipt)? If the answer to that question is yes, the compensation is taxable; if the answer is no, the compensation is not assessable to income tax. In the instant case that part of the compensation which had been apportioned to loss of use of the jetty (1) was paid for the failure of the trader to receive a sum of money, and (2) represented the profit (surplus of receipts over expenses) which would have followed from the use of the jetty during 380 days. So the assessment was correct.

Voluntary payments

A problem which has vexed the courts considerably is the status of a payment made to a trader voluntarily, without a contractual requirement that it be paid. When should such receipts be treated as trading receipts?

INCOME FROM A TRADE OR PROFESSION

It was established by the Privy Council in *Comr of Taxation v. Squatting Investment Co. Ltd* (1954), an Australian case, that the mere fact that a payment was voluntary did not prevent it being a trading receipt. Equally the Court of Appeal in *Simpson v. John Reynolds & Co. (Insurances) Ltd* (1975) confirmed that not all voluntary payments were taxable. That case concerned a payment of £5,000 by clients of the insurance brokers following the discontinuance of use by the clients of the broker's services following a change in control of the clients, a company. Important factors in the decision were that the payment was unsolicited and of an amount not tied to possible future sales, and that the trading relationship between broker and client had ceased. The payment could not relate to future performance. A different Court of Appeal working on different facts, reached a similar conclusion in *Murray v. Goodhews* (1978).

The *Simpson* case was, however, distinguished by another Court of Appeal in *Rolfe v. Nagel* (1982), a case concerning voluntary payments to a diamond broker. It was held that here the sums were compensation for otherwise unremunerated work and were not unsolicited, and were trading receipts. Similar thoughts lay behind *McGowan v. Brown and Cousins* (1977).

TRADING STOCK

It is very important to grasp that trading stock (stock-in-trade) is an essential item in a trader's account—for tax purposes no less than for commercial purposes. Let us take a simple trading account in the modern form in which it is usually presented nowadays.

	£	£
Sales for the year		27,000
Opening stock	2,000	
Purchases	21,000	
	23,000	
Less Closing stock	2,800	
Cost of goods sold		20,200
Trading profit		6,800

Notice that in the account we have used the phrase "trading profit". This account does not deal with expenses such as wages, rent, rates, heating, lighting, telephone, postage. Those matters would be dealt with in a further account, so reducing the trading profit to a taxable profit.

Trading profit is the amount by which the proceeds of the goods sold (£27,000) exceed the cost of those goods (£20,200).

If one omitted stock—both opening and closing—from the trading account one would get a different result. One would get sales £27,000, less purchases £21,000 = profit £6,000. But that would be unreal. This trader has not only made a profit of £6,000 on sales during the year compared with purchases during the year; he has also improved his position by having increased his stock during the year from £2,000 at the beginning of the year to £2,800 at the end of the year, an increase of £800.

The closing stock figure for one year becomes the opening stock figure for the next year.

As closing stock represents expenditure on goods not yet sold, that expenditure is credited to the current year and carried forward to be charged in the subsequent year—as opening stock—in which the stock is to be sold.

In *IRC v. Cock, Russell & Co. Ltd* (1949) the court gave its approval to the accountancy practice of permitting a trader to value stock at its cost price or its market price, whichever is the lower, and to treat each item of stock separately. So, when any item of stock is expected to fetch less than its cost, its market value (or "net realisable value") (instead of its cost) is included in the total of closing stock. The effect is to charge immediately in the current year that part of its cost which is considered to be irrecoverable.

In some of the reported cases on the matter closing stock has been described as being a receipt of the current year, and in other cases it has been described as a notional sale from one year to the next. And the use of a figure of less than cost has been described as an exception to the general income tax principle that an unrealised loss (or profit) cannot be brought into a tax computation. We venture to think that these views are based on a misapprehension as to the nature of the item of closing stock in a trading account, and that the correct view is that put forward by Russell L.J. in the Court of Appeal in *B.S.C. Footwear Ltd v. Ridgway* (1971). Russell L.J. said:

> "In my view the accepted practice of entering stock in hand at cost at the terminal date of the first period and the opening date of the second period arises from the fact that the expenditure has not contributed

anything directly to the figures of gross profit in the first period. It is unused expenditure, to be carried forward into the second period, in which it is estimated that it will contribute on sale to the gross profit of that period. But if it is estimated that on sale it will not contribute to the gross profit of the second period—that is, if it is estimated that it will sell below cost—the shortfall is to be regarded in the course of stock valuation as irrecoverable and may properly be treated as a loss incurred in the first period. This I believe to be the basis of the principle that for tax purposes market value if below cost may be taken as the value of stock in hand."

WORK IN PROGRESS. "Work in progress" is the phrase used to cover such things as goods in the process of manufacture. A manufacturer, at the end of a particular accounting period, will have some items in his factory which are partially but not wholly constructed. Such items are brought into account in the same way (broadly) as is closing stock, although this may not be a simple exercise (see *Duple Motor Bodies v. Ostime* (1961) (H.L.)). And the same principle applies to many other things besides partially manufactured goods; it applies for example to partially performed contracts of a professional person.

The rule in Sharkey v. Wernher. This case established the rule that if you transfer an asset from a taxable activity of yours to a non-taxable activity you must bring in to your accounts the market value of the asset which you have transferred just as though you had sold it. *Sharkey v. Wernher* (1956) (H.L.) concerned Lady Zia Wernher, the wife of Sir Harold Wernher, the owner of Luton Hoo and the Wernher Collection.[5] Lady Zia carried on a stud farm, the profits of which were assessable to income tax under Case I. She also owned horses and ran them at race meetings as a recreation, in respect of which activity no liability to tax arose. In one year she transferred five horses from the stud farm to her racing stables. The House of Lords held that the horses must be treated as having been disposed of by way of trade, and the sum which should be regarded as having been received on their disposal must be a sum equivalent to their market value. Lord Simonds neatly observed that the same point arises when "the owner of a stud farm diverts the produce of his farm to his own enjoyment or a diamond merchant, neglecting profitable sales, uses his choicest jewels for the adornment of his

---

[5] Someone ought to compile a "Who's Who in Tax Cases"; it would be like a tax case itself—long and expensive.

wife, or a caterer provides lavish entertainment for a daughter's wedding breakfast. Are the horses, the jewels, the cakes and ale to be treated for the purpose of income tax as disposed of for nothing or for their market value or for the cost of their production?" And the House of Lords (with one dissentient) answered "Market value."

Some years later the Revenue, very naturally, sought to apply the same rule to an author. In *Mason v. Innes* (1967) (C.A.) Hammond Innes (another celebrity) wrote a book called *The Doomed Oasis* and, before its publication, presented the copyright in it to his father as a gift. The Court of Appeal held that the rule in *Sharkey v. Wernher* did not apply. Their decision was apparently based on two points: first, that the taxpayer was carrying on a profession and not a trade, and that a professional person does not have stock-in-trade; secondly, that his accounts were not on an earnings basis but on a cash basis. (On this point see pp. 95–96, below). Neither of these points seems wholly convincing.[6]

SECTION 770 OF THE TAXES ACT The rule in *Sharkey v. Wernher* is a common law rule, but there is a similar statutory rule in section 770 of the Taxes Act. The section applies to "bodies of persons" (including partnerships). Where the buyer and the seller are under common control ("associated") the Revenue may substitute in the accounts of either party the notional market price of the thing sold for the price in fact charged, thus counteracting a transaction at an over-value or an under-value. The section does not apply where the under-value or over-value will be reflected anyway in the accounts of the benefitted party, which is the case where he (or it) is taxable as a United Kingdom trader.[7] The section is clearly aimed at "transfer pricing" between the United Kingdom and overseas. Bear in mind that where the section does not apply, the rule in *Sharkey v. Wernher* may apply.

TRADING EXPENSES

The legislation relating to trading expenses is couched in very negative terms. There is no section stating what expenses are deductible under Cases I and II of Schedule D. This is very different from Schedule E, where there is a section (section 198 of the Taxes Act)

---

[6] The book ought to have been renamed *The Lucky Oasis*.
[7] The Revenue will not lose any tax in this case, because an over-value will show an inflated plus item in the seller's profit computation and an under-value will show a deflated minus item (expense) in the buyer's computation.

which states positively what expenses are deductible by the holder of an office or employment.

For Cases I and II of Schedule D there are two negative enactments. Section 817(1) of the Taxes Act declares that: "In arriving at the amount of profits or gains for tax purposes ... no other deductions shall be made than such as are expressly enumerated in the Tax Acts." And section 74 of the Taxes Act declares: "Subject to the provisions of the Tax Acts, in computing the amount of the profits or gains to be charged under Case I or Case II of Schedule D no sum shall be deducted in respect of"—and this preamble is followed by 16 lettered paragraphs ((a) to (q)) containing undeductible expenses. If these two enactments (section 817(1) and section 74) had been taken absolutely literally the result would have been that no expenses at all would have been allowable under Cases I and II. A judge once said that the life of the law is not logic but commonsense. And in this case commonsense has triumphed over logic without much difficulty. After all, section 18 (of the Taxes Act) states that tax is to be charged under Cases I and II in respect of the annual profits or gains arising or accruing from any trade, profession or vocation. If you keep a shop and sell goods in a year for £6,000 it would be absurd if you were assessed to tax on £6,000 if you had spent £3,000 on buying the goods in the first place and £1,000 on rent of the shop. Your profit or gain is not £6,000; it is £2,000. It is now absolutely settled law that some expenses are deductible under Cases I and II.

Section 74 presents the reader with a seemingly random list of things. In practice, by far the most important is paragraph (a), which follows the fashion by also being drafted in the negative! It provides that:

> "no sum shall be deducted in respect of ... any disbursements or expenses, not being money wholly or exclusively laid out or expended for the purposes of the trade, profession or vocation ... "

The other items in the list should not be neglected. They separately prevent deduction of expenses amongst other things, for private purposes (para. (b)), deductions for capital (paras. (f) and (g)) and losses (paras. (e) and (k)).

Specific sections elsewhere in the Act (for example sections 83 and 592(4)–(6) sometimes make express provision authorising deductions of particular sums. Other sections (such as section 577) sometimes expressly prohibit the deduction of particular sums.

In the absence of other specific provisions, section 74, aided by the judges, has provided the guidance for what is deductible. In general, three tests must be met:

  (i) the expenditure is revenue, not capital, in nature
  (ii) the expenditure was incurred wholly and exclusively for the purposes of the trade
  (iii) the deduction is not prohibited by section 74.

We say "in general" because there are a few untidy corners. They arise in part from the nature of section 74. It is not clear whether the list of items (a) to (q) is cumulative or disparate, that is, whether a payment which is approved by one paragraph will still be disallowed if it seems to fall foul of another paragraph. Further, interest may be deducted even though it is capital: section 74 (f), and deduction for capital expenditure on the supply of implements appears to be sanctioned by section 74(d): *Hinton v. Maden & Ireland Ltd* (1959) (H.L.). It is for this reason that the whole of section 74 is important. But it is clear that where the other paragraphs are silent, paragraph (a) must be applied.

Revenue, not capital, expenditure

The same distinction falls to be made in regard to expenditure as in regard to receipts. It is not an easy distinction to make. In one case Lord Greene M.R. remarked, "... in many cases it is almost true to say that the spin of a coin would decide the matter almost as satisfactorily as an attempt to find reasons." (*British Salmson Aero Engines Ltd v. IRC* (1938) (C.A.)). But judges do not toss coins, at least not visibly. So we must look at some reasoning.

The first point to be clear about is that (as we pointed out in Chapter 4 above) a payment which is a revenue receipt in the hands of the payee is not necessarily an item of revenue expenditure by the payer. Equally a payment which in the hands of the recipient is a capital item may be a revenue expenditure on the part of the payer. The two things have to be looked at separately. The principles, however, are the same whether one is considering receipts or expenses.

In some cases of expenditure the matter is perfectly clear. If a manufacturer expends money on a new factory that is capital expenditure; if he spends money on raw materials that is revenue expenditure. Adam Smith's distinction between fixed capital and circulating capital is of some help here.

However, in cases where the matter has been less clear–cut reliance has been placed often on the classic statement to be found in the speech of Lord Cave in *British Insulated and Helsby Cables Ltd v. Atherton* (1926) (H.L.): "When an expenditure is made, not only once and for all, but with a view to bringing into existence an asset or an advantage for the enduring benefit of a trade, I think that there is very good reason ... for treating such an expenditure as properly attributable not to revenue but to capital." There is no doubt that this is a helpful general statement, but some qualification is needed. First, it is clear from later cases that "enduring benefit of a trade" must be taken as meaning "a thing which endures in the same way that fixed capital endures": see *per* Rowlatt J. in *Anglo-Persian Oil Co. Ltd v. Dale* (1931), approved and adopted by Lord Wilberforce in *Tucker v. Granada Motorway Services Ltd* (1979) (H.L.). Secondly, there may be expenditure which has an enduring effect, but which, nevertheless, is not deemed to be capital in nature. Thirdly, the identification of an "asset or advantage for the enduring benefit of a trade" may not be easy. For example, if a taxpayer borrows money for a term, is he to be treated as only receiving cash to be used in his business or is he effectively securing a continuance of his trade [and hence an advantage for his trade] for the duration of the loan? (see *Beauchamp v. F.W. Woolworth plc* (1988) (H.L.) in which the taxpayer company borrowed substantial sums in Swiss francs which were then converted into sterling. On repayment of the loans, the taxpayer company, because of the decline in the value of sterling against the Swiss franc, suffered a large loss. The House of Lords held that the loans were an accretion to capital and, therefore, the loss was not allowable [in that, presumably, the loans perpetuated the company's trade rather than being simply a component in the ordinary day-to-day carrying on of the company's business]).

Probably three main factors emerge from the welter of decided cases on the point: the nature of the benefit acquired in exchange for the payment; the manner in which that benefit is to be used; the means by which it is obtained (periodical payments or lump-sum payment). Different weights are to be attached to these three factors in different circumstances. In *Regent Oil Co. Ltd v. Strick* (1966) (H.L.) Lord Reid said:

> "Whether a particular outlay by a trader can be set against income, or must be regarded as a capital outlay, has proved to be a difficult

question. It may be possible to reconcile all the decisions, but it is certainly not possible to reconcile all the reasons given for them ... The question is ultimately a question of law for the Court, but it is a question which must be answered in light of all the circumstances which it is reasonable to take into account, and the weight which must be given to a particular circumstance in a particular case must depend rather on commonsense than on a strict application of any single legal principle."

There is one particular kind of expenditure which deserves to be mentioned separately. This is the setting aside of a sum of money to cover depreciation. It is well settled that such expenditure is of a capital, not a revenue, nature. However, it must not be thought that income tax law gives no assistance in respect of depreciation; it does give such assistance, but it gives it, in the form of allowances, called Capital Allowances, see Chapter 9, below.

Wholly and exclusively ... for the purposes of the trade

The second test that an expense must pass if it is to be an allowable deduction arises from paragraph (a) of section 74, which we quoted at page 84. This paragraph differs from the other paragraphs in section 74 in that instead of referring to some special item of expenditure it is a general test applicable to all expenditure.

It seems that the word "wholly" relates to *quantum*. The whole amount of the expenditure must be laid out for the purposes of the trade, or rather the expense is only allowable up to the amount of it which is laid out for the purposes of the trade. For example, if a company has paid over-generous remuneration to a director, a reasonable amount may be allowed, and the excess over what is reasonable disallowed.

The word "exclusively" has proved difficult to apply. The classic statement of the law is in the judgment of Romer L.J. in *Bentleys Stokes & Lowless v. Beeson* (1952) (C.A.). This case was concerned with business entertainment expenditure. At the time of the case there was no special rule relating to such expenditure; there is such a rule now (in section 577 of the Taxes Act) disallowing it save in the case of a very limited number of exceptions. Romer L.J. said:

"It is ... a question of fact. And it is quite clear that the purpose must be the sole purpose. The paragraph says so in clear terms. If the activity be undertaken with the object both of promoting business and also with some other purpose, for example, with the object of indulging an independent wish of entertaining a friend or stranger or of supporting a charitable or benevolent object, then the paragraph is not satisfied though in the mind of the actor the business motive may predominate. For the statute so prescribes. *Per contra*, if in truth the sole object is business promotion, the expenditure is not disqualified because the nature of the activity necessarily involves some other result, or the attainment or furtherance of some other objective, since the latter result or objective is necessarily inherent in the act."

And so the Court of Appeal allowed the expenditure which had been incurred in entertaining clients.

Lord Justice Romer made it all sound very easy, but in practice it has not proved easy to separate sole purpose cases from dual purpose cases, and one is sometimes left with the feeling that honesty is not the best policy. In *Bowden v. Russell & Russell* (1965) the sole principal of a firm of solicitors visited America and Canada with his wife to attend the annual meeting of the American Bar Association in Washington and the Commonwealth and Empire Law Conference in Ottawa. It was his intention to have also a holiday with his wife. The court held that the expenses incurred in connection with the conferences were not deductible, because they were incurred for a dual purpose, the advancement of his profession and the enjoyment of a holiday.

These rules and the doctrine of "dual purpose" have been applied somewhat unhappily for many years. Unhappily because of the point already made and because they do not allow sums incurred for two purposes (such as telephone rentals and car expenses) to be apportioned. But in practice every accountant knows that they can be apportioned, as long as one is not too greedy, whatever the strict provisions of the law. Take, for example, *Lucas v. Cattell* (1972). This was actually a Schedule E case but, as we shall see, these parts of the deductions rules are the same for both Schedules. Lucas was required by his employers to have a telephone at home, but they refused to meet the expense of the telephone rental. For several years the Revenue allowed Lucas to deduct a small part of the rental. One year he demanded more! One is reminded of Lionel Bart's famous song from *Oliver*. The result was predictable. Lucas ended up with nothing. His payment was not wholly and exclusively for his employment; and the rental payment could not be severed so that part could be said to be deductible. (On this underdeveloped aspect of the rule, see Lord Reid in *Ransom v. Higgs* (1974) (H.L.).)

Then Ann Mallalieu, a barrister and former M.P., gave the courts a chance to make some sense of the rules. They tried, but they found it difficult to resolve the issues and by a four-to-one majority the House of Lords overruled the Court of Appeal and Chancery Division and left the law in as much a muddle as ever: *Mallalieu v. Drummond* (1983) (H.L.).

The facts could not be simpler. Mallalieu claimed £500 for replacement items of court dress, their laundering and cleaning. This was revenue expenditure which she incurred to comply with the official guidance to barristers on dress in court. It was undisputed evidence that, at the time she bought the clothes, her only conscious motive was to comply with these professional requirements.

The judgment of Lord Brightman (for the majority) made clear that there was another source of unease about the rules in his mind. It is often felt that the expenses rules are over-generous to the self-employed as compared with employees. So his Lordship observed, the case was really about "the right of any self-employed person to maintain ... partly at the expense of the general body of taxpayers, a wardrobe of everyday clothes which are reserved for work."

After reciting the dual purpose rule, Lord Brightman reminded himself that the "object" of the expenditure was the decisive factor in applying the dual purpose rule. But, he said, the object of expenditure must be distinguished from its effect. Further, the conscious motive of the taxpayer in making the expenditure was not the deciding factor in establishing the "object". "It is inescapable that one object, though not a conscious motive, was the provision of the clothing that she needed as a human being." He adopted the judgment of Goulding J. in *Hillyer v. Leeke* (1976), which, in effect, rested its conclusion on the "self-evident truth" approach to the question.

Implicitly, this seems to overrule the test laid down in the *Bentleys* case (and cited by Lord Elwyn-Jones in his short, powerful dissent) without mentioning it. So we must now judge the object of an expense objectively, distinguishing its effect. But how do you judge the object of a British medical consultant's flight to the South of France to see a patient (or was it partly to have a holiday?) objectively? Further, for an example of the anomalies to which the application of this test may give rise, see *Watkins v. Ashford Sparkes and Harward* (1985).

Returning to the words of the section, note that it says that the expenditure must be "for the purposes of" the trade. This has been held to mean: "for the purpose of earning the profits": *Strong & Co. Ltd v. Woodfield* (1906) (H.L.), *per* Lord Davey. Damages that were paid by the owners of a licensed house to a guest who was injured when one of the chimneys fell on him were held not to be deductible. Despite criticism, this case and its test were approved by the majority in the *Mallalieu* case.

We want now to make special mention of certain types of expenditure.

TRAVEL TO WORK AND AT WORK. There are no special rules in the Acts governing the deduction of travel expenses by traders, so the general rules apply. However, there seems to be a lot of misunderstanding about expenditure on travel from home to work and from work to home. Some people think that home to work (and return) travel is not allowable for Schedule E taxpayers but is allowable for Schedule D taxpayers. This is not correct. It is quite true that there is a big difference in the rules relating to expenditure under Schedule E and under Schedule D, and we shall be looking at the difference in the next chapter. But in practice the courts have reached, albeit by different routes, similar conclusions about the allowability or otherwise of travel expenses under both Schedules. This is because the phrase in Schedule E, "travelling in the performance of the duties", more or less balances the phrase in Schedule D, "wholly and exclusively for the purposes of the trade" (as applied to travel).

In *Newsom v. Robertson* (1953) (C.A.) a barrister who had chambers in Lincoln's Inn and lived at Whipsnade was held not entitled to deduct the expenses of travelling between the two places. This was so even though he had at his home a library of law books, and worked at home in the evenings and at weekends. On the other hand, in *Horton v. Young* (1972) (C.A.) a self-employed bricklayer was held entitled to deduct the expenses of travelling from his home to the various sites on which he worked. At first glance this may seem to be inconsistent with *Newsom's* case. But this is not so. Mr Horton kept at his home his tools and account books and made his contracts there. It was held that his home was his base, whereas in Mr Newsom's case it was held that his chambers were his base. If your home is your base, travel to work and back home is wholly and exclusively for the purposes of your trade or profession. If your home is not your base then such travel is not wholly and exclusively for the purposes of your trade or profession; it is partly because you choose to live at, *e.g.* Whipsnade.

A later case caused some consternation. This is *Sargent v. Barnes* (1978). A self-employed dental surgeon had a dental laboratory which was on the route between his home and his surgery. He called

The Computation of Profits

at the laboratory on his morning and evening journeys for the purpose of collecting dentures and discussing work with his technician. He claimed to deduct the expenses of travel between the laboratory and his surgery. His claim failed, the judge holding that the expenditure was not wholly and exclusively for the purposes of the taxpayer's profession. The journey did not "cease to be a journey for the purpose of getting to or from the place where the taxpayer chose to live". There is another interesting point in this case—because of a mistake. The General Commissioners were muddled when they heard the appeal, and thought the Schedule E rules applied (see below, p.116–117), and that to travel was necessary.

LEGAL AND ACCOUNTANCY CHARGES. The professional costs incurred in a tax appeal are not allowable. This is because the tax is not an expense in earning a profit—it is the way the profits are spent: *Smiths Potato Estates Ltd v. Bolland* (1948) (H.L.)! But as a matter of practice the fees paid to an accountant for agreeing tax computations with the Revenue are allowed, and so are fees paid for advice on tax liability.

PENSIONS AND PENSION CONTRIBUTIONS. A pension paid by an employer to a former employee will be held to be wholly and exclusively laid out for the purposes of the trade except in so far as it is excessive. Whether annual contributions by a trader to a fund to provide pensions for his employees when they come to retire are deductible depends on the nature of the pension scheme to which the contribution is made. Where such contribution is to an "exempt approved" scheme (see section 592 of the Taxes Act) it is deductible as an expense. Contributions to an "unapproved" scheme are not deductible, unless the employee thereby receives a benefit under the scheme which is chargeable to tax or he is taxable by virtue of section 595 of the Taxes Act on the money paid by the employer (section 76 of the Finance Act 1989).

INTEREST: Interest is quite capable of being wholly and exclusively laid out for the purposes of the trade and, if it is, it is a deductible expense. This is immensely important in practice.

Not prohibited

The third test that an expense must pass if it is to be deductible is that it must not be prohibited by any of the specific paragraphs of section 74. We have now looked at the effect of paragraph (a), and have noted the other paragraphs. We will not deal with them all in detail, but will take a further look at paragraphs (d) and (g).

REPAIRS AND IMPROVEMENTS. Remember that the paragraphs are stating sums which are not deducted. Paragraph (d) says, "any sum expended for repairs of premises occupied ... for the purposes of the trade, profession or vocation, beyond the sum actually expended for those purposes." And paragraph (g) says, "any capital employed in improvements of premises occupied for the purposes of the trade, profession or vocation." So the upshot is that expenditure on repair is allowable, whereas expenditure on improvements is not.[8] In a famous passage Buckley L.J. (in *Lurcott v. Wakely & Wheeler* (1911) (C.A.) said:

> "Repair is restoration by renewal or replacement of subsidiary parts of a whole. Renewal, as distinguished from repair, is reconstruction of the entirety, meaning by the entirety not necessarily the whole but substantially the whole subject-matter under discussion."

In subsequent cases the distinction made by Lord Justice Buckley between repair and renewal has been taken to be the same as the statutory distinction between repair and improvements. His idea of "the entirety" seems attractive, but of course it means that everything depends on what the court regards, in any particular case, as the entirety. In *O'Grady v. Bullcroft Main Collieries Ltd* (1932) the expense of replacing a chimney by another on a different site was held to be not deductible. But in *Samuel Jones & Co. (Devondale) Ltd v. IRC* (1951) the expense of replacing a factory chimney was held to be deductible. In the first case the court regarded the chimney itself as the entirety; in the second case the court regarded the chimney as part of a larger entirety, namely the factory.

The distinction between repair and improvements runs into (in some circumstances it is virtually the same as) the distinction between revenue and capital expenditure. In *Law Shipping Co. Ltd v. IRC* (1924) a trader bought a ship in a state of disrepair. The periodical survey of the ship was overdue, but she was ready to sail, with freight booked, and she did sail. When that voyage was over, the ship underwent survey, and the owners had to spend some £50,000 on repairs, of which some four-fifths was attributable to the

---

[8] See further the useful article by P.F. Smith, "Repair or renewal" [1982] B.T.R. 360.

disrepair of the ship at the time of purchase. It was held by the Court of Session that that latter expenditure was in the nature of capital expenditure and was therefore not deductible. In *Odeon Associated Theatres Ltd v. Jones* (1973) (C.A.) the appellant company bought a large number of cinemas which had not been kept in repair. Some years later they carried out repairs which had been outstanding at the time of purchase. The cinemas were usable in their unrepaired state, but they were not up to the standard set by the new owners. The Special Commissioners made a finding of fact that on the principles of sound commercial accountancy these deferred repairs would be dealt with as a charge to revenue in the accounts of the company. The Court of Appeal held that the cost of the repairs was deductible as revenue expenditure. The *Law Shipping* case (above) was distinguished on three grounds: (1) in that case, but not in this case, the purchase price was less by reason of the disrepair; (2) in that case but not in this case the asset could not (except temporarily) earn profits until it had been repaired; and (3) in that case there was no evidence of accountancy practice, whereas in this case there was such evidence and it pointed towards deductibility.

The Basis of Assessment

Traditionally, tax under Cases I and II of Schedule D has been charged on what is called "the preceding year basis", *i.e.* in each year of assessment the assessment is based (subject to what we say below about the opening and closing rules) on the profits of the accounting period which ended at any date in the preceding year of assessment. However, the demise of the preceding year basis is imminent, as it is in the process of being replaced by a current year basis.

Over the years, reservations have been expressed about the manner in which the preceding year basis operates and the opportunity for tax avoidance offered by some of its rules. Thus, particular criticism has been levelled at the way it operates in the early and latter years of a trade or profession. Special rules (the opening years rules) are applied by which the profits of the opening and second year are taxed on an actual basis (an approach adopted with a view to lessening the tax burden in the formative years of a trade or profession).[9] There are also similar rules for the closing years (the

---

[9] And as an acknowledgment that a trade or profession cannot be taxed on a preceding year basis in its opening year.

last three years) of a trade or profession. The drawback is that the effect of these opening and closing years rules can be to tax the profits of the first year (assuming that the first year is not "loaded up" with losses!) three times and further when the trade or profession comes to an end leave other periods untaxed.

Concern has also been expressed at the use of "the deemed discontinuance" rules to secure a tax advantage. Under the preceding year basis, these rules apply to trades or professions carried on in partnership, and provide that a change in the partners (*e.g.* the retirement of a partner) amounts to an ending of one trade or profession and the setting up of a new one. As a result, such changes in a partnership might be orchestrated to derive the maximum tax benefits from the application of the closing years rules to the "old" trade or profession and the opening years rules to the "new" one. Moreover, where it is fiscally advantageous (which depends on the profits in the relevant years) an election might be made by the partners that the trade or profession be treated as continuing.[10]

However, it would appear that neither of these reservations was the principal reason for the present phasing out of the preceding year basis. Rather, it has occurred in furtherance of the move towards taxing all sources of income on a current year basis; a uniformity which is intended to facilitate the introduction of self-assessment (see above, pp.60–62).

Presently, the position is as follows. A current year basis applies from 1994–95 in respect of trades, professions or vocations commenced on or after April 6, 1994. It *will* apply to trades, professions or vocations existing before April 6, 1994 from April 6, 1997; there are transitional provisions for 1996–97. Trades or professions carried on in partnership are treated similarly, save that where there is a deemed discontinuance (see above) of a trade or profession carried on in partnership, which was in existence before April 6, 1994, and no election for continuance is made the current year basis will apply. (for further consideration of the taxation of partnership income, see below, pp.194–197).

The aim of the new system is to be certain that while the trade, profession or vocation subsists there is equilibrium between the

---

[10] As we shall see (below, p.194–197), these rules and the actions they engendered have no place in the taxation of partnership income under the regime which accompanies the introduction of a current year basis.

profits charged to tax and the profits actually earned (thereby avoiding the idiosyncrasies inherent in the opening and closing years rules under the preceding year basis, see above). Principally, this is achieved by taxing profits are they are earned by which we mean in each year of assessment the assessment is based on the profits of the accounting period (usually a period of 12 months) which ends in that year of assessment (rather than as under the preceding year basis the profits of the accounting period ending in the year before the year of assessment). Under the new system, special rules apply to the opening two years and the year of discontinuance of a trade, profession or vocation (see respectively, sections 61 and 63 of the Taxes Act, as substituted by the Finance Act 1994).

Post-cessation Receipts

The phrase "post-cessation receipts" means sums which are received after the cessation of a trade, profession or vocation for items sold, or services rendered, before the cessation.

It is relevant to this matter to consider the distinction between what is called the "earnings basis" for computing profits and other bases. (And the distinction is relevant to other aspects of income tax as well; see, *e.g. Mason v. Innes* (1967) (C.A.) at p. 83, above.)

The earnings basis is described in section 110(3) of the Taxes Act:

> "The profits or gains of a trade, profession or vocation in any period shall be treated as computed by reference to earnings where all credits and liabilities accruing during that period as a consequence of its being carried on are brought into account in computing those profits or gains for tax purposes ... "

So if a solicitor (to take an example) has, during a particular accounting period, got in, in hard cash, for services rendered during that period £10,000 and has rendered services which he has billed for a further £6,000, his incomings on an earnings basis are £16,000. On an earnings basis there will be brought into account— as well as his prospective incomings—the expenditure incurred for the period, whether paid or owing. The main basis other than the earnings basis is the "cash basis". This means that the taxpayer brings into account only payments actually received in the relevant period of account and outgoings actually paid. This basis is commonly used by barristers (because they cannot sue for their fees) and by authors (because it is impossible to estimate in advance how much they will make out of any particular book).

Any basis other than the earnings basis is called "a conventional basis" (*e.g.* in section 103(2) of the Taxes Act). This is rather a curious phrase, especially as it is the earnings basis which is the most usual. One meaning of "convention", according to the dictionary, is "practice based on consent". So we take it that here the meaning is that the taxpayer and the Revenue have agreed to depart from the earnings basis.

The Revenue does not regard the cash basis as being satisfactory for traders, no doubt because of the extent to which trading stock, and trade debtors and creditors (none of which is reflected in a cash account) can fluctuate from month to month or even from day to day. But the Revenue will accede to the request of a professional practitioner to use a "conventional" basis of accounting, except for the three opening years of a practice, provided he gives an undertaking to render his bills to his clients frequently—and consequently collect his fees promptly.

Until 1960 the post-cessation receipts of a trade, profession or vocation escaped tax. A leading case concerned Leslie Howard, the famous film actor, who was killed in an air crash in 1943. His real name was Stainer and the case is called *Stainer's Executors v. Purchase* (1952) (H.L.). It was held by the House of Lords that royalties which were paid to his executors after his death were not taxable. This result stemmed from the source doctrine; income tax is a tax on what flows from a source; if the source has dried up there is nothing to tax. (see Chapter 2, above.) Another case concerned Peter Cheyney, the celebrated author. In *Carson v. Peter Cheyney's Executor* (1959) (H.L.) it was held that royalties received after Peter Cheyney's death were not taxable, again because of the source doctrine.

This state of affairs, which notably benefited retiring barristers and their estates, was ended by legislation in two bites, one in 1960 and the other in 1968. The enactments are now contained in sections 103–110 of the Taxes Act. Section 103 brings into charge to tax (under Case VI) all post-cessation receipts of a taxpayer who had been on the earnings basis and some post-cessation receipts of a taxpayer who had been on a conventional basis. Section 104 brings into charge (under Case VI) such post-cessation receipts of a taxpayer who had been on a conventional basis as are not caught by section 103. (Certain receipts are expressly excepted and are not caught by either section, *e.g.* a lump sum paid to the executors of an author for the assignment of a copyright.) There is some relief under section 104, but not under section 103, granted to an individual born before April 6, 1917.

Retirement Annuities and Personal Pensions

A self-employed individual does not have an employer to pay him a pension when he retires; he must make his own provision for retirement. Before July 1, 1988, it was fiscally advantageous for such individuals to make provision for their retirement by entering into approved[11] retirement annuity contracts (see sections 619–629 of the Taxes Act). Since that date, as a result of a fundamental re-appraisal by the government of pension provision for both the employed and self-employed, it has not been possible to enter into retirement annuity contracts. They have been replaced by personal pensions (see sections 630–655 of the Taxes Act).

Personal pensions, similarly, receive favourable tax treatment. Thus, tax relief takes the form of deducting from the individual's earnings the amounts he pays as contributions to approved[12] personal pension schemes (see section 639). In other words, he does not pay tax on the amount of the contributions. The relief, however, is limited to a certain percentage of the individual's net relevant earnings, (*i.e.* broadly, income derived from carrying on a trade, profession or vocation), and is determined for 1996–97 as follows, by reference to various age ranges:

Age	Maximum Contribution
to 36	17.5%
36–45	20%
46–50	25%
51–55	30%
56–60	35%
61 or more	40%

[11] "Approved" means approved by the Board of Inland Revenue.
[12] Similarly approved by the Board of Inland Revenue although by using different criteria!

In addition, net relevant earnings are subject to an earnings cap (£82,200 for 1996–97). Effectively this means the *maximum* contribution (qualifying for relief) which the individual can make to personal pension schemes is limited to the percentage for his age range of £82,200. If an individual has unused relief this may be carried forward (section 642), or if he has made excess contributions an election may be made for such contributions to be carried back (section 641).

The relief described above is, of course, directed to the time when the individual is still working helping him to build up provision for when he retires. Such provision is enormously increased by the fact that the scheme itself into which he pays his contributions is exempt from income tax (section 643(2)) and also from capital gains tax (section 271(1)(h) of the Taxation of Chargeable Gains Act 1992).

Save for the earnings cap, broadly similar provisions govern the tax treatment of approved retirement annuity contracts.

Class 4 Contributions

Finally, before we leave the taxation of income under Schedule D, Cases I and II, we must note the effect of Class 4 Contributions under the Social Security (Contributions and Benefits) Act 1992.

Whenever anyone aged 16 or over has income taxable under these two Cases, they are required to pay a "contribution" in addition to income tax on their profits. The contribution is levied as a set percentage of these profits in so far as they exceed a lower limit, up to a higher limit. In 1996–97 the percentage is 6 per cent, the lower limit is £6,860 and the upper limit is £23,660.

No benefits are earned by a Class 4 Contribution. In effect, therefore, the "contribution" operates as a further tax on the taxpayer's profits.

Generally, self-employed earners have to pay Class 2 contributions at a flat rate (£6.05 per week for 1996–97) as well as Class 4 contributions—see Chapter 15.

CHAPTER 6

INCOME FROM AN EMPLOYMENT

INTRODUCTORY

In the last chapter we considered the taxation, under Cases I and II of of Schedule D, of self-employed individuals. Now we have to consider the taxation of employed individuals. Far more people are employed than are self-employed. In 1995, incomes from employment represented 63 per cent of the gross national product, as against 11 per cent for incomes from self-employment. The income tax on employment incomes accounts for some 75 per cent of the whole yield from direct taxes.

The Schedule we are concerned with is Schedule E. It is set out in section 19 of the Taxes Act. The Schedule contains three cases, Cases I, II and III. In this chapter we shall confine the discussion to situations where no foreign element is involved, leaving foreign elements to be dealt with in Chapter 32 below. Cases II and III necessarily involve a foreign element, and Case I can involve a foreign element, though it far more commonly does not. In this chapter therefore we shall be dealing solely with Case I, and with Case I only in so far as it does not involve any foreign element.

Section 19(1) declares:

> "The Schedule referred to as Schedule E is as follows: ... Tax under this Schedule shall be charged in respect of any office or employment on emoluments therefrom which fall under ... Case I: ... for any year of assessment in which the person holding the office or employment is resident and ordinarily resident in the United Kingdom ... "

Two important points are contained in that passage, being the two factors which must be present if tax is to be charged under Schedule E: (1) there must be an office or employment; (2) there must be emoluments which are derived from that office or employment. (The beautiful symmetry of this proposition is broken by the fact that such social security benefits as are taxable are taxable under Schedule E, even although those benefits cannot be said to derive from an office or employment: Taxes Act, section 617. Occupational pensions are also taxable under Schedule E, but that does not militate against the proposition because they *are* derived from an office or employment.)

Office or Employment

"Employment" is a much wider word than "office", but the word "office" fulfils a useful function in that it catches some situations which might not be regarded as employments. An office was described by Rowlatt J. in *Great Western Railway Co. v. Bater* (1920) as "a subsisting, permanent, substantive position which has an existence independent of the person who fills it, and which is filled in succession by successive holders." A good example would be a judge, and that illustrates the point made above: a judge is taxed under Schedule E; it would be disrespectful (and, we think, inaccurate) to describe him as "employed", but he is undoubtedly the holder of an office. Another example is a company director. If he has a service agreement with his company he is probably employed; if he does not he is probably not employed. But in either case he is an office-holder, and he is taxed under Schedule E. This is so even if the company of which he is a director is what is called a "one man company" and he is the one man.

These examples were easy to determine, but what of the status of part-time officials such as inspectors of government inquiries and part-time Rent Assessment Committee or Social Security Tribunal chairmen? The Government takes the view that such people are office-holders in most cases, but the holders frequently disagree, as it would suit them better to regard themselves as still self-employed.

This conflict came before the courts in *Edwards v. Clinch* (1982) (H.L.) and caused them considerable problems. A bare majority of the House of Lords decided that a civil engineer who sat from time to time as a chairman of government inquiries, being appointed separately to separate inquiries, was taxable under Case II of Schedule D and was not an office-holder. The majority broadly endorsed the approach in the *Bater* case, but emphasised that the performance of the office was less important than its existence independent of the holder of the office. It was, it might be added, agreed that the engineer was not an employee.

"Employment" is a very difficult word to define, and the tax legislation does not make the attempt. In one case, Rowlatt J. said: "I thought of the expression 'post'." Perhaps the man on the Clapham omnibus puts his finger on the point when he says: "I used to be employed and work for a boss, but now I am self-employed and I'm my own boss." This question of "employed" or "self-employed" was noted in the last chapter (see p. 70). It is worth nothing just how important the distinction is in tax law. Not only is it of vital importance in distinguishing between Schedule E and Schedule D, but it is also crucial to deciding whether someone is carrying on "his" business so as to be liable to register for VAT. Again it is central to the determination of liability to Class 1 (as against Class 2 and Class 4) National Insurance contributions, and the benefits that follow from such contributions. Much of the early case law about the divide arose from National Insurance contribution cases, such as the *Global Plant* case (1971) and the *Ready Mixed Concrete* case (1968), both against the Secretary of State for Social Services.

However, case law has also developed in the field of employment law. In those cases the status of the individual for tax and National Insurance contributions is sometimes prayed in aid. Not infrequently the same person has claimed to be self-employed for tax and social security purposes, but an employee so as to claim unfair dismissal or redundancy payments or the benefits of health and safety laws.

In *Young and Woods Ltd v. West* (1980) (C.A.) the court drew attention to this and pointed out that corrective action ought to be taken by the tax authorities to reassess individuals who were successful in claiming rights as employees, adding that in such cases, the "employees" themselves might gain little out of belatedly claiming a change of status.

In another employment case, namely *O'Kelly v. Trusthouse Forte* (1983) (C.A.), the Court concluded that the question whether somebody was working under a contract of service was a question of fact to be decided by the competent body. Interestingly, the conclusion that was so reached was in reliance on an income tax case, *Edwards v. Bairstow* (1956) (see p. 56 above). In recent years, the Revenue and the Department of Social Security have worked together to good effect in this area. For example, in March 1994, a joint report entitled *Employment Status for Tax and National Insurance—the Common Approach* was published. There has also been some acceptance by the Department of Social Security of the Revenue lists of types of worker who warrant self-employed status. Another tax case in this field is *Fall v. Hitchen* (1973). The taxpayer was a professional ballet dancer[1] engaged by Sadler's Wells. Under his contract he was paid £18 a week to rehearse, understudy and dance for a minimum period of rehearsals plus 22 weeks and thereafter until the contract was ended by a fortnight's notice on either side. He was permitted to accept outside work when not required by the Sadler's Wells manager. Pennycuick V.-C. held that he had been correctly assessed under Schedule E. The importance of the case is that it decides that the test of whether a person is an employed person is the same in a tax context as it is in a social security or tort context: is he employed under a contract of service as distinct from a contract for services? The judge said:

> "... unless some special limitation is to be put on the word 'employment' in any given expression 'contract of service' appears to be coterminous with the expression 'employment'. I can find no such context in relation to Schedule E. I do not see how it could be said that emoluments arising from a contract of service are not emoluments arising from an employment within the meaning of the charging words in Schedule E."

A person may be a professional person and yet be employed This became clear in the case of doctors (and medicine is one of the traditional learned professions) after the establishment in 1948 of the National Health Service. A full-time hospital doctor is clearly employed. And in *Mitchell and Edon v. Ross* (1960) (C.A.) it was held by the Court of Appeal that a part-time consultant under the National Health Service was assessable under Schedule E in respect of that appointment and at the same time was assessable under Case II of Schedule D in respect of his private practice. (The case went to the House of Lords but not on the above point. In the House of Lords it was held that expenses incurred (but disallowed) under the Schedule E office could not be allowed under the Schedule D profession.)

Another border-line problem with professionals is the "one man service company" where the taxpayer sets up a company, and the company contracts to supply the individual's services. This was

---

[1] It is relief to find that the ballet dancer's name was not Fall, but Hitchen.

queried in *Cooke v. Blacklaws* (1984), but held by the court to be valid for tax purposes.

However, a person cannot hold an office or employment as *part of a* profession for income tax purposes, because the Schedules are mutually exclusive. So if a person is a holder of an office or contract of service, the income must be taxed under Schedule E. This was emphasised in the House of Lords in *IRC v. Brander & Cruickshank* (1971) (H.L.). Although the rule was heavily criticised in that case by Lord Donovan, and is not always strictly observed in practice, it remains the law in income tax cases.

It may also be noted that the Revenue have over recent years made a determined, although not always successful, attempt to extend, Schedule E tax to taxpayers in the "grey areas" between the Schedules where previously taxpayers were treated as taxable under Schedule D. Further, the question of whether a taxpayer should be taxed under Schedule D or E is still very much a "live" issue in the courts—see, for example, *Hall v. Lorimer* (1994) (C.A.).

Emoluments Therefrom

As we have seen, Section 19 of the Taxes Act taxes emoluments from an office or employment. Section 131(1) of the Taxes Act declares: "Tax under Case I ... of Schedule E shall ... be chargeable on the full amount of the emoluments falling under that Case, subject to such deductions only as may be authorised by the Tax Acts, and the expression 'emoluments' shall include all salaries, fees, wages, perquisites[2] and profits whatsoever." Notice that the subsection does not define "emoluments", it merely states what is included in that expression. The dictionary (Concise Oxford) definition of "emolument" is "profit from office or employment, salary". So the idea of the payment being *derived from* the office or employment is inherent in the word "emolument" itself. As Lord Radcliffe said in *Hochstrasser v. Mayes* (1960) (H.L.):

> "... it is not sufficient to render a payment assessable that an employee would not have received it unless he had been an employee ... it is assessable if it had been paid to him in return for acting as or being an employee."

---

[2] The common expression "perk" is an abbreviation of "perquisite".

Income from an Employment

Lord Templeman in *Shilton v. Wilmshurst* (1991) (H.L.) set out the test to be applied in determining whether a payment should be treated as an emolument under section 19. He said:

"Section 181[3] is not confined to 'emoluments from the employer' but embraces all 'emoluments from employment'; the section must therefore comprehend an emolument provided by a third party, a person who is not the employer. Section 181 is not limited to emoluments provided in the course of the employment; the section must therefore apply first to an emolument which is paid as a reward for past services and as an inducement to continue to perform services and, second, to an emolument which is paid as an inducement to enter into a contract of employment and to perform services in the future. The result is that an emolument 'from employment' means an emolument 'from being or becoming an employee'."

In that case, Peter Shilton, the well known footballer, was paid £75,000 by Nottingham Forest on his transfer from Nottingham Forest to Southampton. The question was whether that payment should be treated as derived from his employment with Nottingham Forest (and hence a terminal payment or "golden handshake" as to which see below, p.126) or as an emolument from his forthcoming employment with Southampton. The tax treatment of the payment was dependent on the answer to this question. The House of Lords decided that it was an emolument of his employment with Southampton as it was an inducement for him to sign for Southampton and subsequently to play for that team. It made no difference that the payment was made by a third party, *i.e.* Nottingham Forest which had no interest in how Shilton performed for Southampton.[4]

In the course of his judgment in *Shilton v. Wilmshurst* (1991) (H.L.), Lord Templeman indicated that a payment would not be taxable as an emolument under section 181 [19] if it was attributable to something other than being or becoming an employee, *e.g.* if it was paid to relieve distress. This view was endorsed in *Mairs v. Haughey* (1993) (H.L.) in which it was decided that a payment to employees to relinquish their contingent rights under a non-statutory redundancy scheme was not taxable. This payment took

---

[3] Now section 19 of the Taxes Act.
[4] Except, presumably, when Shilton played for Southampton against Nottingham Forest!

its character from the nature of the payment it replaced, namely, a redundancy payment which might otherwise have been made. Lord Woolf said, "a characteristic of a redundancy payment is that it is to compensate or relieve an employee for what can be the unfortunate consequences of becoming unemployed".[5]

It is central to Lord Templeman's test (and, indeed, to many of the cases in this area) that for an emolument to be taxable it must be a "reward for services". It might be asked, therefore, whether it is conceivable that a payment which is not a "reward for services" can be an emolument taxable under section 19 of the Taxes Act. *Hamblett v. Godfrey* (1987) (C.A.) in which the Court of Appeal decided that a payment of £1,000 made to those employees of GCHQ who agreed to give up their right to belong to a trade union was taxable as an emolument arguably provides (notwithstanding attempts in later cases to suggest otherwise) an example of such an instance.

GIFTS

The most difficult area in which to draw the line between emoluments and non-emoluments is in the field of gifts. There is a mass of decided cases on this matter, and it is not easy to discern in them any clear-cut principle. It is tempting to say that if a payment is made by an employer it must be an emolument and if it is made by other persons it is not an emolument. But the cases do not bear that out; the most one can say is that a payment made by an employer is *likely* to be held to be assessable. In *Ball v. Johnson* (1971) a bank clerk who was paid £130 by the bank which employed him for having passed the examinations of the Institute of Bankers was held not to be assessable on that amount. In *Calvert v. Wainwright* (1947) a taxi-driver was assessed on the tips paid to him by his "fares", who could not be considered to be his employers. Again, it is tempting to say that if a payment is made in pursuance of a term of the contract of employment it must be assessable and if it is made without legal obligation it cannot be assessable. But that again is not borne out by the cases. In *Ball v. Johnson* (above) the £130 was as near as damn-it paid under a contractual obligation; a term of his employment required him to sit for the examinations, and it was stated in the bank's handbook that it was the usual practice to make such a payment. But perhaps *Ball v. Johnson* is rather an exceptional case. We think one can assert that a payment made in pursuance of the contract of employment is almost, but not quite, bound to be assessable. After all, because it is obligatory

[5] However, redundancy payments may be taxed under s.148 of the Taxes Act, see below, p.126.

it is not a gift, so what is it? But the converse is definitely not true; it is not true to say that if a payment is not in pursuance of a contractual obligation it cannot be assessable. In *Wright v. Boyce* (1958) (C.A.) a huntsman was held to be rightly assessed on Christmas presents of cash received from followers of the hunt even though his contract of service conferred no right to the gifts. The payments were made in pursuance of a custom. Custom seems to be a very important factor in this area of the law.

The world of sport has produced some interesting cases in this field. In *Seymour v. Reed* (1927) (H.L.) where a benefit match was held for a professional cricketer on his retirement, the gate money was held not to be assessable. But in *Moorhouse v. Dooland* (1955) (C.A.) money collected from the crowd for a professional cricketer for outstanding performances was held to be taxable. A cynic might think that the distinction between these cases is the distinction between first-class county cricket and Lancashire League cricket, but the Court of Appeal were able to make more orthodox distinctions: in *Dooland's* case there was a contractual right to have a collection made whenever his performance was outstanding; and collections had been made for him not once but several times.

The case of *Moore v. Griffiths* (1972) arose out of England's winning of the World Cup in 1966. The Football Association paid £1,000 to each member of the squad. These payments were held not to be taxable. Brightman J. held that the payments had the quality of a testimonial or accolade rather than the quality of remuneration for services rendered, and he set out a number of factors which pointed to that conclusion. One factor was that "the payment had no foreseeable element of recurrence" (on which one might comment "You can say that again"). Another factor was that "each member of the team, regardless of the number of times that he played or whether he was a player or reserve, received precisely the same sum of £1,000. The sum therefore was not in any way linked with the quantum of any services rendered."

That last factor raises an important and constant theme in these cases. A payment may be unconnected with services rendered, either (as in the *Bobby Moore* case above) because it is given to more than one person without measuring their separate merits, or (more commonly) because it is given to one person precisely as an appreciation of his merits, but his merits as a human being rather than as an employee. There is a flavour of this latter idea in *Seymour v. Reed* (above) and in *Calvert v. Wainwright* (above), where Atkinson J. said:

"Suppose somebody who has the same taxi every day, which comes in the morning as a matter of course to take him to his work, and then takes him home at night. The ordinary tip given in those circumstances would be something which would be assessable, but supposing at Christmas, or when the man is going for a holiday, the hirer says: 'You have been very attentive to me, here is a 10-shilling note,' he would be making a present, and I should say it would not be assessable because it has been given to the man because of his qualities, his faithfulness and the way he has stuck to the passenger."

EXPENSES ALLOWANCES

Generally, if an employee (other than an employee or director to whom section 153 of the Taxes Act applies, see below, p. 120) incurs an expense in such circumstances that it is deductible in calculating his tax liability under section 198 of the Taxes Act (on which see pp. 115–116 below) and his employer reimburses him, the amount paid to the employee by the employer does not form part of the employee's emoluments; so held by a majority of the House of Lords in *Owen v. Pook* (1970). If the employer, instead of reimbursing the employee's expenses after they have been incurred, makes round-sum payments to the employee as expenses allowances the practice of the Revenue is to treat such payments as not being emoluments, provided they are reasonable in amount. In strict law such payments probably are emoluments, but they would be offset by the deductibility of the expenditure in respect of which they are paid. It is important to be clear in one's mind that there is a distinction between an expense allowance that is not an emolument at all and an expense allowance that is an emolument but is balanced by the deductibility of the expense which it represents.

BENEFITS IN KIND

So far we have been talking about payments made to an employee in actual money. But an emolument may take a form other than money. This is clear from the presence of the word "perquisites" in the definition (section 131(1)).

At this point it is necessary to distinguish between what one might call the common law principle and certain statutory modifications of that principle. Legislation has intervened in two ways: (1) it has declared that for *all* employees (and office-holders) certain things shall be regarded as emoluments which under the common law principle would not be emoluments; and (2) it has introduced a separate (harsher) code for employees earning £8,500 or more

Income from an Employment

(known until 1989 as higher paid employees) and directors. Point (2) above must be constantly borne in mind in reading the following pages; you will not have the whole picture until you have read the section on employees earning £8,500 or more and directors beginning on page 119, below.

Let us look first at the common law. (If you still find it strange that we are asking you to look at the "common law" of a statutory subject like tax, just reflect on what the Revenue would do had the judges not intervened).

Even the common law does not confine "emoluments" to money payments. It recognises that benefits in kind, and hence a number of fringe benefits, are emoluments. But it takes the view that benefits in kind are taxable only if they can be converted (although not necessarily are) into money. In the extremely important case of *Tennant v. Smith* (1892) (H.L.) Lord Halsbury said that the benefits which are taxable are "substantial things of money value ... capable of being turned into money". And in the same case Lord Watson used the expression: "that which can be turned to pecuniary account". The dividing line then is convertibility into money. If a thing can be turned into money it is assessable; if it cannot be turned into money it is not assessable. On this principle the following items (by way of examples) are not taxable; free travel, free board and lodging, free meals, free uniforms, free education. None of these can be turned into money. But if an employer, instead of providing, *e.g* a free meal, gives his employee a cash payment with which to buy a meal, that payment is taxable.[6]

A clear example of a benefit convertible into money occurred in *Weight v. Salmon* (1935) (H.L.). The directors of a company by resolution each year gave Mr Salmon the privilege of subscribing for unissued shares at par value, which was below market value. It was held that the difference between par and market value was assessable to tax.

Another good example of a "perquisite" convertible into money is to be found in the case of *Wilkins v. Rogerson* (1961) (C.A.). The employer decided to give certain of his employees a suit, overcoat or raincoat as a Christmas present. The employer made an arrangement with a tailor. The employee went to the tailor and got fitted out

---

[6] The customary free allowance of coal to miners has never in practice been treated as an emolument, even though they might sell it. This practice has been extended by the Revenue Concession number A6 to cover cash payments in lieu of coal.

with a suit. The tailor sent the bill to the employer. It was held that there was an emolument, and that its value was the amount for which the employee could turn the suit into money; that is, the second-hand value of the suit.

If the arrangement had been that the employee should himself contract with a tailor to get a suit made and that the employer should then discharge the employee's obligation to the tailor the value of the emolument would have been the contract price of the (new) suit. This is a general principle; if an employer discharges an obligation of the employee to a third party that constitutes an emolument, the value of which is the sum paid by the employer. For example, if an employer pays the gardener's wages and other expenses of an employee's residence, thus discharging the employee's liabilities in those respects, the employee is taxable on the amounts so paid. This is called "the rule in *Nicoll v. Austin*" (1935).

One particular application of this principle is worth separate mention. Sometimes an employer agrees to pay his employee's income tax or agrees to pay a wage or salary "free of tax". In that case the amount of the tax is an emolument; the employer is discharging an obligation of the employee to a third party (the Revenue). The employer must gross-up the net salary and pay tax on that grossed-up amount.

Before we leave the common law, let us reflect on the state in which the law has been left. The judges have done a thorough job of trying to fill the gaps in the statute, but the end result, for all their efforts, is still confusing.

Take, for example, the provision by an employer of clothes for his employee. He could choose to give the employee a distinctive uniform, or ordinary smart clothing. Alternatively, he could lend the clothing to the employee whilst still technically remaining the owner. Or again, the employer could allow the employee to go out and buy clothes and then pick up the bill, or he could give the employee a sum of money, for the employee to buy clothes himself.

A shrewd employer will seek the most "tax efficient" way of providing the intended result, that is, he will choose the result which costs least when tax is taken fully into account. To see the difference between an employer's choices, let us take a straightforward example. For this purpose, assume that the basic rate of income tax is 24 per cent. Assume also that the employer's and employee's rates of national insurance contributions (see pp.211–213) are both 10 per cent.

Income from an Employment

If the employer chooses to give an employee, say, a clothing allowance of £100 (where the employee has sufficient other income for the allowance to be taxed at the basic rate), what is this worth after tax? The allowance will cost the employer £110 (though that sum can be deducted as a trading expense at the appropriate rate of income tax or corporation tax). The employee will receive £100 less income tax at 24 per cent and contributions at 10 per cent. So the employer pays £110 for the employee to receive £66. If, on the other hand, the employer chooses to lend clothes to the employee (not as daft as it sounds), this will cost the employer £10 less, but benefit the employee £34 more. In "efficiency" terms, the first variant costs 44 per cent more than the second. This simple fact is at the heart of much of the "remuneration packaging" that has come to be the fashionable approach to setting the level of reward paid by private sector employers to their employees.

Vouchers

One way to provide "tax efficient" benefits has been through the use of credit cards, stamp schemes, season tickets and other versions of "plastic" or "paper" money. The Revenue has tackled all these approaches under the title of "vouchers". The legislation distinguishes between cash vouchers and non-cash vouchers.

By section 143 of the Taxes Act a cash voucher (which includes a stamp or similar document) is taxable and is subject to the PAYE system. A cash voucher would have been taxable anyway under the common law principle stated above, and the real purpose of this enactment is to bring cash vouchers into the PAYE system, and ensure that tax is deducted by the employer, thus avoiding the necessity of a separate assessment on each recipient employee.

A cash voucher is any voucher capable of being exchanged for a sum of money greater than, equal to or not substantially less than, the expense incurred in providing the voucher.

Non-cash vouchers are dealt with by section 141 of the Taxes Act. A non-cash voucher is a voucher which is not a cash voucher and which is capable of being exchanged for money goods or services (or any combination of those things). The section has two effects. First, it treats the employee, if he or his spouse or family receives the voucher, as having received an emolument. Consequently certain things that were not previously taxable (because they were not convertible into money) become taxable, *e.g.* free holidays. Secondly, it requires that the emolument be valued at the cost to the employer of providing the voucher and not at the value of the goods or services ultimately received by the employee. So if the employer in *Wilkins v. Rogerson* (above) were now to provide his employee with a voucher exchangeable for a suit, the emolument would be valued (in effect) at the contract price of the (new) suit, and not merely at the suit's second-hand value. But provided no voucher is used in the process of getting the suit, it would seem that the comparatively happy result in *Wilkins v. Rogerson* could still be achieved.

One particular kind of non-cash voucher is the subject of a (not very generous) Revenue concession. Extra-Statutory Concession A2 says that luncheon vouchers will not be taxed if they are non-transferable, used for meals only, available to lower-paid staff, and limited to a value of 15p for each working day.

Share schemes for employees

The simple fact that companies are owned by their shareholders has been seen by some as one solution to the friction that occurs between employees and their corporate employers. If employees become shareholders in their employing companies, they will identify more closely with them and be "better" employees. Since the late 1970's, employee share ownership has been politically a Good Thing (and not just under Conservative governments).

One sure way of making other people indulge in a Good Thing is by making it tax-privileged. To this end there has been a welter of legislation aimed at encouraging employee share ownership, starting in 1978. However, as will be seen, one approach which was perceived to be over generous has been abandoned.

The Finance Act 1978 (a Lib-Lab measure resulting from the then alliance between the Labour and Liberal Parties) introduced approved profit sharing schemes (see now section 186 and Schedules 9 and 10 of the Taxes Act). These are schemes established whereby companies (usually) appropriate part of their profits for distribution to employees in the form of share capital. The shares are paid not direct to the employees but to a trust. If the trustees are allowed by the employee to hold the shares for a period of years (which has been reduced over the years and presently is three) then the benefit of the shares may be received totally free of income tax. There are a considerable number of requirements to be met before a scheme meets the criteria under which it will be approved.

In 1980, a second tax-privileged means of encouraging employee share ownership was approved. This was the Own As You Earn

Scheme, or, as the Tax Acts call it, the Savings-Related Share Option Scheme (see now section 185 and Schedule 9 of the Taxes Act). Employers offer their employees an option, at a discount on market prices, to purchase shares, valid for a period of years. The employee enters a savings contract (also free of tax) to save the cash to buy the shares by regular monthly instalments, usually over a minimum of five years (three year contracts are now permissible), and at the end of the period to use the savings to buy the shares. In such cases, again if the schemes are Revenue approved, there is no charge to income tax.

In 1984, a further scheme was introduced, namely, the approved share option scheme not tied to a savings contract. The approved share option scheme, which is often referred to as the "executive" share option scheme, proved often to be particularly popular not least because it could be directed at selected employees (hence the nomenclature "executive") to whom, under such a scheme, substantial benefits might accrue. However, in 1995, the Chancellor of the Exchequer (possibly influenced by adverse publicity surrounding alleged benefits available under "executive" share option schemes to directors of privatised utilities) decided that these schemes were too much of a Good Thing! Consequently, the income tax privileges associated with these schemes, *i.e.* normally no charge to income tax on the grant or exercise of the option have been withdrawn in respect of "executive" share options granted on or after July 17, 1995. Income tax relief on the exercise of such options will continue to be available to employees who held options on July 17, 1995. The gap left by the resultant demise of the "executive" share option scheme has been filled by what might be described as the "middle manager" share option scheme. The "middle manager" share option scheme must also be approved by the Revenue. Thereafter, it preserves for the grantee of the option(s), *i.e.* the employee the income tax reliefs considered above in respect of an "executive" share option, provided that the value of shares under option held by an employee at any one time does not exceed £30,000[7] and that the option(s) is/are granted at an exercise price not manifestly less than the market value of the shares at the date of grant, *i.e.*, not at a discount.

---

[7] A limit which seeks to prevent the excesses to which the "executive" share option scheme was prone and which fosters, in particular, the aspirations of the middle manager.

Further, an employee may acquire shares under unapproved schemes, *e.g.* a share incentive scheme. A share incentive scheme is a scheme whereby an employee can buy shares in his employing company or, indeed, in any other company, not in the future, as is the case with an option, but immediately and in pursuance of a right conferred on him or an opportunity offered to him as an employee (or director) and not in pursuance of an offer to the public. The tax treatment of such schemes is far from simple and we propose only to draw your attention to the following instances when a charge to tax may arise in respect of shares so acquired and in the light of which the attractiveness of such schemes from a tax perspective may be diminished. Thus, for example, in relation to incentive shares held in the employer's company, section 78 of the Finance Act 1988 charges to tax an increase in value of such shares brought about by an alteration to the rights or restrictions attaching to shares in the company. Also, holders of incentive shares may receive special benefits by virtue of their ownership of the shares, *e.g.* benefits not available to at least 90 per cent of the shareholders of the same class as the holders, which are taxed under section 80 of the Finance Act 1988. Nevertheless, share incentive schemes can be attractive for purposes other than tax and, in particular, provide an effective means by which employees involve themselves with their company (and/or its subsidiaries).

Finally, an employee may benefit from the establishment by his employer of an employee share ownership trust—known as an ESOT—which satisfies sections 67–74 and schedule 5 of Finance Act 1989. Under such a qualifying ESOT an employer sets up and funds a trust. The primary purpose of the trust is the acquisition of shares in the founding employer (using the funds contributed) to be held principally for the benefit of its employees. Particular tax advantages are available to the employer who is entitled to a corporation tax deduction for contributions to the trust (section 67) and, since 1991, for the costs of setting up an ESOT (section 85A of the Taxes Act).

Provision of accommodation

Section 145 of the Taxes Act declares that where living accommodation is provided for a person (or for members of his family or household) by reason of his employment he is to be treated as being in receipt of emoluments of a value equal to the excess of the annual value of the premises over what he actually pays for the premises (if

Income from an Employment

anything). Annual value is defined in section 837 of the Taxes Act, as being (in summary) the market rent on the footing that the tenant pays the rates and the landlord pays for repairs and insurance. This is, broadly speaking, the rateable value.[8] That is the general rule, but if the employer (or other person providing the accommodation) is himself paying rent for the premises (*i.e.* he is not the freehold owner) and the rent which the employer pays is greater than the annual value, the employee's emolument is valued at the excess of the rent which the employer pays over the rent which the employee pays. From any amount to be treated as emoluments the employee can deduct such expenses (if any) as would have been deductible if the employee had paid for the accommodation in full himself. The rules for what expenses are deductible are discussed in the next section.

There are three exceptional situations (section 145(4)) in which the provision of accommodation does not count as an emolument, namely; (a) where it is necessary for the proper performance of the employee's duties that he should reside in the provided accommodation; (b) where the accommodation is provided for the better performance of the duties, and his is one of the kinds of employment in the case of which it is customary for employers to provide living accommodation. In *Vertigan v. Brady* (1988) the taxpayer, who was employed as a nursery foreman, satisfied the court that living accommodation provided by his employer was for the better performance of his duties, but was unable to establish that it was customary for employers in the horticultural industry to provide living accommodation. The court rejected his claim in this respect after taking into account: how many employers in the horticulture industry provided living accommodation (the evidence showed that nearly 70 per cent of key workers in the industry enjoyed this benefit); how long the practice had continued, and whether it had achieved general acceptance; and (c) where, there being a special threat to his security, special security arrangements are in force and he resides in the accommodation as part of those arrangements. Exceptions (a) and (b) do not apply if the employee is a director of the providing company or an associated company unless he has no material interest in the company and either he is a full-time working director or the company is non-profit making or is established for charitable purposes only. Employees earning £8,500 or more who

---

[8] The domestic rating system was abolished in 1989. Estimated values are used for "new" properties.

are not directors have the benefit of the exceptions without any qualification although they may be taxed on associated living expenses (see p. 122).

Where the cost of providing living accommodation exceeds £75,000, the employee may be charged to tax on an *additional* emolument. In essence, the employee is taxed on the additional value to him of the accommodation which is measured by applying the official rate of interest to the amount by which the cost of providing the accommodation exceeds £75,000.

Deductible Expenses

Tax is chargeable under Schedule E "on the full amount of the emoluments ... subject to such deductions only as may be authorised by the Tax Acts" (section 131(1)) of the Taxes Act). There are three differences between the expenses which are deductible under Schedule E and those which are deductible under Schedule D, Cases I and II. The first is a practical difference, namely that whereas profits under Cases I and II do not begin to make sense until one visualises an account with expenses on one side and receipts on the other, expenses play a very much smaller part in Schedule E. Many employed people have no expenses (no deductible expenses, that is) at all. The second difference is that whereas the Schedule D legislation merely states what expenses are not deductible, Schedule E states in a positive form what expenses are deductible. And the third difference is that the rules are much more restrictively worded under Schedule E, so that many expenses which would be deductible under Schedule D are not deductible under Schedule E. One justification for the difference between the two Schedules is that it may be expected that, if an employer requires an employee to incur expenditure on its behalf, it will reimburse the employee. This cannot be so for the self-employed person.

The expenses which are deductible under Schedule E are set out in section 198(1) of the Taxes Act:

"If the holder of an office or employment is necessarily obliged to incur and defray out of the emoluments of that office or employment the expenses of travelling in the performance of the duties of the office or employment, or of keeping and maintaining a horse[9] to enable him

---

[9] They say you can tell the age of a horse by its teeth; you can tell the age of a section by its horses.

Income from an Employment

to perform those duties, or otherwise to expend money wholly, exclusively and necessarily in the performance of those duties, there may be deducted from the emoluments to be assessed the expenses so necessarily incurred and defrayed."

It is noticeable that the words "wholly" and "exclusively" are not applied to the expenses of travelling, but only to other expenditure. The words "in the performance of the duties" relate to both kinds of expenditure, as also does the word "necessarily." The presence of this word "necessarily" is one feature which makes the Schedule E rules more stringent than the rules of Schedule D, from which it is absent. Another feature which has that effect is the presence of the words "in the performance of the duties" which is a narrower phrase than the Schedule D words "for the purposes of the trade, profession or vocation".

We will look at travelling expenses first. The expense of travel from one's home to one's work is not deductible. This basic rule is established by *Ricketts v. Colquhoun* (1926) (H.L.). Mr Ricketts was a barrister residing and practising in London. He was also the Recorder of Portsmouth (a part-time office). He claimed to deduct from the emoluments of his Recordership the expenses of travelling between London and Portsmouth and also his hotel expenses in Portsmouth. It was held by the House of Lords that neither the travelling expenses nor the hotel expenses were incurred in the performance of his duties, but rather before and after,[10] and moreover, the expenses were attributable to the Recorder's own choice of residence and were not necessary to the office as such. This latter, very objective, point was rather softened by a later decision of the House of Lords, *Taylor v. Provan* (1975) (see below).

The cost of travel from one place of work in an employment to another place of work in the same employment is deductible. In *Owen v. Pook* (1970) (H.L.) Dr Owen was a G.P. at his residence in Fishguard, and he also held a part-time appointment at a hospital in Haverfordwest, 15 miles away. Under his appointment Dr Owen was on stand-by duty to deal with emergency cases and he was required to be available by telephone. His responsibility for a patient began the moment he received a telephone call at home. It was held by a majority of the House of Lords that the duties of Dr Owen's employment were performed in two places (where he received the

---

[10] Lord Cave rather sternly said that a person "does not eat or sleep in the course of performing his duties".

DEDUCTIBLE EXPENSES

telephone calls and the hospital) and that he could deduct the expenses of travel between those places.[11] This is akin to the Schedule D cases where a taxpayer is held to have his base at his home. But it is not identical, it is wider; sometimes Dr Owen received telephone calls when he was not at home. It seems to have been regarded as more important when he received the calls than where. But undoubtedly the case does establish that if his home is one of the places at which a taxpayer works (and rightly works) under his contract of employment, then the cost of travel from home to another place of work under the contract is deductible.

In *Taylor v. Provan* (1975) (H.L.) Mr Taylor lived and worked in Canada and the Bahamas. He was a world expert in arranging amalgamations and mergers in the brewing industry. He agreed to become a director of an English brewing company to carry forward such work. He did most of his work on English amalgamations in Canada and the Bahamas, but he paid frequent visits to England. The House of Lords, by a majority of three to two, held that the expenses of travel to England were deductible. Two of the majority based their decision on the view that there were two or more places of work under the contract of employment. Lord Reid based his decision more on the view that "it was impossible for the companies which contracted with him to get the work done by anyone else". Lord Reid felt that this view reconciled the case with *Ricketts v. Colquhoun* (above), but there does seem to be a move away from *Ricketts v. Colquhoun* in that on this more recent view the expenditure does not need to be necessary to the office or employment as such provided it is necessary to this particular contract with the only employee who can fulfil it.[12]

The requirement of being "necessary" applies not only to the fact of the journey, but also to the the *amount* of the expenditure. Only such amount as is reasonable will be deductible (see *Marsden v. IRC* (1965)).[13]

---

[11] This related to that part of the expenses which was not reimbursed to him by the hospital. That part of the expenses which was reimbursed was held not to be an emolument at all (see p. 107, above).

[12] For further discussion of these inscrutable decisions see P.F. Smith at [1977] B.T.R. 290 and [1978] B.T.R. 203, and G. Macdonald at [1978] B.T.R. 75.

[13] The law relating to the deductibility of travelling expenses is under review. See The Inland Revenue Consultative Document entitled *Travel and Subsistence*, dated April, 1996.

Income from an Employment

Let us now look at expenses other than travel expenses. These must be incurred wholly, exclusively and necessarily in the performance of the duties.

"Wholly" and "exclusively" are words which do not occur in relation to travelling expenses. For the importance of that point, remember *Sargent v. Barnes* (p. 90 above). In connection with non-travelling expenses the words proved to be of some importance in *Hillyer v. Leeke* (1976). Mr Hillyer was required by his employer to wear a suit at work. So he bought a suit which he wore at work but on no other occasions. He claimed to deduct the cost of the suit. It was held that the expenditure had not been incurred wholly and exclusively in the performance of his duties. He wore the suit not merely for the purposes of the employment, but also to provide cover, warmth and comfort for himself. This decision was approved by the House of Lords in *Mallalieu v. Drummond* (1983) (see above p. 89).

The word "necessarily" has caused many a claim to founder. Stemming from *Ricketts v. Colquhoun* (above) the test is, as Donovan L.J. put it in *Brown v. Bullock* (1961) (C.A.): " ... not whether the employer imposes the expense ... but whether the duties do." A bank manager was required by his employers (it was "virtually a condition of his employment") to be a member of a London club. It was held that the subscription fee was not a deductible expense. This is a harsh doctrine, and it may in time come to be softened if some of the ideas in *Taylor v. Provan* begin to percolate through. But it will still be the case that the expense must not be necessitated merely by the personal circumstances of the taxpayer as distinct from the necessities of the job. Thus in *Roskams v. Bennett* (1950) Mr Bennett was the district manager of an insurance company. Because of bad eyesight he could not drive a car, and so he found it necessary to maintain an office at home. It was held that the expense occasioned thereby was not deductible.

The phrase "in the performance of the duties" has had similar effects on non-travel expenses as on travel expenses. In *Simpson v. Tate* (1925) a county medical officer of health joined certain medical and scientific societies so as to keep himself up-to-date on matters affecting public health. His claim to deduct these subscriptions was rejected, the court holding that the expense was incurred, not in the performance of the duties, but so that the taxpayer might keep himself fit to perform them. This seems a very restrictive doctrine, and indeed this particular point has been altered by statute. Section 201 of the Taxes Act now permits deduction of (we quote the marginal note to the section) "fees and subscriptions to professional bodies, learned societies, etc." But the doctrine still stands where it has not been changed by statute. In *Fitzpatrick v. IRC (No.2)*; *Smith v. Abbott* (1994) (H.L.) journalists incurred expenditure in purchasing newspapers and journals. They claimed to deduct this expenditure. The House of Lords by a majority (4–1) rejected this claim. Lord Templeman said "a journalist does not purchase and read newspapers in the performance of his duties but for the purpose of ensuring that he will carry out his duties efficiently". The rule surely tends to discourage employees from making themselves better employees.

Employees Earning £8,500 or more and Directors

We must now study the special rules which apply to directors,[14] however much or however little they earn, and to non-director employees who earn £8,500 or more. The rules are statutory and one can think of the relevant enactments as setting up a kind of code and we shall speak of people who are affected by the legislation as being "within the code". In Revenue jargon, those people are often referred to as "P11D" people, by the number of the form used to tell the taxmen about their benefits.

The question whether a person has earnings of £8,500 or more has to be tested on the assumption that the code applies and also that benefits in respect of living accommodation and vouchers are included, and without (at this stage) making any deduction for allowable expenses. So if an employee has a salary of £8,000 and reimbursed expenses of £1,000 he is in the code, even though the bulk of the £1,000 is tax deductible. Also, separate employments with the same employer are treated as one employment, and so are employments with employers who are under a common control. But the code does not catch people just because their total earnings (*i.e.* from other employments or professions) exceed that total.

The code is now set out in sections 153–168 of the Taxes Act as amended by several subsequent Finance Acts.[15]

---

[14] A director is not caught as such if he does not have a material interest (= 5 per cent or more) in the company and either he is a full-time working director or the company is non-profit-making (or charitable). But, of course, he may be caught as being an employee who earns £8,500 or more.
[15] There is a useful guide issued by the Revenue (no. 480) called "Expenses and Benefits: A Tax Guide".

THE PRINCIPLES OF THE CODE

Before going into the details of the code, we want to try to state the main differences in the taxing of people who are within the code as compared with people outside the code. There are three such differences.

First, any sums paid to a person within the code in respect of expenses are to be treated as emoluments; see section 153 of the Taxes Act. For a person outside the code that is not so. We have seen (above, at p.107) that for him a reimbursement of deductible expenses is not an emolument, and in practice a round-sum payment for expenses, if reasonable in amount, is not treated as an emolument. For a person within the code not only a round-sum payment for expenses but even a reimbursement of expenses is an emolument. Mind you, this is not fatal; if he expends, or has expended, the payment in such circumstances that his expenditure is deductible under the ordinary principles, the potential taxability of the allowance is balanced by the deductibility of the expense, so no tax becomes due. But there is an important point here; the onus of proving that a receipt is an emolument lies on the Revenue, whereas the onus of proving that an expenditure is deductible lies on the taxpayer. So for a person within the code the Revenue is relieved of its onus, because the payment in respect of expenses is treated by statute as being an emolument, and the only onus left standing is the onus on the taxpayer to prove that the emolument is balanced by deductibility. This point is illustrated by *Owen v. Pook* and *Taylor v. Provan*. In *Owen v. Pook* the taxpayer was not within the code, and it was held that the reimbursement of his travel expenses was not an emolument at all. In *Taylor v. Provan* the taxpayer was within the code, and it was held that the reimbursement was an emolument. It so happened that Mr Taylor was held to be entitled to an equalising deductibility, but it was a near thing; three Law Lords said yes, two said no. There is an element of absurd circuity about an emolument which is reduced to nil by deductibility, and section 166 of Taxes Act recognises this by permitting an inspector to grant a dispensation to an employer (and hence to his employees) where he is satisfied that the arrangements for paying expenses are such that no tax will be involved. A dispensation carries the great advantage that the dispensed expenses are left out of account in calculating whether a particular employee is within the code.

Secondly, for people outside the code benefits which are not convertible into money are not taxable emoluments. (There are a few statutory exceptions which we have looked at above.) For people within the code the principle of convertibility is irrelevant, with the result that *all* benefits (with a few statutory exceptions and a few extra-statutory concessionary exceptions) whether convertible into money or not are emoluments: section 154 of the Taxes Act. But here again all is not lost; the ordinary principles of deductibility are available to off-set the emoluments where the facts warrant such deduction.

Thirdly, for a person not within the code a benefit in kind is valued (with certain statutory exceptions such as non-cash vouchers) at the value which it has to the employee, and not at the expense to the employer of providing the benefit. For a person within the code a benefit in kind is valued by reference to the expense of the employer in providing it (called the "cash equivalent").[16] This point can be clearly seen by comparing *Wilkins v. Rogerson* (1961) (see p.108 above) and *Rendell v. Went* (1964) (H.L.). It will be recalled that in *Wilkins v. Rogerson* the employee (who was outside the code) was taxed on the second-hand value of the suit which his employer bought for him. In *Rendell v. Went* the taxpayer (who was a director and so within the code) was charged with causing death by dangerous driving, for which he would be liable, if convicted, to imprisonment for a term up to five years. The employing company had special need of Mr Rendell's services at that time, and they were most anxious that his services should not be lost to them by reason of his imprisonment. Mr Rendell at first arranged for the Automobile Association (AA) to conduct his defence, but the company arranged for their own solicitors to defend him (with counsel) at the company's expense. The company paid out £641 in costs. If the AA had conducted the defence Mr Rendell would only have had to pay £50 or £60. It was held by the House of Lords that Mr Rendell was taxable on the sum of £641, because that was the cost to his employers of providing the benefit.

In *Pepper v. Hart* (1993) (H.L.) consideration was given to the method by which the cost of providing a benefit could be measured. The taxpayers were nine masters and the bursar employed by an independent boys' school. The school ran a concessionary fees scheme under which members of its staff were entitled to have their sons educated at the school on payment of 20 per cent of the sum

---

[16] Section 156(1) of the Taxes Act lays down that the "cash equivalent" is "an amount equal to the cost of the benefit, less so much (if any) of it as is made good by the employee ... "

charged to the public at large. The concessionary fees more than covered the additional cost to the school of educating the taxpayers' sons, and, as the school was not full to capacity in the tax years when the taxpayers' sons were educated under the scheme, the school did not lose fees which could otherwise have been obtained. It was not disputed that this was an emolument of the taxpayers' employment: at issue, however, was the cost to the school in providing this benefit.

The Revenue argued that the cost to the school in providing this benefit should be calculated by reference to a rateable proportion of the expenses incurred in running the school as a whole for all the boys, *i.e.* the *average* cost. On this basis, the cash equivalent approximated to the level of school fees paid by the public at large. On the other hand, the taxpayers argued that the only expense incurred by the school in connection with the education of their sons was the *additional* or *marginal* cost. This amounted only to those expenses *directly* attributable to the education of the taxpayers' sons, *e.g.* the cost of their food, laundry and stationery, all of which were covered by the concessionary fees paid by the taxpayers. Consequently, the cash equivalent was nil.

The House of Lords by a majority of six to one accepted the taxpayers' argument. However, it was an argument which was accepted only after the House of Lords had departed fundamentally from previous practice by having recourse to parliamentary materials as an aid to the construction of the predecessor of section 156 of the Taxes Act.

Now let us look at some specific rules of the code.

LIVING ACCOMMODATION EXPENSES

The first point concerns certain expenses connected with living accommodation, and it is dealt with in section 163 of the Taxes Act. This section is a beneficial section because it cuts down (or at least limits) what would otherwise be the tax charge. The section applies where the provided living accommodation comes within the three exceptions stated in section 145(4) of the Taxes Act (see p. 115 above; necessary for proper performance of duties, customary for better performance of duties or part of special security arrangements). In those premises, the provision to the employee of the following things, though it is an emolument, is subject to a tax limit; heating, lighting, cleaning, repairs, maintenance, decoration, furniture, and normal appurtenances and effects. The limit is that the taxable amount of the emolument shall not exceed 10 per cent of the employee's emoluments from that employment for the year (less capital allowances and certain pension contributions). So, if a person within the code, with an income of £9,000, enjoyed such benefits to an amount of, say, £1,500 in a particular year, he would only be taxable (in this respect) on an emolument of £900.

CARS AND RELATED BENEFITS

Traditionally the biggest "perk" from a job is the use of a company car. Under general principles the use of a company car cannot be taxed in the hands of an employee. The employee cannot sell the car, nor can he hire it out, so he cannot convert the benefit into cash. Provided the scheme under which the employee acquired the use of the car did not provide a way of converting the benefit, there was nothing to tax.

The legislation, however, taxes a person within the code on the private benefit he gets from being given the use of a car, *i.e.* he is taxed on the cash equivalent of this benefit as determined by the code. The pertinent provisions emanate from the Finance Act 1993 which in amending section 157 and Schedule 6 of the Taxes Act introduced a fundamental change to the method by which the cash equivalent is calculated. A change which was intended to rectify what came to be seen as the failure of the pre-existing provisions to tax the private use of a company car adequately, notwithstanding the fact that over the years there had been a steady increase in the level of taxation. The provisions apply where there is not any transfer to the employee of the property in the car. (Where there is a transfer of the property in (ownership of) the car its value is taxable on ordinary "common law" principles, and, being convertible into money, it is taxable in the hands of all employees, not only employees earning £8,500 or more and directors.)

Under section 157 and Schedule 6, as amended, the cash equivalent is 35 per cent of the price of the car. Broadly, the price is the list price (which may be provided by the manufacturer, importer or distributor) together with accessories, delivery charge, VAT and car tax (section 168A). The cash equivalent may, however, be reduced by two-thirds if the employee was required by his employment and did use the car for at least 18,000 miles of business travel. It is reduced by one-third if the business travel amounted to at least 2,500 miles but less than 18,000 miles. A further reduction of one-third may be made if the car is four years old or more at the end of the year. In the case of a car which is 15 years old or more and worth £15,000 or more (classic cars) the market value is adopted unless it is less than the list price (section 168F). In any event, there is a limit of £80,000 on the value of any car.

If a car is included in a "car pool" no charge to tax arises in respect of the use of that car. The conditions are that the car was used by more than one employee, that it was not normally kept overnight at an employee's house, and that any private use of it was merely incidental to its business use (section 159).

The Finance Act 1993 also extended the parameters of the code by the addition of sections 159AA and AB, and schedule 6A to the Taxes Act. These provisions tax the employee on the private benefit he gets from the use of a van provided by the employer. The cash equivalent is £500 if the van is less than four years old at the end of the year or £350 if it is older. There are special provisions where the use of a van is shared.

Tax is also levied on persons within the code on what might be described as car related benefits. For example, since 1983–84, the "perk" of free petrol provided by employers for private as well as business use of company cars may be taxed (see now section 158 of the Taxes Act). Further, since 1991–92, persons within the code may be taxed on the benefit of mobile telephones which are provided by employers and available for private use. The cash equivalent of this benefit is £200 for each mobile telephone (see section 159A).

Finally, since 1991, an *employer* may have to pay Class 1A contributions on company cars and fuel provided for the private as well as business use of a company car (see further p. 131 and Chap. 15).

BENEFICIAL LOAN ARRANGEMENTS

Where a person within the code has the benefit of a loan which is obtained by reason of his employment and the loan is either without interest or at a rate of interest less than the "official rate" (*i.e.* the rate prescribed from time to time by the Treasury) the cash equivalent of the benefit is treated under section 160 of the Taxes Act as an emolument. The cash equivalent is the difference between the amount of interest actually paid in the year and the amount of interest which would have been payable at the official rate. However, the tax charge does not arise if the aggregate amount of all such loans at any time of the year does not exceed £5,000 (section 161(1)). Further, certain loans are excluded, *e.g.* loans made to employees on terms comparable to loans made to members of the public at large where the employer's business includes the making of loans. Relief may be available in respect of a loan to the extent that it is used for a qualifying purpose (see section 353 of the Taxes Act).

Where in any year there is released or written off the whole or part of a loan which was obtained by reason of a person's employment, an amount equal to that which is released or written off is treated as an emolument.

EMPLOYEE SHAREHOLDINGS

Section 162 of the Taxes Act applies where a person within the code acquires shares in a company at an under-value in pursuance of a right or opportunity available by reason of the employment. The employee is treated as having an interest-free loan ("the notional loan"), so bringing him within section 160. The loan is treated as outstanding until (a) the whole amount outstanding is made good, or (b) the debt is released, or (c) the shares are disposed of, or (d) the employee dies. In case (a) the tax charge comes to an end; in cases (b) and (c) the employee is taxed as if the notional loan had been written off; in case (d) there is no income tax charge.

Section 162 also imposes a charge to tax where shares are acquired by a person employed or about to be employed as a director or in employment within the code in pursuance of a right or opportunity available by reason of the employment, whether or not they were acquired at an under-value, and the shares are disposed of for a consideration which exceeds their then market value. The amount of the excess is treated as an emolument.

In practice, section 162 is not very important because when shares are held, for example, in an approved profit sharing scheme (on which see p.111 above) a participant is not chargeable to tax under section 162 in any case where the shares are appropriated to him at an under-value.

THE CODE AND LOOPHOLES

Although the code, as the examples we have used show, is wide ranging in its application to benefits provided for directors and employees who earn £8,500 or more, it is not all-embracing. Indeed, some benefits are expressly excluded (see, for example, the provision of certain child care facilities, section 155A). Equally, there are occasions when a taxpayer discovers a loophole in the code, *i.e.* benefits which, perhaps, should be caught by the code but escape it! Of course, it may not take long for such a loophole to be plugged. An intriguing aspect of Finance Acts is to discover what steps have been taken to close a particular loophole (or loopholes). Occasionally, the

Income from an Employment

introduction of such steps is heralded by a Chancellor of the Exchequer with some feeling. Thus in his budget speech in 1991, the Chancellor of the Exchequer, Norman Lamont said:

> "I turn now to one of the great scourges of modern life: the mobile telephone. I propose to bring the benefit of car phones into income tax and simplify the tax treatment of mobile phones by introducing a standard charge on the private use of such phones provided by an employer ... I hope that as a result of this measure, restaurants will be quieter and roads will be safer."

That concludes what we want to say about employees who earn £8,500 or more and directors. The rest of this chapter applies to all employees, whether within or outside the code.

Golden Handshakes

One of the pleasures of studying tax law is that it is bedecked with vivid phrases which start as slang and are then taken into the dictionary, if not into the statute book. One such phrase is "Golden Handshakes." These can, more prosaically, be called "terminal payments".

In the first instance, it is, of course, important to establish that a payment is a golden handshake (something which Peter Shilton singularly failed to do in respect of the payment made to him by Nottingham Forest on his transfer to Southampton (see above, p. 104). However, once this is established it is necessary to distinguish three different kinds of payment on the termination of an office or employment.

First, where there is a contractual provision that a certain sum will become payable if the contract is determined early, that sum is treated as remuneration for past services and is taxed under Schedule E.

Secondly, if employer and employee agree that the employee will stay on at a reduced salary and the employer makes a payment to an employee in connection with this agreement, that payment is treated as being in anticipation of future services and is taxed under Schedule E.

Thirdly, where a payment is made which is not related to services rendered or to be rendered, but is paid as consideration for the release of the employer's obligation under the contract of employment, *it is not taxable under the ordinary principles of Schedule E,* but is taxable under special statutory provisions which were first enacted in 1960. The provisions are now contained in sections 148 and 188 of the Taxes Act.

Section 148 applies to:

"any payment (not otherwise chargeable to tax) which is made, whether in pursuance of any legal obligation or not, either directly or indirectly in consideration or in consequence of, or otherwise in connection with, the termination of the holding of the office or employment or any change in its functions or emoluments, including any payment in commutation of annual or periodical payments (whether chargeable to tax or not) which would otherwise have been so made."

(The words from "including" onwards catch a payment in commutation of pension rights.) The section is clearly very wide in its scope. One important kind of payment which it catches is a redundancy payment. (This point is confirmed by section 580(3) of the Taxes Act.) Some payments (listed in section 188) are exempted from section 148, such as: (a) any payment made in connection with the termination of an office or employment by the death of the holder, or made on account of injury to or disability of the holder; (b) any sum chargeable to tax under section 313 of the Taxes Act (which charges to tax any sum paid to an employee for a restrictive covenant); (c) payments under approved retirement benefit schemes.

Payments which are caught by section 148 are treated as earned income received on the following date: (a) in the case of a commutation payment, the date of commutation; (b) in the case of any other payment, the date of the termination or change in respect of which the payment is made.

Tax is not charged under section 148 on the first £30,000 of any payment. This figure may be calculated by aggregating two (or more) payments from the same employment or from associated employers. Because of this threshold this is one of the rare circumstances where it is advantageous to be a Schedule E taxpayer rather than a Schedule D taxpayer. A similar sort of payment made to a Schedule D taxpayer would in most situations be taxable, and taxable in full without any exemption for the first £30,000. See *IRC v. Brander & Cruickshank* (1971) (H.L.).

The £30,000 exemption raises a point stemming from what is called "the Gourley principle". That principle was laid down by the House of Lords in *British Transport Commission v. Gourley* (1956).

Income from an Employment

Mr Gourley was injured in a railway accident, and was unable to work again. He sued in tort for damages for (amongst other things) loss of earnings. It was estimated that if the plaintiff had not been injured his earnings over the rest of his working life would have come to £37,000. The defendants argued that since the plaintiff's earnings would have been taxed, the damages should be reduced to take account of that factor. It was estimated that Mr Gourley's earnings *after tax* would have been only £6,000. So the issue was whether his damages should be £37,000 or £6,000. The House of Lords decided for £6,000. *Gourley's* case was brought in tort, but the same principle applies to breach of contract. The reasoning of the principle is that the plaintiff ought not to make a profit out of the tort or breach of contract. The principle only applies where two factors are present: (1) what the award represents is lost receipts which, if they had been received, would have been taxed, and (2) the award itself is not taxable. The principle has been applied to awards of damages for wrongful dismissal which fell within what is now section 148. In *Shove v. Downs Surgical plc* (1984) the judge awarded damages well over the £25,000 limit (the threshold at that time). He reasoned that, if liability to pay taxes was not too remote in assessing loss then, likewise, liability to pay tax on the compensation was not too remote. He therefore ordered net damages of £60,000 to be increased to £83,000 so as to provide for income tax payable on the lump sum compensation. For further discussion, see the aptly titled, "Dismissing Employees—Golden Handshakes and the Gourley Confusion" by Roger Kerridge at [1982] B.T.R. 87 and "Wrongful Dismissal: A Taxing Problem" by Robert G. Lee (1984) 47 M.L.R. 471.

Pensions

Many employees, when they come to retire, do not receive any occupational pension. They may get the flat rate state retirement pension ("old age pension") and the state earnings related pension ("SERPS"). Payments received under this state system are taxable under Schedule E and count as earned income.

An increasing number of employees do enjoy an occupational pension. When such an employee retires, and begins to receive periodical pension payments, he is taxed on those payments under Schedule E and they count as earned income.

During his employment such an employee will probably have been subject to some kind of pension scheme, under which he paid contributions and his employer also paid contributions. Two questions arise: are the employee's contributions deductible in computing his emoluments? and are the employer's contributions treated as emoluments of the employee?

The answer to the first question is that the employee's contributions are not deductible unless the pension scheme is what is called an "exempt approved scheme" under section 592 of the Taxes Act or it is a "statutory scheme" (section 594). In either instance, the employee's contributions are deductible up to a limit of 15 per cent. of annual remuneration.[17] In practice, any general scheme will try to be "exempt approved" because of the high degree of tax-privilege accorded such schemes by successive governments. A very important further advantage of an "exempt approved scheme" is that the fund of the scheme is itself exempt from income tax and also capital gains tax (section 592 of the Taxes Act and section 271 of the Taxation of Chargeable Gains Act 1992 respectively).

The answer to the second question is that the employer's contributions are treated as emoluments of the employee unless the scheme is an "approved scheme" (not necessarily an "exempt approved scheme") or a statutory scheme (see section 596 of the Taxes Act).

An employee whose employer does not offer an occupational pension scheme or whose employer runs a scheme which the employee opts not to join may take out an approved personal pension scheme (see further, Chapter 5, p.97). Contributions to such a scheme are treated similarly to those made in respect of the types of occupational pension considered above. Thus, the employee's contributions, within specified limits, are deductible whilst contributions by an employer are not treated as emoluments of the employee (see generally, sections 639–646 of the Taxes Act).

The Mechanics of Schedule E

All income taxed under Schedule E counts as earned income. It is collected by means of the Pay-As-You-Earn system (PAYE). That name indicates two things: first, that the tax is on a current year (not a preceding year) basis, and, secondly, that the tax is collected bit by bit as the year goes on. It is collected by the employer by means of deducting the appropriate amount for tax from each weekly or

---

[17] For those who join schemes set up since March 14, 1989 and for those who join existing schemes on or after June 1, 1989, an earnings ceiling is imposed (£82,200 for 1996–97).

monthly payment that he makes to his employees. The employer is then under a duty to hand over the tax to the Revenue. Every employed person earning over a certain amount (the amount being varied from time to time by statutory instrument in line with variations in the tax threshold) is given a code number by the inspector. This code number tells the employer the amount of allowances and reliefs that any particular employee is entitled to. By applying the code number to the cumulative tax tables with which he is supplied by the Revenue, the employer can know how much tax to deduct from the pay of a particular employee in any particular week (or month) of the tax year. On occasions, a negative code, called a K code, is used. The employer must then, instead of making a deduction from the employee's pay, make an addition to it. This may happen where, for example, an employee receives a benefit in kind which is not within the PAYE system and where it is worth more than his personal allowances.

It is obvious from this (very brief) account that the employer is acting as a collector of tax (unpaid) for the Revenue.

For many years, tax was charged on the emoluments earned by an employee over the tax year (the earnings basis). This often led to problems with regard to emoluments received after the tax year in which they had been earned. Consequently, since 1989–90, emoluments have been taxed on a receipts basis, *i.e.* when they are "received" by the employee (for the meaning of "received", see section 202B of the Taxes Act). Special provision is made for an emolument received after an employment has come to an end, *i.e.* it is treated as an emolument of the last year of employment.

Technically, most benefits in kind are outside the PAYE scheme, because they are not payments of income (although some benefits are treated as "notional payments", see sections 203F–203L of the Taxes Act, inserted by the Finance Act 1994). In practice, however, the Revenue, with a view to increasing the efficiency of the PAYE system, have sought to use it to catch benefits in kind as well as cash, an approach which is no doubt facilitated by the availability of formula to calculate the cash equivalent of such benefits as cars and fuel. Further, there is some judicial support for this practice, see, for example, *Beecham Group Ltd v. Fair* (1984).

In theory the PAYE system should produce the result that at the end of the tax year an individual employee has paid (by deduction) exactly the correct amount of tax. In many, many cases it does so in practice. If it turns out that too much tax has been deducted, the taxpayer can either get a repayment from the Revenue or have the credit taken into account in determining his code number for a subsequent year.

National Insurance Contibutions

Besides income tax, office holders and employees must also pay primary Class 1 contributions on their Schedule E earnings where those earnings reach the lower earnings limit (of £61.00 per week for 1996–97) and to the extent that they do not exceed the upper earnings limit (of £455 per week for 1996–97). Further, their employers must pay secondary Class 1 contributions once the lower earnings limit is reached.

These contributions are, however, not payable on many forms of benefit in kind, and there is no equivalent of the Taxes Act "code" in the Social Security legislation. Nevertheless, recent years have witnessed the introduction of various measures to bring specific benefits in kind within the contributions "net". In particular, since April 6, 1991, a new class of national insurance contribution—the Class 1A contribution—has been payable by *employers* in respect of company cars and fuel provided for employees wholly or in part for private use. The Class 1A contribution is based on the criteria used for measuring the taxable benefit of such items under Schedule E for employees who earn £8,500 or more and directors.
See further Chapter 15.

Tailpiece

Before ending this chapter it is perhaps worth pointing out that payments or benefits in kind which are receipts in the hands of the employee are, looked at from the point of view of the employer, payments out. But the point is this: the question whether a particular receipt in the hands of an employee is taxable under Schedule E is quite independent of the question whether, in calculating the employer's tax liability (under Schedule D) a particular payment out by him is a deductible expense.

CHAPTER 7

CASUAL EARNINGS

This chapter is about Case VI of Schedule D. Case VI is a residuary case or, less politely, a rag-bag. Section 18 of the Taxes Act charges under Case VI "tax in respect of any annual profits or gains not falling under any other case of Schedule D, and not charged by virtue of Schedule A or E". The section does not refer to Schedule F (dividends and similar distributions by companies), but if a receipt does fall within Schedule F it is not assessable under Case VI (see section 20).

Case VI has two aspects, which one might call the "general aspect" and the "particular aspect". By the "particular aspect" we mean that certain kinds of income are specifically directed by other sections to be charged under Case VI. These items include post-cessation receipts, income from settlements which is deemed to be that of the settlor (see Chapter 13), and deemed income from artificial transactions in land (see Chapter 8). But perhaps the commonest example of a Case VI income in recent years has been income from furnished lettings. However, from 1995–96, such income is taxed for income tax purposes under the "new" Schedule A (see Chapter 8).

Turning to the "general aspect" of Case VI, the ambit of this aspect is not as wide as it might at first seem to be. "Annual profits or gains" is the same phrase as that which governs Cases I and II. Indeed the phrase covers the whole of Schedule D. It follows that profits, to be taxable under Case VI, must be of the same kind (*ejusdem generis*) as profits which are taxable under Cases I, II, III, IV or V. Let us remind ourselves of three points about the phrase "annual profits or gains". First, "profits" and "gains" mean the same thing. Secondly, since what is taxable is profits, expenses incurred in earning the profits are deductible. Thirdly, "annual" does not mean that the profits must be recurring, but it does mean that the profits must be income profits and not capital profits. It follows that a profit from buying something and then re-selling it is not assessable under Case VI. If the buying and re-selling is done in the course of trading, the profit is assessable under Case I. If the buying and re-selling is not done in the course of trading, the profit is assessable (if at all) to capital gains tax. In *Jones v. Leeming* (1930) (H.L.) Leeming and three other people obtained options to buy two rubber estates in the Malay Peninsula which they subsequently sold at a profit. The Commissioners found that the transaction was not a concern in the nature of trade. The House of Lords held that on that finding the profits could not be assessed under Case VI.

So what *is* caught by the general aspect of Case VI? In *Scott v. Ricketts* (1967) (C.A.) Lord Denning said that what is caught includes "remuneration for work done, services rendered, or facilities provided". A good example of a Case VI profit is in *Leader v. Counsel* (1942). A group of racehorse owners purchased a stallion. If any member of the group did not have a mare which required the services of the stallion he could sell his nomination to anyone else. It was held that there was not a trade, but that these receipts from the user[1] of property were income receipts and were taxable under Case VI.

Similarly, income from activities which do not form part of a profession or vocation, but would do so if repeated may be charged to tax under Case VI. For example, writing one newspaper article does not make someone into a writer. Case VI also catches income made by selling one's story to the newspapers. The wife of one of the Great Train Robbers sold her story to the *News of the World*. In *Alloway v. Phillips* (1980) (C.A.), the court held that the £39,000 she received derived from her contract with the newspaper, and that her rights under that contract were "property", so that she was liable under Case VI.

Gifts, betting winnings and "winnings" by finding are not assessable under Case VI any more than they are under Case I or Case II.

There are four points to be made about assessment under Case VI.

First, assessment is on a current year basis, and income tax under Case VI is computed on the full amount of the profits or gains arising in the year of assessment (section 69 of the Taxes Act). Secondly, "arising" has been held to mean "received": *Grey v. Tiley* (1932) (C.A.). So assessment is on the cash basis rather than the earnings basis. Thirdly, losses under Case VI are not so favourably treated as

---

[1] "User" is a lawyers' word meaning "use".

Casual Earnings

losses under Cases I and II, because a Case VI loss can only be set off against Case VI profits, not against other kinds of income. Fourthly, income falling within the general aspect of Case VI is, except in rare circumstances, investment income and not earned income: see the definition section, section 833(4)(c) of the Taxes Act. Income falling within some particular aspect of Case VI may or may not be earned income depending on the circumstances. For example, post-cessation receipts are earned income if the profits of the trade which has ceased would have been earned income, but, if not, not: Taxes Act, s.107.

CHAPTER 8

INCOME FROM LAND[1]

"Land", observed Anthony Trollope, "is about the only thing that can't fly away."[2] This is a thought that has occurred to landowners, would-be landowners and the Revenue. The taxation of land has a long and tangled history. Income from land is now taxed under Schedule A, but, as will be seen, there are two versions of Schedule A. This requires some explanation. The first (the old Schedule A) has its origins in the Finance Act 1963 and its rules, although now redundant for income tax purposes, retain their importance because broadly speaking companies pay corporation tax under these rules on their Schedule A income. The second version (the new Schedule A), and the one upon which this chapter concentrates, was introduced by the Finance Act 1995 and its rules generally apply for income tax purposes from 1995–96. The relevant statutory provisions are contained in sections 15 and 21–43 of the Taxes Act. However, before our attention is directed towards these provisions we should look briefly at some history, with a view to, hopefully, throwing some light upon the present position.

History

Originally, Schedule A was a tax on the *ownership* of land. From that it followed that it caught not only landowners who let out their land but also owner-occupiers. It was based on annual values. These annual values were supposed to be revised every five years, but in fact the last revision was made in 1935–36, and after that year they became hopelessly out-of-date and absurdly low. The Finance Act 1940 then introduced a system of taxing landlords (under Case VI of Schedule D) on what were called "excess rents", that is on rents

---

[1] "Land" in tax law, as in law generally, includes buildings (except where the context requires otherwise).
[2] See *The Law Chronicle of Barset*, Chap. 58. Further, as Mark Twain once perceptively remarked, they don't make it any more.

135

received to the extent that they exceeded the annual values fixed under Schedule A.

Then the Finance Act 1963 re-modelled the whole system. Tax on owner-occupiers was abolished. They had, after all, only been subjected to income tax on the basis of a notional income (equal to the annual value) not a real income. And in practice many owner-occupiers had been able to eliminate any tax charge by making a "maintenance claim" in respect of repairs, insurance, etc. So far as non-occupiers were concerned the Finance Act 1963 combined the Schedule A and excess rents provisions into a new taxing code which was labelled Case VIII of Schedule D.

For the next six years there was no Schedule A; that label was vacant. Then by the Finance Act 1969 Case VIII was re-named "Schedule A". Such remodelled Schedule A, which, in essence, taxed the annual profits or gains derived from certain rents[3] and other receipts arising from the ownership of land or an interest in land, then held sway until it was superseded for income tax purposes by the new Schedule A which was introduced by the Finance Act 1995 (at which point it might properly be referred to as the old Schedule A!).

The new Schedule A taxes profits or gains arising from any *business* carried on for the exploitation, as a source of rents or other receipts, of any land or interest in land. Moreover, the income of a Schedule A business is treated, for computation purposes, in a similar way to the income of a trade under Case I of Schedule D. However, these Schedules remain separate and distinct and income of a Schedule A business is neither trading nor earned income.[4]

Finally, for the sake of completeness, it should be mentioned that there was a Schedule B tax until it was abolished by the Finance Act 1988. Originally, this was a tax on *occupiers* of land which was payable in addition to any Schedule A liability. So an owner-occupier paid both with the important exception that dwelling-houses and trade premises were exempted from Schedule B.[5] However, from 1963 until its abolition, Schedule B was confined to

---

[3] This included certain capital payments deemed to be rent—see the treatment of premiums (below, pp.141).
[4] But note the special rules which apply to income from furnished holiday lettings (see below, p.139).
[5] Farms used to fall under Schedule B, until farming was transferred by statute to Case I of Schedule D.

taxing the occupation of woodlands "managed on a commercial basis and with a view to the realisation of profits", and, moreover, an occupier of woodlands might avoid an assessment under Schedule B, which was based on one-third of the annual value of the woodlands, by electing to be assessed under Case I of Schedule D.

The New Schedule A

INTRODUCTION

Before we look at some of the essential features of the new Schedule A it is as well to deal with, albeit superficially, two questions which inevitably arise as a consequence of what we have said thus far. First, why was the new Schedule A introduced and, secondly, why was the old Schedule A retained for companies? The answer to the first question lies primarily in the quest for simplification to facilitate the introduction of self-assessment (see above, pp.60–62). The new Schedule A is undoubtedly simpler in many respects than the old Schedule A and some of the anomalies associated with the latter, *e.g.* the taxation of income from furnished lettings under Case VI of Schedule D rather than Schedule A have been eradicated. It has also been argued that the new Schedule A rules are merely a reflection of Revenue practice preceding the change. The answer to the second question is equally pragmatic in that there are aspects of the old Schedule A rules which favour companies and which were regarded as too beneficial to be lost; a consequence which would have followed if companies had been subjected to the same rules as individuals under the new Schedule A. Hence the existence of the two versions of Schedule A (one for income tax and one for corporation tax) which are simultaneously in force!

THE CHARGE TO TAX

Our starting point for consideration of the parameters of the new Schedule A must be the new basic charging provision enacted in section 39(1) of the Finance Act 1995 and incorporated, for income tax purposes, into section 15 of the Taxes Act. The charging provision says:

> "Tax under this Schedule [A] shall be charged on the annual profits or gains arising from any business carried on for the exploitation, as a source of rents or other receipts, of any estate, interest or rights in or over any land in the United Kingdom".

In short, central to the new Schedule A is the notion of a business carried on for the exploitation of land or an interest in land, *i.e.* a Schedule A business.

SCOPE

Most commonly, the new Schedule A taxes the profits or gains made by an individual from the business of letting property, *i.e.* the rents received or to which the individual is entitled, less any items of allowable expenditure (see further below). However, it also extends to other sources of profits or gains. First, it catches certain capital payments made by a tenant to a landlord and which are referable to the grant of a lease, *i.e.* premiums which may be taxed as if they are payments of rent. The substantive rules relating to the taxation of premiums under the new Schedule A (which are considered below, pp.141–144) are broadly the same as those which apply under the old Schedule A. Secondly, receipts other than rent (actual or deemed) may give rise to profits or gains taxable under the new Schedule A provided, of course, that the receipts are derived from the exploitation of land or an interest in land. Some guidance as to the nature of these "other receipts" is given by *Lowe v. Ashmore* (1971) and *McClure v. Petre* (1988)[6] from which it is apparent that the receipts must be income not capital receipts. In the latter, the taxpayer received a payment in return for the grant of a licence to dump waste on his land. It was held that the payment was a capital receipt and, therefore, not taxable under Schedule A. By granting the licence, the taxpayer deprived himself of a right, namely, the right to dump, which he could otherwise have enjoyed over his land. The payment was the consideration for the disposal of that right. The taxpayer had realised part of the value of his freehold.

It is the treatment of the letting of property, etc., as a business (the profits (or losses) of which, as we have seen, are computed on the same basis as profits under Case I of Schedule D which differentiates the new Schedule A from the old Schedule A. Broadly speaking, under the rules of the latter, each letting of property, etc. by an individual was regarded as an independent and separate source of income and generally taxed as such. However, under the new Schedule A, each source of income, *e.g.* each letting where the

---

[6] Both cases were concerned with the construction to be given to the words "other receipts arising ... from or by virtue of ... ownership of an estate or interest in land or right over ... land or any incorporeal hereditament ... " which appear in the charging provision of old Schedule A.

individual has granted a number of leases is treated as part of a single Schedule A business, and the taxation of the individual in respect of that business is determined by taking into account the income generated and pertinent expenses incurred by such sources as a whole.

COMPUTATION

Section 21(3) of the Taxes Act, as amended by section 39(2) of the Finance Act 1995, provides for the profits and losses of a Schedule A business to be computed (with some exceptions) in accordance with the rules for computing profits under Case I of Schedule D. The Schedule A computation includes all relevant receipts and outgoings of the business for the year of assessment. The charge to tax is calculated on an earnings basis (see above, p.95).

The rules for computing profits under Case I of Schedule D are considered in Chapter 5 (see above, pp.75–93), although some aspects of these rules in the context of the new Schedule A are alluded to in the next section.

PARTICULAR CHARACTERISTICS

The unitary approach to taxation under the new Schedule A means, in principle, that *all* lettings of property by an individual, whether furnished, *i.e.* where part of the rent payable is attributable to the use of furniture, or unfurnished, should be within the parameters of the new Schedule A.[7] Indeed, this is broadly true, although in need of further elaboration in relation to two types of furnished letting, namely furnished holiday lettings and what are known as "rent a room" lettings.

For some time, the commercial letting of furnished holiday accommodation by individuals or companies has been *treated* for certain purposes as a trade. Those purposes are set out in section 503 of the Taxes Act which applies to furnished holiday lettings rules which normally only apply to trades, *e.g.* the loss relief rules for trades (see Chapter 10).[8] However, notwithstanding this close alignment with Case I of Schedule D and the treatment of income from a furnished holiday letting as earned income, the profits or gains of such a letting are *not* taxed under Case I of Schedule D. They are

---

[7] Previously the profits or gains from furnished lettings by individuals were taxed under Case VI of Schedule D.
[8] S. 504 sets out rigorous conditions which must be satisfied before a letting qualifies as a furnished holiday letting for the purposes of section 503.

taxed from 1995–96 onwards in the case of a furnished holiday letting by an individual under the new Schedule A; previously the profits or gains from such a letting were taxed (and continue to be so taxed when the letting is by a company) in accordance with Case VI of Schedule D.

A "rent a room" letting arises where an individual rents out a spare furnished room in his only or main residence (see section 59 and Schedule 10 of the Finance Act (No.2) 1992). This is not a step which an individual would necessarily take without encouragement. That encouragement is provided by a tax incentive. An individual is eligible for relief from income tax if the income from a "rent a room" letting or lettings in a particular year of assessment does not exceed £3,250. If the income exceeds this amount, the individual may choose either to be taxed on the excess over £3,250 or to be taxed on the actual profit made (*i.e.* gross receipts less actual expenses).[9]

Finally, another important facet of the new Schedule A is that in computing the annual profits or gains of a Schedule A business allowable expenses of the business may be set off against any Schedule A income of the business accruing in that year of assessment. An allowable expense is an income expense incurred wholly and exclusively for the purpose of the Schedule A business which does not constitute prohibited expenditure within section 74 of the Taxes Act (see above, pp.84–85, 91–93). This approach can be contrasted with the regime of "permitted deductions" under the old Schedule A, which prescribes, with no small measure of complexity (see, in particular, sections 25 and 28 of the Taxes Act), the conditions which must be fulfilled if certain types of expenditure (principally, maintenance, repair, insurance or management costs)[10] are to be deductible (allowable). In many instances, this means that a "permitted deduction" can only be made from the rents or receipts derived from the property in respect of which the expenditure giving rise to that deduction was incurred and only then in carefully defined circumstances.

---

[9] From 1995–96, liability to income tax in respect of such income arises under the new Schedule A (previously under Case VI of Schedule D), except where the income is trading income taxable under Case I of Schedule D.

[10] For the position with regard to the management costs of investment companies see the generally less rigid section 75 of the Taxes Act.

The New Schedule A

Premiums

The next section may be regarded, with hindsight, as perhaps a well-meant mistake. It is common form with commercial lettings in some areas for the consideration payable by the tenant to come in two forms. The first is the annual rent. The second is a lump sum, usually paid at or before the beginning of the lease. In principle, the lump sum is capital. Nowadays it is liable to capital gains tax. But in 1963 when the first fundamental revision of Schedule A occurred (see above, p.136) there was no capital gains tax, so such sums went tax-free. If premiums were not taxable there would be an obvious and simple tax-avoidance device—don't charge a rent, just take a premium, which, being a capital sum, would not be subject to income tax because it is not an *annual* profit or gain.

The normal meaning of "premium" in relation to land is a lump sum paid for the granting of a lease. But for income tax purposes "premium" has an extended meaning, as we shall see. Presently, the broad principle is that certain premiums are deemed to be income and are charged to income tax. The substantive rules relating to the treatment of premiums under the new Schedule A, which are considered in the remainder of this section, are broadly the same as those which apply under the old Schedule A. The detailed provisions in section 34 to 39 are concerned to stop up various tax-avoidance devices which would otherwise be open. This is an excellent field in which to observe the battle between tax avoiders and the Revenue.

A premium (or part of a premium) which is not caught for income tax may be caught for capital gains tax. Conversely, that part of a premium which is caught for income tax is not chargeable to capital gains tax.

There are three main heads of charge on premium income: (1) under section 34, premiums and like sums are chargeable; (2) under section 35, where a lease is granted at an undervalue the "amount foregone" may be chargeable on a subsequent assignment of the lease; (3) under section 36, where land is sold with a right to reconveyance the difference between the selling price and the reconveyance price may be chargeable to tax.

Let us look first at section 34. Subsection (1) is the provision which catches a "premium" in its normal meaning. It says:

"where the payment of any premium is required under a lease, or otherwise under the terms subject to which a lease is granted, and the duration of the lease does not exceed 50 years, the landlord shall be treated for the purposes of the Tax Acts as becoming entitled when the lease is granted to an amount by way of rent (in addition to any actual rent) equal to—

$$P - \frac{(P \times Y)}{50}$$

where P is the premium and Y is the number of complete periods of 12 months (other than the first) comprised in the duration of the lease."

Notice that the way the subsection taxes a premium is to treat the landlord as being in receipt of rent which is then part of the profits of the Schedule A business. Notice also that a lease for more than 50 years is not caught by section 34, and that the nearer a lease gets to being for 50 years the less income tax is payable. Thus a premium on a lease for 49 years is reduced by 48/50, or 96 per cent, leaving only 4 per cent taxable. A lease for nine years is reduced by eight-fiftieths (or 16 per cent), leaving 84 per cent taxable. A lease for one year enjoys no reduction at all. But remember also that the part of the premium not caught by income tax *is* liable to tax in so far as a chargeable gain arises. Because of this sliding scale there are detailed rules (in section 38) for ascertaining the duration of leases.

We now come to some extended meanings of the word "premium". Section 34(2) treats as a premium a requirement on the tenant to carry out works on the premises (beyond mere maintenance and repairs). The deemed premium is of an amount equal to the increase that the requirement makes in the value of the landlord's reversionary interest. So the premium provisions cannot be avoided by requiring works rather than a cash payment.

Section 34 also deals with other kinds of disguised premium. Subsection (4) deems a sum to be a premium if it becomes payable by the tenant in lieu of rent or as consideration for the surrender of the lease. Subsection (5) deems a sum to be a premium if it becomes payable by the tenant as consideration for the variation or waiver of any of the terms of the lease.

Where a premium (or a deemed premium, as above) is payable by instalments the tax may be paid in corresponding instalments spread over a maximum of eight years, but only if the recipient satisfies the Revenue that he would otherwise suffer undue hardship. This undue hardship test (and the eight-year limit) was introduced in 1972. Before that no such test was required and there was no time-limit, and ingenious leases appeared under which a premium was to be paid over a period of, say 250 years, with the bulk becoming payable in the 250th year.

Section 35 deals with another possible avoidance device. A premium paid on the *grant* of a lease is taxable (as we have seen), but a premium paid on the *assignment* of a lease is not taxable under the provisions we have so far looked at. Therefore, if it were not for this section 35, a simple avoidance would be for A to grant a lease to B (a relative, say, or a friendly company) at a very small premium or without any premium at all and then for B to assign the lease to C (a stranger) at a premium. Section 35 catches this situation. Suppose the market is such that A could have required a premium of £1,000 on the grant of the lease to B, whereas in fact he took a premium of only £200, then £800 is said to be "the amount foregone". If B later assigns the premises for £1,400 he is charged to tax (under the new Schedule A); on the excess of £1,400 over the amount of the original premium (£200), except that the chargeable amount cannot exceed the amount foregone. So on these figures the chargeable amount would have been £1,400 less £200 (= £1,200), but the upper limit is £800, and so the chargeable amount is £800. If B had assigned the premises to C for a premium of £500 the chargeable amount would have been £300. In that circumstance the Revenue would not have collected tax on the whole of the amount foregone, but they would be able to pick up the balance on subsequent assignments by C, D, E, etc.

Section 36 deals with yet another avoidance device, namely selling land subject to a right of reconveyance. If A, a landowner, is minded to take a premium of, say, £7,000, on granting a lease to B, he could, instead, sell the land to B on terms that he, A, could buy back the land from B for the sale price minus £7,000. Section 36 ensures that on such a transaction A is charged to tax (under the new Schedule A) on £7,000. If the sale contains a right for A to take a lease back of the premises from B, the lease back counts as a reconveyance. This lease back procedure is very common in practice, because it is a neat way of solving a liquidity problem or a cash-flow problem, and, as it is not very wicked, section 36 contains a proviso excepting such a transaction from the tax charge if the lease back is granted, and begins to run, within one month after the sale. That seems a very arbitrary way of marking out the exception, but it does enable (as it is intended to do) a genuine lease back arrangement to be free of the tax charge under section 36. But capital gains tax may be chargeable on the transaction; also if the lease back is at more than a commercial rent, only the commercial rent will be an allowable business

Income from Land

expense (section 779 of the Taxes Act); also in certain circumstances a proportion of the sale price may be taxed as though it were income (section 780 of the Taxes Act).

"Artificial Transactions in Land"

These transactions are governed by section 776 of the Taxes Act. It derives from a section first enacted in 1960. Subsection (1) of section 776 states the reason for the section: "This section is enacted to prevent the avoidance of tax by persons concerned with land or the development of land." This is achieved by treating certain capital gains (see below) arising on the disposal of land as income. The rationale of section 776 can be best understood if one looks at its history and antecedents. One must bear in mind that the section dates from 1960, that is, before there was a capital gains tax. In those days an owner of land who sold the land could make a tax-free profit, unless he was a dealer in land. If he was a dealer in land he was taxed on the gain as an item in his trading profit (and still is: see, for example, *Pilkington v. Randall* (1966) and compare *Marson v. Morton* (1986)). He could avoid this tax by forming a company to hold the land and then selling the shares, rather than selling the land as such. That transaction would be tax-free unless he was a dealer in shares. The section took on its present form in 1969 as one of a number of anti-avoidance provisions promoted by the then Labour government.

Section 776 seeks to block this device by a very wide-ranging provision. At first it was little used, and thought to be of little importance, despite its wording. However, a series of largely successful Revenue contests in the courts in the 1980s indicated that it might be potentially a very wide section indeed: see *Yuill v. Wilson* (1980) in the House of Lords, and *Page v. Lowther* (1983) and *Yuill v. Fletcher* (1984) in the Court of Appeal. But these decisions must now, in turn, be read in the light of two significant developments. First, it may be questioned whether the section is needed in view of the approach adopted by the courts in cases such as *Furniss v. Dawson* (1984) (H.L.) (see above, p.42). Secondly, it is inevitable that the importance of the section has been reduced since 1988 by the unification of the rates of tax for capital gains tax and income tax. Notwithstanding these caveats, the section may apply wherever:

"Artifcial Transactions in Land"

   (i) land, or property deriving value from land, is acquired solely or mainly to realise a gain on its disposal; *or*
  (ii) land is held as trading stock; *or*
 (iii) land is developed solely or mainly to realise a gain on disposal when developed,

and a disposal of the land gives rise to a capital gain. The whole of the gain is treated as income taxable under Case VI of Schedule D for the year in which the gain is realised. For this purpose, "disposal" includes disposal of control over land, so covers the case of land owned through companies, where the companies' shares, rather then the land itself, are transferred.

Even more broadly, the gains can be treated as the income of any person by whom the gain is realised or who provides directly or indirectly an opportunity to realise it. This is wide enough to catch a "mastermind" who has taken no actual part in the process of making a gain, as was illustrated in the two *Yuill* cases mentioned above.

The section is unusual even in tax-avoidance law, and almost unprecedented in general statute law, in containing a statement of its purpose in subsection (1). But it is not clear whether this provision adds anything to the operation of the section.

Tailpiece

In considering the taxation of receipts from land, one should bear in mind that as well as income tax (in connection with rents and premiums and section 776 gains) a transaction in land may attract capital gains tax.

CHAPTER 9

CAPITAL ALLOWANCES

When we were considering in Chapter 5 the computation of profits under Schedule D, Cases I and II, we saw that the cost and depreciation of capital assets are regarded as being of a capital not of a revenue character. But this does not mean, as we indicated in Chapter 5, that no relief is given for tax purposes in respect of such capital expenditure. It is given by a separate system of "capital allowances". We consider the manner in which such relief is given later in this chapter. Initially, however, we must determine when capital allowances are available.

Capital allowances are available in respect of the following items:

Machinery and plant;
Industrial and agricultural buildings and structures;
Mines, oil wells, etc.;
Dredging;
Dwelling houses let on assured tenancies;
Scientific research, patents, know-how, etc.

It can be seen from the list that many items of capital expenditure do *not* attract any allowance. Also, all the allowances, with one exception, are confined to income taxable under Schedule D, Case I, that is, the profits of a trade. The exception is the allowances for machinery and plant, which are available to persons carrying on a profession (or vocation) or to persons in employment, as well as to traders: section 27 of the Capital Allowances Act 1990. Allowances can also be claimed for machinery and plant used in estate management: Taxes Act 1988, s.32.

The law relating to capital allowances can be traced back to the Income Tax Act 1945. The system of providing relief for capital expenditure through the availability of capital allowances introduced by that Act is the foundation upon which the present law is based. Of course, that is not to say that the system has not been

Capital Allowances

subject to considerable change over the years. There have been two consolidation Acts in 1968 and 1990 respectively, and the latter, the Capital Allowances Act 1990, as amended by subsequent Finance Acts, is the primary source of the present law.

Before looking at aspects of the substantive law two important questions must be addressed—first, what is the rationale for capital allowances and, secondly, the distinct but interrelated question of the rate(s) at which capital allowances should be available? It is implicit in the opening remarks in this chapter that the availability of capital allowances should in some measure be an acknowledgement of the need to take account of the depreciation in value or obsolescence of capital assets acquired by a business. However, for many years, successive governments perceived capital allowances principally as a means of encouraging businesses to invest, and a system of generous allowances developed which enabled a business to write off capital expenditure markedly in advance of any actual depreciation or obsolescence. Thus, by 1984, a business, if it wished, could set the whole of the cost of buying machinery and plant against its taxable profits for the year of purchase, together with most (and sometimes all) of the cost of industrial buildings. This was achieved by claiming the appropriately named first year and initial allowances respectively. In many instances, however, it was not the desire to invest *per se* which prompted expenditure by a business, but the prospect of claiming these allowances with a view to cutting down taxable profits in the year the expenditure was incurred. Such practices, which were intended to exploit the generosity of the system, brought forth the following lament by Chancellor of the Exchequer, Nigel Lawson, in his Budget Speech in 1984. He said:

> "... Over virtually the whole of the post-war period there have been incentives for investment in both plant and machinery and industrial, although not commercial, buildings. But there is little evidence that these incentives have strengthened the economy or improved the quality of investment. Indeed, quite the contrary ... too much of British investment has been made because the tax allowances make it look profitable rather than because it would be truly productive. We need investment decisions based on future market assessments not future tax assessments."

However, it was a lament which acted as a prelude for a fundamental restructuring of the capital allowances system brought about initially by the Finance Act 1984 and continued by the Finance Act 1985. The general policy was to phase out the generous first year

Capital Allowances

and initial allowances[1] (for machinery and plant and industrial buildings this was achieved between 1984–86),[2] and to provide, thereafter, for the writing down of such capital expenditure solely on the basis of writing-down allowances applicable over a number of years and at rates which bore some resemblance to actual depreciation.[3] Broadly, this policy has been maintained to the present day, although first year and initial allowances were briefly resurrected in respect of machinery, plant and industrial buildings for one year beginning on November 1, 1992 (albeit at rates [of 40 per cent and 20 per cent respectively] substantially below those which had prevailed in 1984).

We will now look at allowances on machinery and plant, and then (much more briefly) at some other allowances.

Allowances on Machinery and Plant

Neither machinery nor plant are defined in the tax legislation, and it is often a matter of some difficulty to decide whether a particular item is entitled to an allowance. The meaning to be given to the word plant has been particularly problematic. This is typified by Parliament's enactment in 1994 (see Schedule AA1 of the Capital Allowances Act 1990, inserted by section 117 of the Finance Act 1994) of a rule that buildings and structures *cannot* qualify as plant (subject to the proviso that buildings and structures already so qualifying would continue to do so). The Schedule sets out those individual items or assets which fall with these expressions and which *cannot* qualify as plant. But, interestingly, it also lists items or assets which although within the definition of these words may nevertheless qualify as plant. In respect of an item in the latter category, it is open to the taxpayer to establish in the light of the meaning given to plant by the courts that it does in fact qualify. It is to the approach of the courts that we now look.

---

[1] Although, this was subject to exceptions, see, for example, below p.154.
[2] The effect over this two-year period was to remove several billion pounds' worth of capital allowances, although this was associated with a drop from 52 per cent to 35 per cent in the main rate of corporation tax.
[3] Writing-down allowances had been available before, but their applicability was dependent on the extent to which a business was entitled to or had utilised a first year or initial allowance. If, for example, a 100 per cent first year allowance was claimed, as was usually the case, no question of a writing-down allowance arose.

Allowances on Machinery and Plant

It is an interesting fact that the case most often cited as a starting point for judicial statements about the meaning of plant is not a tax case at all, but a tort case. The case is *Yarmouth v. France* (1887) (D.C.). A workman brought a claim under the Employers' Liability Act 1880 for damages for injuries caused by a defect in his employer's "plant", namely a vicious horse. Lindley L.J. (in holding that the horse was plant) said:

> "... in its ordinary sense [plant] includes whatever apparatus is used by a business man for carrying on his business—not his stock-in-trade, which he buys or makes for sale; but all goods and chattels, fixed or movable, live or dead, which he keeps for permanent employment in his business."

From that beginning a huge structure of case law has been built up as to what may constitute plant. The item must be a good or chattel; it must have some degree of durability; it must be an item *with* which a trade (or profession) is carried on as distinct from an item which comprises part of the premises or setting *in* which it is carried on.

It is this latter distinction which has often been difficult to draw, although it is established that an item which becomes part of the premises in which the trade is carried on cannot be plant (except in those cases where the premises are themselves plant for example, *IRC Barclay, Curle & Co. Ltd* (1969) (H.L.)),[4] and that this will be so even if the item also has a distinct business purpose, *e.g.* to embellish the premises with a view to pleasing and attracting customers. The determination of whether an item has become part of the premises depends on whether it is more appropriate to describe the item as having become part of the premises as opposed to having retained a separate identity. This is a matter of fact and degree, and a court may take into account whether the item retains visually a separate identity, the degree of permanence with which it is affixed, the incompleteness of the premises without it and the extent to which it was intended to be permanent. In *Wimpey v. Warland* (1989) (C.A.) the court was concerned with whether various improvements including tiling on floors and walls, glass shop fronts, raised and mezzanine floors, staircases and false ceilings which were undertaken at the taxpayer's fast food restaurants were plant. It was conceded that the improvements were designed to attract potential

---

[4] To this extent, Schedule AA1 is declaratory.

customers and to provide a particular atmosphere which the taxpayer considered conducive to the meals served. Nevertheless, the Court of Appeal decided that the improvements were not plant as they had become part of the premises.[5] In circumstances where items have not become part of the premises, it has been accepted by the courts that they may be plant if the taxpayer's business includes the provision of atmosphere and the items are designed to create that atmosphere (see *IRC v. Scottish and Newcastle Breweries* (1982) (H.L.)); a possibility also countenanced by Schedule AA1 of the Capital Allowances Act 1990.

It is obviously easier to apply the ideas inherent in Lindley L.J.'s statement in *Yarmouth v. France* to a trade than to a profession, and in *Daphne v. Shaw* (1926) it was held that law books bought by a solicitor and used in his practice were not plant. However, 50 years later, in *Munby v. Furlong* (1977) (C.A.), *Daphne v. Shaw* was overruled by the Court of Appeal. Mr Munby, a barrister, won his claim for capital allowances in respect of law reports and textbooks bought in his first year of practice. Lord Denning said:

> "Counsel for the Crown ... would confine a professional man's 'plant' to things used physically like a dentist's chair or an architect's table or, I suppose, the typewriter in a barrister's chambers; but, for myself, I do not think 'plant' should be confined to things which are used physically. It seems to me that on principle it extends to the intellectual storehouse which a barrister or a solicitor or any other professional man has in the course of carrying on his profession."

Lord Denning divided what he called "a lawyer's library" into three parts: first, a set of law reports; secondly, textbooks; thirdly, periodicals, including current issues of law reports.[6] Expenditure on this last group was, said Lord Denning, revenue expenditure; expenditure on the first two groups was capital expenditure, and qualified for capital allowances.

---

[5] At first instance, Hoffman J. decided that light fittings installed as part of the improvements were not part of the premises and were plant because the volume of light they gave was important for the furtherance of the taxpayer's business (*cf. Cole Bro. v. Phillips* (1982) (H.L.)).

[6] To which might be added now computer software. Capital expenditure in respect of which may qualify for capital allowances under section 67A of the Capital Allowances Act 1990.

Allowances on Machinery and Plant

If an item constitutes either machinery or plant, capital allowances may be available to a trader who has incurred capital expenditure on acquiring that item wholly and exclusively for the purposes of his trade[7] and where as a result of that expenditure the item belongs to the trader (see section 24 of the Capital Allowances Act 1990). The meaning of the phrase "wholly and exclusively" has been considered in Chapter 5 (see above, pp.87–90), although it might be useful to add that where capital expenditure is incurred for the acquisition of plant or machinery to be used partly for trade and partly for other purposes the system of apportionment in section 79 of the Capital Allowances Act 1990 may be applied. The word "belongs" has an extended meaning for these purposes. Thus, an item of machinery or plant may be deemed to belong to a person even though technically it belongs to another! This is best explained by the following example. Where a lessee of a building incurs capital expenditure on the provision of machinery or plant, which he is required to provide under the terms of his lease, for the purposes of a trade carried on by him (in circumstances where that machinery or plant is not installed or fixed so as to become part of the building or land) then the machinery or plant will be deemed to belong to him and in respect of which he may claim capital allowances (see section 61 (4) of the Capital Allowances Act 1990).

Finally, before we look at how allowances for expenditure on machinery or plant work, we must mention the methods of using the allowances. As we saw at the beginning of this chapter, one of the principal attractions of the system of allowances which operated before the changes introduced by the Finance Act 1984, was the opportunity for a trader, who was subject to income tax, to use capital allowances, particularly in the year of purchase, as a *deduction from profits*. Originally, this method of using capital allowances was adopted because it was considered inappropriate to treat the capital allowances of an individual trader as *expenses* in view of the complications arising from the fact that trading profits were taxed on a preceding year basis. However, these complications will soon be a thing of the past for, as indicated in Chapter 5 (pp. 93–95), the preceding year basis is in the process of being supplanted by a current year basis.[8] Consequently, where the current year basis

---

[7] For the availability of capital allowances in respect of capital expenditure by a trader on machinery or plant used otherwise than in the course of his trade, see section 61 of the Capital Allowances Act 1990.

[8] A change designed to facilitate self-assessment (see above, p.60–62).

applies (and this is so from 1994–95 in respect of trades commenced on or after April 6, 1994 and will be so for trades commenced before April 6, 1994 from 1997–98), capital allowances are no longer a deduction from profits but treated as a trading expense in the computation of profits.[9] This does not mean, however, that capital allowances are to be equated with revenue expenditure. Substantial differences, which emphasise the continued importance of distinguishing between revenue and capital expenditure, remain. Thus, for example, in the computation of profits, allowable revenue expenditure may be generally set off in full and at once against trading income, whereas this is certainly not true of capital expenditure qualifying for writing-down allowances which must be spread over several years (see below).

Allowances

For many years, there were two kinds of allowances on machinery and plant known as first year and writing-down allowances. However, first year allowances are unavailable at present and have been so since 1986, except for a brief renaissance for one year beginning on November 1, 1992 (see above, p. 148). When first year allowances were available they operated in tandem with writing-down allowances. However, as we have already seen (above, p.148), the applicability of a writing-down allowance was dependent on the extent to which a business was entitled to or had utilised a first year allowance. Now the sole entitlement is to an annual writing-down allowance.

Writing-down Allowances

Where a person carrying on a trade incurs capital expenditure on the provision of an item of machinery or plant wholly and exclusively for the purposes of the trade and in consequence of that expenditure the item belongs to him a writing-down allowance may be available on a 25 per cent per annum reducing balance basis. A writing-down allowance may also be claimed by a person who is exercising a profession or vocation, by the holder of an office or employment who purchases an item of machinery or plant "necessarily provided for use in the performance of his duties" and by a

---

[9] Capital allowances are treated similarly in the computation of profits for corporation tax.

Allowances on Machinery and Plant

landlord in respect of machinery or plant purchased for use in estate management (see section 27 of the Capital Allowances Act 1990 and section 32 of the Taxes Act).

A trader (or professional person, etc.) may claim a writing-down allowance at the rate of 25 per cent year by year. Suppose X buys a machine in year one for £1,600. He can have an allowance of 25 per cent of £1,600 = £400. This leaves a balance of £1,200. In year two he can have an allowance of 25 per cent of £1,200 = £300. In year three he can have an allowance of 25 per cent of (£1,200–£300) £900 = £225. And so on in accordance with this reducing balance basis. The £675 at the end of year three is commonly called the "written-down value" of the machine. The legislation calls it the "qualifying expenditure". It is equal to the original expenditure *less* the allowances already given, so it is the amount which "qualifies" for further allowances in the future.

Pooling

The items of machinery and plant belonging to a trader are treated as being in one "pool", except where the item is expressly excluded, *e.g.* certain cars costing more than £12,000 (see sections 34–36 of the Capital Allowances Act 1990), or where at the election of the taxpayer a short-life asset is not pooled in order to allow it to be written down over the period of its prospective useful life (for up to four years): section 37 of the Capital Allowances Act 1990.

Where there is a pool, the 25 per cent is calculated on the qualifying expenditure of the pool as a whole. Each new expenditure increases the qualifying expenditure in the pool. Each disposal of an item of machinery or plant reduces the qualifying expenditure in the pool by an amount equal to the disposal value of the item. If the price obtained for the sale of an item exceeds the amount of qualifying expenditure in the pool, a "balancing charge" is made on the taxpayer. Let us continue our example of Mr X (above) to see how the pooling system works. During the period described above, X only had one machine. Suppose that later on he acquires several more machines, and that at the end of year six he has qualifying expenditure in the pool amounting to £6,000. In year seven he gets a writing-down allowance of 25 per cent of £6,000 = £1,500, leaving £4,500. In year eight he buys a new machine for £3,500. His qualifying expenditure becomes £8,000. In year nine he sells a machine for £8,400. A "balancing charge" is made on him in the sum of £400. A balancing charge is (notionally) a receipt and therefore falls within the income tax net. If X were to sell the machine, not for £8,400 but for £7,600, he would not get a balancing allowance; all that would happen would be that the qualifying expenditure in the pool would go down from £8,000 to £400. When X permanently discontinues the trade there will be a balancing charge or a balancing allowance depending on whether the proceeds of sale of all the machinery and plant in the pool amount to more than or less than the qualifying expenditure.

Industrial Buildings

Allowances have been available for many years for capital expenditure on "an industrial building or structure" which is to be occupied for the purposes of trade.

The kinds of buildings covered are carefully defined (see section 18 of the Capital Allowances Act 1990) and are mainly confined to buildings, *e.g.* mills and factories employed in what might be described generically as productive industries. This tends to exclude commercial office buildings, residential buildings[10] and retail trade buildings, although amendments over the years have seen the definition extended to cover, for example, hotels, commercial buildings in enterprise zones and workshops. Notwithstanding this detailed definition in section 18, definitional problems still exist as epitomised by *Copol Clothing Ltd v. Hindmarch* (1984) in the House of Lords, where an allowance was denied to a warehouse owner (see also *Carr v. Sayer* (1992)). Where capital expenditure is incurred on a building which is not wholly "industrial" as defined by section 18 allowances may still be claimed in respect of that expenditure provided not more than a quarter of the expenditure on the building is attributable to the "non-industrial" part (section 18(7)).

There are two kinds of allowances on buildings, known as *initial allowances* and *writing-down allowances*. Presently, initial allowances are unavailable (save the 100 per cent initial allowance available in respect of capital expenditure incurred on an industrial building [or on machinery or plant therein] in an enterprise zone) and have been so since 1986 except for a brief renaissance for one year beginning on November 1, 1992. The writing-down allowance is 4 per cent of the *original* expenditure, with no pooling, so that,

---

[10] Allowances may, however, be available under Part III (sections 84–97) of the Capital Allowances Act 1990 in respect of certain dwelling houses let on assured tenancies.

since the general demise of the initial allowance, the allowance will apply evenly over 25 years.

Agricultural Land and Buildings

The expenditure concerned here is expenditure on the construction of farmhouses, farm buildings, cottages, fences "or other works". In the case of a farmhouse only a maximum of one-third of the expenditure qualifies for the allowance.

The allowance comprises a writing-down allowance of 4 per cent, which, as with the Industrial Buildings allowance, allows a total write-off over a period of 25 years. An initial allowance of 20 per cent was available for one year from November 1, 1992.

Other Capital Expenditure

The other kinds of capital allowance listed at the beginning of this chapter are merely noted here. Although it is, perhaps, apposite to add in passing that, notwithstanding the generally diminished importance of first year or initial allowances since the middle of the 1980s, it is still possible, in some instances, to enjoy capital allowances which write off capital expenditure in one year (see, for example, the 100 per cent capital allowance available for scientific research).

CHAPTER 10

LOSSES

This chapter is concerned with losses arising in a trade, profession or vocation. This is because, unlike losses arising under Case VI, or under Schedule A, these losses can be set off against taxable income from other sources. The tax position of a trade, profession or vocation is calculated by subtracting from the income the relevant expenses. If that calculation leaves a credit balance there is a taxable profit. But if it leaves a minus quantity there is a loss. Thus far, a loss is calculated in just the same way as a profit is calculated. In particular a trader cannot claim for tax purposes to have made a loss merely because on one transaction he has made a loss. For example, if a builder undertakes to build a house for £25,000 and in the event it costs him £27,000 to build the house, he cannot claim to have made a loss of £2,000. What matters is the overall relationship of trading income and expenses throughout a whole year's operation of his trade.

For many years there has been a very important difference (apart from the obvious!) between a profit and a loss. Profits have been computed (except at the beginning and end of a trade) on a preceding year basis; losses have been computed on a current year basis.[1] However, this dichotomy will disappear shortly, for, as we saw in Chapter 5, the basis of assessing profits under Cases I and II of Schedule D is in the process of being converted from a preceding to a current year basis.[2] It is a change which will apply ultimately to the

---

[1] Thus, a loss is treated as accruing in the year of assessment in which it is incurred and not by reference to some (different) basis period. From this principle two results follow where a trader's accounts for a particular accounting period show a loss: first, there is no profit for the year of assessment for which that period is the base period; secondly, there is a loss for the year of assessment in which the accounting period falls. The odd effect of this latter point is that there can be both a profit and a loss for the same year of assessment from the same trade; the profit being based on a preceding period and the loss being based on the actual period.

[2] A change designed to facilitate self-assessment (see above, p.60–62).

assessment of profits from all trades, professions or vocations from 1997-98. This transition has had some repercussions for the computation of losses and has led, in some instances, to modifications to the ways in which relief for losses is given. The implementation of these changes has been timed to coincide with the conversion of the basis of assessment of profits under Cases I and II of Schedule D from a preceding to a current year basis. Thus, new rules apply from 1994-95 to trades, professions or vocations (businesses) commenced on or after April 6, 1994 (new businesses) and to other businesses, *i.e.* those in existence before that date (existing businesses) from April 6, 1997. There are transitional provisions in respect of such existing businesses for 1996-97, which are predominantly (although, as we shall see, not exclusively) based on the pre-existing or old rules.

In the remainder of this chapter, we shall consider the various ways in which relief for losses may be given and it can be assumed that we are dealing with the new rules, save where specific reference is made, usually for comparative purposes, to the old rules.

There are four main ways in which relief for losses may be given: set-off against general income and capital gains; carry-forward against subsequent profits; carry-back of terminal losses; and a special mode of relief for losses in the early years of a trade. We will look at these in turn.

Set-off Against General Income and Capital Gains

By section 380 of the Taxes Act a person who sustains a loss in any trade, profession or vocation carried on by him either solely or in partnership may make a claim for relief. The relief works by way of setting off the loss in the trade, etc., against profits in some other trade or indeed against any income of the claimant in the same year. If the claimant's income of that same year is not sufficient to absorb the whole of the loss then the balance may be set off against the claimant's income of the preceding year (this also applies to existing businesses during the transitional year). Under the old rules, the balance might be set off not against the claimant's income of the preceding year but against such income for the following year.

The amount of the loss for the purposes of section 380 generally includes capital allowances which are *treated* as trading expenses (see section 140 of the Capital Allowances Act 1990). Under the old rules, capital allowances do not enter into the computation of profits or losses, but are a deduction from profits and might, in such circumstances, be used to create or augment a loss. Thus, under the old rules, if a trader has a profit of £15,000 and a capital allowance of £9,000, his profit is still £15,000 though he will only have to pay tax on £6,000. If he has a profit of £15,000 and a capital allowance of £19,000 he still, technically, has a profit of £15,000, however he can make a claim *as though* he had a loss of £4,000, and this £4,000 can be set off against his other income.

By section 384 a loss is not available for relief under section 380 unless it is shown that the trade was being carried on on a commercial basis and with a view to the realisation of profits. And by section 397 an even more stringent rule applies to farming and market gardening, namely that a loss cannot be relieved under section 380 if in each of the prior five years a loss was incurred. The point of these two sections (384 and 397) is to exclude from loss relief against other income "hobby-trading" and particularly "hobby-farming". Hobby-farming is a pretty popular activity. It arises in this way: a person with a substantial income (say a stockbroker) buys a farm and spends a great deal of money on building it up as a capital asset. If he could contrive to have no farming profits because of vast capital expenditure and set the farming losses against his stockbroking profits he could lay a gigantic nest-egg largely at the expense of the Revenue. The Revenue has disobliged.

Since 1991, a claim for relief under section 380 against general income may be extended to the claimant's capital gains of the same year (see section 72 of the Finance Act 1991). However, the loss must be set off against the general income before relief can be given against capital gains. If the claimant's capital gains of that year are not sufficient to absorb the whole of the loss then the balance may be set off against the claimant's capital gains of the preceding year (this also applies to existing businesses during the transitional year).

Carry-Forward Against Subsequent Profits

Section 385 provides for the carrying forward of a loss in one year against the profits in a subsequent year of the same trade, profession or vocation. Notice that it must be the *same* trade, etc. In that respect this relief is totally different from the relief under section 380. A loss can be carried forward under section 385 indefinitely, but it must be set off against the first subsequent assessment and then, so far as it remains not fully relieved, against the next assessment, and so on. If a loss has been partially relieved under some other provision (*e.g.* section 380), the unrelieved amount may be carried forward. Or, if he chooses, a trader can ignore section 380 and go straight for section 385 relief.

It may happen that the profits of a particular year are not big enough to absorb a loss which is being carried forward into that year. In that case, interest or dividends (if there are any) arising to the trader will be treated as though they were trading profits. This point needs a bit of explanation. If interest or dividends which have borne tax by deduction are received by a trader they are not included in the computation of his profits under Case I. The present point (in section 385(4)) is that those receipts can nevertheless be *treated as* profits, and a carried-forward loss can be relieved against them by means of a repayment of tax.

Another point which may arise under section 385 relates to payments out by the trader under section 349. (See Chapter 11, below.) Section 349 applies where an annual payment is made otherwise than wholly out of profits brought into charge to income tax. This would be so, for example, where the payer had no profits in the year in which he made the payment. Under section 350 he would then have to pay over to the Revenue the tax which he deducted in making the annual payment. The point here is that section 387 says that in such a case, provided the payment was made wholly and exclusively for the purposes of the trade (or profession or vocation) the grossed-up amount of the payment can be treated as a loss and given relief under section 385 (We say "grossed-up" because the section 387 says "the amount on which tax has been paid.".)

Another point on section 385 concerns interest, meaning payments of interest outwards. If a trader makes a payment of interest that will, prima facie, be an expense of his trading. But if he has an overall loss the interest will not get relieved. And if he has insufficient other income, the interest will not get relieved under section 353 of the Taxes Act either. The present point is that by section 390 (of the Taxes Act) the amount of the interest payment may be carried forward under section 385 "as if it were a loss."

The general rules for section 385 relief are that not only must the prior loss and the subsequent profit be incurred in the same trade, but also the claimant must be the person who incurred the loss. However, there is an important exception to these general rules in section 386 which provides that where a business carried on by an individual (or individuals) is transferred to a company, the individual may claim to set off under section 385 any losses which he incurred before the transfer against income derived by him from the

Losses

company after the transfer. The consideration for the transfer of the business must consist solely or mainly of the allotment of shares in the company. The income from the company may take the form of director's remuneration or salary or dividends. Further, a partner does not usually lose the relief available under section 385 when there is a change in the membership of a partnership, *e.g.* when a partner joins or leaves the partnership. This is so because, under the new rules, a partner is deemed to be a sole trader/professional in respect of his share of the partnership profit or loss (see further Chapter 14, p. 196). Therefore, his ability to carry forward his share of any such loss against his share of the partnership profits from the same trade or profession in subsequent years is normally unaffected by a change within the partnership (save where the actual trade/ profession is subsequently carried on by him alone, see below). In respect of existing partnerships and where the old rules apply, the position is complicated by the fact that a change of partners has consequences for each of the partners in that it generates a deemed discontinuance of the business (in the absence of an election that the business should continue). However, conflict with the general rules for relief under section 385 is averted by allowing a person who is a partner both before and after the change to carry forward his share of a previous loss against his share of future profits despite the discontinuance.

Carry-Back of Terminal Losses

By section 388 terminal losses (meaning losses outstanding at the termination of a business) may be set off against the profits of a trade, profession or vocation in the year of cessation and for the three years of assessment preceding the year in which the cessation or discontinuance occurs. This also applies to existing businesses during the transitional year. Under the old rules, terminal losses may be set off against the profits of the trade, profession or vocation for the latter three years only.

If the business is carried on by a partnership the position is as follows. Where the new rules apply a partner may claim relief for terminal losses when his deemed sole and separate trade, etc., is discontinued. Broadly, this occurs when he ceases to be a partner, where the actual trade or profession is subsequently carried on by him alone, or when the actual trade or profession ceases. Under the old rules, where the business was carried on by a partnership, this relief is available on a real discontinuance of the partnership and also on what one might call a statutory discontinuance caused by a change of partners. In the latter case the retiring partner can have relief but the continuing partners cannot. This is fair, because (as we have just seen) they can, despite the discontinuance, have relief against subsequent profits.

Losses in the Early Years

The three heads we have so far looked at provide for relief for losses by set-off against any income or capital gains of the same or the preceding year; against profits of the same trade, etc., in any following year; and (for terminal losses) against profits of the same trade in the year of cessation and for three previous years. This relief, which is provided for in section 381, works by way of a set-off of losses in the year of commencement of a trade, profession or vocation and/or in the next three years of assessment against any income of the taxpayer for the three years of assessment preceding that in which the loss is sustained. The relief applies to sole individuals and to partners. It does not apply to companies. Of course, a new company would not have any previous income, so the possibility of this relief could not arise. But an existing company sometimes sets up a new trade; it will not qualify for this relief. There is a provision to exclude hobby-trading from the relief. This seems a wise precaution on the part of the Revenue. In genuine cases, however, section 381, in effect, provides a subsidy to a loss-making new business.

CHAPTER 11

THE TAXATION OF INCOME UNDER CASE III OF SCHEDULE D

The Scope of Case III

At first glance, Case III looks even more of a rag bag than Case VI. According to section 18(3) of the Taxes Act, it covers: interest, annuities, "other annual payments", discounts and income from public revenue securities. Sections 119 and 120 of the Act add mining rents and royalties and the Finance Act 1996 brings certain discounted securities within case III.[1]

In this chapter we concentrate on the taxation of interest, annuities and annual payments which are the prime examples of what has been called by judges "pure profit income". It is pure profit in the sense that there are no expenses to set against it. This can, perhaps, be best appreciated by contrasting pure profit income with other kinds of income.

Trading income is the best contrast. A sum of money received by a trader in the course of carrying on his trade is a credit item in calculating his profits but it is not in itself in full a profit. Against it there have to be set various expenses; the cost of buying the thing which he has now sold and the overhead expenses of the selling organisation. In short, the receipt is not pure profit.

For many years, a particular feature of the taxation of annuities and other annual payments has been the operation of special rules (now contained in sections 348 and 349 of the Taxes Act) by virtue of which the payer deducts tax when making the payment, so that the recipient (payee) receives the income net of tax, *i.e.* a withholding tax is applied. However, as will be seen shortly, the importance of these special rules has been considerably diminished as a result of changes to the taxation of many annual payments brought about by the Finance Act 1988, although that is not to say, as

---

[1] For corporation tax purposes, profits from certain loan relationships are also taxed under the rules of Case III of Schedule D, see below, p. 289.

subsequent parts of this chapter show, that the special rules are now without significance.

In our consideration of the taxation of interest, annuities and other annual payments, the starting point must be to ascertain what these terms mean.

Interest has been defined as "payment by time for the use of money". There was an interesting discussion about what can and what cannot count as interest in the avoidance case of *Cairns v. Macdiarmid* (1983) (C.A.). Interest on a judgment is taxable. At one time there seemed to be a doubt as to whether interest awarded by a judge as an addition to damages was truly income and so taxable. Now it is well settled that such interest is taxable. There is one exception, by statute. Section 329 of the Taxes Act declares that interest on damages for personal injuries or death under the Law Reform (Miscellaneous Provisions) Act 1934 is "not to be regarded as income for any income tax purpose" (for the taxation of interest, see below, p.175).

An annuity is an income which is paid year by year. Many annuities arise under a will or similar instrument of gift. But it is possible to buy an annuity whereby a capital sum is used to pay for a regular income (for the tax treatment of a purchased life annuity, see below, p.174).

An annual payment is much more difficult to define. We can reduce the difficulty if we confine ourselves to defining such an annual payment *as falls within Case III of Schedule D*.

In some ways, this has been facilitated by the changes introduced by the Finance Act 1988 and incorporated into section 347A of the Taxes Act. The effect of section 347A, subject to the exceptions set out below, is to deny any effect for income tax purposes to many annual payments made by individuals[2]—to effectively ignore such payments for tax purposes and in respect of which, therefore, Case III of Schedule D is redundant. It might be wondered what prompted such a dramatic step. The answer lies in the fact that before this change was made, notwithstanding the existence of fairly wide ranging anti-avoidance rules which sought to counteract tax advantages which might be gained from the use of covenants and other

---

[2] "Individual" has a limited meaning. For example, a trustee is not an individual for these purposes. Therefore, a beneficiary of a discretionary trust who receives income payments from the trustees will be assessed under Case III of Schedule D (see below, p.179).

The Taxation of Income Under Case III of Schedule D

income settlements,[3] this was a fruitful area for tax saving. Thus, in appropriate circumstances, an individual payer could treat the payment as a charge on his income and deduct it computing his total income, whilst a payee, might, for example, not be liable to tax and through the use of unused personal allowances seek to recover the tax paid by the payer (under section 348 or 349) from the Revenue. Where section 347A applies these potential tax savings are no longer possible, for section 347A(1) provides that such a payment shall not be a charge on the payer's income (and that his income shall be computed without any deduction being made on account of the payment) and that the payment shall not form part of the income of the person to whom it is made.

Section 347A is stated expressly *not* to apply to:

(i) a payment of interest;
(ii) a covenanted payment to charity. This means a payment under a covenant otherwise than for consideration in money or money's worth. Such payments must be payable for a period capable of lasting more than three years and the covenant must not be revocable for four years (section 347A(7));
(iii) a payment made for bona fide commercial reasons in connection with the individual's trade, profession or vocation, *e.g.* a payment under a partnership retirement annuity;
(iv) a payment made for a non-taxable consideration (see section 125(1) of the Taxes Act).

To complete the picture, it might be added that annual payments which fall within (ii) or (iii) are not caught by the anti-avoidance rules (as to which see below, p.189). Consequently, such payments continue to be taxed under Case III of Schedule D.

The above discussion gives an insight into some of the annual payments which might, notwithstanding section 347A, still *fall within Case III of Schedule D*; nevertheless it begs the question what *is* an annual payment?! The courts have identified the following five characteristics of an annual payment.

First, the *ejusdem generis* rule of interpretation applies. The context is highly important. Section 18 says: "Case III—tax in respect of— ... any interest of money, whether yearly or otherwise,

---

[3] For the present anti-avoidance rules pertaining to income settlements *not* caught by section 347A, see below, p.189.

or any annuity or other annual payment ... ". A payment, to be an "other annual payment", must be the same kind of payment as is interest and an annuity. Secondly, the payment must be made under a binding legal obligation. A gift, even if it be in money and even if it be one of a series, is not an annual payment. But it is important to appreciate that a payment under a covenant is an annual payment. How can this be, since a covenanted payment is (most commonly) given for no consideration? The answer is that a covenant is a promise under seal, and the seal creates a legal obligation. Thirdly, the payment must have the quality of recurrence. But this requirement is not very exacting. Payments which are variable or contingent are not thereby prevented from being recurrent. Also a payment does not need to be made only once a year; weekly or monthly payments can be annual payments provided they may continue for more than a year. Fourthly, the payment must be, in the hands of the recipient, pure profit income and not merely a receipt which enters into the computation of profit. In *IRC v. National Book League* (1957) (C.A.) the League (which was a charity) decided to raise the membership subscription except that those members who entered into seven-year covenants could continue to pay their subscriptions at the existing rate. Over 2,000 members executed such deeds of covenant, and deducted tax in making the covenanted payments. The League claimed repayment of the tax from the Revenue, arguing that the payments were annual payments within Case III. The argument was not upheld. The subscriptions were not pure income profit (or pure profit income) of the League, because the League had to provide benefits, such as the amenities of a club, in return for the subscriptions. *The National Book League* case left a few questions unresolved because the judges propounded alternative tests for deciding what was pure profit income. However, in *Campbell v. IRC* (1970) (H.L.) the House of Lords (although *obiter*) had another look at the question. They adopted the phrase "pure profit income" to describe Case III, but were at pains to emphasise that non-commercial benefits resulting from a payment, such as having one's name printed in an advertisement or receiving a copy of an annual report, did not count. Fifthly, the payment must be of the nature of income, and not capital, in the hands of the recipient. This is an immensely difficult field and there have been a huge number of decided cases. The point arises when A sells property to B in return for instalment payments. Are the instalments income or capital? A payment may be of a revenue nature from the point of view of the payer and yet may be of a capital nature in the hands of the payee. Conversely, a payment may be of a capital nature from the point of view of the payer and yet be of an income nature in the hands of the payee. If it is of a capital nature in the hands of the payee it cannot be an "annual payment" even from the point of view of the payer. If it is of an income nature in the hands of the payee it may or may not be of a revenue nature from the point of view of the payer. In *IRC v. Ramsay* (1935) (C.A.) Mr Ramsay agreed to buy a dental practice. A primary price of £15,000 was agreed, but it was further agreed that Mr Ramsay should pay £5,000 at once and then pay each year for 10 years a sum equal to one-quarter of the net profit of the practice for that year. No interest was payable. It was held that the yearly payments were capital from the point of view of the payer. In *Vestey v. IRC* (1962) Lord Vestey sold a block of shares valued at £2 million for the sum of £5.5 million payable without interest by 125 yearly instalments of £44,000. It was held that the instalments should be dissected into capital and interest, and that the interest element was taxable income of the payee. In *IRC v. Church Commissioners for England* (1977) (H.L.) the church commissioners sold to their tenant the reversion on a lease in consideration of rent charges payable annually for 10 years and totalling £96,000 a year. The tenant was not willing to buy for a single lump sum. The House of Lords held that these payments were pure income in the hands of the payee and were not to be dissected into capital and interest elements. The church commissioners, being a charity, were entitled to repayment of the tax which had been deducted by the payer from each payment. (The same rent-charges had previously been held—also by the House of Lords—to be capital payments from the point of view of the payer: *IRC v. Land Securities Investment Trust Ltd* (1969) (H.L.).)

The Finance Act 1988 also introduced changes to the tax treatment of certain maintenance payments which would otherwise be treated as annual payments for the purposes of Case III of Schedule D. These changes, which were incorporated into section 347B of the Taxes Act, are considered below, p. 173.

Sections 348 and 349

As we have seen interest, annuities and certain other annual payments fall within Case III of Schedule D.

Broadly, as a result of changes introduced by the Finance Act 1994 and incorporated into section 64 of the Taxes Act, the basis of assessment under Case III of Schedule D is in the process of being

SECTIONS 348 AND 349

converted from a preceding to a current year basis.[4] Thus, the current year basis currently applies to those "new" sources of income which arise on or after April 6, 1994, and will apply to other sources, *i.e.* those in existence before that date from April 6, 1997. There are transitional provisions in respect of such "existing" sources for the tax year 1996–97.

But, on occasions, such payments are not directly assessed under Case III because they are within the special rules mentioned at the beginning of the chapter and as such are subjected to a withholding tax, namely deduction of tax at source under section 348 or section 349 of the Taxes Act. Interest used to be dealt with under those sections but is now dealt with separately.[5] Sections 348 and 349 now apply to annuities and certain other annual payments, *e.g.* to a covenanted payment to charity and to a payment made for bona fide commercial reasons in connection with a trade, profession or vocation annuity and also (with slightly different rules) to patent royalties and certain mining royalties.

The distinction between section 348 and 349 is as follows. Section 348 deals with payments which are made wholly out of profits or gains brought into charge to income tax, whereas section 349 deals with payments which are not made, or not wholly made, out of profits or gains brought into charge to income tax. Notice that the phrase is "income tax", not just "tax": so a payment made by a United Kingdom company cannot fall within section 348 because a United Kingdom company pays corporation tax, not income tax. This point is affirmed by section 7(1) of the Taxes Act.

The basic idea behind section 348 is that the payer has alienated part of his income. If the payer promises to pay the payee £1000 a year in circumstances where the section applies, the law regards that £1000 as being the payee's income and not the payer's. So the payee should pay the tax on it and not the payer. The section empowers the payer to deduct tax at the basic rate from the £1000 and pay the payee the net amount, which at the basic rate of 24 per cent would be £760. The amount deducted is treated as tax paid by the payee. As he is paying out of his taxable income, the payer keeps the amount deducted to recoup himself for the tax which he has paid (or will pay) on the £1000. This is a classic example, indeed *the* classic example (it has been in the tax system since 1803) of a withholding

---

[4] A further change designed to facilitate self-assessment (see above, p. 60–62).
[5] See below at the end of this chapter (below, p. 175).

The Taxation of Income Under Case III of Schedule D

tax operating. The payer is acting as a collector (unpaid) for the Revenue. The *machinery* of section 348 is that the payer pays the tax on the amount of the payment and recoups himself by deducting tax from the payment. The *effect* is that the payee in reality bears the tax and the payer does not. One can state the point in a table as follows (ignoring personal reliefs).

Machinery	Effect
Payer's income............£10,000	Payer's income............10,000
Annual payment	*less*
gross £1000. Deduct	alienated income £1000
tax at 24 per cent.	£9000
Therefore, actual	
payment..............................760	Payee pays tax on £1000 ..240
Payer pays tax on £10,000	Payer pays tax on £9000
at 24 per cent...................2400	at 24 per cent...................2160
Payer has in pocket.........6840	Payer has in pocket.........6840
Payee has in pocket............760	Payee has in pocket............760

(We just want to refer to two rather "olde worlde" phrases in section 348(1)(a). That paragraph says: "the whole of the profits or gains shall be assessed and charged with income tax on the person liable to the annuity or other annual payment, without distinguishing the annuity or other annual payment." The "person liable to the annuity or other annual payment" means the person who is under a legal obligation to pay the annuity. "Without distinguishing the annuity or other annual payment" means without making any deduction for it.

If, on the other hand, the payer pays the payee, not out of taxable income but, *i.e.* out of capital, then a new income springs up in the hands of the payee which has not been taxed. So the payer deducts tax (at basic rate) from his payment to the payee, but this time section 349 applies and he must hand over to the Revenue the amount which he has deducted. This time the payer is doing an even better collecting job for the Revenue because in this situation the Revenue are really interested; they want the tax on what is a new source of income. So the payer *must* deduct tax in making payment to the payee and he *must* hand over the amount deducted, through an assessment, to the Revenue, though the Revenue has an alternative power to assess the payee. In the section 348 situation, by contrast, the Revenue are not so interested because they have got (or will get) the tax from the payer just as though he had alienated any of his income. Consequently, the payer *need not* deduct tax from his payment to the payee; but he may, and if he has any sense he will, in order to recoup himself for the tax he has to pay. If the payer does not make a deduction from his payment to the payee and if, for extraneous reasons, the Revenue cannot get the tax out of the payer they can (since 1971) make an assessment on the payee.

Another difference between the sections is that under section 348 (out of taxable income) tax is to be deducted at the basic rate applicable to the year of assessment when the payment is due, whereas under section 349 (not out of taxable income) tax is to be deducted at the basic rate applicable to the year of assessment when the payment is actually made (see *IRC v. Crawley* (1987)).

If the payee is not liable to tax at the basic rate, the whole or part of the amount deducted may be reclaimed from the Revenue. The system of deduction of tax at source could be seen in all its beautiful symmetry if the basic rate were the only rate of tax. The existence of a higher rate of tax has spoilt the picture a bit. If the payee is not liable to tax at all a full repayment can be obtained from the Revenue, *e.g.* if the payee is a charity which is exempt from paying income tax. If the payee is liable to the higher rate of tax, as may be so, for example, in the case of a person in receipt of a payment made for a bona fide commercial reason etc., the annual payment counts as part of his total income and for this purpose the net amount received must be grossed up (as described at p. 192, below).

If the payer is liable to the higher rate of tax, the cost of the payment can be set against total income for the purposes of the higher rate as well as basic rate. Such a taxpayer, as the following example shows, may by entering into a covenant also "benefit" because of untidiness in the operation of various general provisions of the Taxes Act.

If Barnado, who is paying tax at the higher rate of 40 per cent, covenants to pay to, say, Mencap, £100 a year for four years, this is what happens. Barnado will pay Mencap £76, keeping £24, just as if he was a basic rate taxpayer. Mencap, as a charity, will reclaim the £24. But Barnado can deduct the whole £100 against his total income for tax purposes (sections 835 and 836 of the Taxes Act). However, this reduction, in cutting Barnado's income by £100, will also cut his tax bill by £40. So he has now saved £64 tax in paying the £100. This is too good to be true. The next operation is applied by a little noticed section right at the other end of the Act, section 3.

The Taxation of Income Under Case III of Schedule D

This imposes a charge *at the basic rate only* on the sums which have been subject to double deduction under both section 348 and section 835. The result is that Barnado gets £64 relief, but a tax bill of £24, on his £100 payment to Mencap. At the end of the day, he will pay £76 to Mencap and get back £24 of the £76 from the Revenue. So Mencap's £100 cost Barnado £52, and the Treasury (or you and us) pick up a large part of the cost of Barnado's generosity!

WHICH SECTION?

It is obviously a matter of great importance to the payer that section 348 should apply to his payment because if it does he can keep the tax deducted whereas if section 349 applies he must hand it over to the Revenue. It may also be of some importance to the payee, because if section 348 applies the payment is part of his total income for the year in which it was due, whereas if section 349 applies it is part of his total income for the year in which it was paid, and the rates of tax may vary between those years. Over the years many cases have been fought out on this issue. In *Chancery Lane Safe Deposit and Offices Co. Ltd v. I.R.C.* (1966) (H.L.) the taxpayer company borrowed money to finance the rebuilding of its premises, a fixed capital asset. The interest payable on the borrowings was "capitalised", *i.e.* treated as part of the cost of the asset and not charged to the profit and loss account. Consequently the interest did not reduce the amount of profit available for dividend. It was held by the House of Lords that the company could not subsequently make an inconsistent attribution to revenue account, and so its payments of interest fell outside what is now section 348 and inside what is now section 349. The company must hand over to the Revenue the tax deducted from the interest payments. In 1977 a similar point arose in *Fitzleet Estates v. Cherry* (1977) (H.L.) and the House of Lords declined to reverse the majority decision which the House had reached in the *Chancery Lane* case.

Tax-free Payments and "the Formula"

If A makes an annual payment to B which falls within Case III of Schedule D, *e.g.* where B is a charity, he either may (if he pays out of taxable income) or must (if he pays otherwise than out of taxable income) deduct tax at basic rate in making the payment. In undertaking to make these payments it is important (and difficult) to use words which make it absolutely clear what is to be the position with regard to tax. For many years now a conventional formula has been in use, whereby the payer's undertaking to pay is couched in the following (or similar) words: "Such a sum as after deduction of income tax at the basic rate for the time being in force will amount to the sum of (£100)." The effect of this form of words is that the payer undertakes to pay £100 net to the payee and to notionally gross up £100 at the current basic rate and notionally deduct tax at the current rate. At the basic rate for 1996–97, 24 per cent, the gross of £100 net is £131.58, and basic rate tax on £131.58 is £31.58, leaving £100 net.

If the parties use some form of words radically different from "the formula", difficulties may arise. One difficulty stems from section 106(2) of the Taxes Management Act 1970, which says: "Every agreement for payment of interest, rent or other annual payment in full without allowing any such deduction shall be void."[6] The question has arisen, what is the effect of this subsection on an agreement to pay £100 "free of tax"? In *Blount v. Blount* (1916), Scrutton J. held that the then equivalent of section 106(2) rendered void the words "free of tax" but did not render void the rest of the agreement. Consequently the agreement was to be read as though the words "free of tax" had simply been crossed out and it was construed to mean a payment of £100 gross. This was pretty certainly not the intention of the parties; they meant that £100 to be a net sum. *Blount v. Blount* stood for over 50 years. Then in *Ferguson v. IRC* (1970) (H.L.) *Blount v. Blount* was overruled by the House of Lords. Lord Diplock said that in that case "a Homer nodded". The true effect of an agreement to pay £100 "free of tax" is that it obliges the payer to pay such a sum as after the deduction of tax equals £100. The £100, in other words, is a net sum. Section 106(2) is confined to cases where the agreement uses some such phrase as "without deducting tax", making it plain that the parties really are attempting to state a gross sum and not a net sum. Section 106(2) never applied to wills or voluntary settlements or court orders. This is because the subsection uses the word "agreement". So the effect of *Ferguson's* case is to bring agreements in which the words used are "free of tax" into line with these other obligations.

However, the expression "free of tax" raises another difficulty which may occur in a will, or a voluntary settlement or (since *Ferguson's* case) an agreement. It does not arise in court orders. If

---

[6] The point of this enactment (which goes back to 1803) is to protect the payer against an irate payee who demands his money in full without deduction.

"the formula" is used, the payer fulfils his duty to the Revenue by deducting tax at the basic rate (and, if he pays not out of taxable income, by accounting to the Revenue) and by so doing he also fulfils his duty to the payee. What happens after that between the payee and the Revenue does not concern the payer; if the payee gets a repayment it does not concern the payer, and if, on the contrary, the payee has to pay the higher rate of tax or rate applicable to trusts, as appropriate, that does not concern the payer either. But if the expression "free of tax" is used the position is different. At first sight it might seem (after *Ferguson's* case) that "free of tax" has the same effect as the formula. This is so as regards deducting basic rate tax, but it is not so thereafter. "Free of tax" may mean that if the payee gets a repayment from the Revenue he must hand it over to the payer because if he does not he will have obtained in total more than £100 net. "Free of tax" may also mean that if the payee has to pay at the higher rate of tax the payer must reimburse him, because if he does not the payee will have received in the end less than £100 net. In *Ferguson's* case the House of Lords left open these two points. The matter is complicated, but the position can be broadly stated by reference to two cases: In *Re Pettit* (1922) an annuity was given in a will free of income tax. The annuitant was repaid by the Revenue part of the tax which had been deducted. It was held that he was not entitled to retain the whole of the repayment but must pay a proportion of it to the trustees of the will. The proportion is the proportion which the gross amount of the annuity bears to the annuitant's total income. This is sometimes called "the rule in *Re Pettit*". The rule applies not only to wills but also to voluntary settlements and agreements. It does not apply to any of those obligations if "the formula" is used for the reason stated above, namely that the formula is fulfilled as soon as the payer has paid to the payee the net sum. The rule in *Re Pettit* does not apply to court orders. In *Re Reckitt* (1932) (C.A.) an annuity had been given by a will. The annuitant was liable to tax in excess of the standard rate (broadly equivalent to the basic rate), and it was held that the trustees of the will must reimburse the annuitant for the amount which he had had to pay in tax over and above the standard rate. It is thought that the principle of this case applies, like the rule in *Re Pettit*, to wills, voluntary settlements and agreements but not to orders of a court. It does not apply where "the formula" is used for the same reason that *Re Pettit* does not apply.

Maintenance Payments

In recent years, the tax relief available in respect of maintenance payments made by one party to a marriage (or former marriage) to the other has been considerably reduced.[7] At one time (with certain exceptions), such payments constituted a charge on the payer's income. They were paid after deduction of basic rate tax and taxable in the payee's hands under Case III of Schedule D. This basic structure is now redundant in respect of "qualifying maintenance payments" made under arrangements made after March 14, 1988 and of very limited importance to maintenance payments ("existing obligations") made under arrangements in force on March 15, 1988. Nevertheless, it is a necessary starting point from which to embark on our examination of the present position.

A maintenance payment is a qualifying maintenance payment where it is made to a former spouse (who has not remarried) or separated spouse for the maintenance of that spouse or a child of the family. It must be made *either* under the order of a United Kingdom (or European Union) court, *or* under a written agreement governed by the law of the United Kingdom or that of another Member State of the European Union, *or* in accordance with an assessment made by the Child Support Agency (see section 347B of the Taxes Act, inserted by the Finance Act 1988). If the maintenance payment so qualifies, it is not a charge on the payer's income nor does it comprise part of the payee's income for tax purposes. It is paid gross and effectively operates outside the tax system, save that the payer is entitled to a modicum of relief in respect of the payment by way of a reduction in his tax bill. The reduction to which the payer is entitled is calculated by reference to the married couple's allowance (see below, p.203). For 1996–97, the value of that allowance is £1,790 and the payer is entitled to an amount by way of reduction in his tax bill comprising 15 per cent of that sum, *i.e.* £268.50.

A maintenance payment will be treated as made in pursuance of an existing obligation where it is made *either* in respect of an arrangement entered into before, and operative on, March 15, 1988, *or* under a court order which was applied for before March 16 and granted by the end of June 1988, *or* in respect of an agreement

---

[7] Some have suggested that this may have occurred because of the general reduction in rates of income tax or as a result of a desire to restore family values by increasing the cost of supporting separated families, see *Butterworths U.K. Tax Guide 1995–96*, p.573.

entered into before March 16, 1988 (a copy of which must have been lodged with the Revenue by the end of June 1988). Variations or replacements of these orders or agreements made after March 14, 1988 are also treated as existing obligations. For the purpose of determining the availability of relief in respect of payments under such existing obligations, the payment must be made by one party to a marriage for the other's benefit after the dissolution or annulment of the marriage, or while they are separated by court order or under a separation agreement or in circumstances where the separation is likely to be permanent. The nature of the relief available has been the subject of several changes since the Finance Act 1988 introduced the initial departures from the basic structure we outlined above. Presently, maintenance payments under existing obligations must be paid gross. However, there is some relief in respect of such payments for both the payer and the payee. For the payer, the first £1,790 of the payment is treated in the same way as a qualifying maintenance payment. Thus, for 1996–97, he is entitled to a reduction in his tax bill, which represents 15 per cent of £1,790, *i.e.* £286.50. Where the payment exceeds £1,790, the payer may deduct the excess from his total income (in effect as a charge on income). The amount deductible from the payer's total income, *i.e.* the gross amount of the payment less £1,790 is treated as the income of the payee.

The payer may elect to be governed by the rules for qualifying maintenance payments rather than those pertaining to existing obligations.

Purchased Life Annuities

Many annuities arise under a will or similar instrument of gift. But it is perfectly possible to buy an annuity "in the market". These purchased life annuities, or some of them, have a special rule applying to them. Until 1956 purchased life annuities were taxed as though the annuity payments were wholly income, whereas the commercial reality is that each payment contains a capital element, that is to say, in each payment there is an element which, in effect, goes towards repaying the capital sum for which the annuity was bought. In 1956 the law was changed and the relevant section is now section 656 of the Taxes Act. The capital content of each periodic payment to the annuitant is exempt from income tax. The capital is found (putting it broadly) by dividing the purchase price of the annuity by the normal expectation of life of the annuitant, calculated at the date when the annuity begins. Once the calculation has been made the figure remains constant for every year. Income tax is charged each year on the amount by which the annuity payment exceeds this capital content, whether or not the annuitant survives for the period of normal expectation. Let us take an example. Suppose a widow buys an annuity for £24,000. Her age is 60, and the government mortality tables show that a female at age 60 has a normal life expectation of (say) 20 years. The capital content is £24,000 divided by 20 = £1,200. The annuity brings in say 10 per cent; on £24,000 that is £2,400. Tax is payable on £2,400 less £1,200 = £1,200. The taxable amount counts as unearned (investment) income and, from 1996–97, is taxed as savings income (see below, p. 198). There are some important exceptions where section 656 does not apply. In particular, it does not apply where an annuity is payable under approved personal pension provisions governed by section 630 of the Taxes Act. It will be remembered (from the end of Chapter 5, above) that approved personal pension schemes do have other tax advantages, *e.g.* relief on contributions so it is not altogether surprising that annuities payable under such schemes do not also qualify for this relief under section 656.

Interest

Here we are concerned with interest from the point of view of the payee. We saw at the beginning of this chapter that interest is taxable under Case III of Schedule D. And later on we saw that interest used to be collected at source under the scheme governed by sections 348 and 349. That was so until 1969, but now interest is not within that scheme. There is, however, a somewhat similar provision in section 349(2) which provides for deduction at source; from 1996–97, tax is deducted at the lower rate. But we want to emphasise that section 349(2) only applies to certain kinds of interest and that most interest does not come within this provision. However, as we shall see, sections 477A and 480A of the Taxes Act require collection at source of tax on interest of many kinds; from 1996–97, tax is deducted at the lower rate. All interest is in principle chargeable under Case III, but it may be assessed under Case I where interest is an income item in the computation of the profits of a trade, or it may be collected at source under section 349(2) of the Taxes Act.

Section 349(2) applies only to "yearly" interest, not to "short" interest, meaning interest where the obligation to pay it is to continue for less than a year. And section 349(2) only applies to certain kinds of yearly interest, as follows: (a) interest paid by a company or local authority (in each case, otherwise than in a fiduciary or representative capacity; that is, where the payer is a trustee or is paying on behalf of someone else); (b) interest paid by or on behalf of a partnership of which a company is a member; (c) interest paid by any person to another person whose usual place of abode is outside the United Kingdom. The reason for (a) and (b) is that companies are under a special system of taxation, and the reason for (c) is that the government wants to be sure of getting the tax before the money goes outside its grasp. There are two important exceptions whereby section 349(2) does not apply even though the interest falls within (a), (b) or (c). These are: interest payable in the United Kingdom on an advance from a bank carrying on a bona fide banking business in the United Kingdom; and interest paid by such a bank in the ordinary course of that business.

The limited nature of section 349(2) is made good by sections 477A and 480A of the Taxes Act to the extent that section 477A applies to interest paid by building societies whilst section 480A applies to interest paid by banks, local authorities and the Post Office (National Girobank), on "relevant deposits". These deposits cover money deposited on demand or on such terms as may be agreed subject to an upper limit of £50,000 and other exceptions (as where the depositor is itself a bank).

CHAPTER 12

TRUSTS AND ESTATES

We need to look now at the way in which the income tax system works in relation to trusts and in relation to the estates of deceased individuals.

There is a similarity between income which arises during the administration of the estate of a deceased individual and income which arises under a trust, but there are also differences. It is quite common (though not so common as in the old days of estate duty) for a "dad" to leave his property by will to his wife for her life and then to his children absolutely. On his death there is first a period during which his estate is being administered (or wound-up) and then a period during which there is a trust in operation. In both periods the widow will be entitled to all the income, but the tax rules are somewhat different in the two periods. The executors and the trustees may well be the same people; they are executors during the administration period and then become trustees.

In the general law—quite apart from tax law—there is a fundamental difference between the position of a person entitled to income of a residuary estate and a person entitled to income arising under a trust. The former is not entitled to anything until it is paid to him or at least appropriated to him: see *Corbett v. IRC* (1938) (C.A.). The latter is entitled to his share of the income of the trust from its inception, or, more strictly, to his share of the income of the investments which constitute the trust fund: see *Baker v. Archer-Shee* (1927) (H.L.).

We will look at the two situations in turn.

Trust Income[1]

The existence of trusts causes great difficulties for tax legislators and for everyone else connected with tax, including students of tax

---

[1] For income tax purposes a trust is one kind of settlement, and consequently the reader is advised to look at Chap. 13 (which is concerned with various rules to counteract the use of trusts and other settlements to avoid tax) along with this chapter.

TRUSTS AND ESTATES

law. Tax law would be very much simpler if there were no trusts. Lest that statement sound naive it may be pointed out that trusts fulfil a prominent role in tax planning. Nevertheless, many civil law countries do not recognise the concept of trusts at all. The subject is additionally complicated in Britain because Scottish trusts law is as developed as, but is markedly different from English trusts law. Scottish lawyers rightly resent the fact that the (English-drafted) provisions in tax statutes are often passed in ignorance of Scottish law, although the provisions are supposed to work evenly on both sides of the border. But even confining ourselves to English law, the difficulties in squaring our trusts laws and our tax laws are considerable: for inheritance tax they have proved, as we shall see in Chapter 26, fiendish.

For income tax there is a kind of two-tier system: to some extent income tax is charged on the trustees; to some extent it is charged on the beneficiary.

THE CHARGE ON THE TRUSTEES

Trustees are not "individuals" for the purposes of income tax, but they are "persons". Consequently they are liable to basic rate tax, for example, on the profits of a trade or Schedule A business carried on by them[2] and, on the other hand, they are not entitled to any personal reliefs. (It would be clearer if the so-called "personal reliefs" were called "individual reliefs" since they only apply to individuals). Trustees are not liable to the higher rate of tax, again because they are not individuals and higher rate tax is charged only on individuals.

By section 686 of the Taxes Act a special rate of tax (known as the rate applicable to trusts) is charged on income arising to trustees if it is income which is to be accumulated or which is payable at discretion (whether or not the trustees have power to accumulate income). So, putting it broadly, the rate applicable to trusts is payable by accumulation trusts and discretionary trusts and by trusts which are subject to section 31 of the Trustee Act 1925. (That

---

[2] Of course, trustees may receive income after deduction of tax. In this respect 1996–97 trustees will meet their responsibilities in relation to savings income (see below, p198) so received if they ensure that the beneficiary entitled to such income receives a credit for the lower rate tax deducted at source from such income. This credit will discharge the beneficiary's liabilty to tax in relation to this income other than at the higher rate.
For the taxation of savings income in the hands of an individual (see below, p.207).

is the section which gives trustees power to apply income for the maintenance, education or benefit of an infant). The rate applicable to trusts for 1996–97 is 34 per cent. Not the whole of the income is charged, because expenses of managing the trust are deductible in calculating the liability to tax which arises from the difference between the rate applicable to trusts and the lower rate (if the income is savings income) or basic rate if it is income other than savings income.

The trustees of a discretionary trust may be subject to a further charge to tax when they come to make a distribution of income to a beneficiary. Such a charge will arise if the rate of tax is higher in the year of distribution than it was in the year in which the income arose to the trustees. This matter is dealt with by section 687 of the Taxes Act.

THE CHARGE ON THE BENEFICIARY

A beneficiary's income from a trust forms part of his total income for determining his reliefs and his rate of tax. It would be nice and neat if one could say that one works out the beneficiary's tax bill and then gives him a straight credit for the tax already paid by the trustees. Unfortunately this is not precisely so. There is a case called *Macfarlane v. IRC* (1929) (Ct. Sess.) which held that although trust expenses are not deductible in computing the trustees' income, they are deductible in computing the beneficiary's income. That position now, with the advent of the rate applicable to trusts, is more complicated, because although trust expenses are not deductible in computing the trust's liability to basic rate tax, they are deductible, as we have seen, in computing the trust's liability to tax which arises from the difference between the rate applicable to trusts and the lower or basic rate. Indeed, to further compound this complication, such expenses must, from 1996–97, normally be set off, in the first instance, against savings income. However, one can say this: the tax charge on the beneficiary *takes into account* (to some extent) the tax already charged on the trustees!

Income to which a beneficiary is *entitled* forms part of his total income whether or not he receives it. This follows from the general principle stated above, namely that a beneficiary who is entitled at all is entitled from the very inception of the trust. Of course this principle does not apply to a discretionary trust; if there is a discretion whether to pay any particular beneficiary he has no entitlement until the discretion is exercised in his favour. When a sum is actually paid to such a beneficiary that sum forms part of his total income and is taxed under Case III of Schedule D. Whether one is talking of a fixed trust or a discretionary trust, payments in kind may, just as much as money payments, constitute income. This would be so, for example of a right to occupy a house rent free.

A payment may perfectly well be income in the hands of a beneficiary, even although it is made out of the capital (and not the income) of the trust. However, a payment out of capital does not become income in the hands of a beneficiary simply because it is to be used for an income purpose by that beneficiary (see *Stevenson v. Wishart* (1987) (C.A.).

An important tax point arises in connection with income which is accumulated by a trust. One has to make a distinction here between a vested interest and a contingent interest. This is a matter of general law rather than tax law and it involves some fairly complicated points But broadly the distinction is that a vested interest is one which (generally) cannot be upset, whereas a contingent interest is one which is dependent on some contingency happening. The clearest example is where a trust provides that X is to have a certain interest under the trust when he attains a certain age. As he may never attain that age his interest is until then contingent. When he has attained that age his interest becomes vested. (A person may attain a vested interest in income before he attains, or without ever attaining, a vested interest in the capital of the fund.) For a person who has a vested interest in the income of a trust, that income (as has been said above) forms part of his total income, and that is so even if it is not in fact received by him. But for a person who has only a contingent interest, until that contingency occurs, the income of the trust is not his income. It follows that if the trust's income is accumulated for him it is not his income and it does not become his income even if the contingency occurs (*e.g.* he attains the age of 18) and the accumulations are paid to him. The payments reach him as capital. The leading authority on this point is *Stanley v. IRC* (1944) (C.A.).

Estate Income

What we are considering here is income arising during the period of administration of the estate of a deceased individual. When an individual dies his estate is administered by executors or administrators. The generic name for these is personal representatives; for tax purposes there is no need to distinguish between the two species.

Estate Income

As with trusts, so with estates, there is a kind of two-tier system of income tax. Personal representatives are like trustees in that they are chargeable to basic rate tax, are not chargeable to the higher rate of tax, and do not qualify for personal reliefs. In another respect, however, personal representatives differ from trustees; they are not chargeable to tax under the rate applicable to trusts (section 686(6)).

How is the beneficiary taxed? That depends on the nature of his benefit. If the will gives him an annuity, the annuity payments are part of his total income from the date of death. So far as legatees are concerned it is perhaps worth stating the fairly elementary point that a legacy as such is not subject to income tax because it is not income; it is capital. But a legatee may be entitled to interest or (in the case of a specific legacy) to income from the date of death. In those cases the legatee is chargeable to income tax on the interest or income.

What we have to look at in more detail is the position of a residuary beneficiary.[3] One has to distinguish between a beneficiary who has a limited interest in the residue of the estate and a beneficiary who has an absolute interest in the residue. A person has an absolute interest if he has an interest in the capital, and a person has a limited interest if he does not have an absolute interest. An example of a person with a limited interest is a person who gets a life tenancy. Everything that is paid to him by the personal representatives must be income for the simple reason that he is not entitled to any capital. Therefore very little complication arises in his case. Each sum that is paid to him during the administration counts (grossed-up) as part of his total income for the year of assessment when it is paid. At the end of the administration period any final payment is regarded as the income of the beneficiary in the year of assessment in which the administration ends.

A beneficiary who has an absolute interest has, by definition, an entitlement to capital. Therefore it is by no means certain that everything paid to him during the administration of the estate is income. To get at his tax liability the income element must be sorted out from the capital element. The first step is to calculate the "residuary income" of the estate for each year of assessment during

---

[3] The Finance Act 1995 simplified the tax treatment of residuary beneficiaries in order to facilitate the introduction of self assessment from 1996–97 (see above, pp.60–62). The simplified position, which we discuss above, applies to any estate the administration of which is completed after April 5, 1995.

the administration period. To arrive at residuary income the personal representatives are permitted to deduct certain management expenses. The residuary income of the estate is divided into a residuary income for each beneficiary according to his share. For example, if there are three absolute beneficiaries each with an equal share the residuary income of each is one-third of the residuary income of the estate. Then any sums which are paid to a beneficiary are treated as income for the year of assessment in which they are actually paid in so far as (grossed-up) they do not exceed his residuary income. In so far as they do exceed it they are treated as capital. Finally, if at the end of the administration the beneficiary has not received all the residuary income which is his due, the outstanding amount is regarded as having been paid immediately before the end of the administration period.

CHAPTER 13

SETTLEMENTS: ANTI-AVOIDANCE RULES

This chapter should be read in conjunction with Chapter 11 (taxation of income under Case III of Schedule D) and Chapter 12 (taxation of trust and estate income). It is concerned with the detailed rules relating to settlements in Part XV of the Taxes Act, which are intended to curb the use of settlements for tax avoidance. These rules were redrafted and simplified (although not made simple!) by the Finance Act 1995 with effect from the tax year 1995–96. This was necessary in order to rationalise a series of anti-avoidance rules which had developed ad hoc over many decades and which had been enacted together, most recently in the consolidation of 1988, to produce an unwieldy and unsatisfactory whole. However, notwithstanding this redrafting and simplification, the important wording in the new rules often closely resembles or replicates that used in earlier rules thereby enabling the interpretation of the "new" rules, in this respect, to be influenced, in particular, by the body of case law pertaining to those earlier rules.

Section 660 G (1) of the Taxes Act provides that for the purposes of Part XV a settlement includes "any disposition, trust, covenant, agreement, arrangement or transfer of assets". Broadly speaking, this encompasses two types of settlement, namely, income settlements and capital settlements. An income settlement is a settlement which involves the transfer of income only, *e.g.* a covenant. A capital settlement is a settlement which involves the transfer of income-producing property, *e.g.* a trust. An income settlement is the handing-over of fruits; a capital settlement is the handing-over of a fruit tree. An income settlement may provide for payment to trustees or for payment direct to the beneficiary; a capital settlement necessarily involves trustees. In neither instance, however, can a transaction constitute a settlement unless there is an element of bounty; a bona fide commercial transaction is not a settlement for the purposes of Part XV (see *IRC v. Plummer* (1979) (H.L.) and *Chinn v. Collins* (1981) (H.L.)).

Settlements: Anti-Avoidance Rules

The background to Part XV is that settlements, historically, have been a favourite means of tax avoidance, particularly when individuals have faced high marginal rates of tax. Indeed, in the absence of statutory intervention, the potential for tax-saving through settlements is self-evident—any settlement would enable an individual with a high rate of tax to unload some of his income on to a comparatively poor member of his family to the advantage of the family viewed as a whole, because the poor member has a lower rate of tax or may not be liable to tax at all. Not surprisingly, therefore, governments have over the years sought to counteract the fiscal efficacy of settlements. The rules in Part XV of the Taxes Act, as recast by the Finance Act 1995, are the most recent attempt. Where applicable, the rules in Part XV deem income arising under a settlement during the life of the settlor to be the income of the settlor for *all* income tax purposes. In such instances, the income is treated as arising first in the settlement and then as being transferred to or reverting to the settlor. The important phrase, however, is "where applicable" for, as we have seen in Chapter 11, many income settlements (annual payments) made by individuals are denied any effect for income tax purposes as a result of changes introduced by the Finance Act 1988 and incorporated into section 347A of the Taxes Act. Therefore, in respect of such settlements, the rules in Part XV are redundant (see further, p.189).

The rules in Part XV of the Taxes Act fall into three categories:

(i) rules which apply where the settlor (or his spouse) retains an interest in the settled property (section 660A);
(ii) rules which apply where a benefit is received by unmarried minor children from a parental settlement (section 660B);
(iii) rules which apply where the settlor (or his spouse) has received a capital sum from the settlement (sections 677–678, as amended by the Finance Act 1995).

These rules are now considered first in relation to capital settlements and then, in so far as they may be applicable, with regard to income settlements.

CAPITAL SETTLEMENTS

The order of treatment of the rules is as above.

(I) Settlements where the settlor retains an interest

Broadly, section 660A(1) of the Taxes Act deems all income arising under a settlement during the life of the settlor to be the *income of the settlor* for all income tax purposes unless the income arises from property in which the settlor has no interest. The settlor is treated as having an interest where that property or any derived property (see section 660A(10)) is, or will, or may become, payable to or for the benefit of the settlor or his spouse in any circumstances whatsoever (section 660A(2))—wording which follows closely that used in the "old" section 673. Section 660A(3) provides that a spouse of the settlor does *not* include a prospective or separated spouse or a widow or widower. Thus, it is the existence of the interest which attracts the charge to tax under section 660A and, perhaps, the most compelling example of where such an interest exists is where a settlement can be revoked and, on revocation, property reverts to the settlor or his spouse (but note *IRC v. Wolfson* (1949) (H.L.)). Generally, in determining whether such an interest exists, it is legitimate to expect, in view of the similarity of the wording in section 660A(2) and the "old" section 673, that principles established under the old law will influence how section 660A(1) is applied and, perhaps, more importantly, notwithstanding the potentially wide import of the words "in any circumstances whatsoever", how it may be limited, *e.g.* under the old law no interest was retained if the property reverted to the settlor following an independent act of a third party.

The operation of section 660A(1) is also limited by sections 660A(4) and (5) by virtue of which the settlor is not to be regarded as having an interest if his interest can only take effect on the occurrence of certain specified events, *e.g.* the bankruptcy of a person who is or may become entitled to the property or any derived property or on the death at any age of a child of the settlor who had become beneficially entitled to the property or any derived property at an age not exceeding 25. In addition, section 660A(1) does not apply to the income arising under a settlement by one party to a marriage to provide for the other after divorce, annulment or separation to the extent that the income is payable for the benefit of

185

Settlements: Anti-Avoidance Rules

that other (section 660A(8)). Further, an outright gift by one spouse to the other, of property from which income arises, is not usually treated as a settlement for the purposes of section 660A(1) (see section 660A(6)).

If section 660A(1) applies, the settlor is charged to tax under Case VI of Schedule D, and the income is treated as the highest part of his income. However, the settlor may recover any tax so paid by him from the trustees or any other person to whom the income is payable under the settlement (section 660D(1)).

(II) Benefits received by unmarried minor children from parental settlements

Generally, any income arising under a settlement which is paid during the life of the settlor to or for the benefit of an unmarried minor (including a stepchild or illegitimate child) of the settlor is treated by section 660B(1) of the Taxes Act for all income tax purposes as the income of the settlor. However, section 660B(1) will not apply where the income is treated as the income of the settlor under section 660A, nor will it apply where the income paid to a child under such a parental settlement does not exceed, in total, £100 in any tax year. In addition, if income arising under a capital settlement in favour of the settlor's unmarried minor children is retained or accumulated by the trustees such income is not treated under section 660B as income of the settlor. In certain circumstances, such a capital accumulation settlement can be used to secure tax savings for the family when it is viewed as a whole. For example, if the accumulated income belongs to the beneficiary because he has a vested interest, *e.g.* when capital is settled for a minor absolutely, there may be liability to basic rate tax, but this will, broadly speaking, have been borne by the trustees. Section 686 of the Taxes Act does not apply because the income belongs to the beneficiary (see section 686(2)(b)). Moreover, depending on his other income and allowances, the beneficiary may be able to recover tax paid by the trustees so that the income as long as it remains within the settlement (or is distributed after the beneficiary has reached 18 or married under 18) will in some instances be free of income tax. However, if the beneficiary's interest is contingent, the accumulated income does *not* belong to him. Here the only tax-saving lies in the difference between the tax charged on the income at the rate applicable to trusts, namely 34 per cent, (none of which is recoverable because the income is neither that of the settlor nor the beneficiary) and the tax which would have been payable if the income had been received by the settlor whose marginal rate of tax is 40 per cent. A 6 per cent saving which, in itself, may not warrant the setting up of such a settlement.

Income which is not accumulated but distributed is caught by section 660B. This will be so, for example, where income is applied for the child's maintenance, education or benefit under section 31 of the Trustee Act 1925. And it is no good the trustees thinking that they can avoid section 660B by accumulating income and using capital for maintenance, etc., of the unmarried minor beneficiary. This device is stopped by section 660B(2) which provides that any sum whatsoever paid out for the benefit of an unmarried minor child of the settlor shall be deemed to be income (and not capital) to the extent that there is "available retained or accumulated income". "Available retained or accumulated income" is the aggregate amount of income which has arisen under the settlement since its inception *less* income already treated as income of the settlor or a beneficiary, income paid to or for the benefit of a beneficiary other than an unmarried minor child of the settlor and income properly spent on trust expenses (section 660B(3)).

If section 660B applies, the settlor is charged to tax under Case VI of Schedule D, and the income is treated as the highest part of his income. However, as with section 660A(1), the settlor may recover any tax so paid from the trustees or any other person to whom the income is payable under the settlement (section 660D(1)).

(III) CAPITAL SUMS PAID TO THE SETTLOR

Section 677 of the Taxes Act (as amended by the Finance Act 1995) attacks capital sums paid *to* the settlor (or his spouse) out of the settlement. "Capital sum" is defined to include "any sum paid by way of loan or repayment of a loan" (section 677(9)). This is the key to the understanding of what the section is primarily aimed at. It is designed to stop a settlor (who is a higher-rate taxpayer) making a settlement, causing the trustees to accumulate rather than distribute the income, and causing them to let him (or his spouse) have the income in the form of a loan. For "other" capital sums which fall within section 677, see sections 677(9) and (10).

Where a capital sum is paid by the trustees to the settlor (or his spouse) such sum (grossed up at the rate applicable to trusts) is to be treated for all income tax purposes as the income of the settlor (and charged to tax under Case VI of Schedule D) to the extent that such sum falls within the amount of "income available". "Income available" means, broadly speaking, the aggregate of all income arising to the settlement since its inception which has not been distributed and is not deemed to be income of the settlor under some other provision (section 677(2)). The point of this is that what the section is attacking is the payment out as capital of money which came into the settlement as income.

If in the year in which the capital sum is paid such sum exceeds the income available, the excess is carried forward and charged to the settlor in the following year (in so far as there is income available up to the end of that year) and thereafter, if necessary, subject to a maximum of 11 years. However, if the capital sum is paid by way of loan no charge can be raised in any year after that in which the loan is wholly repaid (section 677(4)).

Section 678 of the Taxes Act stops the dodge of ensuring that the payment of a capital sum was made not by the trustees to the settlor but by an associated company which was in some way put in funds by the trustees. The section deems such sums to be paid by the trustees to the settlor and thus to be within the scope of section 677.

The settlor receives a tax credit for tax paid by the trustees, but cannot recover from the trustees any tax for which he may be responsible as a result of the operation of section 677 (*cf.* the position under sections 660A and 660B).

Summary

These provisions, notwithstanding the redrafting and simplication brought about by the Finance Act 1995, may still seem somewhat daunting. However, it is important to keep their operation in perspective. It certainly should not be assumed that their existence means that trusts cannot be used to effect tax savings. Indeed, we have already seen that where under a capital settlement for the unmarried minor children of the settlor income is accumulated and the settlor does not retain an interest in the settled property within the meaning of section 660A tax benefits may accrue. More generally, a settlor, provided he is willing to give up any interest in the settled property, may make provision for beneficiaries other than his wife or unmarried minor children without falling foul of these provisions, *e.g.* where a grandparent settles property on his minor grandchildren. It should also be remembered that the fiscal efficacy of a trust may not be judged by reference to income tax alone (for the treatment of trusts for capital gains tax and inheritance tax, see Chapters 16 and 25 respectively).

INCOME SETTLEMENTS

As, we saw in Chapter 11, the result of the changes introduced by the Finance Act 1988 and incorporated into section 347A of the Taxes Act was that many annual payments made by individuals were denied any effect for income tax purposes (see above, pp.163–164). This was achieved by effectively ignoring the payment for the purposes of computing the income of the payer and the payee. Thus, section 347A(1) provides that such a payment shall not be deductible as a charge on the income of the payer nor shall it be part of the income of the payee. In such cases, therefore, the anti-avoidance provisions in Part XV of the Taxes Act have no role to play as there is nothing for them to attack. The redrafting and simplication of these provisions by the Finance Act 1995 did not alter the position in this regard.

Where section 347A does not apply to an annual payment (see above, p.164), the income will be treated as the income of the settlor (payer) under section 660A, unless he can show that the income arises from property in which he has no interest or that the income is expressly excluded from the operation of section 660A(1). In the latter respect, section 660A(1) does not apply to income paid under a settlement by one party to a marriage to provide for the other after divorce, annulment or separation to the extent that the income is payable for the benefit of that other (section 660A(8)). In addition, section 660A(9) provides that income which consists of annual payments made by an individual for bona fide commercial reasons in connection with his trade, profession or vocation or covenanted payments to charity as defined by section 347A(7) falls outside section 660A(1); for the treatment of such income under Case III of Schedule D, see Chapter 11.

CHAPTER 14

THE TAXATION OF INDIVIDUALS

We have entitled this chapter "The Taxation of Individuals" because "individual" excludes companies (which, in tax law as in law generally, are "persons" but are not "individuals") and also excludes trustees and personal representatives, to whom special tax rules apply, as we saw in the last two chapters. There are special rules also for partners with which we deal below.

Even when we have been through the process of identifying an individual's taxable income under each charging section in the Taxes Act, the process of working out an individual's tax bill is quite complicated. We will try to state the process here in a series of steps. But it is not easy to reduce it to simplicity, because one has to accommodate "income", "total income", and "taxable income" (which are not the same) and various kinds of deductions (and reductions) which operate at different stages of the process. But here goes:

1. Income is income under any particular Schedule. It is either (see, for example, interest, annuities and annual payments in Schedule D, Case III) pure income or (as, for example, in Schedule D, Case I) the balance of income over expenditure.
2. Total income is the sum of the incomes under the Schedules minus what are called "charges on income", that is, such things as annuities and some annual payments which the taxpayer pays out (see section 835 of the Taxes Act) and certain specified interest payments.
    Until 1990–91, the total income of a husband was deemed to include the income of his wife, where the couple were living together, although the tax bill might be apportioned between them if there was an election for separate assessment. Moreover, the husband and wife might not be taxed as a single entity where there was an election for the wife's earned income to be taxed separately. Since 1990–91, a husband and wife have been taxed as separate individuals.

3. Total income is not the same as taxable income. To arrive at taxable income one deducts from total income certain personal reliefs.
4. To work out the tax bill of an individual one applies to his taxable income the various tax rates. One then deducts the reliefs which are given by reducing that bill, *e.g.* the married couple's allowance. One has now arrived at the "tax payable", being an actual sum in hard cash. One can call this the "tax bill".
Now let us look in more detail at the steps in the process.

1. INCOME

The amounts of income which an individual has under each Schedule are added together to make up his schedular or statutory income. Each Schedule has its own rules for computing that kind of income which falls within it. What requires to be stated here is that some items of receipt are not subject to tax. Important examples are students' grants and scholarships, some social security benefits such as child benefit, and the first £70 of National Savings Bank interest. Brief mention should also be made of two relatively recent innovations, namely, personal equity plans (PEPs) and tax exempt special savings accounts (TESSAs). Both are intended to encourage saving. Under a PEP, an individual may invest up to £6,000 per annum in certain "eligible" shares and investments which are managed by an authorised PEP manager. The income generated by such investments, *e.g.* dividends, is not subject to tax (nor is capital gains tax charged on the disposal of any such share or investment). A TESSA is an interest bearing account which may be opened by an individual at a bank or building society. Interest earned on the amount deposited in a TESSA (up to a maximum of £9,000) is not subject to tax, provided that the amount saved (the capital) is left in the TESSA for five years.

2. KINDS OF INCOME

An individual's income may include items of the following kinds:

The Taxation of Individuals

(a) Income not taxed by deduction before receipt

An important example of this kind of income is income from a trade under Case I of Schedule D. Another example is income from rents under Schedule A.

(b) Income taxed by deduction before receipt

This is where we take account, as we must, of all receipts which were subject to withholding taxes, a deduction at source. One example of this is such income in the form of an annuity or annual payment as continues to be received after the deduction of basic rate tax at source, notwithstanding the effect of the Finance Act 1988. This kind of income, which is taxed under Case III of Schedule D, has been dealt with in Chapter 11.

The point we want to make here is that income taxed by deduction of tax before receipt has to be grossed-up, that is, converted into a gross sum, for the purpose of computing total income. We will explain grossing-up in a moment. The most important example of income taxed by deduction before receipt is salary or wage income which is taxed under the various tax bands (see below, p. 206). Tax is charged under Schedule E and is deducted by the employer under the PAYE system. The gross amount, which includes the tax calculated according to the various tax bands, is included in total income, but of course the employee is credited with the tax deducted by his employer.

Interest received from a building society or a bank is also subject to deduction of tax before receipt (see further, Chapter 11). However, the Finance Act 1996 provides for such interest to be savings income from which, from 1996–97, the lower rather than the basic rate will be deducted.

GROSSING-UP. An employee usually knows what his gross pay is (because his pay slip must state what it is) and so grossing-up does not present any problem. Moreover, it is, perhaps, simpler (and we are very much in favour of simplicity when it is a matter of arithmetic) to consider the mechanics of grossing-up in the case of a covenanted payment to charity. The covenantor will deduct tax at the basic rate. If the charity receives £76 (net), the gross amount is £100. The gross amount is made up of the net payment (£76) plus tax deducted at the basic rate (at present 24 per cent), £24. With less obvious figures, you gross-up by multiplying the net amount by 100 over 76. The explanation (for simple lawyers, not accountants) is

Kinds of Income

that if basic rate is 24 per cent, net income is gross (which is 100 per cent) less 24 per cent of gross, so net income is 76 per cent of gross. Putting it as an equation (or formula), and using N for net and G for gross:

$$N = \frac{76}{100} \times G$$

Conversely,
$$G = \frac{100}{76} \times N$$

One can play around a bit more by introducing T for tax.

$$T = \frac{24}{100} \times G$$

and also
$$T = \frac{24}{76} \times N$$

Summarising the above, three useful points emerge. If you know the net, you can find the gross by multiplying the net by $\frac{100}{76}$. If you know the gross, you can find the net by multiplying the gross by $\frac{76}{100}$. If you know the net, you can find the tax by multiplying the net by $\frac{24}{76}$. Grossing-up where lower rate tax had been deducted at source follows a similar pattern. Thus, if in the tax year 1996–97, an individual receives interest on his bank account the bank will deduct tax at the lower rate. If the individual receives £80 the gross amount is £100. As above, the gross amount is made up of the net payment (£80) plus tax deducted at the lower rate (20 per cent), £20. Similarly, recourse may be had to the equation (formula), suitably adapted, i.e. $N = \frac{80}{100} \times G$ and $G = \frac{100}{80} \times N$.

We have dealt with the arithmetic of grossing-up at some length. The reason is that we want to say to law students that you need not be afraid of tax law because some arithmetic is involved. In fact very little is involved, and if we can do it (which we can, just) anyone can.

Dividends and similar payments from United Kingdom companies

These payments have special features of their own. They fall under Schedule F. The amount to be included in total income is the net amount received (the "distribution") plus the "tax credit" that goes with it. (See further below, pp. 282–285). Broadly, the "tax credit" represents a proportion of the tax paid by the company on the "distribution", *i.e.* advance corporation tax at the rate of 20 per cent. This is imputed to the shareholder and is in satisfaction of his liability to *tax* in respect of that "distribution" (save where he pays tax at the higher rate when more tax must be paid).

Trust income

A beneficiary under a trust has to include in his total income an amount equal to his share of the trust income, grossed-up. He will have received his share after deduction of tax. He will be credited in his tax bill (depending on the circumstances) with all or some of the tax paid by the trustees. The taxation of trust income is dealt with in Chapter 12.

Finally, before we move on to consider the ways in which income may be classified we would like to say something about the special rules which govern the taxation of partnership income.

Partnership income

There are two (fundamentally different) regimes which govern the taxation of partnership income. This has arisen as a result of the adjustments needed to take account of the move towards self-assessment (see Chapter 3) and the related abandonment of the preceding year basis of assessment in favour of the current year basis of assessment (see Chapter 5). Which regime applies depends broadly on when a trade or profession carried on in partnership commenced. Thus, what we shall describe as the old regime applies (subject to there being no change in the partners, or if there is a change no election for continuation made, see below, p.196) to trades or professions carried on in partnership which began before April 6, 1994 (existing partnerships) and generally will continue to do so until the commencement of the tax year 1997–98 when the new regime takes over.[1] The new regime applies to trades or professions carried on in partnership which began on or after April 6,

---

[1] Subject to the caveat that there are transitional provisions for the tax year 1996–97.

1994 (new partnerships). You will see from this timetable that the old regime's days are numbered and its practical importance increasingly limited. We feel, however, that for our purposes it is useful to spend some time looking at its principal features (which we set out below) in order to provide a yardstick against which to measure the degree of change introduced by the new regime. But before we do so it is important to define what is meant by a partnership and to draw your attention to three important non-tax points about partnerships.

A partnership is defined in the Partnership Act 1890 as the relation which subsists between persons carrying on business in common with a view of profit. There is no definition of partnership in the tax legislation, but the existence of partnerships is, as might be expected, acknowledged under both regimes.

The three non-tax points we wish to make are extremely elementary, but we have found that they come as a surprise to some students. First, a partnership is quite different from a company registered under the Companies Acts, of which the main species is a limited company, *e.g.* Imperial Chemical Industries plc. Thus a partnership, unlike a registered company, is not, in English law, a legal entity separate from its members (although, as we shall see, under the old regime it is for purposes of assessment and collection treated as though it were a separate legal entity). Nevertheless, the name of a partnership may contain the word "Company", or "Co.", *e.g.* Price Waterhouse & Co. This does not make it a company in law; it is a partnership. The word "firm" is equivalent to the word "partnership", and should not be used in reference to a company. Secondly, there is no requirement of law or practice that the shares of each partner in the profits (or losses) of the partnership should be equal. Thirdly, a company can be a partner in a partnership.

It is now time to look at the old and new regimes, although we should, perhaps, preface our comments by saying that ease of understanding is not helped by the fact that they are governed, respectively, by the old and new versions of the relevant statutory provisions, in particular, section 111 of the Taxes Act.

The old regime

The old section 111 of the Taxes Act states that:

> "Where a trade or profession is carried on by two or more persons jointly, income tax in respect thereof shall be computed and stated

The Taxation of Individuals

jointly, and in one sum, and shall be separate and distinct from any other tax chargeable on those persons or any of them, and a joint assessment shall be made in the partnership name."

The "precedent partner" (usually the one first named in the partnership agreement) must make a return of the profits or gains of the trade or profession of the partnership. The partnership income is computed as for individuals. Thus a trading partnership has its income computed in the same way as a sole trader, under Case I of Schedule D and on the preceding year basis. (But there are special provisions where one of the partners is a company; this is because corporation tax is on a current basis.) The taxable income of the partnership is allocated to each partner according to the share of the profits to which he is entitled in the year of assessment. There is added to each partner's share any salary and/or interest on capital to which he may be entitled. Personal reliefs are allowed against each partner's share to the extent that they have not been exhausted against non-partnership income. The tax liability of each partner is thus calculated including both basic rate and (where a partner's share exceeds the threshold) the higher rate. The aggregate is then assessed in the partnership name. The tax is payable by the partnership as such. In other words the liability is the joint liability of all the partners. The partners make their own arrangements amongst themselves to recoup the tax from the individual partners. A partner's income from a partnership also forms part of his total income. But of course he gets credit for his part of the partnership assessment.

Where there is a change in the partners, *e.g.* by death or retirement or the introduction of a new partner, the old section 113(1) brings in discontinuance provisions it is as though a new trade had been set up. But if at least one person was in the partnership both before and after the change, there can be an election that the old section 113(1) shall not apply, that is, an election for continuation. Presently, if no election for continuation is made, the new regime will apply.

The new regime

The approach to the taxation of partnership income under the new regime bears little or no resemblance to that which we have considered above. The notion that a partnership might be regarded as an entity upon which an assessment to income tax might be made and from which tax might be collected is swept away. The new section 111 of the Taxes Act provides:

"Where a trade or profession is carried on in partnership, the partnership shall *not*, unless the contrary intention appears, be treated for the purposes of the Tax Acts as an entity which is separate and distinct from those persons." [*emphasis added*]

Broadly speaking, under the new regime, the responsibility for the tax payable on the profits of a trade or profession carried on in partnership lies not with the partnership but with the individual partners. Assessments are made on the individual partners, not on the partnership. Each partner is treated as if his share of the partnership profits is derived from a separate trade or profession carried on by him alone, *i.e.* as a sole trader or professional. This notional sole trade or profession is deemed to begin when he becomes a partner. It comes to an end when he ceases to be a partner or where the actual trade or profession is subsequently carried on by him alone or when it is actually discontinued. The partners are individually liable for tax in accordance with their respective shares in the partnership profits during the period in which the profits accrued.

3. CLASSIFICATION OF INCOME

EARNED, INVESTMENT AND SAVINGS INCOME

For nearly 90 years (since 1907) the law of income tax has made a distinction between two kinds of income, earned income and unearned income, and until 1984 taxed the latter more heavily than the former. At one time the system was to have a "standard rate" of tax applicable to all income, but to have also a relief on earned income. In this respect, the system between 1973 and 1984 was to have a "basic rate" of tax applicable to all income, and also to have a further rate imposed (as well) on unearned income. This further rate was called in the legislation "additional rate", but it has now been repealed. In addition, no differentiation was made between earned and unearned income when a lower rate was introduced from 1992–93.

The legislation does not use the phrase "unearned income", but rather "investment income". And it does not define investment income except to say that investment income is any income other than earned income. Earned income is defined in section 833 of the Taxes Act. Broadly, it includes all income derived from an office or employment which is chargeable under Schedule E and any income which is charged under Schedule D and is immediately derived by an individual from the carrying on of his trade, profession or vocation either as an individual or partner. This definition is consonant with commonsense, but there are some difficult borderline cases.

Income which is charged under the "new" Schedule A (see Chapter 8), notwithstanding its computation according to the principles of Case I of Schedule D, is, with the exception of income from furnished holiday lettings, investment income.

The Finance Act 1996 revives, in part, the notion that earned and investment income may be taxed at different rates. However, its approach is to identify a species of "investment income", which it refers to as "savings income". Savings income includes, for example interest from banks and building societies, interest from authorised unit trusts, interest from gilts and other securities and purchased life annuities. Dividends and similar payments from United Kingdom companies (see above, p.193 and below p.282–285) are also treated as savings income. The taxation of savings income is considered later in this chapter (below, p.207).

4. TOTAL INCOME

It is necessary to find a taxpayer's total income for two purposes: first, to determine whether it is enough to entitle him to the personal reliefs which he claims; secondly, to determine his liability (if any) to the higher rate of tax.

To arrive at total income one deducts what are called "charges on income" and certain payments (outward) of interest.

Charges on Income

A charge on income arises when a taxpayer binds himself by a legally enforceable arrangement to make payments to another person or body on a regular basis. The basic theory is that if a person alienates part of his income it ceases to be his income, and so does not form part of his total income. Instead, it becomes the income of the payee, and he [it] pays the tax instead. The theory of alienation has been drastically cut down by tax legislation, in particular, the Finance Act 1988, but it still stands in a few circumstances. For example, if an individual covenants to pay £x a year to a charity the payments are treated for all tax purposes as income of the charity and not his. He deducts tax at the basic rate from each payment and pays the charity the *net* amount. In calculating his own total income he can deduct the *gross* amount. (He is, however, required to pay to the Revenue the basic rate tax. This is fair, because if it were not so he would get relief twice over; he has had relief once by deducting basic rate tax from his payments to the charity). For further consideration of this matter, see Chapter 11.

Deductible Interest Payments

We are not speaking here of interest paid out as one of the expenses of a business; that is deductible *in computing* the income of that business. We are speaking of payments of interest in respect of which an individual can secure relief from income tax by deducting them *from* income.

Perhaps not surprisingly, these exceptional cases do not include many of the payments of interest with which most people are conversant, *e.g.* on a bank overdraft or under a credit card arrangement or hire purchase contract. Rather they relate to instances where the loan for which the interest is being paid is for one of a number of specified purposes which are discussed below.[2] However, even if the loan is for one of these purposes there are two general restrictions which come into play: first, relief is only given up to the amount of reasonable commercial rate of interest, see section 353(3) of the Taxes Act; and secondly, no relief at all is given if the sole or main benefit that might be expected to accrue to the claimant from the transaction under which the interest is paid was the obtaining of a reduction in tax liability by means of such relief; section 787 of the Taxes Act.

In outline, the rules for the specified purposes are as follows:

1. Loan applied in acquiring an interest in a close company, co-operative, employee-controlled company or partnership

The relief given in each of these instances is intended to encourage the development of small businesses. Broadly, this objective is pursued by granting relief to a claimant where the loan is used to

---

[2] Of course, the class of specified purposes is not closed, but equally the number of purposes which qualify for interest relief may contract, see, for example, the withdrawal of relief in respect of interest on loans taken out after April 5, 1988 and used for home improvements or for the purchase of a main residence for a dependent relative.

invest in or to provide finance for any of the above enterprises[3] and where the claimant is closely associated with that enterprise as an employee, shareholder, or partner as appropriate.

2. Loan to purchase machinery or plant

This relief helps partners and employees. If a partner borrows money to acquire machinery or plant for use by the partnership he can get relief on the interest, and so can an employee who borrows money to acquire machinery or plant which he uses for the purposes of his employment. This relief (both for partners and employees) is limited to three years' interest.

3. Loan to pay inheritance tax

This relief is available to the personal representatives and is some help to the estate in what is often the difficult task of getting together enough ready cash to pay the tax. It may be claimed where the loan in respect of which the interest is paid is used by the personal representatives to pay inheritance tax due on personalty to which the deceased was beneficially entitled. Only one year's interest is deductible.

4. Loan applied in acquiring an only or main residence and Mortgage Interest Relief At Source (MIRAS)

This relief helps owner-occupiers. At the outset, however, two important points must be made. First, it is a relief which is *not* effected by a deduction *from* income unlike the reliefs we have considered so far (nevertheless, we feel this is the most appropriate place to consider it). Secondly, it is a relief which is "out of favour" in that its value has fallen significantly in recent years.

The loan must be applied in acquiring (or for developing land for use as) the claimant's only or main residence. The determination of whether land so qualifies is a question of fact (see *Frost v. Feltham* (1981)). For such an only or main residence, the loan interest (including, for example, interest paid under a mortgage to a building society) in respect of loans taken out after July 31, 1988 is only

---

[3] Close companies are considered in Chapter 21, but, for present purposes, can be loosely described as small, private, family companies.

relievable up to a qualifying maximum loan *per residence*, which for 1996–97 is £30,000; for loans taken out before August 1, 1988 the limit applies to each *borrower*, not each residence.

Once upon a time (that is, before 1983) a person paying interest on, say, a bank or building society mortgage on his house claimed tax relief for that interest by way of *reduction of tax* due to the Revenue. In most cases, this was achieved by adjustment of the taxpayer's PAYE coding. However, the Finance Act 1982 introduced Mortgage Interest Relief At Source (MIRAS) to supersede this. Presently, MIRAS applies to most residential mortgages.[4] Under MIRAS, the tax relief is given to the claimant at source which means that no deduction in respect of the interest is made in computing the claimant's total income. This is how it works. The lender (in many cases a bank or building society) is required to calculate a repayment rate for the borrower which takes account of the tax relief (presently, at the rate of 15 per cent)[5] to which the borrower is assumed to be entitled. The borrower meets his obligation to the lender (and obtains his tax relief at source) by making a payment of interest from which the 15 per cent tax relief has been deducted. The lender then claims the benefit of the tax notionally deducted from the interest payment as if it had been paid by the lender to the Revenue. In many cases, this will entitle the lender to a repayment from the Revenue.

As far as the taxpayer and the Revenue are concerned, MIRAS is a simplification. But it does have the interesting side-effect of giving tax relief to non-taxpayers. As such, it amounts to a subsidy of all those borrowing to buy a house.

The MIRAS scheme may also apply where a retired person borrows money on the security of his house and uses the money to purchase an annuity. In such a case, interest on the loan (to the extent that the loan does not exceed £30,000) is entitled to relief (at the basic rate of tax) if the borrower is aged 65 or more, if at least nine-tenths of the loan is used to buy the annuity, if the loan is secured on land in the United Kingdom or Republic of Ireland, and if the land is his only or main residence.

---

[4] Where MIRAS does not apply, *e.g.* where the loan is made other than by a lending institution (perhaps, by an individual) relief is given by a reduction in tax.

[5] The relief was worth 25 per cent in 1991; 20 per cent in 1994 and now 15 per cent. Rumours of its imminent demise persist!

5. TAXABLE INCOME

Having arrived at an individual's total income, the next step is to convert it into taxable income. This is achieved by the deduction of certain personal reliefs from his total income.

PERSONAL RELIEFS

There are a number of personal reliefs set out in chapter I of Part VII (see sections 257 to 278) of the Taxes Act. As we shall see, the individual's right to claim these reliefs depends in each case (and in each year of assessment) on his personal circumstances, *e.g.* is the individual single or married; is the individual a single parent? Before we look specifically at personal reliefs there are a number of general points we want to make.

First, if an individual's total income in any year is less than the reliefs to which his circumstances otherwise entitle him they are to that extent lost. There is no provision for carrying the balance forward into future years or back into past years. Secondly, personal reliefs may be claimed only by individuals who are resident in the United Kingdom, except that certain non-residents listed in section 278 of the Taxes Act (notably Commonwealth citizens) may claim reliefs in respect of their United Kingdom income. Thirdly, until recently, a feature of the "unified system"[6] of income tax which was introduced in 1973 has been that all personal reliefs operated by way of *deductions* from total income. For most reliefs this system still applies. So if a relief is say £100, it does not mean £100 off the tax bill, but only £100 off the taxable income. In other words, the relief is whatever tax on £100 comes to, according to the tax rate of a particular individual which means, of course, that the relief is worth more to the higher rate taxpayer. However, as a result of the Finance Act 1994, some reliefs no longer operate in this way. Rather they are effected not as *deductions* from total income but as *reductions* in the individual's tax bill. Broadly, where the regimen introduced by the Finance Act 1994 applies, the individual's tax bill is reduced by an amount equal to a percentage (15 per cent for 1996–97) of the value of the pertinent relief. Thus, for example, the value of the married couple's allowance for 1996–97 is £1,790. Any individual who is entitled to claim that allowance receives a reduction in his tax bill for the tax year of £268.50, *i.e.* 15 per cent of £1,790. When we consider the specific reliefs we will make it clear

---

[6] See further, below, p. 205.

which of these alternative means of granting "relief" apply. Fourthly, the value of personal reliefs is adjusted or reviewed each year to take account both of the needs of the Exchequer and the rate of inflation (and, of course, on occasions more political considerations). In theory, the room for manoeuvre is restricted by the requirement that the value of the main reliefs be linked to changes in the retail prices index, *i.e.* to be raised each year by the amount necessary to maintain their true values. In practice, Parliament may determine otherwise (section 257C of the Taxes Act). Finally, there is a matter of terminology. All reliefs are called collectively "personal reliefs", whereas usually, but not exclusively, a specific relief is called an allowance (although it would now be more accurate to refer to a reduction in some instances).

Let us now look at the personal reliefs in more detail.

1. The personal allowance

The personal allowance may be claimed by all taxpayers resident in the United Kingdom. It allows a claimant (for 1996–97) a deduction of £3,765 from his total income. Any such claimant, *however young*, is entitled to the personal allowance and there is every incentive to use it for, as we have seen, if it is not used it is wasted—it cannot be carried forward or back nor can it be transferred to anyone else.

Where a claimant proves that he was during the tax year aged 65 or over the personal allowance is increased. For a claimant who proves that he is between 65 and 74 years of age during the tax year, the allowance increases from £3,765 to £4,910; for a claimant who is aged 75 or over it is increased to £5,090. This extra relief (sometimes called "the age allowance") is reduced where the claimant's total income exceeds £15,200 (section 257(5) of the Taxes Act).

2. The married couple's allowance (reduction)

This allowance may be claimed by a married man whose wife is living with him for any part of the tax year. A husband and wife are treated as living together, unless they are separated under a court order or deed of separation or are in fact separated in circumstances where the separation is likely to be permanent.

Since 1994–95, the claimant's entitlement is to a *reduction* in his tax bill which comprises an amount equal to a percentage (15 per cent for 1996–97) of the value of the allowance (£1,790 for 1996–97).

It is also possible for this allowance to be shared by a husband and wife or for it to be transferred to the wife. Thus, a wife may elect that half of the allowance (reduction) to which her husband would otherwise be entitled should be given to her or a husband and wife may jointly elect that the allowance (reduction) should be given solely to the wife (see section 257BA of the Taxes Act). In either instance, the requisite election must be made before the commencement of the tax year for which it is to have effect.

As with the personal allowance, there is provision for the married couple's allowance (reduction) to be increased on the basis of (old) age (see section 257A (2)–(5) of the Taxes Act).

3. Additional relief in respect of children

This relief is commonly referred to as the "single parent family allowance". It may be claimed by any woman who is not throughout the tax year married and living with her husband, or by a man who is not married and living with his wife for the whole or any part of the tax year or by a married man who is living with his wife but whose wife is, throughout the tax year, totally incapacitated physically or mentally. Any such claimant must show that a "qualifying child" has been resident with him or her for at least part of the year. Only one claim is available for each taxpayer, regardless of the number of children. A man and woman who live together as husband and wife, *i.e.* cohabitees, and who have a number of children are entitled to only one allowance which is provided for the youngest child. A "qualifying child" is, broadly, a child for whom the claimant is responsible and who was born in the tax year, is aged under 16 at the beginning of the tax year, or who is aged over 16 and in full time education (see section 259(5) of the Taxes Act).

The value of this relief is the same as the married couple's allowance (*i.e.* £1,790 for 1996–97) and the claimant's entitlement similarly is to a *reduction* in his or her tax bill of an amount equal to 15 per cent of the value of the relief.

4. Other allowances

Besides the allowances and the additional relief which we have considered so far there are other, less important allowances. A widow's bereavement allowance (reduction) allows a widow (not a widower) to claim the equivalent of a married couple's allowance (reduction) for the year of her husband's death and the following year. Thus, the value of this allowance for 1996–97 is £1,790 and the widow's entitlement is to a *reduction* in her tax bill of an amount equal to 15 per cent of the value of the allowance.

There is relief for blind people (but not for those suffering any other disability). The blind person's allowance for 1996–97 is £1,250 and is available as a *deduction* from the claimant's total income. If a husband and wife are both blind each may claim the allowance; any surplus allowance is transferable between them.

Finally, for the sake of completeness, we should mention an entitlement which is neither a relief nor an allowance, namely, child benefit. This is tax-free payment (usually made on a weekly or monthly basis) to a mother (in most cases) in respect of each of her children who is aged under 16 or who is aged under 19 and in full-time education. In recent years, it has been mooted that this universal benefit should be withdrawn or only be available to those who need it, *i.e.* that it should become a means-tested benefit.

6. THE TAX BILL

Having deducted from total income certain of a taxpayer's personal reliefs, we have arrived at his taxable income. We must now proceed to establish what amount of tax is payable. This is primarily determined by the rate or rates of tax applicable to an individual's taxable income.

THE RATES OF TAX

If one searches for any consistency of application or purpose in the rates of tax which are applied to taxable income one searches in vain as the following brief excursus through recent history shows.

From 1973–74 a new method of charging income tax came into force. This is sometimes called the "unified system", the point of that epithet being that surtax was abolished. Under the new method income tax is all one tax, though it is levied at various rates. Until 1977–78 there were the basic rate, higher rates and additional rates. For 1978–79 to 1979–80 there was a lower rate. The introduction of a lower rate, although at first sight it seemed a very simple point, complicated the system, mainly because of the many cases in which at that time income tax was "deducted at source" at the basic rate. It also greatly complicated the PAYE codes. On the other hand it was thought that the introduction of a lower rate had achieved one very great social good by reducing the number of people caught in the "poverty trap". The poverty trap is the situation in which a family can actually be worse off if the bread-winner gets a rise than they were before. This absurdity arises from the interaction (at a certain low level of income) of income tax, national insurance contributions and means-tested social benefits. It was found, however, when detailed research was undertaken that the main beneficiaries were married women. So it was abolished. From 1984–85 there was another change in the rate structure. The additional rate, levied since 1973–74 on investment income over a certain threshold at the rate of 15 per cent, was abolished. Again, research suggested that in practice it operated in a different way to that which theory suggested. It was mainly paid by retired people. This left a basic rate and a series of progressive higher rates of tax. From 1988–89 a single higher rate of tax of 40 per cent was introduced.

The most significant general change since then has been the resurrection from 1992–93 of a lower rate (levied at 20 per cent) as a first step towards the government's proclaimed goal of achieving a basic rate of 20 per cent; a goal further enhanced from 1996–97, by the taxation of savings income (see above, p. 198) of many taxpayers at the lower rate (see below, p.207).

For the tax year 1996–97, income tax is charged (subject to what we say in a moment about savings income) on an individual's taxable income at the following rates.

Lower rate

The lower rate is 20 per cent and it applies to the first £3,900 of an individual's taxable income.

Basic rate

The basic rate is 24 per cent and it applies to the taxable income of an individual between £3,901 and £25,500.

Higher rate

The higher rate is 40 per cent and it applies to the taxable income of an individual in excess of £25,500.[7]

---

[7] Increases in the bands of taxable income to which the respective rates of tax apply are linked to the retail prices index, save where Parliament otherwise determines.

The Tax Bill

Where an individual's taxable income includes savings income the rate of tax charged on the savings income is the lower rate, save where the individual is liable to tax at the higher rate when more tax is payable. Savings income is treated as the top slice of an individual's income, and an individual with other income will be entitled to set against that other income the totality of the lower rate band. This is illustrated by the following examples taken from the Inland Revenue Press Release issued on November, 28 1995 (Budget Day):

Example 1

An individual with taxable income (after allowances and reliefs) of £5,000, of which £500 is savings income (including the tax deducted at source), will be liable to tax:

— at 20 per cent on the first £3,900;
— at 24 per cent on the next £600; and
— at 20 per cent on the "top slice" of £500 of savings income.

Example 2

An individual with taxable income (after allowances and reliefs) of £27,000 of which £5,000 is savings income (including the tax deducted at source), will be liable to tax:

— at 20 per cent on the first £3,900;
— at 24 per cent on the next £18,100 of non-savings income.

The savings income will be taxed:

— at 20 per cent to the extent that it falls below the basic rate limit of £25,500, so £3,500 will be taxed at 20 per cent; and
— at 40 per cent on the remaining £1,500.

At this point, one might be forgiven for thinking that the computation process is complete and that the individual's tax bill has been ascertained. In some cases this will be so, but in others account must also be taken of reliefs which take effect by reducing the individual's tax bill. Broadly, there are two types. First, such relief may be available to an individual as a "reward" for supporting a government-backed initiative—for example, see the respective reliefs available to an individual, who furthers the government's aim to foster investment in small businesses by acquiring shares in a venture capital trust or in a qualifying company under the enterprise investment scheme. Secondly, as we have already seen (above, p.202), some personal reliefs, *e.g.* the married couple's allowance are effected not as deductions from total income but as reductions in the individual's tax bill. In addition, an individual may be entitled to double taxation relief (see below, pp. 454–458).

CHAPTER 15

NATIONAL INSURANCE CONTRIBUTIONS

Should we have a chapter on contributions in a book on tax? The contributions are (save for one small class) compulsory. They are not saved in a fund, but spent as they are received. While they earn benefit entitlement for some of their contributors, contributors have no option but to pay. What they pay is therefore squarely within the definition we gave in Chapter 1. In the last few years, even the government has quietly accepted this. It has been exploring the extent to which contributions and income tax can be merged.

A second problem is, surprisingly, more difficult. What shall we call the chapter? The difficulty is caused because law and practice have parted company. Just about everyone calls the contributions *National Insurance contributions*. The problem is that technically this name is more than 20 years out of date. The National Insurance Acts were replaced by Social Security Acts in 1973 and 1975. The current law is the Social Security (Contributions and Benefits) Act 1992. According to that Act, the contributions are called "contributions" (see section 1(1) of that Act). If we call the chapter just "Contributions", maybe you think we are not talking about tax. The income tax was called a "contribution on property, profits and income" when first introduced in its present form in 1803, and the company tax was first known as a "national defence contribution", so you would be wrong! It is also wrong to call them National Insurance contributions. The name was changed in 1973 (though the 1992 consolidation artfully avoids this point). But any other title would mislead, so we must continue to perpetrate and therefore perpetuate the error.

Introduction

The authority for levying and collecting contributions is contained in Part I of the Social Security (Contributions and Benefits) Act 1992 (and the identical sections in the almost identical Northern

National Insurance Contributions

Ireland Act of that year). Just 19 sections and two Schedules do much of the work of the Income Tax Acts. Well, not quite. Much of the detail of contribution liability is contained in regulations, of which the Social Security (Contributions) Regulations 1979 (S.I. 1979 No.591) are the most important. Even so, the legislative authority is much less detailed than the equivalent income tax provisions. The reason is that the system works on a much rougher sense of justice. This is combined with wide discretions given to the Secretary of State to deal, for example, with avoidance, in ways which would not be tolerated if given to the Inland Revenue.

The legislation provides for five main classes of contributions. Three classes, called Classes 1, 1A, and 4, are usually collected by the Inland Revenue along with income tax, and are to a large extent parasitic on income tax provisions. The others are collected direct by the Contributions Agency (CA), an executive agency of the Department of Social Security.

Administration of contributions apart from collection, is in the hands of the CA. In practice, matters are handled locally by many of the same staff as work for the Benefits Agency dealing with social security benefits. Appeals are dealt with by a simple procedure which can only be described as archaic compared with the sophisticated systems now available for most taxes. Anyone not satisfied with decisions of the CA or DSS on contribution questions may appeal—to the DSS! Section 17 of the Social Security Administration Act 1992 provides that only the Secretary of State is competent to decide such questions, which cannot be sent to the usual Social Security Appeal Tribunals. To be fair, the Secretary of State usually gets one of the DSS lawyers to hold an inquiry into the matter, and normally endorses the lawyer's opinion as the official decision, but a certain air of natural justice is missing.

Also missing is an elaborate appeal system from the Secretary of State. You are allowed to appeal to a judge of the High Court, but no further: section 18. No higher court can therefore consider contribution law on an appeal, although application on judicial review is possible. This has prevented any form of considered jurisprudence developing for contributions. Perhaps that is why this law has so often been ignored by tax lawyers.

We must now examine in turn the various classes of contribution. In summary they are:

Class 1   contributions from employees and their employers

Class 1A   contributions by employers for employees' cars

Class 2   contributions from the self-employed

Class 3   voluntary contribution from the non-employed

Class 4   contributions from traders and professionals.

Class 1

This class applies to anyone over 16 who is an earner in employed earner's employment and who in any period receives earnings in excess of the lower earnings limit for that period: section 6. That sentence was full of jargon (all quoted from the Act), and needs translating. What it means in practice is that anyone who has earnings that will get taxed under Schedule E will, if those earnings are more than a set minimum limit for any period, be liable for a contribution.

Arriving at that conclusion is not made easy by the exact words of the Social Security Act. That tells us that an "earner" is someone who has earnings. "Earnings" include any remuneration or profit derived from an employment: section 3(1). But it is clear from the Act that the self-employed are engaged in employment as much as employees. The key comes in section 2(1). It tells us that an employed earner is someone gainfully employed either under a contract of service or in an office, with emoluments chargeable to income tax under Schedule E. As the presence of the lower earnings limit prevents a charge to contributions on someone not receiving emoluments from employment, the reference to "gainful" employment seems superfluous.

Ignoring a few loose ends, the charges of Schedule E, as provided by section 19 of the Taxes Act 1988, and Class 1 apply to the same group of people, employees and office holders. We will talk simply of employees.

Where an employee has earnings for a period which exceed a set minimum, called the lower earnings limit, for any period, called an earnings period, contribution liability arises. The liability is of two kinds:

First, there is the primary contribution. This is paid by the employee personally. Then there is the secondary contribution to be paid by the employer. This must not be passed on to the employee.

National Insurance Contributions

Both the primary and the secondary contributions are percentages of the total earnings of the employee for that earnings period, up to a set maximum called the upper earnings limit.

Two things need to be determined so that the contribution can be levied. One is *earnings* and the other the *earnings period* during which those earnings are earned or treated as earned.

Earnings are broadly equivalent to emoluments from Schedule E. But it is only broadly equivalent. The important rule from *Tennant v. Smith* (p.96) about benefits in kind does not operate. Why? In truth, there is no strong reason why, if the terms of the primary legislation are studied, but the case has never been applied to contributions largely because ... it has never been applied. Instead, the matter has been dealt with in the Contributions Regulations. Regulation 19 lists a whole series of payments to be disregarded in working out the total of earnings. In particular, this excludes from charge "any payment in kind or by way of the provision of board or lodging or of services or other facilities": reg. 19(1)(d). Also excluded are tips from third parties (such as those received by employed taxi drivers), pensions, benefits under profit-sharing schemes and other matters. Once these are excluded, the charge is to be on the gross earnings from the employment. There are no provisions about deducting expenses or any equivalent of the deductions from total income available for income tax, such as capital allowances or personal allowances. In summary, if payments or earnings are in cash, or are convertible into cash by surrender (rather than sale), then contributions are payable. If the payment is in kind, no contributions are payable.

Note that the charge is on the earnings from *each* employment. If an earner has two or more employments with the same employer, these are added together. If there are separate employers, the earner must pay a primary contribution separately on the earnings of each job, and each employer must pay a secondary contribution.

There are complicated rules for defining *earnings periods*. The contribution scheme has no equivalent of PAYE coding, averaging out contribution liability through the year. This is because it is felt to be necessary to have the contributions determined at the time they are paid, so as to enable swift decisions to be taken about entitlements to benefits that may be based on those contributions. To enable this to happen, the liability for each period has to be calculated separately, the basic period being a week or month. Detailed rules are needed to stop avoidance, and the Contributions Regulations provide them. They also provide the DSS with extremely wide powers to stop avoidance in individual cases by simply ignoring inconvenient facts: regs. 21, 22.

The rates of liability are adjusted every year to ensure a correct rate of flow into the National Insurance Fund, bearing in mind the outgoing of that year. For 1996–97 the rates were: lower earnings limit—£61 a week; upper earnings limit—£455 a week a year. The primary contribution is payable at a standard rate of 10 per cent on earnings in excess of the lower earnings limit, and 2 per cent on earnings up to that limit. The secondary contribution is payable at various rates depending on the total earnings for the period and ranging from zero to 10.2 per cent.

Note that we called the 10 per cent rate the *standard* rate. This is because there is a *reduced* rate, paid by certain married women and widows. They can only pay at this low rate if they opted out of the scheme before 1978. There is also a *contracted-out* rate, again lower than the standard rate. Despite the names used, this is paid by the majority of employees, particularly those in the public sector. The contracted-out rate applies where the employer is providing employees with an occupational pension payable in place of part of the state retirement pension, or where the employee has opted out of both the state pension and any occupational pension, paying a personal pension instead. In exchange for losing the right to part of the state pension, both employer and employee pay reduced amounts. But they will usually be paying for occupational pensions. Finally, a person over retirement age does not pay a primary contribution, but the employer does.

Class 1A

Eh? This class of contributions is an example of the brilliant art of compromise that is a strength of the British—or, perhaps, an example of why our laws are frequently such a shambolic mess. The Class 1A contribution is in fact a fringe benefits payroll tax. It has nothing to do with social security except that the money is paid into the National Insurance Fund. No entitlement to benefit arises from it. It is a charge on any employer that provides employees with company cars in such circumstances that the employees are liable to income tax on the car (see section 157 of the Taxes Act 1988). If the employee has to pay income tax under that section, then the employer has to pay a Class 1A contribution. If not, not. See section 10 of the Contributions and Benefits Act 1992. Procedure apart, that is the end of the relevant law.

National Insurance Contributions

The contribution was brought in as a compromise. In most countries, social contributions are payable on benefits in kind as well as on cash earnings. The fact that this was not so in Britain meant that considerable tax advantages accrued to those who received benefits in kind. Cars formed the most usual benefit in kind. But the British system cannot readily tax benefits in kind to ordinary contributions because of the special rules on earnings periods. Nor can employers be charged income tax on benefits in kind in the way they do in some states (such as Australia). However, if the tax privilege was to be removed from company cars, an employer levy was necessary. So, what was simpler than to use the one employers' payroll tax that was available?

Class 2

This is payable by those who are ordinarily self-employed and more than 16. There is no definition of "ordinarily", but it is clear that individuals do not cease to be ordinarily self-employed just because they go on holiday for a week. For contributions purposes someone is self-employed if employed gainfully in employment other than employed earner's employment: Social Security Act 1975, ss.2, 7, read with the Categorisation of Earners Regulations (S.I. 1978 No.1689). The distinction between the employed and the self-employed is as important here as anywhere. This is not just because of the very considerable difference in the contributions paid by the employed compared with the self-employed, but because of the differing benefits the two categories can receive. Determining status is a Secretary of State's question, subject only to limited appeal.

Categorisation is the only real problem with Class 2. Note, however, that an employee can also be self-employed at the same time, and pay Class 2 contributions as well as Class 1 contributions, subject to a maximum annual limit (see below). The Class 2 contribution is a flat-rate weekly amount of £6.05 (in 1996–97). Those whose earnings from self-employment are lower than that year's exception level (£3,430 in 1996–97), need not pay the contributions if they wish. This is a voluntary limit. Someone not paying contributions cannot receive benefits either.

Next, we ought to deal with Class 3. This class is a class of voluntary contributions that may be paid by anyone not paying Class 1 or Class 2 contributions. It is therefore not a tax. It may be a good idea to pay them sometimes (and the CA will advise on that), but this is the individual's choice.

Class 4

This is taken out of order deliberately, because it is payable by many of the people who pay Class 2 contributions. Class 4 is entirely separate in law from Class 2, and is entirely parasitic on Schedule D, Cases I and II, so we discuss it there (p.87).

Credits

Several categories of people who are not required to pay contributions are nevertheless treated as having paid them. Much of this topic is beyond the scope of tax law, but it is worth noting that those in receipt of some social security benefits do not have to contribute even if they have enough income to be taxable. Instead, they are treated as having paid the contribution, which is credited to their record. This also applies, amongst other cases, to those undergoing full-time education. This is to prevent unfairness. For example, someone who has just started work and was then sick would not be able to claim incapacity benefit because he or she would not have paid enough contributions. To stop that happening, he or she would be credited with contributions sufficient to make incapacity benefit payable where the reason for non-payment was full-time education: Credits Regulations (S.I. 1975 No.556), reg. 8.

Overlap Between Classes

A person may be required to pay Class 1 contributions on more than one employment, or to pay Class 1 contributions at the same time as Class 2 and Class 4 contributions. While the overlap between Class 2 and Class 4 is deliberate, and is taken into account in setting the rates of those two classes, the overlap with Class 1 may lead to overpayments. To stop excessive payments by individuals with more than one job, or with a job and self-employed status, there is a maximum limit of contributions payable by an individual in any year. In effect, if an employee ends up paying more then the maximum Class 1 contribution for that year (that is, the contribution payable on earnings at the upper earnings level throughout the year), the excess can be reclaimed.

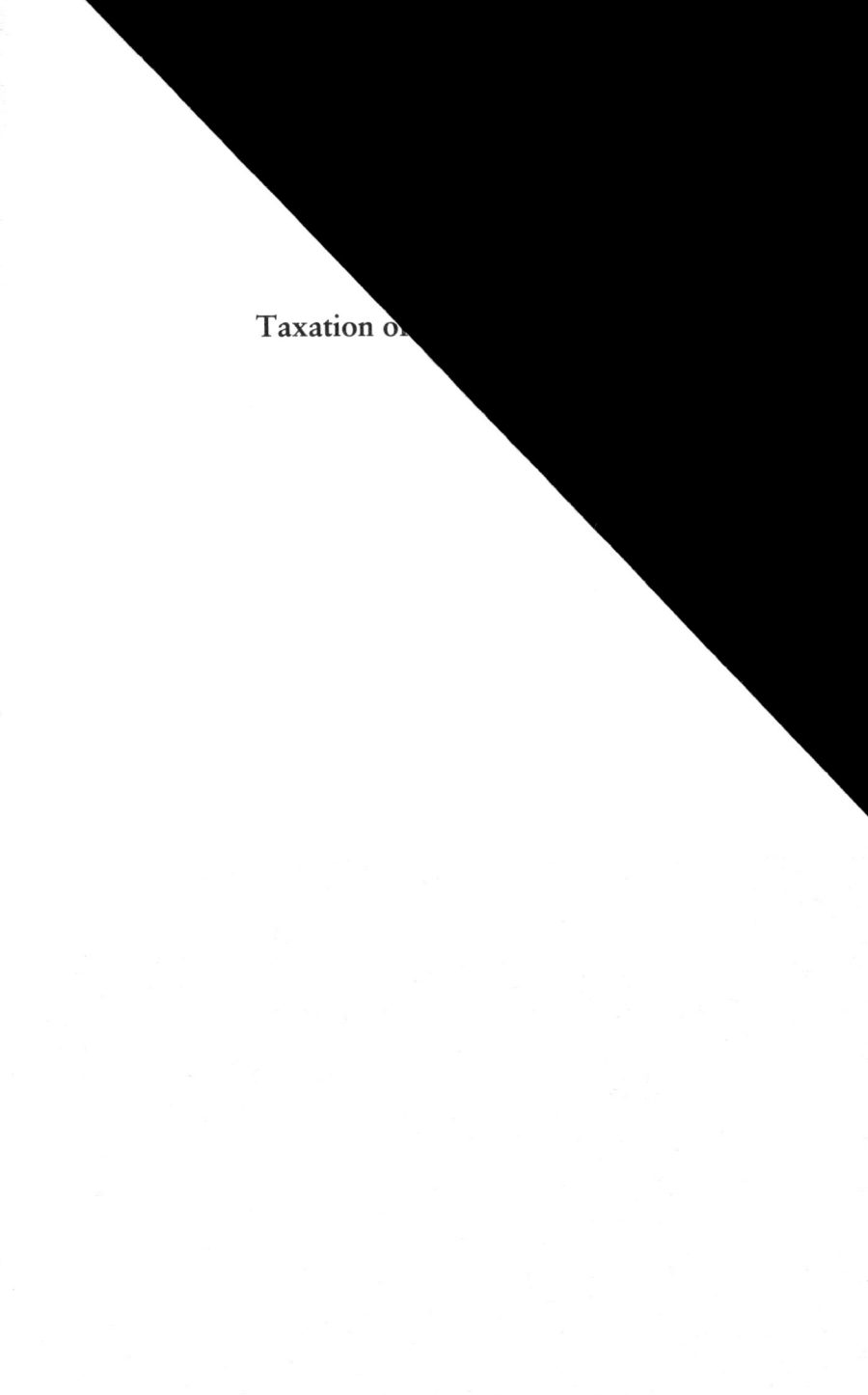

Taxation o

PART THREE

Capital Gains

CHAPTER 16

CAPITAL GAINS TAX

Capital Gains Tax is, not surprisingly, a tax on capital gains. It is not a tax on income and is generally free from any overlap with income tax. Nor is it a tax on capital as such (as a wealth tax would be) but only on gains. It is in this latter point (gains) that it differs from inheritance tax. Both inheritance tax and capital gains tax are concerned, broadly speaking, with the movement of capital from one person to another, but whereas on such a movement inheritance tax charges tax on the whole amount of capital which moves, capital gains tax charges tax only on the gain as between the value it has at the time of this movement (*e.g.* sale by A) compared with the value it had on the occasion of its last previous movement (*e.g.* purchase by A). There are a few occasions when there will be a charge to both taxes where some limited relief is available, but on the whole they are complementary. In general, inheritance tax is designed to tax voluntary transfers whereas capital gains tax is designed to tax commercial transfers. But the changes made to inheritance tax in recent years have led to the general rule that lifetime gifts will be subject to capital gains tax and only rarely to inheritance tax.

The social idea behind capital gains tax is that it is too arbitrary, and therefore unfair, to tax a person on his income (*e.g.* dividends) and not to tax a person on his capital gains (*e.g.* buying shares on the stock exchange and selling them at a higher price). The latter is thought of as being as much a taxable resource as the former.[1]

But the theory was spoiled by inflation. If you bought something in 1978 for £400 and sold it in 1982 the probability is that you would have got around £600 for it. On paper you have made a gain of £200; in real terms you have not made any gain at all. Until 1982 the legislation made no allowance for such a paper gain. In fact the point was tested in court, and in *Secretan v. Hart* (1969) it was held

---

[1] But see "The Meade Report and the Taxation of Capital" [1979] B.T.R. 25.

that no adjustment for inflation (or to put it in another way, for the fall in the value of money) was allowable.

The tax was originally introduced in 1965 by a Labour government and taxed all gains accruing after March 1965. Successive Conservative governments since 1979 have sought to reduce the impact of the tax (by introducing extensive reliefs) and to remedy the perceived injustice of taxing paper gains. In 1982 a form of index-linking was introduced, which was refined in 1985 so that relief is available for all paper gains made after March 1982. Thus if a person bought an asset in 1972 for £1,000 and sold it in 1992 for £11,000 he would be able to discount from his total gain of £10,000 a sum for inflation from 1982 to 1992. But he would still be liable on paper gains incurred before 1982. In 1988, therefore, it was decided to take out of the charge all gains, paper or real, incurred before 1982. Thus in our example the gain would be calculated by taking the market value of the asset at March 1982, say £7,000, and deducting that from the sale price of £11,000. That gain of £4,000 would then also attract relief for inflation between 1982 and 1992. In summary no gain accrued before March 1982 is taxable and indexation relief is available for all gains accrued after that date.

The law relating to capital gains tax was first consolidated in 1979 and again in 1992 in the Taxation of Chargeable Gains Act. **Unless otherwise stated all references to sections in this part of the book are references to that Act.** Most of the amendments made since 1992 are incorporated into that Act. It is, however, quite a technical tax and there have been may cases for the courts to decide. Those which relate to the principles of the tax are included below.

Administration

The administration of capital gains tax is similar to that of income tax. The tax is under the "care and management" of the Inland Revenue. Assessments are made by HM Inspectors of Taxes. Appeals lie to the General or Special Commissioners. The Taxes Management Act 1970 applies to this tax as it does to income tax. Section 57 of that Act empowers the Board (the Commissioners of Inland Revenue) to make regulations concerning capital gains tax appeals.

Thus a taxpayer is obliged to make a return of his capital gains in the same way as his income and the system of self-assessment will apply. The liability to the tax is calculated annually according to years of assessment just like income tax. It is collected by the

Collector of Taxes. Payment is due (until self-assessment) by December 1 of the year following the relevant year of assessment. Under self-assessment that date becomes the following January 31.[2] Interest is payable on overdue tax.

Rates of Tax

Since 1988 the rates of capital gains tax and income tax have been harmonised: section 4. Until then capital gains tax was charged at a flat rate of 30 per cent. A taxpayer's chargeable gains are now treated as if they were the top slice of that person's income and thus the appropriate income tax band, lower, basic or higher will apply. Where the gain straddles two bands it will be taxed proportionately at the two rates. But the two taxes remain separate so that, for example, personal allowances cannot be set off against capital gains tax and capital losses cannot be set off against income tax.

Instead, an individual subject to capital gains tax can take advantage of the "exempt amount" for each year. This is specified by a statutory instrument issued in advance by the Treasury for each tax year and is index-linked unless Parliament decides otherwise: section 3. The amount for 1996–97 is £6,300. Tax is therefore only payable in so far as an individual has taxable gains (chargeable gains less allowable losses) in excess of that amount in the year. The exempt amount is in effect the tax threshold for the year in question and so fulfils the same role for capital gains tax as the personal reliefs do for income tax. Because capital gains tax is charged by reference to a transaction it is therefore possible to limit such transactions between years so as to maximise the use of this exemption. It is not available against income tax liability, however.

Spouses are taxable as separate individuals for capital gains tax as for income tax. Thus they both have an exempt amount. However, there are two consequences for the tax if the spouses are living together. For this purpose a married woman is deemed to be living with her husband unless they are legally separated or the circumstances are such that the separation is likely to be permanent: section 288(3). The first consequence is that a transfer of assets between the spouses is treated as if neither a gain nor a loss has occurred (so that the transferee is deemed to have acquired the asset at the price paid by the transferor) (see below) and the second is that they can only

---

[2] There is a very limited right to payment by instalments for certain charges applicable to settlements.

Capital Gains Tax

have one main residence to qualify for exemption from the tax (see Chapter 18). Thus a cohabiting couple can each have a house which they can sell free of the tax, but not so married couples.

Trustees, who may be liable to pay the tax in relation to changes in the beneficial ownership of the trust property, are only entitled to half the annual exempt amount (Schedule 1, para. 2). Personal representatives, however, are entitled to the full amount for the year of the death and the two following years. After that they cease to have any exempt amount (section 3(7)).

Companies are not liable to capital gains tax as such but they pay corporation tax on their chargeable gains which are computed in the same way as those for individuals. As with individuals, the rate applicable will be the appropriate rate of corporation tax, currently 24 per cent or 33 per cent. There is no exempt amount.

The Charge to Tax

Section 1(1) declares: "Tax shall be charged in accordance with this Act in respect of capital gains, that is to say chargeable gains computed in accordance with this Act and accruing to a person on the disposal of assets."

This subsection contains in summary form the whole of the law relating to capital gains tax. We shall know that law when we know what a chargeable gain is, how the Act requires computation to be made, what a person is, what an asset is, and what a disposal is. This chapter tells us what a chargeable gain is and what amounts to a person, an asset and a disposal; *i.e.* the basic charge. The next chapter concerns itself with the computation of the gain and the final chapter with the various exemptions and reliefs from the tax.

CHARGEABLE GAINS

All gains other than exempted gains are chargeable gains (section 15(2)), but (by Schedule 3) the amount of chargeable gains accruing on the disposal of assets which were owned on March 31, 1982 is restricted in an attempt only to tax gains accruing after that date. A gain accrues on the disposal of an asset. So a disposal after March 31, 1982 may attract the tax even though the asset was acquired before that date. But where the acquisition *was* before that date then, broadly speaking, only that part of the gain is charged to tax which has taken place between March 31, 1982 and the later disposal. We shall look at the ways of achieving this when dealing with computations in the next chapter. The chargeable gain is, again, broadly speaking, the difference between the cost of the asset and the consideration received on its disposal. The cost is usually referred to as the "base cost". It is important to realise that the consideration received by A on a disposal to B will be B's base cost on a subsequent disposal to C. Capital gains tax operates thus by charging the gains on an asset by reference to specific events, known as disposals. In general where an asset was acquired before March 31, 1982, the base cost will be its market value at that date.

Although each asset disposed of in a year of assessment has to be considered separately, the tax is charged on the total amount of chargeable gains in the year after deducting allowable losses (section 2(2)).

The key requirements for a charge are the disposal of an asset by a chargeable person. Let us now examine each of these in turn (in reverse order).

PERSONS

"Person" has the same meaning as in income tax law. So not only individuals are persons but so also are companies and trustees and personal representatives which have been covered above.

Partners

A partnership (or firm) is not a "person" in the law of England. In Scottish law a partnership is a "person". For capital gains tax purposes in all parts of the United Kingdom partners are treated separately as individuals for their share of the gains or losses arising from the disposal of partnership assets or other partnership dealings; section 59. The Board of Inland Revenue have issued a Statement of Practice about partnerships, which is printed in, *e.g.* [1975] B.T.R. at pp. 408–412. When an asset is disposed of by the partnership each partner is treated as making a disposal of his fractional share of that asset. In computing gains or losses the proceeds of disposal will be allocated between the partners in the ratio of their shares in asset surpluses. Where this is not specifically laid down the allocation will follow the actual destination of the surplus as shown in the partnership accounts. If a lump sum is paid to a partner on his leaving the firm that represents consideration for the disposal of his share in the partnership assets. But where a retiring partner receives annual payments instead of a lump sum the capital value of this annuity will not be treated as consideration for a disposal of his share of the partnership assets if it is no more than can be regarded as a reasonable recognition of his past work and effort. The Statement of Practice contains many other detailed rules as well as the above.

Residence, etc.

A person is only chargeable to capital gains tax in respect of chargeable gains accruing to him in a year of assessment during any part of which he is resident in the United Kingdom, or during which he is ordinarily resident in the United Kingdom (section 2(1)). The reference to ordinary residence as an alternative to residence prevents a person normally resident here from escaping the tax by going abroad temporarily and disposing of assets whilst so abroad. The meaning of "resident" and "ordinarily resident" are the same as for income tax.

The disposal of an asset which is situated in the United Kingdom only imposes tax on a person who is not resident and not ordinarily resident here if he is carrying on a trade through a branch or agency in the United Kingdom and the asset is connected with the trade (section 10(1)). An individual who is resident or ordinarily resident but not domiciled in the United Kingdom is taxed only if the proceeds are remitted to the United Kingdom on gains from the disposal of assets outside the United Kingdom (section 12(1)), and losses on the disposal of such assets are not allowable losses (section 10(4)). In *Young v. Phillips* (1984), the disposal of letters of allotment to shares in a United Kingdom company, although taking place in Sark, was held not to fall within section 12(1). The letters carried rights enforceable in the United Kingdom and so were not assets situated outside the United Kingdom.

ASSETS

All forms of property are assets, and this is so whether they are situated in the United Kingdom or not. Thus a United Kingdom resident is liable for disposal of non-U.K. assets. (Section 275 contains rules for determining where certain kinds of assets are situated.) Section 21(1) declares that the following items are included amongst assets: (a) options, debts and incorporeal property generally; (b) any currency other than sterling; and (c) any form of property created by the person disposing of it, or otherwise coming to be owned without being acquired. Notice that head (c) brings into charge things which were never acquired but were on the contrary created by the taxpayer, such as a building, a chattel, the copyright of a book, and (very importantly) the goodwill of a business[3] which of course may have been built up from nothing. Some items, as we shall see later, are expressly stated not to be chargeable assets.

Since assets are defined by reference to all forms of property it is important to note that this will include all interests in property, for example a lease of land is itself an asset as well as the land itself. The major item in practice for capital gains tax is company securities. There has been some doubt as to whether purely personal rights can be assets for this purpose; these include assets such as the right of a protected tenant under the Rent Acts or a right to damages for an action in tort. These cannot be assigned or sold. Damages, but not the right to sue for damages (see the next paragraph), are in fact exempt by virtue of section 19(5), which suggests perhaps that otherwise they would be assets. The point was argued in *O'Brien v. Benson's Hosiery Ltd* (1980) (H.L.) where B was appointed a director of the company in 1968 on a seven-year contract. In 1970 the company released him from this contract in return for a payment of £50,000. The Revenue sought to assess the company on this receipt on the basis that it had disposed of an asset, *viz.* its rights against B under the contract. The House of Lords, reversing the Court of Appeal, held that these rights were assets. The fact that the company could not assign their rights did not matter. The important point was that they could be turned to account, as in fact they had been in this case. As we shall see even the fact that an asset has no obvious market value does not prevent it being an asset—one can always calculate a hypothetical market value.

Non-assignable rights under a contract are therefore assets. Can the same be said of a disputed or moral claim? In *Scott v. Ricketts* (1967), £39,000 was paid by a developer to an estate agent "in consideration for the withdrawal of any claim he may have". It was clear that he only had a moral claim and it was held that Case VI of Schedule D could not apply since it was not "analogous to the sale of an asset". Some assistance may be derived from the decision in *Zim Properties Ltd v. Procter* (1985) that a right to sue for damages in the tort of negligence was an asset on the basis that it could be turned

---

[3] See, *e.g. Butler v. Evans* (1980). In *Kirby v. Thorn EMI plc* (1987), the Court of Appeal held that where a company, having sold three subsidiaries, agreed not to compete with their businesses it had disposed of its goodwill in those businesses. That was an asset. They overruled the judge's opinion that the company was merely fettering its freedom of commercial activity.

to account (*e.g.* by a compromise settlement). The judge, applying the *O'Brien* test, thought that all such actions would be assets unless clearly frivolous or vexatious. "Assets" is a wider concept than "property". Since in practice the question will only arise if the "assets" are turned into account (*e.g.* there is a disposal), the *O'Brien* test suggests that all such rights and claims will be assets if the point arises. Put another way, we can almost say that if you can dispose of it in any of the ways possible under the Act, it is an asset.

Disposals

The basic event on which capital gains tax depends is the disposal of an asset. Whenever a disposal takes place a calculation must be made to see whether there has been a gain or a loss or neither.

The word "disposal" has first of all to be given its ordinary meaning before going on to consider the extended meaning given to it by the Act. In its ordinary meaning a disposal occurs whenever the owner of an asset (which, remember, may be an abstract entity such as a right) divests himself of his entitlement to the asset. Thus the ordinary meaning includes sale, exchange and gift.

It is very important to grasp that the making of a gift is a chargeable event. At first sight this may seem very odd. Clearly the giver of a gift has made a disposal, but how on earth can he be said to have made a gain? The point was challenged in court in *Turner v. Follett* (1973) (C.A.). It was inevitably held that a gift is a chargeable event. In section 17 it is now enacted that where a person acquires an asset by way of gift the disposal of it to him (as well as the acquisition of it by him) shall be deemed to be for a consideration equal to its market value. So if a dad gives to his son an asset which he bought for £10,000 and at the time of the gift its market value is £14,000, dad has made a chargeable (albeit notional) gain of £4,000. But notice that if the gift is a gift of British money there is no charge to *this* tax (though there may be to inheritance tax) because sterling is not an asset; section 21(1)(b). Otherwise, there would be no yardstick to measure gains.

When capital gains tax was introduced there was no other charge on gifts (except those within seven years of a death). Capital transfer tax, introduced in 1975 originally applied to all gifts and there was therefore a potential double charge to tax on a gift. When capital transfer tax mutated to inheritance tax most gifts (except those made within seven years of a death) were again excluded from the charge. Thus the relief from capital gains tax introduced in 1980 to avoid the double charge was substantially repealed.

The market value rule for gifts stated in section 17 applies not only to a disposal by way of gift but also to a disposal "otherwise than by way of a bargain made at arm's length". It may seem surprising that so dignified a document as an Act of Parliament should use the phrase "at arm's length" but that is a phrase well-known to lawyers. The idea is that if two people are closer than arm's length away from each other their dealings may be not wholly governed by commercial considerations, with the result that a deal may be done at less than market value. This might be so, for example, where a young man sells his sailing dinghy to his girlfriend. In such a case the disposal is deemed for the purpose of capital gains tax to be at market value. So if Fred bought a boat for £150 and later sold it to Freda for £180 when its value was really £200, Fred has a chargeable gain of £50 and Freda gets a base cost of £200. In *Zim Properties Ltd v. Procter* (1985) a potential negligence action was held not to have been acquired at arms length or by way of bargain and was thus acquired at market value at the date the right of action accrued.

Where the parties to a transaction are "connected persons" the transaction is automatically treated as a transaction otherwise than by way of a bargain at arm's length; section 18(2). "Connected person" is defined in section 286(2) as follows: "A person is connected with an individual if that person is the individual's husband or wife, or is a relative, or the husband or wife of a relative, of the individual or of the individual's husband or wife." And by section 286(8) "relative" means "brother, sister, ancestor or lineal descendant". There are also definitions in section 286 of "connected person" in relation to trusts, partnerships and companies. In effect, "connected persons" are those kinds of persons who might get together to pull a fast one at the cost of the Revenue.

Where there is a gift or a sale at an undervalue the donor or vendor is primarily liable for the tax, subject to the relief mentioned above, but if he does not pay it the donee or purchaser can in certain circumstances be required to pay it.

Section 17 also applies the market value rule to cases where the consideration cannot be valued, or is connected with the loss of employment, reduction of emoluments or is in respect of the provision or services. In *Whitehouse v. Ellam* (1995) it was said that there must be a direct link at the time of the disposal between the disposal and the loss of emoluments.

Capital Gains Tax

Now we come on to the extended meanings of "disposal" for the purposes of the tax.

Part disposals

First, "disposal" includes a part disposal (section 21(2)). Thus where a person disposes of less than the whole of an asset (or disposes of less than his whole interest in an asset) that counts as a part disposal of the asset and not a disposal of part of the asset (see *Watton v. Tippett* (1996)). For example, a company's holding of shares of the same class in the same company may be treated as a single asset. If some of those shares (but not all of them) are sold, the sale is a part disposal of the total holding. Generally speaking, the gain accruing on the sale is calculated by reference to an appropriate part of the cost of the entire holding. A part disposal also includes the disposal of an interest in an asset, which interest is created by the disposal and did not exist before the disposal. If the owner of freehold land grants a lease (for a premium) over the land the granting of the lease is a part disposal, notwithstanding that the lease only comes into existence at the moment when the part disposal takes place. The freeholder has disposed of part of his interest in the land. While we are talking of leases let us point out that a premium for a lease is only chargeable to capital gains tax in so far as it is not chargeable to income tax (Schedule 8, para. 5(1)). This is part of a wider principle, namely that any sum charged to income tax is not to count as part of the consideration for a disposal for the purposes of capital gains tax (see section 37(1)).

Deriving capital sums from assets

The second extended meaning of "disposal" is this: if a capital sum is derived from assets by their owner there is assumed to be a disposal of those assets, notwithstanding that no asset is acquired by the person paying the capital sum (section 22(1)). The clearest example of this is where a shareholder receives a capital distribution in respect of his shares. This section also applies to fix the charge on those rights and claims, discussed above, which are only assets if they can be turned into account. The "turning to account" is the derivation of a capital sum from the asset, hence the disposal and the charge: *O' Brien v. Benson Hosiery (Holdings) Ltd* (1979) (H.L.); *Zim Properties Ltd v. Procter* (1985). In the latter case it was stated to be a matter for the exercise of common sense as to the asset from which the sum is derived. It might be the right to payment itself or the property giving rise to that demand (*e.g.*, by a vendor of a house). The section was also applied in *Kirby v. Thorn EMI plc* (1987) to a company entering into a restrictive covenant not to compete with the business it had just sold. It had derived a capital sum from an asset (its goodwill).

Section 22(1) then goes on to say that the principle applies in particular to four defined circumstances: (a) Capital sums received by way of compensation for any kind of damage or injury to assets or for the loss, destruction or dissipation of assets or for any depreciation or risk of depreciation of an asset. An example would be compensation for infringement of copyright; another example would be damages paid by a tortfeasor for physical damage done to an asset; (b) Capital sums received under a policy of insurance covering the risk of any kind of damage, etc., to assets. This hardly needs examples; (c) Capital sums received in return for forfeiture or surrender of rights, or for refraining from exercising rights. An example would be a payment received by A for releasing B from his obligation under a contract;[4] (d) Capital sums received as consideration for use or exploitation of assets. This seems to point towards such transactions as the grant of a right to use a copyright. In *Chaloner v. Pellipar Investments Ltd* (1996) it was said that this head could not apply where the owner granted a lease over his property. That would be a part disposal under section 19(2). The head might apply where the owner retained full title to the property, *e.g.* on the grant of a licence. The question might be asked as to why a taxpayer should argue for a disposal under head (d) rather than for a part disposal. The answer is that a disposal under heads (a)—(d) takes place when the capital sum is received (section 22(2)), whereas a part disposal takes place on the grant and, as in the case itself, that can affect the computation of the gain.

Section 22 has produced other problems of interpretation for the courts. In *Marren v. Ingles* (1980) the House of Lords held, demonstrating admirable common sense, that the meaning of "notwithstanding that no asset is acquired by the person paying the capital sum" was "whether or not" he acquired such an asset, *e.g.* absolute title to an asset on payment of a contingent sum. In *Davenport v. Chilver* (1983) the judge decided that if a capital sum was received within one of the specific headings (a—d) the section could apply

---

[4] *e.g.* the disposal of the company's rights in *O'Brien v. Bensons' Hosiery (Holdings) Ltd* (1979), see p.225, above.

even if the capital sum did not strictly derive from an asset as required by the general wording of the section (*e.g.* access to an independant compensation fund).

In *Davis v. Powell* (1977) money paid to a tenant farmer as compensation for disturbance on the ending of his lease as required by the Agricultural Holdings Act 1948 was held not to be *derived* from the lease but from the statutory right to compensation. Nor was it money received under (c) as money received for the surrender of rights under the lease—there was no element of bargain but simply a statutory computation. A similar result has been applied to business tenancies: *Drummond v. Austin-Brown* (1983), but not where the right to compensation is an independent property right, *e.g.* to a compensation fund for loss of foreign appropriated property, see *Davenport v. Chilver* (1983).

Loss, destruction and negligible value

The third extended meaning of "disposal" is set out in section 24(1):

> " ... the occasion of the entire loss, destruction, dissipation or extinction of an asset shall ... constitute a disposal of the asset whether or not any capital sum by way of compensation or otherwise is received in respect of the destruction, dissipation or extinction of the asset."

The *entire* loss, destruction, etc., of an asset would normally mean that it had become valueless, so the deemed disposal is a disposal for a nil consideration. The next subsection—section 24(2)—deals with a situation where there has not been entire loss, destruction, etc., but where the value of an asset has become "negligible". The effect here is that the owner is deemed to have sold and immediately re-acquired the asset at its then market value. The deemed disposal, being at a negligible value, may well give the owner a loss (compared with the price for which he had acquired the asset); the point of the deemed re-acquisition is that if the value of the asset picks up so that there is a gain on its subsequent disposal, that gain is calculated by reference to this new, low, acquisition value. This subsection only applies if the taxpayer makes a claim to the Revenue to that effect.[5]

---

[5] The disposal (loss) cannot be deemed to take effect prior to the claim: *Williams v. Bullivant* (1983).

Disposals

Whether the asset becomes entirely lost, destroyed, etc., or whether it merely becomes of negligible value, if the asset in question is a building it is treated as an asset separate from the land on which it stands. But the owner is deemed to have disposed of the land (as well as of the building) and also to have immediately re-acquired the land at its then market value. The effect of this is that any loss relief that the owner gets in respect of the building will be reduced by the amount of any appreciation in the value of the land itself since he acquired it.

Let us look now at the inter-relation between the destruction, etc., of an asset and the receipt of a capital sum. If an asset is totally destroyed that will produce a loss, because the deemed disposal is for a nil consideration. If the destroyer pays a sum in damages or an insurer pays insurance money that may reduce or wipe out the loss. Suppose A bought an asset for £6,000. Subsequently it was totally destroyed. A is deemed to have disposed of the asset for nothing. That produces a loss of £6,000. A few weeks later an insurance company pays A £6,000. That produces a gain of £6,000. The one balances the other, so all in all there is no loss or gain. Of course, the insurance company may pay A less than £6,000, say £5,500, in which case there is an overall loss of £500. Or the insurance company may pay A more than £6,000, say £7,000, in which case there is an overall gain of £1,000. There are provisions in section 23 whereby in some situations tax on such a gain may be deferred until there is a disposal in the future. This is a kind of "hold-over" relief. ("Hold-over" relief is another splendid piece of tax jargon, to be found nowhere in the dictionary, but everywhere in the Acts. There are several kinds of hold-over relief in CGT, all amounting only to postponements of tax, rather than complete exemptions.) For example, if our friend A spends the insurance money within one year of receipt on buying a replacement asset for £7,000 the £1,000 gain is dealt with by deducting £1,000 from the acquisition cost of the replacement asset. This will have the effect of increasing by £1,000 the gain to A when he comes to dispose of the replacement asset in the future. So A will be in exactly the same position as he would have been in if the asset had never been destroyed. Suppose A sells the asset (the replacement asset) eventually for £9,000. When he sells the asset, he deducts £1,000 from the replacement cost (which was £7,000) so his gain is £9,000 minus £6,000 = £3,000. If the original asset (which cost £6,000) had never been destroyed his gain would equally have been £3,000. These provisions apply not only to insurance money received but also to damages received. A somewhat similar system operates where an asset is not destroyed but only damaged.

We have now dealt with the extended meanings of "disposal," except for some which occur in connection with settled property (on which see below at pp.244 *et seq.*).

What we must do now is to look at some particular disposal situations.

DISPOSALS FOR A DEFERRED OR CONTINGENT CONSIDERATION

Suppose that A sells an asset to B for £500 payable immediately and £100 per month payable for the next 10 months. The consideration received by A for that asset for capital gains tax purposes is £1,500 (£500 + 10 × £100) and he is deemed to have received this amount at the date of sale (date of the contract, unless it is a conditional contract in which case it is the date on which the condition is fulfilled[6], s. 28). Section 48 makes it clear that no allowance is to be made for the fact that A will not receive the full amount at that time. This is an example of a disposal for a deferred consideration (*i.e.* a future payment which will become payable).

The legislation, however, makes no specific provision for disposals for a contingent consideration (*i.e.* a future payment, which may or may not become payable, usually of an uncertain amount). This has caused problems which had to be resolved by the House of Lords in *Marren v. Ingles* (1980). In that case the taxpayer agreed to sell 60 shares in an unquoted company for £700 each, payable immediately, and a stated percentage of the sale price quoted for those shares if the company was floated on the stock exchange. When the company was floated the purchaser became liable to pay the taxpayer £2,825 for each share. Clearly there was a disposal of assets for at least £700 each but how to deal with the additional amount?

The Revenue did not seek to charge the tax by reference to a single disposal on the original agreement but by reference to two disposals—one of the shares on the agreement and one of the right to the contingent payments under section 22(1) as the receipt of a capital sum derived from that right on payment of the extra amount.

---

[6] A conditional contract is one where all the liabilities under the contract are conditional and not where, *e.g.* property is to pass only on payment of all instalments under a contract of sale: *Lyon v. Pettigrew* (1985).

After much technical argument by the judge and the Court of Appeal on the merits of applying section 22(1), the House of Lords held that the section could apply whether the purchaser was thereby acquiring full title to the shares or simply extinguishing a liability to pay an additional sum. The judge, Slade J., also discussed whether section 17 could have applied (*i.e.* a disposal where the consideration cannot be valued is to be charged at market value) or whether it could be regarded as two part-disposals, but expressed no opinion on the matter. It is, however, quite clear that section 48, which we saw relates to deferred considerations, cannot apply—it only applies to quantified and not contingent payments. Thus the argument of the taypayer in *Marson v. Marriage* (1980) that since the original disposal was prior to 1965 (at that time the starting date for the tax) and the contingent payments (in that case for land subsequently developed) subsequent to 1965, section 48 required all the considerations to be regarded as pre–1965 and so out of the charge, failed, and the principle of *Marren v. Ingles* was applied.

APPROPRIATIONS TO AND FROM STOCK IN TRADE

It will be remembered that under the principle of *Sharkey v. Wernher* (1956) (H.L.) where a trader disposes of part of his stock in trade not by sale but for his own use he must, for the purposes of income tax, bring into his accounts as a receipt the market value of the asset at that time. And of course the converse applies—where a trader transfers an item from his own recreational enjoyment into his trade he can show in his accounts the market value of that item as an expense of the trade.

Now, how does capital gains tax bear on these events? Where a person who is a trader transfers a personal asset to his trade that appropriation is treated as a disposal, thus involving a gain or a loss compared with its earlier acquisition cost; section 161(1). But he can, if he wishes, avoid payment of capital gains tax by electing to bring the asset into trading stock not at its then market value simply, but at its then market value reduced by the amount of the chargeable gain or increased by the amount of the allowable loss (section 161(3)). (A partner can only make this election if the other partners concur.) Take the case of a gain: the effect is that the item appears in his trading account amongst "purchases" at a figure below its true value by the amount of the gain, thus swelling his trading profits for that year by that amount.

In the converse case, where a trader transfers an item of trading stock to his personal enjoyment he is treated as having acquired it

Capital Gains Tax

for a consideration equal to the amount then brought into the accounts of the trade in respect of that item for income tax purposes. Thus the closing figure for the item for income tax purposes is taken as the base cost for capital gains tax purposes: section 161(2). For income tax purposes no doubt the trader would like to put a low figure on the item, thus reducing his trade receipts and so his profits. But a low figure for income tax means a low base cost, which will in the end involve him in more capital gains tax.

The practical importance of the provisions we have been discussing is reduced by the presence of an exemption from capital gains tax in the case of a disposal of an asset which is tangible movable property and which is a wasting asset: see below at p.272. But of course not all stock in trade is tangible movable property. It may be tangible without being movable (*e.g.* land) or movable without being tangible (*e.g.* stocks and shares).

CAPITAL DISTRIBUTIONS BY COMPANIES

Where a person receives a capital distribution (other than a new holding, on which see the next heading) in respect of shares in a company, he is treated as if in consideration of that distribution he had disposed of an interest in the shares (section 122). This applies for example when a company makes a "rights" issue of shares[7] and a shareholder sells his rights. Another example of its application is when a liquidator makes a repayment of capital to shareholders in the course of a winding-up. If, however, the inspector is satisfied that the amount of any capital distribution is "small" as compared with the value of the shares he may direct that the occurrence shall not be treated as a disposal, but that instead the amount of the distribution shall be deducted from the expenditure allowable as a deduction in computing a gain when the shareholder comes to dispose of the shares in the future. This of course has the effect of increasing the gain and hence the tax. It is a kind of hold-over relief.

COMPANY ADJUSTMENTS

There are detailed provisions (in sections 126–140) as to the bearing of capital gains tax on the re-organisation of a company's share capital, the conversion of securities and the amalgamation of

---

[7] This is an issue of shares which are offered first to existing shareholders.

companies. We will not go into all the details here. One example is this: where a company makes a "bonus" issue or a "rights" issue of shares and a shareholder takes up the shares (a "new holding") the new shares are treated as acquired when the original shares were acquired, and the acquisition cost of the total holding is the cost of the original shares plus the sum (if any) which the shareholder pays for the new holding. In the case of a company amalgamation (or take-over) then, subject to certain conditions, the exchange of shares in one company for shares in another company does not count as a disposal. This rule led to a great deal of tax avoidance and the relief has been subjected to two conditions, namely that the change must be effected for bona fide commercial reasons and it must not form part of a scheme or arrangements of which the main purpose or one of the main purposes is avoidance of tax liability: see section 137.

TRANSFER OF BUSINESS TO A COMPANY

Where a person (other than a company) transfers a business as a going concern (and with its assets) to a company wholly or partly in exchange for shares, the gain on the transferred assets is computed but not charged to tax. The gain is apportioned between the shares received and any other consideration received. That part of the gain attributed to the shares is not assessed but is deducted from the allowable cost of the shares when the transferor of the business comes to dispose of them in the future. So it is a form of roll-over relief. The part of the gain attributed to the consideration other than shares (*e.g* cash) is assessed at once in the normal way. This matter is dealt with a section 162.

DEBTS

The "satisfaction" of a debt is a disposal by the creditor. "Satisfaction" of a debt includes payment-off of the debt, and it also includes assignment of the debt. It may be worth discussing what the creditor whose debtor pays him a debt is disposing of. The answers is that he is disposing of the debt itself, which is a chose in action—a species of right. There are many circumstances in the law of capital gains tax where it is more obvious that a person is acquiring something (*e.g* money in satisfaction of a debt) than that he is disposing of something. If one looks closely one sees that he is disposing of the right to obtain that which he acquires. Where does the capital gain come in in connection with a debt? The answer to that is that the capital gain is the difference between what the creditor lent and what he gets back as a capital sum.

Although, in general, satisfaction of a debt is a disposal (section 251), so far as concerns the original creditor no chargeable gain accrues on the disposal. And the same is true of the original creditor's personal representative or legatee. At first sight this seems very nice of the Revenue, but the point is really directed against losses. It is a general principle of capital gains tax law that a loss cannot be claimed from a transaction upon which, if there had been a gain, it would not have been a chargeable gain. This principle was to some extent modified for debts which prove to be bad debts by section 49 of the Finance Act 1978. That section was enacted because huge losses had been incurred during the slump of the mid-1970s. The section provides that where a loan or part of a loan *to a trader* becomes irrecoverable the original creditor or a guarantor can claim the loss as an allowable loss. The section only applies where the loan was made (or the guarantee was given) after April 11, 1978 (which was Budget Day). It is notable that the government which insisted on retrospection in respect of the anti-avoidance section 31 of the same Act was not willing to make this relieving section (section 49) retrospective. They agreed to lock the stable door but the horse had already bolted. The provision is now at section 253 of the 1992 Act.

The rule that no chargeable gain (and hence—subject to section 253—no allowable loss) can arise to the original creditor (or his personal representative or legatee) does not apply to a "debt on a security." The exact boundaries of a debt on a security are a matter of judicial controversy, but it is clear from section 132 (3) (b) that an example is loan stock of a company. And, paradoxically, a security is still a security if it is unsecured. On the other hand a mortgage of land is not a debt on security. A debt on security is not the same as a secured debt. However, gains on what are known as "qualifying corporate bonds" (company debentures) are, for individuals, exempt from a charge to capital gains tax but may attract some relief for losses: sections 117, 254.

The assignee of a debt (as distinct from the original creditor) does make a chargeable gain (or an allowable loss) when the debt is satisfied, whether it be a debt on a security or not. This rule (if it stood alone) would open the way to a great deal of tax avoidance, because it is very easy to contrive a loss on a debt. So there are provisions to stop up these possibilities. A loss made by a person on the disposal of a debt is disallowed if he acquired the debt from a "connected person": section 251(4). So if A sells a debt to B for £120 and later X (the debtor) pays up £100 to B, B cannot claim a loss of

£20 if A and B are connected persons. If this were not so, and B *could* claim a loss, it would be a way of B making a gift of £20 to A, to which gift the Revenue would be contributing. Sometimes a creditor takes property instead of money in satisfaction of a debt. In that case the base cost of the property is its then market value and no more. This looks as though it is going to prejudice the creditor when he comes to sell the property. And so it does in the case of a creditor who is not the original creditor, but is a person who has acquired the debt by assignment. So if A assigns to B a debt of £500 for £500 and then X (the debtor) hands over to B in satisfaction of the debt property worth £450, the base cost of the property is £450. So if, later, B sells the property for £520 he has made a gain of £70. But if the *original* creditor (A) (not having assigned the debt) accepts from the debtor in satisfaction of the debt property worth £450 the chargeable gain to A, when he comes to sell the property, is not to exceed the chargeable gain which would have accrued to him if he had acquired the property for a consideration equal to the amount of the debt. So if the debt was £500, the property was worth £450 and A later sells it for £520, A's chargeable gain is £20 (not £70). These matters are dealt with in section 251(3).

OPTIONS

An option is an asset. The grant of an option is treated as a disposal. Where the option is exercised the grant and the exercise are treated as all one transaction. So if A grants to B an option to buy certain property and B subsequently exercises the option and buys the property, the sum paid for the option and the sum paid for the property are added together to ascertain the disposal cost (for A) and the acquisition cost (for B). Supposing, on the other hand, that an option is granted and then abandoned (*i.e.* not exercised): A is left with the gain on the grant of the option; for B the abandonment of the option does not count as a disposal for the purposes of section 24 (total loss, asset becoming of negligible value, etc.)—with the result that, although he has lost money, he does not get any loss relief. On the other hand if the option is abandoned by agreement for a consideration, *i.e.* A pays B to release the option, that will be a disposal by B under section 22(1) (derivation of a capital sum from an asset). Thus if the option is released for a nominal amount loss relief will be available. These and other rules are set out in sections 144–147, as interpreted by Vinelott J. in *Golding v. Kaufman* (1985).

VALUE SHIFTING

This is the dramatic and cryptic heading given to sections 29 to 34. Section 29 begins with a general introduction, and it then proceeds to deal with four specific situations.

First, if a person having control of a company exercises his control so that value passes out of his shares (or other rights) or out of the shares (or rights) of a person with whom he is connected into other shares (or rights) that is a disposal of the shares (or rights). An example would be if A, who holds the only shares which carry voting rights in a company, were to pass a resolution to transfer the voting rights to the shares held by other shareholders. It is, after all, a kind of gift. For a more sophisticated example, see *Floor v. Davis* (1980) (H.L).

Secondly, if there has been a shift of value as above, and subsequently the transferor disposes at a loss of some other asset which has depreciated in value by reason of the shift, that loss is not an allowable loss.

Thirdly, if there is a sale and lease back of land or other property and then subsequently there is an adjustment of the rights and liabilities under the lease which is favourable to the lessor, that counts as a disposal by the lessee of an interest in the property. The idea behind this rule is that the seller has really sold the property for less than its true value. Suppose A, the owner of a factory, sells the freehold of it to B for £100,000 and B immediately leases it back to A at a rent of £5,000 a year. Later an adjustment is made in the terms of the lease in favour of B, so that in effect B is to get £6,000 a year from the property. On this footing the price that A received for the freehold turns out be less than what he could have got for it, with the result that A paid less capital gains tax on the disposal of the freehold than he "should" have done. This present provision, by treating the adjustment in the lease as a disposal by A, enables the Revenue to pick up the lost tax.

Fourthly, if an asset is subject to some right or restriction and then the person entitled to enforce the right or restriction abrogates it, that abrogation counts as a disposal by that person of the right or restriction. An example of this would be if A, who had chartered a ship from B, were to release B from his obligations under the charterparty. That would be a disposal by A of his rights under the charterparty.

Section 30 was enacted (originally in 1977) to strike at some tax avoidance schemes which were based on transferring some of the value of a chargeable asset into a non-chargeable asset. The section is in very wide terms and has the potential to become a general anti-avoidance weapon. It will not apply, if the taxpayer can show that tax avoidance was not the main purpose of the scheme.

Sections 31 to 34 (enacted in 1989) are aimed at preventing a group of companies from selling a subsidiary company with a reduced value, having shifted that value into other companies within the group prior to the sale.

HUSBAND AND WIFE

As we have seen, disposals *between* spouses who are living together are treated (by section 58) "as if the asset was acquired from the one making the disposal for a consideration of such amount as would secure that on the disposal neither a gain nor a loss would accrue to the one making the disposal."[8] Broadly the effect of this is that the transferee takes the asset at the base cost which it had in the hands of the transferor. But it is a little better than that, because the words of the paragraph seem to imply that if there are some incidental costs of the inter-spousal transfer the base cost for the transferee is to include those costs. Thus if H bought an item for £100 and subsequently transferred it to W and the costs of the transfer were £5, the base cost for W (looking to a future disposal by her) would be £105. W's base cost will also include indexation to cover inflation since H bought the asset, or from March 1982 if later.

Death

Until 1971 death was in itself a chargeable event for capital gains tax thus providing a double charge with estate duty (the predecessor of inheritance tax). The Finance Act 1971 abolished the charge. But a person's death still has important consequences—for his survivors. The subject of death is now dealt with in section 62 of the 1992 Act. Section 62(1) provides:

> " ... the assets of which a deceased person was competent to dispose—
> (a) shall be deemed to be acquired on his death by the personal representatives or other person on whom they devolve for a

---

[8] This rule does not apply if (a) the asset is trading stock of the transferor or is acquired as trading stock of the transferee, or (b) the disposal is by way of *donatio mortis causa*.

Capital Gains Tax

        consideration equal to their market value at the date of death; but
  (b) shall not be deemed to be disposed of by him on his death ... '

The main point of the phrase "assets of which a deceased person was competent to dispose" is to exclude settled property in which the deceased had an interest. Settled property is governed by different rules which are discussed under the next heading. To take an example, if, when A dies, he is the life tenant under a settlement, he is not "competent to dispose" of the settled property. One can speak of property of which a deceased person was competent to dispose as being his "free estate".

The effect of section 62(1) is that so far as concerns the deceased's free estate, the death does not give rise to a charge to capital gains tax, but it does give rise to an "uplift" in the base cost of his assets. This, of course, is advantageous for the future. If A bought an asset for £50,000 and later died when its market value was £60,000, the base cost becomes £60,000. On a future disposal of the asset for £65,000, the gain is £5,000 and not £15,000 so that £10,000 gains have been written off. It must be borne in mind, however, that inheritance tax will (or may) be payable on the death of A on the full value of £60,000. Indeed the idea behind the exemption from capital *gains* tax on death is that death should not be an occasion of charge to both taxes. But it goes a bit further than that, because there is no charge to capital gains tax on death even if there is no charge to inheritance tax either, as for instance where assets are left to a surviving spouse. (See p. 337 below.)

The next question which arises is this: when the personal representatives come to dispose of the assets in the course of the administration of the deceased's estate, is that disposal a chargeable event? The answer is that if the disposal is to a legatee that is not a chargeable event, but if the disposal is to anyone else it is a chargeable event.

A legatee gets as his base cost the market value of the asset at the time of the deceased's death; section 62(4). "Legatee" is given by section 64(2) and (3) an extended meaning. It includes any person taking under a testamentary disposition (a will) or under an intestacy or partial intestacy, whether he takes beneficially or as trustee. And where the personal representatives appropriate assets to satisfy a legacy, the person taking under the appropriation is deemed to be a legatee. Also, by section 62, subsections (6) to (9), if the deceased's dispositions are varied by an instrument in writing

Settled Property

made by the persons entitled within two years of the death, the variations do not count as disposals, except such variations as are made for a consideration (other than a consideration consisting of some other variation).

A disposal by personal representatives otherwise than to a legatee *does* involve a chargeable gain or allowable loss. This is so, for example, if they sell an asset in order to pay inheritance tax, or if they simply re-arrange the investment portfolio. There is no provision for personal representatives to offset their losses against gains of the deceased. If the deceased had, in the year of assessment in which he died, an excess of losses over gains these may be "rolled backwards" for the preceding three years: section 62(2).

Settled Property

"Settled property" is defined in section 68 as "any property held in trust[9] other than property to which section 60 ... applies." So the first thing to do is to find out what section 60 is all about. It deals with the situation where one person is nominee for another person or is a bare trustee for another person. Neither a nominee nor a bare trustee counts as a trustee, and the property they hold is not settled property. The property is treated as though it were vested in the person for whom the nominee or bare trustee is holding it, *i.e.* the beneficiary. Unfortunately (from the point of view of clarity) section 60 itself does not use the phrase "bare trustee," but there is an illuminating translation of the phrase used in the section, namely "trustee for another person absolutely entitled as against the trustee, or for any person who would be so entitled but for being an infant or other person under disability (or for two or more persons who are or would be jointly so entitled) ... ". The phrase "bare trustee" does occur in the marginal note to section 60. Section 60(2) says this:

> "It is hereby declared that references in this Act to any asset held by a person as trustee for another person absolutely entitled as against the trustee are references to a case where that other person has the

---

[9] A unit trust scheme does not count as a trust (nor does an investment trust company). Both count as companies, though with some special rules of their own.

exclusive right, subject only to satisfying any outstanding charge, lien or other right of the trustee[10] to person to resort to the asset for payment of duty, taxes, costs or other outgoings, to direct how that asset shall be dealt with."

The words "jointly so entitled" in section 60 do not refer only to persons who are technically joint tenants; they cover also persons who are tenants in common. So *concurrent interests* can exist (whether in the form of a joint tenancy or a tenancy in common) without the property in which the interests subsist being settled property, provided the "tenants" can direct the trustee how the asset shall be dealt with: see *Kidson v. MacDonald* (1974). This point is not confined to real property; the word "jointly" refers to "persons who are, as it were, in the same interest", whatever the subject matter of the trust (*per* Walton J. in *Stephenson v. Barclays Bank Trust Co. Ltd.* (1975)). On the other hand it was held in both those cases that where there are *interests in succession* (*e.g.* where there is a trust for A for life with remainder to B) the trustees can never be bare trustees and the property must be settled property. This is because, although A and B are *together* entitled absolutely as against the trustee, they are not entitled "jointly" and so section 60 can never be satisfied.[11]

If the beneficiaries' interests are contingent they are clearly not absolutely entitled as against the trustees, even if the only contingency is on their obtaining the age of majority. They are not absolutely entitled "but for their infancy" but because they only have contingent interests: see *Tomlinson v. Glyns Executor Co.* (1970).

The essential criteria for a bare trust is that the beneficiary (or beneficiaries) must be able to direct the trustees as to how to deal with the trust property and to give a valid receipt for it. Actual transfer is not required, just the right to do so: *Stephenson v. Barclays Bank Trust Co. Ltd* (1975). This has been applied to what are known as "putting arrangements." Thus where all the members

---

[10] This does not include payment of an annuity under the trust. Thus the presence of an annuity prevents the beneficiaries being absolutely entitled: *Stephenson v Barclays Bank Trust Co. Ltd* (1975).

[11] In *Booth v. Ellard* (1980) it was accepted that the interests of the beneficiaries must be concurrent and all must be the same. See also *Harthan v. Mason* (1980).

of a private company transferred their shares to trustees and subjected themselves to restrictions on transfer they were held to be absolutely entitled since they could collectively end the trust and so destroy or override any discretions or powers vested in the trustees.[12] Similarly where a family entitled to farming property set up a trust in which each member's interest was equivalent to their previous entitlements there was held to be no settlement for capital gains tax purposes.[13] The importance of this is that there is no exit charge if one member takes his interest out of the trust (see. p.244, below). On the other hand, in the case of class gifts, *e.g.* "to such of my grandchildren born within 21 years of my death", the beneficiaries cannot be absolutely entitled until the class has closed, *i.e.* there can be no more potential beneficiaries. Until then the size of each grandchild's share is unknown. Different considerations apply where each potential beneficiary has a defined share, *e.g.* "one quarter to each of my grandchildren on attaining 21". In this case when each beneficiary attains a vested interest (*i.e.* attains 21) the question of whether he becomes absolutely entitled to that part of the settled property depends upon whether he can require the trustee to appropriate that part of it to him. In the case of land held on a trust for sale, for example, the trustees have a power to postpone sale by law, and this can only be overridden by the court or by all the beneficiaries acting together. Thus in *Crowe v. Appleby* (1975) such beneficiaries were held not to be absolutely entitled against the trustees. The position would usually be different if the trust property consisted of money or quoted securities which are easily divisible.

If the trustees are not bare trustees then "any property held in trust" is settled property.

We must now consider the events connected with settled property which count as disposals.

PUTTING PROPERTY INTO SETTLEMENT

A transfer of property into a settlement is a disposal of the *entire property* thereby becoming settled property; section 70. This is so even if the donor takes some interest as a beneficiary under the settlement or is a trustee or the sole trustee of the settlement. This is a pretty harsh rule. Suppose Mr Smith wishes to give his house to his nephew, but to retain for himself the right to occupy the house for

---

[12] *Booth v. Ellard* (1980).
[13] *Jenkins v. Brown* (1989).

Capital Gains Tax

the rest of his life, so that the nephew will only come into occupation when S dies (S for Smith and also for "settlor". S can only carry out this transaction by putting the house into settlement. It is a transfer of property into a settlement and so it is treated as a disposal of the entire property. That means that the deemed consideration for the disposal is the whole capital value of the house. This does not accord with the reality, because in reality all that S has given away is the remainder interest. The same point can occur the other way round: S may want to allow his aged aunt to live in the house for her life. He makes a settlement under which the aunt gets a life interest and he retains the remainder interest. There is a charge to tax based on the value of "the entire property" when this transfer is made. In reality all that S has given away is a tiny fraction of the value of the entire property.

DISPOSALS BY TRUSTEES

Trustees, though they are not "individuals," are "persons", and they are chargeable to capital gains tax. They are chargeable, for example, on gains made in the course of switching investments in the trust's portfolio.

There is also one situation (special to trustees) where they are *deemed* to dispose of assets comprised in the settled property. This is where a person becomes absolutely entitled to settled property and is known as the "exit charge" (section 71(1)). In addition, although there is no deemed disposal, there is a deemed re-acquisition by them where a life interest in possession terminates by reason of a death (section 72(1)). We will look at these situations in turn.

(1) A person becoming absolutely entitled

Suppose assets are held in trust for A contingently on his attaining the age of 25. When A becomes 25 that is an occasion of charge under section 71(1). The assets are deemed to have been disposed of by the trustee and immediately re-acquired by him in his capacity as a bare trustee within section 60(1), for a consideration equal to their market value. After that it makes no difference whether the trustee hands over the property to A at once or keeps it as bare trustee for him. The actual handing over of the property to A is not a chargeable event because it is deemed to be A's already by virtue of section 60(1). The upshot is that the trustees pay tax on the gain represented by the increase in value of the assets between the time when they were put into trust and the time when A became 25, and A takes as his base cost the market value on the day when he attained 25.

Where the event which causes a person to become absolutely entitled is the termination of a life interest[14] by the *death of* the person entitled to that interest no chargeable gain accrues on that disposal (section 73(1)(a)). All that happens is that the trustee is deemed to dispose of the settled property and immediately re-acquire it as a bare trustee. The effect is that there is an uplift of the base cost to the market value at the time of the death. The person who becomes absolutely entitled acquires the property at the up-to-date value. This, of course, is advantageous to him when he comes to dispose of the property in the future. Suppose property is settled on A for life, with remainder to B absolutely. On A's death B becomes absolutely entitled. There is no charge to capital gains tax (even if there is no charge to inheritance tax either) but there is an uplift in line with the general rule on deaths.

There is a special exception to this advantageous rule where there arises what is called "reverter to the disponer". The background to this point is that no inheritance tax is payable on the death of X where X has been given a life interest by S (settlor) in such terms that the property reverts, on X's death, to S. If in this situation S could also get, on the death of X, an uplift in the base cost for purposes of capital gains tax that would be too favourable to S. So he cannot; see section 73(1)(b). If, on the life tenant's death, property reverts to the disponer (settlor), the disposal and re-acquisition shall be deemed to be for such consideration as to secure that neither a gain nor a loss accrues to the trustee. Thus, suppose S grants a life interest to X in property which at the time of the grant is worth £10,000. X dies at a time when the market value of the property is £14,000. The property reverts to S. The trustee is treated as re-acquiring the asset for £10,000 (not £14,000) and that figure (£10,000) becomes S's base cost.

(2) Termination of a life interest in possession by death

This situation is dealt with by section 72(1). Naturally, the termination of a life interest and the absolute entitlement of some person often happen on the same event. If property is held in trust for A for life with remainder to B, the event of A's death brings about the termination of a life interest (A's) *and* the absolute entitlement of some person (B). In this situation it is section 71(1) which applies. Section 72(1) only applies where there is a termination of a life

---

[14] This applies by an extra statutory concession to any interest which comes to an end on a death, even if it is not a life interest.

interest by death but still no one becomes absolutely entitled. This would be so, for example, where property is settled on A for life, remainder to B for life, remainder to C absolutely, and A dies. On A's death there is the termination of a life interest but no one becomes absolutely entitled; B becomes entitled for life and section 72(1) applies. On B's death (or surrender) section 71(1) applies, because C does become absolutely entitled.

Section 72(1) applies only on the death of the person entitled to the life interest and provides that there is no charge to tax, but there is an uplift in the base cost in the same way as section 73 operates in relation to a section 71 charge.[15] There is still an uplift (and no charge to tax) even if the property is exempt from inheritance tax (*e.g.* because the property passes from a deceased husband to his widow). There is no charge under section 72 (or uplift) where the life interest terminates otherwise then on a death, *e.g.* by a surrender. Only section 71 can apply in that case if someone becomes absolutely entitled.

The expression "life interest" includes (*per* section 72(4)) a right under the settlement for the life of a person other than the person entitled to the right. Thus, if A (who is a life tenant) assigns his interest to X, X has an interest during the continued life of A, and X's interest is a "life interest." (The technical description of X's interest is that it is an interest *pur autre vie*.)

This raises an important point. The exemption from charge given by section 73(1)(a) and the base uplift given by section 72 (which we have just been speaking about) only apply where the event causing a person to become absolutely entitled or causing the termination of a life interest is the death of the person *entitled* to the life interest. If A is life tenant (with remainder to B) and A dies still holding the life tenancy, there is no charge to capital gains tax, only an uplift. But if A (life tenant) assigns his interest to X, there is a charge when A dies. B becomes absolutely entitled, and section 71(1) imposes a charge to tax. The charge is not relieved by section 73(1)(a) for the reason that B's becoming absolutely entitled is not caused by the death of the person *entitled* to the life interest because A was not (at death) *entitled* to it. Similarly, if A is life tenant under a settlement for A for life, then for B for life, then for C absolutely. If A is still holding the life tenancy when he dies there is the termination of a life interest and

---

[15] Section 72 applies to a life interest in part of the settled property. This includes any form of joint interest: *Pexton v. Bell* (1975) (C.A.).

an uplift of the base price, because the termination arises on the death of the person entitled. But if A had assigned his life interest to X there is a charge on A's death; section 72(1) does not apply and there is no uplift of the base price.

The charge to tax under section 71(1) which arises on the death of a former life tenant who has assigned his interest will be in addition to a charge to inheritance tax.

Conversely (as explained earlier) where a life tenant dies without having assigned his interest there will be no charge to capital gains tax and there may be no charge to inheritance tax either. This will be so, for example, where the property passes from a husband to his widow.

TRANSFERS BETWEEN TRUSTS

Trustees are liable for capital gains tax in respect of their own settlement. By virtue of section 69 the trustees for the time being are regarded as one body for this purpose, so that there is no charge on a change of trustees. The position is more complex, however, where under a power in the settlement the trustees transfer assets to another trust, of which they may or may not be the trustees. The crucial question is whether the second settlement can be regarded as a separate settlement or as merely a subsidiary part of the first. If they are separate settlements then it appears that the trustees of the second trust will become absolutely entitled as against the trustees of the first, and an exit charge can be made under section 71(1), discussed above. In *Hoare Trustees v. Gardner* (1978) the judge decided that the second trustees need not be beneficially entitled as against the original trustees, nor did the section require them to be absolutely entitled as against the whole world (clearly they were not so as against the second beneficiaries). This was so even though the trustees of both trusts were identical.

If the second settlement is, however, merely a subsidiary of the first trust then the trustees of either trust will be liable for the gains of both but there will be no exit charge. This has been a particularly useful device for the Revenue, where one set of trustees is non-resident and so not chargeable to the tax. In *Roome v. Edwards* (1982) Lord Wilberforce laid down the test to determine whether there are one or two settlements as follows: "The question whether a particular set of facts amounts to a settlement should be approached by asking what a person, with knowledge of the legal content of the word under established doctrine and applying this knowledge in a practical and common-sense manner to the facts

Capital Gains Tax

under examination would conclude." In that case, since the original settlement was still in existence and the second settlement was treated as being held on the trusts of the first as added to and varied by the first, the two settlements could be treated as one.

Each case depends upon its facts and there are no golden rules. Separate administration and separate trust accounts may be relevant.[16] In *Bond v. Pickford* (1983) the Court of Appeal drew a distinction between transferring property under a power which altered the operative trusts of a settlement, thus allowing removal of the assets from the original settlement altogether (*i.e.* powers in the wider form), and powers in a narrower form which do not confer such authority. In that case a power to allocate funds for discretionary beneficiaries which were subject to the rules of the trust was held to be a narrower form power. The trustees of the original settlement continued to be responsible in that capacity for the allocated funds. The Revenue have indicated in a Statement of Practice (SP 7/84) that there will not be a charge under section 71(1) (and so no separate settlement) if there is an exercise of a power in the wider form if either it is revocable or where the trusts declared are not exhaustive so that they may at some time come back into the trusts or reference still has to be made to the trustees' original powers of administration or disposition. There will equally be no deemed disposal if the duties of the trustees of the second settlement fall to the trustees as trustees of the first. Separate identity of the trustees is irrelevant, as is the location of the mechanical powers of the trustees. However, in *Swires v. Renton* (1991), Hoffman J. suggested that even if the funds were transferred under a wider form power the question remained as to whether there was a new settlement or whether it was being "grafted onto" the existing settlement. If any reference back to the original settlement was required then this would indicate that no new settlement had been created.

TAX POSITION OF THE BENEFICIARIES

The legislation is not notably generous to trustees or beneficiaries, but beneficiaries do have one crumb of comfort. It is to be found in section 76(1). If a person is holding an interest under a settlement and that interest was created for his benefit, no chargeable gain arises if he disposes of his interest. Thus, suppose property is held in

---

[16] Vinelott J. in *Ewart v. Taylor* (1983) regarded this as an important factor together with the fact that the transfer to the second settlement was part of a scheme to wind up the first, in finding that the two settlements were separate.

SETTLED PROPERTY

trust for A for life with remainder to B absolutely. If A assigns (*e.g.* sells) his life interest that is not a chargeable event. The same is true if B sells his remainder interest. And if it happens that B dies while A is still alive, B's personal representatives can sell B's remainder interest without tax arising. But a person who acquired an interest for consideration in money or money's worth (other than consideration consisting of another interest under the settlement) and then sold the interest is liable to tax on any gain involved. So if X bought A's life interest (or B's remainder interest) and then sold it at a gain he would be liable to tax. And if X, having bought B's remainder interest and still holding it when A died, would be treated as disposing of the remainder interest in consideration of obtaining the settled property itself and so a charge to tax would arise: section 76(2).

This legislation permits adjustments of the interest of several beneficiaries amongst themselves without a charge to tax arising. "Partition" of settled property is quite a common occurrence. A, a life tenant, may surrender his life interest in part of the trust property in return for an interest in the capital. A is not treated as acquiring his interest in capital for money or money's worth because he has acquired it in exchange for "another interest" (*i.e.* his life interest) "under the settlement" and that does not count as money or money's worth. Consequently if A were to carry out the above transaction and then sell his interest in capital (a remainder interest) at a gain, he would not be liable to tax.

PAYMENT OF THE TAX

A beneficiary may become liable to pay tax which has been assessed on the trustees. This will be so where the tax is not paid within six months of its due date and the asset concerned or a part of it or the proceeds of it are transferred by the trustees to the beneficiary. He can be assessed at any time within two years from the due date on the chargeable gain or, in the case of a transfer of a part, on a proportionate part of the chargeable gain; section 69(4).

CHAPTER 17

COMPUTING GAINS AND LOSSES

Putting it very broadly the amount of a chargeable gain or of an allowable loss is arrived at by comparing the consideration received on the disposal of an asset with the cost of its acquisition. What we must now do is to look in more detail at the way in which the computation is done. If the asset is a foreign asset the consideration received and the costs of acquisition must be converted into sterling at the rate of exchange applicable at each event so that the gain or loss will be affected by fluctuations in exchange rates.[1] And by section 29(1) a loss is to be computed in the same way as a gain.

We will look first at the general rules of computation laid down in Part II, Chapter I (sections 15 to 20) and Chapter III (sections 37 to 52) of the Act. Next we will look at the rules for index linking (inflation relief) in Chapter IV (sections 53 to 57) and then at the special rules where the asset disposed of was owned by the taxpayer on March 31, 1982 (section 35 and Schedule 3) and the further special rules, now much less important, where it was owned on April 6, 1965 (Schedule 2). Finally we look at the position where the computation produces a loss rather than a gain. At this stage it should be remembered that no gains accruing before March 31, 1982 are taxable and that indexation relief is available to offset the effects of inflation after that date.

General Rules

Income receipts and expenditure

First, there is to be excluded from the consideration for a disposal any sum which is taken into account for income tax (section 3). An example would be the whole of the consideration for the sale of an asset by a dealer in such assets. Another example would be that part

---

[1] *Bentley v. Pike* (1981); *Capcount Trading v. Evans* (1993) (C.A.). This is not the position with regard to income taxation.

of a lease premium which was chargeable to income tax. Special rules apply to assets which have enjoyed capital allowances.

Similarly expenditure which would be allowable in an income tax computation is not allowable for capital gains tax (section 39). In making this decision the section requires that the asset is presumed to be a fixed asset of a trade and the question asked whether the expenditure would have been allowable in an income tax computation of that, hypothetical, trade (the statutory hypothesis).[2] Since under income tax law extensive repairs may be carried out to an asset and still be allowable for that tax, (*Odeon Cinemas Ltd v. Jones* (1972)), this, in practice, restricts many claims.

Consideration

This is basically the gross money price paid.[3] If the consideration is in money's worth it can be valued (exchange of assets is a disposal). As we have seen, under section 48, where the consideration is to be paid in instalments the whole purchase price is treated as the consideration at the time of disposal with no discount for the delay in payment or the possibility that it might not be paid at all. Remember also that where the consideration cannot be valued it will be taken to be the market value of the asset. That rule, in section 17, also applies to gifts and sales at an undervalue.

Allowable expenditure

The gain (or loss) is computed by deducting the allowable expenditure from the consideration. As we shall see the expenditure may be increased to take account of inflation. Section 38(1) provides the following heads:

(a) the cost of acquisition of the asset (together with the incidental costs) or, if the asset was not acquired, the expenditure incurred in producing it (*e.g.* the expenditure incurred in writing a book and thereby creating a copyright). Where the taxpayer acquired the asset on a market value disposal to him, *e.g.* a gift, that will form his acquisition cost;

---

[2] See, *e.g. Emmerson v. Computer Time International* (1977) (C.A.).
[3] See, *e.g. Fielder v. Vedlynn Ltd* (1992).

(b) the expenditure incurred for the purpose of enhancing the value of the asset (*e.g.* extensions to a building) and expenditure incurred in establishing, preserving or defending one's title to, or right over, the asset (*e.g.*, the costs involved in taking out probate);
(c) the incidental costs of making the disposal.[4]

The expenditure under (a) and (b) must be "wholly and exclusively" for the acquisition of the asset or for establishing, preserving or defending title to the asset. This has enabled the court to disallow an acquisition cost where acquiring the asset was part of an avoidance scheme,[5] but in *IRC v. Richard's Executors* (1971) the House of Lords, by a narrow majority, held that those words must be given a reasonable interpretation in allowing the costs of obtaining a valuation for estate duty purposes as an expense establishing title since such a valuation was a necessary prerequisite for obtaining their title to the estate.

Expenditure or consideration received on two or more assets may be apportioned between those assets if it is just and reasonable, so that where a company sold the shares of a subsidiary company and agreed to waive a debt owed to it by that subsidiary, the consideration received for the sale of the shares was held to be divisible between the two disposals—the sale of the shares and the waiver of the debt: *Aberdeen Construction Group Ltd v. IRC* (1978). If, however, the consideration for the shares and the waiver are expressed as separate sums no further adjustment can be made: *Booth (E.V.) (Holdings) Ltd v. Buckwell* (1980).

In the absence of fraud or collusion the acquisition cost (base price) is the value placed on the amount provided by the parties in the contract. Thus if an asset is acquired by a company issuing new shares, credited as fully paid up, to the vendor, it is the value placed on those shares by the parties which forms the acquisition cost of the company for any subsequent disposal: *Stanton v. Drayton Commercial Investment Co. Ltd* (1982). The Revenue's argument that market value should apply was rejected. Expenditure, to be allowable, however, must be in money or money's worth. In *Oram v. Johnson* (1980) personal work by the taxpayer on renovating an old cottage was not allowed as an expense as enhancing the value of the

---

[4] Inheritance tax payable on a gift may also be allowable if a claim is made for roll-over relief on a gift of business assets; see the following chapter.
[5] *Eilbeck v. Rawling* (1982).

asset; nothing had passed out from the taxpayer. If he had used a builder the expenditure would have been allowable.

In *Couch v. Administrators of the Estate of Caton* (1996), it was held that whilst the cost of employing a valuer to value shares in a private company was allowable as an incidental cost of their disposal, subsequent costs in negotiating that value with the Revenue and in (successfully) appealing against an assessment were not so allowable.

It will be recalled that there are many instances where there is deemed to be a disposal (and re-acquisition). Can there be incidental costs of such a notional disposal? Section 38(4) says (rather laconically):

> "Any provision ... introducing the assumption that assets are sold and immediately re-acquired shall not imply that any expenditure is incurred as incidental to the sale or re-acquisition."

It has been held in the courts that real expenditure on a notional disposal is allowable (*e.g.* legal costs), but that notional expenditure is not. Real lawyers' fees could arise, for example, in respect of a deemed disposal and re-acquisition by trustees on the death of a life tenant. Such real fees are deductible. But where the deemed disposal and re-acquisition arises because the asset in question was held by the taxpayer on March 31, 1982 (see p. 260 below) the taxpayer cannot say: "If I had really sold and re-bought the shares on the stock exchange on that day I would have incurred brokers' fees and stamp duty, and I claim to deduct those notional expenses."

Certain kinds of expenditure are not deductible, notably expenditure on insuring an asset in respect of damage, injury, loss or depreciation. Another notable non-allowable expenditure is the payment of interest (except as provided by section 40 in relation to loans for construction work taken out by companies where the resulting building, etc. is being disposed of).

A word must be said about Value Added Tax. If VAT has been suffered on the purchase of an asset but that VAT is available as input tax for set-off in the purchaser's VAT account, the cost of the asset for the purposes of capital gains tax will be the cost exclusive of VAT. Where no VAT set-off is available, the cost will be inclusive of the VAT which has been borne. Where an asset is disposed of any VAT chargeable as output tax will be disregarded in computing the capital gain (because the disporter will have to pay over the VAT to Customs and Excise). If the disporter is not selling in the course of a

Computing Gains and Losses

business VAT is not chargeable. VAT which is payable for services (such as stockbrokers' services) is deductible as part of the incidental costs. (See the Revenue's Statement of Practice 8/73.)

Part disposals

Where there is a part disposal the amounts of acquisition or production expenditure (see (a) above) and subsequent expenditure (see (b) above) have to be apportioned between the part disposed of and the part retained (section 42). The apportionment is done by applying to the total of expenditure the fraction

$$\frac{A}{A + B}$$

where A is the consideration for the part disposal and B is the market value of the property retained. To take an example, suppose Mr Smith owns an asset which has a base cost of £10,000 and he sells part of that asset for £7,000 and the market value of the part he retains is £21,000. The "attributable" expenditure is:

$$£10,000 \times \frac{£7,000}{£7,000 + £21,000} = £2,500$$

So the gain on this part disposal is £4,500 (*i.e.* the difference between the sale consideration (£7,000) and the attributable expenditure (£2,500)). The balance of expenditure (£7,500) which was not allowed on this part disposal is carried forward for use on any future disposal of the part of the asset which was retained.

Wasting assets

There is a restriction on the amount of expenditure that may be deducted in respect of what are called "wasting assets". A wasting asset means (*per* section 44(1)) an asset which has a predictable life not exceeding 50 years. Plant and machinery are expressly regarded as having a life not exceeding 50 years. The residual or scrap value of the asset is deducted from the acquisition cost and the resulting sum is written-off on a straight line basis over the life of the asset. Let us take an example. Suppose Mr Jones bought an asset which had a predictable life of 30 years. He paid £10,000 for it. Ten years later Mr Jones sold the asset for £8,000. It has a scrap value of £1,000.

General Rules

The computation for capital gains tax on the occasion of the sale goes like this:

Proceeds of sale		£8,000
Less: cost	£10,000	
Deduct scrap value	£1,000	
	£9,000	
Deduct amount written-off		
$\frac{10}{30} \times £9,000$	£3,000	
	£6,000	£6,000
	Gross chargeable gain	£2,000

Notice that this procedure, on the above facts, converts what at first sight looked like a loss (cost price £10,000; sale price £8,000) into a gain. The idea behind this is that if you buy a wasting asset and use it for a number of years and then sell it you have had the enjoyment of part of its useful life and you have sold it when its prospective useful life is diminished. So the Act deals with this situation by providing that the buying price must be notionally reduced to take account of the enjoyment of the asset which you have used up.

Amongst other things, a life interest in settled property is a wasting asset when the predictable expectation of life of the life tenant is 50 years or less. The legislation is somewhat inconsistent in that it counteracts by these artificial means the inherent depreciation of a wasting asset, such as a life interest, but it charges in full as an ordinary chargeable gain the inherent appreciation in a naturally appreciating asset such as, for example, a remainder interest.

A lease is a wasting asset when its future duration is 50 years or less.[6] But for leases the straight line basis of writing-off is not used. What is used is a fixed Table set out in Schedule 7. On this Table the line of wastage is curved and it accelerates as the lease approaches its end since leases depreciate more rapidly towards the end of their life.

---

[6] Where a lease for less than 50 years could be extended for 50 years under the Leasehold Reform Act 1967 that does not affect the position of the lease which remains as a wasting asset: *Lewis v. Walters* (1992).

Index-linking of Expenditure

Despite earlier protestations that any form of allowance for the effects of inflation would be too complex and unworkable, sections 53 to 57 provide a form of index-linking of capital gains tax. In essence the relief works by calculating the indexation allowance for each amount of allowable expenditure, *e.g.* acquisition costs and enhancement costs, and then deducting that allowance from the "gross gain", *i.e.* the gain as computed without any such allowance. The allowance is therefore the final, and a separate, step in the computation process. There is one major limitation in that the indexation allowance can only reduce a gross gain to nil, it cannot create or increase a loss: sections 53(1) and 53(2A). That had been possible between 1985 and 1994. Where the asset was acquired prior to March 31, 1982 then indexation only applies from that date (as does the gross gain) based on the market value of the asset at that time: section 55.

Calculation of the indexation allowance

Section 54 provides the basic rules for calculating the indexation allowance available against the gain. It is the *indexed rise* in each item of allowable expenditure, calculated seperately.

The indexed rise is $\dfrac{RD - RI}{RI}$

where RD = Retail Prices Index for the month of disposal and RI = Retail Prices Index for the month of the expenditure. Each item of expenditure must therefore be calculated separately. Because of this, RI will vary according to the expenditure in question. For expenditure incurred after the asset was acquired, RI is the month in which that was first reflected in the nature of state of the asset. To prevent too much mathematical labour the indexed rise need only be calculated to the third decimal place and it is then easier to express it as a percentage. If there should ever be a time of negative inflation RD will be taken to be the same as RI so that the allowable expenditure will not be reduced by this calculation!
Two examples may help:

X disposes of an asset in June 1996 having acquired it in June 1990.

Index-Linking of Expenditure

RD = Retail price index in June 1996 which is, let us say, 654.0.

RI = Retail price index in June 1990 which is, let us say, 512.0.

The indexed rise is $\dfrac{RD(654.0) - RI(512.0)}{RI(512.0)}$

which is equal to 0.2578125 or 0.258 to the third decimal place.

Expressing that as a percentage the indexed rise is therefore 25.8 per cent. We can now apply the indexed rise to the disposal. If X disposed of the asset for £50.000 having paid £20,000 to acquire it then his gross gain, *i.e* without the indexation allowance, will be £30,000. The indexation allowance is £20,000 × 25.8 per cent = £5,160. This will reduce the chargeable gain from £30,000 to £24.840.

Suppose, instead, that X disposed of the asset for £22,000 having paid £20,000 for it. His gross gain would then be £2,000. Although the indexation allowance is still £5,160 on the above figures, the gross gain can only be reduced to nil. £3,160 of relief against inflation has been lost. In real terms X has made a loss. This restriction on indexation relief, introduced as part of the original provisions in 1982, is clearly unfair, which was why it was lifted in 1985, only to reappear again in 1994.

Special rules for shares—pooling arrangements

Before index linking was introduced in 1982 shares of the same class in the same company held by a taxpayer were treated as a single asset, *i.e.* a pool of shares. Every time some were bought they were added to the pool (and the acquisition cost added to the acquisition costs of the pool) and when some were sold they were deducted from the pool and charged as a part disposal of the single pooled asset. Thus if half the shares were sold half the allowable expenditure of the pool was available. In 1982 this simple position was destroyed because of the complex indexation rules. In 1985, however, the system of indexation of shares was changed to reinstate the pooling of shares and to accommodate indexation relief.

The present rules are contained in sections 104 to 114. There are in fact two separate sets of rules: (i) for shares of the same class in the same company acquired after April 5, 1982 (new holdings); and (ii) for such shares acquired before April 6, 1982 (old holdings). These two holdings must therefore be kept separate and cannot be pooled.

New holdings are pooled to form a single asset so that on a disposal the appropriate part of the allowable expenditure is available under the pooling system. But how is the indexation allowance to be calculated? The answer is that after the initial acquisition of shares, when a second batch of identical shares are acquired the existing pool of expenditure (the acquisition cost of the initial purchase) is indexed up to that date. The acquisition cost of the second purchase is then added onto to that indexed figure. This process is repeated every time more shares are acquired. When some or all of the shares are disposed of, the pool of allowable expenditure is indexed up from the last time it was indexed up (on an acquisition or previous disposal) to that date. An appropriate proportion of that indexed pool is then available against the consideration for the disposal. In summary, each time shares are acquired the pool is indexed up from the last time it was so indexed and each time shares are disposed of the pool is indexed up from the last time it was so indexed and an appropriate part is used up. The remaining pool is carried forward.

The pool is indexed up on the same principles as the ordinary indexation relief, *i.e.* by a percentage calculated according to the difference between the RPI of the month the pool was last indexed up (or the month of acquisition of the initial purchase) and the RPI for the month of acquisition or disposal, as appropriate. In technical terms these are known as "operative events" and the indexation relief is calculated each time by the fraction

$$\frac{RE - RL}{RL}$$

where RE is the RPI at an operative event and RL is the RPI at the previous operative event.

Again, no loss can be created or increased by such indexing up.
To take a simple example:

> X acquires 100 ordinary shares in Y plc in 1990 for £1,000. In 1993 he acquires another 100 of those shares for £2,000. The original cost is indexed up from 1990 to 1993 (say 10 per cent) so that it becomes £1,100 and the new cost is added on to give an

Index-Linking of Expenditure

indexed pool of expenditure of £3,100. In 1996 X sells 100 of the shares for £2,500. The allowable pool of expenditure (£3,100) is indexed up from 1993 to 1996 (say 10 per cent again) so that it then stands at £3,410. Since half the shares have been sold, half of that figure is available. X's gain is therefore £2,500–£1,705, *i.e.* £795. The remaining £1,705 is carried forward to the next acquisition or disposal when it will be indexed up again.

Old holdings of shares of the same type in the same company (*i.e.* those owned at March 31, 1982) are treated as a separate single asset.[7] Since, by definition, such a pool cannot be increased by subsequent purchases, indexation relief is applied in the normal way on each disposal of those shares. Another example may show how this works:

X owned 200 ordinary shares in Y plc on March 31, 1982. In March 1996 he sells half of them for £400. His gain is calculated as follows: (i) the unindexed pool of expenditure is the market value of those shares at March 31, 1982, say £100; (ii) that figure is then indexed up from that date to March 1996 (say 50 per cent) so that the total indexed pool of expenditure becomes £150; (iii) X's gain will be calculated as £400–£75 (half the indexed pool), *i.e.* at £325; (iv) the remainder of the unindexed pool (£50) is carried forward to the next disposal where the indexation from March 1982 will be calculated again on that figure.

Although, as we have seen, both new and old holdings of shares are treated as a single asset the Act (section 107) provides three identification rules on the disposal of shares within either of the two pools. When such shares are disposed of they are to be identified as follows: (i) with any such shares acquired on the same day; (ii) then with any such shares acquired within the previous 10 days; (iii) and then with any such shares on a last in, first out basis. The effect of (i) and (ii) would be that no indexation is allowable and the practical effect of (iii), which means that the most recently acquired shares are deemed to have been disposed of first, is that where a taxpayer has both old and new holdings of the same shares he is presumed to exhaust the new holding before the old holding.

The wording of rule (ii) allows one simple tax planning device to continue to operate. This is known as "bed and breakfasting". It

---

[7] Those owned on April 6, 1965 are subject to special rules (see below).

involves the sale of a number of shares on the market at the close of business on one day and their repurchase on the market at the start of trading the following day. Thus there will be a disposal which if it gives rise to a gain will have been calculated not to exceed the taxpayer's exempt amount for the year. Thus there will be no actual charge to tax but the taxpayer's base cost will be increased by the repurchase cost. Without this the taxpayer would not be able to take advantage of the annual exemption. The reason why this works is that rule (ii) applies to an acquisition followed by a disposal within ten days, but this is a disposal followed by an acquisition.

No gain, no loss situations

In certain cases, as we have seen, there is a deemed disposal on a no gain, no loss basis—*e.g.* transfer by an executor to a legatee or between spouses. In such cases it is now to be assumed that a gain accrues to the transferor equal to the indexation allowance on the disposal which, higher, figure forms the basic price of the transferee. Where the deemed disposal would otherwise have resulted in a loss no indexation relief is available in forming the base price of the transferee: section 56.

Assets Held on March 31, 1982

Section 35 takes all gains accrued before March 31, 1982 out of the charge to tax. That date was chosen because indexation relief applies from that point. Section 35 (2) accordingly provides that where a taxpayer disposes of an asset which he held on March 31,1982 then "in computing ... the gain or the loss accruing on the disposal it shall be assumed that the asset was on March 31, 1982 sold by the person making the disposal, and immediately reacquired by him, at its market value". Thus the base price of that asset is uplifted to its market value at that date. Thus it can be said to have been "rebased" to March 1982. Where the taxpayer has acquired the asset after March 31, 1982 on a no gain/no loss transfer, *e.g.* as between spouses, from a transferor who owned the asset on March 31, 1982, the transferee is also deemed to have owned it then and rebasing will apply.

Given the constant presence of inflation in the period before 1982, rebasing to March 31, 1982 will almost certainly reduce the gain from what it would have been without such rebasing, *i.e.* by taking the original cost as the base price. But certain assets fluctuate in value irrespective of underlying inflation and it is possible, for

Assets Held on March 31, 1982

example, that an asset was actually worth less in March 1982 than when it was originally purchased. In such a case rebasing would actually increase the gain. There are therefore two exceptions to this rebasing rule.

First, where a computation without rebasing would have produced a loss and a computation with rebasing would produce a gain, or vice versa, then the disposal is treated as one which has made neither a gain nor a loss. Secondly, where a computation without rebasing would have produced a smaller gain or a smaller loss than one using rebasing, then that smaller gain or loss is to be chargeable or allowable as the case may be. In working out the computation without rebasing, indexation relief must be taken into account from 31 March 1982 calculated on the higher of the market value of the asset at that time or the original base cost (section 55 (2)).

To take some simple examples of all this (ignoring indexation relief):

1. A buys a painting for £10,000 in 1976. Its market value in March 1982 is £15,000 and he sells it in 1996 for £20,000. Rebasing will apply so that the gain is £5,000 and not £10,000.

2. B buys a painting for £10,000 in 1976. Its market value in March 1982 is £30,000 and he sells it in 1996 for £20,000. Rebasing would then produce a loss of £10,000 whereas without rebasing there would be a gain of £10,000. Accordingly there is neither a gain nor a loss.

3. C buys a painting for £10,000 in 1976. Its market value in March 1982 is £5,000 and he sells it in 1996 for £20,000. Rebasing would then produce a gain of £15,000 whereas without rebasing there would be a gain of £10,000. Since without rebasing there would be a smaller gain than on rebasing, that smaller gain will be chargeable.

Note that under these rules if rebasing produces a smaller loss than non-rebasing that smaller loss is the only one which is allowable—the non-rebasing alternative is only available if that produces a smaller loss.

Where the asset was held on April 6, 1965 there are special rules for computing the non-rebased gain for comparison with the rebased gain. These are dealt with in the next part of this chapter.

All this is very complex and requires taxpayers to keep records relating to events prior to March 1982. Accordingly any taxpayer may elect that rebasing will apply to all disposals made by him of all assets held by him at March 31, 1982. Once made this election cannot be revoked and it must be a blanket election. It is a matter of mathematics to work out whether any particular taxpayer should make such an election, which must be made within two years of the first such disposal: section 35 (5).

Assets Held on April 6, 1965

Capital gains tax has never applied to gains accruing before April 6, 1965, the date when the tax first came into effect. There have always therefore been special rules where a taxpayer is disposing of an asset which he held on that date and these can now be found in Schedule 2. Obviously, however, since, as we have seen, all pre-March 31, 1982 assets can be rebased to that date, those rules have been largely superseded by the 1982 rebasing provisions. Those provisions do, however, require a computation to be made without such rebasing for comparison purposes so that if the asset is a pre-April 6, 1965 asset the rules in Schedule 2 will be used for that purpose.

The basic rule for computing the comparative gain or loss of a pre-April 6, 1965 asset is known as the straight line apportionment rule. This involves taking the original cost of the asset as the base cost, calculating the gain over the whole period and then apportioning the gain between the period of ownership prior to April 6, 1965 and that after April 5, 1965 on a straight line basis. That gain will then be used as the comparison with the 1982 rebased gain in applying the 1982 rebasing rules. For example:

D buys a painting for £1,000 in April 1955 and sells it for £41,000 in April 1995. The total gain (ignoring indexation relief) is £40,000. This was accrued over a 40-year period, 10 of which were prior to April 1965 and 30 after that date. Thus 30/40ths of the gain is deemed to have accrued after April 1965 and so £30,000 is the chargeable gain. If the painting had a market-value of £50,000 in March 1982 (it was in fashion then) rebasing to that date would produce a loss of £9,000. Accordingly under the 1982 rebasing rules since one method produces a gain and the other a loss there would be neither a loss nor a gain.

One complication in making the straight line apportionment computation is the impact of indexation relief. This must be calculated on the asset's market value at March 31, 1982. But is it to be applied after the gain has been time-apportioned or before? To see the difference, in the example above suppose the indexation relief is £4,000. If that is taken off after the time apportionment it will reduce the gain from £30,000 to £26,000. If it is taken off before then the total gain of £40,000 will be reduced to £36,000 and three-quarters of that will be chargeable, *i.e.* £27,000. In *Smith v. Schofield* (1993) the House of Lords reluctantly held that on the wording of Schedule 2 the latter was the correct procedure despite the fact that it attributed post-1982 inflation relief to gains made before the tax was even introduced.

There are special rules for quoted shares owned since April 6, 1985. For such shares the general rule is that the alternative gain for the 1982 rebasing rules is to be computed by reference to their 1965 values. In effect they are rebased to April 1965. But if using their original cost price would produce a smaller gain or loss that will be used and if it would produce a gain rather than a loss or vice versa then there is neither a gain nor a loss. As a simpler alternative the taxpayer may elect to have all such shares computed on the rebasing to 1965 method in which case the original cost becomes irrelevant. They will then be pooled into a single asset and become an old holding of shares for indexation purposes (see p. 257, above).

There are also special rules for land owned on April 6, 1965 which had development value.

Losses

We want to collect together under this heading certain leading points about losses. Some of the points have been mentioned before; some are new.

Losses are computed in the same way as gains are computed; section 16(1). Remember that indexation relief cannot create or increase a loss, it can only reduce a gain.

If a transaction is such that a gain (if there had been one) would not be a chargeable gain, then if a loss occurs (instead of a gain) that loss is not an allowable loss; section 16(2). This provision has some very important consequences. A good example arises in connection with the disposal of gilt-edged securities or qualifying corporate bonds (see p. 267, below).

Capital gains tax is charged on the total amount of chargeable gains in a year of assessment after deducting any allowable losses. Any surplus of losses over gains in a year of assessment may be carried forward to future years. Both these points are to be found in

Computing Gains and Losses

section 2(2). If in any year a person has a taxable amount (chargeable gains minus allowable losses) (see p. 222, above) not exceeding the exempt amount for that year (see p. 221, above) the accumulated losses of earlier years are not required to be used in eliminating that taxable amount. For example if at the end of year 1 a person has accumulated losses of £5,000, and in year 2 his taxable amount is £4,000, no part of the £5,000 needs to be used in knocking down the £4,000 to nil. He goes forward into year 3 with his accumulation of losses (£5,000) intact: section 3(5)(a). Similarly, if his taxable amount in year 2 had been £8,000, he need only use so much of his accumulated losses as is needed to reduce that taxable amount to the exempt amount (£6,300 in 1996–97). So he would go, on that basis, into year 3 with an accumulation of losses of £2,300: section 3(5)(b). The same principle applies to losses carried *back* from the year in which an individual dies. (See p. 241, above.) Note that in no other circumstances can losses be carried back.

Losses incurred in a disposal to a "connected person" are only allowable against gains made on subsequent disposals to the same connected person: section 18(3).

A loss only becomes allowable when it is realised.[8] On the stock exchange one way of realising a loss is by means of the practice we have already mentioned (p. 259), called "bed and breakfasting". If an investor has made substantial gains in a particular tax year he can neutralise the gains by selling some shares at a loss near the end of the tax year and buying them back the next day.

---

[8] But remember the deemed disposed provisions where an asset has been destroyed, extinguished or became of negligible value where an allowable loss may be claimed. See p. 230, above.

CHAPTER 18

EXEMPTIONS AND RELIEFS

An exemption arises where either some asset is expressed not to be a chargeable asset or some gain is expressed not to be a chargeable gain. A relief arises where although there is a chargeable asset and a chargeable gain the full amount of tax is not exacted or the chargeable gain is postponed. Remember that there is an annual exemption for all gains accruing to an individual up to the exempt amount for the year in question. This chapter deals with the more important exemptions and reliefs.

Hold-over Relief for Gifts Immediately Chargeable to Inheritance Tax

Between 1980 and 1989 all gifts between individuals were eligible for what is known as hold-over relief from capital gains tax. This was because gifts were also subject to inheritance tax and it was thought inequitable to apply both taxes. This general relief was, however, abolished in 1989 on the (slightly flawed) basis that inheritance tax now rarely applies to lifetime gifts. Hold-over relief still applies to gifts of business assets (dealt with at p.277 below) and gifts which attract an immediate charge to inheritance tax. It also applies to some specific types of gift which are exempt from inheritance tax. Before we look at this current relief it is important to understand the concept of a hold-over relief since it applies in other areas we shall come to (gifts of business assets, replacement of business assets, reinvestment relief).

Hold-over relief works by allowing the amount of the chargeable gain which would otherwise be payable on a disposal from A to B to be deducted from the acquisition cost of B rather than chargeable on A. Suppose A buys an asset for £10,000. He disposes of it to B for £15,000. Ignoring indexation relief A would therefore make a gain of £5,000. If hold-over relief is available then instead of charging that gain on the disposal, B will be deemed to have acquired the asset for £10,000 (*i.e.* £15,000–£5,000). If B subsequently disposes of the

EXEMPTIONS AND RELIEFS

asset to C for £20,000 he will therefore be treated as having made a gain (again ignoring indexation relief) of £10,000 (£20,000–£10,000). Thus A's original gain of £5,000 and B's actual gain of £5,000 are chargeable on B's disposal to C. In other words hold-over relief postpones or holds over A's gain, it does not exclude it.

If B's disposal to C had also been eligible for hold-over relief then B's gain of £10,000 would not be chargeable but C's acquisition cost would be reduced by that amount, and so on. Thus whilst the general relief for gifts applied it was possible by simply making a series of gifts of an asset to postpone all the gains. If the final donee died so that the asset passed under his will or intestacy those held-over gains would disappear because of the provisions (already dealt with at p.240) whereby his executors would be deemed to acquire the asset at its then market value but make no chargeable gain on transferring the asset to the beneficiary.

Hold-over relief for all types of gift is now only available where the gift would attract an immediate charge to inheritance tax: section 260. This means that the gift must be a chargeable transfer for inheritance tax purposes. It does not apply, however, to gifts which are potentially exempt transfers, because they will only be chargeable to inheritance tax if the donor dies within seven years of making the gift so that there is no immediate charge to the tax. Even if they do then become chargeable no hold-over relief is available. These concepts are discussed at p.327, below, but the effect broadly is that the relief only applies to the creation or termination of a discretionary trust. The relief is not available to companies or where the donee is neither resident nor ordinarily resident in the United Kingdom. Where it applies the relief for gifts of business assets does not apply. A claim for hold-over relief must be made jointly by the donor and donee and if made entitles the parties to postpone the gain in the way set out above.

The relief also applies to bad bargains taxable on full market value under section 17. In that case the amount which can be held-over is the difference between the price paid and the market value, *i.e.* the gift element. Finally we should note that the relief is available to certain gifts which are exempt from inheritance tax altogether thus taking them outside the tax net. These include gifts to political parties and to maintenance funds for historic houses.

Some Miscellaneous Exemptions

Private motor cars are not chargeable assets. It was just not worth the effort of trying to tax them. Nor are savings certificates or premium bonds chargeable, nor betting winnings.

There is no chargeable gain when a person disposes of foreign currency which he had acquired for personal expenditure abroad.

Sums obtained by way of compensation or damages for any wrong or injury suffered by an individual in his person or in his profession are not chargeable gains. Were it not for this provision, the law might otherwise produce the slightly macabre result that someone who received compensation for, for example, an injury at work, would be regarded as part-disposing of himself for CGT purposes.

There are also exemptions for gains on shares held in a Personal Equity Plan.

Gilt-edged Securities and Qualifying Corporate Bonds

A gain is not a chargeable gain if it accrues on the disposal of certain specified gilt-edged securities: see sections 115, 117 and Schedule 9. The list of specified gilt-edged securities has been added to from time to time by statutory instrument and now comprises virtually all government stocks. At first sight this seems a generous gesture on the part of the Revenue, and it was probably introduced to give a boost to the gilt-edged market, but as things have turned out losses have been much commoner than gains in dealings on the gilt-edged market, and the rule that where no chargeable gain (if there had been a gain) would have arisen there can be no allowable loss has meant that this exemption has mainly operated to prohibit losses rather than to exempt gains. Qualifying corporate bonds are defined to include normal non-convertible corporate debentures. A loss may still be recoverable by individuals on such bonds in certain circumstances.

Life Assurance and Deferred Annuities

In principle the receipt of policy monies under a policy of life assurance, or the receipt of the first instalment of a deferred annuity, is a disposal (a disposal of the right in return for the money). But no chargeable gain arises where the money is paid to the original holder of the policy or his personal representatives or trustees. Nor is there a chargeable gain if he surrenders (or they surrender) the policy. But

EXEMPTIONS AND RELIEFS

if the policy is assigned for money or money's worth (*e.g.* sold) and then the policy money is paid to the assignee (or the policy is surrendered) that is a chargeable event. This matter is dealt with by section 210.

Private Residences

This point is dealt with in sections 222–226. A gain on the disposal by an individual of a dwelling-house or part of a dwelling-house is not a chargeable gain if the house was the individual's only or main residence. This exemption in practice takes most people's main asset out of the charge to capital gains tax and is extremely important in practice in a country where most families now own their own homes. But the benevolence does not extend (as we shall see) to inheritance tax; for that tax a private residence is no different from other property. The capital gains tax exemption does not apply if the house was acquired wholly or partly for the purpose of realising a gain from its disposal: section 224(3).

To get the full capital gains tax exemption the house must have been the individual's only or main residence throughout his period of ownership, ignoring any period of ownership prior to March 31, 1982, except that it does not matter if it has not been such for all or any part of the last 36 months of his ownership. The point of this exception is (we take it) to meet the case where an individual has moved to a new house before he has been able to sell his old one. If the house has not been the taxpayer's only or main residence throughout his period of ownership a fraction of the gain is exempted corresponding to the period of occupation. In certain circumstances a period of absence can be disregarded. These include periods, where the taxpayer was employed abroad and any period not exceeding three years. Where the taxpayer has to live in job-related accommodation the exemption will apply to a house bought as a future main residence even if he never lives in it.

What amounts to a dwelling-house or part of a dwelling-house for this purpose has been the subject of several cases. It has been held to include a caravan (admittedly connected to mains services),[1] but this is always a question of fact.[2]

---

[1] *Makins v. Elson* (1977)
[2] *Moore v. Thompson* (1986), where the caravan was not connected to main services and only occupied sporadically it was held not to come within the exemption.

More difficulties arise as to what amounts to part of a dwelling-house. This has for example been held to include the disposal of a bungalow built in the grounds of a house for the gardener and housekeeper[3] so that a dwelling-house can consist of more than one building. The criteria applied to decide whether the building being disposed of is part of the dwelling house or a separate entity have varied. Initially the question asked was whether the two buildings together formed an entity so that taken together they could form a dwelling-house. Thus in *Williams v. Merrylees* (1987) Vinelott J. held that a lodge built some 200 yards from the main house could form part of a single dwelling-house with the main house, the dwelling-house being split up into different buildings fulfilling different functions. The scale and layout of the buildings was important. But in the same year, Walton J. applied a much more precise (and restrictive) test in *Markey v. Saunders* (1987). To succeed in a claim for relief the taxpayer would have to show that the second building (i) increased the taxpayer's enjoyment of the first dwelling; and (ii) was very closely adjacent to it. Since the employee's bungalow in that case was a long way from the main house and was screened from it, the judge was able to decide that it did not form part of the taxpayer's dwelling-house.

The Court of Appeal in *Lewis v. Lady Rook* (1992) seem to have adopted this narrower geographical (or proximity) approach as opposed to the entity approach. The test set out in that case was to ask whether the building being sold was within the curtilage of, and appurtenant to, the main building so as to constitute an entity which could be described as a dwelling-house. The Court of Appeal were cheerfully of the opinion that everyone would know what the curtilage of a house was, but it is nowhere defined in the tax legislation.[4] Because of this uncertainty more litigation on this issue may follow. In *Honour v. Norris* (1992) the above test was said to be applicable to the "country house" situation but not to the facts of that case. The taxpayer had acquired four separate flats in a block of flats and the fourth, acquired to accommodate their grown up children and their guests, was sold separately. The judge refused to

---

[3] *Batey v. Wakefield* (1981)
[4] There are many cases in other areas as to what amounts to the curtilage of a building. One example, for the purposes of the Housing Act 1980, is the definition laid down in *Dyer v. Dorset County Council* (1988) that the curtilage is a small area of land which is part and parcel of the building it contains or is attached to it.

lay down any general test for such urban cases. On the facts the fourth flat had never formed part of a single entity—it had been acquired as a separate unit conveniently close to the others. It was like a country house owner acquiring a bungalow in the nearby village. The exemption also applies to land occupied and enjoyed with the dwelling house, up to half a hectare in area. If this land is disposed of separately from the house it must be disposed of first, otherwise it will no longer be occupied and enjoyed with the house at the time of its disposal.[5] A larger area may be allowed if it is required for the reasonable enjoyment of the house, given the size and character of the house: section 222.

If the gain accrues from a disposal of a dwelling-house part of which is used exclusively for the purposes of a trade or business or of a profession or vocation the exemption applies only to that part of the gain which falls to be apportioned to the "private" part of the house. (This is a point to be weighed against the income tax advantage of claiming that a part of one's house is being used exclusively for business, etc., purposes.) Similar provisions apply to any reconstruction, conversion or change of use of the property, but it seems that such events will only justify an apportionment if they amount to a change in the taxpayer's occupation[6]: section 224.

If the owner lets his house during his period of ownership the part of the gain attributable to that period is chargeable on a straight line basis (*e.g.* owned 10 years during which it was let for two, one-fifth of the total gain is chargeable). Further relief is available under section 223(4) where the house is let as residential accommodation.[7] The chargeable gain is then reduced by the lower of the exempt gain (*i.e.* four-fifths of the gain in the example above or £40,000. In practice lodgers are not treated as affecting the relief.

The exemption also applies to occupation of a dwelling-house held under a settlement by a person entitled to occupy it under the settlement: section 225. Usually this will be the life tenant but it can include a beneficiary under a discretionary trust where the trustees have a power to allow this.[8]

A married couple can only have one residence or main residence. If they are not separated it is no good claiming that Mon Repos is the

---

[5] *Varty v. Lynes* (1976).
[6] *IRC v. Green* (1982).
[7] This includes taking in hotel guests: *Owen v. Elliott* (1990).
[8] *Sansom v. Peay* (1976).

man's main residence and Dunromin is the wife's main residence: section 222(6). Where a taxpayer, or a husband and wife, have two or more residences, they must choose which is to be the "main" residence. This choice must be made within two years of the acquisition of a second or subsequent residence in which case it will be backdated for that period. In *Griffin v. Craig-Harvey* (1993) the court held that the taxpayer had no right to make an election after two years from the second acquisition, a decision which leaves many taxpayers out of time to make an election. If there is no election the inspector of taxes can decide which is the taxpayer's main residence.

Chattels Disposed of for £6,000 or Less

Section 262 provides that "a gain accruing on a disposal of an asset which is tangible movable property (*i.e.* a chattel) shall not be a chargeable gain if the amount or value of the consideration for the disposal does not exceed £6,000." Section 262 does not apply to a disposal of currency of any description, nor to a disposal of commodities by a person dealing on a terminal market. A terminal market is not defined but it means a market in which you can buy or sell, *e.g.* cocoa, for a price fixed now but for delivery at some future date (*e.g.* three months hence). It is sometimes called a futures market. Notice that the figure of £6,000 refers to the amount of the consideration, not to the amount of the gain.

Where the amount of the consideration exceeds £6,000 there shall be excluded from any chargeable gain so much of it as exceeds five-thirds of the difference between the consideration and £6,000.

These provisions are very generous to such inflation hedges as stamp collecting. It is nice to be able to sell a stamp from your collection for £6,000, making a gain of say £1,000, without attracting tax or biting into the annual exemption.

But the section is far from generous as regards losses. If there is a disposal at a loss, and the consideration for the disposal is less than £6,000, the consideration is deemed to be £6,000. Thus if a chattel was bought for £6,200 and sold for £5,800 the actual loss (£400) is not allowable; the loss relief is limited to £200.

If two or more assets forming part of a set of article (say a set of Chippendale chairs) are disposed of by the same seller to the same buyer (or to different buyers who are acting in concert or who are connected persons) whether on the same or different occasions, the two or more transactions are treated as a single transaction.

EXEMPTIONS AND RELIEFS

The disposals of two (or more) quite separate articles qualify separately for the relief. It is no bar to getting the relief that you have (in the same year) sold a table for £6,000 and a stamp for £6,000, or even for that matter two unconnected stamps for £6,000 each.

Works of Art, etc.

Section 258 lays down the rather complicated and limited circumstances in which a gain on the disposal of a work of art or similar object is not a chargeable gain. Putting it very broadly the exemption applies where the disposal is such that the work of art is likely to be accessible to the public.

Tangible Movables which are Wasting Assets

No chargeable gain (or, more likely, an allowable loss) shall accrue on the disposal of an asset which is tangible movable property (*i.e.* a chattel) and which is a wasting asset: section 45. It will be recalled that a wasting asset is an asset which has a predictable life not exceeding 50 years. This exemption applies (unlike the exemption mentioned next-but-one above) irrespective of the amount of the disposal consideration. The exemption does not apply to disposal of commodities on a terminal market, nor does it apply to assets used solely in respect of a trade, profession or vocation and in respect of which capital allowances have been, or could have been claimed.

Replacement of Business Assets

Section 152 to 159 are the operative sections here. They provide not a complete exemption from tax but a relief in the hold-over form. The relief arises when a trader disposes of business assets (of certain types) at a gain, and uses the disposal consideration to acquire replacement assets. The relief is given by allowing the trader to defer payment of tax on the disposal gain and (instead) to deduct the gain which he makes on the disposal of the old assets from the acquisition cost of the new assets. This will have the effect of increasing the tax payable when he comes (if he does) to dispose of the new assets in the future.

To get the relief the trader must acquire the new assets within three years after the disposal (or within 12 months before the disposal). Once the replacement asset is acquired it must be used in the taxpayer's trade at once. Any gap will prevent the relief applying.[9] In *Watton v. Tippett* (1996) no relief was allowed where a trader disposed of part of an asset and claimed to deduct the gain from the cost of the part retained. The original cost for the whole asset could not be severed.

The relief only applies to assets set out in classes in section 155 (which can be added to by a Treasury Order). These are currently: (i) land and buildings; (ii) fixed plant and machinery[10]; (iii) ships; (iv) aircraft; (v) hovercraft; (vi) goodwill; (vii) satellites, space stations and spacecraft (!); and (viii) certain farming quotas. The old and new assets need not be of the same type, however.

There is no relief for a non-resident where the replacement asset is outside the charge to tax because it is outside the United Kingdom: section 159. In addition there is no relief if the new assets were acquired wholly or partly for the purpose of realising a gain from their disposal. There are further restrictions if the replacement asset is a wasting asset.

Where the whole of the proceeds of sale are not reinvested in acquiring a new asset, the amount not reinvested will be treated as a chargeable gain and only the balance will be held over. Similarly where the new asset is only partially used for the purposes of the business the relief will be restricted to the proportion used in the business.[11]

Transfer of Business to a Company

Hold over relief is also available where an unincorporated business (and not just its assets) are transferred to a company in return for shares in the company; ie where the business is incorporated: section 162. The gains on the disposal can be deducted from the acquisition cost of the shares. The company is deemed to acquire the assets at market value (section 17 will apply).[12] Retirement relief (below) may, if available, be deducted first before this relief is applied.

---

[9] See *Campbell Connelly & Co. Ltd v. Barnett* (1993). There are special rules for groups of companies in this respect.
[10] Thus excluding moveable machinery: *Williams v. Evans* (1992).
[11] For an unfortunate example of this restriction see *Todd v. Mudd* (1987).
[12] See, *e.g. Gordon v. IRC* (1991).

EXEMPTIONS AND RELIEFS

Retirement Relief

Under sections 163 and 164 and Schedule 6 so-called retirement relief is available to an individual who is disposing of his business interests. The relief is always known as retirement relief although it is not limited to retirement situations. There are a mass of detailed rules relating to this relief which is immensely important in practice since it lowers the impact of capital gains tax on the transfer of family businesses between the generations. The relief takes the form of excluding what would otherwise be chargeable gains up to a specified cash amount. The following is an outline of how the relief works.

To qualify for the relief the following three elements must be present:

(i) the taxpayer must be either over the age of 50 at the time of the disposal or retiring on the grounds of ill health and must have owned the property for at least one year;
(ii) the disposal must be either a material disposal or another qualifying disposal; and
(iii) the disposal must be of chargeable business assets.

Thus, provided the taxpayer is over the age of 50 he need not be retiring. There are detailed rules on what amounts to a retirement under that age on the grounds of ill-health and the Revenue's decision on that point cannot be appealed. Provided criteria (ii) and (iii) are met such an individual is entitled to claim the relief provided he has owned the property being disposed of for a minimum of one year. But to claim the full amount of the relief he must have owned it for 10 years. (There are provisions which allow successive businesses and ownership of a business between spouses in succession to be included in this total).

If the taxpayer is entitled to the full relief then the chargeable gain will be totally exempt up to an amount of £250,000 and will be exempt as to half of the gain for the next £1 million. The practical effect of this is that the maximum relief which can be claimed on a gain of £1.25 million or above is £625,000. If the taxpayer does not have ten years of ownership then the relief is scaled down proportionately, losing 10 per cent for each year below 10. Thus if the taxpayer has owned the business for five years (*i.e.* half of the 10 required for full relief), he will have total relief on gains up to £125,000 and the half relief on additional gains up to £500,000 (*i.e.*

half the full amounts). The relief is also available if the assets have been "owned" by the holder of an interest in possession under a trust and the disposal is by the trustees.

What then amounts to a material disposal so as to attract this relief? There are three types of material disposal. The first is a disposal of a business or part of a business, e.g. by a sole trader or a partner. The second is a disposal of assets owned by the taxpayer which at the time when the business ceased were in use in that business,[13] provided the business was owned by the taxpayer either on his own or in partnership with others or by his personal company (see below for what that means).

There can be no material disposal under this second head unless the business has ceased. It follows that if the taxpayer is continuing with the business after the disposal of the assets there will be no relief at all unless the disposal of the assets constitutes a disposal of part of the business so as to come within the first head. What constitutes a disposal of part of a business for this purpose has come before the courts on more than one occasion, each time involving a farmer. In *McGregor v. Adcock* (1977), the taxpayer, a farmer, sold five acres of his farm to a property developer and carried on farming the remaining 30 acres. The court rejected his argument that the five acres could form a separate part of his farming business. Fox J. said that the question was whether the disposal had been such as to be "an interference with the whole complex of activities and assets as can be said to amount to a disposal of a business or part of a business". This test has, however, been criticised in each case since as unhelpful[14] and the later cases have simply asked the question whether an identifiable part of the business has been sold.[15]

The third type of material disposal is a disposal of shares in a personal company by a full time working officer or employee of that

---

[13] In *Clarke v. Mayo* (1994) the court accepted the argument that this need not be construed literally to mean the instant before the business ceased and preferred the test as to whether the assets were being disposed of as part of the taxpayer's withdrawal from the business.

[14] Although it was applied by agreement between the parties in *Atkinson v. Daucer* (1988).

[15] *Pepper v. Daffurn* (1993); *Jarmin v. Rawlings* (1994). In the latter case the court held that disposing of assets relating to dairy farming when the farmer ceased that activity and concentrated on rearing cattle could be treated as a single disposal of part of the business; *cf. Wase v. Bourne* (1996), where such linkage could not be implied, so that the sale of a milk quota could not be regarded as part of the business.

company. A personal company is one in which the taxpayer owns 5 per cent or more of the voting rights.

The relief is also available for "other qualifying disposals". These are disposals of assets held by the taxpayer for the purposes of his office or employment and of business assets held by an individual partner or by a shareholder of a personal company on his withdrawal from that business.

Finally the relief only applies in so far as the disposal relates to chargeable business assets. Thus, for example, if the material disposal is of shares in a personal company there will be no relief for gains attributable to shares held by that company as investments. This is a business and not an investment relief.

Reinvestment Relief

A new relief, originally known as entrepreneurial relief, was introduced by the 1993 Finance Act. It was originally intended to encourage businessmen to reinvest the proceeds of the disposal of a business into another business. The relief was, however, widened considerably in both 1994 and 1995 and given the name of reinvestment relief. It is set out in sections 164A to 164N.

The relief takes the form of a hold-over relief available whenever a taxpayer makes a disposal of any asset and within three years acquires a *qualifying investment*.[16] In such a case the standard hold-over relief applies so that both the disposal proceeds of the disposed asset and the acquisition cost of the qualifying investments are reduced. Unusually, however, the amount to be deducted is limited to the lowest of (i) the chargeable gain on the disposal; (ii) the cost of the qualifying investments; and (iii) the amount claimed. The effect of this is that there is no need to reinvest all the proceeds of the disposal in the acquisition, as say in the case of the replacement of business assets. Reinvesting the gain will suffice both to cancel that gain and attract the relief. The relief may be claimed before retirement relief.

Qualifying investments are ordinary shares (with no minimum amount) in a company carrying on a qualifying trade and which is not linked to a company whose shares were the subject of the

---

[16] The relief is also available if the qualifying investments were acquired one year prior to the disposal.

disposal. Qualifying trades includes property companies but not other investment companies.

This is a very wide and useful relief but there are some restrictions. Thus where the gains on more than one disposal are being held-over into qualifying investments each is to be computed separately so that the amount available for the second gain is reduced by that used for the first. There are also clawback provisions where the investments cease to be qualifying within three years or the taxpayer emigrates.

Gifts of Business Assets

There is a relief for gifts of business assets which is now enacted in section 165. The relief arises where an individual makes a disposal otherwise than under a bargain at arm's length to a person resident or ordinarily resident in the United Kingdom of an asset used for the purposes of a trade, profession or vocation carried on by the transferor or by his personal company or by a trading company which is a subsidiary of his personal company. The relief also applies to a similar transfer of shares of an unquoted company or of the transferor's personal company. The relief is additional to retirement relief (above), but it only applies to the extent that the transfer was not relieved by that relief.

Unlike retirement relief this relief is a hold-over relief so that the amount of the gain can be deducted from the deemed acquisition cost of the donee (market value under section 17). Because the donee will therefore become liable to a potentially higher capital gains tax bill on a subsequent disposal any claim for this relief must be made by both the donor and donee.

Where the relief is available on sales at an undervalue only the amount of that undervalue is available for the relief. If the gift was the subject of a charge to inheritance tax the donee can add that tax paid to his acquisition cost.

Charities

A gain which accrues to a charity and is applicable and applied for charitable purposes is not a chargeable gain: section 256(1). But if property is held on charitable trusts and then ceases to be so held there is a deemed disposal at market value and any gain so accruing is chargeable: section 256(2). Where a charity has an interest under a trust, money paid to it by the trustees on the disposal of surplus

Exemptions and Reliefs

assets are not gains accruing to the charity but to the trustees, unless it is a bare trust.[17]

Turning now to a disposal *to* a charity, such a disposal if by way of gift is exempt from capital gains tax in the sense that neither a gain nor a loss is treated as accruing on the disposal. If the charity subsequently disposes of the property which was given to it, and disposes of it at a gain, the gain will not be a chargeable gain if the gain is applicable and applied for charitable purposes.[18]

---

[17] *Prest v. Bettinson* (1980).
[18] An outright transfer by a charitable company to another charity is deemed to be applied for charitable purposes: *IRC v. Helen Slater Charitable Trust* (1980).

Part Four

Corporation Tax

CHAPTER 19

THE TAXATION OF COMPANIES AND SHAREHOLDERS

A company does not pay income tax or capital gains tax as such; the tax which it pays is corporation tax. Corporation tax is charged on the "profits" of the company, and "profits" means income and chargeable gains; Taxes Act, s.6. The amount of any income shall be computed in accordance with income tax principles (Taxes Act, s.9(1)), and the total amount of chargeable gains shall be computed in accordance with the principles of capital gains tax (Taxation of Chargeable Gains Act 1992, s.8).

So we have already covered a lot of ground but remember that in Chapter 8 we pointed out that there are different rules for corporation tax purposes in computing taxable income from land. The 1995 changes apply only to individuals. The 1996 Finance Act also applies different rules for companies with regard to all forms of debt, known as "loan relationships". This topic is dealt with in the following chapter. In addition, there are many matters peculiar to companies which we have yet to look at.

What is a "company"? It is defined in the Taxes Act, s.831[1] as meaning (except in certain contexts) "any body corporate or unincorporated association, but does not include a partnership, a local authority or a local authority association."[2] (An authorised unit

---

[1] ss.831–842A is a group of sections headed "Interpretation" and it is well worth looking at.
[2] Nor does it include the Conservative Party's Central Office—that is not an unincorporated association. But members' clubs are included: *Conservative and Unionist Central Office v. Burrell* (1982): *Worthing R.F.C. v. IRC* (1985); *Blackpool Marton Rotary Club v. Martin* (1990) (C.A.). In a member's club there is no liability on the members to share profits or losses as there is in a partnership.

281

trust is deemed to be a company, but some special rules apply to it; see Taxes Act, s.46.)

A non-resident company, *i.e.* one not incorporated in the United Kingdom and whose central management and control are located elsewhere, is not within the charge to corporation tax unless it carries on a trade in the United Kingdom through a branch or agency, in which case it is chargeable to corporation tax on trading income from the branch and on income from property held by the branch and on chargeable gains accruing from the disposal of assets within the United Kingdom in the same circumstances as would make an individual chargeable. In so far as it is not liable to corporation tax, a non-resident company is liable to income tax on the same footing as a non-resident individual.

Until 1965 companies in the United Kingdom were subject to income tax and profits tax. That regime was scrapped in 1965 and replaced by a system of corporation tax in what was called the "classical" form. Under that system a company paid corporation tax on all its profits. Then, if it made a distribution, *e.g.* paid a dividend, it deducted income tax at the then standard rate and paid over the tax to the Revenue. Thus distributed profits were fiscally discriminated against compared with undistributed profits. Indeed, distributed profits were taxed twice; once in the hands of the company (corporation tax) and again in the hands of the shareholder (income tax). The company and its members (shareholders) were treated as separate entities. This is, of course, jurisprudentially correct, but it is generally considered to be commercially unrealistic. Retained profits, on the other hand, were only taxed once in the hands of the company, thus producing a tax bias against distributed profits. If, say, the rate of corporation tax is 40 per cent and income tax 30 per cent, retained profits are taxed under this system at 40 per cent, but distributed profits at 40 per cent plus a further 30 per cent on the after-tax balance of 60 per cent (*i.e.* 18 per cent net). Thus every £100 retained by the company leaves £60 after tax, but every £100 distributed leaves only £42.

By the Finance Act 1972 the "classical" form of corporation tax was replaced by the present system which is called the "imputation" system. It remains true that the company pays corporation tax on its profits and the shareholders pay income tax on the dividends, but the two taxes are linked by means of a "tax credit". It is this link which explains the name "imputation" system. Part of the company's liability to corporation tax is "imputed" to the shareholder, that is, is treated as satisfying the basic rate income tax liability of the shareholder.[3] We explain the basics of this system at the end of this chapter.

It may be asked, why have a tax on company profits at all? Why not simply tax, in the hands of the shareholders, what emerges from the company in the form of distributions? The answer originally was because of the different rates of tax between income tax and capital gains tax. Taxing only distributions would have meant that that would enable a company to be used as a kind of receptacle in which profits could be stored up tax-free; distribution (and hence income taxation) could be avoided by storing up the profits for years on end and then eventually selling the shares (causing only liability to capital gains tax at a flat rate). This "receptacle problem" (a problem for the Revenue) is particularly acute in the case of narrowly-owned companies, such as one-man companies and family companies. Special rules were devised to deal with such companies, called "close" companies and, although the harmonisation of income tax and capital gains tax rates has solved *most* of the "receptacle" problems other possible tax advantages remain. These include the use of investment companies to reward higher rate tax and "hidden" distributions. We shall look at these in the next chapter but one.

The question whether a particular individual or partnership would gain (tax-wise) by forming a company is not easy to answer except in very general terms or alternatively in minutely particular terms with a full knowledge of all the circumstances of a particular case. In general, a major pointer is the comparison between the individual's marginal rate of income tax and the relevant rate of corporation tax. This has changed very sharply recently. For example, back in 1979 when the first edition of this book was written the top rate of income tax had just fallen from 98 per cent to 75 per cent. The main rate of corporation tax was then 52 per cent. By 1996 that had dropped to 33 per cent. The "small companies" rate is 24 per cent, the basic rate of income tax. If he does form a company, the individual trader will become a director and be taxable under Schedule E (and PAYE) (instead of Case I or II of Schedule D) and he will be subject to the rules about benefits from higher-paid employment. He will, however, be better off as regards pension arrangements.

---

[3] It is equally true to say that the shareholder's basic rate liability is imputed to the company.

The change from Case I or Case II income tax to corporation tax is done by a discontinuance of the trade (see Taxes Act, s.63); loss relief (income tax) can be carried forward (Taxes Act, s.35); and hold-over relief (capital gains tax) is available.

The decision whether to trade individually or by means of a company is not wholly, perhaps not even primarily, a tax decision. There is one great advantage of incorporation, namely limited liability even for a single member company, although for small companies that may be largely illusory in practice. Also, it is easier for a company to arrange finance (either from inside or outside the business) for expansion particularly by the use of a floating charge. The disadvantage from more (and expensive) paperwork arising from the increasingly stringent requirements of the Companies Acts has to some extent been reduced for small companies in recent years. And, of course, it must be borne in mind that some *professions* do not permit their practitioners to become incorporated.

How the Imputation System Works

We want to conclude this introduction by giving a summary in numbered points of how the current imputation system of corporation tax works.

(1) A company pays corporation tax on all its profits irrespective of whether or not they are distributed. Let us suppose that a company has an income of £100,000. For the sake of simplicity we will look at what happens in respect of each £100 of that income. The rate of corporation tax we take as 33 per cent. So the company's liability to corporation tax is £33, payable nine months after the end of the company's accounting period.[4] This is known as the company's "mainstream" liability.

(2) If the company pays out a dividend (or other "qualifying distribution": see below) it is required to pay to the Revenue (virtually at the same time) advance corporation tax (ACT). This, at present, is at the rate of one quarter, *i.e.* one quarter *of the dividend*. So if the company is minded to pay out the whole of the after-tax balance (namely £67) of the income, it will pay £67 in dividend to shareholders and one quarter of £67 in ACT to the Revenue. One quarter of £67 is £16.75.

---

[4] In this example we suppose that the company is not a "small" company and we put on one side the effect of capital allowances.

How the Imputation System Works

(3) This amount of ACT (£16.75) is set as a credit against the company's corporation tax liability (namely £33 on its income). So what the company has to pay at the end of the year in corporation tax is £16.25, that is £33 less the £16.75 already paid. In other words the company's total tax bill will always be £33 whether that £100 is distributed or not. This set-off of ACT against the company's tax liability is permitted against its liability both on income and chargeable gains. The only "tax bias" against distributed profits now is that ACT is payable earlier than mainstream liability thus affecting a company's cash-flow situation. Part of the company's overall tax bill has been "imputed" to the shareholders.

(4) An individual who is resident in the United Kingdom who receives a dividend receives along with it a "tax credit". That tax credit is the same in amount as the ACT; namely one quarter (in our example £16.75) of the dividend. The individual shareholder (let us call him Albert) is liable to income tax on that dividend under Schedule F on the aggregate of the dividend (£67) plus the tax credit (£16.75). That aggregate is £83.75, of which £16.75 is 20 per cent. But the tax credit is as its name implies a credit against Albert's liability to income tax. So Albert, though liable to tax on the sum of £83.75 is credited as if he had already paid £16.75 (20 per cent) in tax.

The imputation system works by ensuring that that tax credit will in effect cancel out Albert's liability to basic rate income tax so that a basic rate taxpayer will have no actual tax to pay. Since the basic rate of income tax is 24 per cent and the tax credit amounts to 20 per cent it may be asked how this works. The answer is that for income tax assessable under Schedule F (company distributions), the basic rate is fixed at the lower rate of income tax, *i.e.* 20 per cent (Taxes Act, s. 207A). Section 14 of the Taxes Act expressly links the rate of ACT to the lower rate of income tax.[5] This change, from the general basic rate to the special rate for Schedule F, was made in 1993. Companies wanted a lower rate of ACT in order to improve their cash-flow and the principle of covering the basic tax liability of a shareholder could only be maintained in this way.

If Albert is a higher rate taxpayer he will of course be liable to tax on £83.75 at 40 per cent. Thus he will be liable to pay income tax of

---

[5] Thus if the lower rate of tax is reduced to 10 per cent, the rate of ACT would be one-ninth. Thus, on a dividend of £90 there would be ACT of £10, giving a tax credit of £10 (10 per cent) on a grossed-up dividend of £100.

£33.50 on his dividend. But his tax credit of £16.75 will be credited against that so that he will have to pay an additional amount of £16.75 (£33.50–£16.75). In percentage terms he has a tax liability of 40 per cent reduced by a tax credit worth 20 per cent. One effect of the lowering of the basic rate has been therefore to increase the differential between the tax credit and higher rate tax liability. On the other hand, if Albert is not liable to income tax at all, *e.g.* because he is a charitable trustee[6] he can get a repayment of the tax credit from the Revenue.

(5) The legislation makes a distinction between "qualifying distributions" of companies (of which a dividend is the prime example) and "non-qualifying distributions". We must now look to see what happens when a company makes a non-qualifying distribution. There are two kinds of non-qualifying distributions, namely bonus securities and bonus redeemable shares (see p.299, below). Neither of these confer immediate benefit. The company making the distribution does not pay ACT. The individual shareholder does not get a tax credit. The distribution in the hands of the shareholder is not liable to basic rate income tax (*i.e.* a lower rate of 20 per cent for Schedule F). But if the shareholder is within the threshold for higher rate tax, he will be charged on the amount of the distribution. There will be no grossing-up because there is no tax credit. His bill for higher rate tax is reduced by an amount equal to lower rate tax. Thus he is liable to pay tax at 40 minus 20 = 20 per cent.

(6) So far we have been talking about shareholders who are resident in the United Kingdom. A non-resident shareholder is not entitled to a tax credit unless he is (under section 278 of the Taxes Act: see p.202 above) entitled to personal reliefs. But higher rate tax (only) may be charged. He will not be entitled to any tax refund. This is so both for qualifying and non-qualifying distributions. Of course, in any particular case the outcome may be affected by a double taxation relief arrangement.

(7) Now let us consider the situation where the recipient of the distribution is not an individual but a company. After all, a company may receive dividends from other companies in which it is a shareholder. A company which is resident in the United Kingdom and which receives a qualifying distribution is not chargeable to income tax or corporation tax in respect of it. But it has in effect suffered a kind of deduction in that the company making the distribution will

---

[6] *IRC v. Sheppard (No.2)* (1993).

How the Imputation System Works

have paid advance corporation tax in respect of the distribution. Because this is so, the receiving company is described as being in receipt of "franked investment income," and it gets a tax credit. It can set off this tax credit against its liability to ACT when it comes to make a qualifying distribution itself. This process can be spoken of as "franking".

(8) If a company resident in the United Kingdom receives a non-qualifying distribution, that does not amount to franked investment income. The distribution cannot be used by the recipient company to frank its own qualifying distributions, and it does not attract ACT if it is passed on by the recipient company to its own shareholders.

(9) A non-resident company making a distribution is not required to pay ACT, and the recipient does not get a tax credit.

(10) A non-resident company receiving a distribution does not get a tax credit.

Chapter 20

CORPORATION TAX

The corporation tax along with many other taxes including income tax and capital gains tax, is under the care and management of the Commissioners of Inland Revenue, and the detailed provisions for administration set out in the Taxes Management Act 1970 apply to corporation tax. It is important to appreciate, at the outset, that corporation tax *is* the income tax and capital gains tax on companies. Its administration is closely tied in with that of income tax and CGT.

The substantive law of corporation tax is to be found, for the most part, in sections 6–14, Part VIII (sections 337–347), Part X (sections 393–413), and Part XI (sections 414–430) of the Taxes Act (as amended) and in a few sections of the Taxation of Chargeable Gains Act 1992 and Chapter II of Part IV of the Finance Act 1996.

Periods

Corporation tax is levied by reference, not to "years of assessment", but to "financial years". A financial year begins on April 1 and ends on March 31. And each financial year is named by reference to only one calendar year and that is the year in which it begins, not the year in which it ends. So the financial year 1996 is the year from April 1, 1996, to March 31, 1997. Assessment is on a current year basis; the tax assessment for 1996 being based on the profits of 1996. But where a company's accounting period does not correspond to the financial year, the profits of the accounting period are apportioned into the appropriate financial years. This is important in that the rate of tax may differ in the two financial years. Where a company produces a set of accounts covering several years the Revenue may apportion the profits either on a time basis as above or a specific transaction basis. Under a system known as "Pay and File" a company has to pay corporation tax nine months after the end of its accounting period based on its own assessment of its liability. A return must be filed within 12 months of the end of the accounting period (this is sent to the company by the Revenue) and a final assessment will then be made. Any additional time then due is payable within one month, together with interest. If too much tax has been paid the company will receive interest on any repayment.

Rates

Until 1984 the rates of corporation tax for any particular year were set by Parliament in arrear. Now, like those for income tax, they are set in advance. But 1984 also saw a radical change in approach to the rates of corporation tax, with a substantial reduction in the rates of tax being offset by a removal of exemptions and allowances. For a decade the main rate of corporation tax had been 52 per cent as it was for 1982. It was then steadily reduced: 1983–50 per cent; 1984–45 per cent; 1985–40 per cent; 1986–35 per cent; 1990–34 per cent; 1991–33 per cent, which is the current rate. Nonetheless, as we noted at p.147, it was authoritatively estimated that this operation would result in a substantial *increase* in the tax burden on many companies. Alice would have been at home in the tax wonderland! The rate of corporation tax applies to all a company's income and capital gains.

That rate of ACT (advance corporation tax) is set for the current (income tax) year by the appropriate Finance Act. Until 1993 it was directly related to the basic rate of income tax for that year. From 1993 onwards it has been directly related to the lower rate of income tax, which as we saw in the previous chapter is also the rate applicable to income assessable under Schedule F. Section 14 of the Taxes Act applies this link. The reduction in the rate of ACT reflected the fact that ACT is payable earlier than mainstream tax (when the distribution is made) and was intended to improve the cash flow, particularly for smaller companies, where it represents the largest part of the tax actually paid.

For a number of years there has also been a lower rate of corporation tax known as the "small companies rate". This is a bit of a misnomer, as it is based on the level of company profits in *that* tax year, and has nothing to do with average profits levels or assets values. For some years the rate was 42 per cent. In 1982 it was 38 per cent. For the years 1983 to 1986 the rate was set at 30 per cent. From 1988 to 1995 the rate was 25 per cent. The rate for 1996 is 24 per cent.

The rate currently applies to companies with profits not exceeding £300,000. The difference between the two rates potentially gives rise to a severe problem at the threshhold between the rates, as it might be better totally to forfeit profits than incur the higher rate. To avoid this, there are tapering provisions. For a time there was a narrower taper band which effectively meant an intermediate high rate band between the two main rates. Now the taper provisions cover the band of income from £300,000 to £1,500,000. Thus the full rate will only apply after that amount. There are provisions to block the avoidance device of splitting a business into a number of companies in order to get the benefit of the lower rate.

Computation of Profits

A company is charged to corporation tax on its total profits; that is, its income plus its chargeable gains. (Profits = income + chargeable gains). It is declared in the Taxes Act, s.9 that in general a company's income is to be computed on income tax principles, excluding income tax enactments which make special provision for individuals. This, however, does not mean that there are no differences at all. One difference is that the rules for computing a company's income under Schedule A are different from those applicable to individuals. Further, the rules for computing a company's income and gains from either borrowing or lending are different from those for individuals (see below). But the differences are minor compared with the broad principle which (we say again) is that a company's income is computed on income tax principles. If the law of income tax changes during the accounting period of a company, the law which applies for the computation is the law applying to the year of assessment in which the accounting period *ends*.

Similarly, section 8 of the Taxation of Chargeable Gains Act 1992 declares that the chargeable gains of a company are to be computed on the principles of capital gains tax. That is subject to what we say about "loan relationships" below.

The income of a company is allotted to the various Schedules and cases just as is the income of an individual. So, for example, a company's trading income is assessed under Case I of Schedule D and its income from rents under Schedule A (as applied to companies). The rules for determining what expenses are deductible are as for income tax.[1] Under Case I, directors' emoluments are on the

---

[1] Occasionally the problems posed under income tax rules arise from the fact that it is a company which is involved. For example payments made by a holding company to assist a subsidiary company were deductible under Schedule D, Case I from the holding company's profits since they would have been so deductible by the subsidiary and were made purely for the benefit of the holding company: *Robinson v. Scott Bader Co. Ltd* (1981). On the other hand, money spent by a holding company which was for the purpose of a trade carried on by its subsidiaries was not deductible—it was not spent wholly and exclusively for the purposes of the holding company's trade: *Vodofone Cellular Ltd v. Shaw* (1995).

same footing as salaries and wages of the company's employees; they are deductible to the extent that they are reasonable.

The several classes of income of a company together with the total of its chargeable gains constitute the total profits of the company.

Loan Relationships

Chapter II of Part IV of the Finance Act 1996 introduced a new regime for companies in respect of all profits and losses made by companies on loans. In general the idea is to treat all such profits and losses as income, whether or not for individuals they would be treated as capital gains or losses. (The original idea was to apply these rules to individuals as well but that did not find favour during the consultation process). The new rules apply whether the company is the borrower or lender. The most obvious category is the treatment of interest paid by a company on its debentures from the company's point of view. The pre-1996 rules relating to interest payable by a company on its debentures which treated such payments as charges on income and so deductible from total profits (see below) no longer apply to such interest payments.

The 1996 rules apply to what are termed "loan relationships". These are defined in section 81 of the 1996 Act as any relationship in which a company is either a creditor or debtor for a money debt, whether in sterling or another currency, which under the general law is a loan. Thus all forms of bond and corporate debt are covered. In calculating the profits and losses from such relationships companies may use one of two accounting methods (sections 85 and 86 of the 1996 Act): an accruals basis, under which payments and receipts are allocated when they accrue to the accounting periods to which they relate; or a mark-to-market basis, which means that a loan relationship must be accounted for in each accounting period at a fair value. In general companies may use whichever method they use in their statutory accounts prepared for Companies Act purposes.

The central concepts of the new regime (in sections 82 and 83 of the 1996 Act) are: (i) that where companies enter into loan relationships for the purposes of a trade, the profits, losses and expenses relating to those relationships (known in the legislation as debits and credits) will be treated as receipts of expenses of that trade; ie they will form part of the Schedule D, Case I computation; and (ii) in the case of profits and losses arising from other, *i.e.* non-trading, loan relationships any net profit (taking into account the company's other income subject to those rules) will be taxable under the rules of

Case III of Schedule D. Schedule C has been abolished for all purposes so that income subject to that Schedule (largely interest on government securities) is now taxable under Case III and since the new rules apply to all loan relationships, for companies Case IV of Schedule D (overseas interest) can no longer apply.

Any net loss on a non-trading loan relationship, calculated in the same way, may be used to give relief in one of four ways. First, it may be used against any profits for corporation tax of the year in which the loss occurred; secondly by way of group relief (see below); thirdly by way of carry back against similar non-trading profits of the preceding three years; and fourthly by carry forward against non-trading profits generally of the company for succeeding accounting periods.

These new rules apply to all interest payments made by companies (not all such payments were charges on income) but do not apply to payments which are distributions for corporation tax purposes so that the basic distinction remains between dividends payable on shares and interest payable on debentures. The former cannot be deducted from taxable profits but fall into the imputation system described in the previous chapter. The latter are now part of the tax computation as outlined above. Perhaps the most significant feature of the new rules is the general shift from capital gains tax rules to income tax rules for the many forms of corporate and government debt.

Deductions from Total Profits

Having arrived at the total profits of the company the next thing to do is to consider what items are permitted to be deducted in order to determine the amount on which corporation tax is to be charged. There are four kinds of permitted deductions: (1) charges on income; (2) management expenses of an investment company; (3) minor capital allowances; (4) losses. We will deal with these in turn.

CHARGES ON INCOME

It will be remembered from Chapter 16 ("The Taxation of Individuals") that, for income tax, certain payments out are called "charges on income" and are deductible in computing "total income". Those deductions are separate from the deductions which are expenses in earning the income under any particular Schedule or Case. The position is similar for corporation tax. Payments out which are expenses in earning the income under a particular

Deductions from Total Profits

Schedule or Case are deductible in computing the income of a company under that Schedule or Case. That still leaves some payments out which, although not deductible *in computing* income, are deductible *from* (or "against") the total profits of the company. Many payments are not deductible in either way. Those which are deductible against total profits are called "charges on income": see section 338 of the Taxes Act. Of course deductibility is only completely effective if the charges on income are less than the total profits. If the charges exceed the total profits in a particular accounting period, and the charges include payments made wholly and exclusively for the purposes of a trade carried on by the company, then up to the amount of that excess (or of those payments, if less) the charges are deductible as if they were trading expenses of the trade for the purpose of computing a trading loss: Taxes Act, s.393(9). (And see below at p.294 under "Carry-forward of Losses".) Or, where a company is a member of a group of companies, it may in certain circumstances "surrender" its excess of charges on income to another company in the group: Taxes Act, s.403(7).

It is obviously very important to establish which kinds of payments count as charges on income and which do not.

Any payment which amounts to a distribution (whether qualifying or non-qualifying) cannot be a charge on income. This is obvious good sense; if it were otherwise corporation tax would be non-existent, because a company by distributing the whole of its income would escape tax. So the fact that a company has paid a dividend does not entitle it to deduct anything from its total profits. Following the introduction of the new regime for interest payments made by companies introduced by the Finance Act 1996, any payment by a company which is in respect of a loan relationship is no longer a charge on income, although it is deductible in computing profits.[2]

"Charges on income", ignoring for the moment payments to charities, are defined in the Taxes Act, s.338(3) as being:

"(a) any annuity or annual payment payable otherwise than in respect of any of the company's loan relationships, and any such other payments as are mentioned in section 348(2) of this Act but not

---

[2] Thus for tax purposes it is more advantageous for companies to raise money through loan stock than by way of preference shares (both are seen as medium term finance). See Charlesworth and Morse, *Company Law* (15th ed. 1995 Sweet & Maxwell), pp. 235–240.

including sums which are or, but for any exemption would be, chargeable under Schedule A."

Although section 338(3) (above) refers to section 348, that reference is only for the purpose of identifying certain payments, and it must be remembered that a payment by a company can never satisfy section 348 because that section is limited to payments which are made wholly out of profits or gains brought into charge to *income tax*. Thus the payments we are speaking of here fall within section 349 and basic rate income tax must be deducted and accounted for to the Revenue by the paying company. (See Chapter 11 above).

But of course a company, as well as making payments under deduction of tax, may be the recipient of such payments. In that case the company is entitled to set off the amount which has been deducted from its receipts against its own liability to account for income tax deducted on the payments it has made. If this is not possible it may set off the income tax which has been deducted against its corporation tax liability. And if this is not possible because the income tax deducted is more than the corporation tax payable by the company then the company can get a repayment of the income tax deducted.

There are various conditions with which a payment must comply if it is to count as a charge on income. The conditions are set out in section 338. In summary, a payment is not to be treated as a charge on income in any of the following circumstances: if the payment is charged to capital; if the payment is not ultimately borne by the company[3]; if the payment is not made under a liability incurred for a valuable and sufficient consideration (subject to the rules for charitable donation, below)[4]; if (in the case of a non-resident company) the payment is incurred for the purposes of its overseas operations, if it would be deductible in computing the company's taxable profits.

Certain further very stringent rules apply to payments made by companies to non-residents: see Taxes Act, ss.338(4) and 340.

---

[3] Presumably this means if the payment is reimbursed by some third party.
[4] It must be made in *return for* consideration and not just in the hope of receiving consideration. Thus in *Ball v. National & Grindlay's Bank* (1973), money paid under a covenant for the education of overseas employees' children in order to retain their services was held not to be a charge on income. It was a hope of a business advantage only. It is an open question whether payment by the company for the benefit of A with consideration supplied by B will be a charge on income.

DEDUCTIONS FROM TOTAL PROFITS

Payments made by a company under a charitable covenant will be charges on income if the covenant is for a period which may exceed three years and which cannot be ended before the conclusion of that period without the consent of the charity. Such payments must be made after deduction of income tax. In addition a one-off payment to a charity will also be a charge on income provided the donation is a sum of money and the company deducts income tax from the payment and certifies to the charity that it has so deducted that tax. The charity, in both cases, will then generally be able to reclaim that tax. There are special rules for close companies making such donations; Taxes Act, s. 339.

MANAGEMENT EXPENSES OF AN INVESTMENT COMPANY

Another possible deduction from total profits applies to an investment company. Such a company, if resident in the United Kingdom, is permitted to deduct its management expenses: Taxes Act, s. 75. The point of this provision is to make up for the fact that an investment company, unlike a trading company, has no opportunity of deducting expenses of management in the actual computation of profits. "Management expenses" are given a wide meaning by the courts, but they must relate to some act of management and not be part of the cost of acquiring an asset; *e.g.* a commission paid by one investment company to another company in return for that company's guarantee of a loan raised by the first, was held by the Court of Appeal to be an acquisition and not a management expense. It was part of the price of raising the loan.[5] A similar, but more restricted, provision applies to insurance companies: section 76.

MINOR CAPITAL ALLOWANCES

Another possible deduction relates to what one might call the "minor" capital allowances. An example is the agricultural buildings allowance for non-traders. The rules are complicated, but in certain circumstances such an allowance can be implemented by way of a deduction from total profits. (On the other hand what one might call the "major" capital allowances come into the actual computation of profits as though they were expenses: see p. 151 above).

---

[5] *Hoechst Finance Ltd v. Gumbrell* (1983) (C.A.).

CORPORATION TAX

LOSSES

Losses of companies under corporation tax are dealt with in ways similar to losses of individuals under income tax. The reader is referred to Chapter 12, above.

Let us first make the general point that a loss in a trade is computed in the same way as trading income is computed. In other words, the computation process may lead to a plus answer or a minus answer.

There are two main ways in which a trading loss of a company may be relieved: see the Taxes Act, ss. 393, 393A.

Carry-forward

The company may claim, to set off a trading loss of one accounting period against trading income from the same trade in succeeding accounting periods. Relief is given against the first available year and then each successive year as appropriate. For the purposes of this carry-forward relief, if a company in a particular accounting period has an excess of "charges on income" over profits and the charges on income include payments made wholly and exclusively for the purposes of a trade carried on by the company, then, up to the amount of that excess or of those payments, whichever is the less, the charges on income so paid shall in computing a loss be deductible as if they were trading expenses of the trade: Taxes Act, s. 393(9).

Set-off against current and previous profits

The company may claim to set off a trading loss in any particular accounting period against profits of whatever description (including chargeable gains) of that accounting period. If the loss is not in this way completely absorbed, it can be set against the profits of preceding accounting periods, subject to the limitation that the loss can only be carried back for accounting periods falling within the previous three years. Such a claim must be made within two years and relief is given against a later accounting period before an earlier period. The company must have been carrying on the same trade in the carry-back period. Set-off against general profits, but not carry forward relief, is not allowed unless either (a) the trade is being carried on in the exercise of functions conferred by an Act of Parliament or (b) the trade is being carried on on a commercial basis. It will be noticed that (b) above is parallel to a requirement for income tax (section 384) designed to exclude hobby-trading from the relief. And the special rules for hobby-farming (section 397) apply to corporation tax as well as to income tax.

Case VI

Apart from the above modes of loss relief there is also a limited relief for Case VI losses. The company may claim to set off the loss against any other Case VI income for the same or any subsequent accounting period.

Company reconstructions

Where a company ceases to carry on a trade and another company begins to carry it on, the change of company is ignored if the fundamental ownership (*e.g.* by shareholding) is (to the extent of three-quarters or more) the same before and after the change of companies. So if Company A has accumulated losses, and its trade is transferred to Company B (and the common ownership test is satisfied) Company B can use the carry-forward provisions and set off the accumulated losses against profits of the transferred trade[6] (but not against other profits): Taxes Act ss. 343, 344 There are restrictions if Company A is insolvent at the time of transfer.

Change of ownership

Sometimes the converse case arises; that is, the company carrying on the trade remains the same but the underlying ownership changes. There used to be a brisk business in the sale of companies which were bulging with unrelieved tax losses. This commerce was largely struck down by the Finance Act 1969 in a section which is now reproduced in the Taxes Act, s. 768. If in any period of three years there is both a substantial change in the ownership of a company and a "major change in the nature or conduct of a trade carried on by the company" past trading losses will not be available for carry-forward relief. A substantial change in ownership is basically a change in the ownership of more than 50 per cent of the voting share capital. Nor is the relief available if "at any time after the scale of the

---

[6] Company B can merge the trade with another carried on by it, but the relief will only apply to profits of the transferred trade: *Falmer Jeans Ltd v. Rodin* (1990).

activities in a trade carried on by a company has become small or negligible, and before any considerable revival of the trade, there is a change in the ownership of the company." The point of this latter provision is to strike at what was once a common practice keeping a company in existence simply because it was big with losses. Similar rules apply to prevent losses incurred *after* the change of ownership from being carried back against profits incurred *before* the change under the three year carry-back reliefs: Taxes Act, s. 768A.

Group relief

A company which is a member of a group or of companies may "surrender" a loss to another company which is a member of the same group. This enables the transferee company to claim loss relief: Taxes Act, ss. 402 and 403(1). The claimant company must use the relief in the year it was surrendered. A group for this purpose is where 75 per cent of the ordinary shares of one company is owned by the other. The availability of this relief has, however, led to the creation of strange "groups" of companies the object of which is to allow a profitable company to take the benefit of a loss of a company with insufficient profits. This has led in turn to complex anti-avoidance legislation and many complex cases as to what constitutes a group for this purpose.

A similar relief is available within a consortium of companies which together own trading companies. Under the current legislation these companies must be U.K. resident companies but that point has been referred to the European Court of Justice as to whether it is compatible with E.C. requirements.[7]

Distributions

Some payments out made by a company are "distributions" and some are not. A dividend is a distribution; interest on loan stock is not. A distribution which is made by a company resident in the United Kingdom is chargeable to income tax on an individual recipient under Schedule F. A payment which is not a distribution is not subject to Schedule F, though it may be chargeable to tax under

---

[7] *ICI plc v. Colmer* (1996) (H.L.).

DISTRIBUTIONS

some other Schedule. For example, interest on loan stock is chargeable on an individual under Case III of Schedule D.

What is a distribution?

The concept of "distribution" is defined in the Taxes Act, ss. 212 and 218, as amended. The definition is widened where the paying company is a "close company": see Chapter 21, below. A distribution is never deductible from the total profits of the paying company, be it close or non-close.

The definition of "distribution" is involved, but putting the matter broadly it covers (amongst other things) dividends (including capital dividends) and anything else (other than a repayment of share capital) distributed in respect of shares in cash or otherwise out of the assets of the company (meaning that the cost falls on the company) and where the company does not receive any new consideration for that which it distributes. It follows that a bonus issue is not a distribution, because there is no cost falling on the company[8]; and a rights issue is not a distribution, because there is new consideration.[9]

Since, however, in effect a bonus issue turns profits into shares, if a bonus issue is followed by a repayment of share capital, that repayment will be a distribution up to the amount of the bonus issue. For example, if a company has made £10,000 profit and issues 10,000 £1 bonus shares to its members that will not be a distribution—the money is still in the company. But if it then buys back 10,000 £1 shares from the members on a reduction of capital, it has in fact distributed that £10,000 profit and so the reduction will be a distribution (s. 211). Similar rules apply if the company makes a reduction of capital (which remember is not a distribution if it is only returning the original investment) under section 135 of the Companies Act 1985[10] and follows it with an issue of bonus shares. That issue will be treated as a distribution up to the amount repaid on the reduction of capital (s. 210). It is, of course, possible for there to be a reduction of capital, followed by a bonus issue, followed by another reduction of capital, so that both sections could apply. To

---

[8] See Charlesworth & Morse, *op. cit.*, pp. 609–612. In essence the shareholder receives another share(s) in the company but the value of his total holding remains the same.
[9] *ibid*, p. 148.
[10] *ibid*, pp. 173–182.

avoid this double charge, once section 210 has charged the bonus issue as a distribution that bonus issue cannot trigger off a distribution on a subsequent reduction by virtue of section 211. There is a general time limit of 10 years between the bonus issue and the reduction after which the sections will not apply.

What is not a distribution?

The Companies Act 1985 gives companies power to repurchase their own shares and to issue redeemable ordinary shares without requiring a court order.[11] The avowed intention at the time of the introduction of these provisions in 1981 was to provide small companies with shares which would be attractive to an outside investor in that he could resell to the company and not be "locked-in" with no opportunity to sell the shares. (Private companies in general have no open market for their shares.) But such a repurchase or redemption will be a distribution for tax purposes in so far as it amounts to more than the original investment. In 1982 the Revenue therefore introduced an exemption from the distribution rules for certain repurchases and redemptions. We may say, however, that the exemption is extremely limited and in some cases will frustrate the intentions of the companies legislation.

The conditions for exemption are set out in section 217 to 229 of the Tax Act. For a start the exemption is only limited to unquoted[12] trading companies or unquoted holding companies of a trading group. Subsidiaries of quoted companies are also excluded. Secondly, the purchase or redemption must be wholly or mainly to benefit the trade of the company concerned and not be part of a tax avoidance scheme. Thirdly, the shareholder concerned must be resident in the United Kingdom and have owned the shares for at least five years. Above all, however, the shareholder's interest in the shares of that company must be "substantially reduced" (at least by 25 per cent) with a corresponding reduction in his share of the profits. As an alternative to the benefit of the trade it can be shown that the sale is necessary for the payment of inheritance tax as the result of a death and to avoid undue hardship. Purchases and redemptions can be cleared with the Revenue in advance. If the purchase is exempt from the distribution rules no ACT will be

---

[11] *ibid*, pp. 184–195.
[12] Shares traded on the Unlimited Securities Market and the Alternative Investment Market count as unquoted for this purpose.

DISTRIBUTIONS

payable by the company and the shareholder will only be liable to capital gains tax.

There is one other exemption from the distribution rules allowed for by sections 213 to 218 of the Taxes Act. This will be on a "demerger"—*i.e.* splitting up one company into two or more. In certain circumstances an issue of shares by the original company to the members of the new companies will not invoke the distribution rules. As with purchases and redemptions this relief only applies to trading companies when the de-merger is wholly or mainly for the benefit of the trade. Advance clearance is again possible and desirable.

Qualifying and non-qualifying distributions

The legislation draws a sharp distinction between distributions which are "qualifying distributions" and distributions which are non-qualifying distributions. The phrase "qualifying distribution" is not defined except by exclusion. Section 14(2) of the Taxes Act declares that "qualifying distribution" means any distribution other than (a) bonus redeemable shares and bonus securities: and (b) any share capital or security which the company making the distribution has directly or indirectly received from another company in the form of bonus redeemable shares or securities. So there are only two kinds of non-qualifying distributions, both of which confer no benefit on the shareholder immediately (we have seen that a bonus issue on its own confers no benefit) but entitle the benefit to be "cashed-in", *i.e.* redeemed at a future date.

The importance of the distinction is this: if a distribution is a qualifying distribution advance corporation tax (ACT) becomes due from the company and the recipient gets a tax credit: if a distribution is a non-qualifying distribution no ACT is payable and there is no tax credit. The different effects of these two situations have been described above in Chapter 19 under the heading "How the Imputation System Works". It is desirable to go over some of the ground again in more detail, dealing first with qualifying distributions and then with non-qualifying distributions.

QUALIFYING DISTRIBUTIONS

The company making the qualifying distribution (*e.g.* a dividend) becomes liable to pay ACT to the Revenue at the rate (at present) of one quarter of the distribution (dividend). So for every £80 which a company pays to shareholders in dividends it must also pay £20 to

Corporation Tax

the Revenue. The aggregate for the amount of the qualifying distribution and the amount of the ACT which is attracted to it is called "a franked payment": see Taxes Act, s. 238(1). The amount of ACT paid by a company can be set off against its liability to "mainstream" corporation tax on all its income and chargeable gains.

Let us take an example to see how this works out. Suppose a company has profits of £100. It decides not to retain any of it. It must provide for tax as well as paying a dividend. The sum goes like this:

		£
Dividend		67.00
ACT		16.75
Corporation Tax	£33.00	
Less set-off of ACT	£16.75	16.25
		100.00

"Excessive distribution"—surplus AC

It may happen that a company in a particular accounting period distributes more in dividend than it has got in as profits in that period. There are various ways in which that situation might arise, but let us take as an example the case of a company which decides to pay a dividend financed partly from the profits of an earlier period. In this situation there is a limitation on the extent to which ACT can be set off by the company against its mainstream corporation tax. The maximum amount of ACT which can be set off is that amount of ACT which, with the distribution to which it relates, absorbs the whole of the company's income of the accounting period: Taxes Act, s. 239(2). Suppose a company in a particular accounting period has taxable profits of £500. It decides, in view of the very good income it had in recent earlier years, to pay a dividend of £800. ACT amounts to £200 (one quarter of £800). Not all of this £200 can be set off by the company against mainstream corporation tax. The maximum is £100, because a distribution of £400 together with related ACT of £100 (one quarter of £400) would have absorbed the whole of the £500 of company income. This rule boils down to the fact that the amount of ACT which can be set off is equal to the company's income multiplied by the basic rate of income tax for Schedule F: £500 × $\frac{20}{100}$ = £100. Another way of putting it is to say that the set-off of ACT can never reduce the company's mainstream liability on its profits to less than the difference between the rate of mainstream tax and the rate of ACT. Apply that to our example. The difference between mainstream rate and ACT rate is 13 per cent (33 less 20 per cent). The company's liability to mainstream tax cannot be reduced to less than 13 per cent of £500, which is £65. Its mainstream liability, 33 per cent of £500, is £165. Its maximum set-off (see above) is £100. After that set-off its tax liability is £65.

A company in this situation is said to have surplus ACT; *i.e.* it has some ACT which has not been relieved by way of set-off. There are two main ways in which surplus ACT can be relieved. First, it can be carried back to the six preceding accounting periods and used as a credit in those periods. If that does not relieve it in full then, secondly, it can be carried forward into later accounting periods (indefinitely) and used as a credit in those periods: Taxes Act, s. 239. A third way of dealing with surplus ACT is open to a company which is a member of a group of companies; namely, it can surrender the surplus (so far as it relates to a dividend as distinct from other kinds of qualifying distributions) to its subsidiary company: Taxes Act, s. 240. A subsidiary is basically a 51 per cent subsidiary for this purpose.

Section 45 of the Taxes Act contains provisions to prevent a tax advantage arising from the sale of a company which is big with surplus ACT. The provisions are similar to those in section 483 of the Taxes Act dealing with tax losses: see page 295 above.

Tax credits

The recipient of a qualifying distribution gets a tax credit equal to the ACT attributable to the distribution. If the recipient is an individual resident in the United Kingdom he is chargeable to income tax under Schedule F on the aggregate of the distribution and the tax credit. The tax credit (20 per cent of the aggregate) cancels out the lower rate (20 per cent) which is chargeable under Schedule F as the basic rate of income tax. For further details see paragraph (4) at page 283 above. If the recipient is a company resident in the United Kingdom that company is said to be in receipt of "franked investment income."

Franked investment income

A company which has received franked investment income (a distribution plus a tax credit from another company) is not chargeable to corporation tax on that income: Taxes Act, s. 208. But it gets thereby a tax credit. It can in certain circumstances get the amount of the credit paid to it by the Revenue.[13] But more usually it will make use[14] of the credit by setting it off against ACT which it is liable to pay when itself making a qualifying distribution. Suppose a company in a particular accounting period has franked investment income amounting to £10,000 and that in the same period the company makes franked payments amounting to £20,000. Section 241(2) of the Taxes Act declares that where (as in this example) the amount of the franked payments exceeds the amount of franked investment income ACT shall be payable "on an amount which, when the advance corporation tax payable thereon is added to it is equal to the excess." Well, in our example the excess is £10,000. The amount which, when ACT is added to it, equals £10,000 is £8,000. So the amount of ACT payable is that which relates to £8,000. The amount of ACT payable is thus £2,000. The company, instead of having to pay the full amount of ACT relating to a franked payment of £20,000 (which would have been £4,000) receives against that sum a credit equal to the ACT £2,000 related to its receipt (£10,000) of franked investment income. In other words, the amount of ACT now payable is £4,000 less £2,000, which is £2,000.

It is rather heretical to say this, but it may help if one suggests that in a sense the expression "distribution" is a kind of net expression, and the expressions "franked payments" and "franked investment income" are (kind of) gross expressions.

Now, it may happen that a company has in a particular accounting period more franked investment income than it pays out in franked payments. In this situation the company is said to have a surplus of franked investment income. How can it make use of it? First, the surplus can be carried forward indefinitely into succeeding accounting periods and treated as though it were franked investment income of those periods: Taxes Act, s. 241(3). Secondly, the surplus can, by virtue of section 242 of the Taxes Act (as amended), be treated as though it were a like amount of profits. Against the surplus the company can set off among other things, unrelieved current trading losses, charges on income, expenses of management (of investment companies and insurance companies) and minor capital allowances. Suppose a company has a surplus of franked investment income amounting in aggregate to £1,200. And suppose it has unrelieved losses of £400, a charge on income of £300,

---

[13] No interest is payable, however, *Savacentre Ltd v. IRC* (1995).
[14] For example, an incorporated charity can "cash" its tax credit.

management expenses of £200, and capital allowances of £100. Those items together add up to £1,000. The tax credit on £1,000 is £200. The Revenue pays to the company £200. There is £200 left of the surplus of franked investment income. This £200 is carried forward under section 241(3) of the Taxes Act. Similar provisions contained in section 243 of the Taxes Act deal with the set-off against the surplus of franked investment income of losses brought forward.

Groups of companies

Where a United Kingdom resident company pays a dividend (but not other qualifying distributions) to another United Kingdom resident company in the same group, an election can be made (by both companies) under section 247 of the Taxes Act to have the dividend treated as "group income," in which case the dividend is not a franked payment by the payer company and is not franked investment income of the payee company. Similar arrangements apply to payments which are within the phrase "charges on income." The payer company must either be (a) a 51 per cent subsidiary of the other company or of a United Kingdom resident company of which the other is a 51 per cent subsidiary or (b) a trading or holding company owned by a consortium the members of which include the payee company but where the payer company is not itself a 75 per cent subsidiary of another company.

The question as to whether a group should make an election to treat a dividend paid by one company to another member of the group as group income depends upon the circumstances. If a group income election is made then although no ACT is payable by the paying company no tax credit is received by the payee company. Thus when that company in turn makes payments out to its shareholders it will have no tax credit to set off against its liabilty to ACT. In addition the payer company will not have made any franked payments to the payee so if it has franked investment income of its own it will be unable to utilise the tax credits which it has received. Thus if a subsidiary is proposing to pay dividends to its holding company out of a fund consisting of taxable income and franked investment income it may elect to account for ACT on the part of the dividend referable to the franked investment income. Since its franked payments to the holding company will equal its franked investment income the tax credits will cancel out the ACT payable and so none will actually be paid. But the holding company will receive franked investment income from the subsidiary and therefore will be able to use the tax credits conferred against its own ACT on its dividends. In effect the tax credits obtained by the subsidiary will have been passed down the line to the holding company.[15]

NON-QUALIFYING DISTRIBUTIONS

Non-qualifying distributions are (see p. 299 above) bonus redeemable shares and bonus securities, or any share capital or securities which are (so to speak) the proceeds of such.

When a company makes a non-qualifying distribution it is not required to pay ACT and there is no tax credit. The reason is that bonus redeemable shares and bonus securities are not in themselves income, but rather the right to receive income in the future.

If the recipient of a non-qualifying distribution is an *individual* he is not liable to basic rate income tax on it, but he is liable (if he comes within the threshold) to higher rate tax (less the basic (lower) rate for Schedule F) on the net amount of the distribution (there is no ACT and so no grossing-up). If the company subsequently makes a repayment of the share capital or of the principal of the security, that repayment is itself a distribution, but it is a qualifying distribution and higher rate tax will be payable on the grossed-up amount. The individual may be involved again in "excess liability," but he can deduct from it the amount of tax which he paid on the occasion of the non-qualifying distribution. Thus if a higher rate tax payer receives a non-qualifying distribution of £80 he is liable to higher rate tax of (40 per cent less 20 per cent) £16. If that subsequently becomes a qualifying distribution he will be liable to higher rate tax of £20 (40 per cent less 20 per cent of £100). He can set off the £16 already paid.

If the recipient of a non-qualifying distribution is a company resident in the United Kingdom it is not entitled to any tax credit and it cannot use the distribution to "frank" any of its own qualifying

---

[15] Where the subsidiary company has insufficient taxable income to cover its liability to ACT (and so would have surplus ACT if no group income election is made) but wishes to transfer the tax credits from its franked investment income to the holding company it is possible to acquire an intermediate subsidiary which has an accumulated surplus of mainstream tax liability (the previous six years can be used). Then the subsidiary company pays the money to the intermediate company under a group income election (no ACT, no tax credit) and the intermediate company pays it on to the holding company as franked investment income (using its accumulated surplus to offset the ACT and conferring a tax credit on the payee company): *Pigott v. Staines Investments Co. Ltd* (1995).

distributions. The non-qualifying distribution is not part of the recipient company's franked investment income. If the company passes on the distribution to its own shareholders, that event cannot be a qualifying distribution, and consequently it does not attract advance corporation tax.

CHAPTER 21

CLOSE COMPANIES

Over the years there has been a considerable body of legislation creating a special code of rules for companies which are "close companies". We will be considering below the definition of that term. For the moment let us say that they are companies which are narrowly owned or narrowly controlled, notably single member companies and family companies.

The background to the close company rules is that, if nothing were done about them, narrowly controlled companies would give scope for tax advantages to be reaped by their owners. These advantages, which vary according to the changes in the tax system, can be gained along two lines: first, by taking benefits out of the company in tax advantageous ways: and, secondly, by *not* taking out benefits (such as dividends), but using the company as a storehouse[1] and then after many years selling the storehouse at a reduced or nil rate of tax.

It was the latter mode of tax avoidance which first attracted the attention of the legislature. Soon after the First World War, in the early 1920s, measures were introduced to curb the storehouse use of narrowly owned companies. The effectiveness of using a close company as a storehouse depended upon the fact that by not taking anything out of the company by way of dividends, etc., income tax was avoided and so selling the storehouse, with the accumulated gains, created only a capital gain on the sale of the shares. Since initially there was no tax on capital gains this was a very effective tax saving device. Even when capital gains became chargeable to tax there was a substantial disparity between the rates of income tax and capital gains tax which made the latter much more preferable.

---

[1] "Storehouse" is only one of the possible epithets for such companies. They have been called "receptacles", "money-box companies", and "incorporated pocketbooks".

However, under the present system of tax the rates of income tax and capital gains tax are the same for both individuals and companies (who can of course also be shareholders) so that the use of a close company as a storehouse is much diminished and, accordingly, the storehouse legislation was largely repealed in 1989.

That legislation varied over the years, but the basic idea remained constant. In its most recent manifestation it took the form of what were known as the "shortfall" provisions. Under these, where a close company did not pay out in dividend all that it could reasonably be expected to pay given its profits, the shareholders were taxed as if they had been paid the full amount, thus having to pay higher rate tax on income they had not actually received. This process was known as the "apportionment of income of close companies"; *i.e.* the shortfall between what a close company did distribute and what it could have distributed, was apportioned amongst the shareholders. The legislation was extremely complex and will not be missed. Only close investment companies now remain subject to any storehouse impositions. Those rules are dealt with at the end of this chapter.

The tax advantages of taking benefits out of a close company are still mainly intact, however, so it is still important to know which companies are regarded as close companies for tax purposes. (The definition also has a role to play in inheritance tax). We must first consider a number of definitions in order to understand what constitutes a close company. When we have done that we will look at the rules which deal with the taking of benefits from close companies and then at the rules for close investment companies.

The places in the legislation where matters relating to close companies are largely to be found are section 13A and Part XI of the Taxes Act.

What is a Close Company?

Let us first clear the ground by noting that only a company resident in the United Kingdom can be a close company.

A close company is a company which passes the "control" test. This control test can be broken down into two alternatives. A company is a close company if it is under the control of five or fewer "participators" *or* if it is under the control of participators who are "directors" (however many directors there may be). In deciding the control test the interests of a participator's associates are counted as those of the participator.

DEFINITIONS

In order to understand the above test it is necessary to look a little more closely at some of the words used in the test. What follows is only a summary of the very detailed and complex provisions contained in sections 414 to 417 of the Taxes Act (as amended).

"Control"

A person shall be taken to have control of a company if he exercises, or is able to exercise or is entitled to acquire, control (whether direct or indirect) over the company's affairs, and in particular (but without prejudice to the generality of the preceding words) if he possesses or is entitled to acquire:

(a) the greater part of the share capital or issued share capital of the company or of the voting power in the company; or
(b) such part of the issued share capital of the company as would, if the whole of the income of the company were in fact distributed among the participators (without regard to any rights which he or any other person has as a "loan creditor"), entitle him to receive the greater part of the amount so distributed; or
(c) such rights as would, in the event of the winding up of the company or in any other circumstances, entitle him to receive the greater part of the assets of the company which would then be available for distribution among the participators. In applying this test, where one close company (A) is a participator in another close company (B), then the participators of A are deemed to be entitled to the rights in the assets of B held by A in proportion to their interests in A.

There may be attributed to any person all the rights and powers of an "associate" of his and/or all the rights and powers of any company of which he has control either alone or with his associates.

Where two or more persons satisfy any of the above conditions they shall be taken to have control of the company.

It follows from all this that more than one person—or group of persons—may have control of the company at the same time.

Summarising the control test, it comes to this: quite apart from director-controlled companies, a company is a close company if there can be found any five or fewer participators who, together with their associates, have control in any of the senses set out above.

Notice that a person can have control of a company without having a majority of the voting rights.

"Associate"

An associate means, in relation to a participator:

(i) any "relative" (which in turn means husband or wife, parent or remoter forbear, child or remoter issue, or brother or sister);
(ii) any partner;
(iii) the trustees of any settlement in relation to which the participator is, or any relative of his is or was, a settlor; and
(iv) where the participator is interested in any shares or obligations of the company which are subject to any trust (with certain exceptions) or are part of the estate of a deceased person any other person who has an interest in those shares or obligations. For this head to apply, the participator need not have a *beneficial* interest in the shares, etc. It is sufficient if his interest is as a trustee or executor. Thus a co-executor (for example) could be an associate of a participator.

"Participator"

A participator is a person having a share or interest in the capital or income of a company and (without prejudice to the generality of the preceding words) includes:

(a) any person who possesses, or is entitled to acquire, share capital or voting rights in the company,
(b) any "loan creditor" of the company,
(c) any person who possesses, or is entitled to acquire, a right to receive or participate in distributions of the company (construing "distributions" without regard to the extended meaning which relate to facilities, on which see pp. 312–313 below) or any amounts payable by the company (in cash or in kind) to "loan creditors" (see below) by way of premium on redemption, and
(d) any person who is entitled to secure that income or assets (whether present or future) of the company will be applied directly or indirectly for his benefit.

"Loan creditor"

A loan creditor means (i) a creditor in respect of any redeemable loan capital issued by the company or (ii) a creditor in respect of any debt incurred by the company:

(a) for any money borrowed or capital assets acquired by the company, or
(b) for any right to receive income created in favour of the company, or
(c) for consideration the value of which to the company was (at the time when the debt was incurred) substantially less than the amount of the debt (including any premium thereon).

Note that a person can be a loan creditor without, in the narrow sense, lending money to the company. This is so, for example, of a person who sells an asset to the company and leaves the purchase price owing.

Bankers (or banks) are expressly stated not to become loan creditors merely by lending money in the ordinary course of their banking business.

"Director"

One might think that one knows what a director is without needing a definition, but there is a definition and it greatly extends the ordinary meaning. The term "director" includes:

(i) any person occupying the position of director by whatever name called;
(ii) any person in accordance with whose directions or instructions the directors are accustomed to act[2]; and
(iii) any person who is concerned in the management of the company's trade or business and is, either alone or with associates, directly or indirectly able to control 20 per cent or over of the company's ordinary share capital.

The reader may care to re-read, in the light of the above definitions, the passage at page 307, above, headed, "What is a Close

---

[2] This wording has also been used in the Companies Act 1985, s. 741(2), to define a "shadow director." On which see Charlesworth & Morse, *op. cit.*, p.313.

What is a Close Company?

Company?" A company needs at least 11 independent equal shareholders to avoid being such a company.

COMPANIES WHICH ARE NOT CLOSE COMPANIES

Certain kinds of companies are expressly stated not to be close companies even if according to the above definitions they might be. These are as follows.

(1) Non-resident companies

(2) Quoted companies

One can describe these, in broad terms, as companies in which there is a substantial public interest. A company is not a close company if shares (other than any voting shares which are entitled to a fixed rate of dividend, with or without a further right to participate in profits) carrying not less than 35 per cent of the voting power have been unconditionally allotted to, or acquired by, the public, remain beneficially held by the public, and have been dealt in and officially quoted on a recognised stock exchange within the preceding 12 months. There is no definition of "public," but certain holdings (*e.g.* holdings by a resident non-close company) are expressly stated to be public holdings, and certain other holdings (*e.g.* holdings by a director or his associate) are expressly stated not to be public holdings.

(3) Subsidiaries of non-close companies

A subsidiary controlled by one or more non-close companies is generally not a close company. Such a subsidiary is not a close company if it cannot be made a close company without using a non-close company as one of the controlling participators. Thus a subsidiary of a non-close company is not usually a close company.

To stop up what would otherwise be an easy avoidance device, it is provided that a company controlled by a non-resident company is a close company if the non-resident company would be a close company under these rules if it were resident in the United Kingdom.

It is expressly provided that a company which would otherwise be a non-close company does not become a close company merely by taking a substantial loan from a close company thereby giving the lender what one might call "loan creditor control".

CLOSE COMPANIES

Crown-controlled companies

A company controlled by the Crown and not otherwise a close company is a non-close company.

Certain societies

A registered industrial and provident society is not a close company, nor is a building society.

The Taking of Benefits from Close Companies

At the beginning of this chapter we touched on the two possible kinds of advantage that might be reaped from a close company, namely by taking out benefits from the company and by *not* taking out benefits but rather using the company as a storehouse. We must now consider the first possible kind of advantage, the taking of benefits out of the company.

The legislation dealing with such benefits falls under two[3] heads, which we will look at in turn. The method adopted by the legislation for the first head is to extend, in the case of close companies, the definition of "distribution": the second head can be called a quasi-distribution.

EXPENDITURE ON FACILITIES FOR PARTICIPATORS AND THEIR ASSOCIATES

Section 418 of the Taxes Act declares that where a close company incurs expense in connection with the provision for any participator or for his associate or for a participator in its controlling company of living accommodation or other accommodation, of entertainment, of domestic or other services, or of other benefits or facilities of whatever nature, the company shall be treated as making a distribution to him of an amount equal to so much of that expense as is not made good to the company by the participator or his associate. Two benefits are expressly excepted from the tax charge, namely (a) (for a person employed in director's or higher-paid employment) such benefits as are mentioned in sections 145 and 153–168 of the Taxes Act (see p. 119, above)—they will be taxed under Schedule E, and

---

[3] There were formerly three heads, but the provision treating excess interest payments to participators as a distribution was repealed in 1980.

The Taking of Benefits

(b) benefits on death or retirement for the participator (or associate) or his dependants.

Also there is no tax charge if the participator in the company is another close company and one is the subsidiary of the other or both are subsidiaries of a third company and the benefit arises on the transfer of assets or liabilities by or to the company, provided that all the companies are resident in the United Kingdom.

If two close companies have the bright idea that Company A should provide facilities for the participators of Company B and vice versa, well, the Revenue have thought of that; the facility is treated as coming from the company in which each person is a participator.

The expenditure is treated as a distribution. Consequently it cannot be deducted in computing profits nor counted as a charge on income. As it is not stated to be a non-qualifying distribution it must be a qualifying distribution. So ACT is payable and a tax credit conferred.

LOANS TO PARTICIPATORS AND THEIR ASSOCIATES

Certain loans to participators and their associates are attacked by sections 419 to 422 of the Taxes Act. Without some such provision a close company could make money available to its participators on very advantageous terms tax-wise. Under this head the method adopted by the legislation is not (as under the previous head) to make the transaction a distribution. These loans are not strictly distributions. When it makes such a loan[4] the company is required to pay to the Revenue an amount *as if it were* an amount of corporation tax, and the amount is to be such as *corresponds to* the rate of advance corporation tax. So the amount which the company pays to the Revenue is not advance corporation tax and cannot be set off against the company's mainstream tax liability. On the other hand, if the loan is repaid the Revenue refunds tax to the company. The tax is payable nine months after the relevant accounting period unless the loan has been repaid by that date. Similarly, any refund of the tax is due nine months after the accounting period in which repayment took place.

The loan is not treated as income of the borrower at the time it is made, but if the company releases the debt the borrower is treated as

---

[4] It has been held that an appropriation by a sole director of company funds for his own purposes is not a loan or advance *made* by a company and so not within these sections: *Stephens v. T. Pittas Ltd* (1983).

having then received income equal to the grossed-up equivalent of the amount released. Thus if a higher rate shareholder was given a loan of £800 which is released (*i.e.* written off) by the company he will be taxed at higher rate tax on £1,000 (£800 + 20 per cent of £800). He is not liable to basic rate tax (20 per cent in this case) so that he will have to pay £200 (£400–£200).[5]

Loans taxable under section 677 of the Taxes Act (see above) are excepted from the operation of these present sections.

These sections do not apply to a loan made by a close company in the ordinary course of a business which includes the lending of money. Nor do they apply to a loan to a director or employee of the close company or its associated company (one under the control of the same person(s)), if the amount of the loan (with outstanding loans) to the borrower does not exceed £15,000, provided the borrower works full-time for the close company or any of its associated companies and does not have a material interest (usually 5 per cent of the ordinary shares) in the close company or in any associated company.[6] There are provisions to catch the situation where the loan is channelled through a non-participator.

Close Investment-holding Companies

We have seen at the beginning of this chapter that the rules preventing the use of close companies as a storehouse for the purpose of avoiding or limiting tax liability were largely abolished in 1989 as a consequence of the harmonisation of income tax and capital gains tax rates. The Revenue were, however, concerned that close companies might still be used as a way of channelling investment income so as to attract the small companies rate of 24 per cent as opposed to higher rate income tax. The Finance Act 1989 accordingly introduced the concept of the close investment-holding company (see now section 13A of the Taxes Act).

A close company is also a close investment-holding company unless it exists (for the whole of the relevant accounting period) wholly or mainly for one of the following purposes: (i) to carry on a trade on a commercial basis; (ii) to make commercial (*i.e.* non-

---

[5] It has been held that a debt has been released by the company for this purpose where it has been novated from one borrower to another in the company's books, *i.e.* where A has replaced B as the borrower, B will be liable to the charge: *Collins v. Addies* (1992).
[6] Notice that this exception does not apply to participators who are not directors or employees.

personal) investments in land; (iii) to hold shares or make loans to companies within its group; (iv) to provide administration services for a group of companies; or (v) to service the trades or investments in land of a group of companies.

The main consequence of being a close investment-holding company is that the small companies rate will not be available. Standard rate corporation tax will be payable whatever its profits. In addition the Revenue may in certain circumstances restrict the entitlement of certain individuals to a repayment of a tax credit in respect of distributions made by such a company: Taxes Act, s. 231. In essence this will apply where the company is being used as a tax avoidance device to channel investment income to individuals who will have insufficient United Kingdom tax liability to cover the tax credits conferred on a distribution.

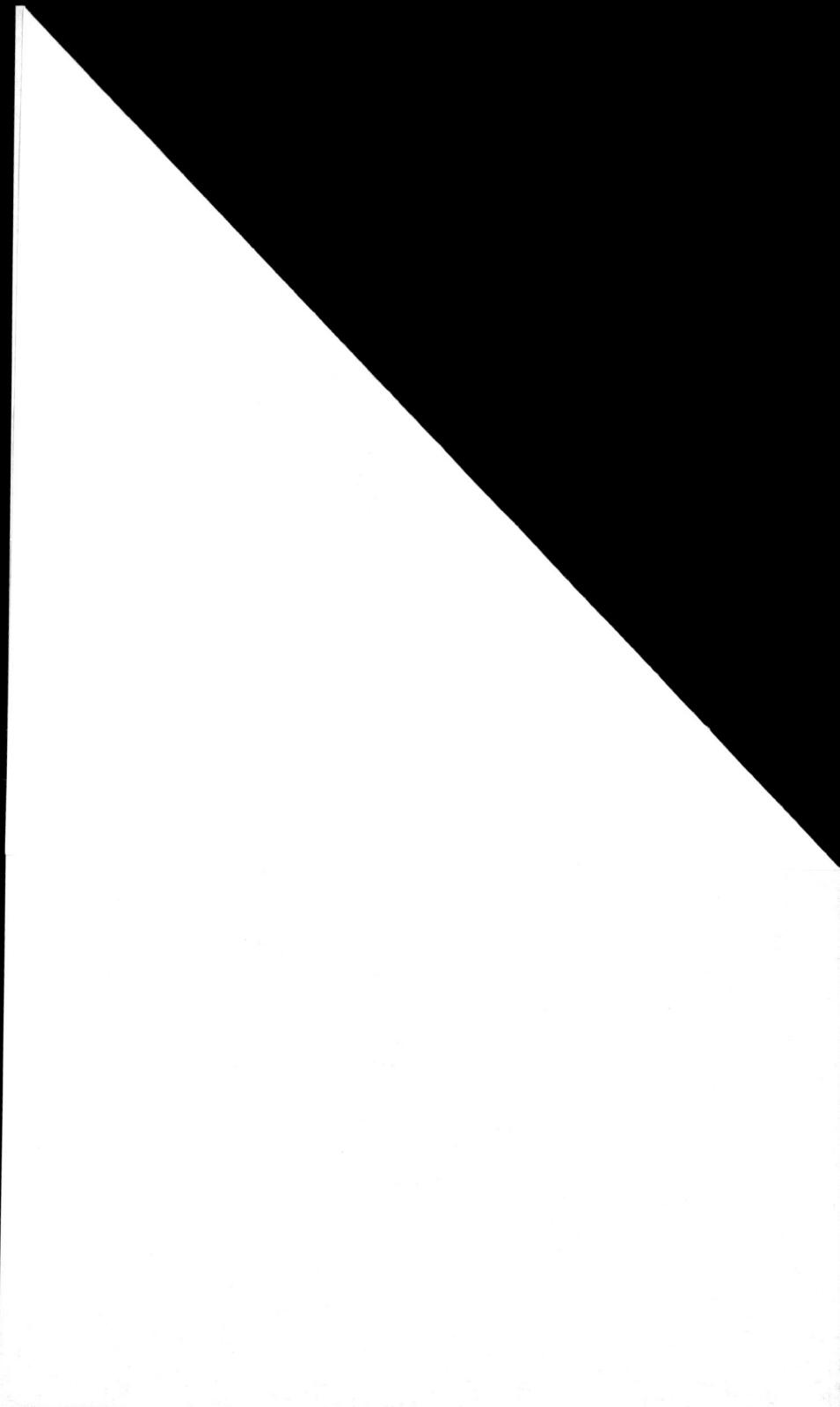

Chapter 22

THE EVOLUTION OF INHERITANCE TAX

Ever since 1894 there has been a tax aimed at non-commercial transfers of capital, charging tax on the whole of the value so transferred. The current version of this tax is known as inheritance tax, although as we shall see it is neither calculated by reference to what a person inherits nor limited to inheritance on a death. It differs from capital gains tax which taxes only the gain on a transfer, does not apply on a death and applies in the main to commercial transfers of capital. The relationship between the two taxes is usually complimentary, although there are overlaps in the area of lifetime gifts, where paradoxically capital gains tax is more likely to apply than inheritance tax.

The evolution of inheritance tax can be traced back to estate duty introduced in 1894. That tax charged all the property of an individual which passed on his death, unless specifically exempted. In its final form this included not only property which the deceased owned at his death and which passed under his will or intestacy but also property which was deemed to pass on his death. Such property included the full value of any settled property in which the deceased had an interest (including certain discretionary trusts) and the value of any gift made by the deceased either within seven years prior to his death or at any time if the deceased had retained any interest in the property given. The whole amount of the property so passing on the death was then aggregated and tax charged on that amount. Thus estate duty was a mutation duty (*i.e.* one charged on the property passing from the deceased) and not an acquisition duty (*i.e.* one charged according to the amount each person acquired on the death). But only a death triggered a charge.

In 1974 the incoming Labour government announced its intention to repeal estate duty, which it finally did in 1975. The replacement was known as capital transfer tax. The central idea of this tax (introduced as the precursor of a wealth tax which never materialised) was to charge all non-commercial transfers of capital (known as chargeable transfers) made by an individual throughout his lifetime, with death being regarded as the final transfer. The important concept was that all such transfers were taxed on a cumulative basis. Thus the rate of tax for each successive transfer was calculated on the basis of the transferor's cumulative total at that time. Thus if X, having already made transfers of £100,000, made another transfer of £50,000, the rate of tax for that transfer would be calculated at that applicable for transfers between £100,000 and £150,000, and so on, until on X's death the rates payable would depend upon his whole cumulative total of lifetime transfers. The value of each transfer was calculated not on the value of the transfer as such but on the loss to the transferor. There were special rules for settlements. The law on capital transfer tax was consolidated in 1984 into the Capital Transfer Tax Act.

But by then this principle of taxing all transfers made by an individual throughout his lifetime had been reduced by the rule that the cumulative principle should only apply to gifts made within the previous ten years. Thus in our example above, if X had made the £100,000 transfers more than 10 years before the transfer of £50,000, the latter would be taxed only on the rates between £0 and £50,000. If only £60,000 of the earlier transfers had been made within the past 10 years, the rate of tax on the £50,000 transfer would be calculated according to the rates between £60,000 and £110,000. More importantly, on a death the deceased's cumulative total would only be those transfers made within 10 years of the death and not those throughout his lifetime. In 1986 even more fundamental changes were made to the structure of capital transfer tax and the resulting product was renamed as the inheritance tax we have today. Even the 1984 consolidation, as amended, was renamed the Inheritance Tax Act 1984[1] and references to sections in the following chapters are to that Act unless otherwise stated.

What then were these changes? Apart from a simplification of the rates of the tax, the major change was to take most lifetime transfers out of the charge to the tax altogether[2]. With one or two exceptions[3] lifetime transfers will only be chargeable if either they were made within seven years prior to the death of the transferor or the

---

[1] Technically the law provides that the 1984 Act *may* be referred to as the Inheritance Tax Act 1984 rather than the Capital Transfer Tax Act, but, in practice, everybody does so.
[2] Thus triggering the reintroduction of the charge on gifts under capital gains tax.
[3] Notably those relating to discretionary trusts.

The Evolution of Inheritance Tax

transferor has retained an interest in the property transferred. Virtually all lifetime transfers are now regarded as potentially exempt transfers which will only become retrospectively chargeable in their own right if the transferor dies within seven years of making them. The cumulative principle for those transfers which are chargeable has been reduced from 10 to seven years accordingly, so that on a death the deceased's cumulative total relates to those transfers charged (at the time or retrospectively) within the past seven years.

Inheritance tax has therefore resurrected the old estate duty concepts that a death rather than a lifetime transfer is the trigger for a charge to the tax and that gifts made within seven years and those with a reservation of benefit (gifts with reservation) become chargeable on that death. But many aspects of capital transfer tax also remain. Charges on a death and on settlements remain much as before, the way in which the value of the transfer is calculated is still the loss to the transferor, there is still a limited form of cumulation and in certain cases there is a charge even though no death has occurred. Thus inheritance tax is a hybrid between estate duty and capital transfer tax, which charges more than just an inheritance on a death and which does so by reference to the total of the transfers made by the transferor and not by reference to the amount inherited; *i.e.* it is still a mutation and not an acquisitions tax. One curious consequence of the changes to this tax is that most lifetime gifts will not be chargeable to inheritance tax (the non-commercial tax) on the full value transferred but to capital gains tax (the commercial tax) on the notional gain made by the donor. Where both taxes are chargeable there is a relief from capital gains tax.

In the following chapters we shall examine the scope and effects of this hybrid known as inheritance tax. The first question which needs an answer is what amounts to a chargeable lifetime transfer so as to give rise either to an immediate lifetime charge or to a retrospective charge if the transferor dies within seven years, explaining as we go the way in which gifts with reservation fit into this. Then we need to examine the charge which arises on the death of the transferor. Having established what is chargeable or potentially chargeable we need to look at the various exemptions and reliefs which are available against this charge. Having thus established the net charge so to speak we then examine how the charge is actually calculated and who ultimately has to account for and pay the tax. Because settlements are the subject of many special rules these are dealt with in a separate chapter.

CHAPTER 23

CHARGEABLE TRANSFERS

Inheritance tax is only chargeable if there is a *chargeable transfer*. These may be made either during the transferor's lifetime or on his death, although, as we have seen, most of the former do not attract an immediate charge to the tax. Instead they may become retrospectively chargeable if the transferor dies within seven years of making them. Until then they are known as *potentially exempt transfers*. There are special rules for lifetime transfers in which the transferor retains some interest in the property transferred, known as *gifts with reservation*. This chapter deals with what is meant by a chargeable lifetime transfer, what is a potentially exempt transfer, the rules for gifts with reservation, transfers on death, and one or two special charges, *e.g.* involving close companies as defined for corporation tax purposes). Settled property, being inevitably the most complex area, is dealt with separately in Chapter 26. Remember that there are many exemptions and reliefs which apply to these various charges—these are set out in the following chapter.

Lifetime Transfers

Section 1 declares: "Inheritance tax shall be charged on the value transferred by a chargeable transfer." What, then, is a "chargeable transfer"? The answer is in section 2(1): "A chargeable transfer is a transfer of value which is made by an individual but is not an exempt transfer."

So we need to know what is a transfer of value, what is the value transferred, what is an individual and what is an exempt transfer.

A "*transfer of value*" is defined by section 3(1) as: " ... a disposition made by a person (the transferor) as a result of which the value of his estate immediately after the disposition is less than it would be but for the disposition: and the amount by which it is less is the *value transferred* by the transfer." The two essential criteria for a charge are therefore a disposition and a loss to the transferor's estate.

The word "*individual*" is not defined by the Act, but of course it is a word well-known in tax law; it does not include companies, nor trustees nor personal representatives. However, as we shall see later, certain dispositions made by trustees of settled property give rise to charges to tax as if they were chargeable transfers, and transfers of value made by companies which are close companies may also give rise to tax liability.

Transfers which are "*exempt transfers*", and therefore not changeable transfers, are dealt with in Chapter 24. They form a very important part of the law.

It is also as well to say here (and we shall see some examples of this later on) that some kinds of property are designated as "*excluded property*", though these are mainly overseas assets. Transfers of such property are not taken into account; section 3(2).

It is very important to appreciate that the *value transferred* by a transfer is measured by the diminution in value of the transferor's estate, and not by the increase in value of the transferee's estate. Of course, in many circumstances the result would be the same whichever measure one took. If Albert gives a motor car to his son Ben, Albert's estate is diminished and Ben's estate is increased by the same amount, namely the value of the car. But there are circumstances in which this is not so, and some of them are very important. For example, if Albert owns 51 per cent of the shares in a company and Ben owns none, and then Albert transfers 2 per cent of the shares to Ben, the diminution in Albert's estate is much greater than is the increase in Ben's estate, because Albert has given up control of the company, and Ben has not obtained control.

One very important aspect of this diminution principle is that if the transferor pays the inheritance tax the tax is itself taxable, because his estate is diminished not only by what he transfers to the transferee but also by what he has to pay to the Revenue. The payment of the tax forms part of the loss to the transferor's estate. So there is a grossing-up process. We will deal with this concept more fully later on.

It will be noticed that the definition of transfer of value includes the word "disposition". There is no general definition of this but it probably includes not only obvious transfers such as sales and gifts

CHARGEABLE TRANSFERS

but also disclaimers[1] and waivers of possible future rights.[2] There have been two attempts since 1975 to charge interest-free loans but both have been repealed and the position remains obscure. It is, however, provided by section 3(3) that a disposition can be merely the omission to exercise a right. This provision prevents many possible avoidance devices. For example, but for this provision Albert could make a tax-free transfer to Ben (his son) by engaging him, for a lump sum paid in advance, to work for a specified time in his (Albert's) business and then standing by and omitting to sue for damages when Ben does not turn up. Section 3(3) only applies, however, if, as the result of an omission by you, your estate is diminished and another's is increased, and it can be avoided if you can show that the omission was not deliberate.[3]

It is stated in section 272 (the definitions section, well worth looking at) that a "disposition" includes "a disposition effected by *associated operations*" and "associated operations" are defined by section 268. They are

"(a) operations which affect the same property ... or
(b) any two operations of which one is effected with reference to the other, or with a view to enabling the other to be effected or facilitating its being effected, and any further operation having a like relation to any of those two, and so on: whether those operations are effected by the same person or different persons, and whether or not they are simultaneous; and 'operation' includes an omission."

For example, if Albert transfers some property to his wife Zoë on condition that she shall transfer it to their son Ben, the transfer to Ben may be treated as if Albert were the transferor. Thus if Albert dies within seven years of the gift by Zoë to Ben, the transfer will be chargeable, even if Zoë is still alive. Equally the transfer will count against Albert's annual exemption limit rather than Zoë's.

The definition of associated operations is very wide and it is interesting to compare it with the *Ramsay* principle devised by the

---

[1] Some disclaimers are expressly excluded from the charge, (*e.g.* of a legacy within two years of death: s.142). So it presumably follows that other disclaimers are included.
[2] Again some waivers, (*e.g.* of future dividends not declared for at least one year afterwards: s.15) are expressly excluded from the charge.
[3] Does this include for example failure to exercise a beneficial option owing to lack of funds?

courts (see p. 41, above). The section has been before the courts on two occasions, both involving settlements. In *Macpherson v. IRC* (1988) the trustees entered into two transactions which together had the effect of lowering the charge to tax on the second. The House of Lords had no difficulty in deciding that these were associated operations but the case is worth noting because their Lordships imposed a restriction on the width of the section by insisting that each operation must be relevant to the scheme which created the benefit for the transferee. In *Hatton v. IRC* (1992) where two settlements were created within 24 hours of each other and the first was set up with a view to the second being created, Chadwick J. also applied the associated operations rules. The consequence was that each settlor was treated as being a settlor of both settlements, which had the effect of negating the sought for exemptions from the tax. It is possible that this approach will also apply to joint and reciprocal settlements.

If the associated operations provision applies then the consequence is that the chargeable transfer is deemed to take place at the time of the last of them: section 268(3). There is one statutory exception in section 268(2). The grant of a lease for full consideration is not to be associated with any operation effected more than three years earlier, *e.g.* a gift of the landlord's reversion.

The word "*estate*" has cropped up several times already. It is defined in section 5(1):

> "... a person's estate is the aggregate of all the property to which he is beneficially entitled, except that the estate of a person immediately before his death does not include excluded property."

Pause to admire the sheer beauty of the last five words—"does not include excluded property." It is quite an important point really, and we shall be considering its significance later on. For the moment the point we want to emphasise about the word "estate" is that it is used in this legislation in reference to a living person as well as to a dead person.

The word "*property*" is stated in section 272 to include "rights and interests of any description." It thus includes (and the importance of this will be seen later) an interest under a settlement such as a life tenancy.

In particular, section 5(2) includes any general power of appointment as being part of a person's estate. The definition of a general power for this purpose seems to continue the estate duty concept[4] of any power which a person can appoint in his own favour, *e.g.* "to such person as X shall appoint", or "to such of X, Y, and Z as X shall appoint". It follows that the exercise of such a power will be a transfer of value (disposition plus loss to the estate) and also in some cases the omission to exercise it (loss to estate and gain to the estate of the person entitled in default of appointment—section 3(3)).

It has been said above that inheritance tax is (in part) a tax on non-commercial transfers, *i.e.* "gifts tax". That phrase is not used in the legislation, but it is made clear by the use of other words "*gratuitous benefit*" that the tax only bites on transfers which contain an element of gift. Sales at market value are not taxable because they do not involve any diminution in the value of the seller's estate. If Albert owns a car which is worth £800 and he sells it to Charles for £800 Albert's estate has the same value after the sale as it had before the sale; he has merely exchanged one asset (the car) for an equivalent asset (cash). But suppose Albert sells the car, not for £800, but for £500. That may occur either (1) because Albert wished to confer a benefit on Charles or (2) because he made a bad bargain. A gift (as in (1), is taxable: a bad bargain (as in (2), is not taxable. This point is dealt with in section 10(1) which declares:

> "A disposition is not a transfer of value if it is shown that it was not intended, and was not made in a transaction intended, to confer any gratuitous benefit on any person and either—
>
> (a) that it was made in a transaction at arm's length between persons not connected with each other, or
> (b) that it was such as might be expected to be made in a transaction at arm's length between persons not connected with each other ..."

The subsection requires two conditions to be met; a subjective non-donative intent *and* the objective fact stated in (a) or the apparently objective fact stated in (b).[5] Where the parties are connected (*i.e.* they are relatives, linked in a trust, partners or involved with a close company) the criterion imposed by (b) of what would be expected to

---

[4] See, *e.g. Re Parsons* (1943).
[5] On a sale of shares in an unquoted company it is also necessary to show that the price was either freely negotiated or one that could have been so negotiated. Thus transfers by close companies are outside the definition.

amount to an arm's length sale was discussed in *IRC v. Spencer-Nairn* (1991). This was an unusual case in that the vendor was unaware that he was selling to a connected person (a company) and had negotiated on the basis that they were unconnected. He sold the property for £94,000 below the market value because he mistakenly thought that he was liable for repairs to the property. The Revenue agreed that he had no gratuitous intention but argued that the discrepancy between the market value and the actual value of the land meant that it was not one which could have been expected on an arm's length sale. The Scottish Court of Session dismissed the argument that any such discrepancy would automatically invoke the section, stating that it was merely one factor which had to be taken into account. They decided that a hypothetical arm's length vendor should be taken to have had the actual vendor's (reasonable) belief that he was liable for repairs and so, since the price was not unreasonable given that belief, they found for the taxpayer. They were impressed by the fact that the price had been negotiated between persons who thought they were acting at arms length. One consequence of this decision is therefore that in assessing what can be expected on an arm's length sale certain subjective factors, such as the reasonable belief in this case, are to be taken into account.

Notice that section 10(1) has the very desirable result that payment for services is nor a transfer of value. If you pay a fee to a solicitor (for example) your estate has been diminished by the amount of the fee but you are saved from tax by section 10(1). You need only pay the solicitor, not the Revenue as well.

Potentially exempt transfers

Lifetime transfers do not necessarily attract an immediate charge to tax. Only those which are not potentially exempt transfers as defined in section 3A become immediately liable to a charge. A potentially exempt transfer (PET) is defined as (i) one made by an individual, (ii) which would otherwise be a chargeable transfer, (iii) which is made to another individual or is made to, or is connected with, a settlement in which an individual has an interest in possession or which is an accumulation and maintenance settlement or is a disabled trust.[6] Thus transfers to companies and the various charges

---

[6] These terms are discussed in Chapter 26, below.

Chargeable Transfers

involving discretionary trusts (other than accumulation and disabled trusts) are not potentially exempt transfers.

In the case of a transfer to an individual the transfer will only be a PET if the property becomes part of that individual's estate or his estate is increased. Thus if David decides to pay his grandson's school fees and does so by paying the school direct he has not made a PET—the grandson's estate has not been increased. It would be a PET if David gave the money to his son who then used the money to pay the school fees as the son's estate will have been increased. Gifts with a reservation, *i.e.* where the donor retains some interest in the property, are the subject of special rules, set out in the following part of this chapter.

We will explain the somewhat tortuous rules for calculating the charges to inheritance tax in Chapter 25. For the moment it is sufficient to note that a lifetime transfer which is not a PET attracts an immediate charge based on the cumulative total of such transfers within the previous seven years. The current rate is 20 per cent on cumulative transfers above £200,000. Thus if Edward, having made no previous transfers, creates two discretionary trusts in 1995 and 1996, each with a value of £200,000—the first will be tax free but the second will be chargeable at 20 per cent.

If the transfer is a PET then there is no immediate charge to tax and if the transferor lives for more than seven years there will be no charge at all. If, however, the transferor dies within that period the PET becomes chargeable at the appropriate rate for deaths (subject to some relief if he has survived at least three years) as laid down at the date of death rather than at the rate in force when the transfer was made unless the former is higher. The effect of a PET ceasing to be exempt because of the death is that it becomes a chargeable transfer. Thus it will have to be taken into account in working out the transferor's cumulative total for other lifetime transfers. This can retrospectively affect the liability for those other transfers. Thus if in our example above, Edward had made a PET of £200,000 in 1994, which subsequently becomes chargeable on Edward's death in 1997, not only is that transfer itself charged to tax but the relevant cumulative total of previous transfers for the discretionary trust transfer in 1995 will change from zero to £200,000 and the latter will become chargeable at 20 per cent.

Gifts with reservation of benefit

With the introduction of the potentially exempt transfer regime in 1986 it was inevitable that measures would be taken to prevent a transferor making a gift, *e.g.* of his house to his son or daughter, whilst retaining a benefit in that property, *e.g.* by continuing to live in the house. If the transferor lived for more than seven years after making the gift he would avoid any inheritance tax and would have passed on his house to his son or daughter tax free, whilst in practice having made no material change in his circumstances. To prevent taxpayers having their cake and eating it in this way the concept of a gift with reservation was introduced by section 102 of and Schedule 20 to the Finance Act 1986. In fact this concept was really reintroduced because it had been necessary for such a provision under estate duty law to prevent exactly the same abuse. The legislation is similar to that for estate duty and some of the cases decided under those rules are relevant here, although of course it is open to modern courts to distinguish them because the wording is not identical.

One problem with using the former estate duty concept of a gift is that it does not always square with the inheritance tax concept of a transfer of value. Thus, whilst a bad bargain may be a transfer of value if it is between connected persons because there will be a loss to the transferor's estate and it will not fall within the gratuitous benefit exemption, it is hard to see that there is any element of bounty so as to classify it as a gift.[7]

Section 102 of the Finance Act 1986 applies when an individual disposes of any property by way of gift and either:

(a) possession and enjoyment is not bona fide assumed by the donee at, or before the beginning of the relevant period; or
(b) at any time in the relevant period the property is not enjoyed to the entire exclusion, or virtually the entire exclusion,[8] of the donor and of any benefit to him by contract or otherwise.

---

[7] It is also arguable that a disposition which is deemed by the 1984 Act not to be a transfer of value, *e.g.* one for the maintenance of the family (see Chapter 24), will still be a gift for this purpose.
[8] This was not present in the original estate duty provisions and is intended to allow *e.g.* the donor of a house to return to it on visits or a short holiday.

Chargeable Transfers

The *relevant period* in which both possession and enjoyment must be assumed and the entire exclusion of the donor is assessed, is seven years prior to the death of the donor. Thus if at any time in the seven years prior to his death the donor was not so excluded or possession was not taken up by the donee, the gift will be regarded as one subject to a reservation. It follows that if any such benefit is given up and possession has been assumed more than seven years before the death then there is no gift with a reservation and in fact no charge to inheritance tax.

There are two possible consequences of a gift being regarded as one subject to a reservation. First, if the gift is still subject to a reservation at the date of the donor's death, the property given is deemed to be part of the donor's estate at death and so chargeable as if he had never given it away. Secondly, if the gift ceases to be subject to a reservation within seven years before the donor's death, the donor is treated as if he had made a PET at that date. Thus the property will be retrospectively charged as if the donor had made a chargeable transfer of the property at the date when the reservation ceased.

Using the old estate duty cases (and one modern one) it is possible to shed some light on how the courts will interpret the various parts of section 102 of the Finance Act 1986. With regard to the concept of the donee assuming bona fide possession in paragraph (a) it is clear that to do so the gift must be a perfect transfer in equity.[9] This was the decision in *Letts v. IRC* (1954). Looking at paragraph (b), it has been held that the donor will not be entirely excluded from possession of the property unless that is the position in fact as well as in law. Thus in *Oakes v. Commissioner of Stamp Duties* (1954), a settlor who settled property in which he had no interest was caught, when he was appointed as a trustee with a right to remuneration, and in *Stamp Duties Commissioner of New South Wales v. Permanent Trustee Co.* (1956), where the settlor borrowed the interest arising from the settlement on his daughter, with no legal entitlement to do so, a similar result applied.

The inclusion of a benefit "by contract or otherwise" is intended to catch collateral benefits to the donor. In *Att.-Gen. v. Seccombe* (1991) it was held that such benefits had to be the subject of a legal

---

[9] Remember that in general equity will not perfect an imperfect gift so that if any formalities required to effect a gift have not been undertaken by the donor, there is no perfect gift.

entitlement. It is doubted whether that would now be the law. Schedule 20 expressly excludes two factual situations from being a reservation of a benefit. Paragraph 6 provides that actual occupation of land by the donor in return for full consideration in money or where the donor comes back into actual occupation of land owing to his incapacity and it is for reasonable provision for his care and maintenance by the donee who is a relative of the donor, are not to be regarded as a reservation of a benefit by the donor.

The most complex of the old cases were those which drew a distinction between a benefit reserved out of the property given away and a benefit retained by the donor which was never given away in the first place. The importance of this is that in the second case the property actually given away has never been the subject of a reservation. This is easier to state than to apply in practice, however. The trick is to separate the part retained by the donor from the part given away. This is sometimes explained by reference to *vertical and horizontal separation.*

> For example if Fred owns two adjoining houses and gives one to Gillian whilst retaining the other this is said to be vertical separation. The fact that Fred has retained one house does not mean that he has retained any benefit in the other which thus becomes a PET.
>
> Suppose instead Fred creates an interest in his property and then gives away the rest, he has horizontally separated the two and so has no benefit in the part given away. It would be different if he gave away the whole property and was then given back the interest in it—he would have reserved a benefit in the property.

With regard to such horizontal separation the timing of the separation seems to be crucial. The original authority for its effectiveness is *Munro v. Commissioner of Stamp Duties* (1934), where the donor gave away land subject to his interest as a partner in its use which had been created prior to the gift. He was held to have given away only the land subject to the partnership interest. He had not reserved his interest as a partner but had never given it away at all. This decision was distinguished in *Nicholls v. IRC* (1975) where the donor gave his land away subject to a condition that it was leased back to him by the donee. He was held to have given away the whole property and reserved the benefit of the lease. The lease had not been created by a prior transaction unlike the partnership interest in *Munro.*

The only case on the new provisions was also directly on this point of horizontal severance. In *Ingram v. IRC* (1995) the donor transferred property to trustees and *at the same time* created the right to a lease of the property to herself. The judge applied *Munro*—there had been a horizontal separation of the lease from the property given to the trustees. The taxpayer had given the trustees the property subject to the lease. The judge stated that horizontal severance would work if it happened before or at the time of the gift as part of the process of defining what was the subject matter of the gift.[10]

The final question involving gifts subject to a reservation is that if they do become chargeable what property is actually subject to the charge. The answers to this are to be found in Schedule 20 to the Finance Act 1986. If the property originally given is still held by the donee unchanged in form then of course it will be that property, valued now, which is chargeable. But if the donee has parted with the original gift an alternative is required. In outline, if the donee sells or exchanges the asset for full consideration then that sum or replacement asset becomes the subject of any charge. In other cases the property with which he parted (including any replacement asset taken in full exchange) becomes the subject of the charge. The same rules apply broadly to gifts into a settlement.

Transfers on Death

Section 4(1) declares that: "On the death of any person tax shall be charged as if, immediately before his death he had made a transfer of value and the value transferred by it had been equal to the value of his estate immediately before his death." It is this enactment which brought in inheritance tax as a replacement of estate duty.

The effect of section 4 is that the deceased is deemed to have made a disposition of all his assets the moment before death. The total of those assets must then be added to the cumulative total of his chargeable lifetime transfers made in the past seven years and charged at the appropriate rate (currently 40 per cent on transfers above £200,000). The rate of tax on a death is twice that on a lifetime transfer, although the former may also be liable to capital gains tax. We have already seen that the death of the transferor will

---

[10] *Nicholls v. IRC* was distinguished on the basis that the decision there was obiter since the case had really been about another provision of the estate duty legislation.

make all PETS made within the past seven years retrospectively chargeable (and part of the cumulative total of previous transfers) and that a gift still subject to a reservation at the death will also become chargeable at the rates for a death. The death will also increase the rate of tax already paid on a non-PET lifetime transfer made within seven years prior to the death. One minor blessing is that since the deceased has transferred all his assets on his death there can be no question of grossing up the transfer to include the tax payable—that must come out of the assets transferred. Questions as to who pays the tax and who ultimately bears the cost (*e.g.* as between the beneficiaries) are the subject of Chapter 27.

What is the point of deeming the transfer of value to have been made "immediately before" the death, not "on" the death? Presumably it is to knock out any argument that at the moment of death certain interests of the person dying cease to exist and therefore do not form part of his estate. This argument could have been put forward, for example, in relation to the interest of a joint tenant which is extinguished "on" the death: section 171(2).

Similarly exercising a power of appointment by will does not affect the fact that such a power formed part of the estate immediately before the death. Estate has the same meaning as for lifetime transfers. Moving the deemed transfer from the moment of death to "immediately before" the death also makes it easier for the legislation to lay down its own code of rules, untrammelled by the general law, as to which assets are to be treated as forming part of the estate and which are not. Such a code is laid down in sections 171 to 177. For example, there is an allowance for reasonable funeral expenses under section 172.

It is important to know what is the tax position if two (or more) persons die (for example in a motor accident) virtually at the same instant. The law of succession to property in such a case is stated in section 184 of the Law of Property Act 1925, namely that the younger person is deemed to have survived the elder person. For tax purposes section 4(2) provides that "where it cannot be known which of two or more persons who have died survived the other or others they shall be assumed to have died at the same instant." Suppose that the two persons are Albert and his son Ben. The effect is that the estate left by Albert to Ben is charged to tax on Albert's death but not also on Ben's death. Similarly, if Ben has left anything to Albert, that estate is charged on Ben's death but not also on Albert's death. Where the order of death *is* known (*e.g.* Albert dies five minutes before Ben) section 4(2) does not apply, but there may be "Quick Succession Relief": see p. 344, below. An alternative is to provide in a will that property will only pass to a beneficiary if he survives the testator by a specified period. Such survivorship clauses if limited to six months will avoid a double charge in such cases: section 92.

Other Charges

This rather curious chapter title is taken from the Finance Act 1975 where "Other Charges" was used as a cross-heading to describe four sections, 39–42, grouped together in that Act as being, broadly speaking, anti-avoidance measures. It is a fair comment on the haste with which the 1975 Bill was prepared that these problems had not been thought through very thoroughly. Indeed, when the Bill was first published the problem of close companies (obvious with hindsight) had not been dealt with at all. When the 1984 consolidation took place some attempts at rationalisation over the 10 years was evident. Section 39 (beefed up in 1976) become sections 94 to 98 *and* section 102 *and* section 202. Section 41 was repealed before it came into effect. But sections 40 and 42 (now sections 262 and 263) still defy classification and were assigned to the "Miscellaneous and Supplementary" part of the 1984 Act.

Close companies

In general, inheritance tax is not charged on companies because they are not "individuals". But, by section 94, where a company which is a close company makes a transfer of value a tax charge may arise. Such transfers cannot be PETs and so attract an immediate charge to the tax. The intention is to prevent such companies from being used to avoid the tax. Tax is charged as if each participator, domiciled here, had made a transfer of value proportionate to his interest in the company.[11] But against this can be set the amount (if any) by which the value of his estate is increased. So (for example) a reduction of capital would be a gratuitous transfer by the company, but no tax would be payable because each member's estate would be increased by the amount received. His estate (for this purpose) does not include any rights or interests in the company.

---

[11] We have come across these terms for corporation tax purposes see p. 309, above. But see section 96 which excludes the ownership of preference shares for this purpose.

Section 98 provides that where there is an alteration of such a company's shares or debentures or rights attaching to them so that there is a loss to a transferor's estate there will be a chargeable transfer by the participators. This is to prevent value being passed in ways that it might be impossible to establish that the transferor shareholder has made a disposition, *e.g.* on a reduction of capital or a purchase by a company of its own shares. The sections are aimed at various avoidance devices, and consequently section 102 provides that a "close company" includes not only a company which is a close company for purposes of corporation tax (see p. 307 above) but also a company which would be such a close company if it were resident in the United Kingdom.

Future payments

This matter is dealt with (in rather obscure language) by section 262. Where a transfer of value takes the form of a disposition for which payments are made (or assets are transferred) more than a year after the disposition, each payment is taxed separately when it is made, the tax being based on a proportionate part of the value transferred. For example, if A buys a property for more than its market value, that is, on the general principles of the tax, a transfer of value by A of the amount by which the price exceeds the market value—the gratuitous element. The effect of this present section is that if A agrees to pay by instalments, each instalment counts as a separate transfer of value. (The rule does not apply to a disposition for no consideration at all, such as an ordinary seven-year covenant.) The point of the section is (presumably) to spread the amount of value transferred. Thus some of the instalments may fall within seven years before A's death, thus attracting a charge, whereas the earlier ones may escape such a charge under the PET rules.

Free loans

This matter was originally intended to be dealt with by section 41 (of Finance Act 1975) but that was replaced by Finance Act 1976, s.115 before it came into effect. That section was itself repealed and there are no specific provisions now to deal with, *e.g.* interest-free loans. The position is therefore covered only by the general provisions of the Act. It follows that a fixed-term loan of money or assets may be a transfer of value. For example, if A lends B £1,000 interest-free for five years, gratuitously, A is making a transfer to B of the then value of using the money for that period. But if the loan was repayable on demand, there would be no value transferred, and no inheritance tax charge.

Annuity purchased in conjunction with life policy

Section 263 imposes a charge to tax where the purchase of an annuity is an associated operation with the issue of a life policy on the life of the annuitant and the policy is vested in someone other than the purchaser of the annuity. The purchaser is treated as making a transfer of value at the time the life policy becomes vested in that other person. The amount of the transfer of value is whichever is the less of the following: (a) the sum paid for the annuity plus premiums paid under the policy up to the time of the transfer; (b) the greatest benefit capable of being conferred at any time by the policy. Such transfers are PETs.

It seems that this special charge to tax is additional to the charge which may arise (if no exemption applies) from the transferor's keeping the policy on foot by paying the premiums, each premium payment being a transfer of value.

The reason why the Revenue are so concerned about back-to-back policies is that a linked contract for life assurance and an annuity with the same company can be obtained on very favourable terms, because if the company loses on the assurance policy it will gain on the annuity contract. Because of this background, it seems that the Revenue will be prepared to treat the arrangements as not being associated operations (and hence not taxable) if the life policy has been issued on no different terms from those which would have been obtainable without the annuity link.

Settled property

The application of inheritance tax to settled property is the subject of Chapter 26, below.

CHAPTER 24

EXEMPTIONS AND RELIEFS

The legislation gives relief from tax in various ways. Some kinds of property are declared to be excluded property. Some transactions are declared not to be transfers of value. Some transfers of value are declared to be exempt transfers, thus attracting no tax. Some transfers of value, though they are taxable, attract a reduced amount of tax. Some apply to lifetime transfers only, some to transfers on a death and others to all types of transfer.

No great benefit would accrue from expounding the exemptions and reliefs under separate heads corresponding to the various modes of relief mentioned above. Until the 1984 Act they were somewhat randomly placed through the legislation, and even the 1984 consolidation has to resort to calling two of its nine parts "Miscellaneous". In order to continue to show how the history of this tax lacks coherence the order in which the exemptions and reliefs are expounded in what follows is based largely (but not wholly) on the order in which they stood in the Finance Act 1975 and then on the order in which further reliefs have been added since. References in this chapter are, however, to the 1984 Act.

We list first those transfers defined as exempt transfers.

Transfers between spouses: section 18

Transfers between spouses are exempt transfers. This is true both of lifetime transfers and of transfers on death. This exemption is obviously of immense importance in family planning, by which *we* mean tax planning from the point of view of the family as a whole.

The exemption is stated in section 18:

> "A transfer of value is an exempt transfer to the extent that the value transferred is attributable to property which becomes comprised in the estate of the transferor's spouse, or, so far as the value transferred is not so attributable, to the extent that that estate is increased."

Exemptions and Reliefs

This is a rather curious phrase. The first part of it gives exemption to the straightforward case where one spouse transfers some item of cash or property to the other spouse. The second part of the phrase deals with less clear-cut cases. An example would be a case where one spouse forgives a debt owed to him (or her) by the other spouse. The forgiveness is a transfer of value, but it is an exempt transfer because, although no property becomes comprised in the estate of the forgiven spouse, that estate is increased by the amount of the debt.

The exemption does not apply if the disposition takes effect on the termination *after the transfer of value* of any interest or period. So if H (husband) leaves property to X (any third party) for life and then to W (H's wife) the exemption does not apply. Similarly if H leaves property to X for 10 years and then to W. Also, the exemption does not apply if the disposition depends on a condition which is not satisfied within 12 months. An example would be if H left property to W provided she survived him by 18 months. But the exemption is not excluded by reason only that the gift is conditional on one spouse surviving the other for a specified period. So a survivorship clause in a will does not knock out the exemption provided the survivorship period is not more than 12 months. In practice wills are commonly drawn with a survivorship period of 30 or 60 days.

As an anti-avoidance measure, the exemption does not apply if the spouse has purchased the reversionary interest in the property: see section 56(2).

There is no requirement that the spouses must be living together. But if the transferor spouse is domiciled in the United Kingdom and the transferee spouse is domiciled abroad, the exemption has a limit of £55,000 (calculated as a value on which no tax is payable. *i.e.* without grossing-up).

Values not exceeding £3,000: section 19

Transfers of value made by a transferor in any one year are exempt to the extent that the values transferred by him do not exceed £3,000. The values are to be calculated for this purpose as values on which no tax is payable; in other words, without grossing up. The year ends on April 5. Unused relief may be carried forward into the next year to be used after the amount for that year. The shortfall cannot be carried forward any further. Thus if in year 1 X gives away £2,500 he can carry forward £500 to year 2. If in that year he gives away £3,200 he uses the £3,000 for that year and £200 from year 1. The remaining £300 is lost.

As husband and wife are separate chargeable individuals for the purposes of inheritance tax, each can make gifts to (for example) their children up to £3,000 per year without either of them incurring any inheritance tax. Compare this to the capital gains tax rules.

Where the transferor makes more than one transfer of value in a tax year the relief is given against earlier rather than later transfers. Where, as in most cases, a transfer is a PET then the relief is first given against any transfers which are not PETs in that year. If the PET subsequently becomes chargeable it will be treated as having been made at the end of the year in which it was made and in so far as the exemption for that year is still available it can be claimed retrospectively against the retrospective charge.

This exemption only applies to lifetime transfers, not to transfers on death.

Small gifts to same person: section 20

Transfers of value made by a transferor in any one tax year to any one person are exempt to the extent that the values transferred by them (calculated as values on which no tax is chargeable) do not exceed £250. This exemption does not apply to transfers on death, and it only applies to lifetime transfers which are "outright gifts", as distinct from gifts in settlement. It does not apply to gifts in excess of £250.

Learned articles have been published arguing that the wording of the legislation is such that this "small gifts exemption" and the £3,000 exemption" (and some other exemptions) are not wholly independent and that in some circumstances they are not cumulative.[1] The position is unclear, however, and there is a good argument that the two exemptions are cumulative. So we think one can say that a taxpayer (Albert perhaps) can give up to £250 to any number of different persons in a year and can also make £3,000 worth of gifts, all exempt from tax: *e.g.* £3,250 to B plus £250 to C plus £250 to D and so on through the alphabet (if his generosity runs so far).

Normal expenditure out of income: section 21

A transfer of value is an exempt transfer if, or to the extent that, it is shown (a) that it was made as part of normal expenditure of the

---

[1] See particularly David Feldman in [1977] B.T.R. 164.

transferor: and (b) that (taking one year with another) it was made out of his income; and (c) that, after allowing for all transfers of value forming part of his normal expenditure, the transferor was left with sufficient income to maintain his usual standard of living.

Some guidance as to what is meant by "normal expenditure" for this purpose was provided by Lightman J. in *Bennett v. IRC* (1995). Mrs Bennett had been given a life interest under her husband's will with her sons taking the whole amount after her death. Initially the income produced by the trust fund was sufficient to meet her needs, which were described by the judge as "modest". Subsequently the income produced by the fund increased substantially and she instructed the trustees that since she did not require any additional income, the surplus income should be paid out to the sons. Her needs did indeed continue to be modest. The trustees did this, although on a conservative basis. Mrs Bennett died unexpectedly two years after giving this instruction and the Revenue sought to charge the payments to the sons as PETs by her, which were activated by her death. The sons argued that the normal expenditure out of income exception applied.

Lightman J. said that for expenditure to be normal, each payment had to be shown to conform to an established pattern of expenditure by the payer. Such a pattern could be established by proof of the existence of a prior commitment or resolve (*e.g.* a regular payment) or by reference to a sequence of payments, *e.g.* by paying the instalments on a life assurance policy. Thus a death bed commitment would not satisfy either requirement. There was no need, however, either for a legal obligation or a minimum period. The amount need not be fixed and the recipient need not be the same, so that, *e.g.* the paying the costs of elderly relatives' nursing home expenses would suffice. The fact that the income was unreasonable or idiosyncratic did not mean that it was not normal for the particular individual. Applying all this to the facts, the judge held that the exception applied in this case. There was a pattern in respect of the surplus income, which she genuinely did not need, and the payments to the sons had been made in accordance with that pattern.

This exemption applies only to lifetime transfers, not to transfers on death.

Gifts in consideration of marriage: section 22

A gift in consideration of marriage is not defined in the legislation. It has been established by case law that a gift is a gift in consideration of marriage if it fulfils three requisites: it is made on the occasion of a marriage; it is conditional on the marriage taking place; and it is made for the purpose of, or with a view to encouraging or facilitating, the particular marriage: see the estate duty case of *IRC v. Lord Rennell* (1964) (H.L.).[2]

Marriage is thought of as an important occasion for tax planners (and for the happy couple), and it is worthwhile to look at the rules set in section 22 in some detail.

Transfers of value made by gifts in consideration of marriage are exempt (if they are lifetime transfers or certain transfers under a settlement, as distinct from transfers on death) to the extent that the values transferred by such transfers made by any one transferor in respect of any one marriage (calculated net) do not exceed:

(a) in the case of gifts satisfying the conditions set out below by a parent of a party to the marriage, £5,000;
(b) in the case of other gifts satisfying those conditions, £2,500; and
(c) in any other case, £1,000.

The conditions which have to be met to obtain the £5,000 or £2,500 exemption are:

(i) it is an outright gift to a child or remoter descendant of the transferor; or
(ii) the transferor is a parent or remoter ancestor of either party to the marriage, and either the gift is an outright gift to the other party to the marriage or the property comprised in the gift is settled by the gift; or
(iii) the transferor is a party to the marriage, and either the gift is an outright gift to the other party to the marriage or the property comprised in the gift is settled by the gift.

There are limits on who can benefit. To qualify for exemption an outright gift must be to a party to the marriage; and a settled gift can only include certain persons (notably the parties to the marriage and their issue) as beneficiaries or potential beneficiaries.

---

[2] Provided these conditions are fulfilled the motive of the donor is irrelevant. See *Re Park Dec'd.* (No.2) (1972).

Gifts to charities: section 23

Transfers of value to charities are exempt transfers. There is no limit as to the amount and the exemption applies to both lifetime and death transfers. There are provisions which prevent the relief applying if the transfer is not an immediate and outright transfer, or if it could be used for other purposes.

Gifts to political parties: section 24

There is a similar unlimited exemption for gifts to political parties defined as one with either two members of Parliament or one member and at least 150,000 votes at the last general election.

Gifts to housing associations: section 24A

There is also a similar unlimited exemption for gifts to housing associations.[3]

Gifts for national purposes, etc.: section 25

A transfer of value is an exempt transfer if it is made to certain bodies (sometimes referred to as "heritage bodies") being certain galleries, museums, libraries, national collections, universities, university colleges, local authorities, or any government department. The bodies given this benefit are listed in Schedule 3. The exemption applies to lifetime and death transfers, and there is no limit in amount. The reference to "any government department" makes it doubly sure that such museums as the Victoria and Albert Museum are within the exemption.

Gifts for public benefit: section 26

Transfers of value of certain types of property (sometimes referred to as "heritage property") are exempt transfers (in life or on death) if the property becomes the property of a body not established or conducted for profit and the Revenue so direct. The types of property include: (i) land of outstanding scenic or historic or scientific interest; (ii) a building (and land and objects associated with the building) for the preservation of which special steps should be taken

---

[3] These are defined by reference to the Housing Associations Act 1985.

Cash Options

by reason of its outstanding historic or architectural or aesthetic interest and the cost of preserving it; (iii) a picture, print, book, manuscript, work of art or scientific collection which the Revenue consider to be of national, scientific, historic or artistic interest; (iv) property given as a source of income for the upkeep of any of the above. The Revenue can require undertakings about preservation and reasonable public access. The restrictions applicable to gifts to charities apply. Where property is transferred which could qualify for this exemption and the transferor dies within seven years (thus activating the PET), the exemption will apply if between the transfer and the death the property has been sold or given to one of the bodies listed in Schedule 3: section 26A.

All the provisions listed above are exempt transfers. The reliefs that follow take several different forms for no particular reasons, so each should be looked at as self-contained.

Cash options under approved annuity schemes: section 152

Where, under an approved annuity scheme, an annuity becomes payable on a person's death to the deceased's widow, widower or dependant and the scheme gave an option for the deceased to require that, instead, a sum of money should be paid to his personal representatives, that option will not involve that the deceased be treated as being beneficially entitled (under section 5) to that sum. In other words, that sum does not form part of his estate.

Death on active service, etc.: section 154

This exemption applies to death on active service against an enemy (or on other service of a warlike nature) and to death arising out of such service.[4] The exemption operates by means of excluding section 4, the section which charges to tax a transfer on death.

Visiting forces and staff of allied headquarters: section 155

This paragraph gives certain exemptions to pay and tangible movables of members of visiting forces (not being citizens of the United Kingdom and colonies) and personnel attached to any NATO military headquarters.

---

[4] This includes service in Northern Ireland.

EXEMPTIONS AND RELIEFS

Relief for successive charges: section 141

This is generally called "quick succession" relief. Prior to 1981 two somewhat confusingly different forms were in operation, one relating to deaths and the other to settlements. Under the new "unified" relief the tax charge on a death or a fixed interest settlement is reduced if the death or settlement charge occurs within five years after some previous chargeable event relating to the same property. For a death the previous charge may be of any type, but for a settlement it must have been a previous charge on that settlement, or the creation of the settlement itself.

The relief operates by way of a "tax credit" against tax payable on the second charge by reference to a percentage of the tax paid on the first. This will be 100 per cent if the gap between the two transfers is one year or less, reduced by 20 per cent for each subsequent year between the transfers, so that if the gap is more than four years it will only be 20 per cent.

Conditional relief for works of art, historic buildings, etc.: sections 30–35 (as amended)

The things to which this conditional relief relates are pictures, works of art, scientific collections, land and buildings which are of outstanding interest. The sections apply to all transfers including discretionary trusts, but the relief can only be sought in relation to a PET if it subsequently becomes chargeable. It is provided (no doubt as an anti-avoidance measure) that for relief to apply to a lifetime transfer the property must have either been owned for six years or the transferor must have acquired the property on a death which was itself a "conditionally exempt transfer" (see below).

To gain the relief the property has to be "designated" by the Revenue, and "undertakings" have to be given concerning preservation, access, etc. A transfer is then called a "conditionally exempt transfer" so that any tax payable will be postponed. It is conditional because if an undertaking is not observed tax becomes payable by reference to the transferor's cumulative total, but at the lifetime rate if the conditionally exempt transfer was not made on a death. Also, tax becomes payable on a subsequent sale or disposal of the property (including disposal on death). There are two cases where a subsequent disposal is not a chargeable event: (a) if the subsequent death or gift is itself a conditionally exempt transfer or the undertaking previously given is replaced by an undertaking given by such

Voidable Transfers

person as the Revenue think appropriate; (b) if within three years of the death the deceased's personal representatives (or, in the case of settled property, the trustees or the person next entitled) give the property or sell it by private treaty to one of the "heritage bodies" listed in Schedule 3 (see p. 342, above) or transfer the property to the Revenue in satisfaction of tax. Where the conditionally exempt transfer loses its exemption on a subsequent gift which is a PET, any inheritance tax triggered will be available as a tax credit against the tax payable if the PET becomes chargeable.

The point of the exemption which has been discussed under this head,[5] as distinct from the heritage bodies exemption and the public benefit exemption discussed above (both at p. 342) is that an ancestral home (for example), or a Rembrandt in an ancestral home, can be kept in the family.

A maintenance fund can be set up under section 27. It is possible for property to be settled on trusts to finance the maintenance, repair or preservation of, or public access to, historic buildings or adjoining land without liability to inheritance tax.

Voidable transfers: section 150

This relief refers to transfers set aside by law. An example would be a gift made within five years before bankruptcy, because such a gift could be set aside (under the Insolvency Act 1986, s. 339) by the transferor's trustee in bankruptcy. If a transfer is so set aside, tax is repaid (with tax-free interest) and also the transfer is wiped out from the transferor's cumulative total of values transferred.

Relief for business property: sections 103–114

This relief was brought in in 1976 in response to claims that without some such relief many small businesses would face closure because of the tax on transfers, *e.g.* from father to son. The relief has been liberalised by subsequent amendments and, in many cases, stands at 100 per cent. Transfers of value in this context include not only lifetime transfers but also transfers on death and chargeable events in relation to settled property.

Where the whole or part of the value transferred by a transfer of value is attributable to the value of any relevant business property,

---

[5] It is sometimes called the "national heritage exemption". So we have the "national heritage exemption" as well as "heritage bodies" and "heritage property".

Exemptions and Reliefs

the whole of that part of the value transferred shall be treated as reduced by either 100 or 50 per cent. The value transferred is to be calculated as a value on which no tax is chargeable, *i.e.* without grossing up. Relevant business property means:

(i) a business or an interest in a business. This includes sole traders and partners disposing of all or part of their interests in a business;[6]
(ii) a holding of shares in or securities of a quoted company which, together with others held by the transfer, gave him control of the company on all questions affecting the company[7];
(iii) a holding of securities in an unquoted company which together with other such securities and unquoted shares held by the transferor, gave him control of the company (as defined above);
(iv) a holding, of any size, of shares in an unquoted company;
(v) any land or building, machinery or plant which was used wholly or mainly for the purpose of a business carried on by a company of which the transferor had control (as defined above) or of which he was a partner.[7]

Certain items are excluded from the definition of relevant business property, *e.g.* shares or securities of a company which is in the process of liquidation.

And, putting it broadly, property is not relevant business property unless it has been owned by the transferor throughout the two years immediately preceding the transfer. But there are provisions adjusting this rule where there have been replacements of property, the incorporation of a business, and acquisitions of property on the death of a spouse.

The relief is given by reducing the value of the net business assets that have been transferred. The relief is given automatically. For

---

[6] In *Fetherstonhaugh v. IRC* (1984) a sole trader who used land owned by a settlement of which he was the life tenant in his business was allowed the relief on that land under this head. In *Russell v. IRC* (1988) the relief was allowed where a legatee was entitled to a cash sum payable only out of the proceeds of sale of a business.

[7] Control is to be assessed at the time of the transfer. In assessing whether the transferor has voting control of a company no account is to be taken of the fact that other shares are held by an individual who cannot in practice exercise his votes, *e.g.* a five year old child: *Walding v. IRC* (1996).

Relief for Agricultural Property

transfers within categories (i), (iii) and (iv) this relief is 100 per cent, so that most family businesses will be outside the tax. For categories (ii) and (v) the relief is 50 per cent. It is generally better therefore for a taxpayer's company to own the plant and machinery, etc., used in its business, rather than the taxpayer.

Where the transferor makes a PET of relevant business property and then dies within seven years so that it becomes a chargeable transfer, the relief will only be available if the transferee still owns the property (or what is known as replacement property) and it would have qualified for the relief immediately before the transferor's death. Similar rules apply where additional tax is payable on a lifetime transfer on the death of the transferor within seven years (see Chapter 25). There is no such provision where a beneficiary sells the business after inheriting it on a death.

In deciding whether the relief applies to a gift subject to a reservation (either one which is still in existence at the transferor's death or which ceased only within the last seven years and so is a deemed PET), the criteria in the various categories are applied to the donee and not the donor, although the ownership of the donor can be added to that of the donee to establish the two year minimum ownership requirement. Paradoxically, however, in assessing whether the shares give control of the company, the shares will be regarded as being owned by the donor.

Business property relief may be available where agricultural relief is also available. In such cases agricultural relief takes priority, through business property relief is also important to farmers and farm owners.

Relief for agricultural property: sections 115–124

This relief applies to lifetime transfers and transfers on death, and it applies to transfers involving settlement as well as to "outright" transfers. It was included in the 1975 Act, but drastically remodelled and extended in 1981.

Short-term purchasers of farms are excluded from the relief; for the relief to apply, both the transferor and the land must fulfil certain conditions. The transferor must have either occupied the land for agricultural purposes throughout the last two years or have owned the land for the last seven years, having been occupied by someone for agricultural purposes during that time. A person who inherits a farm from his or her spouse, provided the spouse fulfilled the above condition, can transfer the farm with benefit of the relief. For the land to qualify it must be agricultural property in the United Kingdom. If one farm has been replaced by another, it is sufficient if occupation of the farms viewed together lasted for at least two out of five years immediately preceding the transfer.

The relief, where it is available, takes the form of reducing the "agricultural value of the agricultural property". "Agricultural property"[8] means:

> "agricultural land or pasture and includes woodland and any building used in connection with the intensive rearing of livestock and fish if occupied with agricultural land or pasture and the occupation is ancillary to that of the agricultural land or pasture; and also includes such cottages, farm buildings and farm-houses, together with the land occupied with them, as are of a character appropriate to the property": section 115(2).[9]

"The agricultural value" is "the value which would be the value of the property if the property were subject to a perpetual covenant prohibiting its use otherwise than as agricultural property": section 115(3). Thus there is no relief for any development value, although business relief may be available for that.

The reduction is either of 100 or 50 per cent. In broad terms owner occupiers are entitled to a 100 per cent reduction, whilst agricultural landlords are entitled to a 50 per cent reduction unless the tenancy began or a tenant succeeds to the tenancy after August 1995 when 100 per cent relief is now available, although of course on the value of the reversion and not the whole farm. The reduction in value because of the agricultural tenancy will, of course, reduce the inheritance tax payable on the land. There are no limits as to size of the farm or as to amount of the relief. As with business relief, this relief is given automatically. It is given in priority to business relief but both may be available. The availability of the relief for PETs and gifts with reservation is governed by the same rules as those for business relief.

---

[8] This includes land used for "Short rotation coppicing" by virtue of section 154 of the Finance Act 1995. In essence this is the planting and harvesting of permanent trees within 10 years.
[9] If the buildings do not fall within that test they cannot be included as agricultural land: *Starke v. IRC* (1995).

Transfers of shares or debentures in a farming company controlled by the transferor can qualify for agricultural property relief.

Relief for woodlands: sections 125–130

Relief is available where any part of the value of a person's estate immediately before his death is attributable to the value of land in the United Kingdom on which trees or underwood are growing but which is not agricultural property. Deathbed purchases of woodland as a tax avoidance ploy will not work. For the relief to apply the deceased must either have been beneficially entitled to the land throughout the five years immediately before his death or have become beneficially entitled to it otherwise than for a consideration in money or money's worth, *i.e.* by a gift or inheritance.

The relief takes the form of leaving out of account, in determining the value transferred on death, the value of the trees or underwood. Notice that the relief does not apply to a lifetime transfer and also that it is only the value of the timber which is relieved, not the value of the land on which it is growing.

The relief is not absolute; a subsequent disposal of the timber can give rise to a retrospective charge to tax at the full rate at the date of disposal. This will be so if the disposal occurs otherwise than on a subsequent death. Tax will be charged on the sale proceeds of the timber if the disposal is for full consideration; otherwise on the then net value of the timber. If the disposal following the death is itself a chargeable transfer, there may be a tax charge on that disposal as well as the retrospective tax charge relating to the death, but the value transferred by the disposal will be calculated as if the value of the trees or underwood had been reduced by the amount of tax charged in respect of the death. Business relief (at 50 per cent) will be available if the growing timber formed a business asset of the deceased at the date of death.

If another death occurs, and there has been no disposal between the first death and the second death, the second death wipes out any possibility of a tax charge arising in respect of the first death.

Dispositions for maintenance of family: section 11

The official Revenue view is that section 11 only applies to lifetime transfers, and not to transfers on death. The point has never been tested in the courts, but the Revenue view is probably correct, for one or other (or both) of two reasons: (1) The section uses the

Exemptions and Reliefs

word "disposition". It is noticeable that the section relating to death (section 4) nowhere uses the word "disposition". It would seem to be a fair inference that wherever in the inheritance tax legislation the word "disposition" occurs the enactment is referring only to lifetime transfers; (2) the section uses the phrase "not a transfer of value", and it may well be (as some commentators assume) that wherever the legislation gives an exemption by saying that such-and-such shall "not be a transfer of value" that exemption is confined to lifetime transfers and does not cover transfers on death.

Section 11(1) declares that a disposition is not a transfer of value if it is made by one party to a marriage in favour of the other party or of a child of either party and is:

(a) for the maintenance of the other party; or
(b) for the maintenance, education or training of the child for a period ending not later than the year in which he attains the age of 18 or, after attaining that age, ceases to undergo full-time education or training.

"Child" includes a step-child and an adopted child. A similar disposition in favour of an illegitimate child is exempt, but in this case only if the child is the child of the disponer (not of the other party to the marriage). A similar disposition in favour of a child who is someone else's child is exempt if the child is not in the care of a parent of his. But in this case, if the disposition is made after the child attains 18 years of age, it is only exempt if the child has for substantial periods before attaining that age been in the care of the disponer.

Also, a disposition is not a transfer of value if it is made in favour of a dependent relative of the disponer and is a reasonable provision for his care or maintenance. Here there is an explicit reference to reasonableness (of amount), whereas in the case of a disposition to a spouse or child there is no explicit mention of reasonableness. However, such a limit seems to be implicit, because it is stated that, where a disposition satisfies the conditions to a limited extent only, so much of it as satisfies them and so much of it as does not satisfy them shall be treated as separate dispositions.

The section gives exemption to a disposition made on the occasion of a decree of divorce or nullity. But it equally applies to a disposition made during an on-going marriage. It is true that so far as a disposition to a spouse is concerned section 11 is not needed because a transfer to a spouse is exempt anyway, but so far as a child is

Alteration of Dispositions

concerned section 11 is very useful as it exempts a payment made by a parent to assist (for example) a child who is a student if the payment is outside the "normal expenditure out of income" exemption (see p.339 above).[10] The section is made to apply to a disposition on the occasion of the dissolution or annulment of a marriage (and to a disposition varying a disposition so made) by subsection (6) which provides that in relation to those events "marriage" (see subsection (1)) includes a former marriage. In *G v. G* (1975) a High Court judge held that the court has power to defer a decree absolute in order to prevent inheritance tax arising.[11]

Alteration of dispositions taking effect on death, etc.: sections 17, 29A, 93, 142–145

The scheme of the sections is this: certain re-arrangements of the deceased's estate shall not be treated as transfers of value and tax shall be charged on the death as if the deceased had left his property in accordance with the re-arrangements. The main provisions can be stated in six numbered points.

(1) By section 142(1), where within two years after a person's death any beneficiary makes an instrument in writing which effects a variation or disclaimer of any of the dispositions (whether effected by will or under the law relating to intestacy or otherwise) of the property comprised in the deceased's estate immediately before his death, the variation or disclaimer shall not be a transfer of value and tax shall be charged as if the variation had been effected by the deceased or (as the case may be) the disclaimed benefit had never been conferred. In the case of a variation, written notice of election must be given to the Revenue within six months after the date of the instrument by the parties thereto and also, where the variation results in additional tax being payable, by the deceased's personal representatives. But the personal representatives can only decline to join in an election if insufficient assets are held by them for discharging the additional tax. Additional tax could become payable, for example, if some item of property which had been left by the

---

[10] The section may not apply if the child leaves school, goes out to work and re-enters full-time education after the age of 18. Has he already ceased to undertake full-time education?

[11] Such orders will usually be exempt under s.10 (no gratuitous benefit).

deceased to his widow is now, by family agreement, to go to his daughter.

The section does not apply to a variation or disclaimer which is made for any consideration in money or money's worth other than consideration consisting of the making of another variation or disclaimer relating to the same estate. For the purpose of this section the deceased's estate includes excluded property but not settled property in which he had an interest in possession. It does not matter whether or not the administration of the estate is complete, and it does not matter that a benefit has been received under the original dispositions, and there is no objection to the variations extending beyond the deceased's family or beyond the original beneficiaries. Where a variation results in property being held in trust for a person for a period which ends not more than two years after the death the disposition at the end of the period is treated as though it had had effect from the beginning of the period.

In *Russell v. IRC* (1988), Knox J. upheld the Revenue's argument that section 142 could not apply where the beneficiaries, having already executed one deed of variation, executed a variation of that deed. The section only allows the first one to count as being read back into the will. On the other hand in *Lake v. Lake* (1989), Mervyn Davies J. held that a deed of disclaimer could be rectified by the court if the wording had failed to give effect to the joint intention of the parties, even though the amended wording would substantially improve the parties' tax position.

(2) By section 144, where by his will a settlor creates a settlement in which there is no interest in possession, but within two years of death the settled capital is paid to a beneficiary, or a person acquires a beneficial interest in possession, or the settlement becomes an accumulation and maintenance settlement then the event in question will not be a capital distribution (see Chapter 26) and tax will be charged on the death as though the event in question had been provided for by the will.

In *Frankland v. IRC* (1996) the section was held not to apply to a variation within the first quarter after the death of the settlor because within that time no capital distribution charge is levied and the section requires that that charge would otherwise apply. The section was not ambiguous and the absurdity not too great!

(3) Section 143 deals with the case where assets are left to a legatee with a request (which is not legally binding) that the legatee should distribute them in accordance with the testator's wishes. If within two years after the death the legatee does so distribute the assets, the

Family Provision Orders

transfers by the legatee are not transfers of value and tax shall be charged in relation to the death as if the property had been bequeathed by the will to the transferees. (Such a provision in a will is called a precatory trust; it is quite common, particularly in respect of household effects, etc.)

(4) Section 145 deals with the case where a surviving spouse elects, under section 47A of the Administration of Estates Act 1925, to redeem for a capital sum his or her life interest which arises under the intestacy rules. Where such an election is made, the election does not count as a transfer of value and tax is charged in relation to the death on the footing that the surviving spouse had from the outset been entitled to the capital sum.

(5) By section 93, where a person becomes entitled (on death or otherwise) to an interest in settled property but disclaims the interest, then, if the disclaimer is not made for a consideration in money or money's worth, the inheritance tax provisions shall apply as if he had not become entitled to the interest.

(6) Section 29A is rather different in that it is in reality an anti-avoidance provision. It applies whenever there is an exempt transfer on a death, *e.g.* to a charity,[12] and the exempt beneficiary subsequently makes a disposition of property which does not derive from that transferred on the death in settlement of a claim against the deceased's estate. In that case the exemption on the death is reduced by the amount transferred by the exempt beneficiary. Thus if Paul agrees with a charity to leave them £100,000 in his will if the charity will then pay £50,000 to his mistress (who may have a claim against his estate), the effect of section 29A will be that only £50,000 of the gift to the charity will be exempt.

Family provision orders: section 146

A court has power, under the Inheritance (Provision for Family and Dependants) Act 1975 to order that provision be made for the family and dependants of a deceased person out of his estate, and for this purpose to change the destination of property. When a court makes an order of this kind the property shall be treated for the purposes of inheritance tax as if it had on the deceased's death devolved in accordance with the order.

---

[12] Other exempt transfers covered are those to spouses, political parties, housing associations, public bodies, maintenance funds and employee trusts.

Dispositions allowable for income tax or conferring retirement benefits: section 12

A disposition made by any person is not a transfer of value if it is allowable in computing that person's profits or gains for the purposes of income tax or corporation tax. It is difficult to think of a disposition which is allowable for income tax (or corporation tax) and yet which would need this section to protect it from inheritance tax; most commonly such a disposition would be a disposition for value and would consequently be excluded from inheritance tax by section 10 (no gratuitous intent). Perhaps certain kinds of business gifts would "fit the bill".

Contributions to approved retirement benefit schemes and approved personal pension schemes for employees and also dispositions to provide in some other way comparable benefits on or after retirement for an employee not connected with the disponer, or, after the death of the employee, for his widow or dependants, are not transfers of value.

Dispositions by close company on trust for benefit of employees: section 13

A disposition of property made to trustees by a close company whereby the property is to be held on trust for the employees is not a transfer of value. The conditions of exemption are very strict and in practice not much use is made of this provision.

Waiver of remuneration: section 14

Sometimes an employee or, more commonly a director, waives (or repays) his remuneration for a period to his employer (company). If nothing were done about it, such waiver or repayment would be a chargeable transfer by the employee or director. Section 14 declares that the waiver or repayment shall not be a transfer of value provided that it is brought into charge in computing the profits or gains of the employer for income tax or corporation tax.

Waiver of dividends: section 15

A person who waives any dividend on shares of a company within 12 months *before* any right to the dividend has accrued does not by reason of the waiver make a transfer of value.

Grant of an agricultural tenancy: section 16

A grant of an agricultural tenancy is not a transfer of value if it is made for full consideration in money or money's worth. Otherwise the almost inevitable reduction in the value of the property (such leases have controlled rents) would lead to a charge.

Tailpiece

After such a long chapter on exemptions and reliefs, the reader may be thinking that there is not much left of the tax, particularly since most lifetime transfers are exempt unless the transferor dies within seven years. But the reality is that, though the exemptions and reliefs are a major factor and the charge to tax is therefore to quite an important extent avoidable, there is still much for the tax to bite on particularly on a death.

In the next chapter we shall look to see the strength of the bite.

CHAPTER 25

COMPUTATION

Inheritance tax is charged on any lifetime transfer of value which is a chargeable transfer, and also on the deemed transfer of value made by a deceased person immediately before his death. Remember that a PET becomes a chargeable transfer on the death of the transferor within seven years and that a gift subject to a reservation still in existence at death is part of the deceased's estate. If the reservation has ceased before then the gift becomes a PET at that time. As we shall see, the existence of PETs complicates the computation rules.

In the case of a lifetime transfer the charge is on the value transferred. In the case of a deemed transfer on death the charge is on the value of the deceased's estate. Section 3 declares that: "... a transfer of value is a disposition made by a person (the transferor) as a result of which the value of his estate is less than it would be but for the disposition; and the amount by which it is less is the value transferred by the transfer." So for a lifetime transfer, one has to compare the value of the transferor's estate (remember that "estate" can refer to a living person's wealth, as well as to a dead person's) before the transfer with its value after the transfer. For a death transfer this comparison does not arise. (The tax charges relating to settled property are discussed in Chapter 26.)

Rates of Tax

As we have already seen the rates of inheritance tax are applied on a cumulative basis so that in essence each chargeable lifetime transfer is charged at the appropriate rate taking into account previous chargeable transfers within the last seven years. This principle is applied equally on a death so that the rate takes into account the chargeable transfers made seven years prior to the death. Only if the transferor lives for more than seven years after making a transfer will it be taken out of the calculation. The effect of the transferor dying within seven years of making a chargeable transfer or a PET is discussed below.

Rates of Tax

The current rates for inheritance tax are very much simplified from those originally introduced. Schedule 1 currently provides that for a charge on a death the rate for the first £200,000 of cumulative transfers is nil. For all cumulative transfers above that amount the rate is 40 per cent. Section 7 provides that for a lifetime transfer the rates are half those on a death, *i.e.* nil and 20 per cent. For peace of mind it is better to regard the band up to £200,000 as being charged at a nil rate rather than as being exempt.

Thus if Fred, having previously made chargeable transfers of £200,000 in the previous seven years makes another one of £100,000, that transfer will be charged at 20 per cent, since he will have exceeded the nil rate band. If his cumulative total had been £150,000, the £100,000 transfer would then have been chargeable at £50,000 × nil per cent and £50,000 × 20 per cent. In effect, therefore, Fred can make up to £200,000 of chargeable transfers in each seven year period without actually having to pay any tax. The position would have been the same if Fred had died and left an estate of £100,000, except that that estate would then have been taxed at 40 per cent. The fact that lifetime rates are half those on death is counterbalanced by the fact that capital gains tax may well be payable on a lifetime transfer whereas it does not apply on a death.

The effect of a death on chargeable transfers and PETs made within the previous seven years

To avoid taxpayers making chargeable transfers shortly before death so as to attract the lower rate of tax, section 7(4) provides that where the transferor dies within seven years of making a chargeable transfer the rates applicable on a death will be retrospectively imposed on that transfer. Since the transfer will have already borne tax at the lifetime rate there is in effect an additional charge to tax (on the transferee) based on the original value of the transfer. That additional charge is computed by working out what the amount of tax would be if the current death rate had applied and deducting from that the tax already paid on the original transfer. However, in making this calculation, if the transferor has survived more than three years after making the transfer, only a percentage of the death rate will be used. This is known as taper relief. Thus if the transferor survives for six years only 20 per cent of the death rate will be used; for five years, 40 per cent; for four years, 60 per cent; and for three years, 80 per cent.

Computation

To take an example.

Suppose that George having already made chargeable transfers of £200,000 in the previous seven years makes a gift of £20,000 (gross) to a company. Tax at 20 per cent will be payable, *i.e.* £4,000. If George dies two years later the Revenue will claim extra tax from the company. The full death rate will be applied to give a figure of £8,000 tax (at 40 per cent) and the company will have to pay the extra £4,000. If George had survived for four years only 60 per cent of the death rate tax would be used to give a figure of £4,800 tax so that the company would only be liable to find an extra £800 tax.

Sometimes the taper relief means that no extra tax is payable on the death (*e.g.* if George had lived for more than five years in the above example, the recalculation at 40 per cent of the death rate would give a total of £3,200, which is less than the £4,000 already paid). There is no refund of any of the original tax, however. Section 131 provides that if the gift has fallen in value between the gift and the subsequent death, the additional tax is calculated on that reduced value,[1] but the original value remains as part of the transferor's cumulative total for the purposes of the transfer of his death estate.

The position is slightly more complicated where the transferor dies within seven years of making a PET (including a gift with reservation where that reservation has ceased within seven years of the death). As we have seen the PET will then become chargeable (on the transferee) in accordance with the transferor's cumulative total at the time when the PET was made on the value then transferred (unless it has since fallen in value, when that lower value can be used). The rate of tax will, however, be the death rate applicable at the date of death (unless the rates have increased in which case the rates at the time of the transfer are used). Once again taper relief calculated as above will be available to lower the amount payable but of course there is no deduction for tax already paid since none was payable at the time. Thus, in the example above, if the gift had

---

[1] This does not apply to wasting assets, *i.e.* those which are inevitably going to decrease in value.

Rates of Tax

been made to Harry instead of a company, no tax would have been payable at the time. Harry would have become liable to tax at £8,000 in the first scenario and £4,800 in the second.

But this activating of the charge has another effect. Since the transfer is no longer a PET it will be treated as if the transferor had always made a chargeable transfer at that time. Thus although it was not originally included in the transferor's cumulative total it will have to be so included retrospectively. Accordingly the tax payable on previous chargeable transfers may have to be recalculated on that basis.

To take a simple example:

> Ian, having made no previous chargeable transfers, makes a PET of £150,000 to John. The next year he makes a chargeable transfer to trustees of £100,000. Ian's cumulative total prior to that (at that time) is nil so that the chargeable transfer is within the nil band. If Ian dies within seven years the PET becomes chargeable so that Ian's cumulative total at the time of the transfer to the trustees is recalculated at £150,000 and that transfer will now fall as to £50,000 into the nil band and £50,000 into the 40 per cent band (death rate applies as it was within seven years of the death).

Where the transferor has made a combination of PETs and chargeable transfers within seven years of his death the recalculations are almost endless.

Transfers of more than one property

It is provided by section 265 that where the value transferred by a chargeable transfer is determined by reference to the values of more than one property the tax chargeable on the value transferred shall be attributed to the respective values in the proportions which they bear to their aggregate, but subject to any provision reducing the amount of tax attributable to the value of any particular property. The "but subject" part of the subsection means that if, for example, on death X leaves a farm to Y and shares in Unilever plc to Z, Z does not enjoy any part of the agricultural property relief. The main part of the subsection means that, for example, if A leaves property worth £60,000 to B and property worth £40,000 to C, the tax is

Computation

spread evenly over the whole value transferred. The gift to B bears 60 per cent of the tax bill and the gift to C bears 40 per cent.

Transfers on the same day

Transfers on the same day by the same transferor present some difficulty. The basic principle is stated in section 266(1): where the value transferred by more than one chargeable transfer made by the same person on the same day depends on the order in which the transfers are made, they shall be treated as made in the order which results in the lowest value chargeable. For example, if on the same day A makes a chargeable transfer to B (A paying the tax) and a separate chargeable transfer to C (C paying the tax), the gift to B will have to be grossed-up, (see p.363, below), whereas the gift to C will not. So it is "cheaper" in tax to count the gift to B before the gift to C, because the grossing-up will come at a point lower down the scale. The legislation permits that. Then, the order of the gifts having been established, section 266(2) declares that there shall be an "effective rate," namely the tax which would have been charged if the transfers had been a single transfer. So A pays tax on the gift to B and C pays tax on the gift to himself, both at the same rate.

Transfers reported late

This is dealt with by section 264. Where an earlier transfer is not notified to the Revenue until after the tax has been paid on a later transfer the position depends upon the gap between the transfers. If the gap is seven years or more there is no problem since they would not be cumulated together anyway and so tax plus interest is payable on the earlier transfer at the rates then applying. If the gap is less than seven years the earlier (unreported) transfer is charged at the rate then applying and the extra tax which should have been collected on the second transfer (because of cumulation) is now charged on the first one (plus interest).

Liabilities

In considering this topic it is necessary to distinguish between liabilities resulting from a chargeable transfer and other liabilities.

LIABILITIES RESULTING FROM A CHARGEABLE TRANSFER

One has to remember that the value transferred is the amount by which the transferor's estate immediately after the disposition is less than it would be if the disposition had not been made.

A chargeable transfer may give rise to inheritance tax and at the same time to two other taxes—capital gains tax and sometimes stamp duty. Also there may be incidental costs of the transfer, such as conveyancing fees. All these items, if paid by the transferor, will diminish the value of his estate immediately after the transfer. So, in the absence of any provision to the contrary, they would all increase the amount of the "value transferred" and so increase the amount of tax payable. The Act does make provisions to the contrary, to some extent. Section 5 provides that in determining the value of the transferor's estate immediately after the transfer, his liability to inheritance tax on the value transferred shall be taken into account, but not his liability for any other tax or duty. And by section 164 the incidental expenses (if borne by the transferor) shall be left out of account.

The great point to grasp is that when one is considering liabilities immediately *after* the transfer, the effect of taking a liability into account is to increase the diminution in value of the transferor's estate and so increase the value transferred and so increase the inheritance tax. Conversely, the effect of leaving a liability out of account is that that liability (*e.g.* liability to capital gains tax or liability to pay conveyancing fees to one's solicitor) does not increase the inheritance tax.

And if the capital gains tax is borne by the transferee, that is treated (for inheritance tax) as actually reducing the value transferred: section 165. And the same is true of the incidental expenses of making a transfer, if these are borne by the transferee: section 164.

There are special rules about debts due to foreign residents (section 162(5)).

Grossing up

The principle of grossing up a lifetime transfer is embedded in section 5. If the transferor is to pay the inheritance tax, his liability to the tax is to be taken into account in calculating the diminution in his estate caused by the transfer. If A makes a chargeable transfer to B of £x in cash or of property worth £x (tax free) A's estate is

Computation

diminished by £x plus the relevant inheritance tax. So £x must be grossed up to find what sum must be paid by A to the Revenue to put £x into the hands of B free from any liability to the tax. If one calls that sum £y, A must pay £x to B and £y to the Revenue.

If A makes a transfer to B, stipulating that B must pay the inheritance tax on it, no grossing up arises. This is because A's estate is not diminished by inheritance tax, since he is not going to pay any of it. Since most lifetime transfers are now PETs, any tax which becomes chargeable will only be due after the transferor's death on the transferee so that no grossing up occurs.

In a general sense there is no grossing up either in the case of a transfer on death. This is because grossing up is, in effect, built into the situation since it is only the sums net of tax which will reach the beneficiaries. However, where a specific gift is left by will "tax-free" a kind of grossing up has to take place to determine the entitlements of other beneficiaries: see Chapter 27 below, under the heading "Incidence".

With regard to the actual process of grossing up, in principle it is just like grossing up for income tax. If A wants to put into the hands of B £40,000, one has to work out what sum, after deduction of tax, will leave £40,000 clear. But in practice it is often very much more complicated than is the income tax process. This is because (a) the tax on any particular transfer has to take account of the transferor's previous tax history under the principle of cumulation and (b) the particular gift itself may cross the rate bands.

The principle of grossing up is perhaps best explained as follows:

If A makes a net chargeable transfer (*i.e.* after tax) of £100,000 to B Ltd the tax is calculated in the following way: tax payable on £100,000 = £x. The loss to A's estate is therefore £100,000 + £x. The tax actually payable is therefore the tax on (£100,000 + £x) = £y. A's cumulative total carried forward for the next transfer is thus £100,000 + £y. £y in effect represents an element of tax on tax (£x).

If, however, A makes a gross transfer of £100,000 to B Ltd, he will actually pay to B Ltd £100,000 less £x (the tax on £100,000). The loss to A's estate will thus only be £100,000 and that will be his cumulative total for future transfers.

The effects of grossing up are therefore to increase both the tax payable on the individual transfer and the cumulative total of the transferor. On the other hand the transferee will receive a set amount, in our example £100,000 and not an amount variable according to the tax payable. As we have seen, however, this concept has been much reduced in importance by the introduction of PETs. It is limited to those lifetime transfers which are not PETs.

OTHER LIABILITIES

What we are talking about here is liabilities other than those which result from a chargeable transfer. The importance of the topic is that it is clearly relevant to the comparison which has to be made in the case of lifetime transfers between the value of a person's estate before and after the transfer (its relevance is to the "before" part) and it is clearly relevant to the valuation of a person's estate on death.

A liability is not taken into account unless it is a liability imposed by law or it was incurred by the transferor for a consideration in money or money's worth: section 5(5). Thus an outstanding mortgage on a house would be deductible but not a voluntary covenant.

In establishing the value of an estate on death section 5(5) is supplemented by section 103 of the Finance Act 1986. This section disallows what are known as "artificial debts". These are defined as debts for which the consideration was either directly derived from the deceased or provided by another person to whose resources the deceased contributed. In the latter case there must be a causal link between the contribution of the deceased and the debt transaction. A simple example of this section applying is where Jane gives away a valuable asset to Kate and three years later she buys it back for full market value but leaves the debt outstanding until the date of her death five years later. The gift to Kate will not be taxable since it was a PET made more than seven years before her death and the debt owed to Kate, having been made for full consideration, would be deductible under section 5(5). But since the consideration for the debt, the asset, derived from Jane's estate it would not be allowable under section 103 of the 1986 Act.

Where an artificial debt is paid off during the deceased's lifetime, the repayment is treated as a PET: section 103(5) of the 1986 Act. Thus if Jane repaid Kate a year before her death it would become a chargeable transfer on her death. This will probably not apply, however, if Jane pays Kate the full amount immediately on buying the asset back—no debt has been incurred.

Where a liability falls to be discharged after the time at which it is to be taken into account it shall be valued as at the time at which it is to be taken into account: section 162(2). In other words its value

COMPUTATION

has to be discounted. This rule does not apply to liability for inheritance tax itself.

A liability in respect of which there is a right to reimbursement shall be taken into account only to the extent (if any) that reimbursement cannot reasonably be expected to be obtained: section 162(1). So if A owes £100 to B but for some reason C is liable to reimburse A, A cannot have his liability taken into account if there is no reason to suppose that C will not pay up.

Before we leave liabilities, notice this general point about them: if it is a question of valuing an estate *before* a transfer (or immediately before death) it is advantageous to the taxpayer if a liability can be taken into account: if it is a question of valuing an estate *after* a transfer it is disadvantageous if a liability is to be taken into account.

Relief Against Double Charges

Section 104 allows regulations to be made to prevent double charges to inheritance tax applying in certain situations. The Inheritance Tax (Double Charges Relief) Regulations 1987 apply such a relief in four situations:

(1) Where A makes a PET of some property to B, B transfers the property back to A (*e.g.* in his will), and A then dies within seven years of the PET. The double charge arises because the property would be chargeable on the gift to B (the PET has become chargeable) and also on A's death (it forms part of his estate). The solution is to either charge the property as part of A's estate at his death and ignore the PET or to tax the PET and ignore the value of the property on A's death, whichever produces the lower amount of tax.

(2) Where A makes a gift subject to a reservation which is also a chargeable transfer, *e.g.* a gift of his house to a company but he continues to live in it, and he dies still enjoying that reservation (or did so within seven years of his death). Since tax will have been paid on the chargeable transfer and the house will form part of his estate on his death (or will be a chargeable PET) there is again the potential for a double charge. The solution again is to take the lower of charging the house as part of A's estate at death and to ignore the gift or to tax the gift and ignore the house as part of A's estate (or as a chargeable PET).

(3) Where A makes a chargeable transfer of money (or chargeable PET) to B and B lends an equivalent sum back to A. A then dies with the loan to B outstanding. The double charge here arises because the debt would not be allowed under section 103 of the Finance Act 1986 as an artificial debt (see above). Thus the money given is chargeable on the transfer and as part of A's estate on death. The regulations provide that the tax payable is to be the lower of taxing the transfer and allowing the debt against the estate or ignoring the transfer and disallowing the debt.

(4) Where A makes a chargeable transfer (but not a PET) and the transferee returns the property to A, which is beneficially owned by A on his death within seven years of the original transfer. The double charge in this case is the additional tax which will be payable on the original transfer because of A's death within seven years and the tax payable on the property as part of A's estate at his death. Again either the original transfer or the value of the property on A's death is to be ignored, although there is no relief for the tax already paid on the transfer.

Valuation

Open market value

The basic principle of valuation is stated in section 160. Except as otherwise provided the value at any time of any property shall be the price which the property might reasonably be expected to fetch if sold in the open market at that time. This is generally called "open market value".

The subsection then goes on to say (perhaps rather inconsistently) that the price shall not be assumed to be reduced on the ground that the whole property is to be placed on the market at one and the same time. So if A owns 100,000 shares in XYZ Ltd the shares are valued (in the absence of an actual sale) without any reduction for the fact that if such a parcel of shares were put on the market at one time the price would be depressed.

The definition of open market value continues the valuation rule which existed for estate duty purposes. The general judicial definition is that it is the best price available from a hypothetical purchaser in the market and not necessarily the highest price.[2] If there are a

---

[2] *Re Hayes W.T.* (1971); *cf. Ellesmere v. IRC* (1918).

range of prices which competent valuers would consider as open market values then the highest is no more likely than the lower. It seems that some account may be taken of the existence of a special purchaser, *e.g.* the owner of adjoining land, who might pay "over the odds" to acquire the property.[3] If there is no open market, *e.g.* there are restrictions on sale, the property is to be valued under what is known as the *Crossman* principle on the assumption that a hypothetical purchaser buys freely in a hypothetical market but, having bought it, becomes subject to the restrictions.[4] This is particularly the case with private company shares which usually[5] have some form of restriction attached to them. Section 168 provides that in such a case the hypothetical purchaser buying in the hypothetical market must be assumed to know all the information which a prudent prospective purchaser might reasonably require to know if he were buying from a willing vendor at arms length.[6] This is in itself an exception to the basic rule that it is the market value of the property and not its intrinsic value which counts, *e.g.* a painting will be valued at its then market value even if it later turns out to be a forgery.

The *Crossman* principle has also been applied where the property is subject to some form of liability other than a restriction on sale. This was the decision of the Court of Appeal in *Alexander v. IRC* (1991). The property was a flat in which the deceased had acquired a leasehold interest at a discount under a statutory scheme. Under the lease the tenant had to repay that discount to the landlord if the lease was sold within five years. The tenant died within the first year. What was the value of the lease? The Court of Appeal held first that the obligation to repay was an incumbrance on the property incurred for a consideration and so fell to be taken into account in valuing the property. They then held that the value of the flat for inheritance tax purposes was what a hypothetical purchaser would pay to acquire the lease subject to the obligation to repay the discount if there was a sale within five years but disregarding the fact that his own (hypothetical) purchase would have given rise to such a liability.

---

[3] *IRC v. Clay* (1914); *c.f. IRC v. Crossman* (1937).
[4] *IRC v. Crossman* (1937); *Re Lynall* (1972).
[5] See Charlesworth, *op. cit.*, pp. 259–266.
[6] *e.g.* whether the company's profits are increasing. The whole concept has a touch of Lewis Carroll about it.

In *Walton v. IRC* (1996) the deceased owned an interest in a tenancy (as a partnership asset). The other interest was held by one of his sons and the landlords were the deceased and his two sons. The court upheld a valuation of that interest on the basis that since it could not be assigned without the landlord's consent and that might be withheld, it could not take into account the value of the land if the lease and reversion were merged. The intentions of the actual landlords could be taken into account; there was no requirement to use a hypothetical landlord.

Restriction on freedom to dispose: section 163

The rule referred to above on restrictions on sale could lead to abuse. To avoid this there is a complex provision which is best understood if we take one particular kind of restriction on freedom to dispose, namely an option. Suppose A grants to B an option to purchase a house. If the option price is the same as the then market price, say £50,000, there is no transfer of value. If the option price, say £35,000, is less than the then market price there is a transfer of value unless B pays for the option a sum (£15,000) equal to the difference between the prices. If, later, B exercises his option and buys the house for £35,000 when it is worth £60,000, the amount of the "value transferred" depends on how much consideration B gave for the option. If B gave no consideration, the "value transferred" by the sale is £25,000 (the gratuitous element). If B gave £15,000 for the option, the "value transferred" by the sale (assuming B pays the tax) is £45,000 (£60,000–£15,000) less £35,000 = £10,000.

Valuation of related property: section 161

The concept of "related property" is an important one. Property is related to the property comprised in a person's estate if (a) it is in the estate of his spouse, or (b) it is (or has been within the preceding five years) the property of a charity etc., and became so on an exempt transfer made by him or his spouse.

Where the value of any property *would be* less than the appropriate portion of the value of the aggregate of that and any related property, it *shall be* the appropriate portion of the value of that aggregate. That is the rather obscure wording of section 161(1). We have italicised "would be" and "shall be" in the hope of making it a bit clearer. But it needs an example. The background is that the enactment is intended to stop up a tax-avoidance device. Suppose A owns 70 of the 100 issued shares in XYZ Ltd. Mrs A owns none. A

Computation

transfers 30 shares to his wife. Controlling shares are worth say £10 each; non-controlling shares are worth say £6 each. The transfer to Mrs A is exempt. The legislation ensures that after the transfer A's holding is valued (*e.g.* on his subsequent death) as being worth not merely 40 × £6 (*i.e.* £240), but $\frac{40}{70}$ of the value of the combined (controlling) holding. The combined value is £700, so A's holding is valued at £400. And Mrs A's holding is valued at £300.

A relief is provided (by section 176) where property was valued on death on the related property basis and is subsequently (within three years of the death) sold for a lesser amount to those who inherited the property on the death on an arm's length sale.

Value of lessor's interest: section 170

In a settlement the life tenant is treated as owning the whole settled property and the holder of the reversionary interest is treated as owning nothing, because his interest is "excluded property" (see Chapter 26). In addition a lease for life, if the lease was not granted for full consideration, is treated (see section 43) as a settlement, but with the modification that the lessor's interest is not excluded property. This present section (section 170) provides that the value of the lessor's interest in the property shall be taken to be such part of the value of the property as bears to it the same proportion as the value of the consideration, at the time the lease was granted, bore to what would then have been the value of a full consideration. So, if L grants a lease for life to T at 75 per cent of full consideration, L's interest in the property is taken to be 75 per cent of the value of the property. (And T's interest is taken by section 50(6) to be 25 per cent of that value.)

Value of life policies, etc.: section 167

This section provides that the value of certain life policies and contracts for deferred annuities shall be treated as not less than the total of premiums paid (minus any surrender value paid, *e.g.* on a partial surrender) where that would be higher that its market value at the time of a lifetime transfer. This does not apply on a death.

Value transferred on death

Inheritance tax is charged on the death of a person as if, immediately before his death, he had made a transfer of value and the value transferred by it had been equal to the value of his estate immediately before his death: section 4. His estate does not include "excluded property": section 5(1). It does include property over which he had a general power to appoint or dispose, and it does include settled property in which he had a life interest (except, in certain circumstances, where the property reverts on the death to the settlor or the settlor's spouse). And it does include his share in a joint tenancy.

On a death, therefore, the whole of the deceased's estate must be valued on the open market basis on the assumption of a hypothetical sale of all the estate immediately before the death. The methods of ascertaining such a value are the same as for lifetime transfers (see p.365, above). One rule which is peculiar to ascertaining the market value on a death, however, is that where by taking a number of items together a higher price could be obtained that must be done, *e.g.* by valuing a set of Hepplewhite dining chairs as a single unit rather than by reference to each chair. (The related property rules, above, prevent this being avoided by transfers of part of such a set to a spouse and part to another). This is known as the process of "lotting"[7]. In *Gray v. IRC* (1994), this approach was applied by the Court of Appeal to aggregate the deceased's partnership interest in a farming business, including a lease of the land farmed, with the deceased's freehold interest in that land. The fact that taking the two together did not form a natural unit of property was irrelevant. The only question was whether a prudent hypothetical vendor would have adopted this course of action in order to obtain the most favourable price without undue expenditure of time and effort.

The Act also lays down some detailed rules, as follows.

An allowance shall be made for reasonable funeral expenses (section 172).

Certain changes (whether increases or decreases) in the value of the estate which occur *by reason of* the death are treated as having occurred before the death. An example of an increase would be the proceeds of a life insurance policy; these proceeds count as part of the estate. An example of a decrease would occur if a restaurant business lost value through the death of its successful proprietor; this fact is to be taken into account in valuing the business as part of the deceased's estate (section 171). An allowance is also made for the

---

[7] That phrase had been used in the House of Lords case which established this principle: *Buccleuch v. IRC* (1967).

COMPUTATION

extra expense of administering or realising foreign property (section 173).

Sections 178 to 189 provide some relief where "qualifying investments" (notably quoted shares and holdings in an authorised unit trust) are sold within the 12 months following the death for less than the value at the date of death.

Sections 190 to 198 provide a similar relief where land (which may include buildings) is sold within three years of the death for less than the value at death.

CHAPTER 26

SETTLED PROPERTY

Part III of the 1984 Act now presents the inheritance tax rules for settled property in a deceptively tidy manner. The original aim of these rules was said to be to ensure that property within settlements bore the same levels of taxation in the longer term as did unsettled property. The general approach adopted has, from the beginning, been to seek to tax the beneficial entitlement or possession of trust property, ignoring the legal title and the status of the trustees. (Compare this with the capital gains tax approach, which concentrates instead on legal title.) However, converting the general aim and approach into workable yet fair legislation has proved a difficult task, not least because politicians' views of what is "fair" taxation of wealth vary widely. In consequence, the 1975 proposals were heavily amended in 1976. They were subject to a substantial review in 1980, and recast in 1982. The impact of the introduction of PETs in 1986 caused additional changes to be made.

"Settled property" is not separately defined; it is simply property comprised in a settlement.[1] What, then, is a settlement, for the purposes of the Act? Section 43 states that it is a disposition whereby property is for the time being:

(1) held in trust for persons in succession; or
(2) held in trust for any person subject to a contingency; or
(3) held on discretionary trusts; or

---

[1] Whether there is one or more settlements has proved to be a problem for capital gains tax (see p. 247, above). Similar problems will arise with inheritance tax. In *Minden Trust (Cayman) Ltd v. IRC* (1985) the exercise of a power under a trust which transferred the entire trust property was held to be a settlement.

Settled Property

(4) held on trust to accumulate the income; or
(5) charged (otherwise than for full consideration)[2] to pay an annuity; or
(6) subject to a lease for life if the lease was not granted for full consideration.[3]

Property subject to provisions equivalent to heads (1) to (5) above under the law of a foreign country can constitute a "settlement." Foreign settled property is, however, excluded property unless the settlor was domiciled in the United Kingdom at the time the settlement was made.[4]

The legislation makes no distinction between a trust for sale and a strict settlement. Neither a tenancy in common nor a joint tenancy is as such a settlement, but either of them will be a settlement if it also falls under any of the heads enumerated above.

Putting property into a settlement

Putting property into a settlement is basically the same as any other lifetime or death transfer for inheritance tax purposes. In the case of a lifetime transfer into a settlement it will be a PET if the trust created is either one in which there is an interest in possession (a fixed interest trust) or it is an accumulation or maintenance trust or a disabled trust. If the trust is a discretionary trust then the transfer is immediately chargeable. If the settlor reserves any interest in a fixed interest trust he will be deemed to have made a PET of the property minus that interest, whereas if he receives remuneration as a trustee he will be regarded as having made a gift subject to reservation (see p. 329, above). The Revenue regard a settlor taking an interest as a potential beneficiary under a discretionary trust as

---

[2] An annuity not charged on property (*e.g.* an annuity purchased from an insurance company) is not a settlement. Even an annuity which is charged on property is not a settlement if it is granted for full consideration. Hence (probably) an annuity granted by continuing partners for a former partner or his dependants is not a settlement.

[3] Presumably the point of this is to prevent a person from seeking to avoid the rules relating to settled property by granting a lease for life instead of a life tenancy.

[4] But not reversionary interests—see the end of this chapter. Domicile here has its extended meaning for inheritance tax purposes.

also amounting to a reservation out of the whole trust property and not a gift of the property minus such an interest.

Classification of settlements for charging purposes

The remainder of this chapter is concerned with the impact of inheritance tax after the property has been put into a settlement. For this purpose the Act makes a sharp distinction between (1) settled property which is held on fixed interest trusts, that is to say, where some person is beneficially entitled to an interest in possession (*e.g.* where there is a life tenant) and (2) settled property in which no one has a beneficial interest in possession (*e.g.* where the property is held on discretionary trusts).[5]

There are also (3) some special kinds of settlement such as accumulation and maintenance settlements which are subject to special rules. We will deal with these three categories in turn, but the reader should bear in mind that some of the property in a settlement may fall within one of these categories and some within another, and that even the same property may change its category from time to time.

The important question therefore is whether there is a beneficial interest in possession in the settled property. The Revenue published a statement on February 12, 1976[6] setting out their understanding of the term "interest in possession." In particular they dealt with the position where a person is entitled to the income of the property subject to a power of revocation or appointment or a power of accumulation. It is generally agreed that it is entitlement to the income as it arises which indicates a beneficial interest in possession (*e.g.* section 50 defines the size of the interest by reference to the proportion of income received). The Revenue's point was that it must be immediate entitlement to the income, so that if there is a power to accumulate income there is no interest in possession, the trustees can withhold current income as it arises, whereas in the case of revocation or appointment over the trustees can only deprive the beneficiary of future income, thus leaving him with a beneficial interest in possession in the meantime.

---

[5] See "Discretionary and Fixed Interest Settlements" by G.F.R. Whitehead [1983] B.T.R. 303.
[6] See, *e.g.* [1976] B.T.R. at 418.

This view was tested all the way up to the House of Lords in *Pearson v. IRC (1980)*. In that case the settlor's daughter was entitled to the income under the settlement subject both to a power of appointment exercisable by the trustees and a power to accumulate the income until appointment. Both sides agreed that the power of appointment did not prevent the daughter from having a beneficial interest in possession until it was exercised. The judge, Fox J., and the Court of Appeal also found that the power to accumulate did not prevent this either. The daughter still had a present right to present possession, the classic meaning of an interest in possession. By a majority of three to two, however, the House of Lords upheld the Revenue's argument that a power to accumulate does prevent the person taking in default of accumulation from having a beneficial interest in possession. Lord Keith, in the majority, concluded that the daughter only had the right to a later payment if the trustees either by inaction or decision did not accumulate the income—she had no absolute right to the income as it accrued.

Several points may be made on this decision. First of all it is a classic example of the working of the English judicial system. In all, six judges found for the taxpayer and only three for the Revenue, yet the Revenue view is the law. Further, the majority of the House of Lords contained not one specialist property lawyer (unlike most of the other judges involved). Secondly, the decision, as Lord Russell (in the minority) implied, is based on two basic misconceptions: (1) as to the nature of a vested interest subject to defeasance; and (2) as to the difference between trusts and powers. What the daughter had was an interest vested subject to defeasance, a perfectly acceptable form of beneficial interest in English law which gives the owner the right to the income until it is taken away. The obsession with it being an "absolute" interest is irrelevant. Powers of accumulation, like powers of revocation or appointment, are only powers, *i.e.* they must be exercised unanimously to take effect. If one trustee disagrees then the power will not apply and the income be paid under the underlying trust, in this case to the daughter. The reader is referred to the speech of Lord Russell for a perfect example of what the law ought to be.

It may be noted, however, that the decision is not all bad for taxpayers. It may be desirable to provide that X receives all the income of a trust but does not have a beneficial interest in possession. That should be possible by giving X a right to the income subject to a power of accumulation which is not intended to be exercised.

Whatever the merits of its application in *Pearson*, the test is still quite clear: does the beneficiary have a present right to present possession, *i.e.* to the income as it arises? This test was applied in *Moore & Osborne v. IRC* (1985)[7] where it was held that the sole member of a class of discretionary beneficiaries could not claim an immediate entitlement to the income unless the class was closed, so that there was no possibility of another member of the class coming into existence. So long as that remained a possibility he was not so entitled and so had no interest in possession for inheritance tax purposes. The potential beneficiaries in this case were himself, any wife he might marry, and any children he might have. In fact he died unmarried and childless, but he did not have an interest in possession immediately before his death.

The entitlement to income being the test, it follows that even if the beneficiary has no right to the capital (*e.g.* he has a contingent interest), a statutory (or agreed) right to the income will suffice. The most common example is a contingent beneficiary's right to the income, once he has attained the age of majority, by virtue of section 31 of the Trustee Act 1925. It is clear that such a right is sufficient to create an interest in possession for this purpose. Thus in *Swales v. IRC* (1984) an appointment to D if and when her eldest child attained 21, operated to give D a right to the income under section 31(i)(ii) of the 1925 Act and so an interest in possession. See also p.377, below.

The effect of powers other than those of accumulation and appointment in relation to the use of income arising under the trust depends upon whether they are classified as administrative (thus not affecting the beneficiary's right to the income as it arises) or dispositive (with the opposite effect). In *Miller v. IRC* (1987) the Court of Session held that a power to use income to maintain the capital value of the fund was an administrative power so that the there was an interest in possession. The criterion was said to be that administrative powers are those relating to the prudent management in discharge of the trustees' duty to maintain the trust estate. A dispositive power is one which diverts income away from one beneficiary for the benefit of others. It is understood, however, that the Revenue are not entirely happy with this distinction and they stand by their subsidiary argument in *Pearson* that a power to use

---

[7] See also *Stenhouse's Trustees v. Lord Advocate* (1984).

income to pay taxes, etc., which would otherwise be payable out of capital prevents an interest in possession from arising.

Where There is a Beneficial Interest in Possession

The basic point to grasp here is that the person holding the beneficial interest in possession is treated "as beneficially entitled to the property in which the interest subsists": section 49(1). So if A is entitled to a life interest in Blackacre he is treated for the purposes of the tax as though he were the owner of Blackacre itself. And if B is entitled to a life interest in a settled fund worth £50,000 he is treated as though he were the owner of £50,000. But if a life tenant is entitled to part only of the income of settled property his interest is taken to subsist in only a proportionate part of the capital. So, if B were entitled to, say, half the income of the settled fund he would be treated as the owner of £25,000.

It follows that a reversionary interest is not an interest in possession. A reversionary interest is defined in section 47 as "a future interest under a settlement, whether it is vested or contingent ... " A future interest cannot be an interest in possession because it is not "*in possession*". An interest in possession means an immediate entitlement: a present right of present enjoyment. There is a distinction in the general law between a reversionary interest and a remainder interest, but the definition quoted above makes no distinction of this kind—both are reversionary interests. So, if property is held on trust for A for life with remainder to B absolutely, A has an interest in possession and B has a reversionary interest.

It was pointed out above that in this situation A is treated as though he were the owner of the settled property itself. If B is also to be treated as owning something there will be some degree of double taxation. So the legislation treats B as owning nothing. This is achieved by declaring a reversionary interest to be "excluded property": section 48. The effect of this is most clearly seen in relation to a death. Section 5 provides that "the estate of a person immediately before his death does not include excluded property". So, if property is settled on trust for A for life with remainder to B, and B dies while A is still alive. B's reversionary interest is not taxed on B's death.

There are three (perfectly reasonable) exceptions to this principle. A reversionary interest is not excluded property if (1) it has at any time been acquired for consideration, or (2) it is one to which either the settlor or his spouse is beneficially entitled, or (3) it is the interest expectant on the determination of a lease for life which is treated as

BENEFICIAL INTERESTS IN POSSESSION

a settlement. The problem of purchased reversions is dealt with at the end of this chapter.

Another kind of interest which is not an interest in possession is a contingent interest. This again is because a contingent interest does not carry an immediate entitlement and so is not "in possession". If property is held on trust for A if he attains the age of 25 years, A's interest in the capital of the trust is contingent upon his attaining that age. Until he is 25, he does not have an interest in possession in the capital. But a very important point arises here. He may well, as we have just seen, become entitled (by statute[7] or otherwise) to the *income* of the trust on attaining his majority, namely 18 years of age. Where that is so, his interest in income vests in possession at 18. And his interest in income is sufficient to make him a person "beneficially entitled to an interest in possession". In other words, a contingent gift of capital which carries what is generally called "the intermediate income" confers an interest in possession as in *Swales v. IRC* (1984).

During the time that the estate of a deceased person is being administered a person who will be entitled to an interest in possession when the administration is completed is treated as having the interest from immediately after the death: section 91. Of course this only matters if the beneficiary dies or disposes of his interest during the administration period.

There is one interest which is an interest in possession under the Act, though under the general law it would not be an interest in settled property at all. This is the interest of the lessee where the lease is treated as a settlement because it was granted for life and for less than full consideration. That the lessee's interest is an interest in possession emerges, by implication, from section 50(6).

THE CHARGING PROVISIONS

We must now look at the circumstances in which a charge to tax arises in respect of settled property where there is a beneficial interest in possession, or (to put it in more popular terms) where there is a "fixed interest settlement," as distinct from a "discretionary settlement". In most cases where these charges arise otherwise than on the death of the life tenant they are PETs and so only chargeable if the life tenant dies within seven years. They will only be immediately chargeable to tax if either a company becomes entitled

---

[7] See the Trustee Act 1925, s.31, as amended.

Settled Property

to the property or a discretionary trust is thereby created. In the discussion below they will be assumed to be PETs.

Death of the beneficial owner

Let us again take the simple case of a settlement by which property is settled on A for life with remainder to B. A, the life tenant, dies. A's life interest is part of his estate (section 5) and is taxed under section 4, just as is his unsettled property. The only special point that arises (and it is one that has already been made) is that (under section 49) A is treated as owning the settled property itself. So, if the subject-matter of the trust is Blackacre, what falls to be valued on A's death is Blackacre itself, and not merely A's life interest in Blackacre. Apart from this (very important) valuation point, there is no difference on the occasion of death between a life interest and any other kind of property (except that the tax is normally payable by the trustees out of the settled property).

We now turn to look at the two circumstances in which a PET may be made during the lifetime of the life tenant.

Termination of an interest in possession

This circumstance is dealt with in section 52(1) as follows:

> "Where at any time during the life of a person beneficially entitled to an interest in possession in settled property his interest comes to an end, tax shall be charged ... as if at that time he had made a transfer of value and the value transferred had been equal to the value of the property in which his interest subsisted."

Notice the valuation point cropping up again in the last few words: what has to be valued is the property itself, not the value of the interest merely. There is no grossing up. The deemed transfer of value will be a PET. An example of an interest coming to an end during the lifetime of the life tenant would be where property is held on trust for X until she shall remarry and she does remarry. Another example would be where property is held on trust for Y for life with remainder to Z, and Y surrenders his life interest to Z.

Disposal of an interest in possession

This depends on section 51. Where a person beneficially entitled to an interest in possession in any property comprised in a settlement disposes of his interest, the disposal is not a transfer of value but is treated as the coming to an end of his interest. So if a section 51 situation arises, it is equated with a section 52 situation: that is to say, disposing of the interest is treated as a coming to an end of the interest. So, if A gives away to X his life interest in Blackacre, a tax charge arises just as if his interest had come to an end. Consequently there is a PET by A (without grossing up) on the whole value of Blackacre.

It is interesting to follow up what happens if A does give away (or, for that matter, sell) his life interest in, say, Blackacre to X. There then arises what is called an "interest *pur autre vie*". This describes the interest which X acquires. He has an interest in Blackacre "for another's life"; that is, his interest lasts only as long as A lives. When A dies, X's interest comes to an end, and a PET arises (under section 52). If X were to die while A was still alive, X's interest (the interest *pur autre vie*) would pass by his will or on intestacy to say, Y. The interest would be part of X's estate and tax would be charged (under section 4) on X's death. Y would then hold the interest and, if A were then to die, Y's interest would end, and a PET would arise under section 52. There might be quick succesion relief: see p. 382, below.

Note that although section 3(4) treats deemed dispositions in the same way as actual dispositions, this subsection is expressly excluded from the operation of sections 19 to 22, so preventing the annual exemption and exemptions for small gifts, expenditure out of income and wedding gifts operating here.

Extension of the termination and disposal rules

If the point were not dealt with in the legislation it would be very easy to minimise the tax by depreciating the value of settled property by various transactions between the trustees and persons connected with the settlement.[8] The point is dealt with by section 52(3). If such a transaction takes place there is a deemed partial termination of the interest and so a PET arises. Thus, for example, if the trustees let a house rent-free to a beneficiary on a lease a tax charge will arise. A depreciatory transaction by an individual is taxable on the ordinary principle that it diminishes his estate. But trustees do not have an estate. That is why it is necessary to have this express rule.

---

[8] See, *e.g. Macpherson v. IRC* (1988).

Settled Property

Qualifications to the termination and disposal rules

We now have to look at a number of qualifications to the disposal and termination rules.

NEW ENTITLEMENT. If A's life interest terminates but he becomes on the same occasion entitled to the property or to another interest in possession in the property, there is no PET unless the later interest is of less value than the former, in which case there is a deemed transfer of value equal to the difference: section 53(2) and section 52(4). This exception is a logical consequence of the principle that the holder of an interest in possession is treated as the owner of the property. If property is settled on trust to pay the income thereof to A for eight years and thereafter to A absolutely, there is no tax charge when the eight years are up and A takes the property absolutely; he was already treated for tax purposes as the absolute owner of the property. Thus there has been no loss to his estate. But if the trust was to pay the income to A for eight years and then to divide the property three-quarters to A and one-quarter to B, there would be a PET on that division. There is a notional loss to A of one-quarter of the settled property. Mind you, it may not be a real loss, because what A has after the eight-year period may well be (and probably will be) more valuable than what he had before. But it is a notional loss (and so taxable) because during the eight-year period he was treated as though he were the owner of the whole trust property, whereas after the division he is the owner of only three-quarters of it. The same point applies to an agreed "partition" between a life tenant and a remainderman, which is quite a common occurrence in practice. The proportion of the property which is partitioned to the remainderman is caught for tax as being property in which the interest of the life tenant comes to an end.

DISPOSAL FOR A CONSIDERATION. If the life tenant disposes of his interest for a consideration (that is, sells it as distinct from giving it away) the value transferred is reduced by the amount of the consideration: section 52(2). So if A, the life tenant of settled property worth £70,000, sells his life tenancy for £20,000, a PET arises not on the whole £70,000 but on £50,000. One might think that this provision would mean that no PET at all would arise if a life tenant were to sell his interest for its full market value. This is not really so because in practice a life interest (except in very rare circumstances) is always worth less than the property itself in which the interest subsists. The full market price of a life interest in Blackacre is almost certain to be less than the value of Blackacre itself. So if the life tenant sells his interest in Blackacre even for the full market price of the interest there may still be a PET on the disposal. A reversionary interest in the property does not count in this connection as consideration. So in a partition (discussed under the previous heading) the fact that the life tenant gets in return for his life tenancy part of the remainderman's reversionary interest does not reduce the amount of tax chargeable on the partition.

REVERTER TO SETTLOR. The word "reverter" is lawyers' old-fashioned jargon for reversion. So what we are talking about here is the situation where S settles property on X with a provision that on a certain event the property is to revert to S. It is provided by section 53(3) that if the interest comes to an end during the settlor's life and on the same occasion the property reverts to the settlor, tax shall not be chargeable. The reason for this exception from charge is that it is considered desirable that a person should be able to provide a life interest (or other interest) for his dependants without a charge to tax when the property reverts to him. An example might occur on a divorce; a husband might want to transfer the matrimonial home to his former wife until the children of the marriage reach (say) school leaving age, with a provision that the house should then revert to him. Section 53(3) ensures that when the reversion takes place no tax charge arises. It is dealing with the situation where the interest comes to an end during the life of the beneficiary—in our example during the life of the former wife. Parallel provision is made by section 54 for the case where the "reverter to settlor" occurs on the occasion of the death of the beneficiary. An example would be where a man gives a life interest in a house to his widowed mother.

The operation of this relief requires the identification of who is the settlor. In *Fitzwilliam v. IRC* (1993) the House of Lords decided that it could include anyone who consciously provided the funds for the settlement but not someone who gave the funds unconditionally to another who then created the settlement.

The relief does not apply if the settlor or his spouse had acquired the reversionary interest for consideration. The point of this rule is to stop an avoidance device. Suppose a settlor (S) were to settle £50,000 on X for life, remainder to Y. If it were not for this rule, S could, when X was old and about to die, buy Y's reversionary interest for £50,000. In this way he could pass the £50,000 to Y without any tax arising.

Settled Property

REVERTER TO SETTLOR'S SPOUSE. A similar exception applies where the property reverts not to the settlor but to the settlor's spouse, provided the spouse is domiciled in the United Kingdom at the time the reversion occurs: section 53(4)

TRUSTEE'S REMUNERATION. Sometimes a trustee is remunerated for his services as a trustee by being given an interest in possession in the settled property (or in some part of it). Section 90 declares that provided the interest does not represent more than reasonable remuneration, no tax charge shall arise on the termination of the interest.

Relief for successive charges

There is "quick succession" relief for successive charges on interests in possession under section 141 in the same way as on a death transfer. Thus if there is a charge on a fixed interest settlement, by the activating of a PET, within five years of a previous chargeable transfer of the property, the value chargeable is reduced by a percentage. If the period since the last chargeable transfer is one year or less the reduction is 100 per cent; if the period is not more than two years the reduction is 80 per cent; if the period is not more than three years the reduction is 60 per cent; if the period is not more than four years the reduction is 40 per cent; if the period is not more than five years the reduction is 20 per cent.

Close companies

We have seen (see p.334 above) that by sections 94 to 98 a transfer of value by a close company can be apportioned to the participators. That provision relates to unsettled property. A close company may be involved in settled property in various ways.

Where a participator in a close company is a trustee of settled property in which the company has an interest in possession a transfer of value by the company can be apportioned to the interest holder. This is effected by deeming there to be a partial termination of his interest: section 99. Such a charge will not be a PET.

Where a close company is itself entitled to an interest in settled property the participators are treated as being the persons beneficially entitled to that interest according to their respective rights and interests in the company: section 101. Again these transfers will not be PETS.

No Beneficial Interest in Possession

Fixed interest trusts and PETS

As we have seen, gifts into fixed settlements and the lifetime charges on such settlements will usually be PETs and so only chargeable if the settlor or the life tenant dies within seven years. However, there will still be an immediate charge where the settlor creates a discretionary trust (other than those specifically protected such as accumulation and maintenance trusts), or where such a trust arises as the result of the termination of the life tenant's interest. A combination of PETs and chargeable transfers may, however, enable a discretionary trust to be set up effectively free of tax. To prevent this sections 54A and 54B were introduced in 1986.

The scheme would work like this:

> Mary, a wealthy settlor with a cumulative total of chargeable transfers of £200,000, settles a further £200,000 on Naomi, who has made no previous chargeable transfers, for one month and then for discretionary beneficiaries. The gift into the settlement by Mary will be a PET. Further, when Naomi's interest terminates, the chargeable transfer will be deemed to have been made by her and so fall entirely within the nil band of tax. Provided that Mary lives for seven years there will therefore be no charge to tax without sections 54A and 54B.

Those sections provide, however, that in this situation tax will be charged on the termination of Naomi's interest as if the deemed transfer of value under section 52 had been made by a hypothetical transferor having the cumulative total of the settlor at the date of the creation of the settlement. Thus such a transferor would inherit Mary's cumulative total and the transfer would then attract tax at the lifetime rate. The sections only apply if the life interest terminates within seven years of the creation of the settlement and during the lifetime of the settlor.

Where There is No Beneficial Interest in Possession

We now turn to look at the totally different regime of tax charges which applies to settled property in which, or part of which, for the time being there is no beneficial interest in possession. The charging provisions are contained in Chapter III of Part III of the 1984 Act, sections 58 to 85. These charges do not fall within the PET regime.

Settled Property

The sections apply to what the legislation refers to as "relevant property". By section 58(1) relevant property means settled property (which we have already defined) in which no qualifying interest in possession exists. Section 59 defines such a qualifying interest as one to which an individual (or a company whose business it is to buy such interests) is beneficially entitled. It follows that with settled property there is either a beneficial interest and Chapter II of the Act applies, or there isn't and Chapter III applies. Section 58(1), however, also excludes from the definition of relevant property certain types of settlement in which there is no interest in possession—these settlements are specially favoured for tax purposes and have special rules of their own. They are dealt with in the next part of this chapter. For the moment it is sufficient to note that these include charitable trusts and accumulation and maintenance settlements for persons under 25. It is also important to remember that a settlement may comprise both relevant and non-relevant property, *e.g.* part may be a discretionary trust and part be subject to a beneficial interest in possession or be a charitable trust.

There are three questions to be answered in relation to relevant property, which we may loosely describe as discretionary trusts. First, when will there be a charge to inheritance tax? Secondly what property will actually be charged? Thirdly at what rate is the tax to be charged? The problem with discretionary trusts is that, unlike fixed interest trusts, there is no person entitled to an interest in possession regarded as owning the whole settled property for inheritance tax purposes, and so there will be no automatic charges on the death of such a person (or on an assignment of his interest, etc.). Fixed interest trusts are, in the nature of things, subject to a charge on the whole settled property at least once every generation (*i.e.* every 30 years or so). Similarly, the rates charged on fixed interest settlements are those applicable to the holder of the beneficial interest in possession—by treating the whole settled property as being in his ownership no special problems arise. Neither of these connecting factors are available for discretionary trusts.

The answer provided is, roughly, to charge a discretionary trust to tax every 10 years in such a way as to provide a charge on the whole settled property every 30 years or so, and to charge any property leaving the settlement in the meantime. The 10-year charge is known as the *principal charge*, the exit charges as *interim charges*. In relation to both types of charge the three questions above must be answered, but it is important to keep them separate in your mind. The rules, particularly as to the calculation of rates involved, are complex, and further difficulties arise because of the more generous treatment of discretionary trusts in existence before March 27, 1974, *i.e.* the date when the tax was introduced. This is because the tax regime for discretionary trusts was altered dramatically from that under estate duty law and it was thought unfair to apply the full rigour to such trusts. In general the basic difference is that a post March 26, 1974 settlement carries with it the cumulative total of the settlor at the date of the settlement whereas an earlier one does not.

It is now time to examine the charges.

THE PRINCIPAL OR TEN-YEAR CHARGE

1. When will there be a charge?

Section 64 provides that on the tenth anniversary of the date on which the settlement commenced and on every subsequent 10-year anniversary, a principal charge to inheritance tax is to be levied. However, section 61 provides that no date prior to April 1, 1983 could be such an anniversary. It follows that settlements created prior to April 1, 1973 could not have a chargeable 10-year anniversary until after April 1, 1983. It therefore became something of a lottery as to how soon such a settlement (created before this tax was thought up) would be taxed. For example, a settlement created on April 1, 1973 will have been taxed on April 1, 1983 but a settlement created on March 31, 1973 will not have been taxed until March 31, 1993! What price tax planning?

It is obviously important to decide when a settlement was created. Section 60 provides that this is when the property first becomes comprised in it, whether it was at this stage a discretionary trust or not, but for post March 26, 1974 settlements where a settlor, or his spouse, has an interest in possession when the settlement is first created, the property is only treated as having become comprised in the settlement when neither he nor his spouse have such an interest (section 80).

2. What is subject to the charge?

A 10-year charge is levied on the value of the relevant property comprised in the settlement, valued at the date of the charge. Since the whole amount is being charged no question of grossing up can arise. It is important to remember that this is all that is being charged

Settled Property

when grappling with the rules as to the calculation of the applicable rates.

3. *What rate is to be charged?*

Here one has to distinguish between pre-March 27, 1974 settlements and others.

(A) SETTLEMENTS CREATED AFTER MARCH 26, 1974. The rate of tax is calculated according to section 66. It is three-tenths of the effective rate of tax payable on a *notional chargeable transfer* made by a *notional transferor* with a *notional cumulative total* charged at the lifetime rates.

The *notional chargeable transfer* consists of:

(i) the relevant property which is actually being charged, valued now;
(ii) other property comprised in the settlement which is not relevant property (*e.g.* in which there is a beneficial interest in possession or which is a charitable trust), valued at the time it entered the settlement; and
(iii) property comprised in any related settlement (section 106 defines that as one made by the settlor on the same day as the settlement except a charitable trust). These should be avoided.

The *"transferor's" notional cumulative* total is:

(i) the settlor's seven-year cumulative total of chargeable transfers at the date of the creation of the settlement; and
(ii) the full amount charged to interim charges (see below) in the 10 years prior to the anniversary.

There is an additional sting in the tail. If the settlor has added property during the 10-year period his cumulative total at that time will be used if it is higher than his total at the time of the creation of the settlement. Conversely, however, if property is comprised in the settlement but has ceased during the 10-year period to be relevant property the amount upon which an exit charge has been made can be deducted from the cumulative ladder (section 67).

In an attempt to display these rules in a different way it may be helpful to give an example.

No Beneficial Interest in Possession

X created a settlement on December 1, 1986, of £100,000. Half is on discretionary trusts and half with an interest in possession. On the same day he made an accumulation and maintenance settlement (not relevant property) worth £50,000. At that time X had a seven-year cumulative total of £200,000.

The 10-year charge will arise on December 1, 1996. Let us suppose that the discretionary half of the settlement is now worth £150,000.
The notional transfer will be
£150,000   (chargeable relevant property)
  £50,000   (value of fixed interest part of settlement at date of settlement)
  £50,000   (related accumulative and maintenance settlement)

£250,000

The notional cumulative total, since there have been no exit charges, is that of the settlor at the date of creation of the settlement, *viz.* £200,000

> therefore calculate the notional tax at lifetime rates on such a transfer of £250,000
> *i.e.* tax on £450,000
> less tax on £200,000
>   = £X

Next, express £X as a percentage of £250,000 to give the effective rate of tax, *i.e.* Y per cent. (Under the current simplified rates this is relatively easy.)
The rate chargeable is then $\frac{3}{10}$ Y per cent.
Remember that rate is then charged on £150,000 only, *i.e.* the value of the relevant property at the anniversary.

Under section 66(2) in applying this rate to the relevant property, if part of that property has not been subject to the discretionary trusts for the whole 10-year period (*e.g.* additions to the property) the tax payable on that part of the relevant property is to be reduced by one-fortieth for each completed quarter of a year prior to its becoming comprised in the settlement.
Thus if a settlement of £500,000 is subject to a 10-year charge of £30,000 under the rules above, but £100,000 was only added two

Settled Property

years prior to that charge, the tax payable on that £100,000 is reduced as follows:

the tax payable on that part is $\dfrac{£100,000}{£500,000} \times £30,000 = £6,000$;

and

that figure (£6,000) is reduced by $\dfrac{32}{40}$, *i.e.* reduced to £1,200.

(B) Settlements created prior to March 27, 1974. Section 66(6) amends the above rules for settlements in existence at the introduction of what is now inheritance tax. The basic concept is, however, the same. *i.e.* three-tenths of the effective rate on a notional chargeable transfer made by a "transferor" with a notional cumulative total.

In this case, however, the notional transfer consists only of the chargeable relevant property and no account is taken of other property in the settlement or related settlements.

The notional cumulative total consists only of the amount subject to exit charges during the 10-year period. The settlor's total is ignored unless he has made an addition to the property after the March 1982 in which case his cumulative total then will be included.

In the example given above therefore the notional transfer would be £150,000 and the notional cumulative total nil. The nil band would therefore apply.

THE INTERIM OR EXIT CHARGES

1. *When will there be a charge?*

Section 65(1) provides that there will be a charge to inheritance tax if either (a) any part of the property ceases to be relevant property (*e.g.* on an advance of capital to a discretionary beneficiary) or (b) the trustees carry out a depreciatory value-shifting transaction which has the effect of reducing the value of the settled property, *e.g.* a loan to a beneficiary at a low rate of interest, etc. (This is similar to the charge on fixed interest settlements under section 52(3)).

No Beneficial Interest in Possession

The gratuitous interest exception in section 10 applies to the second of these charges, as in effect does section 3(3), omission to exercise a right being regarded as equivalent to a transaction[9].

There is no charge in the first quarter after the creation of the settlement or 10-year charge[10] for trustees' costs and expenses, or for income distributions (*i.e.* income in the hands of the recipient). Nor is there a charge if the property ceases to be relevant property because it becomes comprised in a charitable trust (section 76).

2. What is subject to the charge?

Section 65(2) provides that the interim charges are to be levied on the amount by which the relevant property after the event is less than it would be but for the event. This is the standard measure for inheritance tax, in effect the loss to the settlement's estate. It follows that unless the tax is paid by the beneficiary (*i.e.* it is a gross transfer) the transfer will have to be grossed-up for tax purposes.

3. What rate is charged?

In this case it is necessary to distinguish between whether there has been a 10-year principal charge or not. With regard to exit charges prior to the first 10-year charge there was a distinction between pre-March 27, 1974 settlements and others. The former have by now all had such a charge and so those provisions are redundant.

(A) SETTLEMENTS PRIOR TO THE FIRST 10-YEAR CHARGE. Section 68 requires us to apply the *appropriate fraction* of the effective rate of tax on a *notional chargeable transfer* made by a "transferor" with a *notional cumulative total*.

The appropriate fraction is:

$$\frac{\text{number of quarters since the settlement commenced}}{40}$$

except for property which has not been in the settlement for the whole of that time, in which case for that property one uses only the number of quarters since it became relevant property.

---

[9] The associated operations provisions also apply. See *MacPherson v. IRC* (1988).
[10] For an unexpected consequence of this see *Frankland v. IRC* (1996).

Settled Property

The *notional transfer* consists of:

(i) the value of the settled property at the commencement of the settlement;
(ii) the value of any related settlement;
(iii) the value of any addition to the property, valued at the date of entry.

The *notional cumulative total* is the settlor's cumulative total at the date of the settlement, ignoring any transfers made on that day.

To take an example:
A set up a £200,000 discretionary trust on January 4, 1990. He had previously made chargeable transfers of £50,000. Also on January 4, 1990 he set up a £70,000 trust for charity. On February 10, 1996 the trustees advanced £30,000 to F absolutely.

There is an interim charge on £30,000 (ceases to be relevant property). There has been no previous 10-year charge.

To find the rate:
notional transfer

$$= £200,000 \text{ (value of settled property in 1990)}$$
$$+ \underline{£70,000} \text{ (related settlement)}$$
$$\underline{£270,000}$$

notional cumulative total = £50,000 (settlor's total in 1990)
therefore calculate tax on £320,000
less tax on £50,000
= £x

express £x as a percentage of £270,000 to give effective rate = y per cent.

The appropriate fraction is

$\frac{3}{10} \times \frac{24}{40}$ (no. of quarters since 1990 = $\frac{9}{50}$
so the rate chargeable on £30,000 is $\frac{9}{50}$ of Y per cent.

(B) SETTLEMENTS AFTER THE FIRST 10-YEAR CHARGES. In such cases section 69 provides a simpler way of calculating the rates on an interim charge. It is simply the appropriate fraction of the rate charged on the last 10-year charge (ignoring any deduction for added property). We can for once dispense with notional transfer and the like.

The appropriate fraction is

$$\frac{\text{number of quarters completed since the last 10-year charge}}{40}$$

The only complication is if at the time of the interim charge the settlement includes relevant property which was not there at the 10-year charge. In that case the 10-year charge has to be recalculated to include the added property, valued at the time it becomes relevant property.

It may be helpful to read through these provisions again. Perhaps after a good cup of coffee!

Special Kinds of Settlement

As we have said before, some special types of settlement are not relevant property and as such are not liable to the interim and principal charges even though there is no beneficial interest in possession. Similarly, the creation of such a trust is a PET. However, if the property ceases to be held on such trusts there is a flat rate charge which increases according to the length of time the property has been exempt and so avoided the 10-year charge. This is subject to a maximum of 30 per cent and no period prior to March 13, 1975 will be counted.

The list of these trusts can be found in section 58(1). These include trusts for the benefit of employees, superannuation schemes, charitable trusts, and protective trusts. One of the most important is an accumulative and maintenance settlement and this may be used as an illustration of how these settlements are treated for inheritance tax purposes. In general it should also be remembered that if a discretionary trust becomes a specially favoured trust the property will cease to be relevant property and an interim charge will accrue. This does not apply to charitable trusts, however.

ACCUMULATION AND MAINTENANCE SETTLEMENTS

One can think of these settlements as being settlements for the benefit of young people.

Where a discretionary trust comes within the definition of an accumulation and maintenance settlement it is relieved from the normal tax charges relating to discretionary settlements since it is not relevant property. Its creation will also be a PET.

Settled Property

The matter is dealt with in section 71, which applies to any settlement where:

(1) one or more persons ("beneficiaries") will become entitled to the settled property or to an interest in possession in it at some specified age not exceeding 25;
(2) there is no interest in possession in the settled property;
(3) any application of the income must be for the maintenance, education or benefit of a beneficiary;
(4) to the extent that it is not so applied, the income must be accumulated; and
(5) not more than 25 years have elapsed since the latest time when conditions (1) to (4) above became satisfied, except that this rule does not apply if all the persons who are or have been beneficiaries are or were (putting it broadly) grandchildren of a common grandparent.

There has been some dispute as to the meaning of the word "will" in condition (1). In *Baron Inglewood v. IRC* (1983) the Revenue argued that this requires that the beneficiary will *inevitably* become entitled to an interest if he attains the specified age. The taxpayer argued that it was sufficient if *at the present time* someone will and that such things as powers of revocation do not prevent the section applying. The Court of Appeal decided for the Revenue. The settlement has to ensure that one or more of the beneficiaries will attain a vested interest under 25 to come within the section. If his interest is capable of being taken away by the settlement (such as by a power of revocation) that cannot be the case. This involved the Court of Appeal in distinguishing such powers from, *e.g.* the power of advancement under section 32 of the Trustee Act 1925—the latter being classed as administrative powers or auxiliary powers.

There are several tax advantages applying to settlements which fulfil the above requirements. There is no 10-year anniversary charge, no interim charges, *e.g.* on the advancement to a beneficiary, no charge on the death of a potential beneficiary under the specified age or on a beneficiary obtaining an interest in possession by reaching the specified age.

There will be a charge if either (i) the property ceases to comply with the conditions or (ii) the trustees involve themselves in a depreciatory value-shifting transaction (*cf.* similar charges on fixed interest and discretionary trusts). The charge is a tapering charge based on the number of quarters of a year from the time when the conditions were first fulfilled to the date of charge. It is a flat rate charge on the scale set out in section 70.

0.25 per cent for each of the first 40 quarters (10 years—10 per cent).

0.20 per cent for each of the next 40 quarters (11–20 years—further 8 per cent).

0.15 per cent for each of the next 40 quarters (21–30 years—further 6 per cent).

0.10 per cent for each of the next 40 quarters (31–40 years—further 4 per cent).

0.05 per cent for each of the next 40 quarters (41–50 years—further 2 per cent).

Thus if the time lapse is 15 years the rate is 14 per cent. The maximum rate is 30 per cent after 50 years, which cannot occur before March 13, 2015.

It is important to note the effect of section 31 of the Trustee Act 1925 on these rules. That section gives trustees a statutory power to pay maintenance to a potential beneficiary up to the age of 18. It also, unless excluded, gives that beneficiary a right to receive the income between the ages of 18 and the required age. It follows that a gift to X "when he is 30" will give X the right to the income at 18—he will therefore have an interest in possession at that age and so have the right to such an interest at an age under 25. The Revenue have agreed that this will satisfy the conditions for section 71 to apply. Unless section 31 is excluded, such as by a direction to accumulate the income until the beneficiary reaches 30, it does not therefore matter what age is specified as entitling the beneficiary to the capital, he will receive the income, and so get an interest in possession, at 18.[11]

By a further concession the conditions will be fulfilled even if no age is specified in the deed if it is clear that the beneficiary will become entitled to the property, if at all, by age 25, *e.g.* to X in 21 years' time, X being three years old.

The Purchase of a Reversionary Interest

We have seen (notably at p.376 above) that except in certain circumstances a reversionary interest in settled property in the United Kingdom is excluded property, thus giving effect to the

---

[11] This is equally true if the contingency is otherwise than attaining a specific age. See *Swales v. IRC* (1984).

Settled Property

principle that the life tenant owns the whole settled fund and the reversioner owns nothing.

There are a number of special provisions in the legislation, however, some of which are designed to prevent over-charging in respect of reversionary interests and some of which are designed to prevent tax avoidance.

The most important provision is that a purchased reversion is not excluded property: section 48(1)(a). This is to prevent an obvious form of avoidance. Suppose that £200,000 is settled on A for life, remainder to B. C purchases B's remainder for £60,000, which is its market value. This is not a chargeable transfer since there will be no loss to C's estate and in any event no donative intent (protected by section 10). C has depleted his free estate by £60,000 and gained the reversion. If he could thus give the reversion to D as excluded property he would in effect have given D £60,000 free of inheritance tax. Thus there is a charge on the gift to D, a purchased reversion is not excluded property.

The position is more complex if the reversion is purchased by the owner of a prior interest in the settlement.

Suppose that property having a value of £200,000 is settled on A for life with remainder to B. And suppose further that A has free estate (*i.e.* unsettled property) worth £100,000. If A were to die his estate would have a value of £300,000. If A (before dying) were to buy from B the reversionary interest for its full actuarial value (say £80,000) he could do so without any tax charge, because although A's life interest terminates he becomes on the same occasion absolutely entitled to the property: see section 53(2). The reversion merges with the life interest and the property ceases to be settled property. If A were now to die, his estate would have a value of only £220,000, made up of £200,000 (the former settled property) plus £20,000 (his free estate, previously £100,000 but diminished by the £80,000 which he has paid to B). In this way tax would be saved. The "trick" lies in having brought into his estate something which in reality increases his wealth, but which (for the purposes of the tax) he already owned, and in having depleted, by that transaction, his taxable estate.

The legislation meets this avoidance device by treating A as having made a gift to B of £80,000, and so as having made a PET of that amount. This is done by means of section 55 which says this:

> "... where a person entitled to an interest (whether in possession or not) in any settled property acquires a reversionary interest expectant

Purchase of a Reversionary Interest

(whether immediately or not) on the interest, the reversionary interest is not part of his estate ... "

Thus, although A gives full value to B for the reversionary interest, and although there is no donative intent, he is treated as having paid £80,000 for nothing, and so as having made a transfer of value amounting to £80,000. The importance of donative intent is, of course, that the absence of donative intent normally is ground for no charge to tax arising: section 10 (see p. 326).

CHAPTER 27

LIABILITY AND INCIDENCE

In this chapter we deal with two matters which are separate but related, namely liability and incidence.

Liability is concerned with who is to pay the tax to the Revenue. The previous legislation, dealing with Estate Duty, described this duty to pay the tax as "accountability". That was somewhat confusing, because there is also a separate duty to deliver to the Revenue an account. The inheritance tax legislation describes the duty to pay the tax as "liability" which is much clearer.

Incidence is concerned with who is ultimately to bear the burden of the tax. So, for example, an executor may be under a duty to pay the tax to the Revenue. He then looks to the rules of incidence to see against what beneficial interests under the will he is to charge it.

Liability

The following persons may, in various circumstances, be liable to pay the tax: transferor, transferee, trustee, beneficiary, settlor, personal representative. Does anyone feel left out?

The details are set out Part VII, sections 199 to 214, of the 1984 Act.

For *chargeable*[1] *lifetime transfers of unsettled property* the persons liable are: (a) primarily the transferor and then the transferee; and (b) so far as the tax is attributable to the value of any particular property, any person in whom the property is vested (whether beneficially or otherwise) at any time after the transfer or who at any such time is beneficially entitled to an interest in possession in the property; and (c) where by the chargeable transfer any property becomes comprised in a settlement, any person for whose benefit any of the property or income from it is applied.

---

[1] There rules are modified for PETs which become chargeable transfers on the transferor's death within seven years and for any additional "death rate" payable on such a death. See below.

For *chargeable transfers of settled property* the persons liable are: (a) primarily the trustees of the settlement; and (b) any person entitled (whether beneficially or not) to an interest in possession in the settled property; and (c) any person for whose benefit any of the settled property or income from it is applied; and (d) where the chargeable transfer is made during the life of the settlor and the trustees are not for the time being resident in the United Kingdom, the settlor.

For *transfers on death* the persons liable are: (a) in respect of unsettled property and in respect of settled property being land in the United Kingdom which devolves upon them, the deceased's personal representatives[2]; (b) in respect of settled property, the trustees; (c) so far as the tax is attributable to the value of any particular property, any person in whom the property is vested (whether beneficially or otherwise) at any time after the death or who at any such time is beneficially entitled to an interest in possession in the property; and (d) so far as the tax is attributable to the value of any property which, immediately before the death, was comprised in a settlement, any person for whose benefit any of the property or income from it is applied after the death.[3]

Where the transferor dies within seven years of making a chargeable transfer the additional tax which becomes payable (*i.e.* the difference between the lifetime rates and the death rates) is principally the liability of the transferee. Similar rules apply where the transferor dies within seven years of making a PET and the transfer becomes chargeable. But if, for example, the transferee does not pay within 12 months the personal representatives are liable. All concerned are advised to take out insurance against such a contingent liability.

In any circumstances where two or more persons are liable for the same tax, each is liable to the Revenue for the whole of it. But, of course, the Revenue cannot get more tax than is due.

References in the above contexts to any property include references to any property directly or indirectly representing it. So one

---

[2] This liability is a personal liability of the personal representatives and not a liability of the deceased which they assume. See *IRC v. Stannard* (1984).
[3] Liability also extends to anyone who interferes or "intermeddles" in the estate to become an *executor de son tort*. See *IRC v. Stype Investments (Jersey) Ltd* (1982).

Liability and Incidence

does not escape the tax charge merely by selling the original property and investing the proceeds in some other property. (For the tax position of the purchaser, see below.)

Transfers between spouses

Where a transferor is liable for any tax and by another transfer of value made by him any property becomes the property of a person who at the time of both transfers was his spouse, that person is liable for so much of the tax as does not exceed the value of the property at the time of the other transfer. See section 203, which is designed to stop up a rather crude avoidance device—namely, make a transfer of value to someone overseas and make also an exempt transfer of the rest of one's estate to one's spouse, and leave the Revenue to whistle for their money.

Exception of purchaser from liability

A purchaser of property is not liable for tax attributable to the value of the property purchased, unless the property is subject to an Inland Revenue charge (on which see p. 405, below): section 199(3).

Limitations of liability

There are limitations on the extent to which a person is liable for the tax. For instance, a personal representative is liable only to the extent of the assets he has received or might have received but for his own neglect or default. Somewhat similar limitations apply to trustees, beneficiaries and transferees. See section 204.

Incidence

We now come to the question of who is to bear the ultimate burden of the tax, bearing in mind that the person who pays the tax may not be the person on whom the burden should ultimately fall.

Problems of incidence are most acute in relation to tax arising on death. In the case of lifetime transfers it is a matter between the parties as to who bears the tax. The main effect, as we have seen, will be as to whether "grossing-up" is necessary.

Whilst prima facie each item of property comprised in a person's estate at death carries its own burden of tax this general principle is largely reversed by section 211. Tax attributable to the value of property in the United Kingdom which vests in the deceased's personal representatives and which was not, immediately before the death, comprised in a settlement, is to be treated as part of the general testamentary and administration expenses of the deceased, unless the will provides to the contrary. This of course means that, apart from any jointly owned property passing by survivorship which will not vest in the personal representatives, the tax attributed to the bulk of the average testator's estate will be treated as part of the general testamentary and administration expenses of the deceased for it is only in exceptional circumstances that the average estate includes overseas property. The incidence of tax for the average testator is therefore to be determined by the Administration of Estates Act 1925, s.34 and Part II of the First Schedule thereto under which where the deceased has left a will effectively disposing of the residue of his estate the burden will be thrown on that residue.

This process is reinforced by the tendency of testators to include in their wills directions that particular gifts should be paid free of inheritance tax. As we shall see in a moment, such a direction does, however, have another potential effect on the incidence rules on death. There is one exception to this power of testators to make tax-free gifts. Suppose a testator gives his residue equally to his wife and his mother, with a direction that the mother's share is to be free of inheritance tax. The gift to the spouse is exempt, whilst that to the mother is chargeable. Section 41 provides that a chargeable residuary gift must bear its own tax so that the direction that such tax shall be borne by the exempt gift of residue is void.[4]

It is important on a death to calculate the estate rate, *i.e.* the rate of tax which applies to the whole estate, taking into account the nil band. Thus if A dies, having made no previous chargeable transfers, leaving a chargeable estate (ignoring exempt transfers) of £300,000, tax will currently be chargeable at nil on £200,000 and at 40 per cent on £100,000. Thus the tax bill will be £40,000. Applied across all the assets this gives an average rate of 13.33 per cent. That rate will then be deducted from any legacies which have to bear their own tax before the money is paid over to the legatee. Tax-free legacies will be paid in full with the tax coming out of residue. This apparently simple calculation is, however, as in many areas of tax law, not always quite so simple.

---

[4] *Re Benham's Will Trusts* (1995).

Liability and Incidence

Partially exempt transfers on death

In many cases the rule that inheritance tax is a testamentary expense to be paid out of residue causes no problems. Thus where all the legacies are both chargeable and tax free and the residue is also chargeable, the whole tax bill (at the estate rate) is charged on the residue. Similarly, if the legacies are either all exempt, or are to bear their own tax under the terms of the will, the residue and the tax-bearing legacies will simply bear their own tax at the estate rate. But problems arise in three not uncommon cases. These problems are the subject of sections 36 to 42. The following is an outline of the effect of these sections, which in practice involve many complex calculations:

(i) Where the testator leaves a legacy free of tax[5] and an exempt gift of residue; *e.g.* £200,000 to my daughter, free of tax, residue to my wife. In this case, in order to work out how much tax should be charged on the legacy (*i.e.* the estate rate since the residue is exempt) it must be grossed up (in the same way as a net lifetime transfer). The tax then payable on that grossed up legacy is deducted from the residuary gift and the daughter will receive the net £200,000.

(ii) Where the testator makes both tax-free legacies and those which must bear their own tax, together with an exempt gift of residue. Grossing-up only the tax-free legacies would not be enough (since there are other legacies involved in assessing the tax liability) but grossing-up all the legacies would be too much (since those bearing their own tax are not required to be grossed up, just as with a gross lifetime transfer). The solution is to gross up the tax-free legacies at a rate of tax applicable to a hypothetical transfer of the total of the grossed up tax-free legacies and those bearing their own tax. This is known as "double grossing-up".

In essence, the tax-free legacies are first grossed-up in the normal way, then the rate for grossing-up a second time is calculated on a transfer of the total of that grossed-up figure plus the tax-bearing legacies (say 20 per cent). The tax-free legacies are then grossed-up again at that rate. The estate rate of tax is then calculated on the total of those doubly grossed-

---

[5] Remember this will be the case unless the will provides to the contrary.

up legacies and the tax bearing legacies (say 25 per cent). That rate will then be deducted from the residue in respect of the tax-free legacies and from the tax-bearing legacies in respect of their own tax.

(iii) Where the testator leaves both tax-free and tax-bearing legacies, as above, but the residue is partly chargeable and partly exempt. In this case, the tax-free gifts are again subject to a double grossing-up, but the second grossing-up must be at a rate calculated on a hypothetical transfer of the total of the grossed-up tax-free legacies, the tax-bearing legacies and the chargeable part of the residue (divided after deducting the single grossed-up tax-free legacies and the tax-bearing legacies). After the tax-free legacies have been so doubly grossed-up, the estate rate is calculated on the total of the doubly grossed-up legacies, the tax-bearing legacies and the chargeable part of the residue (now divided after deducting the doubly grossed-up legacies and the tax-bearing legacies). That rate is then charged on the residue as a whole in respect of the tax-free legacies. Only after that will the residue be divided and the estate rate applied to the chargeable part. That rate will also be deducted from those legacies bearing their own tax.

CHAPTER 28

ADMINISTRATION AND COLLECTION

Section 215 of the 1984 Act announces that inheritance tax "shall be under the care and management of the Board" (*i.e.* the Commissioners of Inland Revenue). Part VIII of the 1984 Act (sections 215 to 261) provides detailed rules concerning the administration and collection of the tax.

Delivery of an account: section 216

The personal representatives of a deceased person are under a duty to deliver an account to the Revenue specifying to the best of their knowledge and belief all relevant property and its value. And a similar duty rests on a transferor and a trustee[1] of a settlement concerning a lifetime transfer which is not a PET. An account need only be delivered in respect of a PET if the transferor dies within seven years. If there are no personal representatives appointed within 12 months of the death the duty to account falls on those beneficially entitled to the property or an interest in the property (including certain discretionary beneficiaries). There is no duty to account on a death if the estate does not exceed £125,000 and certain other conditions are fulfilled.[2] The phrase "best of their knowledge and belief" means the personal knowledge of the individual. This includes documents in his possessions or custody but he is not required to be an information gatherer.[3]

Personal representatives must deliver their account within 12 months from the end of the month in which the death occurs or

---

[1] This includes a foreign trustee of a foreign trust made by a U.K. settlor: *Re Clore (dec'd) (No. 3)* (1985).

[2] These are: there is no settled property; not more than £15,000 is outside the U.K.; the estate does not include any gifts subject to a reservation; and the deceased died domiciled in the U.K. having made no chargeable *inter vivos* transfer: S.I. 1981 Nos. 880 and 881, as amended by S.I. 1991 No. 1248; made under s.256.

[3] *Re Clore (dec'd) (No 3)* (1985).

404

within three months of the time when they first acted (if this period expires later).

Any other person must deliver his account within 12 months from the end of the month in which the transfer took place, or (if it expires later) the period of three months from the date on which he first became liable for tax. (There are special rules about conditionally exempt works of art, etc., and about timber.)

Personal representatives cannot get probate until they have paid the tax, and they cannot sell any of the estate assets (so as to get cash with which to pay the tax) until they have got probate. That looks like a vicious circle. But the problem can be overcome. The personal representatives can submit a provisional account and pay tax on that, then get probate, then sell off some of the estate assets, then submit a corrective or supplementary account and pay tax on that.

Returns by certain persons acting for settlors: section 218

There is a special provision concerning overseas settlements. Where any person, in the course of a trade or profession (other than the profession of a barrister) has been concerned with the making of a settlement and knows or has reason to believe that the settlor was domiciled in the United Kingdom and that the trustees of the settlement are not or will not be resident in the United Kingdom, he must within three months of the making of the settlement make a return to the Board stating the names and addresses of the settlor and of the trustees of the settlement. This requirement does not apply to a settlement made by will nor to any other settlement if such a return has already been made by another person or if an account has been delivered in relation to it. The provision applies to (amongst others) solicitors and accountants.

Power to require information and inspect property: sections 219 and 220

The Board, with the consent of a Special Commissioner, may by notice in writing require any person to furnish them within such time, not being less than 30 days, as may be specified in the notice with such information as the Board may require for the purposes of inheritance tax. The notice may be combined with a notice relating to income tax. Legal professional privilege is protected except that a solicitor (not a barrister) can be required to disclose the name and address of his client and (in certain circumstances relating to an overseas client) the names and addresses of his client's clients in the United Kingdom.

If the Board authorises any person to inspect any property for the purpose of ascertaining its value for the purposes of inheritance tax the person having the custody or possession of that property shall permit him to inspect it at such reasonable times as the Board may consider necessary.

Assessment and appeals: sections 221 to 225

Instead of the word "assessment" which is the technical term applying to income tax, capital gains tax and corporation tax, the term used in relation to inheritance tax is "determination". The Board make a determination and then serve a notice of determination.

Appeals (which must be made within 30 days of service of notice of determination) go to the Special Commissioners except in two cases as follows: (1) where it is so agreed between the appellant and the Board, or where the High Court (on an application made by the appellant) is satisfied that the matters to be decided are likely to be substantially confined to questions of law and gives leave, the appeal goes to the High Court direct, thus cutting out the Special Commissioner stage; (2) any question as to the value of land in the United Kingdom must be determined by the appropriate Lands Tribunal.

The procedure before the Special Commissioners is similar to that in relation to other taxes.

Appeal lies from the Special Commissioners to the High Court on a point of law only.

Payment of tax: sections 226 to 236

In general, inheritance tax becomes due six months after the end of the month in which the chargeable transfer was made or, in the case of a transfer made after April 5 and before October 1 in any year otherwise than on death, at the end of April in the next year. So in many instances tax is due before the account is due. Tax on PETs is due six months after the death which activates the charge. So is the additional tax payable on the death of the transfers of a chargeable transfer within seven years.

Tax which is due and unpaid attracts interest at prescribed rates and there is no income tax relief for the interest payments. Where there has been an overpayment of tax the repayment by the Revenue carries interest (at the same rates as above) from the date on which

Inland Revenue Charge

the overpayment was made, and this interest is not subject to income tax.

In certain circumstances the tax can be paid by instalments. This facility applies only where the tax is attributable to certain kinds of property: land, controlling shares or securities; other shares or securities which are unquoted and in respect of which certain detailed conditions are satisfied; a business or an interest in a business to the extent of its net value (as defined).[4]

The instalment provisions apply to transfers on death. They also apply, with certain modifications, to lifetime transfers but only if either (a) the tax is borne by the person benefiting from the transfer or (b) the property is settled property and remains in the settlement after the transfer.

Interest on land is payable in instalments from the date on which the first instalment fell due, but in other cases interest only runs if an instalment is in arrears so that there can be interest-free instalments.

Inland Revenue charge for unpaid tax: sections 237 and 238

The word "charge" in this context is being used in the same sense in which a mortgage is a charge. Section 237 automatically imposes an Inland Revenue charge on all property included in a chargeable transfer and, in the case of settled property, on any property included in the settlement. The holder of the property can thus be liable for the tax. On a transfer on death the charge does not apply to personal or movable property in the United Kingdom. Personal property here includes leaseholds and undivided shares in land held on trust for sale (whether statutory or not). A purchaser of land where the charge is not registered and a bona fide purchaser of personal property without notice is not subject to the charge; where this is the case the charge attaches to the proceeds of sale.

---

[4] Rather special instalment provisions apply to timber in certain circumstances.

Part Six

Value Added Tax

Chapter 29

VALUE ADDED TAX

Value added tax is almost always known as VAT. Even the VAT Act calls it that. So shall we. Not only does it save time, it also avoids awkward questions about whether we have the name right! We call it "value added tax", but the Irish call it "value-added tax", and are probably correct. Why? Because the name is a direct translation from the French *taxe sur la valeur ajoutée*—tax on added value. Somewhere we turned the noun "value" into an adjective. It was not the only thing we muddled when transposing the tax into the British context in 1972. Perhaps the New Zealanders had a better idea. They call it the goods and services tax, which is what it is.

Despite the muddles, we have turned VAT from a foreign idea into Britain's second biggest tax in one generation. Why? There are two main reasons: a legal reason and a practical reason. The legal reason is that VAT is the only permissible general sales tax in the European Union. When we joined the E.C. in 1973, we were obliged to adopt the tax. As we see below, many of the details of the tax are a matter of European law.

The practical reason is that the E.U. is, in fiscal terms, a customs union. For many centuries much English, then British, government revenue was earned from customs duties. Now the UK government gets precisely nothing from customs duties—they are a European tax, and cannot be imposed between the Member States of the E.U. We can only tax goods from other European countries to the same extent as we tax domestic production. So we tax both equally—and that is the heart of VAT.

Introduction

VAT is a charge on:

- domestic supplies of goods and services;
- cross-border acquisitions from other states in the E.U.; and
- imports from states outside the E.U.

Value Added Tax

Each of these three charges is a necessary part of the tax. However, we shall first deal with the tax on the assumption that all relevant aspects of taxable transactions take place in the United Kingdom. We then deal with the international issues.

VAT as an E.U. tax

Although we can leave on one side for the moment the problems of taxing transactions where only part occurs in the United Kingdom, we cannot ignore the European nature of the tax. We adopted the tax to comply with European Community Treaty obligations, and they still bind us. Behind the Treaty obligations are detailed directives that lay down the form and much of the detail of the tax.

The principles of the E.C. VAT were laid down in 1967 in the First VAT Directive (Directive 27/227/EEC). Detail was added by a Second Directive, but this was revoked in 1977 and replaced by the Sixth VAT Directive (Directive 77/388/EEC). The Sixth Directive has been amended and extended considerably since 1977. In its embellished version, it forms the main text of the E.C. VAT law. It is also of considerable importance because the European Court of Justice has ruled in a whole series of decisions that those parts of the directive that are clear and unconditional are directly effective in Member States. Much of the directive is drafted in precise terms, so the discretion of Member States in how they apply the tax is limited. The form of VAT had to be tightened up when the single internal market of the E.C. was created. Since then, despite the fashion for subsidiarity, it is only in procedural areas that the individual states have much discretion about how the tax is applied. There is even an agreed minimum main rate of tax throughout the Member States.

It follows that if the British—or French, Italian or Greek—form of the VAT is too far out of line with the E.C. rules, then either the taxpayer or the European Commission can take a case to court to challenge the difference. The European Court has, for this reason, been kept busy dealing with VAT matters in recent years. We shall note some of the key cases as we look at the main features of the tax.

It is in the European Commission's interests to ensure consistent application of VAT for a number of reasons—and not just because it is the law. A major reason is that differences between taxation of domestic supplies and imports can amount to a disguised customs duty or state subsidy, distorting trade. Another reason is that there is an E.U. levy on all national VAT receipts paid into the Community accounts in Brussels. Major reductions in a national tax might therefore reflect in the budgetary receipts of the whole E.U. A third reason is that the complications of different national VATs may make it harder for traders to trade freely outside their own countries.

VAT in the United Kingdom

In the United Kingdom, VAT is imposed by the Value Added Tax Act 1994, a consolidation measure, together with significant provisions in delegated legislation. Partly as a result of a series of cases brought against the United Kingdom Government by taxpayers and by the European Commission, many of the differences that used to exist between the E.C. VAT and its United Kingdom version have been removed or at least reduced. Others have been expressly authorised by derogations from the general rules in the directives approved under E.C. law.

Only a limited number arise from the proper exercise of national discretion.

VAT law is a curious mix of broad principles and considerable amounts of detail. This is because of the nature of the tax. In principle it is a very broad-based tax, much broader than income tax or corporation tax. Potentially it applies to any economic transaction under which anyone adds value to any business activity; that is, under which anyone recovers not only the cost of materials used in a transaction, but also the cost of his or her own labour (or that of employees) or a profit. Of course, both are usually the aim. VAT therefore can apply to any economic activity. Further, it applies directly to those activities, not at one remove in the way corporation tax or income tax do. We must in every case establish not who makes the money, but who makes the supply, to whom, and of what. Easy? No, because checking on those questions can involve almost any aspect of commercial law and intellectual property law and much of real property law as well. If a problem exists in any of these areas of law, it can exist in VAT also.

At the same time, therefore, United Kingdom VAT law has to follow a European paradigm and deal with considerable detail. Both make the traditional pattern of imposition by means only of primary legislation inappropriate. In practice, there are four tiers of operative legislation. The top tier is formed by the European directives. The next tier is the VAT Act and amending Finance Acts. Below that

Value Added Tax

are orders in Council and other delegated legislation. Then comes the fourth layer: official Notices. These Notices (of which there were 59 at the time of writing) are issued by the Customs and Excise Commissioners and, unusually, have legislative status. Taxpayers to whom the Notices are issued are obliged to follow their contents. By this multiple means, the law is imposed. Supported both by considerable use of the appeals process, and also by agreements with trade organisations, extra-statutory concessions, parliamentary questions, press releases, and more than 80 leaflets of guidance, those who need to do so can find out at least what the local VAT offices think they should be doing. Of this wealth of material, you may find it useful to obtain one Notice in particular. Notice No. 700, *The VAT Guide*, is an excellent summary, with worked examples, of the tax for those who have to operate it. It is available free from your local VAT office.

Administration and appeals

VAT administration is the task of the oldest British government department, Her Majesty's Customs and Excise. Perhaps this may seem odd. First, the main job of this department is now running VAT, although that tax is neither an excise tax nor a customs duty. Secondly, the customs duties are not Her Majesty's—they "belong" to the European Union and British customs officers act as agents of the E.U. in collecting duties. A third reason for this seeming odd is that VAT is, in practical terms, collected by the same taxpayers as pay corporation tax and Schedule D income tax. Why is it not then collected by the Inland Revenue?

The answer is that when we adopted VAT it replaced, among other taxes, a sales tax called purchase tax. This left excise officers underemployed, and VAT solved that problem. This had the unfortunate practical effect of emphasising differences between VAT and income tax rather than common areas, particularly in procedural terms. Not all the differences between income tax and VAT are necessary differences. Naturally, the new VAT was fitted into an existing approach. But even now a taxpayer must deal with two lots of officials and sets of powers while in several other European states one team of tax officials deals with both kinds of tax.

The differences between the taxes also extend to the assessment and appeals systems. We will explain the system of the administering of VAT later, but we need to note that the system does not rely on formal assessments in the same way as income tax. Instead, liability to pay arises whenever a taxable supply of goods or services takes place. If the person making the supply cannot agree with the local VAT office about the application of VAT to that supply, then there is a right to refer the matter to a special tribunal. The tribunal has the right to hear appeals on a long list of things: see section 83 of the VAT Act 1994. Apart from disputes about liability, a major subject of appeals is the imposition of penalties.

Appeals are heard by the VAT and duties appeal tribunal (VDAT). Originally set up only to hear VAT appeals, this tribunal now deals with all aspects of the indirect taxes or, in effect, appeals from decisions of the customs and excise authorities. The VDAT has the power to deal with any question of law, procedure or fact in an appeal. Appeals from the VDAT can only be made on a point of law. This right of appeal is part of the general right to appeal to the High Court from a tribunal granted by section 11 of the Tribunals and Inquiries Act 1992.

VAT in Scotland is exactly the same as in England, save that appeals from the VDAT lie to the Scottish courts rather than the English courts. There are, however, not one but two common lines of appeal on Scottish cases and English cases. The first is to the House of Lords. The second is to the European Court of Justice in Luxembourg.

Because many of the key issues in imposing VAT depend on the VAT directives, the interpretation of those directives is at the heart of many appeals. Any court or VDAT which considers that a question of interpretation of European Community law is necessary to a decision may refer the matter to the European Court before reaching a conclusion in a case. This right is contained in Article 177 of the European Community Treaty. It is the right of the judge or tribunal to decide on a reference, not that of the parties to the case. In the case of a court of final appeal, this right becomes an obligation. An example of this is the case of *Apple and Pear Development Council v. CEC* (1988). The case involved a definition of the term *consideration*. While this caused little problem in the lower courts, the House of Lords found that a decision could not be reached without ensuring that the term was interpreted accurately at the European level. The case was therefore referred to the European Court of Justice from the House of Lords. In other cases, the matter has been referred directly from the VDAT. All decisions on such references, whether made from British courts or tribunals or from other E.C. states, bind all British courts and tribunals.

VALUE ADDED TAX

When VAT Applies

The three key questions to be answered in determining the structure of VAT are: who are the taxpayers? on what are they taxed? when, and how much, tax is paid?

In a practical sense, the taxpayers of VAT are the consumers who buy the goods and services subject to the tax. The legal obligation is not placed on them, but on those that supply them. These are called not taxpayers but *taxable persons* in the VAT legislation. This helps us keep in mind that the tax is imposed on transactions rather than persons, although the taxable persons are those required to collect the tax. Who are taxable persons? Section 3 (1) of the VAT Act tells us that "a person is a taxable person for the purposes of this Act while he is, or is required to be, registered under this Act." We will explore below who is in these two categories.

What is subject to VAT? Section 4(1) of the Act says that "VAT shall be charged on any supply of goods or services made in the United Kingdom, where it is a taxable supply made by a taxable person in the course or furtherance of any business carried on by him" while section 4(2) adds that a "taxable supply is a supply of goods or services made in the United Kingdom other than an exempt supply." We must add to this helpful definition the further guidance that *supply* includes all forms of supply, but not anything done otherwise than for a consideration, and that anything which is not a supply of goods but is done for a consideration (including, if so done, the granting, assignment or surrender of any right) is a supply of services (section 5(2)).

But wait a minute. VAT is a European tax. Has the British legislation carried out the requirements of European law? The key provision is Article 2 of the Sixth VAT directive. This provides that "The following shall be subject to value added tax: 1. the supply of goods or services effected for consideration within the territory of the country by a taxable person acting as such ... "

To this we must add Article 4.1 of the directive: "Taxable person" shall mean any person who independently carries out in any place any economic activity specified in paragraph 2, whatever the purpose or results of that activity.

The British provisions say the same thing as the European text. We can say that with authority because if the two differ, the European text prevails—or, rather, it can be made to prevail. The strict position is that where the two texts differ, the Customs authorities follow the British version. However, a taxpayer that wishes to assert the European approach is at liberty to do so. If the VAT office does not accept this, the matter can be referred to the VDAT and, if necessary, to the European Court. Why, then, does the VAT Act not follow the European model? It is, in part, because the intention was to make the United Kingdom version of VAT look more like a familiar set of rules. It was also because in 1972, when VAT was first introduced in the United Kingdom, the European form of VAT was far from complete. Even now, there are major gaps to be filled at national level. Finally, it has to be noted that the British 1972 version differed from the European version in several ways. Many of the gaps and differences have now gone. Others are covered by express, authorised derogations from European law. Other differences remain. For this reason, we must note those differences.

Despite the differences in wording, the structure of the British VAT is that required in European Community law. We should therefore read the British charging provisions in the light of the European provisions—with two cautions. The same words may appear in the two texts, but with different meanings. For example, we shall see that *taxable person* in the European text does not have the same meaning as *taxable person* in the British text. The second warning is that words in the European text may appear to be ordinary English words when they are not. *Consideration* is an example of this, as again we see below. One reason for this is that the European text exists in several equally authoritative language versions. In practice, the French version is the one that is more equal than the others.

Subject to those warnings that—as in any tax law—we must always remember precisely what each word means, we can use the two sets of provisions to state the key structure of the VAT as it applies to supplies internal to the United Kingdom.

The Charge to VAT

VAT applies to:

- supplies

- of goods and services

- for consideration

- other than exempt supplies

Value Added Tax

- in the United Kingdom

- by a taxable person

- as part of the economic activities of that person.

Each of these elements must be present, or be deemed to be present, before the tax operates on a supply. A supply made when one or more of the elements of the tax are missing is said to be outside the scope of the tax. It is a criminal offence deliberately to charge VAT on a supply that is outside the scope of the tax. These seven elements are therefore the necessary criteria for the operation of the tax. They are not sufficient to determine tax liability in full, but we shall examine these key issues first, then deal with the other provisions.

Supplies

The phrase *supplies of goods and services for consideration* should seem familiar to a student of commercial law, and who should therefore have heard of the Supply of Goods and Services Act 1982. Unfortunately, the analogy is not valid. None of the words in that phrase bear the same meaning as in English contract and commercial law, although there is a large area of overlap between the two sets of rules in practice. This is both because VAT is a European tax, and cannot be confined by the commercial rules of any one country, and also because the aim of VAT is different. It is to ensure that the tax is collected regardless of the legal niceties of a particular transaction. See, for example, the case of *CEC v. Oliver* (1980). The High Court had to decide whether a sale through a car auction that was later established to be a void contract was a "supply". Under commercial law principles it was not, but the judge rejected the analogy and found it was a supply. Was that fair? Was it right? The judge decided the matter as an issue of common sense and meaning of words—but he paid little attention to E.C. law. Should he have done so? Indeed he should.

VAT is a tax on trading transactions, and the main base of the tax is commercial sales. More broadly, the tax operates when someone does something that realises value to that person from some other person. The word used for this is *supply*. I supply you with, say, buttered toast or a musical performance, and you pay me. But I cannot, in the ordinary sense, supply myself with the buttered toast. Nor do I supply myself with the butter or the loaf that I use to make the meal. In other words, self-supply is not a supply. Where, for example, a manufacturer makes bolts that are then used by that manufacturer in making windows to sell to others, the manufacturer supplies windows, not bolts. There must be a customer for there to be a supply.

Exceptions to this general rule exist to avoid distortion of competition in certain market sectors. The exceptions are limited, and in the United Kingdom they are confined to: self-supplies of motor vehicles by vehicle manufacturers, self-supplies of commercial buildings by building developers in certain circumstances, and self-supplies of printed stationery.

Neither British nor E.C. VAT laws define *supply*, beyond the vague guidance in the VAT Act that "supply . . . includes all forms of supply". Nor is a general definition possible. This is because the English term *supply*, useful and concise though it is, is a term untranslatable into many western European languages. There is therefore no equivalent of it in the French original E.C. text, or the German, Spanish or other official texts. Indeed, the term was not used as a general term even in the original English text. In the French text we find different terms for supplies of goods and supplies of services. It speaks of a *livraison* or delivery of goods, and a *prestation* or provision of services. Any attempt at defining supply must therefore be made in the context of the kind of supply, of goods or of services.

Despite the warning set out above, lawyers looking at the concept of a supply of goods will be tempted to turn to the commercial law of their own systems to establish when the goods transfer from supplier to customer. Under commercial law rules, that usually occurs when ownership, title, or risk transfers. Of course, if there is title reservation, then ownership does not transfer, although risk may. Is there a supply when goods are handed over, but the ownership is not, and is it relevant that risk passes? For VAT purposes, there are two issues here. First, a supply of the use of goods (for example, equipment leasing) is not a supply of goods at all—it is a supply of services. Secondly, a supply of goods does not always take place if and when the local commercial laws determine that title has transferred. This is because supply is a European concept. The Sixth Directive, having refrained from defining supply, defines instead *supply of goods* as *the transfer of the right to dispose of tangible property as owner* (Article 5.1). Following this, the European Court

Value Added Tax

of Justice has ruled that in the case of a supply of goods, it is not relevant whether title to the goods has passed under the national law: *Staatssecretaris van Financiën v. SAFE BV* (1991).

The definition of *supply* in the context of a supply of services is even more difficult to establish. It is intertwined with two other definitions, that of services, and that of consideration. This is clear from the British law itself: "anything which is not a supply of goods but is done for a consideration (including, if so done, the granting, assignment or surrender of any right) is a supply of services" (section 5(2)). Or, in the words of the law itself, a supply of services can be anything for which someone else pays. To understand this, we must examine the scope of "goods and services".

Goods and services

There is no general definition in the United Kingdom VAT legislation of *goods*. Instead, we must turn to Schedule 4 to the VAT Act. There we are told (in paragraph 1) that a transfer of the whole property in goods is a supply of goods, but anything less is a supply of services. Likewise, the transfer of possession as part of an agreement for sale is a supply of goods, as is transfer of possession where a sale expressly contemplated. A credit sale or hire-purchase is therefore a supply of goods. Equipment leasing, where a sale might occur, is not.

Hidden behind these words is the ghost of the tax systems that VAT replaced. Goods have for centuries been those things that can be stopped at customs barriers. But you will find no generic definition of *goods*. This is because customs duties, like excises and tolls, are essentially specific taxes, not general taxes. The amount of customs duty was (and still is) determined by identifying what kinds of goods have been stopped at the customs post. The argument was not whether the items were goods but whether the article was a Norwegian Blue parrot or not. Services were, by implication, those things that passed invisibly through the customs posts. It is because VAT taxes invisibles that it is such a strong money earner. VAT has, however, inherited the old thinking. If you can't stop it at a frontier post, it is probably a service. For the more legally minded, the technical answer is that goods and services are Humpty Dumpty words. The Treasury can define them as including or excluding anything they want to include or exclude (section 5).

Land is an example of a Humpty Dumpty definition. Land cannot be stopped at frontier posts, so it cannot be goods. But neither is it a service. What, then, do we make of the provision that the supply of a major interest in land is a supply of goods (paragraph 3). For VAT purposes, land has to be deemed to be goods or services. This is because, as we have seen, anything which is not goods is a service. In the binary world of VAT, a sale of land, or of a lease of more than 21 years (a major interest: section 96) is a supply of goods. All else to do with land is a supply of services.

The same is true of other forms of property that do not naturally fit into the deliberately simplified framework of VAT. Supplies of intellectual property, and of the right to use that property are alike treated as supplies of services, even when title is transferred. (This is implied by paragraph 1 of Schedule 5). Supplies of electricity and similar intangibles are supplies of goods (Schedule 4, para. 3).

Tricky problems also occur where a supply is both goods and services. For example, the supply of buttered toast is a supply of the butter, the bread, and the effort of toasting and buttering the bread. Is that goods or services or both? The practical answer may be that it does not matter. The difference between goods and services is only of importance if it changes the amount of tax due, or when the tax is due. The only general difference between goods and service lies in the timing rules about when supplies occur. Otherwise, the problem is the more detailed one of whether a particular supply is charged at one rate of VAT or another. In our example, the tax rate on buttered toast is different to the tax rate on a loaf of bread, so the detail is important. We return to it when we deal with tax rates.

Consideration

A supply is only subject to VAT if it is made *for consideration*, or is deemed to be made for consideration. English lawyers schooled in the fundamentals of contract law often assume that this is because there must be consideration at the heart of any commercial contact. That is not the reason for the VAT rule. Indeed, consideration is a purely English concept, alien not only to continental ideas of contract, but to Scottish contract law as well. The temptation to assume that VAT is modelled on English contract law must be resisted. Consideration is one English translation of the original continental texts. The earlier—and in the writer's view, better—translation was *against payment*.

The idea behind this requirement is an economic one. To be taxable, a transaction must be one that adds value. Consequently, unless in some way value is realised from a supply, there is nothing to tax. In practice, value is realised if the supplier gets paid for the supply. If nobody pays, there is no added value. It is in this way that the rule has been interpreted by the European Court, in a case which nicely illustrates the clash between English thinking and the more general approach required for VAT.

In *Apple and Pear Development Council v. CEC* (1988), the Council carried out two groups of activities. The first group was of ordinary trading activities. The second group comprised activities financed by a statutory levy, and required by the law establishing the Council. The Council claimed that all its activities were for consideration. Much of the argument about this was framed in terms of the English law of contract. Was the statutory levy consideration for the supplies made to those who paid the levy of the statutory services? The case was argued in this way until it came to the House of Lords. The House noted that the point was one of European law, not English law, and found a reference to the European Court of Justice under Article 177 was necessary.

The European Court noted that the question was a general one. Based on a linguistic analysis of the multilingual forms of the texts of the directives, the court laid down the test that there must be a payment for a supply, and that the payment and supply must be directly linked. In accordance with practice, the European Court left it for the national court to determine whether there was a direct link on the facts of the particular case.

The direct link test means that not all supplies for which payments are made are supplies for consideration (or against payment). The European Court itself ruled in another case (*Tolsma* (1994)) that donations made to a street musician do not count as consideration for the supply of the musician's services. Conversely, there must be a supply related to a payment for it to count. Payment of a dividend by a company to a shareholder is not subject to VAT for this reason—the shareholder has supplied nothing to the company linked to the dividend.

A direct link need not be between the supplier and the physical recipient of the supply. For example, if I pay you £10 to send some flowers to a friend, are you supplying the friend or me? The technical answer is that you are making a supply of flowers against payment by me. The fact I do not get the property in the flowers at any time is irrelevant. A less obvious example of this is *CEC v. Professional Footballers Association* (1993) where the House of Lords found that guests paying the PFA to attend a dinner at which the PFA made awards to individuals footballers were being paid by the guests to

present the prizes. VAT therefore had to be charged on the prizes as well as the dinner.
In some cases, a payment is assumed even though none is made. This is to prevent avoidance. For example, if you take some of the flowers from your shop home, or make a gift of flowers to me from your stock, the law treats you as supplying the flowers to yourself or to me for their market value. Were I to give you some buttered toast in exchange for the flowers, the buttered toast would also be treated as being supplied at market value. If I were to give you some tax advice in exchange for the flowers, this would not happen. While supplies of goods without consideration are usually deemed to be made for consideration, the same rule does not apply to supplies of services. Otherwise a practising lawyer acting on her or his own advice is liable to tax on it!

Taxable supplies and exempt supplies

All supplies within the scope of the tax are taxable supplies unless they are exempt supplies (VAT Act, s. 4 (2)). A supply is exempt if, and only if, it is one of the kinds of supply listed in Schedule 9 of the 1994 Act. This copies into the United Kingdom law directly operative provisions of E.C. law. Exemption covers some major kinds of economic activity such as financial supplies and many kinds of health, education and welfare activity. We examine some of these later when discussing liability to VAT.

Supplies in the United Kingdom

This account of the law has been simplified so far by assuming that everything has taken place in the United Kingdom. We shall continue to assume this because there are special rules dealing with both the import and the export of goods. The question of international services is less straightforward and therefore needs attention. Once it has been decided that a supply of services does take place in the United Kingdom, international elements are ignored.

Taxable persons

The structure of European VAT is such that anyone making a taxable supply for consideration can be regarded as a taxable person. United Kingdom VAT does not work this way. Instead, it sets a threshold of activity before the imposition is necessary.

Value Added Tax

Anyone whose level of activities is at or above the level of the threshold is required to register with the VAT office for the locality, and to impose VAT on all taxable supplies made. Those not required to register may do so on a voluntary basis.

For VAT purposes, a *person* is any individual or any body of persons with separate legal personality that is engaged in economic activities. This includes non-profit organisations that do not pay income tax or corporation tax such as charities and clubs as well as companies. It also includes any national or local government body. For this reason, a government department may charge VAT on its supplies. This is to prevent distortions in competition between commercial organisations and other bodies. As a result, many organisations not required to make returns for direct tax purposes have to comply with the VAT rules. In addition, a partnership is also treated as a separate person (unlike the income tax approach). A partnership is therefore separate from the individual partners.

Companies and other large organisations can register divisions or separate parts of the organisation separately. For example, if only part of an organisation is making supplies to which VAT applies, that part can register separately from any other part. This excludes those other parts from the requirements of VAT, but it also means that any supplies made by that part of the organisation to the other parts are subject to VAT.

By contrast, a group of companies can make a common registration for VAT in the name of one of the companies. Where this happens, supplies between companies within the group are outside the scope of the tax. It is only supplies by the group to others that are caught. For this purpose, two companies are in a group if both are based in the United Kingdom and one controls the other or both are controlled by the same third person (VAT Act, s.43). Each of the companies must be involved in an economic activity, so that a company that is purely a holding company has to be left out (*Polsar Investments* (1993)). This sensible idea of grouping has been abused widely. The result is that strict anti-avoidance provisions were introduced by the Finance Act 1996, allowing spurious use of grouping to be counteracted.

A person (in the sense just described) is required to register for VAT if the total turnover from taxable supplies in any period of 12 months is £47,000 or more. (That is the 1996 figure—it is adjusted every year). Any exempt supplies or supplies outside the scope of VAT are excluded from this total. The total is calculated on the assumption that no VAT is charged on the supplies. Note that the amount is for turnover, not profit. It is irrelevant that the person is making a loss, or is not in business to make a profit. It also applies to persons, not to businesses. If I run two businesses, one as a farmer, and one as a sports journalist, I must account for total turnover from both my activities even though they may be treated separately for income tax purposes. The test is applied each month on a rolling basis. However, if the person can show that supplies for the current year are below £45,000 (in 1996), then the requirement to register does not apply. There is some scope for abuse of this provision by dividing turnover between different legal persons to ensure each is below the limit. Where that happens, the VAT office has the right to impose a group registration to bring all the associated avoiders into the tax net.

If registration is required, the person must apply to be registered (by returning a form VAT 1 to the local VAT office) within 30 days of the test being satisfied. Registration is normally put into effect from the end of the next month. A separate test requires a person to register if turnover in the current period of 30 days (from that date) will cross £47,000. In this case the duty to register is immediate, and effect is given to the registration from the date when the test is first satisfied. The rules governing registration are contained in Schedule 1. There are certain additional cases involving foreign elements where registration is also required. These are dealt with below.

A person not required to register under any of these provisions has the right to register on a voluntary basis. Why should anyone want to become a taxpayer voluntarily? In the case of a tax like income tax, there are few, if any, good reasons. VAT is not a tax like income tax. As we shall see below, a VAT payer may actually receive money from the government, rather than pay it. Few businesses can resist a government handout! That is why farmers often seem keen to go out of their way to become registered for VAT, although it seems almost a tenet of faith of some farmers that they avoid income tax as far as possible. Another reason for voluntary registration is that it conceals the fact that total turnover is below £47,000. This encourages some young barristers to register while they are still cutting their teeth!

A further reason is that those who are registered for VAT usually prefer to buy from others who are registered—it is cheaper. Someone who expects to have to register a business in any event may find it advantageous to register before being compelled to do so. Not all traders that could ask for voluntary registration do so. Some refrain from registering in order to avoid VAT. The joke is that they end up paying more VAT by doing so! We see why below.

Value Added Tax

Economic activities

The final element in the structure of VAT is that activities are only relevant if they are economic activities of the taxable person (in the European law) or, in the United Kingdom text, *in the course or furtherance of a business carried on by him*. In this phrase, business is defined as including any trade profession or vocation (section 94). In practice, although the United Kingdom legislation has continued to use the reference to business, it is more helpful to think of the more general, and broader, European phrase. In part, this is because it is clear that VAT is wider than the implicit reference in section 94 to Schedule D, Cases I and II of the Taxes Act might imply. Most things within Schedule A are also within the scope of the tax, as are many things within Cases V and VI of Schedule D. So also are many situations where the charge to capital gains tax or its corporate equivalent will apply.

The other reason for preferring the European test is that VAT applies not only to continuing businesses but also to the sale of business assets, or of the business itself (section 94(5)). After all, selling the business is an economic activity. For example, if Maggie is registered for VAT because of her grocer's business, and she decides to sell the shop fittings or even the entire business, she must account for VAT on doing so. She must also do so if she closes down the business and transfers the stock to her own private account without selling it. This is assumed to be a sale to herself.

There is one exception to the rule about selling the business. If the business, or part of it, is sold to someone who keeps the business on as a going concern, the rules provide that in effect the registration is transferred to the new owner. The supply of the business is deemed to be a supply of neither goods nor services, so excluding it from the charge to VAT. This relief is conditional on the buyer being registered, or registering for VAT, and carrying the business on. It prevents the seller having to add VAT on the whole sale proceeds to the price for the sale where the buyer will be able to claim the VAT back once in control of the business. It is a matter of irrelevance to the VAT office that such a sale takes place as long as the owner for the time being continues to account for VAT.

Are any supplies of goods and services for which consideration is paid outside the scope of the tax? The answer partly depends on the identity of the taxable person. The tax applies to economic activities of taxable persons *acting as such*. An individual buying a house to live in, or buying a car for private use, is not engaging in an economic activity but a private activity. This is true also when the house or car is sold. There is a complication here to which we must return. If a private person sells a car, there is no VAT on the sale. If a car dealer sells it, there is VAT. The same thing applies to antiques, and to horses and ponies. Whether VAT applies therefore partly depends on the identity of the seller, not the kind of goods. This can cause problems, and special rules apply to these occasional or secondhand goods.

A charity that supplies goods to beneficiaries without payment, or for a token fee, is not acting as a business: *Whitechapel Art Gallery v. CEC* (1986), where the running of an art gallery to which free admission was granted was accepted as outside the scope of VAT. By contrast, it will be hard for an ordinary commercial company, a partnership, or a landlord to argue that payments they derive from their activities are anything other than economic. An interesting example of a marginal case is the aptly named decision in *Lord Fisher v. CEC* (1981), which established that shooting (and equally hunting and fishing) one's own land with one's own friends contributing to one's costs is not always an economic activity. You might like to consider how that borderline compares with the borderline for income tax purposes between trading and non-trading transactions.

Another borderline issue related to the definition of consideration. Is a gift a payment in the course of a business? This problem is central to the definition of annual payments for the purposes of Schedule D, Case III. Would the National Book League be expected to charge VAT on the covenanted income it received? If the payments were not consideration, then there would be no VAT liability. Is there a direct link? That depends on the nature of the transaction.

Agents and employees

VAT only applies to the person carrying on the economic activity or business. The most important group of people excluded from VAT by this rule are employees. An employee is carrying on the employer's business as agent, and is not in business by himself or herself. VAT therefore does not apply to the payment of earnings by employer to employee. If the employee's services are supplied to some third party, any VAT is applied to the charge made by the employer to the third party for those services. The effect of this important exclusion is that the added value on which someone is charged includes the total of all payments to employees.

Value Added Tax

The rule applies to office holders such as company directors as well, unless the office holder is holding that office as part of a separate business. For example, a partner in a firm of solicitors may act as a director of a client's business in order to advise the client. Fees paid to the director, or the partnership, should be subject to VAT (section 94(4)). This may be contrasted with the purist view under which such fees can only be subject to Schedule E income tax, not Schedule D (*IRC v. Brander and Cruickshank* (1969)). This also means that a one-person company that pays out its profits to its owner as an employee is in the same position for VAT purposes as a company that pays out the profits to its owner as a dividend (dividends also being outside the scope of the tax).

Behind this rule is a distinction also of fundamental importance for income tax. Is an individual working as an employee or as a self-employed person? The borderline between the two is the borderline between Schedule D and Schedule E for income tax purposes. Nor is there any different definition for VAT purposes than that for income tax purposes—whether taxpayers are in business on their own. Or, as the E.C. Directive has it, a taxable person *acting as such*.

The position is more complex for other agents. By definition, an agent is someone making supplies on behalf of someone else. If the person is an agent rather than an independent contractor, the supply is not made by the agent but by the agent's principal. Take the case of an auctioneer. The auctioned goods are not owned by the auctioneer, but the buyer usually does not know the identity of the seller. The buyer of, say, antique furniture has therefore no way of knowing if the seller is a registered person for VAT purposes, or whether the sale is an economic activity within the scope of VAT. At the same time, the only activity on which an auctioneer is labile for VAT as an agent is the service as an agent. To avoid complications, auctioneers and other agents where the agency is not disclosed are treated as making the supplies themselves. If the agency is disclosed, the VAT is imposed by the principal.

How VAT Works

The rules set out above determine the transactions to which VAT applies. That does not establish the tax as a *value-added* tax. This requires an examination of the way VAT works from the viewpoint of a trader rather than on a transaction-by-transaction basis. Consider this example:

How VAT Works

Alan owns a forest. He sells planks of wood cut from the trees. Beech buys the planks and turns them into chair frames. Caitlin buys the chair frames from Beech, upholsters them, and turns them into chairs. Den buys the chairs from Caitlin, and sells them to customers in his shop. Six of the chairs are bought by Eka for £200 each. How does VAT apply to this series of transactions? Let us assume that A, B, C, and D are all registered for VAT.

A sells the planks from which the parts are made for £10 to B. To this must be added VAT at 17.5 per cent (the appropriate rate). B therefore pays A £11.75. A keeps the £10, but pays the £1.75 to the local VAT office. B sells the chair frames to C for £30, again plus VAT. B therefore charges C £30 plus the VAT, a total of £35.25. Of the £5.25 VAT, B reclaims the £1.75 paid out to A, and hands £3.50 to the VAT office. B's profit is therefore £20. Similarly D pays C £100 plus VAT for the chairs, a total of £117.50. C recoups the £5.25 from the £17.50, handing over £12.25, and keeping a profit of £70.

E pays D £200. VAT is not added to this price, so must be included in it. E is therefore treated as paying D £170.21 plus £29.79 VAT. D keeps £17.50 of the £29.79 VAT, handing the balance of £12.29 over to the VAT office. D's profit is £70.21.

E has therefore paid VAT at the standard rate of 17.5 per cent on the full purchase price paid, the £29.79. VAT has been paid at this rate at each of the four stages of manufacture and sale of the chairs and their components. But at each stage, the seller has kept back the VAT incurred by her or him. The local VAT office has therefore collected only £29.79. A paid in £1.75, B adding £3.50, C adding a further £12.25 and D the final £12.29. This reflects the profits of A (£10), B (£20), C (£70), and D (£70.21). In other words, each has paid VAT on the value-added at that stage of production.

As this example shows, the tax is turned into a value-added tax by allowing each taxable person to collect VAT on the full sale price, but deduct from it any VAT paid out in making the sales. In VAT terms, the VAT collected by a trader is known as the *output tax* (or tax on outputs). The VAT incurred by the trader is *input tax* (or tax on inputs to the business). The VAT payable to the VAT office is the balance of output tax less input tax. How is this balance calculated? This requires accounting rules to determine when VAT is to be collected and returned to the VAT office, and what input tax can be deducted form the output tax. VAT laws have a special language for this as well:

Value Added Tax

- *tax periods* are the periods for which taxable person must make returns to the VAT office

- a *tax invoice* is the formal document required when a supply is made

- the *tax point* is the time when VAT has to be charged on a supply, and therefore determines the tax period in which output tax on a supply must be returned

- the *tax credit* is the amount of input tax that can be set against output tax for each tax period.

Tax periods

All registered persons must make regular returns to the VAT office. In the case of larger traders, this is done on a quarterly basis. For smaller traders, annual accounting is possible. Under this scheme returns are only made once a year and arrangements are made for instalments payments of VAT throughout the year on an estimated basis. Some traders are allowed to make monthly returns. These include exporters because, as we shall see, their returns amount to requests for refunds of tax, and so involve a payment by the VAT office to them.

Each return requires that the trader total up the output tax on all outputs made in the period covered by the return. A tax credit can then be claimed for all input tax incurred during the period, provided that the input tax is claimable as part of the credit.

In each case, the trader must have documentary evidence to substantiate the amounts returned. In the case of most transactions, the required evidence is a *tax invoice*.

Tax invoices

Each taxable supply must be documented in the required way. In most cases, this is by the issue of a special invoice recording the transaction, called a tax invoice. A taxable person supplying goods or services to another taxable person must issue the customer with an invoice recording the key details of the supply. These include the VAT registration details of the supplier (including the VAT number that all registered persons are given on registration), names and addresses, the amount payable for the supply, and the amount of VAT on the supply. In this way, documentary evidence is recorded of the precise details of the transaction, including both the person who should be paying the VAT to the local VAT office, and the person who will be reclaiming that amount as input tax. This is one of the secret efficiencies of VAT: if the purchaser does not have a tax invoice, no input tax can be claimed. If the purchaser produces the tax invoice, the VAT office has the information to check that the supplier has paid in the VAT. When is a tax invoice issued?

Tax points

Tax point is VATese for the time of supply. When does a supply occur? The answer cannot be defined in terms of passing of title. Instead, the rule must be completely practical—it has to be applied by the sales assistant or bookkeeper recording the transaction. In addition, revenue protection requires that the tax point is something that cannot be postposed or avoided.

The solution adopted is a two-tier one. The formal time of supply of goods is either when the goods are delivered (or made available) to the customer, or when payment is made for the supply, whichever is earlier. In the case of services the alternative to payment is when the supplies are rendered. In practice, the tax point is the time when the tax invoice is issued. To tie the two together, the law requires that the tax invoice be issued not later than seven days after the formal time of supply. Normal practice with sales of goods is to issue the tax invoice at the same time as the sale and payment, but the rules give a little flexibility.

All taxable persons must include in their tax returns all supplies where the tax point is within the period covered by the tax return. They will also want to claim a tax credit for all input tax where the tax point is in that period.

Tax credits

A registered person can claim a tax credit for all input tax incurred in a tax period in making taxable outputs. The two key conditions are that the claimant holds tax invoices for the sum of input tax claimed, and that the input tax was incurred *for the purposes of* taxable outputs (E.C. Sixth Directive, Article 17(2)). The Treasury has power to disallow some kinds of input tax regardless of the reason for it is incurred (section 26). This power is not regulated by European law, although the requirement for an input tax credit is. The British rules disallow expenditure on a number of inputs, in particular on private cars (with exceptions such as the purchase of cars for resale), most forms of business entertainment, and expenditure on accommodation provided for staff.

There is an inherent policy conflict in these rules. The tax authorities are concerned to maximise tax revenues. From their viewpoint, input tax is lost tax, and is therefore to be discouraged. But VAT is a tax on value-added, that is, a tax on the differences between inputs and outputs. Any attempt to reduce the entitlement to input tax so as to tax more than the value added is wrong in principle. The dilemma is heightened by the natural temptation of taxpayers to claim as much input tax as possible. I may say that the new power boat I purchased was bought for the purposes of my (taxable) business. The tax authorities, watching me cruising down the river on a Sunday afternoon, may not be entirely convinced that I am doing it to impress my customers. They see an age-old variant of the battle over deductible expenses turning up in a new guise.

There is inevitably a lot of case law building up about this issue, just as there has been in income tax over the wholly and exclusively rule. An early case decided, however, that the test was essentially subjective (*National Water Council v. CEC* (1979). So it is what I say, rather than what the VAT staff think, that counts. The Government has tried to head off endless claims for power boats, racehorses, and the like by amending the appeal section in an attempt to exclude any challenge to what the VAT staff think. It did so by what is now section 84(4)(c) of the 1994 Act. This attempts to bar appeals about withholding input tax credits concerning *something in the nature of a luxury, amusement or entertainment* unless the decision appealed from can be shown to be unreasonable.

The Government adopted this tactic because it cannot change the underlying rule. This derives from E.C. law. Article 17(2) of the Sixth Directive provides that:

> "in so far as the goods and services are used for the purposes of his taxable transactions, the taxable person shall be entitled to deduct from the tax which he is liable to pay ... value added tax due or paid in respect of goods or services supplied or to be supplied to him by another taxable person".

The only relevant proviso to this is paragraph 6, which reads, in part, "Value added tax shall in no circumstances be deductible on expenditure which is not strictly business expenditure, such as that on luxuries, amusements or entertainment" The British government originally intended to make the bar on appeals wider than the present wording, but were forced to retreat before the House of

Commons. Does the current limitation on appeals achieve the purpose? Quite possibly not, because the provisions in Article 17 are directly applicable. You cannot remove a directly applicable right by revoking appeals provisions. In other words, it could be argued to be unreasonable to impose the condition of unreasonableness. The European Court has been asked to decide the point, and the court's judgment is awaited.

The European rule has caused other problems in the United Kingdom too. A major one arises where expenditure is partly for the purpose of a business, and partly for private purposes. Decades of the narrow thinking of the income tax rules tend to make tax officials say that because it is not wholly for the purpose of business, it is not deductible. The European Court thought otherwise in *Lennartz* (1995). In that case, the national tax authorities had refused an input tax credit to the taxpayer for the purchase of a car that was mainly used privately because the business use was less than 10 per cent of the total use. The court ruled that the taxpayer was entitled to a deduction, even if only a small one, unless the national tax authorities had a valid derogation from European Community law to justify the rule. The case is a fascinating glimpse at the practical problems of a VAT. The different practices, and different arguments of, the British, French and German governments in dealing with the case—and the disagreement of the court with all their views—show that there is some way to go before VAT is truly a European tax in all its detail.

Chapter 30

VAT RATES AND PROBLEMS

If the British VAT were a simple form of value-added tax with a single rate, the previous chapter would have covered most of the problems. It is not, and it does not. In this chapter we must examine how the value of a taxable supply is found. We then discuss the rate structure of the tax, the extensive way in which exemptions apply to the tax, some special cases, and international aspects.

The VAT Rate Structure

The simplest form of VAT (such as that found in New Zealand or Denmark) has one rate of VAT applying equally to goods and services. In the New Zealand form of VAT, just about everything including local taxation is subject to the same rate of VAT. Operation of the rate structure of the tax is therefore simple. In the United Kingdom it is complex.

Article 12 of the E.C. Sixth VAT Directive imposes a two-rate structure on the VAT of the Member States: a main rate of not less than 15 per cent, and a lower rate of between 4 per cent and 9 per cent... or so it says. In fact, it allows for several other rates as well. About the only thing it rules out is a rate higher than the main rate, and no Member State now has such a rate. Most, however, resist the approach of Denmark, and have several rates, of which the main rate is the highest.

The United Kingdom rate structure has the following rates:

a standard rate of 17.5 per cent,
a rate on fuel supplies of 8 per cent,
special rates for special regimes, such as the 4 per cent flat rate scheme for farmers,
0 per cent (the zero-rate) for international supplies and a wide range of internal supplies.

The VAT Rate Structure

In addition, there are: supplies outside the scope of the tax, exempt supplies, and supplies deemed not to be supplies or either goods or services.

As a result, the United Kingdom has one of the most complex rate structures for VAT in the developed world. The structure gives scope for many disputes and distortions to competition. The United Kingdom also has the only major system to use its VAT as a subsidy for certain kinds of domestic activity. Why? The zero-rates reflect the exemptions that used to apply to taxes before VAT. However, the zero-rate in VAT is not the same thing as a zero sales tax. It is in reality a subsidy resulting in regular repayments of tax to those who sell zero-rated goods. Add to the predictable consumers' resistance at a rate increase, the pressure to retain the monthly tax rebate paid to those who are zero-rated, and we see why the lobby for the status quo is a strong one. This is so although it makes the British VAT one of the most inefficient around. We see a similar situation in the lower rate of VAT on fuel supplies. The debate over the attempt to increase the VAT on domestic fuel to the standard rate from a zero-rate resulted in a government defeat in the Commons. They intended the 8 per cent to be temporary. Its permanence illustrates the truism that it is never a good idea if people end up paying more tax. It is precisely because of this that we must spend some time looking at the rate structure.

There is a strict order for determining at what rate, if any, VAT applies to a supply:

1. Exclude any supply that is outside the scope of the tax, or deemed not to be a supply of goods or services. If it is not excluded:
2. See if the supply is one of those listed as zero-rated. If it is not listed:
3. See if the supply is exempt. If it is not exempt:
4. See if any special tax regime applies. If it does not:
5. Apply the standard rate.

The order is important because it means that anything to which a special regime does not apply is to be taxed at the standard rate, without exception. We noted the scope of the tax in the last chapter, but we must now explore zero-rating, exemption, and the special regimes.

VAT Rates and Problems

Zero-rated supplies

A supply is zero-rated if it is listed in Schedule 8 to the 1994 Act. The Schedule is divided into (currently) 16 groups, several of which are of considerable complexity. No attempt is made in this introduction to go through the detail, despite its economic and administrative importance and the considerable case law it has generated.

Several themes run through the Schedule. The first is of international supplies: see Group 7 (international services), Group 8 (transport), Group 10 (gold), Group 13 (imports, exports, etc.) and Group 14 (tax-free shops) for the main relevant groups. The policy here is to ensure that no British VAT gets hidden in the cost of any goods or services offered on the international market. Any VAT imposed on a supply or its inputs in the United Kingdom before export is therefore rebated in full, and no VAT is applied on export. The purpose is to keep British goods and services as competitive as possible.

A second theme is that of supplies of a social or community nature. These include: Group 1 (food), Group 2 (domestic sewerage and water supplies), Group 3 (books), Group 4 (talking books for the blind), Group 5 (construction of homes and some other buildings), Group 6 (listed buildings), Group 9 (houseboats and caravans used as homes), Group 12 (medicines), Group 15 (charities), and Group 16 (children's clothes and protective clothing).

The reason for zero-rating these supplies is linked in part to the underlying E.C. law. That lays down those forms of supply that should be exempted, leaving others to be taxed. Most states taxed them at a reduced level, but this has been deemed politically inappropriate in the United Kingdom, so they have been zero-rated. This is, however, expensive to the Treasury. It involves actually paying out money. Governments have been quietly reducing the scope for this since they introduced the tax.

One result of this is that the Schedule is now of considerable complexity. As an exercise in the practical application of the Act, study Group 1, dealing with food. Then take it to your local supermarket and examine how it works in practice. For example, what is the VAT on: a tin of assorted biscuits (some covered in chocolate and some with chocolate filling); bottled water; the food I buy for my pet cat and hamster; a fruit and nut mixture; a warm pasty bought in the cafeteria to eat on the way home, and the identical frozen pasties bought in the supermarket. Then take the details of Group 16 along to a local clothes store, and explain why my wife (age undisclosed!) can buy children's clothes, while my son (12) cannot. After that, take Group 3 to a stationer's and work out which of the following are zero-rated: books, cassettes, sheet music, posters, videos, CDs, pens, biros, ink for a pen, ink for a printer, a newspaper, writing paper and postage stamps. Then prepare a coherent account to justify your findings.

Enough! Not quite. There are then some oddments such as supplies of gold and of banknotes (Groups 10 and 11). We do not advise checking the practical details of these.

Exempt supplies

A supply is exempt if it is within the terms of Schedule 9. The Schedule presents a similar exercise to Schedule 8, and again contains several themes. The chief difference is that behind Schedule 9 are detailed provisions in Article 13 (A, B, and C) of the Sixth Directive. The detail of this schedule is imposed at European level.

One group of exemptions deals with supplies where it has proved extremely difficult to apply VAT. The main group of this kind is Group 5 (financial services), and linked with it is Group 2 (insurance). The chief problem is isolating the value-added in a financial supply such as a loan, or under insurance against a risk. There are also complexities in some kinds of supplies of land (Group 1), and in betting (Group 4). In practice, it can prove easier to put excise taxes on these kinds of supply, and leave them excluded from VAT. This happens in most European countries (including the United Kingdom) with insurance and betting and with many land transactions. The question of VAT on financial supplies also causes a direct overlap with income tax.

A second group of supplies are those made to individuals rather than for commercial purposes, and left out for social reasons. These include education (Group 6), health and welfare (Group 7), burials (Group 8), and community activities including associations (Group 9), sports events (Group 10) and charity fund-raising (Group 12). The oddments include postal services (Group 3, which was slipped into our stationer's example above of the other Group 3). Why add VAT to stamps when the state runs the postal service? Another is works of art (if there is an IHT or CGT exemption applying).

VAT Rates and Problems

Zero-rating and exemption compared

The reason for zero-rating is the need to impose tax on supplies that cannot be exempted under E.C. law. Ironically, however, zero-rating is more advantageous than exemption, so the effect in the United Kingdom of the European rule is the reverse of that intended. For this reason the E.C. Commission objected for many years to British zero-rating. As a result, it forced several previously zero-rated supplies to be either exempted or taxed at the standard rate.

Zero-rating is known in E.C. circles as exemption with credit. They intend this to emphasise the fact that those making zero-rated supplies can claim refunds for input tax incurred for the purpose of those supplies. This is because they are technically taxable supplies, although no new tax will be paid. By contrast, an exempt supply is one for which no input tax credit is possible. The comparative effect of these categories depends on the identities both of suppliers and those being supplied.

It is largely a matter of indifference to taxable persons receiving inputs to make taxable supplies whether the inputs are taxed at the standard rate or at a zero-rate. The only difference is one of cash-flow. They must pay the input tax on the standard-rated supply before reclaiming it. By contrast, an exempt supply to a taxable person is more expensive. This is because the supplier will probably pass on any input tax as part of the non-taxable price for the supply. The recipient therefore pays for that VAT, but cannot reclaim it. In other words, a taxable person would rather buy supplies taxed at the standard rate than exempt supplies. This also explains why taxable persons may prefer to deal with a registered supplier rather than a supplier that chooses to remain unregistered when under the compulsory limit for registration.

An ordinary consumer cannot claim back any VAT. Nor can a claim be made by someone who makes only exempt supplies, or who is not registered for VAT. In each case, they have to bear the cost of VAT whether it is express or hidden. For them, therefore, zero-rated supplies are better than exempt supplies, because there is less total VAT. For them exempt supplies *are* taxed supplies, while zero-rate taxable supplies are not.

Mixed and multiple supplies

What happens when I make a taxable supply at the same time as an exempt supply, or where I mix standard-rated items with zero-rated items? In practice, this happens all the time. For example, I buy a television (standard-rated) on credit (exempt), or I join a club (standard-rated) and get a free guide to its advantages (zero-rated), or I buy a ticket to travel by air (standard-rated) and the ticket includes a meal in flight (zero-rated).

The complexities of both Schedule 8 and Schedule 9 ensure that there are many complicated supplies, but there is little legislative guidance about them. There have, predictably, also been many decided cases, but not much has emerged by way of a clear guiding principle save that it all depends on the facts. While judges may indulge in a little criticism of the attitudes of others (see the *British Airways case* (1990)), they have not done much to alleviate it themselves.

Partial exemption

A problem arises for those who make both taxable supplies and exempt supplies, whether or not they are mixed. The supplier, if registered, is entitled to an input tax credit for input tax incurred for the purpose of taxable supplies. It is not entitled to a tax credit in respect of input tax for exempt supplies. Anyone in this position must therefore take steps to identify which inputs relate to the taxable supplies, and which relate to the exempt supplies. There are special rules to do this. Many traders agree a percentage with their local VAT offices so that, for example, they can claim 60 per cent of the input tax as a fair share of the total inputs.

Special regimes

VAT also lends itself to the development of a multiplicity of special schemes. As with the schedules on zero-rating and exemption, we derive little benefit from a detailed study of these schemes, but they do solve some tricky practical problems.

One series of special schemes (provided for in official Notices in the 727 series) is that for retailers. These are designed to deal with the problems of those selling a mixture of goods that are taxed at different rates, or are exempt. Examples are the supermarket, clothes store and stationer's you are about to visit. They can agree with the local VAT office to avoid having to make separate calculations of VAT on every sale, or having to separate zero-rated goods from standard-rated goods.

Another set of special schemes are those dealing with goods sold by dealers but bought by them from private customers. For example, if I sell my private car to a dealer, I add no VAT to it. But I bought my car from a garage and paid VAT when I did so. If the dealer charges VAT on the whole price of the car when selling it to another customer, it is being double taxed. To avoid this, a *margin scheme* operates. In effect, the dealer has to account for VAT only on the difference between the price paid to me and the price for which the car is sold. Similar regimes apply to antiques.

A further group who get special attention are farmers. The problem here is the assumed aversion of farmers from keeping accounts. Yet someone buying from a farmer wants an input tax credit for any supply, on which the farmer would charge VAT. The compromise, made at European level, is a deemed input tax equal to 4 per cent of the output.

Valuation

The final issue that arises on domestic supplies is the value of the supply. On how much do we impose the VAT? In the most straightforward case, the answer is simple: the value depends on the consideration. Section 19 of the 1994 Act provides that where the consideration for a supply is in monetary form, the value is the amount that, when the VAT is added, equals the consideration. For example, if the price I pay for a supply is £117.50, the VAT rate being 17.5 per cent, then the value of the supply for VAT purposes is £100. Similarly, if the price I pay is £100, then the value of the supply is £85.10, with VAT of £14.90 payable. This suggests that if I offer you a price for a product, the price is VAT-inclusive, rather than VAT-exclusive. The VAT laws are silent on this issue, because it is a matter of contract or consumer law. What price did we agree? The VAT office is not interested in what we agree, only in getting 17.5 per cent of whatever it is.

Where the consideration is not fully in monetary form, the value depends on the monetary equivalent of the consideration. For example, if I agree to a part-exchange deal, the cash will be taken into account along with the value of the goods taken in part exchange.

What happens if goods are sold at a discount, or with a "10 per cent off" voucher, or in a sale? The main answer is a practical one. The solution adopted is one that enables the value to be set at the time of the tax point. Each rule is an application of this approach. For example, if I buy goods "10 per cent off", then the value is based on the reduced price. If I hand in a voucher that entitles me to £10 off, the value for VAT purposes takes account of the £10 reduction. This is so although I would have to pay more if I did not have the voucher. Less obviously, if the price is £100 "but £90 for immediate cash sales", and I buy the item but do not pay immediately and therefore pay £100, the VAT price is still £90.

What if I set an artificial price—too high or too low—for some ulterior purpose? Usually this is irrelevant to VAT. If the supplier and the recipient are both registered for VAT, the only effect is that the input tax credit changes with the output tax. Nothing is lost to the Government. It is only where one party is not registered for VAT that avoidance issues may arise. In those cases, the VAT office has the power to replace the actual consideration with the market value of the supply if the supplier and recipient are associated. The market value rule also applies if for any reason the monetary value of the consideration cannot be established by any other means.

International Aspects

The European Community adopted VAT partly because it deals better than most forms of indirect tax with two problems. The first problem is the GATT (the General Agreement on Tariffs and Trade). GATT, and its successor GATT 1994 (now operated by the World Trade Organisation), require that all Member States reduce their customs duties. They also require that they do not replace them with discriminatory forms of internal indirect taxation. In other words, indirect taxes must not discriminate on grounds of the origin of the goods or services. Imports must be taxed no more heavily than internal goods. The second problem was ensuring not only non-discrimination but also neutrality. Items sold in a Member State must be subject to no more tax in total when made in another state than when made locally. This was not just a case of ensuring tax neutrality in the importing state, but throughout the production process.

VAT can be both non-discriminatory and neutral in some forms. The E.C. adopted a form of VAT that meets both these tests: the destination-based VAT. VAT operates at the destination of a supply, where it is consumed or received, not at its origin, where it is created.

To achieve this objective, all goods coming into a state must be subject to VAT on the value when they arrive in the state. This is why the two alternative charges to VAT occur for goods coming into

VAT Rates and Problems

the United Kingdom, on cross-border acquisitions from other member states, and on imports from third states. In both cases, VAT is payable when the goods come into the country.

For imports, this is done by charging the VAT at the same time as customs duty, and using the same rules to do so. This applies to all imported goods, whether imported by registered persons or others. VAT is payable without there being any need for registration. There are exceptions to the charge to VAT. The main one, for individuals, is the traveller's personal allowance, or "duty-free" as it is usually but inaccurately called.

For cross-border acquisitions, the rules are more complex. This is because there are no internal frontiers between Member States. So the customs rules cannot apply. Instead, anyone bringing in goods is obliged to register (if not already registered) if total acquisitions from other Member States exceed the limit applying for internal supplies. The key difference is that registration is related not to supplies made, but to acquisitions. (The rules are in Schedule 3). The reason for the registration is that those receiving cross-border acquisitions are required to report them to the VAT office, and to pay the VAT due on them at their value on receipt. For example, I buy goods for my business from Denmark subject to VAT on delivery here. I must report the delivery of the goods to me on arrival, and pay VAT on their value as delivered to me.

The converse of the charge to tax on imports and acquisitions is that VAT is relieved on exports and outward goods. This is done by zero-rating all exports and cross-border sales. An exporter is entitled to claim a refund of all input tax incurred for the purpose of exporting taxable goods. The VAT is refunded to the exporter, so enabling all indirect taxes to be taken out of the price of exports.

Within the E.C., this rule is strengthened by allowing an overseas trader who buys goods in this country to take them home to reclaim the British VAT by registering here. Traders involved in trading in several Member States can, for this reason, register in each of the states in which they trade.

Several special rules deal with cross-border acquisitions to make the overall rules work better without a frontier. To prevent avoidance, a trader engaged in cross-border trade such that supplies made into or in this country are not made by someone registered in another state must register here if turnover exceeds £70,000 a year (Schedule 2). Most other special rules are exceptions to the destination-basis of VAT. They prevent a rebate being paid by the state from which the goods are acquired, or impose VAT in another state. One exception is for mail-order goods. These are usually purchased from a taxable person, but may be bought by a non-registered person in another state. The purchaser will not pay VAT in her or his own state, but must bear the VAT of the state of the supplier. Even so, if VAT rates vary significantly, mail order purchasing saves tax. Another exception is for cars. VAT is paid on cars where they are first registered. This avoids a new car being driven around to avoid VAT, or to make unjustified VAT refunds. The most common exception is the allowance for travellers and the "duty-free" shops that encourage travellers to make maximum use of these allowances. Likewise, British trippers buying goods in France for personal use, on which VAT is paid in France, cannot make a reclaim in Britain. They pay French VAT not British VAT.

The rules dealing with goods may seem awkward, but the rules dealing with exports, imports, and cross-border acquisitions of services are far more complex. We cannot treat services in the same way as goods. Nor does the destination basis work well. This is because the services cannot be impounded to ensure payment of the VAT at the frontier, and the supplier is of course in another state to the state wishing to collect the VAT. Nor, in the ordinary sense, can services be exported.

Instead of the usual rules for goods, the general approach is to locate the service either where the supplier is based or where the recipient is based. If the location is that of the supplier, it is often provided that the services are zero-rated. In other words, the service provider is entitled to claim a refund on input VAT, and incurs no new VAT. If the service is taxed where it is received, a self-supply charge has to be imposed. This means that the recipient of the service has to declare receiving the service, and account for the VAT on its value. If the service is received for the purpose of making taxable supplies, the recipient will seek a tax credit equal to the amount of the self-supply charge. However, VAT will be payable in whole or in part by those whose supplies are exempt or partially exempt.

For the future, it is the intention of the E.C. Commission to propose that the basis of the E.C. VAT system be changed from the destination basis to what they term an origin basis. This was supposed to happen in 1997, with economic union. Until then, the present basis of VAT is regarded as transitional (the term used in the current version of the Sixth Directive). On present predictions, it is likely that the transition will be a long one—perhaps as long as the life of the "temporary" income tax.

Part Seven

Stamp Duties

CHAPTER 31

STAMP DUTIES

General Survey

The law relating to stamp duties was last consolidated by two Acts passed in 1891: the Stamp Duties Management Act 1891 and the Stamp Act 1891. At that time the tax was already two centuries old. Those Acts have been amended and supplemented many times by subsequent Finance Acts, but the law has remained unconsolidated for over a century. During that time most forms of stamp duty were to be abolished. Indeed, the whole tax has been threatened with abolition. As yet, it has not been abolished, despite the fact that the spread of information technology means that the use of official documents may be disappearing! Instead, we now have a stamp duty reserve tax as well, taxing transactions where there is no document. The stamp duty reserve tax was introduced by the Finance Act 1986, section 87 imposing the principal charge. We also have an excise duty—the insurance premium tax—being used to tax transactions that used to be taxed by stamp duty. This was introduced by the Finance Act 1994, the stamp duty having been abolished in 1989.

The Stamp Duties Management Act 1981 deals, as you will guess, with the administration of stamp duties. Section 1 places them under the care and management of the Commissioners of Inland Revenue. Day-to-day administration is delegated to the Controller of Stamps. There is a separate Controller for Scotland. This is because the different property laws in Scotland require different rules and practices to those in England and Wales.

The Stamp Act 1891 is in three parts. Part I contains the charging section (section 1) which charges duty on the instruments listed in the First Schedule to the Act. Part I also contains provisions applying to stamping instruments generally. Part II explains and amplifies particular heads of charge in the First Schedule. Part III contains miscellaneous supplemental provisions. *Instrument* is not (in a strict sense) defined, but section 122 declares that: "The expression *instrument* includes every written document". In the First Schedule there

Stamp Duties

used to be a long list of particular instruments in alphabetical order. Against each was listed the duty charged on it. Now only a few remain. These are the *heads of charge*.

Each instrument is charged either to *fixed duty* or to *ad valorem duty* (Latin for "according to the value"). Fixed duties are often sweeping-up duties. They are usually charged a duty of 50 pence.

An instrument that is liable to duty usually has to be taken (or posted) to a Stamp Office. There a stamp is *impressed* upon it by means of a die (usually red). It is this process of impressing a stamp on a document that is the key to the success of stamp duty. If a document that requires to be stamped is not stamped, it cannot be used officially. English law requires that certain transactions, such as transfers of land, take place by formal deed, so the stamp duty can only be avoided by avoiding the transaction. In days gone by that was hard to achieve. Modern technology, however, can be in conflict with these objectives. Little is achieved by trying to impress a red stamp on a computer memory. Further, the process of stamping may hamper ordinary commercial transactions. Therefore, many kinds of document that used to require stamping are now not in the list. An example is that of cheques. Most of the documents liable to fixed duty were removed from the list in 1985. The Finance Act 1990 prospectively abolishes several remaining heads of charge on "abolition day", but abolition day has not yet been named.

Stamp duty principles

There are several basic principles in stamp duty law. The most fundamental is that the duty is charged on *instruments* (documents). If there is no instrument there is no duty. If a transaction can be carried out by spoken words or by conduct, there is no document and consequently no duty. To take a straightforward example, the sale or gift of a chattel can be made entirely validly by delivery of the chattel to the transferee.

Other basic principles may be summarised as follows. Duty is charged in accordance with the substance of an instrument, not its mere form. If more than one instrument is written on the same paper (or other material) each must be separately stamped. If one instrument contains (or relates to) "several distinct matters" it is to be stamped as if it were a separate instrument in respect of each of the matters. Nevertheless, it has been established by case law that "all that is required is that the instrument should be stamped for its leading and principal object, and that this stamp covers everything accessory to this object": *Limmer Asphalte Paving Co. v. IRC* (1872). For example, the stamp on a lease covers an option to purchase the reversion, but it does not cover an option to purchase other property. If one transaction is effected by more than one instrument, only one *ad valorem* duty is charged. This is helpful in relation to the formation of a settlement, which is often effected in practice by two instruments.

The reason for some of these principles is that the heads of charge in the First Schedule are a list rather than part of a structured charging provision. It is easy for one document to fall within two or more heads of charge. If it does, the Revenue can choose whichever head involves the most duty.

Ad valorem duty is payable on whatever sum may be calculable at the date of the instrument as the maximum consideration that *may* arise. We call this the contingency principle. For example, payments by a tenant under a lease may be subject to VAT at the option of the landlord. The *ad valorem* stamp duty on those payments is therefore based on the assumption that the landlord may collect VAT. This is unusual—not a tax on a tax so much as a tax on an option to tax!

Sanctions for the payment of duty

Payment of stamp duties is enforced primarily by an indirect means. The legislation makes unstamped instruments useless to the parties. Section 14(4) of the Stamp Act 1891 provides that:

> "an instrument executed in any part of the United Kingdom, or relating, wheresoever executed, to any property situate, or to any matter or thing done or to be done, in any part of the United Kingdom, shall not, except in criminal proceedings, be given in evidence, or be available for any purpose whatever, unless it is duly stamped ... "

You cannot even use it for a lampshade if it is not stamped! This rule compels the stamping of, for example, conveyancing instruments. Because an unstamped instrument would be inadmissible as evidence of title a purchaser can insist that every instrument that forms a link in the vendor's title be duly stamped. Further, the Land Registry will refuse to complete the transaction by registration if instruments are unstamped.

To be on the safe side, the law backs this in three ways. First, penalties are imposed for stamping out of time. Secondly, there are fines for offences relating to stamp duty. For example, a company

Stamp Duties

secretary who registers a share transfer that is not properly stamped can be fined. Thirdly, the Revenue may sue for the duty under some heads of charge in the High Court.

In many circumstances getting a *denoting stamp* is necessary or desirable. This ensures that the denoted document effectively records the transaction, though the stamp for the transaction is on another document. Sometimes the duty on an instrument depends on the duty paid on another instrument. If so, a blue impressed stamp denotes that duty has been paid for one instrument on the other instrument. There are two kinds of denoting stamps. The first is a *duplicate denoting stamp*. The duplicate or counterpart of an instrument is not duly stamped unless either it is stamped as an original or it is denoted. There is one exception to this: the counterpart of a lease does not need to be denoted if the lessor does not execute it. As well as the denoting stamp, a duplicate or counterpart must bear a fixed (red) stamp of 50 pence, then the same stamp as on the original.

The second kind is a *duty paid denoting stamp*. This is used on a conveyance if *ad valorem* duty has already been paid on the agreement for sale. It is also used on a lease, if *ad valorem* duty has already been paid on the agreement for the lease. For a conveyance an alternative procedure is for the Stamp Office to transfer the *ad valorem* duty to the conveyance.

Adjudication

Stamping is not conclusive that the instrument is *duly* stamped. The Commissioners (in practice, the Stamp Office) can be required to express their opinion whether an executed instrument is chargeable with any duty and, if so, how much. If they decide that the instrument is not chargeable with duty, it is stamped "Adjudged not chargeable with any duty." If they decide that the instrument is chargeable, they *assess* the duty. The instrument is then stamped as assessed, and an adjudication stamp (stating "adjudged duly stamped") is added. An appeal can be made direct to the Chancery Division against an assessment, by way of case stated.

Adjudication is compulsory for some instruments, in the sense that without adjudication the instrument is not duly stamped. An example is a voluntary disposition. Some instruments, even if they have been adjudicated, are not duly stamped unless they are produced to the Stamp Office and stamped with a stamp denoting that the instrument has been produced: Finance Act 1931, s.28. We call this a *produced stamp*. It confirms that a *particulars delivered* form has been produced. This is because anyone producing to the Commissioners an instrument transferring land must produce with it a document giving certain particulars, including the consideration. The rule applies to transfers on sale of the fee simple of land, grants of any lease of land for a term of seven or more years, and transfer on sale of any such lease. If the document does not need stamping, but does need registering, the particulars delivered form must be sent instead to the Land Registry. The effect is to ensure that the government has, at the expense of buyers, a complete record of land transfer values. This can then be used, for example, to enforce other taxes.

General exemptions

Some instruments are exempt from all stamp duties. The following are more important examples: transfers of government stocks; transfers of ships; wills; *inter vivos* gifts; transfers on divorce; training contracts; contracts of employment; transfers and covenants to charities; transfers of loan capital; transfers of shares in unit trusts; bankruptcy documents.

Foreign elements

The territorial limits of the Stamp Act 1891 are in effect laid down by section 14(4), set out above. As a result, stamp duty is charged (1) on instruments executed in the United Kingdom whatever they relate to, and (2) on instruments executed abroad which relate to "any property situate, or any matter or thing done or to be done" in the United Kingdom.

Particular Instruments

We now turn to look separately at some more important heads of charge. The current heads of charge to *ad valorem* stamp duties are: bearer instruments; bonds, and covenants (of certain kinds); conveyances or transfers on sale; partitions; leases—rent and premium, and agreements for leases. The current fixed stamp duties are: conveyances or transfers except on sale; declarations of trust; duplicates or counterparts of stamped documents; partitions; some minor leases; releases and surrenders. In each case the fixed duty is 50 pence, and the only appropriate comment is that it should either be abolished or set at a sensible level.

Conveyance or Transfer

This description covers two heads of charge. Head (1) deals with *conveyance or transfer on sale of any property*. It carries *ad valorem* duty. It links with several other heads, notably a contract for sale, and a transfer in contemplation of a sale. The head relates to any kind of property: personal property and intellectual property; things in action and things in possession; shares and land. Of course, there must be a conveyance or transfer, or at least some instrument to be stamped. A purely oral agreement is not dutiable. There must be a conveyance or transfer of property. A revocable licence will not transfer property. So duty is normally only paid on land and share transfers. There must also be a sale. So there must be a consensus, a price in money and a transfer of property (or, as with a declaration of trust, a vesting of property).

We must say a word about the formation and dissolution of a partnership. A partnership agreement is charged to conveyance on sale duty in respect of any price paid by an incoming partner for his share. It is not charged on assets brought in by him as capital of the business. A dissolution agreement incurs conveyance on sale duty in respect of any price paid to the outgoing partner for his share of the business by the continuing partners. This duty is not incurred if the sums paid to the outgoing partner come out of the assets of the business. This would be a "partition" and under that head of charge the duty would be a fixed duty of 50 pence.

Where conveyance on sale duty does apply, the full rate of *ad valorem* duty is 1 per cent of the amount or value of the consideration. There is no duty where the consideration does not exceed £60,000, if the instrument has *a certificate of value* worded as follows:

> "It is hereby certified that the transaction hereby affected does not form part of a largest transaction or of a series of transactions in respect of which the amount or value or the aggregate amount or value of the consideration exceeds £60,000."

Exchanges are treated as sales at market value. A conveyance or transfer by gift or voluntary disposition has been exempt from *ad valorem* duty since 1985. It is also exempt from the 50 pence duty and the need to have the deed adjudicated if an appropriate certificate about the exemption is added.

Contracts for sale

Section 59 of the Stamp Act 1891 deals with a possible avoidance device. In many circumstances a purchaser could be content with the vendor's contract to sell property to him without going on to take an actual conveyance on sale duty. The section was aimed particularly at the sale of a business. It provides that any contract or agreement for the sale of certain kinds of property shall be charged with ad valorem duty as if it were an actual conveyance on sale. The kinds of property caught by the section are as follows:

(1) any equitable estate or interest in any property whatever; or
(2) any (legal) estate or interest in any property except;
    (a) land;
    (b) property located outside the United Kingdom;
    (c) goods, wares or merchandise;
    (d) stocks and shares;
    (e) marketable securities;
    (f) ships or shares of ships.

Items of property caught by the section that are likely to be involved in the sale of a business are: goodwill, book debts, cash on deposit, patents, copyrights, the benefit of pending contracts, tenants' fixtures, trade fixtures.

There is still, however, considerable scope for saving duty on the sale of a business. For example, book debts need not be transferred. There can instead be a provision that the purchaser is to collect the book debts as the vendor's agent and apply the proceeds in discharging them. If sold to a limited company it seems that duty may be avoided by first selling the business for cash by an oral contract and then using the cash to subscribe for shares: see *Spargo's case* (1873).

Transfer in contemplation of sale

An avoidance device of transferring property, *e.g.* shares, without a sale, but in contemplation of a future sale was stopped up by the Finance Act 1965, s.90(1):

> "any instrument whereby property is conveyed or transferred to any person in contemplation of a sale of that property shall be treated ...

Stamp Duties

as a conveyance or transfer on sale of that property for a consideration equal to the value of that property."

Exemptions from conveyance on sale duty

There are several exemptions of which the most important in practice are reconstructions and amalgamations of companies and transfers between associated companies. For example, a company is formed or has its capital increased for the purpose of acquiring the whole or part of the undertaking of another company or of acquiring not less than 90 per cent of the issued share capital of another company. Any instrument made in connection with the transfer of the undertaking or of the shares in connection with a reconstruction or amalgamation is exempt from duty. The conditions for the exemption are strict.

Exemption from duty is given in respect of transfers between associated companies. This exemption is also subject to strict conditions. Either one of the companies must own beneficially 90 per cent or more of the issued share capital of the other, or another company must own beneficially 90 per cent or more of the issued share capital of the transferor company and of the transferee company. Further, there must be no arrangement under which the consideration for the transfer is to be provided or received by any person other than a company that is associated (in the sense set out above). And there must be no arrangement for the transferor and transferee companies to cease to be associated (in the above sense).

Leases

Leases of land are charged to stamp duty under the heading in the First Schedule "Lease or Tack". (Tack is the Scottish equivalent of lease). This head of charge applies only to leases of land. It does not apply, for example, to the hiring of chattels in consideration of periodical payments. Land, of course, includes buildings.

In general, leases are charged to *ad valorem* duty. One important exemption is a lease for a definite term less than a year of a furnished dwelling; in this instance there is a fixed duty. For other leases there is a charge on the premium (if any) and a charge on the rent. The duty on the premium is *ad valorem*. It is the same as conveyance on sale duty for the same amount. However, no duty is payable where the average rent does not exceed £300 per annum (and a certificate of value is included in the lease). The duty on the rent is also *ad valorem*. Section 75(1) of the Stamp Act 1891 provides that an agreement for a lease for any term is to be charged with the same duty as if it were an actual lease.

Stamp Duty Reserve Tax

The Finance Act 1986 introduced this tax as a backup to deal with cases where stamp duty could be avoided by not having a document to stamp. It is prospectively abolished, along with the heads of charge of stamp duty that is it designed to back, by the Finance Act 1990. The prospect is not immediate! Curiously, when SDRT was extended in 1996, the legislation included provisions to repeal itself.

An attempt was made, in introducing the tax, to use modern drafting techniques. The charging section is, by itself, meaningless: "A tax, to be known as stamp duty reserve tax, shall be charged in accordance with this part of this Act" (section 86(1)).

Section 87 (as amended in 1996) confirms that section 86(1) has no independent meaning: "(1) This section applies where person (A) agrees with another person (B) to transfer chargeable securities ... for consideration ... (2) there shall be a charge ... " unless the agreement is to transfer the securities to B, and two conditions are met. These are: (1) that an instrument is executed transferring the securities to B and (2) the instrument is duly stamped. There is an exemption to avoid charging agreements made by market makers in the ordinary course of their business of dealing in securities. Unit trusts, public issues, and transfers to charities are also exempted. Conversely, where the agreement to transfer is by a renounceable letter of allotment then, unless exempted, the charge is immediate.

Tax is charged at 0.5 per cent of the amount of the consideration for the agreement. The agent who carries out the transaction normally collects this, although formal liability rests on B. This reflects the amount that would be paid if the conditions for avoiding SDRT are met. SDRT is charged at a higher rate of 1.5 per cent where a depositary receipt is issued for the securities, and on certain clearance services.

The chargeable securities to which these charges apply are stocks, shares, loan capital, or interests in or rights (including dividends) arising from, or rights to subscribe for or acquire, them, and units in a unit trust. The definition (in section 99) excludes anything exempt from stamp duty or tax and foreign securities that cannot be traded in the United Kingdom.

Stamp Duties

A transfer of any of these items amounts, or can amount, to a transfer of property within the head of conveyance or transfer above, but restricted to those kinds of property dealt with by the Stock Exchange and by securities and investments dealers. A depositary receipt is a receipt or other instrument that acknowledges that stock or shares, or instruments under which someone can receive stock or shares, have been deposited and that some person has rights in relation to stock or shares of the same kinds.

Insurance Premium Tax

This new tax—introduced by the Finance Act 1994—is an interesting example of pragmatic tax raising. There used to be stamp duty on insurance and assurance policies. They have been abolished. Another way of taxing insurance is to impose VAT on it, but that is not possible because of the Sixth VAT Directive. This tax is a compromise: an *ad valorem* tax imposed on the premiums, much like a withholding tax under the income tax, but collected by the recipient of the payment and called an excise duty. It is therefore administered by the Commissioners of Customs and Excise. It was introduced at a rate of 2.5 per cent of the amount that, with the addition of the tax, equals the amount of the premium. Sounds simple? Maybe, but by 1995 there were 30 sections of primary legislation, four schedules, three statutory instruments, six required forms and three extra-statutory concessions already in operation. Plus ça change, plus c'est la même chose.

Part Eight

International Aspects

Chapter 32

INTERNATIONAL ASPECTS

We must now turn our attention to an aspect of tax law left on one side in our earlier discussions. This is the question of the effect on our taxes of a foreign element being present. Arguably this is the most fascinating area of our tax laws. It is certainly one of the most complicated. It is also one to which much attention is now devoted in the United Kingdom. This is because of the ease with which money and other assets can be moved in and out of the United Kingdom. Since the creation of the single internal market in the European Union, funds may be moved as freely as goods and people around the member states.

What makes the international side of tax so fascinating? It is in part because it involves a complex study of comparative law. Everywhere else (bar the Cayman Islands) has tax laws of some kind. Just as our domestic history and politics have shaped our own tax laws into particular forms, so the tax laws of all other states tend to differ for individual reasons. The chances are also that when there is a foreign element to a British tax problem, there will also be foreign tax to pay. This gives rise to the problem of *double taxation*, where the same income or property gets caught within the tax jurisdictions of more than one country at the same time. The effect is that, unless special rules apply, punitive rates of taxation are applied to international trade. The consequent distortion of trade benefits no one in an open economy. To avoid problems, rules to prevent double taxation have been developed, and they are another aspect of the fascination of the subject. The problems are, in practice, most severe in the area of income and corporation taxes, and we deal with these first.

Behind double taxation and the treatment of any foreign elements in tax liability is an elementary rule of housekeeping. It suits the Exchequer to regard income or property as covered by United Kingdom taxes wherever possible for financial reasons. What we look at in this part of the book is the way in which our tax laws tackle those foreign elements, and how they deal with the problems of double taxation.

We tackle these issues in reverse order, dealing first with the occurrence of double taxation. There is a reason for this. The rules dealing with double taxation may override and replace the United Kingdom's usual rules for dealing with a foreign element. Further, the special rules apply more often than the underlying national legislation. So the prior question must be: what double taxation rules apply here? Only then should we look at the United Kingdom's own rules. They deal with two broad issues: whether a person is regarded as covered by the tax laws, and whether those laws reach to the form of income or property, or to the transaction or arrangement, which it is sought to tax here. But before we deal with either of these rules, we must answer another question: Whom does the United Kingdom try to tax?

Who Is Caught By United Kingdom Tax?

The first factor in deciding whether United Kingdom tax is payable by a potential taxpayer under either a DTA or general United Kingdom law is the territory or territories to which the person is regarded as attached.

In deciding whether a person should be regarded as "attached" to the United Kingdom or some other country, or both, the United Kingdom follows general world practice in ignoring the nationality of a taxpayer and concentrating instead on where the person is based or lives. For this purpose the law deals with individuals separately from businesses. For individuals it uses three concepts: residence, ordinary residence and domicile. In summary, residence may be regarded as where the taxpayer is living now, ordinary residence as where the taxpayer is normally living, and domicile is where the taxpayer has his permanent home. But these are misleadingly brief summaries, and we must expand them further.

In looking at these terms, we should bear in mind a warning given by the House of Lords in *Shah v. Barnet London Borough Council* (1983) (H.L.), a case about the entitlement of overseas students to British education grants. The case involved the House of Lords in interpreting the concept of "ordinary residence". The Lords made it clear that, unless special rules were laid down by Parliament in particular cases, this and similar concepts had the same meaning throughout the law and not separate meanings for each different kind of law. They are also largely a question of looking at the facts. There are few special rules in United Kingdom tax law.

Residence

Residence is of pervasive importance in every income tax situation in which there is a foreign element. This is because the general rules are that:
(a) someone who is resident in the United Kingdom is liable to income tax on worldwide income, but
(b) anyone not resident here is only taxable in the United Kingdom on income arising here.

Despite the importance of the concept of residence, the legislation on the meaning of residence is a mixture of a few statutory pronouncements to which have been added a considerable body of case law. Apart from law, the *practice* of the Revenue is important in this field. The general idea is that someone is resident where they are living for a time in *that* tax year. The problem of applying the concept of residence to the facts of individual cases engaged the courts in some of the earliest tax appeals, such as in *Re Young* (1875) (Court of Session). Since then, elaborate rules have evolved in a mixture of law, concession, and practice.

Section 336 of the Taxes Act declares that a person who is in the United Kingdom for some temporary purpose only and not with a view or intent of establishing his residence here, and who has not actually resided in the United Kingdom at one time or several times for a period equal in aggregate to six months in any year of assessment is not chargeable as a United Kingdom resident, but that a person who has so actually resided shall be so chargeable for that year. This is the United Kingdom version of a general international rule known as the "183 day rule"—that someone comes within the local tax jurisdiction after having been there for 183 days. It is implicit in the section that a person may be held to be resident here even though he has been present for less than six months, provided his presence has what is called a "residential quality". There are three main aspects of this.

First, a person who has a home here (a residence, but use of that word confuses things!) may be treated as resident in a tax year of assessment if present here only for a short period—or possibly even if not present at all. There is a statutory qualification to this rule. It is declared by section 335 of the Taxes Act that if a person works full time abroad the question of residence in the United Kingdom must be determined without regard to any place of abode (residence?) maintained here. Also, (with regard to Schedule E) where the employment is in substance one of which the duties fall to be performed outside the United Kingdom, merely incidental duties performed here are treated as performed abroad.

Secondly, a person who does not maintain any home here, but pays regular visits to the United Kingdom, is regarded as resident if these visits form part of the individual's habit of life. This vague test, based on the case law, is interpreted by the Revenue in its code on residence (published as IR 20) as meaning more than 91 days in each of four years.

Thirdly, section 334 of the Taxes Act states that when a Commonwealth citizen or citizen of the Republic of Ireland, whose ordinary residence has been in the United Kingdom, leaves the country for the purpose only of occasional residence abroad, actual residence in the United Kingdom treated as continuing.

In applying these tests, it is important to remember that an individual may be resident in the United Kingdom and another state—possibly more than one other state—at the same time.

Residence of companies is as important to decide for tax purposes as residence of individuals. For many years this was decided by a judicial test, offered by Lord Loreburn in *de Beers Consolidated Mines v. Howe* (1906) (H.L.): "A company resides ... where its real business is carried on ... and the real business is carried on where the central management and control actually abides." This was a common sense application of the idea of residence to something which is purely a creation of the law. But it has a distinct disadvantage for tax purposes in the days of faxes and executive jets. The central management and control of a company can be wherever the directors chose to meet to take their decisions. So, if the directors of a British-registered company, all of whom are resident in Britain, decide to take the corporate jet together for a trip to Bermuda once a month for their monthly board meeting at a small office they maintain there, where is the company resident? Bermuda may be British, but it is also a tax haven outside the British tax jurisdiction.

The common law rule was therefore supplemented in 1988 (by FA 1988, s. 66) by a second rule, adopting a prevalent international rule into the United Kingdom. This is that any company incorporated under the laws of the United Kingdom is resident here for tax purposes. This rule applies alongside the old rule. Any foreign incorporated company with central management in the United Kingdom is also resident here.

Because many states operate double tests like those now applying in the United Kingdom, it is common for a company to have more than one residence, although this can be inconvenient for some companies and also for the tax authorities. To avoid both these sets of problems, both tests are overridden by a rule relating to our double taxation rules. If under those rules, which we note below, the company is to be regarded as resident outside the United Kingdom, then it is not a United Kingdom resident for any tax purposes (FA 1994, s. 249).

Ordinary residence

In 1928 in *Levene v. IRC* (H.L.) Viscount Cave said " ... I think that [ordinary residence] connotes residence in a place with some degree of continuity and apart from accidental or temporary absences". In 1983 in *Shah v. Barnet London Borough Council* (H.L.) Lord Scarman, giving judgment on behalf of all their Lordships, noted that the words bore the same meaning in 1983 as they did in 1928, and that that was their ordinary meaning, He added his own description, that the words refer to "a man's abode in a particular place or country which he has adopted voluntarily and for settled purposes as part of the regular order of his life for the time being, whether of short or long duration".

We have noted that the Revenue has based its "four year rule" on its own view of this case. Following these tests, it is possible for a person to be ordinarily resident in two places, and therefore two countries, at once. It is also possible for a person to be resident here without being ordinarily resident here, and the reverse.

Domicile

Domicile also has no special meaning in tax law. Internationally, it is a confusing term because it is the French equivalent of "residence", but the French and English meanings of domicile are far removed from each other. The nearest equivalent is permanent residence, but the individual's permanent home would be a better way of putting it. An individual can only have one domicile, and at birth that is where the person is born. The domicile of origin, as this is called, can be replaced by a domicile of choice, but not easily, and only if both the intent of the individual and the factual pattern of the individual's life, dictate this. The result is that a person may spend many years away from home but still be domiciled there.

Double Taxation Relief

United Kingdom tax laws provide for a relief called double taxation relief to apply to any case where a person has to pay income tax, capital gains tax, corporation tax or inheritance tax at the same time as paying a similar foreign tax. This is subject to exceptions based mainly on the grounds that a foreign tax is not of the same kind as these taxes. Relief is provided by two means. By far the more important means is through application of bilateral treaties with other states known in the United Kingdom as double taxation agreements (DTAs). Where there is no agreement, the tax authorities here provide a foreign tax credit against United Kingdom taxation, known as unilateral relief.

Double Taxation Agreements

The best practical answer to double taxation problems between the United Kingdom and any other state is for the authorities of both states to sit down and work out what to do about the various problems of overlap individually. They are greatly assisted in doing this by the existence of standard forms of agreement which most states follow closely. The most important model is the OECD Model Tax Convention (OECD is the Organisation for Economic Cooperation and Development, based in Paris, and of which the United Kingdom is a very active member). Another model, that the United Kingdom uses when negotiating with developing states, is the United Nations Model Double Tax Convention.

Once the treaty negotiators have worked through problems thrown up by both sets of tax laws, and sorted out the answers, they draw up an agreement which binds the two states to follow the answers whenever the problems arise. The United Kingdom authorities do not need legislative powers to do this, because agreeing treaties can be done on the authority of the royal prerogative. It would be possible to deal with individual foreign problems by individual provisions in Finance Acts but, with only rare exceptions, this does not happen. The necessary legal authority to require the authorities—and taxpayers—in this country to comply with the answers is given under a general provision. You will find it in section 788 of the Taxes Act 1988, with equivalent provisions in the TCGA 1992, and the IHTA 1984.

Section 788 provides that if Her Majesty by Order in Council should declare that arrangements have been made with the government of any overseas territory with a view to double taxation relief, "then, subject to the provisions of this Part of this Act, the arrangements shall, *notwithstanding anything in any enactment*, have effect ... ". The words in (our) italics mean what they say. Anything in an Order in Council can override anything in any of the taxing Acts—or, indeed, any other Act except the European Communities Act 1972 (which contains the same words referring to E.C. law). Orders in Council are quite common, and the United Kingdom has concluded more than 100 DTAs with other governments. Most follow the standard patterns of the Model Tax Conventions.

Individual DTAs are negotiated in the form of Conventions binding in international law on the two states. In practice parts of each Convention need renegotiating from time to time as the tax systems of the two states are amended. Parts of DTAs are revised by Protocols.

The United Kingdom has concluded DTAs with many states, including all our European Union partners and main trading partners. Most of these agreements are aimed to be comprehensive, dealing with most—usually all—the problems likely to arise. We note the individual answers given in the standard forms of DTA below.

Until recently, it was an aim of many states to reach agreements with all their neighbours. But this has given rise to a practice known as "treaty shopping" and has also encouraged "tax havens". If a country has a DTA with the United Kingdom, overlap of taxes is usually avoided. If at the same time the other state has very low, or nil, tax rates applying to income protected from United Kingdom taxes, it will become fiscally very attractive. A place with a favourable (to the taxpayer) tax regime is often called a "tax haven"—though "no tax haven" or the French term "paradis fiscal" might be more accurate. Recently some countries have started to take action against tax havens, by terminating or limiting DTAs.

They have also been adopting special provisions in their treaties or national laws to stop "treaty shopping". This is the use by a taxpayer of a treaty between states of which the taxpayer is not a resident. This can be done, at least in theory, by the taxpayer setting up a company in one of the states and using it as a "conduit" company to pass income through the state under the treaty provisions. Treaties concluded by some states, particularly the United States (and to a lesser extent the United Kingdom) therefore contain provisions designed to ensure that the treaty provisions can only be used by those who are genuine residents of the two states for income that genuinely relates to the states.

The forms of relief from double taxation

The first form of relief offered by a DTA that follows the usual form of the Model Conventions is a series of "tiebreaker" provisions designed to ensure that an individual or company that is treated as a resident for national tax purposes by both states has resident status in just one of the states. In the case of companies, this is done by replacing the national rules by a single rule: the company is resident in the state (of the two) where its centre of effective management is to be found. Note that this is different to either of the British rules, but overrides both of them. The centre of effective management is where the day-to-day management decisions are taken—usually the same place as its head office.

The tiebreaker rules for individuals consist of a series of rules that give preference in turn to the centre of economic interests of the individual, the individual's real home, and the individual's nationality.

The effect of these rules is to ensure that only one of the two states has a worldwide claim to tax over any taxpayer. But it also creates a problem. Companies and individuals may have genuine strong economic links with both states. By removing the residence link between the taxpayer and one of the states, that state's claim to tax may be removed or reduced excessively compared with the income being earned by the taxpayer in that state. To deal with this, DTAs have special rules about "permanent establishments" (or PEs as they are usually termed). A PE is a branch or agency of the taxpayer established on a continuing basis in the other state. If a PE exists, the state where the PE is has extended rights to tax income of the taxpayer effectively connected with the PE. At the same time, the tax paid with respect to the income of a PE in one state is available for foreign tax credits in the other state, to limit the maximum level of taxation that can be imposed.

The second form of relief given by a DTA is a series of provisions that attribute the rights to tax different forms of income between the two states to reduce the scope for double taxation. The rights to tax some forms of income are attributed primarily to the state where the income arises (the source state). This applies to taxation of income and capital gains from land. The rights to tax cross-border transfers of income are often shared between the two states, with the source state having a limited right to tax. For example, many DTAs provide that both states can tax interest paid by a lender in one state to a borrower in the other state, but they limit the source state to a maximum of perhaps 10 per cent tax. Yet other forms of income can be taxed in the state where the taxpayer is resident (the state of residence)—remembering that the taxpayer is for these purposes only resident in one state. This is true of trading income (see below).

The third form of relief given by a DTA is by requiring states to limit any double taxation that does occur. This can be done in two ways. Where the source state taxes a form of income, the state of residence may either exempt the income from further tax, or give a foreign tax credit for the tax paid in the source state against any tax payable in the state of residence. The United Kingdom rarely gives relief by way of exemption, relying instead on the granting of foreign tax credits. For example, where a source state is entitled to levy a 10 per cent tax on interest paid to a taxpayer resident in the United Kingdom, the United Kingdom tax authorities allow the taxpayer to set the tax paid in the source state directly against tax due here. The United Kingdom therefore only collects the difference between the total tax payable in the United Kingdom and the tax already paid in the source state. It grants this foreign tax credit in accordance with the provisions of United Kingdom law. These are the same whether or not a DTA exists.

Unilateral relief

Where we have no DTA with another territory, or where the agreement does not apply to a particular foreign tax (for example a local income tax), unilateral relief is available under United Kingdom law, by section 790 of the Taxes Act 1988 and equivalent provisions in the TCGA 1992 and IHTA 1984. These sections empower the authorities to grant relief unilaterally as if there were a DTA in effect.

As already noted, the actual relief is given in the form of a foreign tax credit, whether the entitlement to the relief arises under a DTA that has been incorporated into our law by an Order in Council, or where it is being granted under the more general authority of section 790. The taxpayer has to show that the tax has actually been paid to the foreign tax authority, that the tax is either a tax expressly covered by a DTA or a similar tax to the United Kingdom income tax, corporation tax or capital gains tax, and that the tax relates to

International Aspects

the same income as the United Kingdom charge to tax. Where a credit is allowed, the tax due in the United Kingdom will be reduced by the amount of foreign tax paid. This relief prevents the tax paid being more than the higher of the rates of tax of the two territories. If the United Kingdom rate is higher than the foreign rate, only the difference between the two is payable here.

The rules allowing a foreign tax credit prevent the taxpayer claiming back excessive foreign tax credit. In particular, if the United Kingdom tax on a form of income is lower than the foreign tax, so that the tax credit is potentially greater than the United Kingdom tax bill, the credit is limited to the amount of the United Kingdom tax bill. Also, the taxpayer cannot add two or more claims for foreign tax credit from different countries or different sources together to achieve a cross-subsidy from lower foreign tax bills to higher foreign tax bills. The credit rules have to be applied separately to each form of income and each foreign state.

Finally, if neither of the above forms of relief operate, section 811 may come to the aid of those subject to a double charge to income or corporation tax. This section allows relief by way of deduction. It treats the amount of income taxable in the United Kingdom as equal to the gross income less the amount of overseas tax paid. For example income of £100 is subject to foreign income tax at 30 per cent. For these purposes, the income will be treated as equal to £70 only, liable to United Kingdom income tax at 24 per cent totalling £17. Note that this is less beneficial than relief by credit, where *no* United Kingdom tax would have been due.

Foreign Incomes and Gains

We now look in turn at how each of the schedules and main charging sections deal with foreign elements, remembering of course that in any individual case a double taxation agreement of the kind discussed above may override the general rules. For this reason, we shall also examine how the OECD Model Tax convention (MTC) and, where it differs, a typical British double tax agreement (DTA) deal with the issues.

Schedule A

Schedule A is charged expressly on land in the United Kingdom, so the only foreign element that could arise is the identity of the taxpayer. However, any foreign association of the recipient of a rent or the occupier of woodlands is irrelevant under the rules of the

Schedule. Article 6 of the MTC (which is followed in most DTAs) provides that tax may be collected by the state where the land is, authorising taxation under Schedule A of foreign landowners. Income from foreign land is taxed under Schedule D.

Schedule D, Case I and II

At first sight it would seem that trades or professions carried on abroad are within Case I or Case II. Section 18(1)(a)(ii) of the Taxes Act relates to "any trade, profession or vocation whether carried on in the United Kingdom or elsewhere." Despite these words it is clear from case law that if a trade is carried on *wholly* outside the United Kingdom it is not within Case I. Instead it will be caught in Case V. This is equally true of a profession or vocation. See *Colquhoun v. Brooks* (1889) (H.L.) But if the trade or profession is carried on *partly* here, then Case I or Case II applies to the full profits. Case I and Case II apply even if the taxpayer is not resident in the United Kingdom, and whether or not the taxpayer is a British national. Note that all corporate profits of a resident company are regarded as being under Case I, and that Case V does not apply to corporate trading profits. If the company is not a United Kingdom resident, then it is taxed in the United Kingdom to corporation tax on any profits of a branch or agency here, but to income tax on any other United Kingdom source profits.

The Schedule D rules are normally overridden by rules in our DTAs. Article 7 of the MTC provides that a trade is to be taxed in the state where the trader is resident, unless the trader maintains a permanent establishment (PE) in the other state. (On PEs see above). If so, then the state where the PE is may tax trading income effectively connected with the PE. If it does so, the state of residence of the trader must give double tax relief for that tax against any tax it levies on the same income. British DTAs broadly follow this approach. On this basis, the Inland Revenue is authorised to impose tax on the worldwide trading profits or British residents, and on the British trading profits of foreign residents. Problems tend to arise mostly in deciding in which of the two states the expenses of the business are to be claimed.

Schedule D, Case III

The Case applies to interest, annuities or annual payments "payable within or out of the United Kingdom": section 18(2). In practice much of the income falling within this part of the charge of Case III is dealt with by withholding taxes, most of which apply whether or not the recipient is linked to the United Kingdom. For example, interest paid to a foreign recipient is usually subject to a 24 per cent withholding. The level of withholding is normally set by the DTA. The MTC recommends a withholding tax of 10 per cent, but an increasing number of British DTAs provide for exemption at source, leaving the interest be to taxed in the county of the recipient only.

Schedule D, Cases IV and V

These are the only main charging sections aimed specifically at overseas income. Case IV taxes "income arising from securities out of the United Kingdom", and Case V deals with income from "possessions" out of the United Kingdom, except where the income is emoluments caught under Schedule E. "Securities" and "possessions" are not defined. It may be noted that the words go back to the start of income tax, when a possession probably consisted of a sugar plantation, no doubt manned by slave labour. The terms certainly predate that revolutionary new concept called the joint stock company. In practice these terms cause little difficulty. There is no difference of importance between Case IV and Case V. The alternatives to the two cases will be charged under other Schedules or Cases. These may well end up with the same tax "take", because in most cases the charge under either case is on the whole of the income for the relevant year, whether or not it has been received in the United Kingdom. The application of either case to companies is limited. Case IV does not apply to companies since 1996. Either Case I or Case III applies. Case V, as we have already noted, does not apply to profits of resident companies, and foreign profits of non-resident companies are outside the scope of the tax.

If a Commonwealth or Irish citizen is not ordinarily resident in the United Kingdom, or if any other national is not domiciled in the United Kingdom, then he or she will only be charged under these Cases on what is termed a "remittance basis". That means United Kingdom tax will only be charged if the income is received (in any form) in the United Kingdom. Such a person can avoid a United Kingdom tax charge by keeping the income out of this country. This is widely used by wealthier foreign residents in Britain to reduce their exposure to British tax.

Again, these Cases may be overridden by the rules of DTAs. Several rules are relevant. Article 10 of the MTC covers dividends, and provides for a limited withholding tax of 5 per cent to 15 per cent of the dividend for the state where the dividend is sourced. There is no withholding tax in Britain, so our DTAs do not follow this provision for the United Kingdom However, the other state may follow the provision, imposing a limited withholding. The rule for foreign rents and trades have already been noted. "Other income" not specifically mentioned elsewhere in a DTA is usually taxable in the state of the resident only.

Schedule D, Case VI

This is the "rag-bag" provision, but, as we have already seen that Cases IV and V are a sort of "overseas rag-bag" there is in practice no point under Case VI of importance here. Nonetheless, we shall see that Case VI is used to cover specific overseas antiavoidance provisions. If these catch income already taxed in another state, then double tax relief is usually required either by a DTA or by our own rules.

Schedule E

Schedule E is divided into three Cases which are set out in section 19 of the Taxes Act. That section used the phrase "foreign emoluments" and that phrase is relevant to all three cases. "Foreign emoluments" are "emoluments of a person not domiciled in the United Kingdom from an office or employment under or with any person, body of persons or partnership resident outside and not resident in, the United Kingdom." Notice that there are two factors here, one turning on the domicile of the employee and one on the residence of the employer.

CASE I

Case I applies where the person holding the office or employment is resident and ordinarily resident in the United Kingdom. The charge to tax is on the *whole* of the emoluments. That is the basic position but there are two possible exceptions. First, there is a deduction in respect of earning from work done abroad during an absence from the United Kingdom of 365 days or more. The deduction is the whole of the amount of the emoluments attributable to that period. Secondly, where the duties of an office or employment are performed wholly outside the United Kingdom and the emoluments are foreign emoluments the emoluments are excepted from Case I.

CASE II

Case II applies where the person holding the office or employment is not resident, or if resident, is not ordinarily resident, in the United Kingdom. Tax is charged only on emoluments for the year of assessment in respect of duties performed in the United Kingdom. This case can only apply to a person who performs duties here but does not become resident or alternatively does not become ordinarily resident here. Case II is not strictly in line with the principle that a non-resident can only be taxed on a United Kingdom source of income, unless we regard the United Kingdom duties as a "source".

CASE III

Case III applies to a person who is resident in the United Kingdom (where ordinarily resident here or not) in either of two situations. The first is where the emoluments are from an employment whose duties are performed wholly outside the United Kingdom and the emoluments are foreign emoluments. Because the duties are performed wholly outside the United Kingdom, this situation is not caught by Case II, and because of this—and also that the emoluments are foreign emoluments—the situation is not caught by Case I. The second situation is where the emoluments are for duties performed outside the United Kingdom and the employee is resident but not ordinarily resident in the United Kingdom. Because the duties are performed outside the United Kingdom Case II does not apply, and because the taxpayer is not ordinarily resident here Case I does not apply. Case III is designed to apply, and does apply, only where Cases I and II do not apply. The charge to tax under Case III is only on emoluments received in the United Kingdom (the remittance basis).

In most cases, this complex set of rules is overridden by the DTA rules. Article 15 of the MTC sets out the rules for taxing foreign employees. The main rule is known as the "183 day rule". Tax on employment income is levied in any year only by the state of residence of an employee working temporarily in another state, unless the employee is in the other state for 183 days or more in the year (or that year and a previous year), and the pay for the work comes from an employer in the state where the work takes place. For example, if I work in another state for two three-month periods, it must be calculated whether or not those periods total 183 days. If they do, I can be taxed in the other state. If the Inland Revenue can also tax me under any of the cases of Schedule E, I will be given double tax relief for the foreign tax.

Schedule F

This applies expressly only to payments by companies resident in the United Kingdom. In practice the liability is covered by the ACT payments made by the paying company. If the recipient is non-resident, the ACT can sometimes be reclaimed from the Revenue. This depends on the terms of the DTA made with the other state. In the absence of a DTA, a foreign shareholder may not be entitled to a reclaim. Dividends from foreign countries received in the United Kingdom by individuals are taxable under Case V of Schedule D.

Capital gains tax

The general charge to capital gains tax applies to all assets whether situation in the United Kingdom or not. However, a person is only liable to the tax on a gain if during part of the relevant tax year he is either resident here or ordinarily resident here: TCGA 1992, s.2. Where a person is resident or ordinarily resident here, but is not domiciled in the United Kingdom, then gains from foreign assets will only be charged to tax when received (if ever) in the United Kingdom. Conveniently, section 275 provides a list of rules to identify the location of assets such as debts or shares (why is there not a similar list in the income tax legislation?).

The MTC, Article 13, (followed by many DTAs) provides a series of rules for deciding which state may tax capital gains. Gains on land may be taxed in the state where the land is. Most other forms of capital gain may be taxed in the state of residence of the taxpayer. However, many states still do not charge capital gains tax, or restrict it to gains made in the state. Consequently, the British rules create something of a tax haven for foreign investors here if they realise their profits in the form of capital gains rather than income, and they do not get taxed in their own states.

Anti-Avoidance Provisions

The full story of this chapter has not been told until we look at special anti-avoidance provisions aimed at catching transaction and arrangements designed to avoid United Kingdom tax. We will note four of these measures, where a determined attempt was made to tackle the "leakage" of taxable income overseas.

Transfer of assets abroad

Section 739 of the Taxes Act was enacted (to quote the near-unique statement of legislative purpose in the section):

> "for the purpose of preventing the avoiding by individuals ordinarily resident in the United Kingdom of liability to income tax by means of transfers of assets by virtue ... whereof ... income becomes payable to persons resident or domiciled out of the United Kingdom...."

Originally enacted in 1936, these provisions were given an extremely wide interpretation in 1948 in *Congreve v. IRC* (H.L.). They proved to be oppressively effective until the House of Lords reinterpreted the sections in *Vestey* in 1981, which gave the sections their present shape.

The sections give the Revenue wide powers to deem an individual to be receiving income (chargeable under Schedule D, Case VI) where that individual has power to enjoy overseas income which would be taxable if it were received here. The individual can escape the charge if he can show "to the satisfaction of the Board" that either avoidance of tax was not one of the purposes behind the transactions or that the transactions were bona fide commercial transactions not designed for tax avoidance reasons.

Migration of companies

Section 765 contains power for the Treasury to stop a company resident in the United Kingdom becoming non-resident and thus slipping round the tax net. Two brief comments are warranted. First, as a Royal Commission observed as long ago as 1954, this provision has no place in a Taxes Act. Secondly, the fact that companies cannot migrate does not stop assets migrating to associated, but foreign, companies.

Controlled foreign companies

Sections 747 to 756 of the Taxes Act contains proposals originally entitled "Tax Havens", and this summarises their purpose. Their methods are better summarised by the present title: controlled foreign companies.

ANTI-AVOIDANCE PROVISIONS

These provisions apply potentially to any company resident outside the United Kingdom in a low tax area but which is controlled by persons resident in the United Kingdom. They are only applied to individual companies if the Board of Inland Revenue so directs. Until recently, few directions were made because the Revenue could not so direct if the company was quoted (using the same 35 per cent test as for close companies), if it followed an acceptable distribution policy, if it engaged only in exempt activities (broadly, that it is trading or operating locally and not mainly with the United Kingdom), or if its profits did not exceed £20,000. The Finance Act 1996 modified the "acceptable distribution" test and makes use of this provision more likely.

If the Board directs that a company is to be treated as a controlled foreign company, then the profits of the company will be apportioned among those who have an interest in the company in broadly the same way as with a close company, so that income will be deemed to be received in the United Kingdom by those with interests in the controlled foreign company, and will be taxed accordingly. A crucial question here is the residence of a company, but in general the ordinary rules apply.

Offshore funds

This is the rather vague title given to sections 757 and following of the Taxes Act. An offshore fund includes any overseas company, any overseas unit trust or any other overseas method for co-owning property. Introduced in 1984, these measures attack certain material interests in non-qualifying offshore funds. A material interest means any interest which allows the owner to get the market value of his investment back in some way within seven years of investment. A fund is non-qualifying unless the Board of Inland Revenue certifies that the fund is following a full distribution policy, and that the fund does not have a significant investment in other offshore funds or other companies.

Where someone is regarded as having a material interest and the "fund" is non-qualifying, then the provisions treat any gain made by an investor resident or ordinarily resident in the United Kingdom (and calculated along the same lines as gains for capital gains tax) as an income gain chargeable under Schedule D, Case VI.

INDEX

Accommodation, provision of, 113–15, 122–3
Accountants, 19, 20, 76, 405
'Accounting Standards and Taxable Profits' (BTR), 77
Accounts, importance of, 75–7
Accumulation trusts, 178
Acquisition duty, 321
Addington, Henry (1st Viscount Sidmouth), 23
Administration
  Capital Gains Tax, 220–21
  Corporation Tax, 288
  Income Tax, 51–6
  Inheritance Tax, 404–7
  Stamp Duties, 447–48
  VAT, 412
Advance Corporation Tax (ACT), 284–5, 286, 287, 315
  distributions and, 300, 301
  non-qualifying, 306–7
  groups of companies, 305–6
  non-resident companies, 473
  rate, 289
  surplus, 302–305
Agency workers, 71
'Annual', meaning of, 65
Annuities, 162–3, 174–5, 267, 338
Appeals, 17–19, 28, 43–6
  Capital Gains Tax, 220
  Income Tax, 53–6
  Inheritance Tax, 406
  NI Contributions, 210
  Stamp Duties, 450
  VAT, 413
Arm's length transactions, 227, 328-9

Assessment, 52–5, 58, 93–5, 288, 406, 412–13
  see also self-assessment
Assessments, alternative, 31, 32
Assets
  defining as trading expenses, 86
  transfer of
    abroad, 474
    market value, at, 82–3
  see also Capital Gains Tax
Auditors, 76
Avoidance, 9, 42, 43, 45, 141, 143
  anti-avoidance, 183–4, 421, 473–5
  Corporation Tax, 290, 300, 313, 317
  NI Contributions, 212
  Stamp Duties, 448, 453
Avoision, 9

'Badges of trade', 72–3
Barristers, 89, 95, 150, 405, 423
Base, 7, 13–14
Beneficiaries, taxation of, 179–82, 197, 248–9
Benefits, defining as trading expenses, 86
Benefits Agency, 210
Benefits in kind, 107–15, 121–5, 130, 212, 214
Betting winnings, 133
Bill of Rights (1689), 27, 32, 34, 39
Black economy, 8
British Tax System, The (Kay and King), 6, 24

476

INDEX

Budget statement, 37
Business entertainment expenditure, 87–8

Calendar, reform of, 23
Capital allowances *see* Income Tax
Capital allowances, minor, 295
Capital and income distinguished, 66–7
Capital Gains Tax (CGT), 12, 13, 25, 31, 473
  arm's length transactions, 227
  assets, 224–6
    business, 235, 272–3, 266, 277
    capital sums derived from, 228–30, 231
    foreign, 250
    held on 31 March 1982, 260–62
    held on 6 April 1965, 262–63
    loss, destruction and negligible value, 230–32
    rights as, 215
    wasting, 254–5, 272
  background, 219–20
  base cost, 223
  beneficiaries, tax position of, 248–9
  Capital Transfer Tax and, 226
  charge to, 222
  companies, 222
    adjustments, 234–5
    capital distributions, 234
    transfer of business to, 235, 273
  compensation, 229, 230, 267
  computation, 250, 255
    allowable expenditure, 251–4
    consideration, 251
    income receipts and expenditure, 250–51
  connected persons, 227, 236
  consideration, 232–3, 251
  Corporation Tax and, 222, 281

Capital Gains Tax—*contd*
  damages, 229, 231, 267
  death and, 239–41
  debts, 235–7
  disposals, 226–32
  dwelling house, 268–70
  exchange rates, 250
  'exempt amount', 221
  exemptions and reliefs
    betting winnings, 267
    business, transfer of to a company, 273
    business assets
      gifts of, 277
      replacement of, 272–3
    cars, 267
    charities, 277–8
    chattels disposed of for £6000 or less, 271–2
    compensation, 267
    currency, foreign, 267
    damages, 267
    deferred annuities, 267–8
    gilt-edged securities, 267
    hold-over relief, 231, 265–6, 172, 277
    life assurance policies, 267–8
    PEPs, 267
    premium bonds, 267
    private residences, 268–71
    qualifying corporate bonds, 267
    reinvestment relief, 276–7
    retirement relief, 274–6
    roll-over relief, 235
    savings certificates, 267
    tangible moving wasting assets, 272
    works of art, 272
  gains
    chargeable, 222–3, 263
    meaning of, 219
    taxable, 221
  gifts, 226–7, 265–6, 277
  husband and wife, 221–2, 239

INDEX

Capital Gains Tax—*contd*
  Income Tax and, 220–21, 224, 228
  incorporeal property, 224
  index-linking, 220, 221, 256
  indexation allowance
    calculation, 256–7
    no gain no loss, 260
    share-pooling, rules for, 257–9
  inflation and, 219–20, 260–61
  Inheritance Tax and, 219, 226, 245, 247, 265–6, 277
  insurance and, 229, 231
  land with development value, 263
  law, 220
  lease premiums, 228
  legatee, 240
  life interest, termination of, 245–6
  losses, 263–4
  market value rule, 227
  material disposal test, 275–6
  O'Brien test, 225–6
  options, 237
  overdue tax, 221
  part disposals, 228
  partners, 223–4
  payment of tax, 249
  personal representatives and, 222, 240–41
  persons, 223–4
  qualifying investments, 276
  qualifying trades, 277
  rates, 221–2, 283
  rebasing, 260–61
  reliefs, *see* exemptions and reliefs
  residence, 224
  self-assessment, 220, 221
  settled property, 240, 241
    absolutely entitled, 241–2, 243, 244–5
    bare trustees, 241, 242–3
    beneficiaries, tax position of, 248–9

Capital Gains Tax—*contd*
  settled property—*contd*
    concurrent interest, 242
    interest *pur autre vie*, 246
    interest in succession, 242
    nominee, 241
    payment of the tax, 249
    'putting arrangements', 242
    reverter to disponor, 245
    termination of life interest, 245–6
  settlement, putting property into, 243–4
  shares, 235, 257, 259, 263
  spouse, 221–2, 239
  stock in trade, 233–4
  straight line apportionment rule, 262
  trusts, transfer between, 247–8
  trustees, 222, 244
    disposals by, 244–7, 275
    exit charge, 243, 244, 247
  uplift, 240, 245, 246
  value shifting, 238–9
  VAT and, 253–4
  'wholly and exclusively', 252
Capital settlements, 185–9
Capital Transfer Tax, 26, 226, 321–22, 323
Cars, 123–4, 213, 214, 267, 443
CD-Rom versions
  commercial consolidations, 35
  Inland Revenue instruction manuals, 38
Charities, 277–8, 295, 344
Chartered Institute of Taxation, 20, 38
Chesterfield, Lord, 23
Close companies, 199–200, 283, 295, 297
  see also Corporation Tax; Inheritance Tax
Clothing, provision of, 109–10, 118

Index

Code, The, *see* Income Tax, employees earning £8500 or more and directors
Codification Committee (1936), 23
Commissioners of Income Tax, 54–5, 58, 61
   appeal from on point of law only, 18, 56–7, 72
   see also General Commissioners; Special Commissioners
Commissioners of Inland Revenue *see* Inland Revenue, Board of
Committee on the Structure and Reform of Direct Taxation, 24
Community Customs Code, 28, 34
Companies, 76, 161, 462–3, 474–5
   close *see* close companies
   holding, 290n, 305–6
   investment, 295
   non-resident, 282, 313
   'one man service', 102–3
   quoted, 313
   small, 283, 284, 289, 300, 317
   subsidiary, 303, 305–6, 313
   see also Capital Gains Tax; Corporation Tax; Inheritance Tax
Companies Acts, 76
Consolidation Acts, 32
Consolidations, commercial, 35
Contributions Agency (CA), 14, 15, 38, 210
Contributions Regulations, 212
Corporate bonds, qualifying, 267
Corporation Tax, 12, 25, 26, 29, 31
   accounting periods, 288
   accruals basis, 291
   advance *see* Advance Corporation Tax
   building society, 314
   Capital Gains Tax and, 281, 284, 300, 301
   charge to, 281
   charges on income, 292-95, 305

Corporation Tax—*contd*
   charity, payment to, 295
   'classical form', 282
   close companies
      associate, 309, 311
      background, 308–9
      benefits, 314–16
      control, 309, 310
      defined, 309, 313
      director, 312
      facilities for participators and associates, 314–15
      loan creditor, 312, 313
      loans to participators and associates, 315–6
      participator, 311
   close investment-holding companies, 316–17
   common ownership test, 297
   companies, 281
      change of ownership, 297–298
      groups of, 305–307
      resident in UK, 286–7, 298, 305–6
      see also close companies; close investment-holding companies
   company reconstructions, 297
   computation of profits, 290–1
   covenant, charitable, 295
   Crown-controlled companies, 314
   debentures, 291, 292
   deductions, 292–97
   demerger, 301
   directors, 283, 290
   distributions, 282, 283, 292, 293, 298–307
      non-qualifying, 286, 287, 306–7
   dividends, 284, 292, 298, 299, 305
   excessive distribution, 302–303
   exemptions, distributions rules, 300

INDEX

Corporation Tax—*contd*
  expenses, 290n, 292–93
  financial years, 288
  franked investment income, 287, 303–305
  franked payments, 302, 304, 305
  group income election, 305
  higher rate taxpayer, 285–6
  holding company, 290n, 305–6
  imputation system, 282, 284–7
  Income Tax and, 281, 284, 285, 289, 290, 296, 298
  individuals, non-resident, 286, 294
  Inheritance Tax and, 300
  insolvency, 297
  interest, 291, 292, 298
  investment company, 295
  land, 281
  law, 288
  loan relationships, 281, 291–2, 293
  mainstream liability, 284, 285, 301, 302
  management expenses, investment company, 295
  mark-to-market basis, 291
  minor capital allowances, 295
  'Pay and File', 288
  PAYE, 283
  pensions, 283
  periods, 288–9
  profits, defined, 281, 291
  rates, 289–90
    small companies, 283, 317
  redemptions, 300–1
  registered industrial and provident society, 314
  reliefs
    carry-back, 303
    carry-forward, 296, 297, 303, 304
    Case VI losses, on, 297
    change of ownership, 297–
    company reconstructions, 297

Corporation Tax—*contd*
  reliefs—*contd*
    double taxation, 286
    group, 298
    set-off, 296–7
  Schedule A, 290
  Schedule D, 283, 284, 290, 291, 297, 299
  Schedule E, 283
  Schedule F, 285, 298, 303, 306
  shares issues, 299
  subsidiary company, 303, 305–6, 313
  surrender, 293, 298, 303
  tapering provisions, 289
  tax credits, 282, 303, 315
    groups of companies, 305–6
    imputation system, 285, 286, 287
  trustee, charitable, 286
  unit trust, 282
Court orders, 171, 172
Covenants, 163, 165, 167, 169, 183, 192–3
  charitable, 295
Current year basis, 93
Customs and Excise, HM, 14, 15, 19, 38, 412, 456
Customs duties, 3, 5, 10, 22, 28

Damages, 89–90, 163, 229, 231, 267
Delegated legislation, 33
Depreciation, money set aside for, 87
Directors, 114, 117, 119–26, 283, 290, 426
  close companies, of, 312
Divers and diving supervisors, 71
Dividends, 191, 193–4
  see also Corporation Tax
Doctors, 102, 117
Domicile, 460, 463
Double taxation, 459, 460
  relief, 208, 286, 466–7
  unilateral, 467–8

INDEX

Double Taxation Agreements (DTAs), 34, 460, 464–6
  foreign incomes and gains, 468–73
Dowell, Stephen, 22
Dual-purpose doctrine, 88, 89

Earnings, casual, 132–4
Earnings basis, 130
Earnings cap, 98
ejusdem generis, 132, 164
Emoluments, 65, 99, 103–15
Employed or self-employed, 70–71, 101
Employee share ownership trust (ESOT), 113
Employment, defined, 101
Employment Status for Tax and National Insurance – the Common Approach (IR and DSS), 101
'Enduring benefit of trade', 86
Enterprise investment scheme, 208
Equity, horizontal and vertical, 6–7
Escape to Victory (film), case study, 43–6
Estate duty, 26, 321, 323, 328, 331
Estate income, 180–82
Estates of deceased individuals, 177, 180
European Community Treaty, 10, 18, 34
European Court of Justice (ECJ), 18, 19, 41
European Union, 459
  customs duties and, 3, 28
  law, 15, 18, 34, 41
  VAT and, 10, 25, 409, 410–11
  see also VAT
Evasion, 8, 9
'Excess rents', 135–6
Excises, 10, 22
Executors, 177

Expenditure, revenue, 85–7
Expenditure tax, 10, 24
Expenses
  allowances, 107
  deductible, 115–26
Expenses and Benefits: A Tax Guide (IR), 119n
Extra-statutory concessions (ESCs), 34, 36, 111, 121

Farmers and farming, 75, 423
  see also Income Tax, capital allowances; Inheritance Tax
Fees and subscriptions, 118–19
Financial Forecast, 37
Financial reporting standards (FRSs), 76
First year and initial allowances, 147–8
Foreign elements, 459, 460
Foreign incomes and gains, 468
Form not substance, 42
Fraud, 58
'Free of tax', 171, 172
Fringe benefits, 108
Furnished lettings, 132, 139, 140

GATT (General Agreement on Tariffs and Trade), 441
General Commissioners, 17, 54, 55, 56, 57, 91, 221
Gifts, 105–7, 133, 165
  see also Capital Gains Tax; Inheritance Tax
Golden handshakes, 104, 126–8
Gourlay principle, 127–8

Higher rate taxpayer, 169
History of Income Tax (Sabine), 22
History of Taxation (Dowell), 22
Hobby-trading, 161

481

Index

Husband and wife, 190, 203,
  221–2, 239, 339–40, 400

Income
  alienated, 167
  capital distinguished, 66–7
  casual earnings, 132–4
  Corporation Tax charges on,
    292–95, 305
  earned, 197–208
  employment, from, 99–131
  estate, 180–82
  husband and wife, of, 190
  individual, of, 191–2
  investment, 197–208
  land, from, 135–45
  meaning, 65–6, 190
  partnership, 194–7
  pure profit, 162, 165
  savings, 192, 197–208
  schedular or statutory, 191
  taxable, 202–5
  total, 190, 191, 198–201
  trade or profession, from, 69–98
  trust, 194
Income Tax, 9, 11, 13
  allowances *see* capital
    allowances; personal reliefs
  annual payments, 162–3, 164–5,
    165–6
  annual tax, 26–7
  annuity, 162–3
  artificial transactions in land,
    144–5
  'back duty' cases, 57
  beneficiary, charge on, 179–82
  benefits in kind, 107–15, 130
  capital allowances
    agricultural land and
      buildings, 155
    first year, 147–8
    industrial buildings, 154
    machinery and plant, 148–54
    pooling, 153–4
    scientific research, 155
    writing-down, 148n, 152–3

Income Tax—*contd*
  Capital Gains Tax and, 51, 70,
    145, 191
  cars, 123–4
  case, steps in, 52–62
  case stated, 56
  casual earnings, 132–4
  charges on income, 198–9
  close company, loan to acquire
    interest in, 199–200
  closing years rules, 93–4
  compensation, 78–9
  computation of trading profits,
    75–7
  co-operative, loan to acquire
    interest in, 199–200
  criminal proceedings, 59
  dates for payment, 59, 61–2
  deductible interest payments,
    199–201
  deduction at source, 167, 175,
    192
  directors and employees earning
    £8500 or more, 119–26
  discontinuance, 161
    deemed discontinuance rules,
      94
  dividends, 193–4
  double taxation relief, 208
  earned income, 197–8
  emoluments, 103–5
  employee-controlled company,
    loan to acquire interest in,
    199–200
  employees earning £8500 or
    more and directors
    beneficial loan arrangements,
      124–5
    benefits in kind, 121–2
    benefits not convertible into
      money, 120–21
    cars and related benefits,
      123–4
    Code, The, 119
    loopholes and, 125–6
    principles of, 120–22

482

Income Tax—*contd*
  employees earning £8500 or
    more and directors—*contd*
    emoluments, 120–21
    employee shareholding, 125
    living accommodation
      expenses, 122–3
    'notional loan', 125
  employment, on, 99–131
  employment or office, 100–103
  enquiries, Revenue power to
    make, 61
  errors, correction of, 61
  estates of deceased persons,
    177–82
  expenses, 107, 115–19
  'Formula, The', 170–72
  gifts, 68, 105–107, 133
  golden handshakes, 104, 126–8
  grossing-up, 192–3
  Inheritance Tax, loan to pay, 200
  inspectors' powers, 52–3
  interest, 91, 163, 175–6, 199
  investment income, 134, 197
  land, income from, 135–45
  law, 25
  lease premiums, 141–4
  legal and accountancy charges,
    91
  losses, 156–7
    carry-back of terminal,
      160–61
    carry-forward of, 158–60
    early years, in, 161
    set-off of, 157–8
  maintenance payments, 173–4
  market value rules, 82–3
  mechanics, 51–63
  MIRAS, 200–201
  office or employment, 100–103
  opening years rules, 93
  ordinary time limit, 58
  partnership, 160, 194–7, 199
  PAYE, 129–31
  penalties, 57–8
  pensions, 97–8, 128–9

Income Tax—*contd*
  personal reliefs, 202–3
    age allowance, 203
    blind person's allowance, 205
    child benefit, 205
    married couple's allowance,
      203
    single parent family
      allowance, 204
    widow's bereavement
      allowance, 204–5
  post-cessation receipts, 95–7,
    134
  profession or trade, on, 69–98
  purchased life annuities, 174–5
  rates, 205–8
  records, duty to keep and
    preserve, 62
  repairs and improvements, 92–3
  retirement annuities, 97–8
  returns, 52, 60
  savings income, 198
  Schedule A, 135–6
    new, 137–40
  Schedule B, 136–7
  Schedule D
    Case I, 69–70
    Case II, 70
    Case III, 162–76
    Case VI, 132–4, 145
    Case VIII, 136
  Schedule E, 99–100, 129–31
  self-assessment, 51, 60–62
  settlements, 183–4
    capital, 185–9
    income, 189
  Sharkey v. Wernher, rule in,
    82–3
  Shilton v. Wilmshurst, test in,
    104, 105
  tax bill, 205–8
  tax-free payments, 170–72
  taxable income, 202–5
  Taxes Act (1988)
    sections 349 and 349, 166–70
    section 770, 83

Index

Income Tax—*contd*
  time limits, 58
  top-slicing relief, 207
  total income, 198–201
  trade or profession, on, 69–98
  trading receipts, 77–80
  trading stock, 80–82
  traditional approach, 52–9
  travel to work and at work, 90–91
  trustees, charge on, 178–9
  trusts, 177–82, 197
  unified system, 70
  unpaid tax, Revenue sanctions, 53
  voluntary payments, 79–80
  work in progress, 82–3
Individuals, 163n
  taxation of, 190–97
Inheritance Tax (IHT), 12, 13, 26, 178, 200
  account, delivery of, 404
  active service, death on, 345
  agricultural property relief, 349–51
  agricultural tenancy, grant of, 255
  annuity, 338
  appointment, power of, 327–8, 335
  arm's length transactions, 328–9
  associated operations, 326–7
  back-to-back policies, 338
  bad bargain, 328, 331
  benefit 'by contract or otherwise', 332
  business property relief, 347–9
  Capital Gains Tax and, 323, 359, 363
  cash options, annuity schemes, 345
  chargeable transfers, 324–38, 363
  close companies, 336–7, 356, 384
  collection, 404–7

Inheritance Tax—*contd*
  computation, 358–72
  conditionally exempt transfers, 346–7
  connected persons, 328–9, 331
  contingent interest, 379
  Crossman principle, 368
  death
    alteration of dispositions on, 353–5
    change in value due to, 360, 363, 371
    partially exempt transfers on, 402
    same instant, at, 335
    transfers on, 334–336
    value transferred on, 334, 335, 370–72
    within seven years after transfer, 359–61
  debts, artificial, 365
  determination, 406
  diminution principle, 325
  disposition, 325–6, 328
  dividends, waiver of, 356
  double charges, relief against, 366–7
  double taxation, 378
  employees, disposition by close company for benefit of, 356
  estate, 327, 335
    in course of administration, 379
  estate duty and, 331, 332
  evolution, 321–23
  excluded property, 325, 339, 374, 378
  exempt transfers, 330, 339
  exemptions and reliefs, 339–57, 400
  family maintenance, relief for, 351–53
  family provision orders, 355
  fixed interest trusts, 385
  foreign aspects, 325, 363, 374, 405

484

INDEX

Inheritance Tax—*contd*
 free loans, 337
 future payments, 337
 gifts, 328, 341, 342–44
  lifetime, 324–34
  with reservation, 323, 331–334
 gratuitous benefit, 328, 331
 grossing-up, 363–5
 heritage bodies exemption, 344
 historic buildings, 346–7
 horizontal separation, 333–4
 housing association, gifts to, 344
 incidence, 400–403
 Income Tax, allowance dispositions for, 356
 individual, 325, 331
 information, Revenue power to require, 405–6
 joint tenancy, 335, 374
 lease, grant for full consideration, 327
 lessee, interest of, 379
 lessor, interest of, 370
 liabilities, 362–66
 liability for tax, 398–400
 life policy, annuity with, 338
 life policy, value of, 370
 'lotting', 371
 marriage gifts, 342–43, 381
 national purposes, gifts for, 344
 normal expenditure out of income, 341–42, 381
 open market value, 367–9
 'other charges', 336–8
 partially exempt transfers, 402
 payment of the tax, 406–7
 political parties, gifts to, 344
 potentially exempt transfers (PETs), 323, 329-30, 332, 338, 349, 385
 precatory trust, 354–5
 property, 327, 334
 public benefit, gifts for, 344–5
 quick succession relief, 336, 346, 381, 384
 Ramsay principle, 326

Inheritance Tax—*contd*
 rates, 358–9
 related property, 369
 relevant period, 331
 relevant property, 348, 349, 386
 reliefs, 339–57
 remainder interest, 378
 remuneration, waiver of, 356
 restriction on freedom to dispose, 369
 retirement benefits, allowance dispositions for, 356
 returns, 405
 reversionary interest, 378–9
 settled property, 373–95
 settlement
  accumulation and maintenance, 374, 386, 393–5
  beneficial interest in possession, 375, 378–9
  beneficial owner, death of, 380
  classification of for charging purposes, 375–8
  definition, 373–4
  disabled trust, 374
  discretionary trusts, 374, 375, 379, 380, 385
  disposal for a consideration, 382–83
  entitlement to income test, 375–7
  fixed interest trusts, 374, 375, 379, 385, 386
  gifts into, 334
  interest in possession, 375–77, 379
   disposal of, 380–81
   termination of, 380
  interest *pur autre vie*, 381
  new entitlement, 382
  no beneficial interest in possession, 385–7
   interim charge (exit charge), 390–93

485

INDEX

Inheritance Tax—*contd*
  settlement—*contd*
    no beneficial interest in possession—*contd*
      principal charge (ten year charge), 387–90
      putting property into, 374–375
      reversionary interest, purchase of, 340, 395–7
      reverter to settlor, 383–4
      special, 393–7
      termination and disposal rules
        extension of, 381
        qualifications to, 382–84
  small gifts, 341, 381
  spouses, transfers between, 339–40, 400
  Stamp Duties and, 363
  successive charges, relief for, 346, 385
  taper relief, 359–60
  tenancy in common, 373
  transfers
    chargeable, 324–38, 363
    conditionally exempt, 346–7
    death, on, 334–336
    exempt, 325, 339
    lifetime, 321–23, 324–34
    more than one property, of, 361–62
    partially exempt, 402
    potentially exempt (PETs), 323, 329–30, 332, 338, 349, 385
    reported late, 362
    same day, on the, 362
    spouses, between, 339–40, 400
    value, of, 324–6, 329
    voidable, 347
  trust for sale, 374
  trustee's remuneration, 384
  unpaid tax, Revenue charge for, 407
  valuation, 367–72
  value transferred, 325

Inheritance Tax-*contd*
  values not exceeding £3000, 340–41
  vertical separation, 333
  visiting forces, 345
  voidable transfers, 347
  waiver, 356
  woodlands, relief for, 351
  works of art, 346–7
Inland Revenue, Board of, 14, 19, 219, 288
  conduct of, how controlled, 63
  discretion to mitigate penalties, 58
  functions, 15
  guidance and information from, 36, 37–8, 43
  Inheritance Tax and, 405–6, 407
  residence, practice on, 461
  Stamp Duties and, 447, 450, 451
Inspectors of Taxes, HM, 15, 52–3
Institute of Chartered Accountants of England and Wales, 20, 38
Institute for Fiscal Studies, 24
Institute of Indirect Tax Practitioners, 20
Interest, 91, 159–60, 163, 175–6
  bank or building society, 192
  overdue tax, on, 54, 61–2, 221
Interest payments, deductible, 199–201
Internet, 37

Judges, 16, 39–40, 45
Judicial review, 62, 210

Land Registry, 449, 451
Land tax, 23
Landfill tax, 5
Lands Tribunal, 406
Law
  accounting, relationship with, 76
  applying, 41–3

INDEX

Law—*contd*
  charging sections, 28–9
  finding, 35
  geography, 27–8
  history, 22–7
  improving, 46–7
  interpreting, 38–41
  nature, 21
  official view, 36–8
  purpose, 13, 33
  using, 35–6
Law Society, Revenue Law Committee, 38
Lease premiums, 141–4
Legal and accountancy charges, 91
Legislation, 32–4
Legatees, 181, 240
Life assurance relief, 14
Life tenants, 181
Lifetime gifts *see* Capital Gains Tax; Inheritance Tax
Loans, held to be accretion of capital, 86
Losses, 156–61
'Lump, The', 71
Luncheon vouchers, 111

Machinery and plant, 146, 148–54, 200
Maintenance payments, 166, 173–4
Mallalieu, Ann, 88–9
Management expenses, 181
Market gardening, 75
Market value, 82–3, 367–9
Married couple's allowance, 173
Meade, Sir James, 24
Mining royalties, 167
Minors, unmarried, benefits received by from parental settlements, 186–7
MIRAS (Mortgage Interest Relief At Source), 200
Model Tax Conventions, 465, 466
Moonlighting, 8

Mutation duty, 321
Mutual exclusion rule, 31–2, 103

National Insurance Fund, 13, 213
National Savings Bank, interest, 191
'Necessary' expenditure, 117
Negligence, 58
NI Contributions, 11, 13, 14, 25, 101, 131
  benefits in kind, 212, 214
  cars, 213, 214
  classes, 210–15
    Class 2, 98
    Class 4, 98
    overlap between, 215
  Contributions Agency (CA), 210
  Contributions Regulations, 212
  credits, 215
  earner, defined, 211
  earnings period, 212, 214
  fringe benefits, 213
  Inland Revenue, Board of, and, 210
  judicial review, 210
  law, 33, 209–10
  National Insurance Fund, 213
  pensions, 213
  primary contribution, 211–12, 213
  rates, 213
  secondary contribution, 211–12, 213
  self-employed, 214
  tribunals, 210
  voluntary contribution, 214–15
Nicoll v. Austin, rule in, 109
Northern Ireland, 19, 28

OECD Model Tax Convention (MTC), 464, 468, 469, 470, 472, 473
Office or employment, 100–103

Index

Office-holder or self-employed, 100
'One man service company', 102–3
Offshore funds, 475
Ombudsman *see* Parliamentary Commissioner for Administration
Orders in Council, 34
Organisation for Economic Co-operation and Development *see* OECD
Own As You Earn scheme, 111–12

'P11D' people *see* Income Tax, employees earning £8500 or more and directors
Parliamentary Commissioner for Administration, 19, 37, 63
Part-time office holders, 116
Patent royalties, 167
Path to Tax Simplification, The (IR), 46
PAYE (Pay As You Earn), 8, 13, 192, 201, 205
Pensions, 91, 97–8, 128–9, 213
PEPs (personal equity plans), 191, 267
Permanent establishments (PEs), 466
Permitted deductions, 140
Perquisites, 107–9
Personal allowances, 164
Personal equity plans (PEPs), 191, 267
Personal reliefs, 202–5, 208
Personal representatives, taxation of, 58, 181, 222, 240–41
Petroleum revenue tax, 13, 28
Pitt, William, 22
Poll tax, 4, 7
Pollution tax, 5
Pooling
  capital allowances, 153–4
  shares, 257–9
Post-cessation receipts, 95–7

Poverty trap, 206
Practitioners, 19
Preceding year basis, 93
Profession, meaning of, 75
Profession or vocation, meaning of, 69
Profit and loss accounts, 77
Profit-sharing schemes, approved, 111, 125
Profits, meaning of, 64–5
Property, letting as a business, 138–40

Qualifying corporate bonds, 267
Qualifying expenditure, 153
Qualifying investments, 276
Qualifying trades, 277

Rates, 13, 205, 206
Re Pettit, rule in, 112
Receipts, casual, 67–8
Receipts basis, 130
Reconveyance, 143
Recurrence, 106, 165
'Red book', 37
Redundancy payments, 105
'Rent a room' lettings, 138, 140
Residence, 460
  companies, of, 462–3
  individuals, of, 461–2
  law, 461
  ordinary, 460, 463
Retail prices index, 203
Retirement annuity contracts, 97
Revenue, The *see* Inland Revenue, Board of
Revenue Adjudicator, 19, 63
Revenue Bar, 20
'Revenue code', 38
Repairs and improvements, 92–3
Reward for service, emolument and, 105
Royal Commission on Income Tax, 23

Sabine, Basil, 22
Schedules, 29–31
  see also Corporation Tax, Income Tax
  Schedule A, 142, 192, 198, 468–9
  Schedule D, 101, 116, 117, 127
    Case I, 136, 146, 156, 157, 175, 192, 469
    Case II, 100, 156, 157, 469
    Case III, 175, 179, 189, 192, 469–
    Case IV, 470–
    Case V, 470–
    Case VI, 135, 186, 187, 471
  Schedule E, 101, 116, 126, 127, 192
    Case I, 471–2
    Case II, 472
    Case III, 472–3
  Schedule F, 132, 473
Scholarships, 191
Scotland, 19, 28, 178
Self-assessment, 15, 35–6, 94, 220, 221
  see also assessment
Set-off relief, 157–9
Settled property see Capital Gains Tax; Inheritance Tax
Settlements
  capital, 185–9
  income, 189
  parental, 186–7
  voluntary, 171
  see also Capital Gains Tax; Inheritance Tax
Share incentive scheme, 113
Share option schemes, 111–12
Share-pooling, 257–9
Sharkey v. Wernher, rule in, 82–3, 223
Shilton v. Wilmshurst, test in, 104, 105
Simons Tax Cases Special Commissioners' Decisions, 18
Smith, Adam, 5, 6, 7, 10, 85

Social Security, Department of
  see Benefits Agency; Contributions Agency
Social Security Appeal Tribunals, 210
Social security contributions
  see NI Contributions
Solicitors, 150, 405, 426
Source doctrine, 27, 67, 96
Special Commissioners, 17, 18, 54, 55, 56, 221, 406
Stamp Duties, 12, 13, 22
  ad valorem duty, 448, 449, 450, 456
    charge to, 451, 452, 453
  adjudication, 42–3
  certification of value, 452
  charge to, 447, 448–49
  contingency principle, 449
  contract for sale, 452, 453
  conveyance or transfer, 452–3
  Customs and Excise, HM, and, 456
  denoting stamps, 450
  dissolution agreement, 452
  exchanges, 452
  exemptions, 451, 452, 454
  fixed duty, 448
    charge to, 451
  foreign elements, 451
  heads of charge, 448, 449, 451
  Inland Revenue, Board of, and, 447, 450, 451
  instrument, 447–48
  insurance premium tax, 447, 456
  land, transfer of, 451
  Land Registry, 449, 451
  law, 447–48
  leases, 449, 454–5
  particulars delivered from, 451
  partnership, 452
  principles, 448–49
  produced stamp, 451
  sanctions, 449–50

INDEX

Stamp Duties—*contd*
  transfer in contemplation of sale, 453
Stamp Duty Reserve Tax, 12, 447, 455–6
Stamp Office, 448, 450
Statements of standard accounting practice (SSAPs), 76
Statutory interpretation, 39
Stock-in-trade, 80–82
Student grants, 191
Surcharge, 62
Surtax, 205

Tax
  assessment, 15
  collection, 8, 10, 15
  defined, 3
  incidence of, 14
  neutral, 6
  parliamentary authority needed for, 27
Tax authorities, 16, 17
Tax bill, 205
Tax Bulletin, 37
Tax cases, reviews of, 19
Tax competition, 10
Tax exempt special savings accounts (TESSAs), 191
Tax-free payments, 170
Tax havens, 11, 465, 474
Tax and Judicial Review (Woolf), 62
Tax Law Review Committee, 46
Tax planning, 35, 42
Taxable income, 191, 202
Taxation
  administrative law of, 16
  effects, 9
  efficiency, 8–10
  fairness, 6–8
  hidden costs, 8–9
  international aspects, 10–11
  principles, 5–6
  purposes, 4–5
  reform, 10

Taxes
  annual nature of, 26
  assessed, 12, 13
  charging provisions and, 31–2
  comprehensive, 27
  direct, 10
  hidden, 3
  parliamentary authority needed for, 32
  schedular, 27
  territorial application of, 27
  transactions, 12, 13
  when to be charged, 13
Taxes Act (1988), sections 348 and 349, 166–70
Taxpayer's Charter, 63
Taxpayers, 14, 16, 17, 58
Terminal payments *see* golden handshakes
TESSAs (tax exempt special savings accounts), 191
Tiebreaker provisions, 466
Tips, 67–8
Trade tax, 23
Trading, criteria for defining, 73–4
Trading expenses, 83–92
Trading profit, 80, 81
Trading stock, 80–82
'Transfer pricing', 83
'Treaty shopping', 465
Trusts
  accumulation, 178, 374
  disabled, 374
  discretionary, 178, 179, 374, 375, 379, 380, 385
  fixed interest, 375, 379, 385, 386
  precatory, 354–5
  subject to s. 31 Trustee Act (1925), 178
  venture capital, 208
Trustees, taxation of, 178–9

Undue hardship test, 142
Unified system, 144, 201, 205

Index

Unilateral relief, double taxation, 467–8
United Kingdom
  composition of for tax purposes, 27–8
  constitution, 34
  principal taxes in, 3
United Nations, Model Double Tax Convention, 464

VAT (Value Added Tax), 8, 9, 10, 11, 13, 75, 101
  agents, 425–8
  background, 25–6, 27
  cars, 443
  charge to, 409, 414, 415–16
  consideration, 415, 419–21, 425
  cross-border acquisitions, 442
  Customs and Excise, HM, and, 14, 15–16, 412
  destination base, 441, 442, 443
  direct link test, 420, 425
  Directives, 410, 411, 413
    Sixth, 410, 414, 417, 426, 430, 443
  'duty-free', 442, 443
  economic activities, 424–5
  employees, 426
  European Union and, 28, 409, 410–11
  exemption, partial, 439
  goods, 418–19
    mail-order, 442
    occasional and secondhand, 425
  imports, 442
  international aspects, 441–3
  law, 33, 41, 411–12
  liability, 413, 414
  market value, 441
  mechanics, 426–7
  nature, 416, 418
  partnership, defined, 422
  person, defined, 422

VAT—*contd*
  persons, taxable, 414, 415, 421–23
  rate structure, 434–35
  registration, 422–23
  services and goods, 418–19
  special régimes, 439–40
  supplies, 416–18
    exempt, 421, 437
    mixed and multiple, 438–9
    taxable, 421
    United Kingdom, in, 421
  supply, must be customer to be, 417
  tax credits, 429–31
  tax invoices, 428–9
  tax periods, 428
  tax points, 429
  tribunals, 413
  valuation, 440–41
  zero-rating, 436–7, 442
    exemption compared, 438
VDAT (VAT and Duties Appeal Tribunals), 18
Venture capital trust, 208
Vocation, meaning of, 75
Voluntary payments to traders, 78, 79–80
Voluntary settlements, 171
Vouchers, 101–11

Wealth of Nations, The (Smith), 5
Wealth tax, 10, 13
'Wholly and exclusively', 87–90, 116, 151, 252
Widget, 78
Widow, 177
William of Orange, 22, 26
Wills, 171, 172
Withholding tax, 12–13, 14, 167
  see also deduction at source
Woolf, Lord, 62
Work in progress, 82
Works of art, 272, 346–7